Letters of

GROVER CLEVELAND

1850–1908

CLEVELAND, Grover.   Letters of Grover Cleveland, 1850–1908; sel. and ed. by Allan Nevins.   Da Capo, a div. of Plenum, 1970 (orig. pub. by Houghton Mifflin, 1933).   640p   70-123752.   17.50. SBN 306-71982-7

CHOICE   MAY '71

History, Geography &
Travel

North America

Virtually all the significant letters extant which Cleveland wrote. Nevins, author of the still valuable biography of Cleveland (1932), graced the *Letters* with an interpretative introduction, chapter summaries, and brief informative footnotes as needed. Whether or not Nevins was right in seeing Cleveland as a courageously independent leader (Merrill's biography in 1957 depicted him as a dutiful spokesman for conservative businessmen), any student of the Gilded Age can profit from reading the *Letters*, for there is ample evidence therein to construct his own interpretation. The correspondence reveals a stubborn President ever seeking approval from a narrow circle of associates, and consequently quite unresponsive to needs of less favored groups. One finds little beyond a mixture of Social Darwinism, Calvinistic beliefs, and ante-bellum Democratic shibboleths when looking for his political philosophy. Cleveland was most human in writing about his social and recreational interests.

Letters of
GROVER CLEVELAND

1850–1908

Selected and Edited by

ALLAN NEVINS

Boston and New York

HOUGHTON MIFFLIN COMPANY

The Riverside Press Cambridge

1933

The Riverside Press
CAMBRIDGE · MASSACHUSETTS
PRINTED IN THE U.S.A.

PREFACE

IN MAKING this selection from the great mass of copies of Grover Cleveland's letters which I have gathered, my principal aim has been to secure both an autobiographic and an historical interest. The latter demand has been more easily answered than the former. It was characteristic of Cleveland that he wrote many letters about public business, few about his personal affairs or personal feelings. Only in his last years, when his life had taken on a broad margin of leisure and he had a half-dozen friends — Commodore E. C. Benedict, Richard Watson Gilder, ex-Secretaries Olney and Vilas, Joseph Jefferson, Dean Andrew F. West — whose affection meant much to him, did he try to express what was close to his heart as well as to his mind and hand. In order to furnish a biographical thread, it has been necessary to give each of the chapters of the book a brief introduction, tracing Cleveland through the appropriate month or years. Again and again, in studying his life, we must find ourselves wishing that he had set down an exact indication of his thoughts regarding this or that incident, his feelings regarding this or that person; but that was not his way. It is significant that I have not found it necessary to omit a single letter because it expressed too intimate a view of his private life (for some parts of every man's life are essentially sacred to himself and his family), or too frank an opinion of others.

Cleveland's correspondence after he became President was naturally considerable. It was as extensive as that of Rutherford B. Hayes or Benjamin Harrison; more extensive than that of the inarticulate Grant. But compared with the letter-writing of later Presidents, like Theodore Roosevelt and Woodrow Wilson, it was for several reasons modest. Cleveland's range of interests was narrow; he wrote when affairs required it, but seldom spontaneously and never discursively, for the love of writing; he never learned to employ stenographers or use a typewriter, and the number of letters he could indite with his own heavy fist was limited; and he transacted most business with Congressmen and Cabinet officers orally. Of his correspondence much has been lost. It was not his habit to keep copies of his letters, and many must have been destroyed by the recipients. The largest number of those remaining are now in the Cleveland Papers in the Library of Congress, for after his death his family and Dr. Robert McElroy systematically collected what papers they could. Other letters are in the Lamont Papers, the Manning Papers, the Olney Papers, and like groupings in the same library. Still others are scattered widely — in the Hoke Smith Papers in Atlanta, the Vilas Papers in Madison, Wisconsin, and in the hands of hundreds of individuals. But the total body of letters is by no means unmanageable.

It is my belief that this book contains nearly all of Cleveland's letters that are important to the student of his life or times. It is impossible to say *all*, for no one knows when a significant letter will yet turn up from some hidden nook. The excluded materials fall into three or four broad groups. There are a large number of brief and trivial notes upon private affairs: trains to take, dinners to eat, speeches to write, and fish to catch. There are a large number upon appointments to petty offices: collectorships, postmasterships, marshalships, and the like, all over the American map. There are a number of the meaningless and tiresome letters which every public man writes between sleep and waking: letters to Tammany Hall to be read at its annual celebration of the Fourth, letters to associations met to honor Shakespeare, Washington, or Colonel Mulberry Sellers, letters of regret to be droned by toastmasters at banquets. Two or three such letters have been included as specimens of the rest, and no one will want more. Excluded also are a few official letters, which may be found in that sparkling collection known as Richardson's *Messages and Papers of the Presidents;* and the so-called 'letters of acceptance,' in which Cleveland acknowledged his nominations by a semi-epistolary campaign speech.

To list one-half or one-tenth the men and women, from England on the east to Honolulu on the west, who have sent me copies of letters or other aids toward this collection, would be impossible. Dr. McElroy generously lent me his whole body of transcripts. As for the others, I can only thank them all; thank those whose letters have not been used as warmly as those whose letters have been printed; thank them not merely for myself, but for all who find any pleasure or profit in these pages. To scholars one word may be said about the editing of these letters. Every effort has been made to give Cleveland's meaning in full, with an accurately transcribed text and without any alteration or softening whatever. But small corrections have been made in spelling and punctuation, uniformity has been sought in capitalization and the use of proper names, and in many letters the amount of paragraphing has been reduced; for Cleveland sometimes made almost every sentence a paragraph, and in print this is irritating. It may be added that the fullest commentary on these letters is provided by the author's recent book *Grover Cleveland: A Study in Courage,* which offers also a summary of much correspondence in reply to them.

ALLAN NEVINS

COLUMBIA UNIVERSITY, *September* 15, 1933

CONTENTS

INTRODUCTION: GROVER CLEVELAND IN HIS LETTERS

THERE is always something inspiring in a perusal of those documents which reveal, no matter how imperfectly, the texture and range of a courageous soul. They help us to define the line between the noble and ignoble; they remind us of our most valuable heritage, the heritage of character; they challenge our own manhood. We realize as we read how chilled and faint-hearted we are, how selfishly intent on petty aims, how vain, shallow, and puny. Our demands upon the newer race of leaders are heightened, and our hopes for the future are lifted to a higher level. Historians may dispute endlessly about the merits of many great transactions of the past; critics of letters and art may wrangle still more heatedly over questions of taste and intention. But in weighing certain authentic expressions of stubborn human integrity there can be no dispute over values. When we read some of the state papers of Cromwell, or the letters which Dr. Samuel Johnson wrote under great emotion, or the Second Inaugural of Lincoln, we understand at once that we are in the presence of a man of heroic mould. They are men as truly human as ourselves; they had to push their way through a world which offered plenty of mud and even blood, and their clothes were stained and their feet soiled; but they found opportunity for gallantry and heroism in life, and their words prove it. Of such records of truth and courage, great and small, we cannot have too many.

Grover Cleveland possessed his measure of faults, and was pent in by even more limitations than usually afflict the race of politicians. But he had a soul that in its simple and unpretending fashion was truly heroic, and to touch his garment is to receive virtue. In his own day, for all the hatred he inspired and all the abuse he received, he became a symbol of civic staunchness. Men knew that he made mistakes, that his vision was restricted, and that he was too conservative to be a great constructive statesman. But they knew also that he was immovable in his honesty, that he was unflinching in his fortitude, that his faith in democracy was a part of his very being, and that his aims never stopped short with personal, or partisan, or sectional advantage, but embraced nothing less than the whole national welfare. They knew that this sturdiness of character was a great national asset. They turned from cleverer, better-informed, and more imaginative leaders to place their trust in it. To intelligent Americans of the nineties any revelation that Cleveland had done an unworthy political act would have been a stunning shock. The shock never came, for Cleveland was simply incapable of any such action. He was Bunyan's Valiant-for-Truth transferred to a scene which sorely needed all his valor.

It is for their disclosure of a steadfast heart, an unfaltering character, that the letters of Grover Cleveland are chiefly interesting. And this disclosure is by no means as choked and difficult as some might suppose. Fluency of speech is often used to conceal rather than express personality. Cleveland, whose works reached his pen with such difficulty, was quite unable to dissemble his ideas and emotions. Even when he tried to employ some innocent stealth, like a schoolboy plotting a surprise, he let his secrets escape by the very ponderosity of his precautions. Many volumes of letters written by masters of language, full of the chosen coin of fancy, tell us little of the writer — little, at least, of his inner nature as distinguished from his mental activities. But it is impossible to read a hundred pages of Cleveland's letters without knowing in considerable degree the man himself. Between the formal style of his state papers and the humble everyday style of his letters to friends there is fortunately a wide gulf. His messages and speeches are involved, awkward, and stiltedly ponderous. One reason for this is that he was a man of action, reserved of speech, and men who are doers instead of talkers are usually labored when they turn to words. Another is that in his law office he formed his style on Blackstone, Lord Mansfield, Kent, and other jurists who wrote in a heavy eighteenth-century fashion. But in his letters to friends, or in most of them, Cleveland fell into an easier vein. He said simply and directly what was in his mind, without pretence or artifice. In a letter which he once wrote in irritation he burst out that he was not a man to beat about the bush or be on his guard with friends, and this was true. The result in these pages is the simple, direct expression of an extraordinarily simple, direct man.

Indeed, the primary impression which the letters produce is that of a forthright bluntness. They are the work of a man who had the courage to say what he thought and say it plainly. When as governor he wanted to prevent the renomination of a hostile State senator, he did not go through the pretence of appealing to the electorate. He wrote a frank letter to the boss of Tammany Hall. Midway in his second Administration, though he knew that he was being accused of disrupting his party, he unhesitatingly published his famous letter declaring that Gorman, Brice, and other high-tariff Senators were guilty of 'party perfidy and party dishonor' in their treatment of the Wilson Tariff Bill. He put into the few trenchant lines of his 'silver letter' just before the campaign of 1892 such a complete repudiation of free silver that he later confessed himself half afraid to open his friend Vilas's next missive — fearing that even Vilas would reproach him. He wrote William Randolph Hearst in blunt terms in 1898 that his 'patriotism' was hypocritically assumed to gain circulation and money. He did not hesitate for a moment, in a hard-fought campaign for re-election, to send to Henry Watterson letters which made that influential editor his lifelong enemy. When a Methodist minister in Massachusetts repeated some fables about Cleveland's intemperance, he came out with a scorching indictment of this 'disseminator of wholesale lies and calumnies not less stupid than they are cruel and wicked.'

This forthrightness was based upon a stubborn independence of mind and soul which he cherished above all other possessions. He held friends without capitulation or not at all, and he faced enemies without compromise. 'Whatever you do,' ran his famous telegram of 1884 to the Buffalo associates who were stunned by the scandal suddenly published there, 'tell the truth.' A little later he was writing one of them that the policy of *not cringing* had been the only possible course. To the men who advised him that year to conciliate the Greenback-Labor candidate who was covertly supported by Tammany, he declared that 'I would rather be beaten in this race than to truckle to Butler or Kelly.' He never truckled then or later. When in 1892 his principal campaign manager, the brilliant William C. Whitney, besought him to make a tactful appeal to the hostile Tammany-David B. Hill group, his resentment and anguish were extreme. His letters on the subject show that he was willing to go to any length rather than abate his self-respect by a single concession, and that he even thought of the unprecedented step of resigning the nomination. Again and again, when beset in some way, he speaks of his grim resolution almost as if it were that of some person or force outside himself. Thus during the struggle of 1883 to enforce the State civil service law he wrote: 'I hope I shall hold fast. I believe I shall.' Having an inner conviction of the right, lack of support from others never shook him. 'God,' he wrote Gilder thankfully late in his career, 'has never failed to point out to me the path of duty.' And again in the stormy second term: 'I am sure I was never more completely in the right path of duty than I am now, and I never did better public service than now; but it is depressing enough to have no encouragement from any quarter. I believe I shall hold out.' He always held out.

His candor, which was one of his great public merits, early became an ingrained habit with him. The story is familiar of the journalist who, after trying to get something from him, declared: 'He is the greatest man I ever met — and he wouldn't promise to do a single thing I wanted.' So is the story of Cleveland's remark when he heard that his young son Richard had himself, one day in school, pointed out an error in his work that the teacher had overlooked, and that ruined his perfect mark. The boy, said Cleveland, seemed to be taking after his father, 'because untruthfulness appears to be no temptation whatever to either of us.' This honesty shines all through his letters. In our entire collection there seems to be but a single possible exception to it. In one letter of his first term Cleveland comments angrily upon Governor Hill's attempt to win the faithful Daniel Lamont away from his side, and adds some biting words about Hill being a whelp morally and politically. Not long afterward he is writing Hill an invitation to come visit him at the White House. But in the meantime he may have found that the charge against Hill was baseless, or that there was some justification for the governor's course. In any event, the frank truthfulness of every word of the letters is remarkable. He flatters nobody; he never evades or palters; he never writes in one sense to Peter and another to Paul. Caution is often evident in his epistles, for Cleveland was naturally conservative, but it is always an honest caution.

James Russell Lowell, who knew Cleveland slightly, remarked that 'With all his firmness he has a very tender and sympathetic nature, or I am much mistaken.' This tenderness, which appears in both his public and private relations, is illustrated by a large proportion of his letters. It animates his resentment over abuses, and his sympathy with the abused — for example, with the Indians. It is displayed in letters expressing his deep family affection. He never mentions his mother except with reverence. When he was inaugurated governor he wrote his brother an extraordinary communication. He spoke of her constant prayers for his success, and declared that now that she was gone he wished William, who was a minister, to help him in the same way. When McKinley was inaugurated in 1897 he had his mother on the stand beside him, and Cleveland was manifestly touched. He would have given anything, he said, to have had *his* mother with him when he entered the White House. A similar emotion comes to the surface in his frequent references to his married life. 'My wife sits by me,' he confides to Bissell in 1888. 'I tell you, Bissell, I am sure of one thing. I have in her something better than the Presidency for life.' Even more fervently, he pours out to Bissell his feelings over his first baby. He has 'just entered the real world'; he sees 'in a small child more of value than I have ever called my own before'; in short, he is transported. His affection for other children, such as Gilder's, was always marked. Any helplessness caught at his heartstrings. The story is still told in Albany of how he came on New Year's Eve in 1884 to a friend's house asking to be cheered up. That afternoon a stranger had brought his little boy to the Executive Chamber, saying that he had promised the lad a visit to the President-elect. The man had lifted the little fellow up — and he was blind! There had rushed upon Cleveland's recollection his own days as a teacher in an institution for the blind — the days when, in a bleak asylum in New York City, he was surrounded by the poor and unfortunate; and in thinking of this and the little youngster he had fallen into a fit of profound depression.

Like all men who have to fight the world, he had to be harsh at times. But he nevertheless maintained an unusual vein of sentiment, both deep and fine. It comes out repeatedly in his references to his public duties. 'It seems to me,' he writes when new to the Presidency, 'I am as much consecrated to a service as the religionist who secludes himself to a sacred mission.' He showed a keen sensibility to the meaning of death. Few men had done more for his early rise than E. K. Apgar, who died at an untimely age. Cleveland writes soon afterward that he finds it hard to believe that Apgar is dead, 'but sometimes it comes upon me with dreadful distinctness' — a telling phrase. He was capable of the warmest kind of affection for the few men that he really cared to call friends. They were all but brothers to him. Unquestionably he meant it when he wrote Bissell in 1884 that if he had the world he would give his old partner half of it at least. More than once in these letters he speaks wistfully of the Buffalo years as 'days of simple, honest, hearty friendship.' He was cut to the heart in 1885 by evidence that some of his associates of those days thought him cold and selfish simply because he now refused them offices, and he eloquently expressed his hurt to Bissell and Lockwood. As late as 1891 we find him writing a less intimate friend, D-Cady Herrick, that 'I feel very badly and blue, for the only thing in the world I am timid about is the charge of ingratitude.' In both his Administrations his Cabinets became true families, bound closely together by ties of affection and loyalty. None felt those ties more strongly than he. He was genuinely grieved, as difficulties thickened in his second term, that he had dragged so many good men into a sea of trouble and vituperation. And we find him writing Bayard, with a burst of gratitude: 'You don't know what a comfort Gresham is to me, with his hard sense, his patriotism and loyalty. It is but little for me to say that I would trust my life or honor in his keeping at all times. I have some other good men about me, and I am constantly thinking that enmity and evil and misfortune must overcome eight more good true ones before my discomfiture can be accomplished.'

It is easy in these letters to pick out many expressions of irritation, scorn, or condemnation. To Cleveland politics was often a hair-shirt, and he squirmed under what he called 'influences not always akin to the best sensibilities.' He was always ready to give battle for a principle. 'I am not anxious to be beaten and cuffed about too much,' he writes in one of his letters; and after a buffet or two, he would give back blow for blow. But it is extraordinary to note in this collection how much there is also of a large, easy tolerance. This tolerance was a compound of willingness to let other people differ from him so long as they differed honestly, and of a patient faith that while God often moves slowly and mysteriously, in the end the right triumphs. His tolerance in religious matters he illustrated by a favorite story of the Hard-Shell Baptist whom certain Presbyterians tried to cajole into their church, and who replied: 'No, you folks are Presbyterians, and if I should go over to your church *I couldn't enjoy my mind.*' Wishing to enjoy his own mind, he was ready to let others enjoy theirs. In matters political the tolerance crops out in a letter written early in his governorship: 'I sometimes think the people of this State act like "a passel of boys."' What could be more indulgent than that phrase? And in one of his letters written from the White House, he tactfully admonishes a friend that while the citizens of the United States might not always act just as he or others wished them to act, they were after all a pretty good people, and in the long run did right. There is no trace of intolerance in the plaintive letter which he wrote Bayard in 1895 when everyone seemed to have deserted him: 'You may be surprised to learn,' he remarks, 'that in all the darkness I have never lost the feeling that the American people and I have a perfectly fair understanding.'

This tolerance was largely nourished by a fundamental good humor which is strewn all through his letters, as it is through all accounts of his relations with friends. He dearly loved all fun except practical jokes, which struck him as undignified or painful; and to the end of his life he retained that boyish quality which gleams from his eye in the Zorn portrait. Many of his sayings cannot be interpreted without this twinkle in the eye; for example, his remark to the reporter who was trying to worm out of him a statement on a question of foreign policy — 'That, sir, is a matter of too great importance to discuss in a five-minute interview, now rapidly drawing to its close.' In the letters of his earliest years we encounter a gay persiflage. He indulges in self-depreciatory fun — 'my homely, burly face'; in observations on the social customs of Buffalo — 'the last night of the old year, when Methodists dolefully sing its requiem and the Dutchmen fire their guns'; in mere boyish exuberance — 'I'm a regular chatterbox, ain't I?' When he sets forth on his vacation in 1883 he flings back a sally to his secretary: 'Two things must be done, to wit: the Republican party must go, and Arthur must be beaten as a fisherman.' Sometimes he smiled at his own juvenile qualities. His old partner Lyman K. Bass came to the White House and they went for a drive. 'I was so boyishly glad to see him that when I was obliged to bid him good-bye to go and make postmasters, I felt like giving up the Presidency and going with him.' And in the letters of the last years we can see him and Commodore E. C. Benedict and 'Bob' Evans in the intimacy, not of grave men, but of high-spirited youths. The joviality creeps into even his letters on investments. He proposes to Benedict that they make a moderate investment in some stock, and then bet heavily against the fall in the market which invariably follows!

Tolerance and humor both depend, in their separate ways, upon a sense of proportion, and it is clear from a hundred of his utterances that Cleveland developed this sense in a fashion that was extremely valuable to the head of a state. In his second Administration some men, like Watterson, complained that he showed touches of arrogance and conceit. But we can see from his private communications how completely erroneous was this impression. He never thought highly of his own abilities;

at least, he never exaggerated them. As governor he wrote frankly to a friend that he did not believe he had the material to do more for the people than he could in that office — that is, he did not believe that he had the capacity to make a President. A little earlier he had not even been sure that he had the qualifications for a successful governor. 'The question is whether I know enough to accomplish what I desire,' he confided to his brother. In the Presidency he gradually developed a conviction that he had been called there to do a special work. The hand of Providence, he felt, had selected him as a humble instrument. 'God,' he writes Gilder after the surgical operation in 1893, 'has put the belief in my mind that I can still be of use to my country.' In all his letters to former Cabinet associates after both the first and the second Administrations there shines a touching pride in their joint achievements. But it is the pride of a man who was singularly lacking in self-complacency, and who was pleased merely that what talents he possessed had not been laid away in a napkin. 'If I only knew as much as Abram S. Hewitt I might amount to something,' he once remarked to Gilder, and he meant every word of it.

And yet at times, as we have said, he displayed a capacity for the fiercest and most devastating anger — the anger of a just man slowly but completely aroused. For three memorable examples of it, the reader need only turn in this volume to the short letter to Mr. Leo Oppenheim and the longer one to Mr. George Cary Eggleston, and to Cleveland's public statement on the slanders propagated by the Rev. Mr. Lansing.

We may trace in these letters, as in those of almost every man, a series of psychological stages. In the fragments which have been preserved from his correspondence as a young lawyer there is a lightheartedness, an ebullient jocularity, that naturally appears but seldom in his later life. When he first assumes office his sense of duty and responsibility is fully developed. But he is still uncertain of himself, for he realizes that his preparation has been defective and his rise to power singularly rapid. While still new in the White House he said, 'Sometimes I wake at night and rub my eyes and wonder if it is not all a dream.' That wonderment appears in his letters, and so does a constant anxiety lest he should make grave mistakes. He was slow to comprehend the necessity of becoming a national leader; he thought at first of holding to a 'constitutional' view of the Presidency, and abstaining from all interference with Congress. The error of this view gradually dawned upon him, and he realized that a President ought to give Congress, his party, and the whole country a definite programme. With his tariff message of 1887 he became a full-fledged leader, and the letters of the next ten years must be read in the light of that fact. They have a more masterful tone than before, and breathe a sense of responsibility for the guidance of the nation.

But during the ceaseless and almost crushing troubles of his second Administration, a new note appears. Cleveland at that time had to learn to take punishment as few Presidents have ever taken it, and the almost ceaseless procession of disasters produced interesting effects upon him. One of the most striking is a marked deepening of his religious instinct, for as men forsook him he relied more and more upon God. When he left office in 1897, it was with a sense of having been driven into exile. His own party had abandoned him with taunts and reproaches; the opposition party regarded him with contemptuous indifference. The result is that we find in his correspondence of the next few years, for the first time, a somewhat querulous note. Rusting like an outworn suit of mail on the wall, he felt grieved and even slightly embittered. But little by little this mood disappears from his letters. He gradually learns that the country still admires and increasingly appreciates him, and in his last years the central note struck in his correspondence is a high serenity. It is a happy fact that it can end on such a note.

But the dominant chord in this volume is something finer and more disciplinary. Cleveland probably never read *Sartor Resartus*. But he and the grimly honest Scotchman who wrote that book had learned the same fundamental truths, and his career is one of our best exemplifications of Carlyle's noble sentence: 'Too early and too thoroughly we cannot be trained to know that Would, in this world of ours, is a mere zero to Should, and for the most part as the smallest of fractions even to Shall.' The word always in Cleveland's mind was 'Should.'

The Letters of

GROVER CLEVELAND

I

THE BUFFALO YEARS

CLEVELAND was thirteen when, visiting his uncle Lewis F. Allen at Black Rock, then just outside Buffalo, he wrote his sister Mary the first of his letters which has been preserved. He had been born at Caldwell, New Jersey, on March 18, 1837, fifth among the nine children of the Reverend Richard Falley Cleveland and Anne Neal Cleveland. His father, as a Presbyterian minister and as district secretary of the American Home Missionary Society, lived successively in Caldwell, Fayetteville, New York, Clinton, New York, and Holland Patent, New York, dying in the last-named village in the autumn of 1853. Cleveland's education was abruptly broken off. He spent a year, 1853–54, teaching with his older brother in the New York Institution for the Blind in New York City. In May, 1855, he reached Buffalo on his way west, but was persuaded by his uncle to remain there; and after a summer of work on a Shorthorn Herdbook which his uncle was compiling, he entered a law office as clerk and student. In 1859 he was admitted to the bar. For more than twenty years thereafter his career in Buffalo was comparatively uneventful. Partly because he was compelled to help support his mother and younger sisters, he remained unmarried. He formed various legal partnerships, and in the middle seventies became virtual head of the firm of Bass, Cleveland, and Bissell. Little by little he rose at the bar until he became recognized as one of the leading attorneys of western New York, and one of the most substantial and trustworthy men in his city. He served one term each as assistant district attorney and sheriff, but manifested little political ambition, and apparently had his hopes fixed chiefly on one of the judgeships of the State Supreme Court. Throughout these years he was a 'man's man'; mingling little in general society, and, caring nothing for travel, he had a comparatively narrow range of interests, and devoted himself with extraordinary single-mindedness to his legal work. However, he was warmly attached to his mother and sisters, and spent much time in visits to the family home at Holland Patent; he was devoted to a few good friends, chief among them his

partner Wilson S. Bissell and a fellow-attorney, Oscar Folsom; he
was an ardent fisherman and hunter; and especially in early manhood, he read more widely than most of his associates supposed.

To MARY CLEVELAND

Black Rock, *October 29,* 1850

After so long a time I seat myself in the dining-room to answer your
kind letter, which was duly received. You can better imagine than I can
describe, how it gladdened my heart. My journey here was a very slow
one, as by many hindrances the boat was much later than usual. And on
account of this I had to stay all night in Rochester, and take the morning
boat. I did not arrive here till Sabbath morning. I have a great many
adventures to tell you when I get home (for you must know my journey
has been adventurous). I long to be with you there, although I do not
feel at all homesick. How could I when all appear to take an interest in
my happiness? I have enjoyed myself at a great rate since my stay here.
I am very much pleased with the place and the people and would like to
stay the longest allotted time. I find Cleveland [1] to be a very pleasing
companion, and Aunt, Uncle, and all appear to aim at my enjoyment.
Richard's health has been very good until lately he has been suffering
with one of his spells of derangement. But we hope for his speedy restoration. Gertrude is perfectly healthy and as full of fun as ever. She
sends her love to you and says: Tell her about my pony. Which is one of
the prettiest little creatures I ever saw. Tell Father to say in his next
letter whether he would be willing to have me stop at our old home as I
return and spend a day or two, as it would afford me great pleasure. Tell
Fred [2] the stump of Pat O'Dagon is still left and will be with him shortly,
for I after the manner of Dagon was laid low before an ox by the introduction of his foot a short time since. Tell Ditcher hunting here is good.
Patrick has killed 14 black squirrels during his stay.

I have not yet been to see the Falls, but expect to go tomorrow (Thursday). I think if I were to have my own way I should not be ready to
come home till the middle of the month. It seems a great while since I
saw you, and I long to get home and spend a Sabbath with you. As far
as money is concerned my funds are low, but I do not know as I wish for
more. I have received a letter from Cecil in which he says he is contented

[1] Cleveland Allen, Richard Allen, and Gertrude Allen were cousins.

[2] Lewis Frederick Cleveland, younger brother of Grover; Cecil, mentioned below, was
Richard Cecil Cleveland, an older brother.

and quite happy. It will seem very queer to leave Fayetteville to go home. Tell Father the captain of the boat upon which I came says he will let me come back for the same price, $2. On my way I was fortunate enough to get a berth each night in which I slept as soundly as if I had been at home. Aunt thinks it is queer, she says, why she don't hear from you. Tell Anna [1] it is a cause of great wonder with them (Aunt and Cleveland especially) why John and her were not a long time since joined by Hymen's silken cord, to which marvel I generally reply, I don't know anything about her matters. Tell Mother those mittens have lasted first rate, for on opening my bag I found them as well as some collars minus. However, I get along very well as everything else was O.K., but my stock of news has nearly run out and as Cleveland will soon be in to have me take a ride with him, and as I have a letter to write to Louise, I think I must close this interesting epistle with a wish for your contentment and happiness. Pass over in this what perhaps you would notice in others and remember me....

To MARY CLEVELAND

Holland Patent. (No date; winter of 1853–54.)

As Mother is despatching a letter to you, I cannot let it go without writing a little, although it will not amount to much. I received a letter from you some time since which as yet is unanswered. But the fact is, Mary, I have to study very hard and it takes most all my time to prepare to confront Bradin. We heard from William [2] last night after a long silence. *He is well.* That's all I learned from the letter and I had to conjecture that. Did you ever see such a fellow to write?

As for myself, Mollie, I am kind of fooling away my time here, I think. To tell the truth, I am heartily sick of studying at home. 'Tell it not in Gath, publish it not in' — the other place. I don't want Bill to know it, but I mean to get into some business again next spring *at least*, if not before. I have used all the rules in *my* arithmetic, and I have not solved the problem yet, viz., How is a man going to spend four years in getting an education with nothing to start on and no prospect of anything to pay his way with? Until I see how I am going to get through you don't catch me inside of college walls. 'That's gone up.'

[1] Anna Cleveland did not marry 'John,' but (in 1853) the Reverend Eurotas P. Hastings.

[2] William Neal Cleveland, oldest of the children, was now a student in Union Theological Seminary.

Lizzie Dwight is greatly troubled about you, Mother says. I wonder who it was that made such a discovery. Somebody that can see farther into a *millstone* than most folks. For my part I thought I never saw you look better than you did last July. But you know my opinion ain't good for anything. So don't allow yourself to be flattered. I too am getting to be a 'dignified old pate.' People all asked me if I had voted at the election. I ascribe it all to my whiskers — oh, perhaps you don't know that my beard has become so unmanageable that I have been under the necessity of letting it take its own course, and in consequence I now sport quite — indeed a *very* — respectable goatee. I should love to see you dearly. There are lots of things I want to say to you, and then the advice of such an *aged* person as yourself would be of immense advantage to me. You must try and visit us soon.

To MARY CLEVELAND HOYT

Buffalo, *October* 18, 1855

I have laid Blackstone aside for a few minutes,[1] for I don't feel like study this afternoon, and I do feel like writing to some of my friends. I believe I don't owe any of them a letter, but you know that doesn't make much difference with me.

I suppose by this time you are fairly under way in your new responsibility as housekeeper. How does it go? I don't doubt but that you will make a model housewife. Aunt and Uncle have gone West, but we expect them back in a few days. We have had quite a party of 'young folks at home.' I am trying to find a place to board in the city, but am so far unsuccessful. I have to work pretty hard just at present, as the senior clerk is absent. But it is better for me, as the more I do the more I learn. As you say, I find oftentimes 'Jordan a hard road to travel,' but for the most part feel pretty well encouraged. I think and hope that I shall have no trouble, that is, any more than is the unavoidable concomitant of poverty.

I have had but one letter in (I think) two weeks. I am a favorite with all my friends, ain't I? But I don't care much and every day I am growing more regardless of little things — like letter-writing, receiving, etc.

My employers are very kind to me and promise me promotion again soon. They at present pay my board or an equivalent, which is very

---

[1] Cleveland was now a student in the office of Rogers, Bowen and Rogers. His sister Mary had married M. E. Hoyt.

satisfactory. How is little — what's-his-name — *the boy?* When I get to be an *old lawyer* and he wants to study the profession I'll take him in my office — then you need not thank me — I'll do it with the greatest pleasure. Consider that a fixed arrangement.

If you see 'that feller' (you know who) just tell him I've *got my eye on him* — he'd better look out how he performs. But here! I haven't made any wishes in your behalf as housekeeper, have I?

Accept (Mrs. Hoyt) my sincere and heartfelt wishes for entire success in your capacity as housekeeper. May your heart and bread be always light and your purse always heavy. May your tea be always strong and your butter always mild. May your husband be sociable but your baby be dumb. May rats, company, and trouble be scarce and comfort and quiet plenty. And last and most important — next summer (when I come up there) may you have a spare room with an extra bed in it. May you have a big table with an extra plate on it. May you have a nice garden with lots of 'stuff' in it. And welcome *your friends* to stay and *enjoy* it.

Louise [1] says Charley Hoyt is going to Chicago to live.

Now, Mary, I spun off quite a yarn, although I haven't got off much either. I am a regular chatterbox, ain't I? I'm going to see about my boarding-place tonight. You must write to me soon, won't you? I am quite ashamed that I can't write you a better letter, but you'll have to take it for better or for worse. Remember me to Will.

To MARY CLEVELAND HOYT

Buffalo, *November* 14, 1855

Your kind, affectionate, dutiful, obliging, but alas, disappointed brother has shown a commendable zeal as well as a homely, burly face in searching this town from Lake Erie to the end of shopkeeping, in search of *said* trimming. I enclose a bit which comes the nearest of any found in our 'Gotham.' It is a fact that stands unparalleled in the annals of history, that in this great city the exact thing cannot be found. I am well assured that the trouble is not in the *trimming*, but in the dress *material*. They ought to have known more than to make such stuff of such a color.

I am very busy nowadays — have just 'moved' to town — health good — heart and pocket light — but all right. I don't know about my writing to you again before you do.... If that stuff should answer (very unlikely) you can have some of it.

[1] Margaret Louise Cleveland was a younger sister.

To Mary Cleveland Hoyt

Buffalo, *December* 31, 1855

On this last evening of the year when poor '55 shall be consigned to the shades of reminiscence and the new year shall take its place — when Methodists dolefully sing its requiem and the Dutchmen *fire their guns* — on this evening, I say, I have seated myself at my table and am determined that your last shall be forthwith answered. I have no news that I suppose *is* news to you to communicate, and shall have to (for aught I see) resort to my never-failing substitute — nonsense, etc.

We are having beautiful sleighing and I am reminded that others besides myself inhabit this terrestrial globe by the constant and merry jingle of sleigh-bells and the explosion of guns — for you know there are a great many Germans in Buffalo, and with them the firing of cannon is a common and delightful manner of celebrating the advent of the New Year. You know I am such a matter-of-fact old bachelorish body that New Year's is almost as good as any other day to me and no better. And here let me, by way of parenthesis and conforming to the usual custom in such cases 'made and provided,' wish you a Happy New Year.

You received the paper I sent you containing an account of Richard Allen's death. He was found dead in his room, having just died in a fit. We were all very much attached to him for his kindness and amiability, and while we cannot but mourn his departure, we have to console us that it is well with him and that his sufferings are over forever. You must write to Aunt.

Cleveland is expecting to go to Michigan on an engineering tour soon. Gertrude is at home and I believe intends to avail herself of the advantages afforded by Buffalo Female Seminary, this winter. I am intending to go down to Black Rock tomorrow.

I was most happy to learn that your experiment in housekeeping is much more than successful. I promise myself the pleasure of testing your model housewifery next summer. I suppose you are experiencing freezing cold weather in your section of the country just at present. It's dreadful cold here and we have to apply the anthracite largely to keep up the necessary supply of carbon.

Supposing that my situation, prospects, etc., are at all times interesting to you I shall proceed to inform you in regard to these items. I am still living along as I have always done, sustaining life and energies by means of eating, drinking, and sleeping. Indeed, I am so addicted to these habits that I find it impossible to forego them for any length of time. I must have my *provender* three times a day and eat and drink in proportion: It's lamentable, isn't it?

I am boarding at a second-class hotel [1] and paying at the rate of $4 a week. I am not very much pleased with my situation in this respect and contemplate a change soon. My employers are very kind to me, and all things taken into consideration, I try to be happy, though I sometimes find it pretty hard.

Do you hear from your other brothers often? I don't have many letters nowadays. I haven't heard from Cecil in quite a long time, and I have no idea where he is. Can you inform me in regard to him? I don't believe any of your brothers are as conscientious as I am in the matter of letter-writing.

I am aware, my dear Mary, that I have inflicted a miserable scrawl upon you, but I can't help that. I've written already more than I know. The next time maybe I shall have more news and better materials every way. Tonight I feel stupid at best, and now with a wish to hear from you soon and assurances of love I bid you good-bye.

To MARY CLEVELAND HOYT

Buffalo, *February* 14, 1856

After studying this evening until a quarter past eleven, I have pushed aside my lawbooks to write you a short valentine, and I shall also take occasion at this time and place to inform you of two or three things of which you seem to be in entire ignorance. 1. You have a young brother in this city (who by the way is a *very* worthy young man), who is just at this time languishing and pining away by reason of the incomprehensible neglect and scorn of *a much-loved sister*. 2. The said brother is not aware of any just cause for such neglect on the part of his said sister, and in much seriousness propounds: 'Are you *maad* at me?' The belief, my dear Mary, that the fact that I have not heard a word from you for months is attributable to some fortuitous circumstance other than premeditated neglect on your part, has induced me to write you the *second* time. You know you promised quite largely in your last that my poor mean scrawls should receive attention. May I not expect a fulfillment of so reasonable a promise?

You are, I believe, already informed that 'I still live.' I am happy to

[1] This was the Southern Hotel, at the corner of Seneca and Michigan Streets, Buffalo.

inform you that I am doing well — that is, well *considering*. I flatter myself, and my employers assure me, that if I keep on, I'll make a lawyer — 'a circumstance devoutly to be wished,' I assure you.

I received a *beautiful* valentine this morning from Buffalo, and I ave endeavored to repay my sweet *incognita* without delay. I have sent two and am quite assured that one of them will hit the mark. Excuse me, my dear Mary, for entering somewhat into a description of one of these last-mentioned documents. Its total size was just about a quarter the size of this note-paper. Upon the first page was a beautiful and highly-colored and ornamental picture suggestive of love, etc.: underneath was a short verse of *appropriate* ideas; and on the inside I thought it quite *recherché* to insert that beautiful and matchless verse, familiar perhaps to you, and commencing: 'How doth the little busy B,' etc. The other valentine, I assure you, was no less perfect and unobjectionable. The reception of such a matter was very unexpected to me, but having received one, I thought I must in return do something worthy of myself.

I am leading a very quiet life and tread day after day in the same old track. I have very few 'blue' turns, but 'tis not for the want of those little trials that induce blueness; but I *strongly* suspect 'tis owing to a fixed determination on my part not to yield to such things.

I am anticipating much pleasure from a visit home next summer. May I not add to my other pleasing expectations, the hope that I shall see you then? May I not expect to hear from you soon? Will you remember me to your husband? Will you rest assured that none of all your brothers loves you more than yours very affectionately, S. Grover Cleveland?

To MARY CLEVELAND HOYT

Buffalo, *January* 1, 1858

A happy New Year from the bottom of my heart to you and yours, my dear Molly!

I have been moping all day and have spent most of the time at the office; and after revolving...

(Sunday morning)

I had just written 'revolving' last night when a friend stepped in and we, after a little more revolving, revolved to the theatre and saw the wonderful revolutions of the wonderful Revels. And so the evening passed and my letter was unfinished.

On this Sunday morning, *in* the office of Rogers, Bowen, and Rogers, with no fire, *at* 9 o'clock A.M., I sit with full purpose of and endeavor after a full discharge of epistolary duty to youward. The holidays are over and I am glad. They don't amount to anything, so 'What's the use?' I didn't get no presents and I am glad of *that*.

I have made a new arrangement with the firm here and have engaged to work for them another year for the enormous sum of $500. 'O God! That bread should be so dear, and *work should be so cheap*.' I am so ashamed of myself after allowing such a swindle to be practised upon me. It shows how selfish the men I have to do with are, and how easy it is to fool me. I ought to have a great deal more, and from the bottom of my soul I curse the moment in which I consented to the contract. But it's over now and I don't propose to whine.

Aunt is greatly troubled because Gertrude keeps up a communication with her beau by letter and otherwise. I don't know what will come of it, I'm sure. It would be a perfect deadener to them if she should marry him. I don't know but I shall go down and help Uncle about his herd-book next month. I want to go for the sake of the pay, and I don't want to go for any other reason.

If I knew of any pretty music I'd send it to you, but I never hear any and am not posted. If you can suggest anything new and pretty and if I can find it I'll send it. But my fingers are growing cold and I must emigrate to my room. Let me hear from you soon....

To MARY CLEVELAND HOYT

Buffalo, *May 27*, 1858

I have just put aside my law papers, many and voluminous, and am determined to write you this evening at all hazards.

'Twas only yesterday that I learned through Louise of the death of your babe. Be assured, my dear sister, that you have my most sincere sympathy and condolence in this your affliction. Though of course I cannot fully appreciate the poignancy of your grief as a mother, upon the death of your child, yet I know you are greatly afflicted; and though I am sure all my efforts to comfort you at this time must be in a measure unavailing, yet I cannot forbear assuring you that I sympathize with you to the furthest extent of the strongest brotherly love.

I am sorry to hear that your health is not at all good. I trust it will speedily amend and that you will accept Mother's invitation to spend some time with her this summer. I don't suppose the people at Black Rock know of the death of your child. I wanted to go down there last evening, but could not, and this evening I have spent at work in the office. I shall try to go tomorrow night.

I was thrown from a horse a week ago tonight and somewhat injured. I am still very lame. My hurts are not serious and yet quite uncomfortable.

You must have wondered occasionally why you never heard from me lately; but the truth is I have a very great deal to do nowadays and am getting quite out of the habit of writing letters. And then, besides, I know that your attention must be fully occupied of late. Hereafter I shall write you oftener. I propose now to take my vacation about the middle of July. I am afraid I can spend but little time away from the office, and though I mean to visit you if possible, yet I may be disappointed. Perhaps you intend to be away from home at that time yourself. Remember me very affectionately to Will and tell him his kindness to me last summer is all treasured up....

To INGHAM TOWNSEND

Buffalo, *January* 23, 1867

I am now in condition to pay my note which you hold given for money borrowed some years ago.[1] I suppose I might have paid it long before, but I have never thought you were in need of it and I had other purposes for my money. I have forgotten the date of the note. If you will send me it I will mail you the principal and interest. The loan you made me was my start in life, and I shall always preserve the note as an interesting reminder of your kindness. Let me hear from you soon. With many kind wishes to Mrs. Townsend and your family....

To DENNIS BOWEN [2]

Buffalo, *August* 14, 1867

I am a trifle hard up today. I wonder if you can send me $15 Referee's fees in the matter of selling some lunatic's real estate where Callender was committee. I've forgotten the name.

---

[1] Townsend, a wealthy Presbyterian elder of Holland Patent, had lent Cleveland $25 in the spring of 1855 for his trip to Buffalo.

[2] Of the three partners in the law firm which Cleveland entered as clerk, Dennis Bowen exerted the most influence upon him.

To WILLIAM WYSE

Buffalo, *August* 13, 1873

I am amazed and dumfounded, but I congratulate you from the bottom of my heart. A long life of perfect bliss and married contentment I hope may be yours. I go to find Bissell, with whom I drink the health of the newly-married. Please present my compliments to the other side of the firm.

To DENNIS BOWEN

Buffalo, *November* 29, 1875

The size of prisoners' boxes in the new courtroom should depend upon the manner in which they are used.[1] If you propose that all prisoners shall be *arraigned* from the boxes, there should be room for eighteen or twenty persons at least. If you propose that they shall be occupied only by such as are awaiting *trial* or *sentence*, they should be large enough to hold eight or ten persons. My notion would be to arraign from seats near the boxes and use the boxes as last above indicated.

Anything contraband is usually handed prisoners when they are occupying the box waiting for trial or sentence; and this should be guarded against by the *location* and manner of construction of the boxes. I think they should be somewhere near the Court and officers, and the sides which are exposed to the contaminating influences of the wicked outside world should be pretty high and very close. The side in view of the officers, etc., might well be so constructed as to expose any 'hocus-pocus' that might be going on inside.

But I have answered more than you asked me. I was absent when your note came and have just returned.

To THE HONORABLE E. B. A. TAYLOR

New York, *May* 5, 1880

In reply to your letter of April 19 addressed to John S. Darling[2] the undersigned begs leave to call your attention to the stipulation in the lease just expired which provides that if the lessees shall be desirous at the end of the term thereby granted to take a further lease of the premises

[1] Cleveland was writing from his experience in 1871–73 as sheriff of Erie County.

[2] Cleveland's brother, Lewis Frederick, while lessee and manager of the Royal Victoria Hotel at Nassau in the Bahamas, perished in the burning of the steamer *Missouri* in October, 1872. As an executor of the estate Cleveland held the lease and was here writing the colonial authorities.

therein described, they shall '*have a preference over all persons desiring to lease the same*, on such terms as the commissioners for the time being shall decide on as proper terms for the further leasing of the said hotel.' It is suggested [by us] that the *preference* secured by this provision is not made available to the lessees by calling on them for tenders of rent for the hotel; but the intention rather was, that when the commissioners had determined upon the price which they deemed proper terms for the further leasing of the property, whether this price was determined on by the invitation for tenders or otherwise, the lessees should have an opportunity to secure the further lease at such rate, before negotiations are closed with any other party.

In further answer to your communications, but without in any manner waiving our rights under the stipulations alluded to above, it is proposed: 1st, to pay as an annual rent for the renewal of the lease for the term of five years, the sum of two thousand dollars with satisfactory security for its payment, or, 2d, to take a lease of five years, paying to the Government annually one-fourth of the net profits of the business. In either case the Government to paint and keep the premises in repair. These propositions are made after consultation with Mr. Morton,[1] and in the expectation, if another lease is secured, that he will continue to manage the hotel.

To JOHN S. DARLING

Buffalo, *August 29*, 1880

Immediately upon the receipt of your letter with the draft of lease I sent for Morton and he came up and spent a day here, leaving yesterday morning. We went over the lease very carefully and the changes desired are interlined in pencil or contained in riders attached. I send it in this way instead of having the whole thing copied so that the Board of Works may the more easily see the extent to which their draft is changed.

1st. I propose that the term shall be six years instead of five. That carries the lease to the end of the present annual contract....

2d. I propose that the rent should be paid in two instalments instead of four and that the payments should be made on the first days of February and May. At the beginning of every season there is quite an outlay necessary, and I desire that the first payment of rent shall be postponed till the business of the season may pay it. And as the lessors would prob-

---

[1] James M. Morton of New York had operated the hotel.

ably in any event not think of regaining the first quarterly payment before January 1, I suggest that payment be postponed a month longer and then pay half instead of a quarter. . . .

3d. I think it better that the time for which the hotel is to be kept open should be specified. And I have prepared an announcement covering that item. Experience has shown that the seasons in which the opening of the hotel before December 1 has resulted in any profit to the lessees or advantage to the Government (if any) are exceedingly rare. And the opening and maintaining of the hotel during the month of November has, since my connection with the business, invariably resulted in a loss to the management, which sometimes the whole season has not made good. . . . As to the closing of the hotel my suggestion is not different from the way it has been managed in years past. And I only wish to say that the proprietors will probably keep open as long after May 1 as they can make it pay.

4th. In case of any epidemic I am not willing to open the hotel or to pay rent. Mr. Morton handed me the *Herald* of last Wednesday, August 25, which contained the slip I send herewith. Besides these reports in the papers there are plenty of people in this country from Nassau and their friends who are constantly spreading the news of yellow fever. With all this we must also regard the unfriendly disposition of the Florida people who, it has been demonstrated, can create a great stir out of much less material than they now have or may hereafter have. It would be bad enough to open the hotel in the midst of reports without foundation. But to open when yellow fever was actually epidemic there would be ruinous to the proprietors and almost as disastrous to the island. . . .

5th. I think the same provision as to a renewal of the lease should be in this, that was contained in the old lease. . . .

I have thus explained and commented on all the changes in the lease which I deemed desirable. . . . I wish you to make known my notions on these subjects to the Board of Works and to present such other arguments or suggestions as will tend to my protection. Of course I expect to hear by next mail.

II

MAYOR AND GOVERNOR

In 1881 Cleveland, then at the head of the firm of Cleveland, Bissell, and Sicard, was asked by the New York Central to become its chief counsel in western New York. His refusal was more important than anyone realized; for if he had accepted the position, he would never have consented to run for mayor, and would never have become President. In the fall of 1881 there was a general revolt in Buffalo against the corrupt government of a bi-partisan ring. Cleveland, who as a bachelor was in a position to drop most of his law practice temporarily and take a $2500-a-year office, was elected mayor. He gave the city an administration marked by blunt honesty and energy, particularly distinguishing himself by his veto of numerous bad bills, his exposure of a scheme to rob the city of more than $100,000 on a street-cleaning contract, and his insistence upon building a new sewage system without politics or graft. Before his first year as mayor ended Cleveland was brought forward for the governorship. The Republican State Convention in 1882, under the dictation of the Arthur Administration, nominated a candidate who was felt to represent the Conkling-Arthur machine and the interest of Jay Gould. A great body of Republican voters immediately rebelled, and the way was opened for a reform candidate. Cleveland was elected by a majority of more than 192,000, and on January 1, 1883, became governor. Again he worked hard, vetoed more bad bills than any predecessor, and treated his office as a business commission which he had received from the people of the State. In his appointments he gave little weight to political considerations, and refused to grant the slightest 'recognition' to Tammany Hall, which had been deprived of many of its former officers in New York City by the County Democracy there, and was hence hungry for spoils. The result was a partial breach between Cleveland and Tammany Hall in the last days of the first legislative session. Cleveland made it complete that autumn, when he took steps to defeat the re-election of Thomas F. Grady, the legislative leader of the Tammany forces in the State Senate. Thereafter Grady and the boss of Tammany Hall, John Kelly, fought him at every step.

To SHERMAN S. ROGERS

Buffalo, *April* 15, 1882

I am deeply sensible of the compliment implied by my employment to assist in the suit of Smith vs. Matthews.[1] And by virtue of my employment I take the liberty of suggesting to you that our client be advised to go a little slow in his paper anent this suit. Our conduct from this time should be steered to win, I think; and on this theory I am sure we can dispense with any appearance of bravado in any publications which can be construed as proof of malice. A lawsuit, like a gun, is a dangerous thing 'without lock, stock, or barrel.'

To SHERMAN S. ROGERS

Buffalo, *May* 10, 1882

It's kind of a ridiculous thing for me to do, but I have just returned from the cornerstone-laying, pretty hot and uncomfortable; and I want to say to you right here — hot as I am — that your address was the best thing I have ever heard of the kind, and I want to thank you for it.

To EDGAR K. APGAR[2]

Buffalo, *August* 29, 1882

Your letter of the 23d is received, and was read with much satisfaction. I am gratified with the interest you take in my candidacy, and I think not the less impressed with the sentiments contained in your letter, so much in accord with my own, touching the Democratic cause generally, and the condition of our party's affairs.

You are quite right in believing that I am not actively seeking the nomination for governor. The efforts of my friends and neighbors in that direction were begun in my absence from the city; and the unanimity and heartiness of the demonstration have been extremely pleasant. I know that neither my acquaintance in political circles, nor my standing in the State Democracy, would for a moment suggest my name as a proper one to head the ticket in the coming campaign. And if it were not for my abiding faith in the success of an honest effort to perform public duty, I

[1] J. N. Matthews, editor of the Buffalo *Express*, had provoked a libel suit.

[2] Edgar K. Apgar, a brilliant young lawyer and politician who became deputy secretary of state and deputy treasurer, was the first prominent man in Albany to support Cleveland for the gubernatorial nomination.

should at times distrust my ability to properly bear the responsibilities of the place in case of election.

I am entirely certain that if there is anything of my candidacy, it rests upon the fact that my location, and an entire freedom from the influence of all and any kind of factional disturbances, might make me an available candidate. If my name is presented to the convention, I should think it would be presented upon that theory. And I am sure, if I were nominated, and could be the instrument of bringing about the united action of the party at the polls, I should feel that I had been of great value to the people and to the party.

When an interview with Mr. Manning[1] was first suggested some time ago, my impulse was at once to find my way to him by way of showing my respect for his position in the party, and the regard I have learned to entertain for him as a gentleman. Upon reflection, however, it has occurred to me that if we meet by appointment, it will of course be known that we have been together, and it will not the less surely be falsely *alleged*, that an understanding has been arrived at between us, and pledges made which make me his man.

Would not this lying interpretation be used in answer to the claim that I am free from any alliances? Might not the friends of other candidates claim, that one who was proclaimed as a free candidate, and yet had an understanding with Mr. Manning, or his friends, ought not to be nominated? What would be the effect of such an appeal on the convention, or afterward on the election?

There ought not, of course, to be any foundation for apprehensions of this kind; but I cannot rid myself of these reflections. I ask you then, as one who has kindly said that he favors my nomination, whether it is not more likely to occur, and whether, if it does, the chances of our election will not be better, if this visit is not made as you suggest.

May I not in this way avoid even the appearance of being anything except what I really am; and may I not thus absolutely preclude the pretence that I am not a sound, plain, uncomplaining Democrat, and an absolutely free man?

[1] Daniel Manning (1831–87), who had been in control of the influential Albany *Argus* since 1873, and was long one of Tilden's political lieutenants, was Democratic State Chairman 1881–84.

To WILSON S. BISSELL [1]

Buffalo, *September* 19, 1882
One o'clock A.M.

John B. Manning has been in to see me tonight and has much to say about treachery, etc. I listened to all.

He talks Congressman-at-large. I still listened.

Now do just as I tell you without asking any questions.

When Dan and Scheu [2] get there, have them go the first thing to Daniel Manning and urge with the *utmost vehemence* my nomination.

Never mind what he says — have them pound away.

I am quite sure he thinks these two good friends are cool and jealous and don't want to see me nominated. And I am sure he has in his head the idea of Congressman-at-large and I think it is based upon what he thinks as to the real feelings of some of my friends — or that we think are friends.

Of course I know how it is, but I want Manning to be convinced that he is wrong in his premises.

I heard the same old song — if I had come to see him my nomination would have been assured, etc., Flower has much money, etc.

I think that if Dan and Scheu would go separately to see Daniel Manning they could soon convince him he was reckoning without his host.

You may be sure the thought is that I will not get governor, but the western part of the State may be placated by Congressman-at-large.

To WILLIAM N. CLEVELAND

Buffalo, *November* 7, 1882

I have just voted. I sit here in the mayor's office alone, with the exception of an artist from *Frank Leslie's Newspaper*, who is sketching the office. If Mother were here I should be writing to her, and I feel as if it were time to write to someone who will believe what I write. I have been for some time in the atmosphere of certain success, so that I have been sure that I should assume the duties of the high office for which I have been named. I have tried hard in the light of this fact to properly

---

[1] Wilson Shannon Bissell (1847–1903) was Cleveland's law-partner and at this time his closest friend. At the time this letter was written he was attending the Democratic State Convention at Syracuse in an effort to promote Cleveland's nomination as governor.

[2] Daniel N. Lockwood (1844–1906), a Democratic attorney in Buffalo who had nominated Cleveland for mayor, and Solomon Scheu, an ex-mayor of the city, were promoting Cleveland's candidacy.

appreciate the responsibilities that will rest upon me, and they are much too much to be underestimated. But the thought that has troubled me is, can I well perform my duties, and in such a manner as to do some good to the people of the State? I know there is room for it, and I know that I am honest and sincere in that desire to do well, but the question is whether I know enough to accomplish what I desire.

The social life which seems to await me has also been a subject of much anxious thought. I have a notion that I can regulate that very much as I desire, and, if I can, I shall spend very little in the purely ornamental part of the office. In point of fact, I will tell you, first of all others, the policy I intend to adopt, and that is to make the matter a business engagement between the people of the State and myself, in which the obligation on my side is to perform the duties assigned to me with an eye single to the interests of my employers. I shall have no idea of re-election or any higher political preferment in my head, but be very thankful and happy if I can well serve one term as the people's governor. Do you know that if Mother were alive [1] I should feel so much safer? I have always thought her prayers had much to do with my success. I shall expect you to help me in that way.

To DANIEL LAMONT

Buffalo, *December 26,* 1882

I have received today the copies of the inaugural speeches, and shall try to construct mine between this and next Monday.

The message is in the hands of my stenographer to be copied. It will be done on a printing machine, which I think may facilitate the setting it up. It will be finished tomorrow.

The stenographer which I have employed, I believe intends to start for Albany Thursday night. If I am right in this, he will bring the message to you. The colored servant will also start Thursday night, and report to Colonel Farnsworth [2] Friday morning.

I hope I shall employ a pardon clerk tomorrow morning. If the one goes that I hope to secure, we shall have a good one. I shall try to have him go down early so that he will take his place January 1st. I will send you a dispatch tomorrow in which I will call him 'the gentleman.'

The young man that has been helping me is to go down too. I shall

[1] Cleveland's mother had died July 19, 1882.
[2] John G. Farnsworth was adjutant-general of the State.

need him for a while at least, and if he will do, we can make a messenger of him. If not we will do something else with him, or send him back. The young man Apgar spoke of will go in as one of the executive clerks. He might be breaking in.

I believe you think it best to retain one of the present clerks for a while. If you adhere to that opinion, we will keep the one which you think would be most useful. If not I can bring down the young man in my office of whom I spoke.

Gov. Cornell [1] is to meet Colonel Farnsworth Friday at 12 o'clock to surrender up the house.

I now expect to start Saturday morning at eight o'clock. I think I arrive at Albany about 4:30 P.M. and should like to have you meet me. Let me hear from you.

To SHERMAN S. ROGERS

Albany, *January* 6, 1883

I return to you the letter of Mr. Frederic; [2] and I assure you that its perusal has been a comfort to me for two reasons. 1st, Because of its own good spirit and friendship. 2d, Because it develops the fact that you sort of came to the rescue of your old pupil and townsman.

Brown makes me thus far a first-rate clerk. I think in point of fact that my establishment is pretty well officered all around.

Thus far I think I have succeeded pretty well. Next week I expect to send in some nominations and then I suppose things will be cut loose again.

I sometimes think the people of this State act like '*a passel* of boys.'

I shall be glad to hear from you at any time.

To SUPERINTENDENT BAKER *of the New York Prisons*

Albany, *February* 2, 1883

I deem it proper to call your attention to the provision of section 108 of the Laws of 1847, which prohibits the infliction of blows upon any convict in the State prisons or by the keepers thereof, except in self-defence or to suppress a revolt or insurrection; and also to chapter 869 of the Laws of 1869, abolishing the punishments commonly known as the 'shower bath,' 'crucifixion yoke,' and 'buck.' I suppose these latter

---

[1] Alonzo B. Cornell (1832–1904), son of Ezra Cornell, was governor of New York 1880–82 inclusive.

[2] Harold Frederic (1856–98), later noted as a novelist, was editor of the Albany *Evening Journal*.

forms of punishment were devised to take the place of the blows prohibited by the law of 1847. Both of the statutes above referred to seem to be still in force and in my opinion they are in no manner affected by the constitutional amendment giving the Superintendent 'the superintendence, management and control of the prisons,' or by sections 1 and 5 of chapter 1,079 of the Laws of 1877, providing that the Superintendent shall have the management and control of the prison and of all convicts therein... and that he shall make such rules and regulations for the government and punishment of the convicts as he may deem proper.

I respectfully desire to avoid any injurious interference with the maintenance by prison authorities of efficient discipline, but I insist that, in the treatment of prisoners convicted of crime, the existing statutes of the State on that subject should be observed.

To THE REVEREND CHARLES WOOD [1]

Albany, *March* 21, 1883

I was much gratified to learn that you had called to tender your congratulations on my forty-sixth birthday. It was thoughtful and kind and I am exceedingly sorry that I did not see you. It seems to me that such things are more grateful than ever, now that I am so surrounded by influences not always akin to the best sensibilities.

I took my card home Sunday so that I might consider what I ought to do annually to meet the objects spoken of in the sermon. I enclose it signed. I want to pay the amount quarterly with my pew rent. The two will make $35 every three months, which is easy to remember.

I probably shall not be in the city next Sunday and so trouble you with it.

To THE REVEREND CHARLES WOOD

Albany, *April* 14, 1883

I have had an unexpected arrival in the person of my old partner and friend, whom I call the Assistant Governor.[2] He has but a few hours here. I want to see all I can of him, not perhaps so much to visit, as to consult with him in relation to official matters. This long preface tells the story, and presents the reason why, with much regret, I ask to be excused from lunching with you today as proposed.

[1] Minister of the Fourth Presbyterian Church in Albany, and a former Buffalonian.
[2] Wilson S. Bissell, whose advice Cleveland greatly prized.

To MRS. FRED H. MARTIN

Albany, *April* 14, 1883

I have today received a card, from which I learn that I have a new namesake. I am very much flattered by this token of esteem, and trust that Grover Henry Martin's name may in the future be connected with a pure life and useful career. I hope above all things that he will be a joy and comfort to his mother, and at all times regard her as his best earthly friend.

I shall feel it more important than ever to behave myself in such a way as not to cast discredit on his name.

To WILSON S. BISSELL

Albany, *April* 22, 1883

I have just received the enclosed letter from Robbins [1] which I know you will be glad to read. I was glad to hear from you yesterday. I am quite sure that the appointment of Mike amounts to drawing the other half of a 'twenty.' George made his appearance and called to say to me that he was disappointed at the salary offered him and asked me if I thought there would be a chance for promotion. I told him what I thought and like the Wayne County delegation I have not seen him since.

I received by telegraph this morning an invitation from Whitelaw Reid asking me to dine at his home with ex-President Hayes next Thursday. I don't see how I can go, as I hope that the legislature will adjourn Friday or Saturday.

I will tell you as the deadest secret in the world, that for the last few days I have felt the effects of long hours, steady work, and worse than all, incessant pester about offices. I honestly think I can't stand it more than two weeks longer. My head a good deal of the time don't feel right, and when a man begins to talk about office I begin to get irritable and my head begins to ache.

Lamont acts and looks as if he needed rest too.

I shall enter upon this next week with apprehension that I may make a mistake before it closes. Remember me to Charley [2] and other friends.

P.S. I enclose check for $100.45 to pay my life insurance as per notice enclosed.

[1] Mort Robbins had been a clerk in Cleveland's law-office.
[2] Charles W. Goodyear, one of Cleveland's closest friends in Buffalo.

To SHERMAN S. ROGERS

Albany, *May* 20, 1883

I have just read with pleasure your letter. I am exceedingly glad to be able to state that the plan proposed by you in the matter of filling the vacancy in the Civil Service Commission is the one I am determined to pursue. I am waiting now to hear the views of the very class of men to which you refer. Richmond [1] knows all about it and set the machinery in motion.

I must not fail to give expression to the satisfaction I feel upon the approval of such friends as you have always been of my course thus far. I sometimes feel that the fight for the good against the bad is a discouraging contest with odds on the wrong side; this is where it seems to me that the people and the press are unwilling to give aid and encouragement. But I straightway become ashamed of my unbelief when I receive a word of acknowledgment and appreciation from men who *I know* are right.

I look for better things. I am where I *must* and *have* and *shall* feel the strain and wrenching of the change. I hope I shall hold fast. I believe I shall. It is exceedingly unfortunate that those who in public place battle with the jobbing and dishonesty confronting them must constantly feel that malice, uncharitableness, and misrepresentation are treacherously fighting them in the rear.

I don't know but this is a foolish letter; but it is written.

To DANIEL S. LAMONT [2]

Buffalo, *June* 24, 1883

I received the letters last night. Two of them have reference to appointments and I therefore return them. I am having a very good time and have already a very respectable burn on my neck and face. I think by the time I return to the shop I shall beat your nose to death.

I don't hardly think a letter for Rich would reach him before he left and I guess I won't write one.

I want to stay here all the week if I can. I don't want as long a furlough as the girl said that Pierson had, but I think if I bring up at Albany next Sunday morning that ought to do. If, however, there is anything

---

[1] Cleveland this spring appointed John Jay, Augustus Schoonmaker, and Harry Richmond as State Civil Service Commissioners under a newly passed law.

[2] Daniel S. Lamont (1851–1905), formerly a member of the Albany *Argus* staff and secretary of the Democratic State Committee, had become Cleveland's private secretary.

which requires my presence there before that time, let me know. I am very much pleased with what you write me about Hill and the Capitol matters. Let me hear from you.

To DANIEL S. LAMONT

Buffalo, *June* 26, 1883

You will see by the enclosed that I am doing business here and don't propose to entirely neglect executive duties. There is so much danger of the department running short of applications for fish and game protection and applications for pardon that I send additional papers on these subjects. I wish you would tell me how long I can stay here. I have much to do yet in the way of fishing, etc., and a great many fish are waiting for me.

P.S. Webster has just come in and says you were considerably 'under the weather' Saturday. Don't fail to let me know by telegraph if I am needed.

To DANIEL S. LAMONT

Albany, *July* 15, 1883

I leave this with you. It is as I think I shall 'get it off.' If you think it won't do at all, *telegraph me to kill it.* If you approve it, and think it is best, it may be handed to the *Argus* for publication Tuesday morning, unless something to the contrary is heard from me.

I have told Colonel Rice [1] to speak to you about publishing the game protection districts and such other information in regard to that business as will be calculated to explain the situation to applicants and at the same time I hope may discourage many of them. Put in about their being under the control of the Commission and that it must approve their conduct and accounts and make regulations for their guidance.

To DANIEL S. LAMONT

Holland Patent, *August* 17, 1883

I have just received the last grist of papers and enclose them herewith all signed. . . . I have no doubt that you have selected the best man, but I wish you would hold the [Fish and Game] Commission in its present shape and not put the appointment on the blotter till you hear from me by telegraph or letter.

[1] Colonel William Gorham Rice (1856–   ) was secretary first to Governor Cleveland and then to Governor Hill (1883–89).

In the Brooklyn matter I don't want to be boyish and personal and will not set myself up against the other good friends there. But I don't want them to run their legs off to make the *nomination referred to* to please me. In this as in all other political matters anything personal to me should be absolutely secondary except so far as it affects the party good.

I think something is going on. Dan Lockwood was at Saratoga a week ago last Saturday. George C. Gunn expected to be there but was not, and you know Parcher was there.

Maxwell's fear is, I am sure, a creature of his imagination and anxiety. I have always said that Maxwell had made a good and faithful officer and have, in that way, favored his renomination, and I don't think anyone has said to the contrary.

I should like to have you see the Brooklyn man and tell him just how I feel. I will write you again soon.

To DANIEL S. LAMONT

Forestport, *August* 20, 1883

I have just received the commutation sheets and signed them. They are returned herewith. I received at the same time a letter, a copy of which I enclose, accusing me of stealing bait. I think this is pretty mean treatment to begin with and suspect that this is a pretty tough country. At this rate, I am liable to be accused of rape before I get back. . . .

I went to church three times yesterday and had big audiences on all occasions. It's raining quite hard now, but I don't think it makes any difference, because I have a rubber overcoat for just such things.

I understand arrangements have been made for me to kill a deer (this game is spelled differently from that I am accustomed to), and the only difficulty I now have is to fix upon the kind of a story to be agreed upon as to the size of the deer and the weight and number of the trout. Two things *must* be done, to wit: the Republican party must go, and Arthur [1] must be beaten as a fisherman. You may be sure I feel deeply the responsibility of my share in this work. . . .

I hope to hear from you again soon. You may if you think best make an item of the bait-stealing business. It may not be best and don't do it if this is your idea. In any event omit names. With regards to Manning and Apgar.

[1] President Chester A. Arthur.

To DANIEL S. LAMONT

Camp Corlies, *September* 3, 1883

I send by the mail which takes this the Civil Service classification with my approval and adoption endorsed thereon; also the papers in the Kaler requisition case with an endorsement declining to issue a mandate. In connection with this matter I send a slip cut from a newspaper, which I want Brown to keep with the rest of the papers. I have not been away from here at all and shall start for civilization tomorrow morning and expect to land in Buffalo Thursday morning. Friday or Saturday morning I shall be in Albany unless you hear further from me in the meantime. I am a good deal concerned about the political situation but don't know what to say about it. I am not anxious to be beaten and cuffed about too much, and yet I want to subordinate all things except honor and consistency to the good of the party if rightly guided.

I am in disgrace, with myself at least, just at present. I had a beautiful shot at a deer Saturday and *missed him*. We are now preparing to start again for my last chance.

To WILSON S. BISSELL

Albany, *October* 7, 1883

Your letter containing a check for $1000 is just received and it with the newspaper accompanying the same was most pleasantly gobbled up. I am very firm in the conviction that the Buffalo & Southwestern Railroad is the best in the world and that its management, past and present, is entitled to entire confidence.

I have just written a long letter to Dick Fassett in which I explained the reason of my inability to attend the Engineers' Convention on the 17th to be the necessity of my being at Newburgh on the 18th. Things of this description are pouring in thick and fast just at present, and of course the most of them have to be declined.

My foot got no better very fast after you left and I did not go out of the house till half-past one o'clock Thursday morning when I rode to the train. But I was not bothered at all during my absence and regard myself all right now. I had a great time up North and am very glad I went. After everything else was over at Ogdensburg, Metcalf pulled me into the dining-room of the hotel, where about 75 or 100 had a sort of a lunch and lots of fun. He is a regular lunatic. At Watertown there was a big crowd awaiting my arrival and the business places were all decked with flags and bunting. I am sorry to say, however, that the thing was managed just exactly in the wrong way, in my judgment. I was driven at once to the home of Mr. Lansing, a very nice man, and kept in the custody of a few men all day. An attempt was made to have a reception there and of course the hard-fisted Democrats would not attend. When I got to the depot to leave, there were a lot of people there, and till the train started I held a reception that I liked better than all the rest of the performance.

Tom Brown and Dan Lockwood came here night before last and stayed over yesterday to see me. Tom brought Dan for the express purpose of making things up. He said that they had all felt badly about the position of affairs between Dan and me and especially *his father*, who insisted upon the visit. They went to lunch with me and to dinner too, and after dinner Dan and I played a game of billiards. I enjoyed the visit very much. I said some things to Tom which I hope he will repeat to his brother-in-law, but Dan and I proceeded as if nothing had happened. I told him about the vacancies upon the staff and asked him to find out if Schenck still wanted a position. He asked me to come and see him when I came to Buffalo and I asked him to make my house his home when he next came to Albany. He seems to think it quite likely that Bob will consent to run for the Senate when the time comes. I should be pleased to have him, for I am sure he would be a better senator next winter than he was last.

You know your own business best, but sometimes I think it would be a good idea for you and Charley to let the rest do the talking this fall as far as local affairs are concerned except so far as good hearty help in general principles is concerned. These people will all be coming out of the trees to you in State matters, I think.

The course of the *Courier* is, I think, simply damnable and it is the theme of much comment. If Erie County lags this fall, the proprietor will not be allowed to escape the responsibility. I have a strong inclination to write McCune [1] a letter with a little United States language in it.

I hope you and Charley will try to run up against Dan. We can afford to be magnanimous.

I want to go to Buffalo dreadfully. You needn't laugh. I am not thinking about what you are. Yesterday I was absolutely homesick to get there. I think I'll go up next Friday or Saturday.

[1] Charles W. McCune, editor of the Buffalo *Courier*, a Democratic newspaper, was one of the men who had induced Cleveland to run for mayor. He was a member of the Democratic State Committee.

I am thinking some of inviting the Democrats who will be here next Friday for consultation to my house in the evening to a kind of reception. They will include, I suppose, the editors of our papers, chairmen of the county committees, and some others of the faithful. Perhaps if the reception is given, a serenade will be shot off at me in the midst of it when I will have a chance to give my ideas on the 'incongruities of the opaque humors.' If you are lucky enough to get an invitation you had better come. I wish Colonel Doyle [1] would come too.

I think I'll write to Lang. I am sorry I cannot write you a longer letter, but I have not in mind any other important facts to communicate. Give love to Charley [Goodyear] and George [Sicard].

To Mrs. John V. L. Pruyn

Albany, *October* 16, 1883

I am really and truly very sorry that I cannot accept your kind invitation to dinner today. I rode all night, slept but little, feel very stupid, and, which is as bad or worse than all, have an official engagement, which must be kept.

To Daniel Manning

Albany, *October* 17, 1883

I desire to contribute the enclosed ($500), towards the payment of the necessary and legitimate expenses of the pending State campaign.

To Wilson S. Bissell

Albany, *October* 19, 1883

Your letter was received this morning. I read it mostly to Lamont. Dan Manning says I understand that he don't care how soon that brother of his gets 'knocked out.' . . .

I think the *Courier* has been a trifle better for the last two or three days. I haven't even any doubt as to who will be the candidate for mayor.

The reports we get here for the State are good — though someone has told here that Scheu said in Rochester that all the saloonkeepers in Buffalo are going against Maynard. I said I didn't think Scheu said such a thing. I wish you'd ask Charley Miller if my name is registered. Can't you see my friend McLeod and touch him up a little on the whiskey and Catholic questions?

[1] Peter C. Doyle was chairman of the Democratic County Committee in Buffalo.

To JOHN KELLY [1]

Albany, *October* 20, 1883

It is not without hesitation that I write this. I have determined to do so, however, because I see no reason why I should not be entirely frank with you. I am anxious that Mr. Grady should not be returned to the next Senate. I do not wish to conceal the fact that my personal comfort and satisfaction are involved in the matter. But I know that good legislation, based upon a pure desire to promote the interests of the people, and the improvement of legislative methods, are also deeply involved. I forbear to write in detail of the other considerations having relation to the welfare of the party and the approval to be secured by a change for the better in the character of its representatives. These things will occur to you without suggestion from me.

To ALFRED C. CHAPIN [2]

Albany, *December* 18, 1883

Thanks for your letter and the kind interest thereby evinced.

I have thought entirely different. My idea has been to deal lately with the practical things relating to State affairs and in which my people are interested. The fact is, I am growing to be a kind of crank on all that pertains to this commonwealth and the citizens of New York. I will confess that I want to be a good governor. I haven't the material, I think, to do more for the people, the party, or myself than I can do in that rôle.

However, I have considered the topics of your letter and should be glad to hear further from you. You will see Mr. Manning and I hope you will talk with him on the subject. We have expected to see you here long before this.

To WILSON S. BISSELL

Albany, *December* 27, 1883

I arrived safely at six-thirty and have been here in the office since eight. O Boy! What a nice dressing-gown I found here! It fits like paper on the wall.

William [3] had my room all trimmed up so that it looked beautifully.

I send the statement you spoke of. Henry Richmond has just come in.

[1] John Kelly (1822–86), was leader of Tammany Hall from the downfall of Tweed in 1871 to his death, when he was succeeded by Richard Croker.

[2] Alfred Clark Chapin (1848–   ), at this time Speaker of the Assembly, later mayor of Brooklyn and member of Congress, 1891–92.

[3] William Sinclair, Cleveland's mulatto house steward in Albany and Washington.

To WILSON S. BISSELL

Albany, *December* 31, 1883

I cannot resist the temptation to write you tonight and congratulate you upon another birthday; and like Blind Tom, I congratulate myself upon the close of my first year of gubernatorial life — and a close, I'll say to you and myself, which brings no disgrace or regret. My dear fellow, I feel the utmost kindness to all men and the rest of mankind and especially do I feel most affectionately toward you, my best friend. The messages have gone by mail and all is ready for tomorrow. Most all of my staff will be here and dine with me in the afternoon. I'll receive here from twelve to two. I wish you were to be here. Apgar and Lamont are both here and desire me to congratulate you on your birthday, and for them to wish you a Happy New Year. Apgar says he thought you would certainly be here to see the close of the first year as you saw the beginning.

Things are beginning to assume a serious shape politically. They say that Hewitt [1] is Kelly's candidate and that I am the man to hold the delegation against him and if I don't run to direct the vote somewhere else. It makes me feel uncomfortable, but if I am necessary to prevent a wrong drift there is but one thing to do. You know how strictly this is between us. With love to Charley and George.

P.S. I want you to read the message and tell me what you think of it.

To WILSON S. BISSELL

Albany, *January* 8, 1884

Yours received. I should have said the tax was paid at first sight; but I guess it is not. If you will pay it you may take it out of my *corn-crib* or I will pay you when I sell my dog. I opened the Bar Association meeting this morning and Milburn is now (half-past three P.M.) I suppose, delivering his oration. I mean to get Apgar and Chapin over to dine with him. I wish you were here....

To WILSON S. BISSELL

Albany, *February* 11, 1884

It is almost twelve o'clock and I have closed business for the day. My appointees for Convict Labor Commissioners were confirmed tonight on the spot, and you will probably see my little message to the Senate before

[1] Abram S. Hewitt of New York City (1822–1903), the eminent iron manufacturer and Congressman, now chief leader of the County Democracy.

you read this. If you do not I want you to look it up. I think it is pretty good when all the facts are known, but of course they will not be by any of the New York papers except the *Herald*, and so I expect to be pretty thoroughly pitched into and called imprudent, presuming, sensational, oversensitive, undignified, etc. But the *Herald* ought to have it right.

I am settled down to the old gait again and feel first-rate. I enjoyed your visit very much, and my only grief now is William has been making me eat the remains of the reception. I've worked like the devil and am told that my redemption is near. I've written everything but that which I started to write, which is that I understand that you are to tender one of the review tickets to George Hayward. 'Be I right?'. . .

To CHARLES S. FAIRCHILD [1]

Albany, *March* 17, 1884

I have delayed expressing my gratification which the receipt of your letter gave me much longer than I expected to, but I hope this will not be cause for a suspicion that I am at all indifferent to the friendly interest which you exhibit in my welfare personally and politically.

It is absolutely true that I have always regarded any suggestion of my candidacy for a place higher than that I now occupy as a serious mistake on any ground except merely personal ones; and on such latter grounds as *entirely inadmissible*. I should long ago have made such declarations in public as I have privately, had I not been restrained by good friends who seemed to think my silence on the subject had better be longer maintained. I know I am right on this subject and will not yield my convictions to any amount of superior political wisdom which may be brought to bear against my position. I don't want to appear to assume that I may be nominated — but I think such a complexion need not be given to my acts or declarations. I should not feel, perhaps, that I ought to refuse to do what the sentiment of my party shall require of me — but I believe there is no such sentiment that will embarrass me; and if there is it can be guided in the proper direction and enlightened.

I have but one ambition and that is to make a good governor and do something for the people of the State, and by such means to benefit the party to which I belong. I feel now that I shall desire to retire from public life at the close of my present term; and, making any allowance for a

---

[1] A lawyer and financier of New York City (1842–1924), who had helped Tilden prosecute the canal ring and served as attorney-general of the State, and was a close friend of Manning.

change in sentiment, it is absolutely certain that an endorsement by the offer of a second term will satisfy any wish I can possibly entertain, at all related to political life. You see I tell you frankly not only what I don't want but what possibly I may want. My expectation is firm that I shall be able to somewhat prepare the way for better things, and that then I shall be relieved as one who has performed his purpose in political affairs. With this I shall be content.

I haven't received a letter in many a day that pleased me as much as yours.

I shall sign the Roosevelt Bill [1] today and file with it a memorandum of my reasons for so doing. If they are published I wish you would read them and give me your opinion about them. I want to see the good Democrats in New York in accord with the new scheme so that they shall not be entirely left. I suppose in the next contest for mayor the Tammany men and the bad Republicans will be together and that there will be a movement on the part of the citizens. I believe the latter will be so strong that I should be glad to see the decent Democrats in such an attitude to them that they may get some credit and advantages from their success if they succeed. If the bad element, through divided counsels among the good, succeed in electing a mayor, God help us all.

I should be very glad to see or hear from you at any time.

To MARY CLEVELAND HOYT

Albany, *March* 23, 1884

Your letter was received and I was much pleased to have my birthday so pleasantly remembered by you. I had a letter from Louise too, which with yours made me feel that the event was not forgotten by the family.

I somewhat expected Lizzie and Miss Nelson here today, but the visit is postponed until next Wednesday. I shall not stop your *Argus*. I want you to have it so that you can see what I am up to. I have had all sorts of nice things said of me and to me during the last week for signing the law called the Roosevelt bill in relation to the government of the city of New York. Congratulatory letters and dispatches have been arriving by the score and most of the papers have been praising me for merely doing my duty. Still I do not object to it, for it is about the only satisfaction I derive from the office I hold.

[1] Theodore Roosevelt had carried through the legislature three bills reorganizing the governments of New York City and New York County; Cleveland signed all three.

I sometimes get a little worried about the Presidential question — that is, when it looks as if it might come my way. I wish I might not hear my name mentioned in connection with it again.

I am getting on splendidly at the Mansion. I congratulate myself every day on having such good help. I work hard but keep well in the main, though for the past week I have been just a little out of sorts. I shall be all right tomorrow morning, I think. The weather has been dreadful, and I don't see how anybody keeps well.

I haven't thought of my arrangements for the summer, but should be pleased to have you and the girls here as you and they were last summer.

Mrs. Lamont has had a hard time, but we have thought she was getting on nicely with a setback once in a while. Within the last few days, however, she has not done so well, and yesterday the Colonel took her to New York to see a physician who makes a specialty of such cases.

To COLONEL ROBERT TOWNSEND [1]

Albany, *March* 27, 1884

I received the oysters in due time and in splendid condition. . . . As the time for the adjournment of the legislature approaches and as I think of the comparative freedom from the perplexities of official life which summer brings, I find myself calculating upon all sorts of visiting and excursions; but last year's experience has so fully shown me the delusive character of such calculations and the speed with which the summer passes that I am determined not to make elaborate plans for the future.

To MARY CLEVELAND HOYT

Albany, *May* 7, 1884

I avail myself of a moment or two when I am not overwhelmed with people to write a note the length of which will depend upon the length of the period of such non-interruption.

I suppose you are beginning to think of moving eastward about these days, and I expect you and the nieces will make your home with me again this summer. Mrs. Eggleston has been changing the house a room at a time, but I think has now suspended operations till you can be consulted in regard to carpets, etc. I expect I need some new ones, and have thought best to wait until I can have your assistance in their selection. Aside from the purchase of carpets, I suppose I shall do little or nothing at this time

[1] An officer of the State militia resident in Oyster Bay, New York.

toward the renovation of the mansion. The lawn looks very nicely, and the clematis shows signs of life. Some people think that a little should be done in the way of interior decoration, but I like the present old-fashioned style unless it be the sides of the dining-room. I don't like that a bit.

Let me hear from you soon and tell me if you are coming and when. We have a new girl who does the laundry work and helps Mrs. Eggleston upstairs. I guess she is pretty good, but think she is not quite up to attending to the door well.

I am very busy and perplexed, and begin to wish for the adjournment of the legislature. I think of no plans for the summer, and feel a good deal of the time as if I did not care to leave Albany at all. With love to the boys....

To WILSON S. BISSELL

Albany, *May* 8, 1884

Superintendent Payne of the Bank Department is here now talking about bank examiners. If there is a good man among our friends I think he can get the place. The salary would be $1800 or thereabouts, and the most important prerequisite is that he should be a good accountant. The rest will be easily learned. Would it not be well to see Sweet or Martin or some of our bank men with a view of furnishing such a man? . . .

To MRS. JOHN V. L. PRUYN

Albany, *May* 13, 1884

Your very kind invitation to dine this evening is just received, and I am very sorry to be obliged to decline this time. I am in these last days of the legislature in a whirl of perplexity and confusion, with a flood of things that must be done today. I had my lunch brought to me and have directed my dinner to be also brought, and with this economy of time I am afraid the night will not be long enough to do all I have on hand. Need I say any more — except to assure you that 'it's fun to be governor'?

III

NOMINATED AND ELECTED

SAMUEL J. TILDEN, who had suffered a stroke of paralysis, made
it clear early in 1884 that he could not stand for the Presidency,
and the old Tilden organization, now headed by Daniel Manning
of New York, threw its strength behind Cleveland for the nomination. His principal rivals were Thomas F. Bayard and Allen G.
Thurman, but neither rallied many delegates. The enthusiasm of
the West and South had been awakened for Cleveland by his battle
with Tammany; when the Chicago Convention met, the opposition
of Kelly and Grady added to his strength, for as Edward S. Bragg
of Wisconsin said, men loved him for the enemies he had made; and
he was nominated on the second ballot. The campaign that followed was one of the most desperately waged in the history of
American politics. The nomination of James G. Blaine had been
the signal for a secession of reformers from the Republican party.
These 'Mugwumps,' under the leadership of Carl Schurz, George
W. Curtis, E. L. Godkin, Moorfield Storey, and others, were
instrumental in bringing to light a fresh series of the so-called
'Mulligan letters,' throwing a discreditable light upon Blaine's
railroad transactions while Speaker of the House. Supporters of
Blaine retaliated by attacks upon Cleveland's private life, and
declared that he was the father of an illegitimate child born in
Buffalo ten years earlier. The fact that the principal assailant of
Cleveland's private record was a Buffalo clergyman, and that
many of his townsmen proved willing to believe additional stories
that were utterly false, filled Cleveland with resentment and gave
him a lifelong distaste for the city. Under John Kelly Tammany
Hall made only a thin pretence of supporting Cleveland, its members dividing most of their strength between Ben Butler, the
Greenback candidate, and Blaine. As the campaign of almost un-
exampled bitterness and quite unprecedented scandal drew to its
close, it seemed almost certain that the covert opposition of Tammany would defeat the Democratic ticket in New York and hence
in the nation. A series of events in the last week, however, dra-
matically acted to Cleveland's advantage; the chief being the
memorable 'Rum, Romanism, and Rebellion' speech of the Reverend Samuel D. Burchard. Cleveland was elected with 219 electoral
votes to Blaine's 182. He retained the governorship of New York
until just after New Year's, and then set to work in earnest to

organize his Cabinet. Even before he went to Washington, events forced him to take a decided stand on the silver question, and he came out in favor of repeal of the existing Silver-Purchase Law.

To DANIEL S. LAMONT [1]

Albany, *June* 18, 1884

I wish a dispatch could be sent to Bissell asking him if he will come here and go to Buffalo with me. A dispatch just received from Doyle informs me that Scheu and Lockwood are elected delegates and that 'everything looks good.' I am considerably better today.

To DANIEL MANNING

Albany, *June* 30, 1884

I have determined to put in writing some of the ideas which I have heretofore, without reservation and in full reliance upon your friendship and good judgment, expressed to you in conversation.

I am entirely content to remain at the post of duty which has been assigned to me by the people of the State of New York. No one has a better appreciation of the greatness of the office of President of the United States, and of the supreme honor that attaches to the citizen holding the same. And the fact that my name is mentioned among those deemed worthy of the place is a source of the highest possible gratification, because I interpret it as an endorsement of my official course, and a manifestation of the greatest kindness and consideration on the part of my political friends.

And yet I have not a particle of ambition to be President of the United States. Every consideration which presents itself to me tends to the personal wish on my part that the wisdom of the Democratic party in the coming convention may lead to a result not involving my nomination for the Presidency. If, however, it should be otherwise and I should be selected as the nominee, my sense of duty to the people and my party would dictate my submission to the will of the convention.

But there is another subject which has frequently been a topic of conversation between us, upon which I desire here to particularly express myself. I should not, in any condition of affairs, or under any imaginable

---

[1] William Dorsheimer had written Cleveland from Washington on June 9 that 'The nomination of Blaine renews the interest in yourself'; 'there is much conversation here about you and Bayard'; 'No one else is in the people's minds.' Cleveland's friends were redoubling their efforts to win him the Presidential nomination.

pressure, deem it my duty to relinquish the trust which I hold for the people of my State, in order to assume the duties of the Vice-Presidency; and the nomination for that office, I could not accept under any consideration whatever.

To JOSEPH L. HABERSTRO

Albany, *July* 14, 1884

I was very much pleased to receive your letter of congratulation of yesterday. It seems to me that nothing will gratify me more than to receive a good support at my home and from my German friends there. It is quite true that three years have brought great changes, and I think if anyone had talked about my being President when you were trying to get me to run for mayor we should have thought him crazy. I should be glad to receive any suggestions from you.

To DANIEL N. LOCKWOOD

Albany, *July* 15, 1884

I received your dispatch this morning and thank you for your courtesy. But I am decidedly of the opinion that this is the place for me to receive the notification, and I am afraid that my going to Buffalo to welcome the committee in the house of even as good a friend as you would be misinterpreted and be made the subject of comment. And then, too, I suppose the Buffalo people themselves might not be all pleased with the arrangement, since I see by the papers that Charles McCune is to offer me his house and General Rich has already done so. In this condition of affairs I think the best way to manage the matter is to have you with me here when the thing comes off; and in this I hope you will not disappoint me.

I want you to do another thing for me. Bowman and Whitney [1] were here this morning by their appointment to talk about Rochester affairs. They came to say that there were a number of good fellows and Democrats who in the fight between Raines and Purcell [2] got on to the anti-Raines side but who will not go with Purcell and are my friends.... I can't write all I want to say, but I wish you would go to Rochester, call on George Raines, and tell him you want for me to see the good fellows together, and then send for Bowman and talk it all up and see such others

---

[1] William C. Whitney (1841–1904), of New York City, a wealthy attorney, former corporation counsel, and one of the leaders of the County Democracy, helped direct Cleveland's campaign.

[2] George Raines and William Purcell, prominent in up-State politics.

as you think best. Let the matters between Purcell and me be as personal matters, but see if there is not something that can be done to get the Democrats who ought to pull together into line. Bowman talks first-rate, and I think and so does he that a visit from you managed in this way would do great good to the cause. If you are dead against all this thing let me know why.

To CARTER H. HARRISON

Albany, *July* 21, 1884

Your letter of the 18th is received and its contents will be duly considered. The opposition of the labor element is, I am sure, most unjust and rests upon no foundation so far as I know. This being the case, I expect it will not bear the test of investigation at all. We shall try to get the facts before the people by the distribution of information by documents and direct representations. There will be pamphlets printed in a few days on this and other subjects concerning which I have been grossly misrepresented, and I will take the liberty of sending some to you. I hope you will come this way and that I may see you soon.

To CHARLES W. GOODYEAR [1]

Albany, *July* 23, 1884 (telegram)

Whatever you do, tell the truth.

To DANIEL N. LOCKWOOD

Albany, *July* 31, 1884

How did you succeed or rather what did you do at Rochester? I was very much gratified upon the receipt of your dispatch yesterday. There were a good many good men here from all the States, and I am going to tell you (as a cool matter of information and with no vanity in it) that they were all — well! what shall I say? — more than satisfied.

I don't know but I am all 'out,' but I am going to be frank enough to say to you that it does not seem to me that things are getting into just the right shape at Buffalo. What is the matter with Rohr?

I learned last night that McCune had started the story and told it to

---

[1] The Buffalo *Telegraph* had just published in exaggerated form the story of Cleveland's supposed son, born in 1874 and named Oscar Folsom Cleveland. The friends of Cleveland in Buffalo were eager to take steps to check the flood of filthy misrepresentation which followed.

newspaper men (one at least) that I had nothing to do really with the subject of the *Telegraph* story — that is, that I am innocent — and that my silence was to shield my friend Oscar Folsom. Now is this man crazy or does he want to ruin anybody? Is he fool enough to suppose for a moment that if such was the truth (which it is not, so far as the motive for silence is concerned) that I would permit my dead friend's memory to suffer for my sake? And Mrs. Folsom and her daughter at my house at this very time!! I am afraid that I shall have occasion to pray to be delivered from my friends.

How often I wish that I was free and that some good friend of mine was running instead of myself.

I wish I knew what if anything is the matter. Can't you tell me frankly some things I want to hear?

This story of McCune's of course must be stopped. I have prevented its publication in one paper at least.

Let me hear from you.

To CHARLES W. McCUNE

Albany, *August* 4, 1884

I must not interfere with your business at all; but it is represented to me that I am held responsible to a very great extent and very injuriously for the trouble existing between you and the printers' union. Of course I know nothing of the merits of the controversy, but I wish it could be settled. Can you not yield a point to remove what I am told is the chief if not the only cause of complaint on the part of the workingmen of the State?

I wish you would come down and see me Wednesday of this week to talk the matter over. Telegraph me if you will come.

To DANIEL S. LAMONT

Plattsburg, *August* 8, 1884

We arrived last evening after a very pleasant trip and I have risen early in the morning according to custom. I am writing this before breakfast. I merely speak of these things to show you that 'though on pleasure I am bent,' I shall tinge the trip with a spice of industry and early rising.

But I sat down to merely write you that I have not seen Develin, as he was in bed when I went to the hotel. He says he will see me at Paul Smith's tomorrow (Saturday). Now I come to the point (at last). I want you to send copies of the letters we spoke of to him at 'Paul Smith's, St. Regis Lake,' and that is all there is about it — except to tell you to take good care of yourself and make things as easy for yourself as you can.

To DANIEL S. LAMONT

Upper Saranac Lake, New York, *August* 10, 1884

We arrived here this afternoon and have had our dinner. We dined yesterday at Loon Lake. When we drove up all the guests (about 150) were assembled on the verandah and we were taken in charge by a committee composed of Judge Comstock, Judge Andrew Montgomery Throop, and a Mr. Vanderhoff (I think). When we entered the dining-room all the guests had assembled and rose to receive us, etc. We went to Paul Smith's in the afternoon, arriving I guess about six o'clock. We were then taken in charge by another committee, composed of Mr. Hoguet, chairman, John Develin, and James Lynch, and conducted to the parlor, where an address of welcome was delivered by the chairman and responded to by the governor in his *usual* happy style. This morning we started for this place. It looks as though I should find the quiet here which I want, but which thus far is just exactly what I have not had. I hope that brass bands and such nonsense are over for a time.

I had a good talk with Develin and told him he would receive the letters and he said he would write a suitable reply. I like Lynch very much. Weed has been just as kind and attentive as he possibly could be. He and six young people from his home came to Paul Smith's with us.

I received last night the dispatch which I enclose. I suppose it was sent with some idea on the part of somebody to get me in some kind of a hole. If you think it is worth while to pay any attention to it you had perhaps better send a copy of the dispatch to somebody in New York and find out what there is of it. Of course keep the original, which I send.

I have just partially unpacked my trunk. From the appearance of the stationery supply, etc., which it contained, I imagine you must have thought I intended to establish the Executive Chamber here.

Take matters as easily as you can and don't pledge me to be back at any particular time. I don't want to feel that I cannot stay beyond two weeks if I desire.

To Daniel S. Lamont

Upper Saranac Lake, *August* 11, 1884

I return the order removing County Treasurer Sperry and the abstract of the evidence upon which I acted prepared by Newcomb.

I am having a good time and find this place very quiet and nice. Nevertheless, I worked on the letter till two o'clock this morning and was up at half-past six. I don't know whether I like it or not, but such as it is, I regard it as nearly complete. I told Develin and Weed pretty nearly what it would be and they both approved it. I think I may send it down pretty soon.

Now this is for you privately. I want to tell you just how I feel. I had rather be beaten in this race than to truckle to Butler [1] or Kelly. I don't want any pledge made for me that will violate my professions or betray and deceive the good people that believe in me. Of course I appreciate my relations to the party and the earnest desire on the part of many good men to win at almost any price. But I cannot forget that a stiff upper lip may be the best means of bringing about a united action nor that if such a thing is not accomplished the chance to win without the element that threatens trouble is only a forlorn one.

I don't like the suggestion of Orestes Cleveland to say in my letter that I am in favor of aggressive organization of labor, and I don't quite like the tone of Randall's letter. But we shall see what we shall see. In the meantime give my affectionate regards to Manning and tell him I am relying on him to keep me in the right shape. He knows well how I feel.

Take good care of yourself and look a little after the people at the mansion. I wrote you to send the Ireland letter to Develin, but it is just as well that it came to me, for some people are coming here tomorrow from Paul Smith's and I can send them to him when they return.

Tell me how things are going at the Chamber.

Remember me to Apgar.

To Daniel S. Lamont

Upper Saranac Lake, *August* 14, 1884

I send you with this the letter of acceptance which I have just finished (twelve o'clock). You will receive it, I expect, Saturday morning. The

---

[1] Benjamin F. Butler (1818–93), of Massachusetts, nominee of the Greenback and Anti-Monopoly parties for President and closely connected with Tammany, was making a campaign for the labor vote and cutting into Cleveland's strength.

subjects I have treated of I have tried to get in upon the theory that they are very clearly connected with the very framework of the government and that their treatment does not constitute a commentary on the platform.

I travelled seventeen miles and back today in a buckboard to show it as I finished it last night to Mr. Develin, and he and I altered it some, so that he fully approves it in its present shape.

I wish both Mr. Tilden and Mr. Hendricks[1] should be consulted about it or that it could be read to them. Can't Mr. Manning see them both Saturday?

I want the thing to suit those who are wiser than I, but I have given it quite a good deal of thought and sincerely hope that it will not be deemed necessary to change it. If, however, it is thought best to change the form of expression it may be done, but if the substance must be changed of course it must be submitted to me. If Mr. Hendricks is not seen and consulted about the letter and the time of its appearance, he must at all hazards be notified in advance of the time it will appear in the papers.

I want to have it off my hands as soon as possible. I hope Manning can take it Saturday or Sunday. Telegraph me something about it. If anyone wants to see me in regard to it I will, if necessary, meet the party at some convenient point. But Au Sable is, I think, more than forty miles from here — a stage-ride taking all day.

I send with this the papers I received tonight which I have executed. I cannot help saying again I hope the letter will answer. If it goes *don't forget to put in the date, which I have left a blank.*

I wonder where Hudson[2] is. I am glad you wrote as you did in regard to the Blaine scandal. I am very sorry it was printed and I hope it will die out at once.

To DANIEL S. LAMONT

Upper Saranac Lake, *August* 19, 1884

Your dispatch was received; and though I was much pleased to learn that the thing was considered good enough to ship in the shape it left my hands, I occasionally think that if I had it to do over again I might improve it.

[1] Thomas A. Hendricks (1819–85) of Indiana, Democratic nominee for Vice-President.

[2] William C. Hudson (1843–1915), Albany newspaperman, was active in Cleveland's campaign, and gives valuable glimpses of it in his *Random Recollections of an Old Political Reporter.*

I have just read Butler's address and think that it is very funny. It ought not to be dangerous, but in these days 'you can't most always tell.' I am glad that it is out this early so that it and its author can be well sifted.

I think unless you think I ought to be in Albany before that I will extend my vacation till the last of next week. What do you think? I am to get up at half-past five o'clock tomorrow morning and go a-fishing for big fish. Let me hear from you soon.

To WILSON S. BISSELL

Albany, *September* 11, 1884

I am determined to write you a little letter tonight anyway. I shall not make the usual display of copper plate probably, for I think I shook hands with at least 2500 people yesterday. And as for the matter of the letter, I hardly know what it will be, for I am always thinking that you know all that I can write and that anything I can put down has already come to you through the press. I returned last night after three days of heat and crowd and discomfort. I must not say that the trip was altogether uncomfortable, for there were many and I may say constant manifestations of kindness that were exceedingly pleasant, and I am thoroughly convinced that there are a number of people in the State that will vote our ticket.

I hope, now that the scandal business is about wound up, that you have a little freedom from the annoyance and trouble which it necessarily brought in its train. I think the matter was managed in the best possible way, and that the policy of not cringing was not only necessary but the only way. King's interview made me trouble. And now Cochran has published something just as bad in a Chicago paper. I don't see what possessed him to do it. I had a letter from Ambrose Butler of the *News* today asking me when I was to be in Buffalo. I answered him that the time was to be fixed by my friends there. Was that right?

I send you with this my check on Albany for $3500 and on Buffalo for $1500, making up my subscription to the National Committee, which I wish you would deposit to your account and then give your check to Locke,[1] if that is the thing to do, so that my mite may go with the rest to the National Committee. I want to help swell the amount sent from Erie County and yet I don't want the Committee to know that I contrib-

---

[1] Franklin D. Locke, Buffalo attorney and close friend of Cleveland.

uted that much. I will try to help the State Committee too, and do something for the people at home if possible. . . .

To JOSEPH PULITZER [1]

Albany, *September* 13, 1884 (telegram)

If your dispatch refers to the allegation that I have written letters to Congressmen to influence their action on tariff measures or legislation you may deny it in distinct terms on my authority.

To CHARLES W. GOODYEAR

Albany, *September* 14, 1884

Since you left me last night I have been thinking and much of the time feeling very blue and wishing that the Presidential nomination were in —— or on some other shoulders than mine. I am very clear that if I can go to Buffalo the parade should not be accompanied by any meeting. . . .

To COLONEL ROBERT TOWNSEND

Albany, *October* 4, 1884

Your delicious present or *presents* came to hand in due time and I have enjoyed them very much. . . . All the reports I receive concerning the canvass are encouraging and I think if we do all we ought we shall win. The chances are that I shall review the 1st and 2d divisions this month.

To WILLIAM F. VILAS [2]

Albany, *October* 4, 1884

Mr. Manning has shown me your letter to him of October 1 and I am much pleased with its contents. I have had no idea of making any answer or statement touching the matters referred to in your letter — at least until the condition of affairs is very much changed. An answer was given by the people of Buffalo two nights ago which I think is the best the subject admits of.

I desire to thank you for your words concerning my course in remaining at the post of duty. It will take great pressure to induce me to

---

[1] Joseph Pulitzer (1847–1911) had assumed in 1883 the ownership and management of the New York *World*.

[2] Vilas (1840–1908), was a Wisconsin Democrat of reform stamp, a leader of the Northwestern bar, and a noted orator, who had been chairman of the Democratic Convention in 1884.

change it. The reports I hear are much favorable to our cause. I shall be pleased to hear from you at any time.

To WILSON S. BISSELL

Albany, Sunday evening, *October* 5, 1884

We arrived here safely yesterday morning and I did a good day's work. All our party agreed that the trip had been a pleasant one and that the ovation was much beyond anticipations and in point of fact the largest thing they have ever seen. I was very much pleased that Corning thought so well of it. He said: 'O hell! Of course the procession could be gotten up with money, but a man don't decorate or illuminate his house unless he wants to.' The people here seem to be as much pleased at the success of the demonstration as I am and express themselves freely on the subject. I attended a very nice dinner party this evening and I was handsomely congratulated by some of the best people here.

The Catholic question is being treated and so well treated in so many different ways that I should not be at all surprised if what has been done by the enemy should turn out to my advantage.

And now that the Buffalo rumpus is over, I want to tell you how fully I appreciate all that you and Charley [1] have done to make it a success and how grateful I am to all my friends in Buffalo who had the management of the affair. There really were a number of ladies that wanted to go up and I heard considerably about it tonight. Mrs. Pruyn told me she was to have Lord Ross at her house this week and she wanted me to dine with him.

What I should like to do now above all other things is to go to Buffalo in my old way and be on the streets and see the people quietly. I wonder if I cannot spend a Sunday there before election. I think I could do the cause some good — don't you?

Remember me to Robbins and to Charley and tell them both how I appreciate their kindness. If you go to New York this week can't you stop off?

To WILSON S. BISSELL

Albany, *October* 9, 1884

We received today a copy of the Buffalo Catholic papers; and are bound to say that your efforts as a newspaper writer do you much credit.

---

[1] Bissell, Goodyear, and John G. Milburn had capably handled the Buffalo scandal in the campaign.

Lamont thinks that your order of 1000 copies will be abundant for all needs. But seriously, did you ever see such a thing in your life? I tell you they are not right and don't propose to be right.

I am impressed with the idea that there should be prepared a statement concerning the scandal derived from the sources which are available to us and have it all ready for publication in case the thing is published again enlarged and amended, which I think will be done just before election. I still hear that there is an intention to publish letters of a very dreadful kind written by me to the woman. If any such appear they will be forgeries and I propose to be ready for them.

I may want the letters I have and perhaps I will go to Buffalo Saturday afternoon or night and return Sunday night to get them. If such a statement is prepared who would be a good man to do it? I have thought of Willcox.[1] How would it do to send a stranger there? If I start so as to reach Buffalo at midnight I will telegraph, 'Documents will be there tonight.' If I start from here at 10:20 at night I will say, 'Documents will be there in the morning.' In either case I want to see you if I come, at my room at ten o'clock in the morning. Give my love to Charley and George.

To MRS. HENRY WARD BEECHER [2]

Albany. [No date; about *October* 20, 1884]

Your letter, as you may well suppose, has affected me deeply. What shall I say to one who writes so like my mother? I say so like my mother, but I do not altogether mean that, for she died in the belief that her son was true and noble, as she knew he was dutiful and kind. I am shocked and dumfounded by the clipping from the newspapers that you sent me, because it purports to give what a man actually knows, and not a mere report, as the other four or five lies do, which I have read or heard, about my life in Albany. I have never seen in Albany a woman whom I have had any reason to suspect was in any way bad. I don't know where any such woman lives in Albany. I have never been in any house in Albany except the Executive Mansion, the Executive Chamber, the Fort Orange Club House — twice at receptions given to me and on, I think, two other occasions — and the residences of perhaps fifteen or twenty of the best citizens, to dine.

[1] Ansley Willcox, a well-known Republican of Buffalo, who had joined with fifteen other Republicans of the city in a report exonerating Cleveland from the general charges against his character.

[2] This letter was read by Henry Ward Beecher before a large Brooklyn mass meeting on October 23, 1884.

Of course, I have been to church. There never was a man who has worked harder or more hours in a day. Almost all my time has been spent in the Executive Chamber, and I hardly think there have been twenty nights in the year and nine months I have lived in Albany — unless I was out of town — that I have left my work earlier than midnight to find my bed at the Mansion. I am at a loss to know how it is that such terrible, wicked, and utterly baseless lies can be invented. The contemptible creatures who coin and pass these things appear to think that the affair which I have not denied makes me defenceless against any and all slanderers.

As to my outward life in Buffalo, the manifestation of confidence and attachment which was tendered me there by all the citizens must be proof that I have not lived a disgraceful life in that city. And as to my life in Albany, all statements that tend to show that it has been other than laborious and perfectly correct are utterly and in every shape untrue. I do not wonder that your good husband is perplexed. I honestly think I desire his good opinion more than any aid he is disposed to render me. I do not want him to think any better of me than I deserve, nor to be deceived. Cannot I manage to see him and to tell him what I cannot write? I shall be in New York Wednesday and Thursday morning, I suppose, of next week. Thursday afternoon and evening I shall spend in Brooklyn. Having written this much it occurs to me that such a long letter to you is unnecessary and unexpected. It is the most I have ever written on the subject referred to, and I beg you to forgive me if your kind and touching letter has led me into impropriety.[1]

To GEORGE W. CURTIS [2]

Albany, *October* 24, 1884

While my letter of acceptance in that part devoted to civil service reform, has verbal reference to subordinates in public office, I am of the opinion that there are other officials of a non-political character, to whose retention in place, during the time for which they were appointed, the same considerations should apply.

---

[1] About the time Cleveland mailed this letter, Brooks Adams wrote him that 'the dignity and patience with which you have borne the most disgraceful attacks ever made, I believe, upon a candidate in America, have won my admiration,' and that in Quincy and Boston 'the same feeling prevails among most of the men I meet, Republicans or Democrats.'

[2] The editor of *Harper's Weekly*, who supported Cleveland, had been the principal defender of civil service principles in New York politics.

I am, of course, a Democrat attached to the principles of the party; and if elected, I desire to remain true to that organization. But I do not think partisan zeal should lead to the 'arbitrary dismissal for party or political reasons' of officials of the class above referred to, who have attended strictly to their public duty and have not engaged in party service, and who have not allowed themselves to be used as partisan instruments or made themselves obnoxious to the people they should serve, by the use of their offices to serve party ends.

To MR. GEORGE F. DEGE

Albany, *October* 24, 1884.

Your letter of the 23d, enclosing copy of a circular issued at Buffalo for distribution to the veteran soldiers of the State, is received, and I thank you for calling my attention to this new development of political mendacity. So far as this circular has any reference to me, it is in all respects calculated to deceive and in all prejudicial statements it is absolutely false.

I was drafted the first day the draft was put in operation. Being then assistant district attorney, I had plenty of opportunity to secure a convict substitute with no expense, and, in fact, was urged to do so. I refused, however, and hired a man to go who was a sailor on the lakes, and who had just arrived in port and been paid off. I don't know that he was ever arrested, and I am sure he was not a convict. I borrowed the money to pay him for going as my substitute, and I think before I paid him he had more money than I had. I often heard from him while he was in service, and I saw him quite frequently after he returned.

If he is alive yet, I don't think either of the noble veterans who signed this circular would care to meet him after he had read it.

I know Mr. Lyth and Mr. Oatman, whose names are appended to the circular, and I am astonished to find them in such business.

To WILSON S. BISSELL

Albany, *November* 13, 1884

I suppose I may now address you as the President-elect. We have just heard that eleven of the twenty-four districts in New York have been canvassed with no reduction in our majority.[1] These include that part

---

[1] Cleveland had a majority of less than 1200 votes in New York State, and the election was in doubt for a number of days.

of the city in which informalities and mistakes our friends think would be found if anywhere. So I should think the count might be concluded tomorrow or Monday at furthest.

As I look over the field I see some people lying dead whose demise will not harm the country, some whose wounds will perhaps serve to teach them that honesty and decency are worth preserving, and some whose valor, fidelity, and staunch devotion are rewarded with victory and who have grappled themselves to me with 'hooks of steel.' In this last array stand my true Buffalo friends. You don't, I am sure, want me to be invidious, but you must trust me to appreciate all that you have done. I am busy all day long receiving congratulations of friends in person, while through the mail and by telegraph they are counted by the thousand. It's quite amusing to see how profuse the professions are of some who stood aloof when most needed. I intend to cultivate the Christian virtue of charity toward all men except the dirty class that defiled themselves with filthy scandal and Ballism.[1] I don't believe God will ever forgive them and I am determined not to do so.

I look upon the four years next to come as a dreadful self-inflicted penance for the good of my country. I can see no pleasure in it and no satisfaction, only a hope that I may be of service to my people.

I had a very queer but very confidential letter from Crandall. Is there any chance of having a decent and ably conducted Democratic paper in Buffalo?

I ought to have some money. Is there anything among my traps that can be sold?

There are a good many things that I want to talk to you about and I think I must manage to go to Buffalo pretty soon if possible, and if that is not possible I must get you down here.

I think S. S. R.[2] has made a fool of himself — as usual. I don't believe he need worry himself about his senatorial chances. How I hate all this self-righteous hypocrisy!

This is not much of a letter, but I want to hear from you and perhaps it will do to accomplish that object. Give my love to Charley, Frank, J. G., and all the other good friends.

---

[1] The Reverend George H. Ball, D.D., of the Hudson Street Baptist Church in Buffalo, had taken the lead in disseminating false and scandalous reports concerning Cleveland.

[2] Sherman S. Rogers.

To WILSON S. BISSELL

Albany, *November* 23, 1884

I have just opened and read the enclosed letter from Bass,[1] which I know you will be glad to see. I hope you will return it to me, as I naturally value it very much. How delightful it is to find among all the common and usual congratulations one like this. I tell you what it is: 'it takes me back' to days of simple, honest, hearty friendship of which there are few bonds that reach me now.

Dorsheimer has been here with Congressman Herbert[2] of Alabama ever since noon and they have just left. I should have sent for you if I had been alone, but I did not think you and I could have had just the time we wanted under the circumstances. If I find I am to have no company and do not go to Buffalo next Sunday, I shall send you a dispatch to come here and shall expect you to put in an appearance. You will remember, I hope, that the President's invitation is an order and must be obeyed. I have learned that much already. Mrs. Hibbard was here yesterday morning before I was up and she and her son took breakfast with us. She came all the way down here to extract from me a promise that I would spend the time with them between my resignation and my leaving for Washington. Of course I did not promise anything of the kind. Did you ever see such work?

Bacon was here yesterday and I suppose is with you today. I told him to say to you not to pay another cent to the Committee. Lamont is going with me to Washington. All kinds of receptions, etc., are now being tendered to me. I don't know what to do about them. Hendricks was here yesterday and a number of the members of the National Committee and a delegation from the Chamber of Commerce who wanted to act as escort, etc. I don't know what in the world I will do with all these things. I shall resign the minute the legislature meets, which I think is January 6.

How much would it cost to start an evening Democratic paper in Buffalo? Something ought to be done, but I suppose the expense will stand in the way. It's pretty tough to start an Administration without a friendly paper of any size at home. Can't I come up next Saturday,

[1] Lyman K. Bass (1836–89), Cleveland's law partner and for four years (1873–77) Republican member of Congress from the Buffalo district, now resident in Colorado for his health.

[2] Hillary A. Herbert (1834–1919), Confederate veteran and later Secretary of the Navy in Cleveland's second administration. William Dorsheimer (1832–88), of a wealthy Buffalo family, had been Lieutenant-Governor 1875–80, and was now (1883–85), a member of Congress from New York City.

quietly arriving at midnight, and leave Sunday night? Let me hear from you.

To WILLIAM J. LEADER

Albany, *November* 27, 1884

Day before yesterday when I arrived here in the evening from the Executive Chamber I found in the house a fine Newfoundland dog; and yesterday I learned through your letter that the dog was intended as a gift from you. I hope you will not deem it affectation on my part when I write you that I am very averse to the receipt of gifts — especially in the relation of strangers which you and I sustain to each other.... The acceptance of presents of value which could involve an obligation, I should deem in my present position entirely inadmissible. And I confess I should feel better if all gifts of any description were discontinued.

I have determined to assure you most heartily of my full appreciation of your kindness in sending me the dog and that I do not at all distrust your motive in doing so; and while thanking you for the friendliness which prompted the gift I ask you to permit me to return the same.

I shall please myself and I hope not offend you, by sending the dog by express to your address tomorrow at my expense.

To WILSON S. BISSELL

Albany, *December* 5, 1884

Yours just received. I shall not come to Buffalo — just yet at all events. As I feel this moment I would never go there again if I could avoid it.

Elected President of the United States, I feel that I have no home *at my home*.

There are some things I want to do — some business matters I feel that I ought to attend to. I don't like to bother you with them. I honestly feel that I have taken so much of your time and labor I ought to take no more. I know that I have been and am a dreadful nuisance.

I want to make some financial arrangements. Perhaps it would be safe for me to arrive there some morning and leave at night.

I wish you'd try to put yourself in my place and imagine how all this thing seems to me.

Bayard[1] is coming here tomorrow night and will spend Sunday with me.

---

[1] Thomas F. Bayard (1828–98), Senator from Delaware, veteran Democratic leader, and shortly to be Secretary of State in the first Cabinet.

I am overwhelmed with all kinds of things and perplexed more than I can tell you; but nothing is so annoying to me as my thoughts connected with Buffalo.

I wish I could take all I have got and turn it into money. I'll write Henry Martin and if he will loan me five thousand dollars for three or six months perhaps I'll have to ask you to endorse my note.

You know how much I appreciate your kindness in offering me a stopping place at your house and how much I thank you for it.

To WILSON S. BISSELL

Albany, *December* 25, 1884

I mean to spend my holiday here at work, and I expect the most of that work will be writing letters. Of course you are the first on the list.

First. I wish you a very 'Merry Christmas' from the bottom of my heart.

Second. I want to confess to a tremendous amount of stupidity in that, both by word of mouth and by letter, I failed to make you understand that the trifle sent you at your house a short time ago, and which you are afraid will be moth-eaten, is your Christmas present. If I had the world I'd give you half of it at least. But as I have not much but anxiety and labor and perplexity, I propose to give you the least possible share.

I have accepted George Sawyer's invitation to dine with him the evening of the ball. This will oblige me to leave here the day before, I suppose.

You have doubtless heard all about the reception. I am very proud of my Buffalo friends and they have abundant reason to be gratified as I am at the very favorable impression they left upon the best people of Albany.

The plot thickens. I am sick at heart and perplexed in brain during the most of my waking hours. I almost think that the professions of most of my pretended friends are but the means they employ to accomplish personal and selfish ends. It's so hard to discover their springs of action and it seems so forlorn to feel that on the question as to who shall be trusted, I should be so much at sea. I wonder if I must, for the third time, face the difficulties of a new official life almost *alone?*

I have no doubt you think I had better stop. I think so too. Good-bye.

P.S. Did you ever think to look after the Goodemote will?

To GEORGE W. CURTIS

Albany, *December* 25, 1884

Your communication dated December twentieth, addressed to me on behalf of the National Civil Service League, has been received.

That a practical reform in the civil service is demanded is abundantly established by the fact that a statute, referred to in your communication, to secure such a result, has been passed in Congress with the assent of both political parties; and by the further fact that a sentiment is generally prevalent among patriotic people, calling for the fair and honest enforcement of the law which has been thus enacted. I regard myself as pledged to this, because my conception of True Democratic faith and public duty requires that this and all other statutes should be, in good faith and without evasion, enforced, and because in many utterances made prior to my election as President, approved by the party to which I belong and which I have no disposition to disclaim, I have in effect promised the people that this should be done.

I am not unmindful of the fact to which you refer, that many of our citizens fear that the recent party change in the National Executive may demonstrate that the abuses which have grown up in the civil service are ineradicable. I know that they are deeply rooted, and that the spoils system has been supposed to be intimately related to success in the maintenance of party organization; and I am not sure that all those who profess to be the friends of this reform will stand firmly among its advocates when they find it obstructing their way to patronage and place.

But fully appreciating the trust committed to my charge, no such consideration shall cause a relaxation on my part of an earnest effort to enforce this law.

There is a class of government positions which are not within the letter of the civil service statute, but which are so disconnected with the policy of an administration that the removal therefrom of present incumbents, in my opinion, should not be made during the terms for which they were appointed, solely on partisan grounds and for the purpose of putting in their places those who are in political accord with appointing power.

But many now holding such positions have forfeited all just claim to retention because they have used their places for party purposes, in disregard of their duty to the people, and because, instead of being decent public servants, they have proved themselves offensive partisans and unscrupulous manipulators of local party management.

The lessons of the past should be unlearned; and such officials, as well as their successors, should be taught that efficiency, fitness, and devotion to public duty are the conditions of their continuance in public place, and that the quiet and unobtrusive exercise of individual political rights is the reasonable measure of their party service.

If I were addressing none but party friends, I should deem it entirely proper to remind them that though the coming Administration is to be Democratic, a due regard for the people's interest does not permit faithful party work to be always rewarded by appointment to office; and to say to them that while Democrats may expect all proper consideration, selections for office not embraced within the civil service rules will be based upon sufficient inquiry as to fitness, instituted by those charged with that duty, rather than upon persistent importunity or self-solicited recommendations on behalf of candidates for appointment.

To A. B. Farquhar [1]

Albany, *December* 25, 1884

I return you my sincere and heartfelt thanks for the picture of Mr. Black which arrived yesterday. I had never seen him or his picture before, and I shall prize your gift with all the enthusiasm which should characterize an ardent admirer of the original.

I must also be permitted the pleasure of acknowledging the great satisfaction your two letters lately received have afforded me. There is that about them which leads me to believe that I have an unknown and non-political friend in York, who understands me pretty well. I should be very glad to see you or hear from you at any time.

To Wilson S. Bissell

Albany, *December* 31, 1884

I have stopped on my way to the afternoon's perplexity and annoyance to answer in the 'den' your last letter, which was received this morning.

I am glad to learn that the chances of the ball [2] being a success are so good. You don't know how hard it will be for me to absent myself from duties and occupations which claim my presence here (to say nothing of pleasures which all the good people of Albany vie with each other in pro-

[1] A large farm-implement manufacturer of York, Pennsylvania, a devoted Democrat, and henceforth Cleveland's lifelong friend. The Black here mentioned was Jeremiah S. Black (1810–83) of Pennsylvania, Attorney-General under Buchanan.

[2] The annual Charity Ball in Buffalo.

moting) for the purpose of aiding a charity and seeing my old friends at my *former* home.

I do hope that in such circumstances I may be protected from any unnecessary annoyance which might be caused by contact with the dirty and contemptible portion of the Buffalo population. I am very glad that there will be no reception in either club.

I have accepted an invitation to dine with Sawyer the 9th. Mr. Humphrey has invited me and proposed the 8th, but said any other time which suited me better would be satisfactory. I have therefore told him that I would dine with him the 10th. I received Hamlin's cards this morning for the 13th. That is a reception and can be accepted, if at all, after I am in Buffalo. I want to spend an evening with Dr. Brown, though I have not yet any special invitation. Richmond tells me he wants to give a dinner and George Sicard writes me a very cordial and tempting letter to the same effect. So you see I don't know where I shall come out, and the trouble is this dinner business ought to be settled early. My sister will go with me. She has had three very kind invitations to stop with good people there — Mrs. Metcalfe, Mrs. Utley, and Mrs. Sicard. She has accepted this morning the latter. I thought the fact that George is my old partner, etc., made it the best, as it certainly is the pleasantest thing to do.

I shall stop at the Geneva and I wish in due time you would engage me a modest and not expensive parlor and bedroom. I do not insist upon their being too accessible.... It would be nice if I could get there at seven o'clock of the 8th and spend the rest of that evening with a half-dozen good friends.

To Wilson S. Bissell

Albany, *January* 5, 1885

Your letter is just received. I like the idea of meeting a few good friends at the club the evening of my arrival, and think the idea of having Lockwood and Titus there a good one. I expect Robbins will be with me — also my sister. She will go directly to George Sicard's house, I suppose. I don't know what to do in regard to the invitations I have received to dine, etc. I have one to breakfast from Sprague. Milburn wants me to dine, Sicard too, Utley and Henry Richmond, and I want to go to Brown's. I have only accepted Sawyer's for Friday and Humphrey's for Saturday, both dinners. What shall I do with the rest? I want to go to Sprague's and think I will breakfast with him at twelve Monday.

One trouble is that I don't like to set any pins down as to the time I will stay in Buffalo. If I don't like it I want to be free to skip. Let me hear from you.

To SAMUEL J. RANDALL [1]

New York, *February* 9, 1885

I have received your letter containing a copy of an amendment in relation to the coinage of silver, which it is proposed shall be inserted in a bill now pending in Congress, and asking my judgment upon the subject.

I have some delicacy in saying a word that may be construed by anybody as interfering with the legislation of the present Congress. But, so grave do I deem the public emergency, that I am willing as a private citizen to say that I think some legislation of the character suggested is eminently desirable.

To THOMAS F. BAYARD

Albany, *February* 11, 1885

When we met in Albany a few weeks ago, you, with the utmost kindness and consideration, asked me to determine after deliberate reflection, in what position you could do the best service to the incoming Administration, and to frankly express to you my conclusion. I remember too with peculiar satisfaction your assurance that in any station you might occupy you would at all times be prepared to aid and advise me in the performance of my official duty.

I have given the subject the consideration which you enjoined upon me, bearing in mind all the conversation which has taken place between us. As the result of serious thought as well as a strong personal desire which I am not able to relinquish, I have determined to ask you to accept the position of Secretary of State in the new Cabinet.

I hope to receive an early and favorable response; and if you accept the position tendered, I shall be glad to confer with you as soon as possible.

To WILSON S. BISSELL

Albany, *February* 19, 1885

... While your letter was waiting for me unopened I had a call from Frank Locke and my interview with him has done me much good. I

---

[1] Randall (1828–90) was Democratic Representative from one of the Philadelphia districts, former Speaker, friend of Tilden, and sound-money advocate, who had besought Cleveland to come out for repeal of the Bland-Allison Silver-Coinage Act of 1878.

have asked him to carry you my thoughts which have been frankly given him. It is a serious thing to die; but a man in my position learns with emphasis how serious a thing it is to live. I think so often of the legend over the head of my bed at home.

I shall write you again soon. I am wrestling most actively, but not with the best results, with my inaugural speech.

To THE HONORABLE A. J. WARNER [1] *and others*

Albany, *February 28, 1885*

The letter which I have had the honor to receive from you invites, and indeed obliges, me to give expression to some grave public necessities, although in advance of the moment when they would become the objects of my official care and partial responsibility. Your solicitude that my judgment shall have been carefully and deliberately formed is entirely just, and I accept the suggestion in the same friendly spirit in which it has been made. It is also fully justified by the nature of the financial crisis which, under the operation of the Act of Congress of February 28, 1878, is now close at hand.

By a compliance with the requirements of that law all the vaults of the Federal Treasury have been and are heaped full of silver coins, which are now worth less than eighty-five per cent of the gold dollar prescribed as the unit of value in section 16 of the Act of February 12, 1873, and which, with the silver certificates representing such coin, are receivable for all public dues. Being thus receivable, while also constantly increasing in quantity at the rate of $28,000,000 a year, it has followed of necessity that the flow of gold into the Treasury has steadily diminished. Silver and silver certificates have displaced and are now displacing the gold in the Federal Treasury now available for the gold obligations of the United States called 'greenbacks.' If not already encroached upon, it is perilously near such encroachment.

These are facts which, as they do not admit of difference of opinion, call for no argument. They have been forewarned to us in the official reports of every Secretary of the Treasury from 1878 till now. They are

---

[1] Warner (1834–1910) was Democratic Representative from the Marietta district in Ohio and a lifelong leader of the silver forces in the House, who with 94 other Representatives had begged Cleveland not to yield to those who demanded suspension of silver coinage. This letter was written by the former editor of the New York *World*, Manton Marble, and signed by Cleveland.

plainly affirmed in the last December report of the present Secretary of the Treasury to the Speaker of the present House of Representatives. They appear in the official documents of this Congress, and in the records of the New York clearing-house, of which the Treasury is a member, and through which the bulk of the receipts and payments of the Federal Government and country pass.

These being the facts of our present condition, our danger, and our duty to avert that danger, would seem to be plain. I hope that you concur with me and with the great majority of our fellow-citizens, in deeming it most desirable at the present juncture to maintain and continue in use the mass of our gold coin, as well as the mass of silver already coined. This is possible by a present suspension of the purchase and coinage of silver. I am not aware that by any other method it is possible. It is of momentous importance to prevent the two metals from parting company; to prevent the increasing displacement of gold by the increasing coinage of silver; to prevent the disuse of gold in the custom-houses of the United States in the daily business of the people; to prevent the ultimate expulsion of gold by silver. Such a financial crisis as these events would certainly precipitate, were it now to follow upon so long a period of commercial depression, would involve the people of every city and every State in the Union in a prolonged and disastrous trouble. The revival of business enterprise and prosperity so ardently desired, and apparently so near, would be hopelessly postponed. Gold would be withdrawn to its hoarding places, and an unprecedented contraction in the actual volume of our currency would speedily take place.

Saddest of all, in every workshop, mill, factory, story, and on every railroad and farm the wages of labor, already depressed, would suffer still further depression by a scaling down of the purchasing power of every so-called dollar paid into the hands of toil. From these impending calamities, it is surely a most patriotic and grateful duty of the representatives of the people to deliver them.

SAMUEL J. TILDEN *to* CLEVELAND [1]

Graystone, Yonkers, *February* 28, 1885

Your silver letter is absolutely perfect. It is the only silver thing I know of that transmutes itself into gold.

[1] Tilden knew that his friend Manton Marble had written the letter for Cleveland.

To Mother O'Rorke [1]

Albany, *March* 2, 1885

I send by my good friend Mr. McCall something which I hope will cause the little ones of the Convent to know that, while they are thinking of me, they are not forgotten by the man who in the midst of their holiday is undergoing the most perplexing ordeal that his life can bring to him. With many kind thoughts of you and of all the good people....

[1] This letter to the Mother Superior of the Convent of the Sacred Heart in Washington was accompanied by a check for $50.

IV

OFFICES AND OFFICESEEKERS

CLEVELAND'S principal labors and worries during his first ten months in the White House — that is, until the beginning of 1886 — related to the filling of Federal offices. More than one hundred thousand places were subject to the decisions of himself or his immediate subordinates. Of these the postoffices constituted by far the largest group. The Democratic party, finding that the national service was staffed almost entirely by Republicans, was eager to seize the fruits of its first victory since 1856. Politicians, and especially the Democratic Congressmen, were ready to make a rush for the jobs. On the other hand, the reformers, banded together in the National Civil Service Reform League and controlling, through such men as E. L. Godkin of the *Nation*, George W. Curtis of *Harper's Weekly*, and Samuel Bowles of the Springfield *Republican*, some of the most powerful organs of opinion, bent a critical eye upon the President. He had pledged himself to maintain the Civil Service Act passed in the Arthur Administration; going beyond this, he had also promised to protect many other positions ('disconnected with the policy of the Administration') from the spoilsmen. His first spring and summer in Washington witnessed an incessant fight with the politicians. He was simultaneously much worried by the demands of personal friends in New York State, and especially in Buffalo, for appointments which they felt they had 'earned.' With a vigor which won the praise of the reformers, he stood firm against most of the onslaught. In the end, however, he was faced by the danger of an actual schism in the party, and had to yield part of his ground. He was also deeply interested during his first months in Washington in reforming the various departments of the Government. It was found that the Treasury Department, Navy Department, and Interior Department had become the scene of gross inefficiency and abuse. Cleveland and his Cabinet set on foot many reforms in the handling of naval contracts, Western lands, the rights of the Indians and homesteaders, and the management of Treasury business.

To WILSON S. BISSELL

Washington, *March* 14, 1885

Your note was received Thursday.... General Walker of Connecticut wants the place of which you write[1] and it has been spoken of to me as

[1] The place in question was the consul-generalship in London, which by virtue of its fees paid about $40,000 a year.

a nice thing to do for him; but I am in no way committed to the appointment, though I suppose it is calculated on by some of our friends. I will go through most anything to give you what you desire. There is a vacancy in the South American Commission to visit that country and examine its resources, etc. The Commission consists of three and the vacancy is in the Presidency of the Commission ($7500). If you desire the London business I will at once begin to trim my sails to sail in that direction.

I am much surprised to hear of McCune's death. What will become of the *Courier*? I am extremely busy and reminded of the first few months in Albany. When are you coming down to see me?

To POSTMASTER-GENERAL VILAS

Washington, *April* 4, 1885

In answer to your inquiry as to the disposition to be made of the case of the postmaster at Rome, Oneida County, New York, which was presented to the Senate on the 26th day of March with a proposition that he be removed for cause, and which proposition was not acted upon prior to the adjournment of that body on the 2d day of April, I have to say that to me it clearly seems to be my duty to exercise by prompt action in this case all the power which the present condition of the law has left in my hands, so far as it may be done independently of the Senate,[1] to protect the interests of the Government, to vindicate the laws which have been enacted for the regulation of the postal service, and to impress upon Federal officeholders the fact that no indulgence will be granted by the Executive to those who violate the law or neglect public duty.

This postmaster, under section 4044 of the United States Revised Statutes and the regulations of the Postoffice Department, was required to transmit to the Department weekly a report of the business done by him in the money-order branch of his office.

It appears from the official report of an inspector of the Postoffice Department now before me, and which was submitted to a committee of the Senate while the proposition to remove this official was before it, that an examination of his office was ordered on the 24th day of January, 1885, in consequence of the fact that no such weekly report had been made since the 6th day of December, 1884. It further appears from this report that such examination developed the most disgraceful confusion

---

[1] The Tenure-of-Office Act gave the President power to suspend delinquent officials, but not to dismiss them without the consent of the Senate.

in all that pertained to the accounts and financial conditions of the office, that there had been no entry in the money-order cash book since July, 1884, and that, as might have been expected, there was a deficiency in the money-order account of more than seven hundred dollars and in the postal accounts of more than four hundred dollars.

There is, I think, no dispute touching these facts. The deficiency has been refunded to the Government under an arrangement with one of the sureties of the delinquent official; and he attempted to excuse the wretched condition of his office by alleging that his assistant had the entire charge of the money-order business as well as all other details of the office.

In making such an excuse this officer admits, it seems to me, a violation of plain duty in turning over the operations of his office to an assistant without any pretext of the sickness or unavoidable absence of the post-master, which is contrary to a reasonable construction of section 4031 of the Revised Statutes, which provides that 'in case of the sickness or un-avoidable absence of the postmaster of any money-order postoffice, he may with the approval of the Postmaster-General authorize the chief clerk or some other clerk employed therein, to act in his place and to dis-charge all the duties required by law of such postmaster.'

By the claim now made that the assistant having had full charge is re-sponsible for the delinquencies and irregularities complained of, the post-master also appears to contradict his own sworn statement made to the Department as late as September 30, 1884, to the effect that he himself had performed for the preceding quarter the money order business in his office except when necessarily absent.

I shall do all that is in my power to rid the public service of officials who exhibit such loose ideas of their duty to the Government.

The fact that I have before me documents signed by many residents of the city where this postmaster is located, and who belong to both political parties, asserting their entire confidence in his honesty and fidelity, demonstrates the unfortunate facility with which such papers may be obtained and gives rise to an unpleasant suspicion touching a too pre-valent standard of political honesty.

If I cannot remove this delinquent postmaster I can surely suspend him. This I have determined to do promptly; and I desire you at once to present to me the papers necessary for that purpose with a designation of James B. Corcoran to perform the duties of postmaster in place of the official thus suspended.

To DANIEL S. LAMONT

Washington, *April* 26, 1885

I wish that you would seriously consider the proposition for you and your family to come and stay with us awhile. I am sure we can arrange matters in quite a nice way and I should certainly be much pleased if such a scheme could be consummated. My sisters leave here Wednesday to be absent a week or more and I should be especially glad to have you here then, and Mrs. Lamont could boss the job in the internal arrangements. I wish you'd give this some sober thought and see what you conclude, taking into account my wishes as well as yours. We are getting on nicely here. Don't hurry.

To LIEUTENANT-GENERAL PHILIP H. SHERIDAN [1]

Washington, April ?, 1885

In view of the possible disturbance that may occur among the Indians now in the Indian Territory, and the contemplated concentration of troops in that locality, I deem it desirable that you proceed at once to the location where trouble is to be apprehended, and advise with and direct those in command as to the steps to be taken to prevent disorder and depredations by the Indians and as to the disposition of the troops.

Your acquaintance with the history and the habits and customs of these Indians leads me also to request that you invite statements on their part as to any real or fancied injury or injustice toward them, or any other cause that may have led to discontent, and to inform yourself generally as to their condition. You are justified in assuring them that any cause of complaint will be fully examined by the authorities here, and if wrongs exist they shall be remedied. I think I need hardly add that they must be fully assured of the determination on the part of the Government to enforce their peaceful conduct, and by all the power it has at hand, to prevent and punish acts of lawlessness and any outrage upon our settlers.

To MARY CLEVELAND HOYT

Washington, *April* 30, 1885

Your letter is just received. Of course I shall want you to come here next fall and winter, and at all other times and seasons you can make it

---

[1] Written at a time when Indian discontent with the irregular 'grass leases' under which powerful ranching interests were using much of the best land of the Indian Territory was rising to a peak.

possible. The only limit to the time I should like to have you spend here is made by your own necessities and inclination. Of course I don't know what Libbie's ideas are, and perhaps there may be something in the May Hastings scheme. Libbie went to New York yesterday and I hope she will have a little rest. She'd had a pretty hard time here. Annie,[1] I expect, will return with her and stay a short time. I hope the newspapers will not spoil her.

I am pretty well. All the Lamont family came to stay with us yesterday, and I expect to enjoy the children first-rate. I know it will do the Colonel good and I am glad to have Mrs. Lamont here to look after things while Libbie is away. I don't take to the Soldier's Home idea much. I have got a nice team and I expect the carriage next week.

To JOHN G. MILBURN [2]

Washington, *June* 14, 1885

I am lately informed that the papers in Ball's suit against the *Evening Post* were delivered to my personal friends in Buffalo with the expectation that the defence should be managed by them, and that you and Locke are doing the fighting without, as I infer, exactly knowing whether you have a client or not. In this condition of affairs, I especially desire that I may be considered responsible to you for your professional compensation; and I beg of you that you should never hereafter feel that you have not behind you a backer, perfectly able and willing to see you through. You know my good friends have helped me to a first-rate salary — a part of which I am sure cannot be better expended than in the way indicated.

I have not heard from you or Locke in such a long time that I fear you have abandoned this Administration. I hope this is not so, for I need all the good friends I have strongly on my side. Give my kindest regards to Locke.

To EDGAR K. APGAR

Washington, *June* 19, 1885

I *will* take the time now, which I have thought from day to day would come to me, to thank you for your splendid letter to Mr. ——, a copy of

---

[1] Cleveland's oldest sister, Mrs. E. P. Hastings; 'Libbie' was his youngest sister, Rose Elizabeth.

[2] A rising Buffalo attorney, once clerk in the office of Cleveland and Bissell. He successfully defended E. L. Godkin, editor of the New York *Evening Post*, against a libel suit brought by Dr. Ball.

which Colonel Lamont showed me.[1] It was so exactly the thing, I wish it could be published in every newspaper in the land. I want to say much in its praise, but believe I can sum the matter up to my satisfaction, when I say it was just like you in your very best mood. Perhaps other people know how much that means, better than you.

I am getting on pretty well, though I mean to forego the handshaking in the East Room today, on account of a good deal of stiffness in my right hand, which I am fearful means the approach of my unpleasant friend rheumatism.

The clock has just struck ten, and the doors must be opened to the waiting crowd. The question with me is, When (if ever) will the thing stop? You know I am always glad to hear from you.

To DANIEL MANNING
Washington, *June 20*, 1885

There are, I think, eighty-five Internal Revenue Collection Districts in the United States. Since our accession to power we have replaced all but twenty-five. This has been done, with not more than three exceptions, by removing such as had occupied the office more than four years, and by suspending others upon charges and filling the places of such as required it. Seven still remain, who have held for four years and afterwards; and when they are disposed of (as I suppose they soon will be) we shall have turned out, or got out, all the Collectors but *eighteen*, in the first four months of our reign. I think this is about as far as we ought to go at present, in the absence of any complaints against present incumbents.

My idea has been that those officials who have held their places for four years should as a rule give way to good men of our party, that those who have been guilty of offences against our political code should go without regard to the time they have served, and that we should gladly receive all resignations offered to us and fill the vacancies thus created by our friends. I think this will work first-rate and enable us to avoid dangers and obstruction.

To WILSON S. BISSELL
Washington, *June 25*, 1885

It is nearly twelve o'clock. Lamont just brought in your letter (we have a mail at eleven o'clock now) and after reading it, I have put aside my work to reply.

[1] In this letter Apgar had peremptorily refused to use his influence with Cleveland in behalf of an officeseeker.

Somehow this letter has impressed me with the suspicion that in one quarter, at least, there is an idea that I owe something to friends for political aid, which I am not ready enough to acknowledge. Perhaps this is true. At all events I tell you now, with the utmost sincerity, that I cannot rid myself of the idea that I owe so much to the country, that all other obligations shrink almost to nothingness before it — though I must confess that sometimes I am much comforted by the reflection that I may serve the country well and still serve my party. My ability to do either of these things depends, of course, upon the approval of the people. The people I have to deal with — that is, the people of the country — are not perhaps just what I wish they were, and they perhaps have ideas which are not useful or correct, but their ideas to a very great extent must be met or my efforts to do good must miscarry.

Your letter indicates that you appreciate partly the extent and perplexity as well as the delicacy of my work. For three months I have stood here and battled with those of my party who deem party success but a means to personal advantage. They have been refused and disappointed; and you are able today to write as you do, that my Administration is strong and popular, because those thus refused and disappointed cannot say that I have refused them in order to make place for personal friends, and have bestowed patronage in payment of personal political debts. I have often thought how solemn a thing it is to live and feel the pressure of the duties which life — the mere existence in a social state — imposes; but I have never appreciated the thought in its full solemnity till now. It seems to me that I am as much consecrated to a service as the religionist who secludes himself from all that is joyous in life and devotes himself to a sacred mission.

I think you know how much of all that has had anything of comfort in my life has grown out of my love for my friends and the hope that I had earned some real unselfish attachments. And if in carrying my present burden, I must feel that friends are calling me selfish and doubting my attachment to them and criticising the fact that in the administration of my great trust I am not aiding them, I shall certainly be unhappy, but shall nevertheless struggle on. The end will come; and if on that day I can retire with a sure consciousness that I have done my whole duty according to my lights and my ability, there will be some corner for me where I can rest.

You must not think that I am always blue and always unhappy. In the midst of all I have to do, daily and hourly come the assurances from the people in all parts that they are satisfied and pleased. If I could only, by giving up all I have or expect, liquidate the debts and obligations to my friends, a terrible load would fall from my shoulders. You say they were very few and could be counted upon the fingers of one hand. I am sure five thousand have claimed that they have spent in my behalf to an extent that can never be compensated.

What a nice thing it would be if my *close* friends could see a compensation in my successful Administration.

Of one thing you may be certain. I shall bear with me to my dying day a heart full of gratitude for all that you have done for me.

To P. Henry Surgo, *Grand Sachem of Tammany*

Washington, *July* 1, 1885

I beg leave to acknowledge the receipt of your invitation to join the Society of Tammany in its ninety-seventh celebration of the Fourth of July, the birthday of the Republic. I regret that the pressure of official duties and engagements prevents the acceptance of this kind invitation.

Of the purposes sought to be accomplished by the people in their recent choice of a Chief Magistrate, referred to in your note of invitation, I am seriously mindful. In order that the hopes of the people may be fully realized, every member of the party entrusted with power should yield a cordial support to all efforts on the part of the Administration to restore a pure, free and just government.

The statement contained in your note that 'the Administration should so discharge all its functions as to merit not only the approbation of the people but at the same time insure a harmonious party united in Jeffersonian Democracy' meets my approval, although my conception of the true purposes and the mission of my party convinces me that if the present Administration merits the intelligent approval of the people, this result of itself certainly should 'insure a harmonious party united in Jeffersonian Democracy.'

While the coming celebration will revive and keep alive the memory of patriotic devotion and sacrifice for the sake of free institutions, no occasion is more propitious for a renewal of our pledges to a true and progressive Democracy, so essential to our country's safety and prosperity.

To MALCOLM HAY [1]

Washington, *July* 1, 1885

I appreciate with sincere sorrow the fact that the Administration is no longer to have the benefit of your association and assistance — both of which have been of very great value.

The high and noble patriotism which induced you at great sacrifice to enter the service of the Government, and the gallant struggle you have made, against terrific odds, to continue to use the advantage of your sacrifice, have caused me to regard you with affection and tender consideration; your just and exact conception of the policy of the Administration as related to the work you had to do, and the firm and resolute pursuit of the path marked out by that policy have largely increased my admiration for your qualities of mind and heart, while the great aid which you have been able to render, during your short stay in office, to the cause of improved methods in the public service, I acknowledge with hearty gratitude.

You bear with you to your retirement the kindest wishes of those with whom you have been lately associated and their earnest hope for your restoration to health as well as the lasting friendship and esteem of Grover Cleveland.

To GEORGE HALL

Washington, *July* 8, 1885

I am not sure that I understand fully your letter of the 7th, purporting to give the opinion and the desire of the St. Lawrence County Democracy, as reflected by their County Committee. Every member of the Administration is working very hard to do the things which in the canvass the party pledged should be done, if the Democracy was entrusted with the management of the executive branch of the Government. The policy of the Administration regarding appointments to office and removals therefrom is, or ought to be, well known. This will be adhered to; and I trust that St. Lawrence County does not expect a special rule to be applied to that particular locality.

Removals when they should be made, and the appointment of reputable and fit persons to fill vacancies, would be much aided and the Democracy of the different localities might find reason to be better satisfied, if those

---

[1] A public-spirited attorney of Pittsburgh, who had almost worn himself out in supporting Cleveland during the campaign, and had been appointed First Assistant Postmaster-General, in which office he vigorously resisted the spoilsmen.

having their interests in charge, and acting as Country Committees, etc., would co-operate with us in furtherance of our plans, instead of breeding dissatisfaction by meeting for the purpose of grumbling and finding fault.

To WILSON S. BISSELL

Washington, *July* 16, 1885

... As I was reading the clipping which you sent me Lamont handed me the Springfield *Republican* of yesterday containing something which I have just now read and take the liberty of enclosing.

Bass and his wife called to see me yesterday afternoon. We took a ride together and they dined with us. I don't know when I have enjoyed a visit so much and I was delighted to find him so well. It seemed so like old times and he appeared so really glad to see me and I was so boyishly glad to see him that when I was obliged to bid him good-bye to go and make postmasters, I felt like giving up the Presidency and going with him.

Attorney-General Garland [1] has just arrived and I must go to work. Give my love to Charley and George, and let me hear from you soon.

To GEORGE W. HAYWARD

Washington, *July* 21, 1885

Your letter was received and I immediately became an officeseeker. I applied in the most approved style to the Postmaster-General [2] and thought my chances were good. Tonight he brought me some papers by which it appeared that two applicants had filed petitions, one a man endorsed by considerably more than a hundred citizens and a number if not all of the local committee, another a woman with over a hundred signers. There was not a word in all the papers for my candidate. Of course I suppose I have the power to do this thing, but it seems to me that there ought to be a little local support. If Mr. L—— has friends to come to you for help those friends ought to appear here in the papers.

I do not say I will not do it, but to make an appointment in the face of the wishes of the people of the place as they are expressed here seems a little high-handed for a man who believes this is the People's Government. I will examine the matter further, and in the meantime would it

---

[1] Augustus H. Garland (1832–99) of Arkansas, former governor of that State and United States Senator, served as Attorney-General 1885–89.

[2] William F. Vilas was Postmaster-General.

not be well to intimate to the friends of Mr. L—— that he is not represented by any papers on file?

ORDER TO DISTRICT EMPLOYEES

Washington, *July* 23, 1885, 11 o'clock A.M.

Ex-President Ulysses S. Grant died this morning at 8 o'clock.

In respect to his memory it is ordered that all the offices of the Executive Departments in the City of Washington be closed today at one
o'clock.

To MRS. U. S. GRANT

Washington, *July* 29, 1885

Notwithstanding my desire that you should be as free as possible
from the consideration of the details connected with the obsequies of
your deceased husband, I am constrained to submit to you my thoughts
relating to the selection of the bearers at the funeral to the end that in
the performance of the part which I have undertaken nothing may be
done which by possibility might jar your sensibilities or add an iota to
the sadness of your surroundings.

The following persons, it seems to me, may be appropriately selected:
General Sherman; Lieutenant-General Sheridan; Admiral Porter; Vice-
Admiral Rowan; Gen. J. E. Johnston; Gen. S. B. Buckner; Hon. Hamilton
Fish; Hon. George S. Boutwell; George W. Childs, Philadelphia; A. J.
Drexel, Philadelphia; E. B. Washburn, Chicago; George Jones, New York.

These represent the highest officers in the Army and Navy, the Confederate service by two of its most distinguished generals, the two Cabinets of the deceased when President, by its two most prominent survivors,
and the personal friends of General Grant in the last four names.

May I ask you to frankly tell me by telegraph if these persons, all of
them, meet your approval, and to make any suggestion of changes that
occur to you?

To A. BUSH [1]

Washington, *August* 1, 1885

I have read your letter of the 24th with amazement and indignation.
There is but one mitigation to the perfidy which your letter discloses and
that is found in the fact that you confess your share in it. I don't know

---

[1] An adviser who had recommended an unfit appointment, and when it was made, had
confessed the fact.

whether you are a Democrat or not; but if you are, the crime which you confess is the more unpardonable. The idea that this Administration, pledged to give the people better government and better officers, and engaged in a hand-to-hand fight with the base elements of both parties, should be betrayed by those who ought to be worthy of implicit trust, is atrocious; and such treason to the people and the party ought to be punished by imprisonment.

Your confession comes too late to be of immediate use to the public service; and I can only say that while this is not the first time I have been deceived and tricked by lying and treacherous representations, you are the first one that has so frankly owned his grievous fault. If any comfort is to be extracted from this assurance you are welcome to it.

To CHARLES W. GOODYEAR [1]

Washington, *August* 6, 1885

I return you Bissell's letter, and am exceedingly surprised at it, as also by the statement in your letter that you have wanted to tell me 'of ——, ——, ——, ——, and others who were your (my) warm-hearted friends,' etc., etc. I think I understand it; and the truth that I have been attempting to crowd back is forced upon me. What have these friends to complain of?

Has Bissell made up his mind that he is justified in withdrawing his friendship, because he was not appointed as a member of the Cabinet or consul to London? These two things he will see some day were impossible; and from one he withdrew himself. I would not demean myself to speak of the pleasure it has given me to do every other thing which I thought he wanted.

Is —— offended because I forgot to insist in the Cabinet (and I would not have done it if I had remembered it) that the banking business should be continued in the hands of the most pronounced Republicans, who were fleecing the Government right and left?

Has —— ceased to be a friend because I did not appoint him to a place in the diplomatic service, and thus offend my party and give the lie to my declaration that the Administration was to be Democratic, and weaken myself by giving public places to reward personal friends?

---

[1] This somewhat peevish outburst, elicited primarily by Bissell's ill-humor, emphasizes the fact that Cleveland, unlike Grant or McKinley, sternly refused to appoint mere friends to office.

Has —— made up his mind that our long friendship should be broken and interrupted, because I did not insist upon his taking the Paris consulship, or because I am now hesitating about an attempt to find something of personal and professional interest to him, which I am convinced by my present lights ought not to be done?

I can think of nothing else which should interfere with the relations I have been so delighted to maintain with these gentlemen. Of all the 60,000,000 people in the country, high or low, my Buffalo friends when here have been treated with the utmost consideration and hospitality, so far as I have been able to do it, and so far as my knowledge of proper and handsome treatment went. It may be that public business has prevented my devoting as much time to them as I desired, but I did the best I could.

I have been here five months now, and have met many people who had no friendship for me, and were intent on selfishly grabbing all they could get, without any regard to the country, the party, or to me; but I have managed to get along with them apparently as well as with my Buffalo friends. And now I am done. I feel sick at heart. I don't want to let these friends go; but I am tired of this beating about the bush and all this talk about 'second-handed invitation' and 'holes in a plank' and that sort of thing. If people lie in wait for me to discover things that may be construed into slights and offences, they will find plenty of them. I am not much on my guard with friends.

I have no complaints to make. Of course I thought it a little strange that with the hundreds of invitations to visit hundreds of places during my vacation, my friends in Buffalo did not seem to care to see me; but I am not going to say that I can get along without Buffalo or Buffalo friends. I care much — very much — for the latter. But by God! I have something on hand here that cannot be interfered with; and if my Buffalo friends or any other friends cannot appreciate that, I can't help it.

I am getting in that condition where any demonstration of kindness touches me deeply; and therefore I thank you for your kind words and offer to attend to any matter for me in Buffalo. I hope to receive the tin box very soon; and after that I will try to be real good and make as little trouble as possible.

For God's sake, Charley, don't think that I am any way out of sorts with you.

To A WESTERN POLITICIAN [1]

Saranac Lake, *August* 25, 1885

I have lately received a letter signed by you and Mr. —— setting forth the importance of a change in the incumbents of Federal offices in the State of ——, and suggesting the political propriety of making such changes promptly. I have much faith in your judgment and political sagacity, and am fully convinced of the patriotic motives which have instigated your recommendations to office in your locality; and because I entertain these sentiments, with a firm conviction of your friendliness and kind wishes toward me, I am constrained to remind you of the conditions which surround the subject referred to in your letter.

Nothing, it seems to me, could be more distinct than the promise I made to the people during the campaign, and since its close, that officers whose duties are purely executive should not be displaced during the continuance of their terms merely and solely to make way for those who are in affiliation with the party to which I belong.

This promise was not made with any lack of appreciation on my part of the importance of party organization, nor with any disregard and failure to recognize the value of the services of party associates in the struggle for the ascendancy of Democratic principle. But it seemed to me at the time that there was no sentiment so nearly uppermost in the minds of the people as the belief that a wholesale and indiscriminate change in the public officers should not necessarily and inevitably follow a change of Administration.

This sentiment was based, I suppose, upon a natural regard on the part of the people for their interests as distinguished from the benefit which would accrue from such changes to those who make a profession of politics, and who are not always in full sympathy with the things that pertain solely to the public good.

I understand that the party which succeeded to the Administration in the last election is a progressive Democracy; and it should be really and truly in full accord with the wishes of the people, and willing to base its hopes of a continuance in power upon popular approbation. During the campaign we certainly claimed to stand in that position, and it was only because the people trusted in our professions that they gave into our hands the administration of their Government.

I would not have you understand that the pledges to the people which

[1] This letter was never sent. It was first published in Mayes' life of L. Q. C. Lamar.

I thus personally acknowledge were given on my part merely to achieve success, and that I feel bound to redeem them because they were made. On the contrary, I fully share in the sentiments to which I have referred, and sincerely believe that a change of Administration should not be the signal for an entire change in the servants who are employed to do the people's work.

It follows that honor, good faith, and my conviction of what is right and just, all combine to cause me to remain firm and steadfast in the line of conduct which has been marked out for the guidance of the present Administration. All officers connected with the furtherance of the political policy of the Government should be of the same political creed and party as the Administration; but faithful and honest officers not thus related, and whose removal is not deemed necessary to the proper consummation of needed reforms, and having fixed terms, will not be removed merely upon the allegation that such officers belong to the party lately defeated at the polls.

Of course there should be no protection for officeholders who have used, and are now using, whatever of influence and power their offices afford, to carry out partisan designs, and who sacrifice the interests of the people to partisan zeal; nor to them who, in their discharge of official duty, wilfully offend their fellow-citizens of another political faith.

These unworthy officials and offensive partisans should be promptly removed; but the enjoyment, in a decent manner, of their political privileges and rights, should not be made a pretext for removal for the purpose of putting in their place our political friends.

There can be no doubt, it seems to me, that every member of the Democratic party is in honor bound to sustain the present Democratic Administration in fulfilling the pledges made to the people in its behalf, with the approval and endorsement of the party. These promises and assurances constituted the conditions upon which the party was entrusted with power, and common honesty demands that they should be faithfully kept and preserved.

It can be only those who suppose that, under a code of morals peculiar to political affairs, promises can be made when the people's suffrages are solicited and easily forgotten afterwards, who can find fault with the course which I have determined to pursue.

To DORMAN B. EATON [1]

Washington, *September* 11, 1885

I am in receipt of your letter tendering your resignation as a member of the Board of Civil Service Commissioners.

I cannot refrain from expressing my sincere regret that you have determined to withdraw from a position in the public service, where your intelligent performance of duty has been of inestimable value to the country.

The friends of civil service reform and all who desire good government fully appreciate your devotion to the cause in which you early enlisted; and they have seen with satisfaction that your zeal and faith have not led you to suppose that the reform in which you were engaged, is unsuited to the rules which ordinarily govern progress in human affairs, or that it should at once reach perfection and universal acceptance. You have been willing patiently to accept good results as they step by step could be gained, holding every advance with unyielding steadfastness.

The success which thus far has attended the work of civil service reform is largely due to the fact that its practical friends have proceeded upon the theory that real and healthy progress can only be made, as such of the people who cherish pernicious political ideas, long fostered and encouraged by vicious partisanship, are persuaded that the changes contemplated by the reform offers substantial improvement and benefits. A reasonable toleration for old prejudices, a graceful recognition of every aid, a sensible utilization of every instrumentality that promises assistance, and a constant effort to demonstrate the advantages of the new order of things, are the means by which this reform movement will in the future be further advanced, the opposition of incorrigible spoilsmen rendered ineffectual, and the cause placed upon a sure foundation.

Of course there should be no surrender of principle, nor backward step; and all laws for the enforcement of the reform should be rigidly executed but the benefits which its principles promise will not be fully realized unless the acquiescence of the people is added to the stern assertion of a doctrine and the rigorous execution of the laws.

It is a source of congratulation that there are so many friends of civil service reform marshalled on the practical side of the question, and that

[1] Veteran civil service reformer, author of a profoundly influential report to President Hayes on the subject, and appointed by Arthur head of the first Civil Service Commission under the Act of 1883.

the number is not greater of those who profess friendliness for the cause, and yet mischievously and with supercilious self-righteousness discredit every effort not in exact accord with their attenuated ideas, decry with carping criticism the labor of those actually in the field of reform and, ignoring the conditions which bound and qualify every struggle for a radical improvement in the affairs of government, demand complete and immediate perfection.

The reference in your letter to the attitude of the members of my Cabinet to the merit system established by the Civil Service Law, besides being entirely correct, exhibits an appreciation of honest endeavor in the direction of reform, and a disposition to do justice to proved sincerity, which is most gratifying. If such treatment of those upon whom the duty rests of administering the Government according to reform methods was the universal rule, and if the embarrassments and perplexities attending such administration were fairly regarded by all those professing to be friendly to such methods, the avowed enemies of the cause would be afforded less encouragement.

I believe in civil service reform and in its application in the most practicable form attainable, among other reasons, because it opens the door for rich and poor alike, to participate in public officeholding. And I hope the time is at hand when all our people will see the advantage of a reliance for such opportunity, upon merit and fitness, instead of a dependence upon the caprice or selfish interest of those who impudently stand between the people and the machinery of their Government. In the one case a reasonable intelligence and the education which is freely furnished or forced upon the youth of our land, are the credentials to office; in the other the way is found in favor secured by a participation in partisan work, often unfitting a person morally, if not mentally and physically, for the responsibilities and duties of public employment.

You will agree with me, I think, that the support which has been given to the present Administration in its efforts to preserve and advance this reform by a party restored to power after an exclusion for many years from participation in the places attached to the public service; confronted with a new system precluding the redistribution of such places in its interest; called upon to surrender advantages which a perverted partisanship had taught the American people belonged to success, and perturbed by the suspicion always raised in such an emergency that their rights in the conduct of this reform had not been scrupulously regarded, should receive due acknowledgment and should confirm our belief that there is a sentiment among the people better than a desire to hold office and a patriotic impulse upon which may safely rest the integrity of our institutions and the strength and perpetuity of our Government.

I have determined to request you to retain your present position until the first day of November next, at which time your resignation may become operative. I desire to express my entire confidence in your attachment to the cause of civil service reform and your ability to render it efficient aid; and I indulge in the hope and expectation that, notwithstanding the acceptance of your resignation, your interest in the object for which you have labored so assiduously will continue beyond the official term which you surrender.

To WILSON S. BISSELL

Washington, *September* 15, 1885

I enclose you a report of Superintendent Jackson (a copy) touching the successor to Jack White, from which you will see that Werrick will not do.... I know these are little matters to bother you with, but they come to me and I have to refer them to someone on the spot. If you suggest it and want to be rid of the annoyance I will have all such things referred to the County Committee or somewhere else....

It's nearly one o'clock. Colonel is gone and William [1] too. If I did not keep one of the waiters here I should be absolutely alone in the upper part of the house. That's splendor for you! — sleeping alone in the White House — barring a colored servant.

The weather here and all is very pleasant now and I think you would enjoy a few days' visit. Why don't you come? With love to Charley and George....

To DANIEL MANNING

Washington, *September* 18, 1885

Of course the talk about my writing such a letter to Peck (or any other letter) is false, and if true that he is showing such a thing it is a very bold proceeding. It might be well enough to answer Faulkner's letter, saying as little as possible, except perhaps that the matters forcing themselves constantly upon our attention prevent us from taking any part in the political movements in New York even if inclined.

[1] Daniel S. Lamont and William Sinclair.

Whitney will come to me for dinner at seven o'clock and we have cooked it up so that you shall be there too. We three must have a talk. Will you come?

To WILSON S. BISSELL
Washington, *September* 19, 1885

Yours was one of the three letters received this morning referring to the employment of Theodore Tyson in the Treasury Department. I have never heard of his employment in that or any other department. Mr. Manning says he never heard of such a thing and that no such name appears on his books. So I suppose this is one of the lies manufactured out of whole cloth which are at this time being circulated with so much relish by the press, and which, if they were pursued by the Administration, could well engage the attention of a good-sized department in the attempt to hunt them down.

To MISS JENNIE HUMPHREY
Washington, *September* 21, 1885

I suppose that I should feel complimented by the special invitation you sent me to attend your wedding; and I expect I should thank you — which I accordingly do most sincerely. But has it never occurred to you that the dropping off, one by one, of those who in a way have been with me in single misery might possibly cause the least little twinge? But we must not be selfish; and you may be sure that if I could, I should witness the ceremony.

I do not need to wish for Mr. Jones the utmost happiness, for that is assured; and you need hardly be told how much and how sincerely I wish that your married life may daily and to the distant end bring increasing joy and comfort.

To WILLIAM GORHAM RICE
Washington, *September* 23, 1885

I have received the copy of Shakespeare's works which you sent me at the request of Mr. George W. Apgar, as a memento of my dead friend, and I am grateful to you for the part you assumed in putting in my hands something which I shall prize so much. I find it hard to realize that Apgar is dead, and when sometimes it comes upon me with dreadful distinctness, it seems to me that his place in my life will never be filled by so true, sincere, and unselfish a friend.

I suppose you are full of politics in these days. I hope that we shall have a safe deliverance.

To WILLIAM S. BISSELL

Washington, *September* 24, 1885

I have just heard (12:30) of the nomination of Hill.[1] I hope that he will pull through, though I am afraid of it. I was surprised to hear by one of the dispatches that Lockwood's speech seconding the nomination was supposed to voice the President's sentiments. I think our friends the enemy did the shrewdest thing possible yesterday.

I have been very much worried about the Bacon-Sterling affair[2] and that was on my mind when I wrote you last Saturday. It looks now as though with my usual luck I was to wiggle out of it all right and perhaps turn the whole thing to profit. I don't object to telling you confidentially that I expect to have an entirely new Civil Service Commission on the first of November. I want two of the best Democrats I can find — men who are real genuine civil service reformers, full of practical sense. I am quite sure that I have made a mistake in the selection of Collector and Surveyor of the Port of New York, and I came very near taking the bit in my teeth and making a grand dump. I haven't given it entirely up yet. I think Thompson[3] is played out. I understand he drinks a good deal and I believe he is in a condition to damn any man that ties to him. If this Collector business comes to a crisis I should like to put in a close personal friend of my own, and depending upon my own recommendation; and so of the Civil Service Commission. The latter don't pay but $3500 and it's hard to get just the man for that sum. I think the people would be pleased and feel safe if I should put two of my own friends in these positions. I can make Codman stand for Civil Service Commis-

[1] David B. Hill (1843–1910), who as lieutenant-governor had succeeded Cleveland when the latter resigned the governorship, was now nominated and in November elected for the three-year term.

[2] Cleveland's newly appointed Collector of the Port of New York, E. L. Hedden, had removed Captain Bacon, for fifteen years chief weigher of the Brooklyn customs district, and appointed George H. Sterling, a local politician, in his stead. Sterling was regarded as an unfit politician and a loud outcry followed.

[3] Hubert O. Thompson, one of the leaders of the County Democracy, who had urged Hedden's appointment. He was a favorite of Manning's, but his administration of the Public Works Department in New York City had been lax and extravagant.

sioner, though he begs like a dog. He, you know, is a Mugwump and way up in civil service circles. He lives in or near Boston. I think it will stand two Democrats besides, though it might be considered a little strong. I've a good notion to call Schoonmaker. He stands well, though he is not as strong a man as people think. My God! What a strike it would be if I had you there. There's lots in this civil service reform and there's lots to do to make it more perfect and more practical. It's come to stay and the men that oppose it will leave their corpses on the field. What do you think of the letter to Eaton? I am congratulated on it from all sides.

Now they are pressing me from Pennsylvania to put out Postmaster Huidekooper at Philadelphia. I can't see it quite yet.

I wish I had you down here where I could talk with you. I have a first-rate Cabinet, but after all the best things have to be worked out alone.

I have all the time bearing down upon me, besides the ordinary things, some special perplexities — but they all work out. God is good to me, and after all the American people are pretty nearly right. At any rate, while I scold a good deal I love them and am grateful to them.

Tell me all you think. I wish I dared ask you to be a Civil Service Commissioner — that is, if I succeed in reorganizing the Board. If Eaton is the only one that goes I think I had better put Codman [1] in his place, don't you? It would be a dreadful sacrifice for him, and sense of duty has impelled him to say he would take it if I must have him, at the same time exacting a promise from me that I'd let him off if I possibly could. He is George W. Curtis's brother-in-law, I think, and a hard-headed business man. I know he has talked to Curtis and advised with him and I think a few others; and though personally he would be glad to be left out, I think if he was it would be misconstrued in some quarters.

To EDWARD M. SHEPARD [2]

Washington, *September* 29, 1885

I was glad you wrote to me regarding the Bacon-Sterling affair. Since the receipt of your letter I have caused the suspension of Sterling pending an examination. I cannot afford to be unjust even towards a man so

---

[1] Charles R. Codman of Boston, a prominent Mugwump and reformer.

[2] A well-known New York attorney, reformer, and author (1856–1911). He is best remembered now as the author of an admirable biography of Martin Van Buren.

promptly and vigorously assailed. In such cases as this we are all apt to go a little fast. I want you now in cooler moments to help me investigate this affair — and especially the character of Sterling. The rest I can attend to.

I have received letters from very excellent sources representing that Sterling is and always has been a good son to a widowed mother and exemplary as a husband and father, and much more very much to his credit. I wish you would take a little pains to inquire concerning him and his associates, and all that will aid me in making up a judgment, and write to me the result of your investigation. Mr. James How, of the Morris White Lead Manufacturing Company, knows him well, and he had the endorsement of Arbuckle Brothers and other prominent business houses before he was appointed. Vicar-General Keegan knows him well, and I think can say something of his life and habits.

The people I have mentioned are no doubt ready to speak well of him. It is in your power to give me the names and opinions of others perhaps who speak ill of him. You can readily see that I am not in a position to act now on general denunciation.

To HERBERT P. BISSELL

Washington, *September 30*, 1885

Please accept my thanks for the pamphlet you sent me containing papers read before the Cleveland Democracy of Buffalo. The collection gives excellent proof of the amount and value of the work already done by the organization. I know of nothing which could better engage the endeavor of such an association than its declared objects — 'to foster and disseminate Democratic principles,' and 'to promote and secure the political education and Democratic fellowship of its members.'

A marked improvement in our politics must follow, I think, a better understanding of the reasons for the existence of parties, and a clearer apprehension of their relations to the welfare of the country and the prosperity of our people. Membership in a party might as well rest less upon a blind, unreflecting enthusiasm for a certain continued partisan companionship as the hope of personal reward and advantage, and more upon a deliberate attachment to well-defined and understood party principles. And this better condition is to be realized largely as the result of such work as the Cleveland Democracy has undertaken.

The Democratic cause need have no fear of the most complete discussion of its principles, and the history of its great leaders and their achievements cannot fail to inspire the members of the party with pride and veneration. It is well in these latter days to often turn back and read of the faith which the founders of our party had in the people—how exactly they approached their needs and with what lofty aims and purposes they sought the public good.

The object of your organization should arouse the zeal and continuous effort of every member, and its usefulness should insure its encouragement and prosperity.

To Collector E. L. Hedden

Washington, *October* 1, 1885

A consultation with the Civil Service Commissioners yesterday, and a re-examination of their decision in regard to the status of weighers under the law, resulted in an agreement that their prior decision was wrong and that weighers should be examined and passed before appointment. It has been determined that such an examination may be had at once.[1] I suppose that it will be of quite a practical character. *It has also been determined that all who pass the examination shall be certified to the appointing power at the same time* — thus giving a wide range of selection and an opportunity for inspection.

Special rule 2 providing that those parties examined prior to July 16, 1884, should remain on the register for two years was repealed, and a new rule adopted dropping on the 1st of November, 1885, all persons from registers in the postal and customs service who had been on the register one year or more. This leaves rule 16 as the limit for eligibles in full force, and solely controlling the matter, and rids the lists of those kept on by special rule 2, and by the resolution passed by the Board extending the eligibility of certain persons till January 1, 1886.

I think the matter is in such condition as should remove from the execution of the law certain features which were irritating and troublesome; and I do not see why it should not operate now without friction and annoying criticism. You will doubtless receive a letter from the Civil Service Commissioner; but I have thought this might not be amiss in addition.

[1] This decision by the Civil Service Commission extricated Cleveland from the vexatious Bacon-Sterling affair. It was declared that the position of chief weigher properly came under the classified service; an examination was held; Mr. Sterling came out twenty-second in a list of forty-five; and the man with the highest mark, a Republican of long experience as assistant weigher, was given the place.

To DON M. DICKINSON

Washington, *October* 11, 1885

The time has now come to you when you are called upon to make a sacrifice for your country. I want you to summon all the patriotism you have and all your love for party, for the Administration, and for myself, and consent to accept the office of Civil Service Commissioner at the minimum salary of $3500 per annum and all travelling expenses paid. This is the first offer I have made of the plan to any member of my party and I think it is the best position in the country to do good — to say nothing about gaining fame. I expect to reorganize the Commission entirely, and if you will take it I will promise you two first-rate assistants.

Will you come? I am anxious to know as soon as possible and I wish you would answer me by telegraph.

To COMMISSIONER JOHN M. GREGORY [1]

Washington, *October* 12, 1885

Soon after my inauguration as President, you frankly expressed your entire willingness to retire from the office of Civil Service Commissioner whenever I should desire to reorganize the Board; and repeated declarations of a like character since that time have proved your disposition upon this subject to be unaltered. Deeming such reorganization at this time to be desirable for the promotion of the cause which we both have so much at heart, and appreciating fully the patriotic motives which prompted your professions, I beg to say that I am now ready to accept your resignation to take effect upon the appointment of your successor.

To REPRESENTATIVE ABRAM S. HEWITT [2]

Washington, *October* 12, 1885

I should not be frank with you if I did not confess that I read your last letter with much surprise, and that after a second and third reading my comprehension of it caused me positive sorrow. I do not speak of this because I suppose my emotion is a matter of any concern to you, but rather as an excuse for adding that the complaining tone of your letter

---

[1] Gregory (1822–98), formerly the head of the Illinois Industrial University (University of Illinois), had been appointed to the Federal Civil Service Commission by Arthur.

[2] Hewitt, the respected iron-master and philanthropist, a member of Congress 1875–79 and 1881–86, and later mayor of New York, had written Cleveland urging him to appoint Richard Henry Dana, Jr., a government inspector of the Union Pacific Railroad. Cleveland objected because Dana was a friend of the president, Charles Francis Adams, Jr.

forced me to the conclusion that I have in some manner ignorantly offended one whose good opinion and friendship I desire on all accounts to
retain.

As for the special matter of which the letter treats, it is utterly impossible for me to see that I am properly performing my duty when I
appoint, as one of the three persons to inspect and report to the Government the condition of an extension of a railroad, when the directors of
said road upon a favorable report have a right to claim valuable government grants, the most intimate friend and associate of the president of
such railroad company.

I beg you to believe that I regret exceedingly my inability to appoint
Mr. Dana as one of the inspectors referred to, which you seem so much to
desire. I wish we could see this matter in the same light. I am not at all
comfortable in an attitude of difference with you nor in the reflection
that I have in any way lost your friendly feeling.

To Collector E. L. Hedden

Washington, *October* 14, 1885

I have received and read your letter dated October 8 with such satisfaction as grows out of my belief that you intend honestly to do your duty,
and thus aid the Administration in the difficult task it has undertaken,
which is to give the people better government in all departments.

I fully appreciate the difficulty of your position; and you will perhaps
remember that I warned you of some of the perplexities which awaited
you, the first time we ever met, which was just after your appointment.
In the Sterling matter I am prepared to believe that you acted upon
recommendations which you thought to be honestly given. And yet I
venture to say that some of them, if not a majority, would appear upon
inquiry to have been given with good-natured contempt and with no
sense of responsibility incurred.

I feel that I have had the experience which justifies me in advising you
that the ordinary recommendations which are presented by those seeking
office are but snares and delusions.

I am not at all inclined to differ with you as to the manner in which
work was being done by Mr. Bacon, nor the injustice to you involved in
the howl at his removal. But his removal, taken in connection with the
fact that the new appointee apparently gained his place more on account
of his value as a local politician than for any other reason, formed a

combination of circumstances which gave to the transaction a bad complexion, and put you in a position which I frankly say to you should have been avoided. I honestly think you were injured by it to such an extent that it will take time and good works to regain for you a first place in the confidence of the people whose good opinion you desire.

You would not read these words from my pen, if I did not think that you would yet vindicate my action in your appointment and give the people of New York greatly improved Custom House service. I am extremely anxious that this object should be fully gained. And my anxiety leads me to assure you, with the utmost friendliness and seriousness, that it can only be done by hard and continuous work, by an unyielding determination to at all times aim at the good of the service in every endeavor, and by a clear perception that if you are saved from failure, it will be through your own efforts, and your own work, guided by your own patriotic judgment. Advice and counsel of course you will need; and it should be sought of those who appreciate your condition and all you have to contend with, and who are willing to help you, rather than of those who seek to gain a selfish advantage — not caring for any consequences which may be visited upon you, and having no sympathy with your aims and purposes. There are those all about you, who desire only to compass personal and unworthy ends; and depend upon it, if in yielding to them you fall into trouble and disgrace, they will be utterly powerless to help you, and entirely careless of your fate.

I approve of your plan to reform the details of your office, so far as it is outlined in your letter, and I shall watch your progress with much interest — hoping for the best results.

To LEVERETT SALTONSTALL [1]

Washington, *October* 15, 1885

I have had upon my mind for some time, a matter regarding which I desire to confer with you, but have hesitated to do so because of the pendency of the question of the Collectorship at Boston, with which your name has been very prominently connected. I have determined, however, at last to write to you frankly and rely upon you to believe, that the proposition herein contained is in no way connected with the subject above referred to, or your relation to the same.

---

[1] This prominent Boston Mugwump refused the civil service commissionership here offered him, and was appointed Collector of the Port of Boston.

I am really in trouble and perplexity. And the fact that the good people of my party have generally been kindly and patriotically willing to help me in such emergencies, has caused me to come to you at this time.

I have undertaken, you know, to entirely reorganize the Board of Civil Service Commissioners, in the hope that I may do nothing to endanger the firm and rigorous enforcement of the law, while I popularize the Administration, and exact from the people, and especially those of my own party, a more willing and hearty support of the reform. This is, I think, the most delicate and important undertaking I have had in hand during my Administration; and I know of nothing yet to come, embracing such far-reaching consequences to the country, to the party, and to the present Administration. The men who are to compose the new Board must of course be firm and sincere believers in civil service reform, and such as by their very names, when announced, will give the friends of the movement everywhere the fullest assurance that the cause is safe in their hands. I am such a firm believer in this reform, that I firmly am of the opinion that there is nothing in public life with which a man can be connected, that promises such a field for doing good, and at the same time gives such an opportunity for distinction and fame of the best sort.

Will you come to me and make one of the new Commissioners? I have an impression that the duties of the place will not preclude the ability of paying some attention to private affairs; and while I desire to appeal in this matter to your patriotism and the desire I know you have, for the good of the country and the success of the Administration, I cannot forbear expressing to you the pleasure and satisfaction it would bring to us all, to have you connected with the work here, in such an important way.

I am anxious to learn your decision upon this proposition as soon as possible and yet I hope that you will not decline, in the absence of any circumstance connected with the question which might influence your judgment. I should be especially pleased to have you signify your acceptance by telegraph.

To ALTON B. PARKER [1]

Washington, *October 22,* 1885

I send with this a contribution towards defraying the expense of the pending Democratic campaign in the State of New York.

---

[1] Parker (1852–1926) a leader in Ulster County, New York, was helping direct Hill's campaign.

If I thought you needed any advice I should strongly urge upon you to enjoin upon any person pretending to desire the success of the ticket, and at the same time howling about the Administration and claiming that it should '*speak out,*' that campaigns are successfully fought by pushing the merits of candidates and principles, and not by a foolish attempt to discredit an Administration which is doing all that is possible to assist the canvass. I think the greatest enemy to the success of your ticket today is the man and the paper which is constantly yelling to the Administration to come to its rescue. And if you know of anybody that has any influence with the New York *World* you should, I think, ask that manifestation of its unfriendliness to the Administration be restrained till after election. As for the professed friends of the ticket who are constantly drumming at the Administration, their motives and purposes ought not to be misunderstood and they should not be permitted to conceal their misdeeds by the cry of 'stop thief.'

You see I do not claim any decent treatment for myself, though I am not able to see where I have forfeited it.

To Wilson S. Bissell

Washington, *October 23,* 1885

The matter in the sub-treasury at California presents a very awkward and embarrassing question. The change has been made, it appears, and the presumption is that a good man in sympathy with the Administration and the choice of the local Democracy has been appointed. To change back now, it seems to me, would make great trouble, especially for the reasons which would have to be given if the truth was told. I am very much annoyed and will see Manning about it.

I can see that it is going to be very difficult for me to be in Buffalo on election day, but am glad that through your thoughtfulness and the kindness of our Lehigh Valley friends the trip promises, if undertaken, to be as easy and pleasant as possible. I think I should like it if the train reached Buffalo in the night at one, two, or three o'clock so that I could have an excuse to spend the rest of the night *in my room.* You understand what that means. Do you think it can be accomplished?

I think your friend Kinney is making a mistake to vote for Davenport for governor if he believes in me. He and the rest of the Republicans are very sweet now, but when they have elected their tickets no time will be lost in shouting that the Administration has been repudiated and rebuked.

I wish I might know the railroad arrangement as early as possible. Give my regards to Charley and George.

To POSTMASTER-GENERAL WILLIAM F. VILAS
Washington, *October* 24, 1885

With the sincere expression of sympathy and condolence I desire you, of course, to drop all your departmental work and hasten to your poor afflicted mother. Convey to her my heartfelt condolence, and I pray you don't think of your work at all.

God bless you, my friend, and comfort all who are within the shadow of the affliction.

To WILSON S. BISSELL
Washington, *October* 24, 1885

Your letter dated yesterday is just received and I hasten to reply.

I am afraid that I ought not to have calculated upon going to Buffalo to vote. I am frightened when I reflect upon the near approach of the session of Congress and of the work I have to do before it assembles.

I must return the same day I arrive there, and with many thanks to any of my friends who are inclined to offer me social attentions, I am obliged to decline all. I suppose I shall want something to eat while I am there and if I can have that with as little fuss as is possible, I shall be quite content. It would be very pleasant to see some of my good friends but I don't know what suggestions to make.

One thing I know. I can't go to anybody's house to dine unless it is yours.

I wrote you a letter a day or two ago relating to the trip. You don't know how I wish I could do as other people do. Please say to Gorham how much I appreciate his kindness and let me hear from you as soon as possible.

To ABRAM S. HEWITT
Washington, *October* 25, 1885

I return you the letter of Mr. Harris which I received with yours yesterday. I think Mr. Harris writes in a manly way; and his letter and my correspondence with you upon the subject to which he refers only illustrates the truth that two or more sincere and fair-minded men may be very differently impressed by the same state of facts.

I can't think it is necessary to assure you that I should have been glad to please you — and Mr. Harris too.

You speak of some appointments that have been made which you recommended, and among them Mr. McMullen. Perhaps it is hardly worth mentioning, but your letter advising his appointment was shown to me and upon that alone the appointment was *at once*, and with no further inquiry, made. I desire to thank you for suggesting this selection, and I should be glad always to have your advice in such matters. I certainly shall not consider any recommendation you may make as the solicitation of a personal favor or my following it as granting a favor to you; for I believe you have at heart the public good and the success of the present Administration.

SECRETARY WHITNEY *to* CLEVELAND

Washington (no date)

My dear Mr. President:

I am clearly of the opinion that that executive order holding these lands within the indemnity limits for the railroad company to exercise its choice *when it gets ready* is illegal.[1] If legal it would be a gross abuse of power to hold it for a series of years. I wish to read the Supreme Court cases and shall take them home this afternoon and go them through.

I will keep Sparks'[2] and Montgomery's arguments and the copy of Garland's opinion and return you the other papers.

I wish to let it settle in my mind a little before talking with you.

STATEMENT TO THE PUBLIC

Washington, *October 27,* 1885

For nearly eight months, a large share of the time of the President has been devoted to the hearing of applications for office, and the determination of appointments. Much of the time thus spent has undoubtedly subserved the public good; some of it has been sacrificed to the indulgence of people in their natural insistence upon useless interviews, and some of it has been unjustifiably wasted.

---

[1] Cleveland had submitted to his Cabinet the case of the farm of Guilford Miller in Washington Territory, claimed by the Northern Pacific as part of its grant. Attorney-General Garland supported the railroad's position, but Cleveland agreed with Whitney that Miller should be protected in holding his land.

[2] William A. J. Sparks of Illinois (1828–1904) was Commissioner of the General Land Office, and displayed great zeal and energy in conserving the public resources, protecting defenceless settlers, and resisting corporation encroachments.

The public welfare, and a due regard for the claims of those whose interests in the government are entirely disconnected with office-holding, imperatively demand that in the future the time of the President should be differently occupied; and he confidently expects that all good citizens will acquiesce in the propriety and reasonableness of the following plan adopted to that end:

After the first day of November, the President will decline to grant interviews to those seeking public positions or their advocates. On Mondays, Wednesdays, and Fridays during that month, from ten to eleven o'clock in the morning, he will receive such other persons as call on strictly public business; and on the same days at half past one in the afternoon he will meet those who merely desire to pay their respects. On all other days and times during that month, he will receive only Cabinet officers and heads of Departments.

To Patrick A. Collins

Washington, *October 29,* 1885

I fully intended when I saw you last to dispose of the *hard question* relating to Massachusetts appointments,[1] but I have been in as great uncertainty as ever. I want very much to please you, and yet all the time my judgment and inclination lead me in a direction which thus far you have not approved. I am drawn in the same direction at least as strongly as ever now; and if I do the thing which you do not want done, you must put yourself in my place. You will never know how I have tugged at this thing.

I heard yesterday (I think) that you were quite ill. Your letter I take as an agreeable denial of the rumor.

Melville W. Fuller [2] *to* Cleveland

Chicago, *October 29,* 1885

Your message came upon me like a thunderbolt out of a clear sky. The pecuniary sacrifice would be about $20,000 a year (less, of course, if practice in the Supreme Court could be retained), but that would not stand in the way if I could so adjust my private affairs as to be able to come to

---

[1] The 'hard question' was whether Peter Butler or Leverett Saltonstall should be appointed Collector of the Port of Boston. Collins (1844–1905) was a political leader of Massachusetts and sat in the House of Representatives 1883–89.

[2] Fuller (1833–1910), later Chief Justice, was at this time merely a prominent attorney of Chicago.

Washington. I assume that the members of the Commission are practically obliged to reside there, and it must be so as to the Chief Commissioner. Then I have fixed engagements that I cannot without great difficulty get rid of. If I could accept I would, as you have my entire sympathy in your determination to do right because it is right, which Tennyson correctly says, 'is wisdom, in the scorn of consequence.' No matter what the politicians say, you have the people personally at your back beyond any doubt, and this civil service reform question is having a much more serious effect than the party ostriches, sticking their heads in the sand and thinking their tails are hid, seem to comprehend. . . .

To WILSON S. BISSELL

Washington, *November* 4, 1885

I arrived here this morning in due time after a very comfortable trip. I enclose you a draft for five thousand dollars to be used as suggested by you yesterday. Of course you will do all the business in your own name. I have received plenty of congratulations upon the election yesterday, all hands seeming to think that the results endorse my Administration. Two little things please me very much — to say nothing of the great results. One is the destruction of that very great nuisance Mahone [3] in Virginia, and the other is the burying of that cheapest and most impudent of all demagogues Cass in New York.

Of course I am much more gratified than either Rogers or Matthews can possibly be by their inevitable reflections.

Will you let me know what you do in the business matter we have in hand?

To COLLECTOR E. L. HEDDEN

Washington, *November* 8, 1885

I was much pleased by the report that Mr. Lamont brought me of his conversation with you and the full appreciation you seem to have of the position of affairs in the weigher matter. I regard the action that may be taken by you in filling the place of the utmost importance to you, to the cause of civil service reform, and to the strength and success of the Administration.

The statement I made and which was published in the newspapers,

---

[3] Senator William Mahone of Virginia (1826–95), whose single term ended in March, 1887, was elected as a 'Readjuster' — i.e., an advocate of partial repudiation of the State debt.

I have supposed would aid you somewhat by setting forth the status of the question as I understand it.

Some things have taken place in connection with the matter which I regret, and which are calculated to make me feel a little annoyed and irritated. (I refer to things connected with the examination, with which you are in no way related.) I hope that you do not feel in the same way. But if you do we must both put all that aside and not allow any prejudice and feeling to interfere with the course that seems to be right, just and judicious. Other things will adjust themselves, but now the important thing is to avoid action that can be justly criticised. I see by the papers that of those who have passed the examination, four or five are discharged soldiers, entitled to preference in appointment under an express provision of section 1754 of the Revised Statutes, a recognition of which statute is found in section 7 of the Civil Service Law.

It is exceedingly important that the force of this law should be scrupulously regarded. Indeed this *must* be done. O'Brien, the first upon the list of eligibles, is fully, and so far as I can hear very honorably, entitled to the preference; and it seems to me that his selection would furnish a way out which would rob those, who I am inclined to think are anxious to cavil and find fault, of a much desired opportunity to do so. And especially would this course be one calculated to put you upon a good footing if the whole list is certified to you — as not unlikely it will be. This would be proof that though you had ample opportunity to choose differently, you implicitly followed both the statute giving soldiers a preference and the Civil Service Law too, in their spirit as well as their letter.

Of course I would not have you appoint this man, who seems to me so fortunately to stand in this position, if you are entirely certain that he is after all unfit; but I desire to hint to you that it will be nearly impossible to explain your course if he is rejected. And in view of the fact that you have the advantage of a six months' probation to fully test all his qualifications, I can hardly see why he should not be tried.

I have written you a long letter: but I know, better than you can, the importance of the matter I have touched upon. I am very much interested in your success and I want this settled in such a way that you will hold a stronger position to do other things which I think ought to be attended to.

To SILAS W. BURT [1]

Washington, *November* 8, 1885

The information which Mr. Lamont brought me in relation to the estimates both you and Mr. Godkin [2] have of one of the old Civil Service Commissioners, and two letters received from you since then, have filled me with astonishment. The same afternoon that Mr. Lamont returned from New York I heard something in the same direction, but I looked in the face of the man who addressed me and thought he was lying — God forgive me for such uncharitableness!

Up to the very day that I issued to him a new commission, I had been left to an unbroken belief that Mr. Eaton was the incarnation of civil service reform. When Mr. Godkin came to me to urge the reappointment of Mr. Pierson he brought Mr. Eaton with him to represent, I supposed, the civil service reform idea involved in the subject. I have consulted him at all times in matters connected with this reform and have had the utmost confidence that if I kept near to him I was safe. I have found no fault with any idea of his which seemed to me perhaps a little impractical and have thought I did God and the cause good service when I agreed with him. I have tried to convince many people that 'Old Eaton' was not a bad man at all, and that he was endeavoring to do his whole duty — all this because I believed it, and for the good of the cause. Not a word, not a hint to the contrary of the belief I entertained as to the high place he held in civil service reform circles, did I receive until less than three days ago. It's rather a rude awakening, this.

I am entirely aware that the enforcement of the Civil Service Law rests largely with me. Those who do not believe I am sincere in my efforts to do this, I may perhaps be pardoned for saying, ought not to be found among the prominent friends of the reform.

I hope that we are all seeking the same result. If we differ let us be tolerant. You will not take it amiss, I hope, if I say that it is absurd to claim that if it is thought best to send all those who have passed the weighers' examination to the Collector, that civil service reform will thus receive a fatal wound; and the dogs of criticism ought not to be let loose on me if I think differently.

I have heard it objected to the methods of the law that they were too

---

[1] Cleveland had restored Burt, a Republican of long service, to the post of Naval Officer of the New York Custom House.

[2] Edwin Lawrence Godkin (1831–1902), editor of the *Nation*.

secret, and it has been suggested that more publicity as to those who have passed the examination would not be hurtful. I am not prepared to say that there is anything in this tack; certain it is, however, that heretofore the policy has been against such a course until the present examination for a weigher on the Brooklyn waterfront. And now the names and the standing of those passed are not only known but published. Not content with this, the person to be appointed is selected for the Collector, civil service reformers are interviewed on the subject, and the whole matter seems to have been taken in charge by a self-constituted committee, entirely outside of the Commission and regardless of the instrumentalities which the law provides for its enforcement.

If this is well intended it certainly implies a distrust which is ungenerous; and in any event it threatens mischief.

Let us have things done decently and in order.

I confess to writing in a mood of annoyance; but nothing has yet occurred which ought to disturb the regard I have for you and other good friends of civil service reform.

To PETER BUTLER [1]

Washington, *November* 22, 1885

The question of the Collectorship of Boston having been lately settled, I feel a desire to address you this letter. If it serves no other purpose than to assure you of my regard for you, and my hope that I shall before long have the satisfaction of your personal acquaintance, it will not be written in vain. The course pursued by both of those prominently named by their friends for the office which has just been filled impressed me as so manly, and so far from the unpleasant personal jealousy too often characterizing candidates for place, that I feel very anxious to count them both among my friends. There never have been two better candidates for a position pressed upon me; and never have I been more embarrassed in making a selection. I know that you will not take it amiss if I congratulate you from the bottom of my heart upon the number and character of the friends you have gathered about you. I should not write this to a man less generous than you, nor to one whom I suspected of a disposition to misconstrue and misinterpret my motives and purpose. I take it for granted that you will suppose there is no intention on my part, simply by

[1] A well-known Boston business man, candidate of organization Democrats for Collector of the Port of Boston.

a few complimentary words, to mitigate any feeling of disappointment which I suppose you to harbor, nor by a cheap and thin assurance of interest to regain your kind feelings which I suppose you are holding in abeyance. I do not suspect you of entertaining either sore disappointment or unkind feelings; and if I did I should not hope in this way to change your condition, and should think too well of you to attempt it....

It is not at all surprising that I should especially claim that such a man take part with me in the administration of public affairs; and I have determined to ask you to accept the position of Assistant Treasurer at Boston.   Of course this is a place of great trust and importance and I should be exceedingly pleased to have you fill it....

To SECRETARY MANNING

Washington, *November* 25, 1885

The meeting is merely to consider the death of Mr. Hendricks and we can get on without you. This catastrophe will crowd us all for time, or some of us at least, who will have to attend the funeral. I suppose we shall know the day appointed for that, soon. But I'll spare you all I can as I appreciate fully your condition.

To WILSON S. BISSELL

Washington, *November* 25, 1885

Your letter is received. I don't think I shall remove the Internal Revenue Collector immediately in the third district of New York and if I should I honestly don't see the least chance of appointing Mr. Scheu's son.... I enclose a check I want collected. I haven't finished my message by a good deal and am about crazy over it. I am afraid it will be a bad one; the d——d everlasting clatter for offices continues to some extent, and makes me feel like resigning, and *HELL* is to pay generally....

I expect to set out for Indianapolis at 2 P.M.

To JOSEPH KEPPLER [1]

Washington, *December* 12, 1885

I have just received your letter with the newspaper clipping which caused you so much annoyance.

---

[1] Keppler (1838–94), a native of Vienna, was the founder and editor of the humorous magazine *Puck*, which did valiant service for the Democratic party in these years.

I don't think there ever was a time when newspaper lying was so general and so mean as at present, and there never was a country under the sun where it flourished as it does in this. The falsehoods daily spread before the people in our newspapers, while they are proofs of the mental ingenuity of those engaged in newspaper work, are insults to the American love for decency and fair play of which we boast.

I hasten to reply to your letter that the allegation contained in the slip you send me, to the effect that you ever asked a personal favor of me, is entirely and utterly false. You have never in the slightest manner indicated a wish, claim, or preference touching any appointment to office, or any official act of mine, and the only occasion I remember when I ever had any conversation with you was during a short and very friendly call you made upon me in Albany, during my term as Governor. If I ever received a letter or message from you on any subject I have forgotten it — a thing I should not be apt to do.

While I am sorry that any friendliness you may have felt or exhibited to me has been the cause of embarrassment to you, I cannot refrain from saying that if you ever become a subject of newspaper lying, and attempt to run down and expose all such lies, you will be a busy man, if you attempt nothing else.

Hoping that the denial which I send is sufficiently explicit, I am...

To WILSON S. BISSELL

Washington, *December* 14, 1885

Your letter of the 13th is just received.

In the matter of the assessment for personal property in Buffalo, I expect that as long as I am a resident there I am liable to be assessed for such property wherever it may be; and I don't want it to appear that the claim of a change of residence was made *after* an assessment is made and with the apparent purpose of avoiding its payment. You know pretty well what personal property I have and its value except what I have saved as President; and you know that I have been assessed wrongfully for three years. If I am liable here I shall see that I am properly assessed here; but I don't see any sense in paying in the city of Buffalo because I used to live there. I certainly have determined not to remove my residence there.

Somebody sent me a copy of the Buffalo *Times* which contained extracts from all the other papers concerning the message. I was very much surprised and exceedingly gratified.

I own a billiard table in the Executive Mansion at Albany. I mean to write to Hill and see if he wants it. If he does not, have you any use for it?

I had rather an impudent letter from Gluck about the manuscript of the inaugural. I answered him yesterday and then wrote to Lamont and sent him the draft of the Thanksgiving proclamation. It was the best I could do.

I am delighted to hear of the prosperity of the old firm and I tell you that your share of the business is much better than being President.

Things move on very well. I think the Senate, if discreetly treated, will do better than many suppose. There hasn't been a time since I came here that I have stood stronger and had the people so nearly with me as now, and I think I see chances of doing good — and that's a good thing.

I must go to dinner. I wish it was to eat a pickled herring, Swiss cheese, and a chop at Louis' instead of the French stuff I shall find.

To WILLIAM E. W. ROSS *and* ROBERT G. KING

Washington, *December* 18, 1885

Your letter calling my attention to the discharge of Captain S. S. Baker, an inspector attached to the custom house in the city of Baltimore, and citing in opposition to such a discharge the provisions of the statute giving preference to certain honorably discharged soldiers in making appointments in the public service, has been received. At my request a report of the facts connected with the discharge referred to has been furnished me by the Treasury Department.

It appears that a recent examination of the Baltimore custom house and its operations, resulted in the conclusion that a considerable reduction in the number of its employees could be made, without detriment to the service, and that the employment of four inspectors could profitably be discontinued....

I cannot think for a moment that you intend to claim that the statute giving preference of employment to honorably discharged soldiers should be so construed as to prevent a reduction of the force in any branch of the public service, when a due regard for economy demands the same. And though I have adopted the theory that the spirit of the law requires that the same preference should be applied to the retention of soldiers when a reduction is necessary, as to their appointment, I do not suppose you claim that this preference should be carried so far as to retain those who are unworthy or inefficient. The law which you quote was not expected, in its operation, to impair the public service, but to secure the recognition in public employment, by a preference in selection, of such discharged soldiers and sailors mentioned in the statute as could and would furnish faithful and efficient work.

It is well that associations should exist such as you represent, organized for the purpose of protecting and enforcing the rights thus guaranteed by law. The statute is based upon justice, and a proper and generous appreciation of the services of those who risked their lives for the safety of their country in her time of need. The letter and spirit of its provisions should be fairly and in good faith observed. But it should always be remembered that service in the army or navy does not of necessity fit applicants for the proper discharge of duty in all public employment; and the unwelcome fact must also be conceded, I suppose, that discharged soldiers and sailors may sometimes prove themselves unworthy of employment or retention in public positions.

Thus while your association may with perfect propriety insist that the letter and the spirit of the law should be scrupulously complied with, may it not be suggested that a due regard for the public welfare and the success of government business should require a careful consideration of cases of alleged violation before complaint is made?

I believe that the present Administration has furnished abundant proof of sincerity in its adherence to the principle upon which preference given to the soldiers and sailors is founded. But I beg you to consider the limitations which necessarily surround the rule, and which must be observed if we seek its just and fair application. And my words should not be misconstrued when I add that the persons intended to be benefited by the statute are not found exclusively in one political party, nor necessarily within the membership of the useful and beneficial veteran organizations with which you are officially connected.

Above all, let us constantly be reminded that the good of the people and the protection of their interests is the supreme duty of all public officers.

To SECRETARY ENDICOTT [1]

Washington, *December* 22, 1885

I received the within dispatch tonight. I want to talk with you about its contents and wish you would come to me early, as soon as you can

[1] William C. Endicott (1826-1900) of Salem, Massachusetts, was Secretary of War.

after the receipt of this. I go to bed tonight very much dejected and wondering if something cannot be done to better protect our citizens on the frontier and put a stop to these dreadful murders.

To WILSON S. BISSELL

Washington, *December* 24, 1885

I received today your beautiful Christmas present, and I need not tell you how deeply I am touched by your thoughtfulness and kindness. The 'thing,' as you call it, will all my life be a reminder of the best of the friendships that have found their way to me.

Last week I went with the Cabinet and we had our photographs taken. They are the best I ever saw in a group, and the first one finished up (I suppose) was sent to me. It goes by express to you today.

I had a letter from Charley today recommending Crocker for Commissioner of Education. Of course I understand that Charley don't think for a moment that such a thing is proper, and that he wrote the letter to satisfy the applicant.

I don't suppose the Senate would permit the removal of the Internal Revenue Collector if I desired to do so. In case there should be a vacancy, Hanlon of Orleans County would be very strongly urged. I declare I am astonished that Scheu turns up for that. With a number of other German candidates in Buffalo, all with the pretext they have for jealousy of the name of Scheu, it does not seem to me that the appointment would be very good politics....

I received a letter today advising me that a package from Pittsburgh had been sent to me here.

In about a week the social phase of this thing will be upon me. I dread it and most of all I begrudge the time which it will take. I mean to do just as little of the social business as is possible and not be shabby. I regard all this as a feature of the job.

It don't look as though Congress was very well prepared to do anything, but maybe it will get into shape. If a botch is made at the other end of the Avenue, I don't mean to be a party to it. And yet I desire more and more that the *party* shall demonstrate its usefulness and fitness to hold the government.

You know how sincerely I wish you a Merry Christmas and a Happy New Year.

To WILSON S. BISSELL

Washington, *December* 27, 1885

Manning has just left me, 11:45. We have been talking about you. I said, 'What a splendid thing it would be if we could get Bissell to take the place of Comptroller of the Currency.' He grabbed at it so earnestly that he made me promise to write you and see if you'd take it, which I now do. I need not tell you how delighted I would be to have you say 'yes.' Cannon, the present incumbent, has either resigned or wants to resign as his time is out, I am not sure which. At any rate, there is no question of removal in the case. The salary is $5000, with Manning says about $1000 more connected in some way with the Freedmen's Savings Bank. This latter will last but a short time longer, as the thing will soon be wound up. Why can't you come down and spend New Year's with me? There will be quite a show here and I should be delighted to have you here. Think of this and let me know. Whitney gives a dinner to the Cabinet (I suppose) Thursday evening and if you could be here then *I think I could get you in.* I know he would be pleased to have you come.

I see Hill has taken all the Buffalo people off his staff but Field. I do not suppose he will stay on.

Tell Charley that I will forward my resignation as trustee of the Normal School immediately.

I don't want you to bother about the billiard table at all. I thought if you had a place to put it, I'd give it to you. I don't see why Hill should wear it out. He told Lamont no one played on it and that he had two or three of his own. He was inclined to offer you the place of Judge Advocate General, but Lamont didn't encourage it a bit. He professes to want to do all that we desire here, but I guess he means to paddle his own canoe.

Things are working here. I think some men are pretty busy digging their political graves. I tell them I shall keep right on doing executive work. I did not come here to legislate. Let me hear from you soon, and come down if you can.

V

THE CROWDED YEAR: 1886

THE first months of 1886 brought upon Cleveland a grievous succession of problems, burdens, and attacks. He had emerged from his worst battles with the spoilsmen, but Congress was on his hands; a Congress which, with the Senate Republican and the House silverite though Democratic, was hostile to him and eager to make trouble. The Senate majority first attempted, on the basis of the Tenure-of-Office Act passed in Johnson's Administration and amended in Grant's, to block Cleveland's suspension of officeholders whom he considered unfit or partisan. Senator Edmunds and his followers miscalculated their powers, which were decidedly less than they supposed, and the result was a complete victory for the President, vindicating his conception of Executive authority. There immediately followed the attempt of the silver majority in the House to attack the gold reserve and pave the way for bringing the country to a silver basis for its currency. Early in this 'silver blizzard' Daniel Manning, the ablest member of the Cabinet and Cleveland's most trusted adviser, broke down, and the administration of the Treasury passed into the hands of Charles S. Fairchild. The silver *démarche* was defeated, thanks to the conservative Republicans in the Senate, but all Cleveland's efforts to stop the continued coinage of silver under the Bland-Allison Act of 1878 were thwarted. Meanwhile, Cleveland had torn open a hornets' nest by his veto of scores of special or private pension bills. He was accused of a partisan hostility to the veterans of the Civil War, and the Grand Army of the Republic opened an unremitting fire upon him, in which it was supported by most of the Republican press. As the session of Congress in 1886 drew to a close, Cleveland tried to take a vigorous hand in the tariff struggle which was raging in the House, with the low-tariff Democrats under William R. Morrison arrayed against the high-tariff Democrats under Samuel J. Randall. The President employed his influence in behalf of the Morrison Bill, which proposed a moderate reduction of duties, but Randall nevertheless succeeded in blocking action upon it. In the midst of the whole hurly-burly Cleveland was married to Miss Frances Folsom, the daughter of his long-time friend in Buffalo, Oscar Folsom, and at the beginning of June took a five-day honeymoon. The disgraceful efforts of the press to spy upon him and his bride, and the mendacious gossip which it soon began printing upon his private life, outraged his feelings. The closing months of 1886

were marked by the Congressional elections, in which the Democrats maintained their control of the House, and by another unsuccessful effort by Cleveland to bring the Morrison Tariff Bill to a vote.

To GEORGE W. HAYWARD
Washington, *January* 6, 1886

Yours of yesterday is just received and I am glad that your memory is
so good touching your engagement with me, and I do not propose to let
you off. But on the 20th of this month some guests are to arrive for a
week's stay. With them in the house I cannot have the kind of a time
I want with you. And they will pretty well fill up the house. I am sorry
for this but am going to ask you to postpone your visit. The next time
you arrange it there will, I am sure, be nothing in the way.

I thank you for the picture of the namesake. I honestly think he is
the handsomest of them all. I hope the next attempt to visit us will not
be long postponed. With love to your mother....

To SECRETARY MANNING
Washington, *January* 11, 1886

With this you will find a letter addressed to you in the matter of Mr.
Bassemain, cashier in the San Francisco Sub-Treasury. He has been there
a great many years. The man proposed to succeed him is, I think, a brother of a Congressman (Henley, I suppose), and this man is trying to
learn the business under Mr. Bassemain's instructions — the latter, I believe, still receiving the salary. Now it seems to me that while we are contemplating the vast and important responsibilities of offices such as this,
and the necessity there is of absolute fidelity and tried integrity, it is a
good time for you and me to make a stand for this man. I have written
the letter I send with this in such a way that I don't care if Bryan sees it
— the Assistant Treasurer.

I don't exactly see why my wishes in this matter, coupled as they are
with my regard for the public welfare, should be put aside to gratify somebody belonging to the class of whom we so freely conversed last night.

To WILSON S. BISSELL
Washington, *January* 30, 1886

Yours of the 28th is received. I am surprised to find the statement
you make so favorable, as I certainly thought the thing had gone much

worse, though to tell the truth I have paid but little attention to it. I am glad that it is closed out, for convenient as it really is, I shall feel a good deal better not to be, as long as I hold this office, concerned in anything of the kind. A man is apt to know too much in my position that might affect matters in the least speculative.

I wish you would pay the amounts needed to settle the enclosed — $30 to the City Club and $50 on my subscription to Music Hall — and send me the balance of the money belonging to me in your hands, which according to my calculations will be $4626.96. I hate to bother you with these little things, but I have been trying for a number of days to send the money to pay these things and the temptation is too strong to resist to saddle the labor upon you....

I am glad to read in your letter to the Colonel that you may stop over here in March; but I want to see you very much earlier than that. I'll invite you now to come to the Supreme Court dinner next Thursday. Let me know by telegraph immediately whether you will come. If you do not you must hold yourself in readiness to come to some other dinner or reception — say to the Diplomatic Corps. Give my love to Charley and the rest.

To WILLIAM DORSHEIMER [1]

Washington, *February* 9, 1886

I have received with regret your letter announcing a desire to be relieved from duty as United States Attorney for the Southern District of New York. When at my request you undertook the discharge of the duties of that office, I anticipated with much satisfaction your faithful and intelligent labors in the public service during the term for which you were appointed. My expectation fails of realization only in the period of your incumbency....

To SECRETARY MANNING

Washington, *March* 8, 1886

I enclose you what I think would be a sale, and I am inclined to think a satisfactory, answer to the urging of the Committee on Finance of the Senate.[2] In its present shape it seems as though if it is satisfactory to

[1] Dorsheimer had become editor of the New York *Star*, a Democratic newspaper affiliated with Tammany.

[2] The Committee, in trying to apply the Tenure-of-Office Act, had demanded an explanation of suspensions and new appointments under the Treasury Department.

'our friends the enemy' in one case it can be in all. I have submitted it to Garland, Lamar, Vilas, and Senator Beck, and they all approve. The committee, Mr. Beck tells me, will meet tomorrow, Tuesday morning. I suppose you will have replies ready for their consideration. I think there had better be no discrimination, but the three in Kentucky, two in Ohio, and one in Iowa are ready to be reported. My assumption would be to have all the replies of this class before the committee tomorrow morning.

To A Little Girl

Washington, *March* 18, 1886

I thought my birthday would be a pretty dull affair, and I didn't suppose that anyone would care enough about such a dreadfully old man to notice the occasion. But when I read the nice little message in which you sent, with your mother's, 'compliments and love,' I began to think that birthdays were pretty good things after all.

I shall enjoy the roses very much. They are nicer than any I am in the habit of seeing or smelling. And then you know in such cases a great deal depends upon the way you get flowers and the person from whom you receive them. I hope, Mollie, that in the years to come and when you are a pretty old girl, all the flowers which are given you will bring to you as much pleasure as I enjoyed through this morning's floral gift.

To Mary Cleveland Hoyt

Washington, *March* 21, 1886

... I expect to be married pretty early in June — very soon after Frank [1] returns. I think the quicker it can be done the better and she seems to think so too. You know she can hardly be said to have a home, and if the event was delayed long after her return the talk and gossip which would certainly be stirred up could not fail to be very embarrassing to her. I find it very hard to settle the question as to the manner in which the thing should be conducted. It will, I suppose, be impossible for me to go on a trip at that time or until Congress adjourns, which it seems to be the general impression will not take place until July or August.

I want my marriage to be a quiet one and am determined that the American Sovereigns shall not interfere with a thing so purely personal to me. And yet I don't want to be churlish and mean or peculiar for the sake of being peculiar. But if the example of the President is worth anything I

[1] Miss Frances Folsom of Buffalo, to whom Cleveland had become engaged in August, 1885.

want it in this matter to be in the direction of sense and proper decency. I have thought of having no one but the family, hers and mine, present at the ceremony; but maybe there are but few that would come. Hers is not large. Her mother has two sisters and two brothers and her mother. Then I have thought that it might be well to have the Cabinet people at the ceremony. They have all been so devoted to me all through and on all occasions that it seems almost as though they should be with me there. As far as the ceremony proper is concerned I do not feel like extending the attendance beyond that above indicated. I have thought that after the ceremony and on the same evening I might have a card reception, or that might be postponed to an evening or two later, or it might be given up entirely. A more democratic and popular thing, and what I would like on some accounts better, would be a public reception; but it seems rather hard to subject Frank to such an ordeal at that time. I wish you'd think of all these things and let me know how they strike you. Of course I can't get along without you and I shall utterly refuse to go through the thing unless you are about. I have calculated that you would come to me about the first day of May and stay through, and the sooner you can come the better.

I believe I shall buy or rent a house near here where I can go and be away from this cursed constant grind. I have thought it would be rather nice if Mrs. Folsom could live there and keep up the establishment, but I don't know as I could make that work.

It has occurred to me that it would be nice to have the little room adjoining mine which William occupies fixed up for a dressing-room, etc., for Frank, or a place where she could sit and stay during the day.

You can see from all this that I have been pretty busily thinking, though I have not settled on much. This is the first time I have suggested any of these things to a human being. I suppose my bridal present for my new wife is in process of manufacture. I am almost afraid I shall make a mistake there and have something too expensive. I have my heart set upon making Frank a sensible, domestic American wife, and I should be pleased not to hear her spoken of as 'The First Lady of the Land' or 'The Mistress of the White House.' I want her to be happy and to possess all she can reasonably desire, but I should feel very much afflicted if she lets many notions in her head. But I think she is pretty level-headed.

Let me hear from you as soon and as fully as possible upon all the topics touched upon in this letter....

To Mrs. Minnie Scott

Washington, *April* 4, 1886

Your letter, portraying a condition which greatly excites my sympathy, is received. I have many such and find it utterly impossible to comply with the requests for aid which they contain in a great many cases. I am so well convinced of your truthfulness and good faith that I am constrained to send you a small sum, which I hope will add to your comfort and that of the young triplets. I am so unaccustomed to matters of the kind that I must ask to be excused from the attempt to give names to the three little girls.

To Wilson S. Bissell

Washington, *April* 12, 1886

I have just received the enclosed notice. My first impulse was to write to the Board of Assessors at once; but when I recalled your statement, as I understood it, that they had agreed that this assessment should be dropped, I thought better of it. I have paid more personal taxes into the City Treasury since the year that I was mayor, in proportion to the personal property I owned, than any other man — and that too for three years when I was not a citizen or resident at all. Take it all in all, that municipality seems determined to punish me pretty severely.

I will pay no more personal tax to the city of Buffalo. I don't live there and never shall again; and if there is any way to shake off my allegiance I want to do it. I should prefer, of course, to prevent the assessment of this tax, to a refusal to pay it after it is assessed; but I certainly will pay no more. I want the exemption I claim to be put expressly upon the ground of non-residence. If my affidavit of that fact is necessary I will furnish it. May I trouble you to attend to this?

P.S. I am alone with the Colonel. I wish you were here.

To Mary Cleveland Hoyt

Washington, *April* 14, 1886

I must before I go to bed write you a little letter and tell you that I received yours of a late date and how pleased I am at the prospect of your being here soon. I want to talk with you about the event which is soon to take place. You know as it draws near there are lots of little things which I begin to stew over a little, and I can't talk to anyone about them except the Colonel. He and I canvass the matter and I expect we could get it pretty nearly right, but probably there might be something in which you could help us.

It looks now as if Frank would reach New York about the 28th of May, stay there a few days, and then come here and be married the next day or the day of her arrival — say the 2d or 3d of June.

We have sort of planned the thing in this way: Have the ceremony at 7 o'clock, with no one present but the two families; have a dinner immediately after the ceremony; have the members of the Cabinet and their families come about 8:30 o'clock, and have a reception *by card* from 9 to 11.

I had a letter from Libbie tonight.... Let me know just as soon as you can when you will probably be here.

To REPRESENTATIVE JOHN B. WEBER [1]

Washington, *April* 19, 1886

Allow me to thank you personally, as well as in the interest of a due regard for woman and decency, for the words atrributed to you in the newspaper this evening. This is the first glimpse I have had of American manhood, since the scandalous press and thoughtful people of the country began to hunt down an absent and defenceless girl, as if she were a criminal.

To MARY CLEVELAND HOYT

Washington, *April* 19, 1886

I have changed my ideas entirely in regard to the wedding. I am decidedly of the opinion now that the affair should be more quiet even than at first contemplated. The time when Frank will arrive in this country is not entirely certain, and for that reason the day of the wedding cannot be fixed, with no chance of postponement, long enough in advance to permit of all arrangements on the part of the families to attend. If they should attend, they will be subjected from the time of their arrival to the impudent inquisition of newspaper correspondents, and if this latter dirty gang were not entirely satisfied, our friends would probably be dished up in a very mean way; and the newspapers and the people have acted in such a mean way that I don't care to gratify either of them.

[1] John B. Weber (1842–96), an old Buffalo friend who had succeeded Cleveland as sheriff, was a member of Congress 1885–89. He was a Republican.

My notion now is to have you and Libbie [1] and Bissell (if he will come) and Miss Nelson on my side, and Frank's mother and perhaps one or two of her aunts and one or two others on her side, and be married by Dr. Sunderland [2] with no reception the same night or any other time unless we choose — which we can decide when we get ready. I should like to have Colonel Lamont at the ceremony, but am not strenuous about that. He and I have canvassed the whole matter and agree that the plan above outlined is the best that offers. I have written the whole scheme to Frank and from something she wrote in her last letter I think she will be pleased with it. If she is not, I will accede to her wishes; but I am of the opinion that after she sees the newspaper clippings I sent her yesterday she will feel more than ever like falling in with my ideas.

The good people of the country will, I am sure, be satisfied to have their President behave on such an occasion like anyone else and dispense with all nonsense and flummery.

I want you to approve of the manner in which I am inclined to have the thing arranged. It would be hard to do so with your preconceived notions, but you must put yourself in my place as nearly as you can and try to see how much that may be unpleasant will be avoided. I am very indignant at the way Frank has been treated and mean to give the 'gang' as little chance at us hereafter as possible.

I believe I shall make no change in the house until she is here, when I expect I shall be better able to tell just what we want. So I don't want you to write to any members of the family about it — at any rate until I give you the word.

To Mary Cleveland Hoyt

Washington, *April 26*, 1886

. . . I have written to Frank more than a week ago giving her my new scheme and I am inclined to think she will agree to it. I have lately thought of adding to the very few family and intimate friends, the Cabinet, General Sheridan and wife, Admiral Porter and wife, Chief Justice Waite and wife and daughter, and such, making about fifty or more.

It would not do at all to invite all my family and omit her uncles and

---

[1] Rose Elizabeth Cleveland, previously mentioned as the President's youngest sister.

[2] The Reverend Byron Sunderland, minister of the First Presbyterian Church in Washington.

aunts. They are all the relatives she has and she has lived with them so much that they are precisely as near as her brothers and sisters. I would not propose making any distinction between them and my sisters and brothers. It will work out some way, but I would like to talk with you about it. I can't write all I want to say.

Do you happen to remember what was done with the key I had to cable messages? I can't find it. It's awkward fixing this business because it takes about a month to get an answer to a letter.

Let me hear from you again very soon. You see, Frank is entering a life where she can have all the excitement she wants, and she can afford better than a good many girls to have a quiet wedding.

To Mary Cleveland Hoyt

Washington, *May* 5, 1886

I was pleased to hear from your last letter that you were to be with me next week. On the strength of your coming Libbie writes me that she will probably leave Holland Patent the last of next week and stay over Sunday in New York and arrive here probably the first of week after next. She seems to think it too bad not to have all the brothers and sisters at the wedding, and yet she thinks I ought to go to Frank somewhere and be married and take my bride to the White House. If Frank would agree to it, I think I would be quite willing to be married in New York with no one present but the witnesses....

To Mary Cleveland Hoyt

Washington, *May* 20, 1886

I think I shall have very nice arrangements perfected for a short stay at Deer Park after the performance; but I don't know how all our plans may be changed by the death of Frank's Grandfather Folsom [1] yesterday. I should think the wedding might go on as planned very quietly. And an additional reason is afforded for quietness which may seem to cut off some guests which have heretofore been calculated upon — Miss Grigg, for instance.

The news from the ship office in New York is that the vessel will arrive not earlier than Tuesday afternoon nor later than Thursday. I have just received a letter from Mrs. Welch, the aunt, asking me what the arrangement now is by which, according to letters from the traveling party, they

---

[1] John Folsom of Folsomdale, near Buffalo.

propose to circumvent people. I don't know what to write to her, and think I will put off a reply to such time as it will reach her just about as the ship arrives.... Let me hear what effect you think Mr. Folsom's death will have on the plans and what Louise says.

To POSTMASTER-GENERAL VILAS
Washington, *May* 28, 1886

On Wednesday next at seven o'clock in the evening I shall be married to Miss Folsom at the White House.

We shall have a very quiet wedding, but I earnestly desire that you and Mrs. Vilas will be present on that occasion.

To MARY CLEVELAND HOYT
Washington, *May* 28, 1886

... Mrs. Lamont was just here (9:15 A.M.) and says she has just received a dispatch from the Colonel that he is on his way from New York and will arrive at 10:40. I heard from him last night to the effect that at half-past five there was no news. I think now that the ship came in later. And just this very moment a dispatch is handed me from Ben dated this morning saying: 'Arrived safe. All in good health.' So that I guess now that the Colonel is hurrying home to complete arrangements for the wedding to take place at the time contemplated.

I think you may safely calculate on that.

To WILSON S. BISSELL
Washington, *May* 29, 1886

I was yesterday for the first time able to fix positively the 2d day of June as the date of my wedding — that is, it was the first day that I was sure, in view of certain events, that we could be married on the day we had selected some time ago.

I don't know that you expect anything in the way of an invitation, but this is to say, what you already know, that your presence has always been, in contemplating the event, one of its important features, and I should be delighted if you will be one of the very few who are to witness the ceremony. I know you will be here unless you are deterred from coming by the death of your sister, which I know was a great affliction to you; and while any discussion involving the influence of that event upon your conduct is entirely out of place, I cannot help telling you how much I want you at my marriage.

I must add that the affair will be extremely plain and quiet, with nobody but the members of the Cabinet and their wives, a very few members of the families, and one or two friends on each side perhaps — not more than twenty-five in all.

To SECRETARY MANNING

Washington, *May* 30, 1886

I have not before made answer to your letter tendering your resignation as Secretary of the Treasury, [1] because it was a subject which at best I was loath to entertain, and for the further reason that I hardly knew at once how to treat it.

It affects me greatly, my dear friend, to think of separating you from my official life, and from a pleasant intercourse in *every* relation of life; but I conceive it to be my duty in view of the sacrifice which your entrance to my Cabinet involved on your part, to consider the question so reluctantly met with a view entirely to your claims and needs instead of my own.

I propose this for your consideration, earnestly hoping that it will meet your views. Let us permit the matter to remain as it is, and entirely confidential between us and those already informed till the first day of next August. Then we will take it up again. Of course in the meantime you are the head of the Department, and I will as the head of every Executive Department of the Government insist upon only one thing on the part of my Secretary of the Treasury; and that is, utter and complete idleness and rest during the next two months. Go when and where you please — subject to the direction and control of the two 'jailers,' your wife and your physician — and let the rest of us manage your department; but you must banish it from your thoughts as well as from your efforts.

At the date above indicated I promise now to consider the main question in a spirit of sacrificing friendship, with my judgment entirely undecided by any selfish interests or inconsiderate preferences.

Let me hear on Tuesday, if you can perfectly well, whether or not you will be perfectly easy and satisfied to consent to the arrangement proposed *in all conditions.* In the meantime believe me, more than ever, your sincere friend.

[1] Secretary Manning had suffered a stroke of apoplexy on March 23, and though he attended Cleveland's wedding, was too enfeebled to return to his desk. Assistant Secretary Charles S. Fairchild acted in his stead.

To SECRETARY MANNING

Washington, *June* 1, 1886

I have received your letter in which your resignation is tendered as Secretary of the Treasury. The sentiments therein contained are entirely in keeping with the devotion to public duty and the loyalty to the interests of the Government which have characterized your relations to the present Administration. I am not surprised, though much impressed, by the concern you evince for the correction of the abuses and the inauguration of the reforms to which in your letter you allude, and which have been so often topics of our anxious consultations.

I have hoped that the day was at hand when the party to which we belong, influenced largely by faith and confidence in you and in the wisdom of your views, would be quickened in the sense of responsibility and led to more harmonious action upon the important questions with which you have had to deal.

In considering your proposed resignation, I should be strongly inclined by my personal regard and friendship and by the value of your services to the country to beg you to at once and entirely abandon your inclination to relinquish your path of arduous duty. But I am convinced that I should not do this, and that in all I suggest and ask I should have much at heart in your welfare and safety.

You have placed your resignation in my hands. My responsibility here begins and I know that the responsibility will be met and the wishes of the people of the land fully answered, when I ask you to postpone for a while any insistence upon the acceptance of your resignation and that your final conclusion thereon may be delayed until the effects of continued rest and freedom from official care upon your condition may be better tested. I therefore earnestly request you to accept a leave of absence until the first day of October next, when, if you desire it, the question of your resignation may be resumed with, perhaps, better means of judging all the facts and probabilities which should be considered in its determination.

Hoping that you will consent to this suggestion and trusting that your encouraging progress towards restoration to health may continue, I am...

To DANIEL S. LAMONT

Deer Park, Md., *June* 3, 1886

We arrived this morning at four o'clock and were immediately domiciled in a beautiful cottage where we already feel quite at home.[1] William and Lena have matters well in hand and it certainly looks as if in selecting this place for a few days' sojourn we had achieved a 'triumph of genius.' Mr. John Davis came up with us and has been indefatigable in his efforts to do anything possible for our comfort and pleasure. He brought up with him eight or nine men to act as a patrol charged with the duty of protecting us from newspaper nuisances. He has established certain limits within which such animals are not allowed to enter, and these limits are to be watched and guarded night and day. There are a number of newspaper men here and I can see a group of them sitting on a bridge which marks one of the limits, waiting for some move to be made which will furnish an incident.

I find that a coach and *four* horses have been sent here for my use. Mr. Davis said the man from the *Tribune* asked him all about that and much more. Of course the four horses and the fact that the cottage belongs to the Baltimore & Ohio Railroad Company, etc., etc., will be subjects of comment peculiar to that sheet. I — that is, *we* — mean to ride this afternoon, but propose to make two horses answer our purpose. In climbing some of the mountains hereabout four horses are necessary; and when we need them we shall use them.

A gentleman in the neighborhood has just sent us a nice lot of brook trout.

I come now to the real purpose of this letter.

Everything thus far is so very nice and the place appears to be so beautiful that I wish you and your wife and Mr. and Mrs. Vilas could come here and spend Sunday. We can take care of you first-rate and I know that you would all enjoy the visit. This may and probably will be handed to you by Mr. Davis, who will tell you when you can start and how well you can be accommodated en route and when you arrive. I wish you would see Vilas and fix it up. If he and his wife cannot come, I do hope you and Mrs. Lamont will come. If you can do so let me know by telegraph and we will have you met at the train. Our carriage is here and I must break off.

[1] Deer Park is in the Blue Ridge Mountains of Garrett County, western Maryland, not far from the headwaters of the Potomac.

am sorry to see the determined effort made, in any form, to do in Congress what I think can better be left to the Treasury Department.

To FRANCIS LYNDE STETSON [1]

Washington, *July* 15, 1886

You said when you left me a few days ago that if I desired it you would see the Collector and tell him of my determination to have a change in the administration of his office. I have thought of the matter a good deal and my determination grows stronger — that is, my mind is absolutely made up. There is no use in trying to dissuade me for I cannot dissuade myself; and I have tried to do so sincerely and faithfully. The only question is as to the manner in which the change is to be brought about.

At present I am able and very willing to acquit the present incumbent of any wilful act or deliberate fault, and I desire to keep my mind in that condition. And while it is in that condition I want to have the change effected in such a way as to save Mr. Hedden as much as possible. Therefore it is that I desire him to tender his resignation without my asking him for it — which I shall certainly do unless it is immediately offered.

As I said above, I have no specific charge that I want to make against him, but my resolution to make a change is based upon the conviction that Mr. Hedden is in the wrong place and is not calculated to do the things necessary for a successful administration of the office. Sending any person here to expostulate or coming here himself for that purpose will make matters infinitely worse, and there is nothing to be done for his comfort and mine except for him to take the instructions.

Will you please see the gentleman immediately and with as much consideration as possible for his feelings tell him the condition of affairs? I shall await very impatiently the result and wish you would telegraph me something.[2]

To C. H. JONES

Washington, *July* 25, 1886

I confess to some surprise at the tenor of your last letter to me and a later one to Colonel Lamont. There are several millions of people in the

---

[1] Stetson (1846–1920) was an important corporation lawyer of New York City and friend of Tilden, who advised Cleveland on local appointments.

[2] Hedden resigned August 7, 1886, and was supplanted by Daniel Magone of Ogdensburg, New York.

granting a pension to Carter W. Tiller, as the dependent father of George W. Tiller.

My veto was based upon the non-dependence of the claimant upon the deceased soldier, though the fact of his son's desertion was mentioned in a way which quite plainly led to the inference that it was of itself sufficient reason for the rejection of the bill.

Representations were made to me last evening, and papers and statements furnished, for the purpose of convincing me that I had erroneously determined both questions which the case involved. Of course I want to do exact justice to the applicants for pensions. And my idea of justice in their consideration involves the exercise of the utmost liberality and the determining of doubts in favor of the soldier or those claiming through him.

Fully convinced that you are governed by the same considerations, and as you have the best means available for a thorough examination of these matters, I have determined to ask you to review the case, not only upon the papers now on file in your office, but with the aid of any additional evidence or information within your reach, and act upon it. If you feel constrained to affirm the action of your predecessor in office, will you please furnish me with the reasons which lead you to an adverse conclusion upon the application?

To SAMUEL J. RANDALL [1]

Washington, *July* 14, 1886

You know, I think, that I am not at all inclined to meddle with proposed legislation while it is pending in Congress.

My object in sending this is to express in writing, to avoid all misunderstanding, my regret that any of our friends in the House should deem it necessary to aid in such legislation as is contemplated by the resolution now pending. I am unable to see why the Treasury Department should not be trusted as previously it has been, under other Administrations. There was nothing on Mr. Manning's mind so much as the fear that something might be done in the direction now proposed.

I do not speak of these things as presenting any reason why wise legislation should not be passed. It is because I deem it dangerous that I

---

[1] Randall was the House leader in opposing the so-called Morrison Resolution, which required the Treasury to employ all its reserves over $100,000,000 in the redemption of government bonds, and which Cleveland feared would menace the gold standard.

(Later)

We have had our first ride in this country and in its course I was constantly reminded of the rides about Washington. I want to say in continuation of the subject of your visiting us here that if you should come on the same train we did you could probably remain on the car and have your sleep out before coming to our cottage.

You have had so much to do with all that concerned our marriage that we should be glad to have you the first to see us in our new relations. Frank and I have been talking a good deal today about the wedding and in recalling the details of the affair we have run against you so often that I think we are both willing to admit that if it hadn't been for 'poor Colonel Lamont' (as Frank calls you when she recounts all you had to do) we couldn't have been married at all.

And I want to assure you of another thing: of all that was done for us by kind friends in the way of remembrances nothing has touched and pleased us more than the beautiful flowers which through the thoughtfulness and kindness of yourself and Mrs. Lamont accompanied us here and now decorate our cottage.

Upon reflection I think it would be better not to invite anyone to come with you here. It might cause comment or surprise on the part of other members of the Cabinet to invite Vilas and I am sure we would rather see you and Mrs. Lamont here alone.

If you can't spend Sunday here (but you can if you want to), perhaps you and Mrs. Lamont can come up and go home with us. But we have our hearts set on your seeing us here.

I hope that we shall receive newspapers giving accounts of the wedding. With love from the new firm to yourself and Mrs. Lamont....

To THE PEOPLE OF CHARLESTON, SOUTH CAROLINA
Washington, *June* 18, 1886

I have asked the privilege of thus communicating our joint acknowledgment of this present, because this delicate and thoughtful attention to my wife has naturally given rise to grateful emotions, and because it affords me an opportunity to express my appreciation of the kind words with which the donors refer to myself and my performance of public duty. You and your associates who have united in the letter accompanying your gift can hardly realize the comfort I derive from the assurance therein contained of confidence and esteem. The letter and the gift take their places in my new household, and for all time will serve as reminders not only of the happiest incident of my life as a citizen, but of the further fact that in my official character, the humble efforts I have made to assure good government to the people and complete reconciliation between all sections of the land, are considerately and pleasantly recognized by my fellow-countrymen.

To DR. S. B. WARD

Washington, *June* 21, 1886

You don't know how I sometimes am perplexed when thinking of my vacation. Occasionally I almost feel like giving the thing up and remaining here where I know what I must meet rather than fly to ills I know not of.... You have no idea how I fairly yearn to be *let alone*. I'll fly from any spot where the poor privilege of being no trouble to any human being is denied me.

To JAMES FREEMAN CLARKE

Washington, *July* 5, 1886

I have been hoping for a little leisure which would permit me to reply to your letter more at length than I find myself able to do. And as I see no chance of my doing better I have determined to send you a report made in answer to my inquiries touching the discharge of your friend.

The heads of these Departments work very hard themselves, the people expect much of us all, and we must have good assistants. In many cases when changes are made the parties dismissed have good friends who in all sincerity and honesty cannot see why the change should be made. I have been quite a good deal afflicted by these things, but I do hope that in this case my good friend will see the matter, as nearly as possible, as if he were on the ground.

With many thanks for your kind words to me in your last and with assurances of the highest esteem....

To COMMISSIONER JOHN C. BLACK [1]

Washington, *July* 8, 1886

On or about the 19th day of last month, I transmitted to the House of Representatives a message giving reasons for my disapproval of a bill

---

[1] Black (1839–1915), an attorney of Champaign, Illinois, and a colonel in the Civil War, had been appointed Commissioner of Pensions in March, 1885.

United States who have much more time to write letters to the President than he can possibly find time to reply.

I have not written, as you requested, any explanation of the manner in which something claimed to be a letter from you to me, but which you declared was not a true copy, found its way into print, because I knew I could not account for its appearance, and for the further reason that I did not exactly see why I should become in any way involved in a newspaper war over the publication of a letter which you said was not a copy of one in my possession....

I am surprised that newspaper talk should be so annoying to you, who ought so well to understand the utter and complete recklessness and falsification in which they so generally indulge. When, after one of your interviews with me, kind friends put under my eye what purported to be an account of some dreadfully foolish things which you had said, I did not allow them to disturb me at all, feeling perfectly confident that the alleged interview was false.

To Dr. S. B. Ward

Washington, *August* 8, 1886

...A proprietor of a Chicago newspaper has written the Colonel practically asking permission for a representative of his newspaper to go with us.

My destination will be pretty well known, I suppose, and I begin to fear that the pestilence of newspaper correspondence will find its way to our retreat. And Mrs. Cleveland's presence will I presume increase this probability. I am thinking a little of selecting some gentleman of the craft and inviting him to go and impart to the Associated Press all that can by any possibility interest any decent citizen of the United States, and giving it out that all other reports are spurious. One thing is certain. If the newspaper men get there *I shall leave.* I will not have my vacation spoiled by being continually watched and lied about, and I won't subject my wife to that treatment. Let me hear from you as the plans mature.

P.S. If we could have some sort of bathing facilities in the cottage I would gladly pay the expense. Do they have those india-rubber bathtubs in Albany?

To WILSON S. BISSELL

Washington, *August* 12, 1886

I enclose you check for $25.75 with thanks for standing between me and an accusation of dead-beatism. I plan to start for the woods next Monday, but believe that if arrangements were not all perfected and I could keep people off me here that I would not go at all. I could do lots of good things here during the next month.

I thank you for telling me about the governor trying to get away my secretary.[1] What a whelp, morally and politically, he is! I send you a letter just received to show you a sample of what I get. I've just opened it, and if I knew who to suggest I would send a name to the writer.

My address in the woods will be 'Saranac Inn, Upper Saranac, Lake Bloomingdale, Essex County, New York,' and you may be sure I should be glad to hear from you.

To WILSON S. BISSELL

Washington, *August* 14, 1886

Colonel Vilas will arrive in Buffalo next Tuesday between 11 A.M. and 12 M. and will stop at the Tifft House. I write this thinking and hoping that you and perhaps some of my other good friends would like to meet him. He will stay all the afternoon and take a boat to go up the lake in the evening. If you don't look him up he will call on you — or at least he expressed his intention of doing so. You know I think he is one of the most complete men, mentally, morally, and politically, I ever met.

I leave for the woods Monday morning. I hate to leave, and yet this very day I was obliged to acknowledge that my vacation came just in time.

To THE CONFEDERATE HOME OF CHARLESTON, SOUTH CAROLINA

Washington, *September* 3, 1886

A circular just received informs me of the object and purpose of the Home for Mothers, Widows, and Daughters of Confederate Soldiers at Charleston, as well as its present need, caused by recent misfortunes. Though constantly appealed to from all sides and upon all manner of occasions for pecuniary aid, I cheerfully enclose a slight contribution to the sum necessary to make such repairs as will enable this useful and benevolent institution to again open its doors to the mothers, widows, and

[1] Governor David B. Hill had attempted to secure the services of Daniel Lamont.

To THOMAS PARKER

Washington, *September* 23, 1886

I find your letter of the 16th instant awaiting my return to the Executive Mansion.

Your exceedingly ill-natured reference to the 'Irishman' and the 'Catholic' who you say has succeeded you in your work detracts very much, I think, from the claims you base upon 'twenty-two years of honest and fruitful service in the Brooklyn postoffice and ten years as a soldier with an honorable discharge,' and demonstrates that you have but little idea of the impartial treatment due to American citizenship.

You send me a newspaper clipping containing a published letter written to you by George William Curtis which contains so much good sound sense upon the general subject of removal of subordinates by their immediate superiors that I recommend it to your careful re-perusal.

To FREDERIC R. COUDERT [1]

Washington, *September* 30, 1886

You are informed, I suppose, of the arrangement that has been made touching the part which the Government shall take in the matter of invitations to foreign guests to attend the inauguration of the Bartholdi Statue.

I have reflected upon the suggestion which has been made that a special invitation be sent by me to Mr. Bartholdi himself, and I confess that it would be a pleasure to accede to that proposition. It has seemed to me, however, that such a departure from the plan adopted, which contemplates the giving of all invitations abroad through our minister to France, might not, for obvious reasons, be satisfactory in all quarters or properly understood.

I think Mr. Bartholdi's presence cannot but be regarded as the main feature of a successful inauguration of his great work; and I should be extremely sorry to have him suppose for a minute that the manner in which his invitation is transmitted to him can be regarded as the slightest indication of a want of interest, or lack of appreciation of all that he has done for us, on the part of the Government. I earnestly hope that he will be present at the inauguration ceremonies.

[1] Coudert (1832–1903), a noted New York attorney, was a warm admirer and supporter first of Tilden and then of Cleveland.

daughters for whom it was intended, and whose condition presents such an urgent appeal to the sympathy of every American citizen.

To QUEEN VICTORIA

Washington, *September* 4, 1886 (cable)

Your Majesty's expression of sympathy for the sufferers by the earthquake is warmly appreciated and awakes grateful response in American hearts.

To DANIEL S. LAMONT

Saranac Inn, *September* 8, 1886

It's after twelve o'clock and I am to rise at half-past six to join a deer hunt; but I must write you tonight how pleased I am to learn from your dispatch of today that you will come here next week and stay till I go out, which will be the 21st.

Ward will be in Albany next Saturday and arrange for the car, etc.   I wish you would see him if you can without losing a train, for he will have something to send by you.   Manning has sent me a dispatch saying that it is very important that he should see me before I go to Washington and I have replied that I will meet him on the way home.

You will take the train at Albany about 11 o'clock P.M.; get a ticket there if you can for Paul Smith's Station or Smith's Station — the sleeping-car goes right through.   You arrive there about 11 A.M.   Paul has asked the privilege of bringing you up here and I have told him he might do so.   You must telegraph me when you will be there and who will be with you and he will be prepared to bring you here more comfortably than you can come in any other way.   Let me know as early as possible.

We shall try hard to save you some good fishing, though this is not just the season for it.   If there is any point in all this matter which is not just clear the Doctor will be posted fully and if you are cramped any for time in Albany you had better ask him to meet you at the depot.

Give my love to Mrs. Lamont and the children and come up as soon as you can and get a little of this mountain air if nothing else.

My wife would send her regards if she was not in bed and asleep.

VI

A WESTERN TOUR: THE TARIFF ISSUE

CLEVELAND began the year 1887 by signing the Interstate Commerce Act and selecting a capable list of men, under Thomas M. Cooley as chairman, for places on the new Commission. He also witnessed the full initiation of a reform still closer to his heart when he signed the Dawes Severalty Act, empowering the President, whenever he determined the time was right, to break up any Indian reservation, allot the land to the inhabitants, and endow the Indians of that tribe with American citizenship. After Congress adjourned in March, the President had a comparatively quiet spring and summer. It was marked by renewed difficulties with the G.A.R., accentuated by Cleveland's well-meant but unfortunate order in June, 1887, for the return of all battleflags, Union and Confederate, to the various States — an order which Cleveland had to revoke; and by a partial reorganization of the Cabinet, Charles S. Fairchild taking the place of Manning at the Treasury, and William F. Vilas succeeding Lamar as Secretary of the Interior. Most of the month of October was spent by Cleveland and his wife in a tour of the West and South. They went as far in the one direction as St. Paul and Omaha, and in the other as Atlanta and Montgomery; and they were greeted with much cordiality as well as curiosity. On their return Cleveland found a grave and urgent problem confronting him — that of the Treasury surplus. Thanks to a redundant revenue, it had swollen to unmanageable proportions, and threatened to impound enough of the nation's currency in Washington to produce a monetary stringency. The principal source of this surplus was the tariff, which was also objectionable in that it placed an unfair burden on the farmers and the workingmen. At the famous Oak View Conferences early in September, Cleveland, Speaker Carlisle, Representative Roger Q. Mills, and others determined to make a frontal assault upon the tariff law. This was executed by Cleveland in his annual message to Congress at the beginning of December, 1887. Breaking all precedent, he devoted the entire message to the single subject of the tariff, demanding a marked reduction in the duties on articles of necessity. A bill embodying his views, the Mills Bill, was at once introduced. Up to that moment his reelection in 1888 had been taken for granted. But the opposition to his tariff stand among manufacturers and other business men gave the Republicans new heart, and they prepared for a vigorous fight in the campaign of 1888.

sults of Administrative endeavor to be reached with such agencies as these.

Upon a full consideration of all I have before me, I am constrained to decline the application of Mr. Stone for his reinstatement.

I enclose his letter with this, and desire you to acquaint him with my decision.

To GOVERNOR DAVID B. HILL

Washington, *December* 19, 1886

Your letter to Colonel Lamont in relation to your long contemplated visit to Washington and to me, is now before me.

I note with pleasure the inclination it evinces towards a comfortable visiting sort of a time, though you know it is perfectly easy to get up a hurrah here upon the slightest occasion. And the suggestion you make as to the time is also full of sense. If you can get away between Christmas and New Year's it would be a first-rate time to come here to visit. And if you find you can cut loose then, suppose you come Tuesday or Wednesday of that week.

Of course I shall want you to meet my Cabinet and perhaps a few others at a dinner; but I will promise not to bore you much in that way. Mrs. Manning gives a dinner on Monday the 27th, and if you want to come as early as that, I think if you are longing for such a thing, I could get you an invitation.

So the gist of this rambling letter is, that I hope very much that you can visit me for a while at the White House during the holiday week — leaving the exact days to your selection. Please let me hear from you as early as you can determine this question. A fellow who has his message off his hands ought certainly to wish the other fellow who has his in the pains of parturition 'a safe deliverance,' and I do this most sincerely. But I have neither patience nor indulgence for the likes of you, who calmly write that 'Mrs. Hill will not accompany me.' [1]

[1] Governor Hill was of course a bachelor.

the purpose of advancing partisan interests, and conducted upon the avowed theory that the Administration of the government was not entitled to the confidence and respect of the people. There is no dispute whatever concerning the fact that Mr. Stone did join others who were campaigning the State of Pennsylvania in opposition to the Administration. It appears, too, that he was active and prominent with noisy enthusiasm in attendance upon at least two large public meetings; that the speeches at such meetings were largely devoted to abuse and misrepresentation of the Administration; that he approved all this and actually addressed the meetings himself in somewhat the same strain; that he attended such meetings away from his home for the purpose of making such addresses, and that he was advertised as one of the speakers at each of the said meetings.

I shall accept as true the statement of Mr. Stone that the time spent by him in thus demonstrating his willingness to hold a profitable office at the hands of the Administration which he endeavored to discredit with the people, and which had kindly overlooked his previous offences, did not result in the neglect of ordinary official duty. But his conduct has brought to light such an unfriendliness toward the Administration which he pretends to serve and of which he is nominally a part, and such a subsequent lack of loyal interest in its success, that the safest and surest guaranty of his faithful service is, in my opinion, entirely wanting. His course, in itself such as should not have been entered upon while maintaining official relations to the Administration, also renews and revives, with unmistakable interpretation of their character and intent, the charges of offensive partisanship heretofore made and up to this time held in abeyance.

Mr. Stone and others of like disposition are not to suppose that party lines are so far obliterated that the Administration of the government is to be trusted in places high or low to those who aggressively and constantly endeavor unfairly to destroy the confidence of the people in the party responsible for such Administration. While vicious partisan methods should not be allowed for partisan purposes to degrade or injure the public service, it is my belief that nothing tends so much to discredit our efforts, in the interest of such service, to treat fairly and generously the official incumbency of political opponents, as conduct such as is here disclosed.

The people of this country certainly do not require the best re-

To ATTORNEY-GENERAL GARLAND

Washington, *November* 23, 1886

I have read the letter of the 18th instant written to you by William A. Stone, [1] lately suspended from office as District Attorney for the Western District of Pennsylvania, and the subject matter to which it refers has received my careful consideration. I shall not impute to the writer any mischievous motive in his plainly erroneous assumption that his case and that of M. E. Benton, recently suspended and reinstated, rest upon the same state of facts, but prefer to regard his letter as containing the best statement possible upon the question of his reinstatement.

You remember, of course, that soon after the present Administration was installed, and, I think, nearly a year and a half ago, I considered with you certain charges which had been preferred against Mr. Stone as a Federal official. You remember, too, that the action we then contemplated was withheld by reason of the excuses and explanations of his friends. These excuses and explanations induced me to believe that Mr. Stone's retention would insure a faithful performance of official duty; and that whatever offensive partisanship he had deemed justifiable in other circumstances, he would, during his continuance in office at his request under an Administration opposed to him in political creed and policy, content himself with a quiet and unobtrusive enjoyment of his political privileges. I certainly supposed that his sense of propriety would cause him to refrain from pursuing such a partisan course as would wantonly offend and irritate the friends of the Administration who insisted that he should not be retained in office, either because of his personal merit or in adherence to the methods which for a long time had prevailed in the distribution of Federal offices.

In the light of a better system, and without considering his political affiliations, Mr. Stone, when permitted to remain in office, became a part of the business organization of the present Administration, bound by every obligation of honor to assist, within his sphere, in its successful operation. This obligation involved not only the proper performance of official duty, but a certain good faith and fidelity which, while not exacting the least sacrifice of political principle, forbade active participation in purely partisan demonstrations of a pronounced type, undertaken for

---

[1] Stone, the Federal Attorney for the Pittsburgh district, had also made campaign speeches and been suspended; he was a Republican, and Cleveland regarded his real offence as his disloyalty to the Administration, for he had attacked it in abusive terms.

To EARL M. VANSLYCK

Washington, *January* 10, 1887

On behalf of Mrs. Cleveland I return with this the certificate for fifty shares of stock in the Cleveland Milling and Mining Company, which was sent to her a short time ago by you and the president of the company. However these officers of this corporation may justify themselves in thus donating its stock, Mrs. Cleveland can see no reason why she should be the recipient of the same. I write to you because I am not certain that I correctly read the name of the president of the company.

To COLONEL JOHN I. ROGERS

Washington, *January* 26, 1887

I have received from you, as one of the committee of the Catholic Club of Philadelphia, an invitation to attend a banquet to be given by the Club on Tuesday evening, February 8th, in honor of His Eminence Cardinal Gibbons.[1] The thoughtfulness which prompted this invitation is gratefully appreciated; and I regret that my public duties here will prevent its acceptance. I should be glad to join in the contemplated expression of respect to be tendered to the distinguished head of the Catholic Church in the United States, whose personal acquaintance I very much enjoy, and who is so worthily entitled to the esteem of his fellow-citizens.

I thank you for the admirable letter which accompanied my invitation, in which you announce as one of the doctrines of your Club: 'that a good and exemplary Catholic must *ex necessitate rei* be a good and exemplary citizen,' and that 'the teachings of both human and divine law, thus merging in the one word duty, form the only union of Church and State that a civil and religious government can recognize.'

I know you will permit me, as a Protestant, to supplement this noble sentiment by the expression of my conviction that the same influence and result follow a sincere and consistent devotion to the teachings of every religious creed which is based upon Divine sanction. A wholesome religious faith thus inures to the perpetuity, the safety and the prosperity of our Republic, by exacting the due observance of civil law, the protection of public order and a proper regard for the rights of all; and thus are its adherents better fitted for good citizenship and confirmed in a sure and steadfast patriotism. It seems to me, too, that the conception of duty to the State which is derived from religious precept involves a sense of per-

---

[1] James Gibbons (1834–1921), had been elevated to the rank of Cardinal in June, 1886.

sonal responsibility, which is of the greatest value in the operation of a government by the people. It will be a fortunate day for our country when every citizen feels that he has an ever-present duty to perform to the State which he cannot escape from or neglect without being false to his religious as well as his civil allegiance.

To EDWARD M. SHEPARD

Washington, January 30, 1887

I have not had an opportunity till this evening to read the argument 'privately printed' which you kindly sent to me.[1] I have just finished it and hasten to thank you for it with all my heart. It is superb, and has given me new ideas, while the concluding pages contain precisely what I have been longing to say and hoping that someone would say for me. Your words come like rays of light in the midst of storm and clouds, which my independent friends have for a short time past been blindly and with inconsiderate ruthlessness launching into the atmosphere of my political life.

I am perfectly astounded at some recent occurrences and very much irritated to more than suspect that some of these friends have, like a coroner's jury, been sitting upon my body and endeavoring to agree whether a verdict should be rendered of 'Found dead' or 'Died by his own hand and disgraced by broken pledges.'

They seem to be inclined to hold on to promises I have never thought of making and to expect me to perform miracles at once and now. I have thought of the strange situation which would be presented by these and the *World*, the *Sun*, and the worst spoilsmen of both parties standing together. And yet extremes do thus sometimes meet.

You would not, I think, be at all afraid of my weakening at this stage. I can see too much accomplished and too much of encouragement in the future to be discouraged — and if I was ever so much cast down I think too much of the value of the results to the people and the country of the things I am striving to accomplish, to abate a particle of effort.

I have had two years of hard fighting in front. Of course I should be better pleased if I had support instead of attack in the rear, but — I shall get on.

If you have a stock on hand can you send me a few of your pamphlets?

[1] A defence of Cleveland's course with regard to the patronage and civil service.

I should be glad to have at least enough to give one to each of my Cabinet, unless you choose to hand them direct to these parties.

And I want to see you too very much. When can you come over and have a chat? The sooner the better.

To THOMAS M. COOLEY [1]

Washington, *February* 8, 1887

Ever since the duty of appointing Commissioners under the law to regulate Interstate Commerce was devolved upon me, and the subject has challenged the attention of the public, your name more than any other has been in mind and has the oftenest been mentioned in connection with such a place.

I have had an idea that you could be induced, upon considering the public contributions which would be accomplished by you as a member of the Board, to consent to your selection as one of these Commissioners. It is almost necessary to a successful administration of this law that the confidence of the people in the men to whom it is entrusted should be gained at the outset. This will be secured very largely by your appointment, and I earnestly wish you to consent to serve us all in the capacity mentioned.

If this involves a sacrifice I beg you to make it for the public good. I will give you, if you consent, a long or short term as you desire, and will do my very best to associate with you able and patriotic men.

I should be glad to be informed of your decision as early as possible; and in view of the desirability of completing the organization of the Commission speedily, I should be glad to receive your answer by telegraph.

To SECRETARY MANNING

Washington, *February* 15, 1887

Your formal letter of resignation which I have received, though not entirely unexpected, presents the reality of a severance of our official relations and causes me the deepest regret.[2] This is tempered only by the knowledge that the frank and friendly personal relations which have unbrokenly existed between us are to still continue. I refer to these

---

[1] Cooley (1824–98), long a judge of the supreme court of Michigan and a professor of law at the University of Michigan, had recently acted as receiver of the Wabash lines east of the Mississippi. He accepted Cleveland's appointment.

[2] Charles S. Fairchild now became Secretary of the Treasury. Manning died a few months later.

because such personal relations supply, after all, whatever of comfort and pleasure the world affords, and because I believe it to be almost superfluous to speak of the aid and support you have given me and the assistance you have furnished to the administration of the Government, during the time you have directed the affairs of the exacting and laborious office which you now seek to surrender. Your labors, your achievements, your success and your devotion to public duty are fully seen and known, and they challenge the appreciation and gratitude of all your countrymen.

Since I must at last relinquish my hope of your continuance at my side as counsellor and co-laborer, and since I cannot question the reasons upon which your request to be relieved is based, it only remains for me to accept the resignation you have tendered and to express my profound thanks for all that you have done for me in sharing manfully my labors and perplexities of the past two years.

I feel that I may still ask of you that the first day of April next be fixed as the date on which your resignation shall take effect, and that you will so regulate what remains to you of official duty in the meantime, as to secure that maximum of freedom from vexatious labor which you have so justly earned....

To WILSON S. BISSELL

Washington, *February* 22, 1887

I am almost crazy over the things that crowd upon me. I am interrupted so much that the days and the nights do not give me time to do all....

To WALTER H. ROGERS

Washington, *April* 1, 1887

I acknowledge with thanks an invitation extended to me by the Association of the Army of the Tennessee, to attend the unveiling of the equestrian statue of General Albert Sidney Johnston, on the 6th instant, at your cemetery. I regret that, owing to engrossing official duties which demand my attention, I cannot be present on that occasion.

That General Johnston was a great soldier, and that from the time he left West Point to the hour of his death on the field at Shiloh, he was conspicuous for valor, for military ability, and for the highest personal character, must be freely conceded by all his countrymen. The erection of a monument for the perpetuation of his name is a fitting testimony to the affection and respect in which he is held by his comrades of the Civil War, and may well be to them a work of the greatest interest and satisfaction.

The patriotic sentiments accompanying the invitation which I received and the fraternal feeling therein expressed, I gladly recognize as proofs that in personal convictions, every American citizen may share in the pride implied by the illustration, in any circumstances, of the traits which have ennobled American character.

With my best wishes for the success and prosperity of your Society, I am...

To GEORGE STEELE [1] and others

Washington, *April* 7, 1887

I have received your letter lately addressed to me, and have given full consideration to the expression of the views and wishes therein contained, in relation to the existing differences between the Government of Great Britain and the United States, growing out of the refusal to award to our citizens engaged in fishing enterprises the privileges to which they are entitled, either under treaty stipulations or the guarantees of international comity and neighborly concession.

I sincerely trust the apprehension you express, of unjust and unfriendly treatment of American fishermen lawfully found in Canadian waters, will not be realized. But if such apprehension should prove to be well founded, I earnestly hope that no fault or inconsiderate action of any of our citizens will in the least weaken the just position of our government or deprive us of the universal sympathy and support to which we should be entitled.

The action of this Administration since June, 1885, when the fishery articles of the Treaty of 1871 were terminated under the notification which had two years before been given by our Government, has been fully

---

[1] President of the American Fishing Union. Congress had abrogated a treaty which gave American fishermen distinct rights in Canadian inshore waters in return for the free entry of Canadian fish into the United States. As a result, Canadian authorities during 1886 and 1887 treated American fishing vessels with unfriendly rigor. Congress passed legislation empowering the President to retaliate against Canada by closing our ports to Canadian ships and fish. Such a measure would have been highly advantageous to New England fishing and shipping interests. Because he believed it a partial and unfair measure, and because he was attempting to negotiate a new treaty with Canada, Cleveland refused to act under the law.

disclosed by the correspondence between the representatives and the appropriate Departments of the respective Governments, with which I am apprised by your letter you are entirely familiar. An examination of this correspondence has doubtless satisfied you that in no case have the rights or privileges of American fishermen been overlooked or neglected, but that on the contrary they have been sedulously insisted upon and cared for, by every means within the control of the Executive branch of the Government.

The Act of Congress approved March 3, 1887, authorizing a course of retaliation through Executive action, in the event of a continuance on the part of the British-American authorities of unfriendly conduct and treaty violations affecting American fishermen, has devolved upon the President of the United States exceedingly grave and solemn responsibilities, comprehending highly important consequences to our national character and dignity, and involving extremely valuable commercial intercourse between the British Possessions in North America and the people of the United States.

I understand the main purpose of your letter is to suggest that, in case recourse to the retaliatory measures authorized by this Act should be invited by unjust treatment of our fishermen in the future, the object of such retaliation might be fully accomplished by 'prohibiting Canadian-caught fish from entry into the ports of the United States.'

The existing controversy is one in which two nations are the parties concerned. The retaliation contemplated by the Act of Congress is to be enforced, not to protect solely any particular interest, however meritorious or valuable, but to maintain the national honor and thus protect all our people. In this view, the violation of American fishery rights and unjust or unfriendly acts towards a portion of our citizens engaged in this business is but the occasion for action, and constitutes a national affront which gives birth to or may justify retaliation. This measure once resorted to, its effectiveness and value may well depend upon the thoroughness and extent of its application; and in the performance of international duties, the enforcement of international rights, and the protection of our citizens, this Government and the people of the United States must act as a unit — all intent upon attaining the best results of retaliation, upon the basis of a maintenance of national honor and duty.

A nation seeking by any means to maintain its honor, dignity, and integrity, is engaged in protecting the rights of its people; and if in such efforts particular interests are injured and special advantages forfeited, these things must be patriotically borne for the public good.

An immense volume of population, manufactures, and agricultural productions, and the marine tonnage and railways to which these have given activity, all largely the result of intercourse between the United States and British America, and the natural growth of a full half century of good neighborhood and friendly communication, form an aggregate of material wealth and incidental relations of the most impressive magnitude. I fully appreciate these things, and am not unmindful of the great number of our people who are concerned in such vast and diversified interests.

In the performance of the serious duty which the Congress has imposed upon me, and in the exercise upon just occasion of the power conferred under the act referred to, I shall deem myself bound to inflict no unnecessary damage or injury upon any portion of our people; but I shall, nevertheless, be unflinchingly guided by a sense of what the self-respect and dignity of the nation demand. In the maintenance of these and in the support of the honor of the Government beneath which every citizen may repose in safety, no sacrifice of personal or private interests shall be considered as against the general welfare.

To DANIEL MANNING

Oak View,[1] Washington, *April* 16, 1887

...For the past few days I have been staying here nights with my wife and her mother. We all enjoy it very much and I put on great airs looking after my farm. We don't get good settled warm weather here yet, but are expecting it any day. I have two old horses, a cow without horns that gives twelve quarts of milk a day, and some hens. I am thinking about a pig, but can't quite settle on one yet....

To TERENCE V. POWDERLY [2]

Washington, *April* 19, 1887

I am glad to learn through your letter of the 12th that your attention has been directed to the topics therein referred to. I am fully of the opin-

---

[1] Cleveland had purchased a house and twenty-seven acres of land on the Tenallytown Road (now Wisconsin Avenue), two miles north of Georgetown. The house, enlarged and improved, he called Oak View, though the popular name was Red Top. Here he spent much time in warm weather.

[2] Powderly (1849–1924), was an attorney and head of the Knights of Labor.

ion that there has been in the past far too much heedlessness and recklessness in the management and disposition of our public domain. So far
as the results you deplore arise from abuses in departmental methods, I
feel that every effort of the Administration should be employed for
their correction. Though a burdensome legacy has descended to us, I am
extremely gratified at the progress we have made in this direction. Of
course much of our trouble arises from legislation which has either been
enacted in the interest of those whose grasp is relentless or in entire
disregard of the rights and interests of those who, upon all theories
attached to the possession of the public domain, are entitled to first
consideration.

Thus hedged in by bad administrative operations and precedents, the
interposition of rights innocently acquired therefrom, and by laws which
we must all obey, our progress may at times seem exasperatingly slow.
But with a long pull and strong pull and a pull all together, very much
can be done to remedy the present condition of this subject.

In the representative position you hold and to which you refer in your
letter, a great responsibility is put upon you. You will remember I spoke
of this when I once had the pleasure of meeting you, and I have thought
much of it since and recalled the sincerity with which you expressed your
appreciation of that responsibility. I should be very glad to confer with
you upon the subject of your letter, and hope that you will soon find it in
your way to come and see me for that purpose. If you could make it
convenient to come to me next Saturday at two o'clock in the afternoon,
I will set apart that time for a conference....

To HENRY E. YOUNG

Washington, *April* 19, 1887

I am sorry that I must decline the invitation which I have received
to be present at the unveiling of the monument erected to the memory
of John C. Calhoun on the 26th instant.[1] The ladies of the Monument
Association have good reason for pride and congratulation in the complete success of their efforts to fittingly commemorate the virtues and
services of this loved and honored son of South Carolina. I believe it
would be well if all he did and even all he believed and taught and all his
aspirations for the welfare and prosperity of our Republic were better
known and understood. If this were so, much would be found to enlighten

[1] In Charleston, South Carolina.

and encourage those charged with public duty, and much to stimulate patriotic enthusiasm. The ceremonies attending the unveiling of the monument erected by his ardent admirers in the State which bears the impress of his renown should furnish an occasion for such an instructive illustration of his character as shall inspire in the minds of all his countrymen genuine respect and admiration for his courage and self-abnegation, toleration where approval of his actions is withheld, and universal pride in the greatness of this illustrious American.

To WILSON S. BISSELL

Washington, *April* 21, 1887

When you were here I spoke to you of the difficulty I had to select a United States Treasurer. I did not ask you to take it then because I had an idea that you did not want to be bothered with any offers of that kind; but if I remember rightly I spoke of the kind of man I was looking for in such a way as pretty plainly indicated you. In canvassing the matter with a few of our friends I have said that the man I had rather have than any other was you and all have replied that of all things the best was to induce you to take it. The last one was W. L. Scott tonight; and under the influence of his enthusiasm upon the subject I have determined to ask you to take the position.

You know about the office, that it is equal in dignity to a Cabinet place, that in the eyes of the people it is fully as prominent, and the salary is six thousand a year. You remember how well Spinner and his crooked signature became known to the people who saw his name on all the greenbacks.

I need not tell you how glad I should be to have you here, a part of the most important Department of the Government and an adviser upon all our financial policy and one of those whose counsel I should rely upon if stormy weather overtakes us.

The place ought to have been filled before and I should like to hear from you as soon as possible after the receipt of this by telegraph. I am afraid I am taking serious risks by allowing this vacancy to remain so long. So if you take it I should want you to qualify immediately and perhaps settle other matters after that. The bond is $150,000.

Fairchild has indicated that he had rather have you in the place than anybody else. I think you would be pleased at the reception you would meet.

To SECRETARY LAMAR [1]

Washington, *April* 25, 1887

I have examined with much care and interest the questions involved in the conflicting claims of Guilford Miller and the Northern Pacific Railroad Company to certain public land in Washington Territory.[2] The legal aspects of the case have been examined and passed upon by several officers of the Government, who do not agree in their conclusions.

Miller claims to be a settler upon the land in question, whose possession dates from 1878. He alleges that he has made substantial improvements upon this land and cultivated the same, and it appears that he filed his claim to the same under the Homestead Law on the 29th day of December, 1884.

The railway company contends that this land is within the territory or area from which it was entitled to select such a quantity of public land as might be necessary to supply any deficiency that should be found to exist in the specific land mentioned in a grant by the government to said company in aid of the construction of its road — such deficiency being contemplated as likely to arise from the paramount right of private parties and settlers within the territory embracing said granted lands — and that the land in dispute was thus selected by the company on the 19th day of December, 1883.

A large tract, including this land, was withdrawn by an order of the Interior Department from sale and from pre-emption and homestead entry in 1872, in anticipation of the construction of said railroad and a deficiency in its granted lands. In 1880, upon the filing of a map of definite location of the road, the land in controversy, and much more which had been so withdrawn, was found to lie outside of the limits which included the granted land, but its withdrawal and reservation from settlement and entry under our land laws were continued upon the theory that it was within the limits of indemnity lands which might be selected by the company as provided in the law making the grant.

The legal points in this controversy turned upon the validity and effect of the withdrawal and reservation of this land and the continuance

[1] Lucius Quintus Cincinnatus Lamar (1825–1893), was a Representative in Congress 1857–60; colonel in the Confederate army; a Representative again 1873–77; Senator from Mississippi 1877–85; Secretary of the Interior 1885–88; and Associate Justice of the Supreme Court 1888–93.

[2] For a full history of the Guilford Miller case see the editor's *Grover Cleveland: A Study in Courage*, 359 ff.

thereof. The Attorney-General is of the opinion that such withdrawal and reservation were at all times effectual and that they operated to prevent Miller from acquiring any interest in or right to the land claimed by him.

With this interpretation of the law and the former orders and action of the Interior Department, it will be seen that their effect has been the withdrawal and reservation since 1872 of thousands if not millions of acres of those lands from the operations of the land laws of the United States, thus placing them beyond the reach of our citizens desiring under such laws to settle and make homes upon the same, and that this has been done for the benefit of a railroad company having no fixed, certain or definite interest in such lands. In this manner the beneficent policy and intention of the Government in relation to the public domain have for all these years to that extent been thwarted.

There seems to be no evidence presented showing how much, if any, of this vast tract is necessary for the fulfilment of the grant to the railroad company, nor does there appear to be any limitation of the time within which this fact should be made known and the corporation obliged to make its selection. After a lapse of seventeen years this large body of the public domain is still held in reserve to the exclusion of settlers, for the convenience of a corporate beneficiary of the Government and awaiting its selection, though it is entirely certain that much of this reserved land can never be honestly claimed by such corporation.

Such a condition of the public land should no longer continue. So far as it is the result of Executive rules and methods these should be abandoned, and so far as it is a consequence of improvident laws these should be repealed or amended.

Our public domain is our national wealth, the earnest of our growth and the heritage of our people. It should promise limitless development and riches, relief to a crowding population and homes to thrift and industry.

These inestimable advantages should be jealously guarded and a careful and enlightened policy on the part of our Government should secure them to the people.

In the case under consideration I assume that there is an abundance of land within the area which has been reserved for indemnity, in which no citizen or settler has a legal or equitable interest, for all purposes of such indemnification to this railroad company — if its grant has not already been satisfied. I understand, too, that selections made by such corporation are not complete and effectual until the same have been approved by the Secretary of the Interior or unless they are made in the words of the statute, under his direction.

You have thus far taken no action in this matter and it seems to me that you are in a condition to deal with the subject in such a manner as to protect this settler from hardship and loss.

I transmit herewith the papers and documents relating to the case which were submitted to me at my request.

I suggest that you exercise the power and authority you have in the premises upon equitable considerations, with every presumption and intendment in favor of the settler, and in case you find this corporation is entitled to select any more of these lands than it has already acquired that you direct it to select in lieu of the land upon which Mr. Miller has settled other land within the limits of this indemnity reservation, upon which neither he nor any other citizen has in good faith settled or made improvements.

I call your attention to sections 2450 and 2451 of the Revised Statutes of the United States as pointing out a mode of procedure which may perhaps be resorted to if necessary for the purpose of reaching a just and equitable disposition of the case.

The suggestion herein contained can, I believe, be adopted without disregarding or calling in question the opinion of the Attorney-General upon the purely legal propositions which were submitted to him.

To MRS. HENRY WARD BEECHER

Washington, *May 22, 1887*

I have been asked to furnish a contribution to a proposed memorial of your late husband.[1]

While I am by no means certain that anything I might prepare would be worthy of a place among the eloquent and beautiful tributes which are sure to be presented, this request spurs to action my desire and intention to express to you more fully than I have yet done my sympathy in your affliction and my appreciation of my own and the country's loss in the death of Mr. Beecher.

More than thirty years ago I repeatedly enjoyed the opportunity of hearing him in his own pulpit. His warm utterances, and the earnest interest he displayed in the practical things related to useful living, the

---

[1] Henry Ward Beecher died in Brooklyn March 8, 1887.

hopes he inspired and the manner in which he relieved the precepts of Christianity from gloom and cheerlessness, made me feel that though a stranger, he was my friend. Many years afterward we came to know each other; and since that time my belief in his friendship, based upon acquaintance and personal contact, has been to me a source of the greatest satisfaction.

His goodness and kindness of heart, so far as they were manifested in his personal life and in his home, are sacred to you and to your grief; but so far as they gave color and direction to his teachings and opinions, they are proper subjects for gratitude and congratulation on the part of every American citizen. They caused him to take the side of the common people in every discussion. He loved his fellows in their homes; he rejoiced in their contentment and comfort and sympathized with them in their daily hardships and trials. As their champion he advocated in all things the utmost regulated and wholesome liberty and freedom. His sublime faith in the success of popular government led him to trust the people, and to treat their errors and misconceptions with generous toleration. Our pardonable pride in American citizenship, when guided by the teachings of religion, he believed to be a sure guaranty of a splendid national destiny. I never met him without gaining something from his broad views and wise reflections.

Your personal affliction in his death stands alone, in its magnitude and depth. But thousands wish that their sense of loss might temper your grief, and that they, by sharing your sorrow, might lighten it.

Such kindly assurances, and your realization of the high and sacred mission accomplished in your husband's useful life, furnish all this world can supply of comfort; but your faith and piety will not fail to lead you to a higher and better source of consolation.

To QUEEN VICTORIA

Washington, May 27, 1887

Great and Good Friend:

In the name and on behalf of the people of the United States I present their sincere felicitations upon the arrival of the fiftieth anniversary of Your Majesty's accession to the crown of Great Britain. I but utter the general voice of my fellow countrymen in wishing for your people the prolongation of a reign so marked with advance in popular well-being, physical, moral, and intellectual.

It is justice and not adulation to acknowledge the debt of gratitude and respect due to your personal virtues for their important influence in producing and causing the prosperous and well-ordered condition of affairs now generally prevailing throughout your dominions.

May your life be prolonged, and peace, honor and prosperity bless the people over whom you have been called to rule. May liberty flourish throughout your empire under just and equal laws and your government be strong in the affections of all who live under it, and I pray God to have Your Majesty in his holy keeping.

To SECRETARY ENDICOTT

Washington, *June* 16, 1887

I have today considered with more care than when the subject was orally presented to me, the action of your Department directing letters to be addressed to the governors of all the States, offering to return, if desired, to the loyal States the Union flags captured in the War of the rebellion by the Confederate forces and afterwards recovered by government troops, and to the Confederate States the flags captured by the Union forces, all of which for many years have been packed in boxes and stored in the cellar and attic of the War Department.[1]

I am of the opinion that the return of these flags in the manner thus contemplated, is not authorized by existing law nor justified as an Executive act.

I request, therefore, that no steps be taken in the matter, except to examine and inventory these flags and adopt proper measures for their preservation. Any directions as to the final disposition of them should originate with Congress.

To JOHN W. FRAZIER

Washington, *June* 24, 1887

I have received your invitation to attend, as a guest of the Philadelphia Brigade, a reunion of ex-Confederate soldiers of Pickett's Division who survived their terrible charge at Gettysburg, and those of the Union army still living, by whom it was heroically resisted.[2]

The fraternal meeting of these soldiers, upon the battlefield where

---

[1] The order for the return of these flags had originated with Adjutant-General Richard C. Drum, a Republican and a member of the G.A.R. Cleveland had given his verbal assent and Secretary Endicott a written endorsement. The idea of returning 'rebel' flags to the South aroused a Northern storm.

[2] This reunion occurred July 4, 1887.

twenty-four years ago in deadly fray they fiercely sought each other's lives, where they saw their comrades fall, and where all their thoughts were of vengeance and destruction, will illustrate the generous impulse of brave men and their honest desire for peace and reconciliation. The friendly assault there to be made will be resistless because inspired by American chivalry; and its result will be glorious, because conquered hearts will be its trophy of success. Thereafter this battlefield will be consecrated by a victory which shall presage the end of the bitterness of strife, the exposure of the insincerity which conceals hatred by professions of kindness, the condemnation of frenzied appeals to passion for unworthy purposes, and the beating down of all that stands in the way of the destiny of our united country.

While those who fought, and who have so much to forgive, lead in the pleasant ways of peace, how wicked appear the traffic in sectional hate and the betrayal of patriotic sentiment. It surely cannot be wrong to desire the settled quiet which lights for our entire country the path to prosperity and greatness; nor need the lessons of the war be forgotten and its results jeopardized, in the wish for that genuine fraternity which insures national pride and glory. I should be very glad to accept your invitation and be with you at this interesting reunion; but other arrangements already made and my official duties here will prevent my doing so.

To WILSON S. BISSELL

Oak View, Washington, *June* 30, 1887

My wife came out here yesterday to stay, I hope, some time, and I mean to try driving out and in every morning. I have bought a new light kind of a road wagon and drove out in it for the first time tonight. I don't know how it will go but I know I can do lots of work here if I can bring it out. The weather is delightful and I honestly think I have one of the handsomest places in the United States....

To MAYOR DAVID R. FRANCIS [1]

Washington, *July* 4, 1887

When I received the extremely cordial and gratifying invitation from the citizens of St. Louis, tendered by a number of her representative

---

[1] Francis (1850–1927) was successively mayor of St. Louis, governor of Missouri, and Secretary of the Interior in Cleveland's second Cabinet. He had presented Cleveland a monster invitation of 200,000 citizens to visit his city. But after the outburst over the 'rebel flag order,' he wrote the President (June 22) that it would be better not to come at the time of the G.A.R. Encampment, as first proposed.

men, to visit that city during the national encampment of the Grand Army of the Republic, I had been contemplating for some time the acceptance of the invitation from that organization to the same effect, and had considered the pleasure which it would afford me if it should be possible to meet not only members of the Grand Army, but the people of St. Louis and other cities in the West, which the occasion would give me an opportunity to visit. The exactions of my public duties I felt to be so uncertain, however, that when first confronted by the delegation of which you were the head, I expected to do no more at that time than to promise the consideration of the double invitation tendered me, and express the pleasure it would give me to accept the same thereafter, if possible.

But the cordiality and sincerity of your presentation, reinforced by the heartiness of the people who surrounded you, so impressed me that I could not resist the feeling which prompted me to assure you on the spot that I would be with you and the Grand Army of the Republic at the time designated, if nothing happened in the meantime to absolutely prevent my leaving Washington.

Immediately upon the public announcement of this conclusion, expressions emanating from certain important members of the Grand Army of the Republic, and increasing in volume and virulence, constrained me to review my acceptance of these invitations. The expressions referred to go to the extent of declaring that I would be an unwelcome guest at the time and place of the national encampment. This statement is based, as well as I can judge, upon certain official acts of mine involving important public interests, done under the restraints and obligations of my oath of office, which do not appear to accord with the wishes of some members of the Grand Army of the Republic.

I refuse to believe that this organization, founded upon patriotic ideas, composed very largely of men entitled to lasting honor and consideration, and whose crowning glory it should be that they are American citizens as well as veteran soldiers, deems it a part of its mission to compass any object or purpose by attempting to intimidate the Executive or coerce those charged with making and executing the laws. And yet the expressions to which I have referred indicate such a prevalence of unfriendly feeling, and such a menace to an occasion which should be harmonious, peaceful, and cordial, that they cannot be ignored.

I beg you to understand that I am not conscious of any act of mine

which should make me fear to meet the Grand Army of the Republic or any other assemblage of my fellow citizens. The account of my official stewardship is always ready for presentation to my countrymen. I should not be frank if I failed to confess, while disclaiming all resentment, that I have been hurt by the wanton and unworthy attacks upon me growing out of this matter, and the reckless manner in which my actions and motives have been misrepresented both publicly and privately, for which, however, the Grand Army of the Republic as a body is by no means responsible.

The threat of personal violence and harm in case I undertake the trip in question, which scores of misguided, unbalanced men under the stimulation of excited feeling have made, are not even considered. Rather than abandon my visit to the West and disappoint your citizens, I might, if I alone were concerned, submit to the insult to which it is quite openly asserted I would be helplessly subjected if present at the encampment; but I should bear with me there the people's highest office, the dignity of which I must protect, and I believe that neither the Grand Army of the Republic as an organization nor anything like a majority of its members would ever encourage any scandalous attack upon it. If, however, among the membership of this body there are some, as certainly seems to be the case, determined to denounce me and my official acts at the national encampment, I believe they should be permitted to do so unrestrained by my presence as a guest of the hospitable city in which their meeting is held. A number of Grand Army posts have signified their intention, I am informed, to remain away from the encampment in case I visit the city at that time. Without considering the merit of such an excuse, I feel that I ought not to be the cause of such non-attendance. The time and place of the encampment were fixed long before my invitations were received. Those desirous to participate in its proceedings should be first regarded, and nothing should be permitted to interfere with their intentions.

Another consideration of more importance than all others remains to be noticed. The fact was referred to by you when you verbally presented the invitation of the citizens of St. Louis that the coming encampment of the Grand Army of the Republic would be the first held in a Southern State. I suppose this fact was mentioned as a pleasing incident of the fraternal feeling fast gaining ground throughout the entire land, and hailed by every patriotic citizen as an earnest that the Union has really and in fact been saved in sentiment and spirit, with all the benefits it vouchsafes to a united people.

I cannot rid myself of the belief that the least discord on this propitious occasion might retard the progress of the sentiment of common brotherhood which the Grand Army of the Republic has so good an opportunity to increase and foster. I certainly ought not to be the cause of such discord in any event or upon any pretext. It seems to me that you and the citizens of St. Louis are entitled to the unreserved statement of the conditions which have led me to forego my contemplated visit and to withdraw my acceptance of your invitation.

My presence in your city at the time you have indicated can be of but little moment compared with the importance of a cordial and harmonious entertainment of your other guests. I assure you that I abandon my plans without the least personal feeling except regret, constrained thereto by a sense of duty, actuated by a desire to save any embarrassment to the city of St. Louis, or their expected guests, and with a heart full of grateful appreciation of the sincere and unaffected kindness of your citizens.

Hoping the encampment may be an occasion of much usefulness, and that its proceedings may illustrate the highest patriotism of American citizenship, I am...

To WILSON S. BISSELL

Washington, *July* 25, 1887

Assistant Secretary of the Treasury Hugh S. Thompson, ex-Governor of South Carolina, will be in Buffalo Thursday evening of *this week* and will stop at the Genesee. He will arrive about five o'clock. He is a splendid fellow, funny and nice in every way and a perfect gentleman. I have said nothing to him about writing you, but think perhaps you would like to meet him.

To JOHN TEMPLE GRAVES [1]

Washington, *July* 30, 1887

I am glad to hear through Colonel Lamont how you express yourself touching the matters contained in Mr. Burt's letter to you which has been read to me.

[1] Graves (1856–1925), a progressive-minded Democrat of Georgia, was at this time editor of the Atlanta *Journal*. The Burt here named is Silas W. Burt.

I have heard nothing of any improper conduct in Maryland by any Federal officeholders, but I am assured by those who know and whom I can trust that the ticket presented is a good one, composed of honest upright men.

Of course in any event the Civil Service League will be told that something dreadful has happened and the old Higgins Treasury business will be again served up and our friends in attendance will deem their confidence in the Administration sorely tried — and all this because one faction of the Democratic party cannot have control in Maryland to the exclusion of another. I do not say that some things in Maryland are not as they should be, but I know that much of the influence of our civil service friends in that State amounts to their being used to aid a faction in the Democratic party the aims and purposes of which are, to say the least, not as disinterested at all times as they appear.

I insist upon officeholders, who make no special pretence as civil service reformers, attending to the duties of their offices and not interfering improperly with the political actions of others. The thing which I judge is sure to be done at Newport amounts in my view to just that; and I disapprove strongly of the course of any public officer who has a large and important department or bureau in his charge and who yet proposes to leave his place to interfere in the politics of another State.

Mr. Burt has plenty to do. He cannot in any way do so much for civil service reform as by demonstrating in the conduct of his office the good there is in such reform and proving to Democratic cavillers that his selection...has been vindicated by its benefit to the public service. This has all been done with wonderful success in your case, and I thank you for all you have done to support and strengthen me.

Of course there is a question of good taste and propriety involved in all this matter which must be left to Mr. Burt's consideration; but I feel like saying that I am not likely to permit him any sooner now than any other officeholder to embarrass or discredit me in what I know and you know and he knows to be honest efforts to give the people good government.

You may if you desire communicate as much of this letter as you see fit to Mr. Burt.

To DR. GEORGE H. MOORE

Washington, *July* 31, 1887

Please accept my thanks for that little book you sent me entitled 'Washington as an Angler.' I am much pleased to learn that the only element of greatness heretofore unnoticed in the life of Washington is thus supplied. I am a little curious to know whether the absence of details as to the result of his fishing is owing to bad luck, a lack of toleration of fish stories at that time among anglers, or to the fact that, even as to the number of fish he caught, the Father of his Country could not tell a lie.

To POSTMASTER-GENERAL VILAS

Washington, *August* 1, 1887

The ladies have all left Oak View and I propose to establish stag quarters there at once. The Colonel and Mrs. Lamar are already located and I want you to join the band. Tonight especially I expect to have some of the Cabinet there — most all of them — for consultation, and you must be there.

So you had better pack up a little grip-sack and be here with it about five o'clock today prepared to go out with me and make your home there for awhile. I know it will be a relief to you after the heat and labor of the day and you can work there if necessary.

To AN UNIDENTIFIED CORRESPONDENT

Washington, *August* 23, 1887

I am sorry that I cannot help you at all respecting the coin you sent in and which is herewith returned. And I can help you but very little concerning Aaron Cleveland, of whom you write. I have had but little time to study genealogy, having been all my life kept very busy in an attempt to fulfill the duties of life without questioning how I got into the scrape.

There was a Cleveland — Aaron I think — who started, I believe, to go to Halifax, sent by a Missionary Society, but who died before he reached there at the home of his friend Benjamin Franklin in Philadelphia. The latter wrote an obituary which I have seen published several times. He may have preached in Halifax temporarily before the journey spoken of. There used to be a man in Elizabeth, New Jersey, named Edmund Cleveland, who had studied the Cleveland tree a good deal.

To WILSON S. BISSELL

Washington, *August* 25, 1887

I received your letter and receipted tax bill this morning, and thank you for your attention to the matter. If I could get $100 a foot I'd sell the Butler Street lot.

Have you seen any of the vile wicked lying stuff the papers are printing about me in connection with Charley Macomber? I send you a specimen sent me and which of course was in the Buffalo *Express*, and came to me without a signature from Buffalo. He never asked me for office and I know of nothing of the kind. Of course I saw him very seldom. This little fellow Billy Woods has known him for a long time....

To G. A. SULLIVAN

Washington, *August* 27, 1887

Your letter of inquiry regarding the truth of the report that I approved a bill while Governor authorizing mixed schools in the State of New York, is received.

The only bill that I know of being passed and affirmed on that subject while I was governor was one affecting the city of New York, and has precisely the contrary effect — that is, its purpose and object was to retain the colored schools separate and distinct from the whites. Mr. Nelson J. Waterbury of New York City, I think, drew the bill; and Professor Rasin, Superintendent of the Colored Schools, and the Reverend Mr. Derrick, both of New York City, advocated it strongly. The school board of New York City had determined to consolidate these schools with the white schools; and the bill took them out of the control of the board so that it should not be done. It was strongly urged before me that separate schools were of much more benefit to the colored people than mixed schools. I suppose in the city of New York colored schools are separately maintained today by virtue of its provisions.

I have thus given you all I remember on the subject of your inquiry. I have been much surprised at hearing, before the receipt of your letter, that this matter has been so grossly misrepresented.

To WILSON S. BISSELL

Washington, *September* 2, 1887

I was especially glad to gain the intimation, from the last clause of your letter which I received yesterday, that you would not deem it an imposition for me to urge you to accompany us upon our Western and Southern trip. So I am going at that the first thing.

This trip is to be solely a social affair and the idea which I desire to have pervade all the arrangements of it is that there is no swinging about the circle and no political tour. I shall take no one from here but Lamont and Mrs. Cleveland's maid and I have insisted that in the cars we are to have a family party with every freedom from restraint which that implies. Our first stop will be Indianapolis four hours, and then Terre Haute a half hour — then St. Louis three days, including a Sunday — Chicago one day and night — Milwaukee part of a day and a night — Madison nearly three days, including a Sunday (stopping with Vilas) — St. Paul a night and part of a day — Minneapolis part of a day — Omaha an hour — Kansas City one day and night — Memphis part of a day — Sunday and part of Monday at Nashville, spending Sunday at Belle Mead, Judge Jackson's beautiful stock farm — Monday night at Atlanta and stay, I think, three days — after that one day at Montgomery and then home by the beautiful Kenesaw Mountain route — arriving home the 21st or 22d of October — making the trip three weeks long and starting from here September 30. I shall make Vilas and his wife join the party when we leave Madison if I can. It will be time for him to come back here.[1]

Now nothing would so much improve my idea of a social trip and everyday-kind-of-visit-to-the-people upon the affair as to have my nearest and best personal friend along. Think of this. We shall see a wondrous country. Your friend Bannard will be present among the managers at Chicago.

Another thing. There must now be no mistake about retaining Doyle on the committee[2] through the action of the delegates to the convention. Such an issue as has been presented having been forced, it must be met and there should be no failure. What can I consistently and properly do? I don't understand some of the votes reported unless they were given upon something entirely separate from the choice of persons.

How is Lockwood in the matter? I hardly think Mr. Hill is in it, but of course he may be pulled in by his friends — the same as I am. But the question is among my friends and neighbors. That makes the differ-

[1] The trip to the West and South was made almost precisely as outlined in this letter. Melville W. Fuller begged Cleveland to deviate from his schedule to visit Lincoln's tomb at Springfield, but he declined to do so. The journey began September 30 and ended October 22, 1887.
[2] The Democratic State Committee in New York.

ence. I believe I told you I wrote to Walker. He knows how I feel. But of course the question the next time will be with you delegates. Tabor surely cannot afford to interfere. Let me hear what you think about the trip.

To GEORGE J. HEPMOUTH
Washington, *September* 9, 1887

I have just read your letter and hasten to reply. In the first place, you are dreadfully at fault in supposing that the mere fact that I was not invited made the basis of Mrs. Cleveland's declination.[1] I have not the slightest doubt that I would have been very welcome; and besides I don't think it is my fault that I strike upon things purely personal. I am entirely clear, too, that no sort of neglect or slight has been intended; and I am not sure that I would have done any differently if I had been managing the invitation.

But the fact remains that the proposition was that my wife, because she is my wife, was expected to appear before the city of New York, in its streets, in the most public way possible, and assume a prominent rôle without reference to the presence or absence of her husband and without the least participation on my part. Now you would see how different the case would have been if I had been invited to do something — like reviewing the parade or something of that kind — and she, accompanying me, had as a pleasant incident of the affair passed over the flags to the firemen.

The people of the country insist upon having everything nearly that their President can give — all his time — all his strength and as much as they can get of his home life. I do think he ought to be allowed to have his wife, perhaps not so fully as the humblest citizen, but to some extent.

You know how heartily I entered into the sentiment of your plan when it was proposed and how I suggested reasons why the thing might be properly done; and you will remember that the most prominent was the fact that as Mayor I had become interested in the firemen of my city and that as governor I had become much interested in the New York Department and that both my wife and I were New Yorkers. If I had sent for you (which I thought of) you could not have made the arrangement

---

[1] Mrs. Cleveland was invited by friends of the New York Fire Department to visit the city and make the presentation of a set of flags purchased for that department.

presented satisfactory; and I did not feel in all the circumstances of the case that I ought to suggest any modifications.

I am very sorry that all this has happened; but in the present condition of affairs I think the matter had better be dropped.

To MAYOR ABRAM S. HEWITT [1]

Washington, *September* 11, 1887

It seems to me that I run up against more 'flag incidents' than I deserve. The last one has annoyed me very much on account of what some people and newspapers have professed to infer from it; and the thing which has made me feel especially uncomfortable is the hint I have had that in some quarters it has been suggested that Mrs. Cleveland's decision of the matter presented to her was in some degree influenced by supposed unfriendly relations existing between the mayor and myself.

I feel great hesitation in regarding such talk of sufficient importance to write about it; and yet I shall be better satisfied after assuring you that on my part there is no sentiment which can furnish any pretext for a suspicion of the insinuation mentioned, and that if there was, it would not be manifested in such a manner.

Congratulating you upon the success of your patriotic labors in the perplexing office which, I believe for the good of your great city, you have assumed, I am...

To JOHN E. HALL

Washington, *September* 13, 1887

Your letter of the 9th instant enclosing a copy of a letter from Bartholomew Burke of the Bath Soldiers' Home is received.

I have of course seen references in the newspapers to the fact that I had a substitute in the army and have occasionally seen something insinuating that I had not done all I should have done for him, or that in some way I was at fault in the affair. I have not thought it worth while to notice these things as long as they rested entirely upon improper statements; and the receipt of your letter is the first occasion that these matters have been brought to my personal attention.

I presume that the date of the transaction between George Benninsky

---

[1] Hewitt had been elected mayor of New York City in a three-cornered battle of 1886, Henry George and Theodore Roosevelt being the other contestants.

(as I always understood his name to be) and myself, when he enlisted as my substitute, is correctly given in the statement of Mr. Burke, though I thought it occurred earlier.

Mr. Benninsky was brought to me by George A. Reinhart, who still lives in Buffalo, I suppose, who told me that Benninsky was a sailor on the Lakes and was willing to enlist as my substitute for one hundred and fifty dollars. The bargain had been made before I saw the proposed substitute, as Mr. Reinhart had known him a long time. The terms, however, were distinctly repeated by me and perfectly understood. There was no hint or suggestion of anything more being paid or of any additional obligation on my part. At this time (whatever the date may be) plenty of substitutes were obtained at the price named and even less. Indeed, being then the Assistant District Attorney of Erie County, I had abundant opportunity to secure without expense a substitute from discharged convicts and from friendless persons accused of crime if I had desired to do so.

Benninsky went to the war, and in the first battle at which he was present he claimed that he fell and hurt his back. I saw him when he was home on a furlough still complaining of this injury and during his service I wrote to him a few times and sent him postage stamps, at his request. After the war closed, I saw him but very seldom and years have passed since that date during which I neither saw him nor heard of him. I never saw his discharge, I am certain that I had nothing to do with his naturalization (I supposed he was a citizen when he enlisted), and I have no idea where he was nor how he voted when I was elected Sheriff. I now know that he was in the poorhouse.

My impression is that while I was governor or since I have been President he wrote me a letter asking me for a place: I know that while I was in Albany or since I have been here, an attorney somewhere in Pennsylvania wrote me that Benninsky was in some kind of trouble and requested me to write what I could concerning his character. This letter I am quite sure I answered.

When I was at Buffalo on election day in November, 1885, I saw Benninsky for the last time. I spent but one day in the city and as I sat in my office with a number of my old friends he came in. I talked with him in the kindest possible manner. He told me that he had been sick, and that he was poor and in need, but he said nothing about the poorhouse. I had no suspicion as to his condition at the time, and without any hesitation or question I gave him five dollars, which he received with expressions of gratitude and immediately left.

Never at any time nor in any form has he uttered a complaint to me of my treatment of him, there is no obligation of mine to him that has not been more than fulfilled, and there has not been in my relations with him any omission of duty or kindness which upon any decent theory ought to subject my conduct to criticism.

To DANIEL S. LAMONT

Washington, *September* 13, 1887

Your letter is all right, but I don't want the stops at Pittsburgh and Harrisburg to be of such a kind as will induce the people there to make great preparations and elaborate arrangements for us.

However, I suppose we can arrange that and I think your letter does not convey the idea that arrangements for these stops must be made a part of the necessities of the transportation.

I send you a letter I have written to a Mr. Hall who sent me a copy of a letter from the Bath Soldiers' Home about my substitute. My judgment is that this reply should be made — and made now.

I saw within a few days a statement in the papers that my old substitute was dead. If this is so they will be accusing me, if I answer by and by, of waiting till he could not dispute me.

You will see that I ignore the fact of his death if it is a fact, and state that Mr. Hall's letter is the first time the matter has been brought to my attention. His letter is dated only four days ago.

Unless you want to differ with me about the judgment of sending the letter please copy and mail it. Hall's letter is with it which I wish you would carefully preserve.

To HENRY R. BEEKMAN

Washington, *September* 13, 1887

Since Mrs. Cleveland's reply to the invitation extended to her to assist in the presentation of certain flags donated to the Fire Department of your city, both of us have been greatly annoyed by what seems to be a determination in some quarters to lend to her declination a significance never for a moment intended.

Your note to me, received this morning, recognizing the existence of a misapprehension of the true meaning of Mrs. Cleveland's action, gives me an opportunity of saying for her and for myself that we have not had the slightest idea that any discourtesy to me was either intended or appeared in the form of the invitation, nor was the reply intended to in any way recognize or admit the existence of any such intention or the appearance of it.

It is also true that the manner and form of the invitation was not criticised as a matter of etiquette. We do not know that any of its rules were violated and, if we were sure of it, I hardly think that would have determined our action.

The question presented to Mrs. Cleveland was whether she was willing to assume such a public rôle, entirely independent of her husband, and not as an adjunct or incident to something he was to do. Her judgment and feeling were against it and she declined the invitation.

I am very glad she did because, if the plain meaning of her declination is distorted, I am sure her conduct would have been if she had accepted. With this explanation, the regret common to us both is that the good people of New York and the members of her grand Fire Department should be in the least disappointed.

To POSTMASTER-GENERAL VILAS

Washington, *September* 14, 1887

I have just been made acquainted with what has passed between you and Mr. Lamar.[1] I am here alone stuck up with my own thought except that I have availed myself of consultation with Mr. Carlisle and Mr. Scott, who have both been here. It is curious that both of them have pitched at once upon you as the very best and safest successor in the Interior Department. To me of course it seems providential that a man so exactly fitted and so familiar in a general way with the duties and the policy of the office was at hand. Mr. Lamar, I think, has not told you that I hesitated to suggest your relinquishment of a position which you have so absolutely conquered and your transfer to another where there is so much to do, because I was afraid you would think it a kind of an imposition, and not sufficiently appreciative of your past labors and your rights to the more easy conduct of the Department which you have caused by getting it so well in hand.

[1] Lamar's resignation from the Department of the Interior to accept a seat on the bench of the Supreme Court left a vacancy to which Cleveland appointed Vilas. But Vilas left the Postmaster-Generalship with reluctance, pointing out that his Department had suffered greatly from a too-rapid succession of heads, and that he had just fully mastered its business.

And yet I shrink from putting a new man at the head of the Interior Department just at the time when so much is expected of it and when it can do so much for the success of the Administration. So there is nothing but considerations which are related to your personal comfort and ease which stand in the way of the only adjustment which will be perfectly satisfactory to me. And if without a mental reservation you cast these aside I shall regard the matter settled and shall address myself to the selection of a new Postmaster-General. And here too you have made my task a difficult one — since the men are few who can maintain that Department in the splendid shape it now is in. I have thought of Pattison of Pennsylvania — a splendid, honest, Christian man and very industrious. I don't know that he would take it. Then there is Williams, the third auditor, who has made in his present position a first-rate officer and comes from a State which we must have our eye on. I have thought of Proctor Knott, a firm friend of us all, an honest man and a good executive officer, but for some reason unpopular in his State and living in a State which needs no further recognition than it has.[1] Stevenson,[2] I suppose, might think he ought to be chosen except for some reasons which he couldn't be made to understand connected with the number of places Illinois already has or something of that kind. You see from all this that I am in a state of perplexity and with the provision I can so satisfactorily make as to the Interior Department, I feel that I should not determine these questions till I can see you, which according to present plans will be pretty early in October. This leaves me to contemplate leaving the vacancy on the Bench unfilled until after the beginning of the next session of the Court, which, though contrary to my original intention, will do no harm.

I come now to another topic in which I am greatly interested. I have rather taken it for granted that we should see you in Chicago and that you will go with us to your home. And I have calculated upon more than this, to wit: that you and Mrs. Vilas will keep with our party during the rest of the trip and reach Washington when we do about the 21st or 22d of October. Will you do this? The party will be one of close friends instead of political associates. Lamar will go. I have just heard that Bissell will go — and that is all. I don't see how anyone will get my swinging around the circle out of that.

[1] Knott (1830–1911), after long service in the House from Kentucky, was governor of that State 1883–87.

[2] Adlai E. Stevenson (1835–1914) had served two terms in Congress from Illinois, and was now First Assistant Postmaster-General.

I am at Oak View and have written this in great haste while a messenger is waiting to take it into the mail. When you receive it cannot you telegraph me? With kind regards to Mrs. Vilas.

W. L. SCOTT [1] *to* CLEVELAND

Erie, Pa., *September* 16, 1887

On my return from Bethlehem, N.H., on Tuesday evening of this week, I found Mr. Randall was registered at the Fifth Avenue Hotel; in fact, as I passed into the hall I saw him standing in the crowd. As this was a new departure for him, [he] having for the last twenty years always put up at the New York Hotel on Broadway, I felt confident he had some object in view in coming to the Fifth Avenue. About eight o'clock in the evening I made up my mind that it was policy for me to leave my card for him in his box, as he was not in the hotel that evening. Wednesday morning about half-past six o'clock I was wakened with a note from him stating that he would leave at eleven o'clock and would like to see me, and I met him about nine. The interview was not of any special importance, although it lasted an hour or more, except giving me an opportunity of judging what his policy is to be and where he thinks he stands.

So far as his professions for the Administration go, no one could speak more favorably of it. He is, however, thoroughly impressed with the idea that he is the master of the situation; that he can carry through the House his ideas of revenue reform, and he stated to me that he knew that he could accomplish this, for he had Virginia, North Carolina, Tennessee, and Kentucky with him. I did not dispute this fact with him, but when we came to discuss the policy of the future and I urged upon him harmony and united action of the party as an absolute necessity and endeavored to arrive at what his views were, I soon discovered that his plans were by no means matured. When I put it to him that the question was one of the reduction of the surplus revenue and not of protection or of free trade, and asked him if he proposed to take the internal tax off of whiskey and beer and leave the duties on the necessaries of life, he immediately replied that more revenue could be obtained on whiskey at 40c or 50c than at the present tax of 90c, evidently proving to my mind that he has abandoned the idea of abolishing internal revenue, and that his scheme will be to take off all the tax on tobacco and reduce the tax on

---

[1] William Lawrence Scott (1828–91), an important industrialist and railroad-builder of Erie, Pennsylvania, and a firm believer in tariff reduction, was at this time Representative.

whiskey and beer and thereby accomplishing a reduction of about sixty millions of revenue, hoping thereby to catch not only the tobacco men of the South, but the moonshiners of North Carolina and Eastern Tennessee, and by such a policy to escape the hue and cry that would be raised against him should he favor free whiskey. When I spoke to him about sugar and wool and salt, he virtually said he was opposed to any reduction of the present duties on imports. I suggested to him that you would be glad to see him, and he said that he intended to have called, but that you were out at Oak View and he could not very well go out there. The impression created on my mind, growing out of this interview, is that today Mr. Randall feels very confident of his position and believes in his ability to defeat any programme which our party may bring forward in connection with revenue reform. It is possible he may not be as confident as he appears to be, but this is my impression. I have no doubt he has had assurances from Virginia and North Carolina that make him more confident than he otherwise would be.

Now from my standpoint, there is but one policy to be pursued: We have got to take Mr. Randall by a flank movement, and if possible draw his supporters from him one by one. This can only be done by systematic work. Everyone we get away from him will weaken him, and if he stands alone in the next House or only with a few Democratic supporters, his opposition will become a farce.

But this work should be taken in hand by someone competent to do it, and whose position in public life should carry some weight with it. I don't know whether Mr. Carlisle [1] is the man or not; being a candidate for the Speakership it might possibly interfere.... It appears to me that someone should take the members from North Carolina and Virginia in hand at once so that we would know just where they stand and what they will or will not do. Governor Vance [2] of North Carolina ought to be able to do this, and if Vance will not, then General Cox [3] ought to be a good man to see the members from North Carolina individually; and you will excuse me for saying here that Cox lost his seat, as I understand it, mainly through his advocacy of civil service reform and his opposition

[1] John G. Carlisle (1835–1910), of Covington, Kentucky, was Representative in Congress 1877–90, Senator 1890–93, and Secretary of the Treasury throughout Cleveland's second Administration.

[2] Zebulon B. Vance (1830–94), the Confederate governor of North Carolina, was United States Senator from 1879 to his death.

[3] William Ruffin Cox (1831–1919) was a Representative from North Carolina 1881–87.

to Vance, and he ought not to be forgotten. John S. Barbour[1] of Virginia, living in Washington, is unquestionably the best man to look after Virginia.

You will excuse me for making these suggestions, but I am so confident this is our line of policy to pursue that I cannot refrain from suggesting it.

I may possibly be in Washington before you leave on your trip. I was truly gratified at the action of the Treasury Department day before yesterday on New York. I was there and it appeared as if a heavy load had been taken off of the business community.

I hope you will pardon this long letter and be able to find time to read it.

To M. P. PELLS
Washington, *September* 27, 1887

In the matter of the Maxwell land grant, referred to in your communication, as in every other, the law of the land must be supreme. The judgment of the Supreme Court of the United States on the subjects involved therein is authoritative and conclusive. This judgment must be respected and obeyed. Those who counsel resistance to the law or by false and inflammatory statements such as are made in the handbill submitted to me, attempt to impose upon the ignorant by advising an appeal from the highest court in the land to lawless force, are the worst enemies of those they so mislead. Any unlawful overt act committed in pursuance of such counsel will, of course, be visited with the penalty appropriate to the crime. If any wrongs are done, their redress can be obtained through the peaceful method of the law, which is fully adequate to protect every right of the citizen. Its faithful enforcement is due alike to the poor and the weak, the wealthy and the strong. I sincerely trust the incendiary material in the handbill will not produce the baleful effect for which it was intended, and that those in whose favor the court has determined these vexed questions of title will not attempt to extend their rights to cases not determined, and that insisting upon their rights, they will deal kindly and generously with those who have mistakenly acted upon an invalid title.

[1] John Strode Barbour (1820–92) was a Representative from Virginia 1881–87, and Senator from that State from 1889 to his death.

To E. W. FOSNOT [1]

Washington, *October* 24, 1887

... I do not know what your idea is as to the thing which we should send, and do not care to assume that anything which we might contribute to be 'voted off' would be of especial value to the cause for which the fair is to be held. But it is so refreshing in these days, when the good that is in the G.A.R. is often prostituted to the worst purposes, to know that at least one post proposes by its efforts to increase its efficiency as a charitable institution, that I gladly send a small money contribution in aid of this object.

No one can deny that the Grand Army of the Republic has been played upon by demagogues for partisan purposes, and has yielded to insidious blandishments to such an extent that it is regarded by many good citizens whose patriotism and firmness cannot be questioned as an organization which has wandered a long way from its original design. Whether this idea is absolutely correct or not, such a sentiment not only exists, but will grow and spread unless within the organization something is done to prove that its objects are not partisan, unjust, and selfish.

In this country, where the success of our form of government depends upon the patriotism of all our people, the best soldier should be the best citizen.

To MRS. H. T. ELLETT [2]

Washington, *October* 25, 1887

I cannot resist the impulse to express my deep and sincere sympathy with you in the terrible affliction you have sustained in the sudden death of your loved and honored husband. I know I can write nothing which will comfort you in this trying hour, since consolation at such a time can only come from the heavenly source which permitted the grievous blow. My immediate relation to your deceased husband, at the moment of his fatal stroke, seems to connect me so nearly with his death that the sad scene is indelibly fixed upon my mind.

The death of so good and useful a man is an affliction to the entire community in which he dwelt, and if there is any solace in the knowledge that many share your grief, or if there is consolation in the fact that the

---

[1] In response for an appeal for a donation from Post 176 of the G.A.R., Lewiston, Maine.

[2] Henry Thomas Ellett, who had served in Congress from Mississippi before the Civil War and had later removed to Tennessee, died while delivering an address of welcome to President Cleveland in Memphis on October 15, 1887.

last words of the lamented dead, spoken in the presence of his neighbors and fellow-citizens, were full of noble patriotism and love for all his countrymen, this solace and this consolation you have in full measure. In this hour of your bereavement may God give you his support and the peace of mind which passeth all understanding. Mrs. Cleveland also desires me to convey to you her heartfelt sympathy and condolence.

To REPRESENTATIVE JAMES B. WEAVER [1]

Washington, *October* 25, 1887

Your letter of the 20th instant regarding the eviction by proceedings in the State Court of certain parties from lands in O'Brien County has excited my interest and sympathy. Such results are sure to bring distress oftentimes upon those entirely innocent who have settled upon lands in entire good faith. I very much fear there will be much of this consequent upon the loose and wasteful method in which our public domain has been heretofore managed.

I find upon consultation with the Secretary of the Interior and the Attorney-General that the cases to which you refer were some time since considered by them, and they concluded that the United States could not interfere in these controversies because in any event its title to the land was gone; and I am obliged to concur with them in the opinion that in these circumstances the United States would have no standing in the contest and could demand no redress for itself.

I think you will see the difficulty with a little reflection. I am afraid the two claimants in these cases must fight out their respective rights in the State Courts; but I suppose the determination then may be submitted to the Supreme Court of the United States upon appeal for final adjudication. If any legal way can be suggested by which the general Government can aid in the settlement of the questions involving so much hardship and vexation it will be considered.

To DR. S. B. WARD

Washington, *October* 25, 1887

I have not heard from you for a long time and I have lately often wondered why I have not received from your facile pen some of the won-

---

[1] James Baird Weaver (1833–1912) of Iowa, who had been the candidate of the Greenback party for President in 1880, was elected to Congress on the Democratic and Greenback-Labor tickets for the terms 1885–89. He was Populist candidate for President in 1892.

drous tales that are apt to follow your annual Adirondack outing. I am afraid that the camera has superseded the gun and rod — a mighty poor exchange, I think.

For myself I feel that I have made a mistake in passing the summer with so little vacation and I should feel much worse about it if I did not have a consciousness that the curtailment of my usual recreation was to some extent at least the result of the requirements of official duty. And since my return from the Western and Southern trip, I am more than ever fearful that I have not laid up enough of rest to last me through the long and trying winter before me. Still I feel real well and know of no reason why I shall not be able to 'see it through.'

We often talk of our experiences in the woods and as we call up pleasant pictures you may be sure that in all you are a central figure.

We all hope that another winter will not pass without welcoming you as a guest at the White House.

Mrs. Cleveland and Mrs. Folsom have bade me give you their regards when I wrote; and I wish when you have leisure you would let me hear from you.

To William Steinway

Washington, *October 28*, 1887

I am surprised to learn that the *Staats-Zeitung* demurs somewhat in its support of Mr. Fellows,[1] the candidate for District Attorney in the city of New York. I do not know the reason for this but regret it very much indeed. Mr. Fellows is the man upon whom dependence has been placed for a number of years, to do the hard and important work of bringing criminals to justice; and in all important cases he has had the laboring oar. His voice may almost be said to still ring in his denunciation of the men in public place in the city of New York who betrayed their trusts and disgraced the community — none of whom have escaped the condemnation which he demonstrated they deserved. Of course he only did his duty; but in these days that should not be discouraged. I am afraid the objections now made against him are not put forth in good faith by those who originated them. His indebtedness has been made the most of; but I am told that is greatly exaggerated, that its contraction involved no disgrace and that the extent to which it has been paid shows no disposi-

---

[1] John R. Fellows (1832–96), a veteran of the Civil War, was assistant district attorney in New York City 1885–87, district attorney 1888–90, and a Representative 1891–93.

tion to defraud anyone. One charge which I have seen made against him I know to be wicked, false, and I think, malicious. It is said, I believe, that he left town at the time one of the indicted aldermen was tried upon the plea of sickness, and that this was a pretense. I saw him just as he was leaving on that occasion and his appearance was abundant proof that he had sought rest from the exacting and straining work forced upon him, none too soon. I feared that he had delayed too long, for he certainly then appeared like a broken down man. Upon his return apparently fully restored, he entered upon the most important case of all that class, and the conviction of Sharp followed. It's a curious fact that the only time conviction failed, was upon the trial in which on account of sickness, he took no part. It is now claimed that this man is unfit for the head of the office in which he has had so important a part; and the reasons given so far as I am acquainted with them, seem to me to be insufficient. I honestly believe that in some quarters (one at least) the opposition to Mr. Fellows has a much wider scope and range than appears upon the surface — looking to the defeat of the Democracy in the State in the pending campaign, and its anticipated effect upon the Presidential campaign next year.

Since I began this letter it has been decided that Colonel Lamont will be in New York tomorrow, and will endeavor to see you. I therefore will not write more but as the Colonel starts within an hour or two, will hand this to him as a memorandum of part of the things I want him to communicate to you — only adding that I am convinced that anybody desiring the ascendancy of Democratic principles in the State and nation, and the failure of treacherous schemes to defeat those principles, will make a great mistake in opposing the election of John R. Fellows.

To EDWARD COOPER [1]

Washington, *November* 2, 1887

I don't think the newspaper clippings you send and now before me amount to enough to even raise a doubt concerning my desire for the success of both the State and the New York local tickets in the coming election. You know that I am very much inclined to abstain from any interference with New York City campaigns, fully believing the people of that city to be quite competent to manage their affairs. It surely ought not to be considered any interference, however, when I say, in reply to

[1] Edward Cooper (1824–1905) was a son of Peter Cooper, brother-in-law of Abram S. Hewitt, and one-time mayor of New York City.

your letter, that the newspaper tracts which you enclose totally mis-represent my wishes and hopes in regard to the fate of your Democratic local ticket. I shall be very much pleased to see it entirely successful.

I know nothing which, if I were a voter in the city of New York, would prevent my support of Mr. Fellows' candidacy without the least misgivings and with considerable personal satisfaction. Please present my congratulations to Mr. Hewitt upon his excellent letter published this morning.

HORACE WHITE [1] *to* CLEVELAND

New York, *November* 6, 1887 (telegram)

At the time of writing your recent letter in behalf of Colonel Fellows, were you aware of his solicitation of pecuniary favors from Tweed and his repudiation of gambling debts? Please telegraph answer.

To HORACE WHITE

Washington, *November* 7, 1887 (telegram)

For your personal information I answer to your telegram of last evening I did not.

To SECRETARY FAIRCHILD

Washington, *November* 7, 1887

I should like to know the surplus in the Treasury June 30, 1885, after the contribution to the sinking fund during the year then ending, and the amount of such contribution. (I believe nothing was paid that year on the debt except for sinking fund; but if there was I should be glad to have it stated.)

Also the surplus June 30, 1886, after contribution to sinking fund and the amounts of such contributions and the amounts paid for bonds reclaimed, from the surplus — showing what the surplus would have been after sinking fund payments, if no bonds had been taken up. Also the same for the year ending June 30, 1887. Also the transactions since that date until now, with kinds of bonds, amounts of each, and the average premium paid.

[1] Horace White (1834–1916), friend of Lincoln and former editor of the Chicago *Tribune*, was at this time associated with Godkin in editing the New York *Evening Post*.

To COMMISSIONER WILLIAM A. J. SPARKS [1]

Washington, *November* 15, 1887

I have read your letter of resignation left with me today, and also the communication addressed to you by the Secretary of the Interior, accompanying the same.

In the present situation I do not feel called upon to determine the merits of the controversy which has arisen between the Secretary and yourself further than to say that my impressions touching the legal question involved incline me to rely, as I naturally would do even if I had no impression of my own, upon the judgment of the Secretary. It presents a case of interpretation where two perfectly honest men may well differ.

The intent you have shown in the operation of the Land Department and your zealous endeavor to save and protect the public lands for settlers in good faith, induce me to believe that you will be pleased to receive the assurance that this policy upon which we are all agreed will continue to be steadfastly pursued, limited and controlled, however, by the law and the judgment of the courts by which we may be at times unwillingly restrained but which we cannot and ought not to resist.

I desire to heartily acknowledge the value of your services in the improved administration of the Land Department which has been reached, and to assure you of my appreciation of the rugged and unyielding integrity which has characterized your official conduct. I am constrained to accept the resignation you tender with assurances of my continued kindly feeling toward you and with the earnest wish that wherever your future way of life may lead, complete success and satisfaction may await you.

GEORGE HOADLY [2] *to* CLEVELAND

New York, *November* 22, 1887

Your letter of November 20 is just at hand. Thanking you for the confidence manifested in your suggestion that you would like to confer with me regarding your message, I have to reply by expressing absolute confidence that the message will be as well without the conference as with it. I have no faith in my own wisdom to advise under the present

---

[1] Commissioner Sparks had quarreled with Secretary Lamar upon the interpretation of certain laws pertaining to the public lands.

[2] Hoadly (1846–1902), was a prominent attorney and Democratic politician, who had been governor of Ohio in 1884–85 and was now practising in New York City.

circumstances, and I have unlimited trust in the wisdom and sagacity of the powers that be. I would only make this suggestion, namely, that in the matter of the revision of the tariff, you 'go slow.' Not to be misunderstood, I mean that I think it a perfectly safe proposition to stand on before the country, that you seek to reduce the duties on raw materials and to impose duties on luxuries. The danger of alienating large bodies of workmen, whose ignorance is crass, who are thoroughly organized, and whose employers are extremely jealous of any danger of loss or profits, is to my mind the danger of the situation. You have both the manufacturer and the Knight of Labor to be afraid of. I do not believe you need this suggestion. Nevertheless your letter justifies me, I think, in making it. I am, theoretically, as radical a free-trader as Mr. Hurd, but above all things I am in politics what the French call an Opportunist. I think you have now the opportunity to make a very great success, but that, if the counsels of Henry Watterson and Frank Hurd were fully followed, the success would be converted into defeat. *In medio tutissimus ibis.* Pardon my having enlarged so greatly. It is the only thing I am afraid of.

To WILLIAM R. GRACE [1]

Washington, *November 29*, 1887

You surely need not doubt Mrs. Cleveland's inclination to aid, in any way possible, Father MacGlynn's noble undertaking. It certainly deserves the aid and sympathy of all the truly benevolent.

But after quite some reflection we beg you to agree with us that it would not be exactly the thing to comply with your request. Mrs. Cleveland has just declined to present some flags to the New York firemen. She has often to decline propositions to aid by her presence and participation numerous projects which appear, to those in charge, of paramount merit. She hardly dares to open a door to further solicitation, which after compliance with your requests she could hardly refuse. Her social duties here, very exacting, and just now rapidly accumulating, cause her to shrink from a contemplated visit to New York with all the bustle and excitement which must attend the programme you suggest, and to tell you the truth, I cannot think that it ought to be put upon her. She has a long and trying season before her and will need all the strength she can muster.

Hoping that in some other way the occasion you have so much at

[1] Grace (1832–1904), was a prominent New York merchant, shipowner, and local Democratic leader, and was mayor of the city 1881–86.

heart may be very successful, and with assurances of sincere regret from us both...

To WILSON S. BISSELL
Washington, December 1, 1887

Archie Allen has been here bothering me about a place. He wants me to say a good word for him to Arthur, or Hanlan or Cutter. Is there anything in this? Doyle and Wiley were here a few days ago. I put out the postmaster at Tonawanda and put in the man they wanted. I guess it's the greatest stretch I have ever made between you and me....

My message is done. I think it is pretty good, but you will be surprised when you see it. Things are improving here and I think we can do some good legislation.

I want more and more to get out of this thing. When Doyle and Wiley said that Sheehan was about the country trying to get delegates for Hill, I did not feel half so bad as they thought I did.

To DR. S. B. WARD
Washington, December 23, 1887

Your note is just received. I shall be here, of course, both Tuesday and Wednesday and very glad to see you. As to hotels, the best one I know of is the Hotel Cleveland, sometimes called the White House. I know the proprietor will be much offended if you do not stop with him.

Seriously, Doctor, if you don't come to us, we will not forgive you. Telegraph me the train you will be on. You must not expect a great deal of time from me, but you can do as you please in my house and that is something.

VII

THE FIRST TERM ENDED

As THE year 1888 opened, it was evident that the tariff question would dominate all political discussion. Cleveland had determined that his message upon the tariff must be translated into a bill reducing the duties, especially upon raw materials and articles of general necessity. The Mills Bill, named after the Texan who headed the Ways and Means Committee, was debated in the House during April and May, and on June 21 passed by a narrow margin. The Senate, which was Republican, of course blocked it. But the President had succeeded in his purpose of converting his party to an uncompromising espousal of low-tariff principles, and in making the tariff problem the central issue of the Presidential campaign. It was generally expected that the Republicans would nominate James G. Blaine against him on a protectionist platform. But Blaine, who was in a hypochondriacal frame of mind, refused to be considered, and Benjamin Harrison was named in his stead. Agricultural interests in the Northwest were shocked by the completeness with which the Republican party went over to high-tariff doctrines, but actual bolters there were few. In the East the protected interests, led by the American Iron and Steel Association, raised large sums of money to defeat Cleveland and vigorously urged their employees to vote against him. The President, who was renominated by acclamation at the Democratic Convention in St. Louis, entered the campaign with the odds slightly against him. He labored under several severe handicaps. His running-mate on the ticket, Allen G. Thurman, was so aged as to be a liability, and broke down ludicrously when he tried to make a campaign speech in New York. Cleveland felt that the dignity of his office required him to refrain from stumping any part of the country, and so kept silent while Harrison was making scores of brief and highly effective speeches. The complicated fisheries dispute with Canada and Great Britain reached a crisis during the summer with the Senate's rejection of a treaty drafted by the Administration; and when the British minister, Sackville-West, committed the error of writing the so-called Murchison letter implying that Cleveland was more favorable to England than the Republicans, many Irish-American voters showed resentment. Above all, the management of the Democratic campaign proved weak and apathetic, while the Republican management under Chairman Matthew S. Quay was signally efficient. The Democratic national chairman, William H. Barnum, and the campaign chairman, Calvin S. Brice, were at heart opposed to tariff reductions, and put little energy into their fight. As a consequence, in November Cleveland was defeated, receiving 168 electoral votes to Harrison's 233; but his popular plurality exceeded 100,000, and the election gave no verdict against tariff reduction. He prepared with a light heart to return to private life.

To Dr. S. B. Ward

Washington, *January* 6, 1888

Yours is received. I was glad to hear that you arrived safely home and hope that if you derived no other advantage from your visit at the White House, you have some new ideas concerning the game of sixty-six.

The Manning story is too absurd for any attention. I know Mr. Manning never said I asked him to resign unless he was insane. Why, after he was stricken down he tendered his resignation and I insisted that he should take a long leave of absence instead in the expressed hope that he might possibly be able to go on. And all that correspondence is published and dated about the first day of June, 1886. If any such story as you refer to is afloat, I think I understand it. The absurdity of the thing is apparent when you reflect that when the President asks a member of his Cabinet to resign he does so. But Mr. Manning remained in the Cabinet a year or more after his stroke.

To Secretary L. Q. C. Lamar

Washington, *January* 7, 1888

When I determined to nominate you to a position upon the Bench of the Supreme Court, the personal gratification afforded by the tender to you of so honorable and suitable a place and the satisfactory conviction that an important Executive duty would thus be well performed, led me almost to forget that my action involved the loss of your conscientious and valuable aid and advice in Cabinet counsel, which for nearly three years I have so much enjoyed and appreciated.

Your note of today forces me to contemplate this contingency with the most profound and sincere regret. But since I know that the separation you now insist upon arises from that conception of public duty which has always so entirely guided your conduct in our official relation, I am constrained to accept the resignation you tender, hoping that it only anticipates your entrance upon the discharge of higher and more congenial functions than those now relinquished.

What I have thus far written seems very formal indeed. I intended this, because I am sure that the close confidence and the relation of positive affection which have grown up between us need no expression or interpretation. And yet I find it impossible for me to finish this note, without assuring you that the things which have characterized your conduct and bearing in the position from which you now retire — all your devotion to your country and Chief — all your self-sacrificing care and solicitude for public interests — all the benefits which your official services have conferred upon your fellow-countrymen, and all the affection and kindness so often exhibited toward me personally — I shall constantly remember with tenderness and gratitude.

To WILSON S. BISSELL

Washington, *January* 13, 1888

Peter Doyle was so persistent about having something done for Nicken that I spoke to Jewell about a place among the customs special inspectors. The day I telegraphed you Jewell wrote me a note saying he had selected him and would send his papers off that day. But before that the Colonel had shown me in the *World* a long account of Nicken's going to see some man's wife and being caught there, etc. So you may be sure I was not long in stopping the papers and hence my dispatch. It looks to me as if the thing must be given up....

Doyle in his last letter was quite peremptory in his suggestion of some good German to a place, but he didn't quite mention the German and upon my life I don't know him. Nearly three years of my term have passed and I honestly think as much of my time is taken up in hearing applications for office as at any other period. I cannot understand it.

I want to find a pretty prominent ex-soldier for Pension Agent. I don't get my eye on him.

I am quite fully convinced that schemes are on foot for an anti-Administration control in New York.[1] Every day brings confirmation of that belief. I suppose you have your full share of it in your locality. It extends further than the State of New York, but you know my feelings well enough to be satisfied that it will not keep me awake at all. I do think,

---

[1] Governor Hill and Tammany were eager to take control of the party in New York, and, capitalizing the dislike of many politicians for Cleveland, bring Hill forward for the Presidency.

however, that a move ought to be made towards organization for the sake of the best interests of the party — whatever they are.

To the ALBANY Argus

Washington, *January* 16, 1888

For more than two years I daily read the Albany *Argus*, deriving therefrom my information of passing events, and gathering abundant reasons for my Democratic faith. Of course, long before this intimate acquaintance, I was familiar with the paper as an influential expositor of party principles and policy. But when a person reads a newspaper every day, for even no longer a period than two years, it grows to be like a companion and friend whose existence and prosperity become matters of interest. It is for these reasons that I most heartily and sincerely congratulate the managers of the *Argus* upon the seventy-fifth year of its establishment. Its history has been honorable; its influence has been great; its loyalty to political principle in days of newspaper inconstancy has been steadfast, and its success has been fully deserved. I hope it may continue for many years to demonstrate that courage and loyalty and honesty are profitable, as well as right.

To POSTMASTER-GENERAL DON M. DICKINSON [1]

Washington, *January* 23, 1888

Confidential.

I will work with you tonight. Come about eight o'clock.

I hope that none of the Michigan people will vote today to do anything else but seat Mr. Carlisle. Any other course will only play into the hands of those who work for political advantage to prolong the sham of a contest. The thing has gone too far to do anything else except seat Mr. Carlisle, leaving the consideration of an investigation to be treated separately.

I cannot explain further, but a failure to end the matter on the committee's reports today will be, I fear, very bad.

---

[1] Donald M. Dickinson (1846–1917), a Michigan attorney, succeeded Vilas as Postmaster-General in January, 1888. He was one of Cleveland's most loyal friends, and took a leading part in his reëlection in 1892.

To WILSON S. BISSELL
Washington, *January* 31, 1888

Sackett and Runcie and Ferguson were in this afternoon with the same old story — discontent and discouragement. The matter of [the] chairmanship of the County Committee was talked of and Runcie was urged to take it strongly. I said they couldn't do better than take him and that I'd like to see him there, etc. I did not have your letter then, but received it before they got out of the house, I think. I don't know as I could have said any more if I had had it before me when they were in. Runcie said he had thought it all over and had fully made up his mind not to take it again — that he had served six years and that was all that ought to be expected of him — that there had never been a man appointed for him, etc.

Of course I did not know exactly how far to go with these people, and had to talk pretty severely with them so far as other people in Buffalo are concerned. I don't know exactly where the jealousies are. Of course they complained of Hanlen. I told them I thought all hands were a little at fault in the matter of the lack of co-operation with him. Then of course they complained of Arthur and I pinned them down to say particularly what was the matter. They spoke of Fiske, Reynolds, Chase, Blossom (?), and another man, I think Arthur or some such name.

Sackett said but very little indeed on these subjects, but apparently sympathized fully with the others.

I think I suggested some things to them which they had not thought of, but there is trouble there about the distribution of patronage. I said among other things that an official hesitated about dismissing a man when he feared that for the vacant place someone would be crowded upon him whom he could not appoint and that I thought the way to do was to select good, clean, honest men and offer them to the appointing officer so that he could see just how he would come out....

When are you coming here?

To WILLIAM A. FURSY
Washington, *February* 2, 1888

I acknowledge with sincere thanks the invitation extended to me on behalf of the Kings County Democratic Club, to attend a banquet to be given in the city of Brooklyn, on the ninth instant, in commemoration of the birthday of Samuel J. Tilden....

The birthday of Samuel J. Tilden is fittingly celebrated by the Democracy of Kings County, for he found there in all his efforts to reform the public service and to reinstate his party in the confidence of the American people firm and staunch friends, never wavering in their willing and effective support. Let these friends now remind all their fellow-citizens of the patriotic and useful career of their honored and trusted leader and let everyone professing his political faith proclaim the value of his teachings.

He taught the limitation of Federal power under the Constitution; the absolute necessity of public economy; the safety of a sound currency; honesty in public places; the responsibility of public servants to the people; care for those who toil with their hands; a proper limitation of corporate privileges, and a reform in the civil service.

His was true Democracy. It led him to meet boldly every public issue as it arose. With his conception of public duty he thought it never too early and never too late to give battle to vicious doctrines and corrupt practice. He believed that firm and sound Democracy flourished and grew in open, bold and honest championship of the interest of the people, and that it but feebly lived upon deceit, false pretences, and fear. And he was right. His success proved him right, and proved, too, that the American people appreciate a courageous struggle in their defence.

I should certainly join you in recalling the virtues and achievements of this illustrious Democrat on the anniversary of his birth if in the arrangements of the social events connected with my official life, an important one had not been appointed to take place on the evening of your banquet. This necessarily detains me here.

To GEORGE W. HAYWARD

Washington, *February* 8, 1888

Your letter is received and I hasten to tell you that I am much gratified by the prospect of seeing you so soon. But the main point of my letter is to tell you that of course you will come to the White House and stay while you are here and you can come when you please. I shall find time enough to have a good visit with you, and when I am busy with other affairs I know you are quite able to take care of yourself. Miss Folsom of Buffalo, a cousin of my wife, will be here and no more, and it would be ridiculous for you to put up at any other hotel. So send me a dispatch telling the train you will arrive on and we will see that you reach your hotel with speed and in safety.

To COLLECTOR DANIEL MAGONE

Washington, *February* 20, 1888

It is exceedingly important that Steinway accept temporary place on National Committee. We must have the use of his name. He can avoid the labor if necessary and terminate his tenure at date of Convention. See him at once, explain all, and urge his acceptance.

To COLLECTOR JOSEPH S. MILLER

Washington, *March* 3, 1888

An old lady (Mrs. Mayhew) has been here asking assistance to collect a claim of about $300 which she has against Mr. James J. Jarboe, a Deputy Collector of Internal Revenue, District of Maryland. The claim is repre-sented by a judgment and appears to be a just one. I don't think we ought as a general rule to attempt the collection of debts owing by employees of the Government, but this old lady's case has excited my sympathy and I wish there was a way suggested to you to aid her in the collection of this claim.

To JAMES SHANAHAN [1]

Washington, *March* 7, 1888

Private

I received your letter today and assure you that I was very much pleased with the hearty friendship contained in every line of it. I think this response will prove to be the longest letter I have written since I have lived in Washington.

I hardly think that you will be surprised to hear that my feelings, tastes and inclinations are such that if I felt justified in following their lead and doing precisely as I personally desire I would insist that my public life should end with the fourth of March next; and if any person authorized to speak for our grand party would today give me my discharge to take effect on the day I have named, I should be a very happy man. But I am daily and hourly told that the conditions are such that such a course is not open without endangering the supremacy of the party and the good

---

[1] While governor, Cleveland had appointed James Shanahan, a professional engineer, as superintendent of public works, and Shanahan remained his staunch political friend.

of the country. Occupying the position I do on this subject, having no personal ambition, willing to obey the command of my party and by my own act being in no man's way, I confess I cannot quite keep my temper when I learn of the mean and low attempts that are made by underhand means to endanger the results to which I am devoted. And when I see such good staunch friends as you with their coats off and sleeves rolled up, I feel like taking a hand with them.

Much of what you say in your letter corroborates what I have heard before concerning certain parties and influences which you mention. Many friends have been here since the Albany meeting of the committee, and I think plans have been pretty well made in different parts of the State. There is no slumbering and if the Albany fiasco did nothing else it roused up a lot of first-rate men and led them to see the danger of inaction.

I think the convention will be called early and I should not be surprised if the notice should be issued pretty soon. The New York and Brooklyn people appear to be inclined in the direction you desire and the districts in the country are the ones that should be looked to.

What you say about the men in Orleans County is just what I have insisted on. They are trying to fool my friends in Erie County and I think they may succeed even against my warning. I understand they have offered to permit them to name two of the delegates. Whether this is for the purpose of securing one of their own kind surely, or whether they hope that having certainly secured that one a part or the entire of the remainder will also happen to be of their kind I do not know, but I am sure there is mischief in the proposition. You know my Buffalo friends and Hanlen are not on speaking terms.

I am told that there is no danger of Sheehan's [1] doing anything in Erie County or Buffalo. We expect Maxwell here in a few days. I am very much pleased with your assurance that you will see me soon — the sooner it is the better I shall like it.

Now, Uncle James, I want to say to you that there has been enough of lying since the meeting of the State Committee to damn the world; and it has amused us a good deal here to see certain people protesting either that they had nothing to do with some queer transactions or that they

[1] William F. Sheehan (1859–1917), a Buffalo lawyer, and an important member of the Hill group, was member of the State Assembly 1885–91, Speaker 1891, and lieutenant-governor 1892–95. In 1895 he removed to New York City, and became an important ally of Tammany.

didn't mean anything. Ex-Mayor Grace was here and said to me, 'Don't let them give you any sleeping doses' — and I have not.

I think I know a man who will before a great while be asking such men as you for the nomination for governor and will be protesting that all his manipulation was for the general good and for the purpose of keeping certain discontented persons in line, etc.

I have written very frankly to you and said more about my feelings and inclinations than I intended; and some of what I have written is of course intended for you alone.

My position is this: I should personally like better than anything else to be let alone and let out; but although I often get quite discouraged and feel like insisting upon following my inclinations I shall neither go counter to the wishes of the party I love and which has honored me nor shall I desert my friends....

To RICHARD WATSON GILDER

Washington, *March* 11, 1888

We should be very glad to see the authors who propose to infest the National Capitol next Saturday [1] within the doors of the White House; and we have given the subject a little attention and thought.

We hear that Mrs. Hearst proposes a reception on Saturday night. What kind of a job would it be to have the party visit us after the reading, Monday night the 19th? I suppose the reading would be finished by ten o'clock or a little after. If you think this plan would operate, please let me know as soon as possible. If you know of a better scheme I beg you to suggest it. We shall have to transmit our invitation through you or someone else who is in the Ring.

With love to Mrs. Gilder (my own with Mrs. Cleveland's).

To GEORGE W. BISHOP

Washington, *March* 14, 1888

I am in receipt of a letter relating to Mr. Jacob R. Tucker, now employed under you, in which it is stated that his resignation will be requested upon party grounds and to satisfy partisan claims. In view of Mr. Tucker's meritorious service in the war as well as for other reasons

---

[1] A deputation appearing in behalf of international copyright legislation. Gilder (1844–1909), poet and editor of the *Century Magazine* from 1881 to his death, was after 1888 one of Cleveland's close friends.

connected with the good of the service, this removal should not take place for the reasons stated.

Mr. Tucker has not written to me and I doubt his knowledge of the fact that his case has been presented to me; but to discharge an ex-soldier with a record like Mr. Tucker's, merely because he does not belong to our party, would be directly contrary to the spirit if not the letter of the law giving preference to discharged soldiers, as well as an offence to the patriotic sentiment of the country. If Mr. Tucker is an efficient and faithful employee of the Government, and our party friends are finding fault with his retention, you may put the blame and responsibility of such retention upon me.

To WILSON S. BISSELL

Washington, *March* 21, 1888

I have read George Raines's letter with quite some satisfaction and enclose the same. It's mighty hard to get along with the Democrats of a locality when different factions are tattling and finding fault with each other like a mess of schoolboys. I think, however, that Monroe County will straighten out after a while.

I expect the next thing will be an attempt to fasten Grace's candidacy for governor upon me. 'About these days expect' all manner of lies and nonsense.

P.S. I received a letter from Jake Schenkelberger today thanking me for his nomination. His letter proves that he must have some good men about his office.

To THE FEDERAL CIVIL SERVICE COMMISSION

Washington, *March* 21, 1888

I desire to make a suggestion regarding Subdivision C, General Rule III, of the Amended Civil Service Rules promulgated February 2, 1888. It provides for the promotion of an employee in a department who is below or outside of the classified service to a place within said classified service in the same department upon the request of the appointing officer upon the recommendation of the Commission and approval of the President after a non-competitive examination, in case such person has served continuously for two years in the place from which it is proposed to promote him and 'because of his faithfulness and efficiency in the position occupied by him,' and 'because of his qualifications for the place to which the appointing officer desires his promotion.'

It has occurred to me that this provision must be executed with caution to avoid the application of it to cases not intended and the undue relaxation of the general purposes and restrictions of the Civil Service Law.

Non-competitive examinations are the exceptions to the plan of the Act, and the rules permitting the same should be strictly construed. The cases arising under the exception above recited should be very few, and when presented they should precisely meet all the requirements specified and should be supported by facts which will develop basis and reason of the application of the appointing officer and which will commend them to the judgment of the Commission and the President. The sole purpose of the provision is to benefit the public service, and it should never be permitted to operate as an evasion of the main feature of the law, which is competitive examinations.

As these cases will first be presented to the Commission for recommendation, I have to request that you will formulate a plan by which their merits can be tested. This will naturally involve a statement of all the facts deemed necessary for the determination of such applications, including the kind of work which has been done by the person proposed for promotion, and the considerations upon which the allegations of the faithfulness, efficiency and qualifications mentioned in the rule are predicated.

What has already been written naturally suggests another very important subject to which I invite your attention.

The desirability of the rule which I have commented upon would be nearly, if not entirely, removed, and other difficulties which now embarrass the execution of the Civil Service Law would be obviated if there was a better and uniform classification of the employees in the different departments. The importance of this is entirely obvious. The present imperfect classifications, hastily made, apparently with but little care for uniformity, and promulgated after the last Presidential election and prior to the installation of the present Administration, should not have been permitted to continue till this time.

It appears that in the War Department the employees were divided on the 19th day of November, 1884, into eight classes and sub-classes, embracing those earning annual salaries from $900 to $2000.

The Navy Department was classified November 22, 1884, and its employees were divided into seven classes and sub-classes, embracing those who received annual salaries from $720 to $1800.

In the Interior Department the classification was made on the 6th day of December, 1884. It consists of eight classes and sub-classes and embraces employees receiving annual salaries from $720 to $2000.

On the second day of January, 1885, a classification of the employees in the Treasury Department was made consisting of six classes and sub-classes, including those earning annual salaries from $900 to $1800.

In the Postoffice Department the employees were classified on February 6, 1885, into nine classes and sub-classes, embracing persons earning annual salaries from $720 to $2000.

On the 12th of December, 1884, the Bureau of Agriculture was classified in a manner different from all the other departments, and presenting features peculiar to itself.

It seems that the only classification in the Department of State and the Department of Justice is that provided for by section 163 of the Revised Statutes, which directs that the employees in the several departments shall be divided into four classes. It appears that no more definite classification has been made in these departments.

I wish the Commission would revise these classifications and submit to me a plan which will as far as possible make them uniform, and which will especially remedy the present condition which permits persons to enter a grade in the service in the one department without any examination, which in another department can only be entered after passing such examination. This, I think, should be done by extending the limits of the classified service rather than by contracting them.

To MRS. MORRISON R. WAITE [1]

Washington, *March* 23, 1888

I am shocked and appalled by the intelligence I have just received of your husband's death. I cannot close my mind entirely to the nation's loss and my own affliction, the results of this terrible visitation; but above all and beyond all at this moment is my sympathy for you, thus suddenly cast to the lowest depths of sorrow and grief.

In my utter helplessness, when I would gladly furnish earthly comfort

---

[1] Morrison Remick Waite of Ohio (1816–88) had been appointed Chief Justice by President Grant.

if I could, I can only pray that God in His infinite mercy may bind up your broken heart and strengthen and sustain you.

To the REVEREND JAMES MORROW, D.D.

Washington, *March 29,* 1888

I have received from you certain resolutions passed at the Annual Conference of the Methodist Episcopal Church held at Philadelphia on the 20th instant. I am not informed how to address a response to the officers of the conference who have signed these resolutions, and for that reason I transmit my reply to you.

The action taken by this assemblage of Christian men has greatly surprised and disappointed me. They declared 'that this conference earnestly protests against the recent action of the Government in excluding the use of native languages in the education of the Indians, and especially the exclusion of the Dakota Bible among those tribes where it was formerly used. That while admitting that there are advantages in teaching English to the Indians, to compel them to receive all religious instruction in that language would practically hinder their receiving it in the most effective way, as the line of power travels with the human heart, and the heart of the Indian is in his language. That it is in harmony with the genius of our country — a free church in a free state — that the operations of all missionary societies should be untrammelled by state interferences.'...

The Government seeks, in its management of the Indians, to civilize them, and to prepare them for that contact with the world which necessarily accompanies civilization. Manifestly nothing is more important to the Indian, from this point of view, than a knowledge of the English language. All the efforts of those having the matter in charge tend to the ultimate mixture of the Indians with our other people, thus making one community in all those things which pertain to American citizenship.

But this ought not to be done while the Indians are entirely ignorant of the English language. It seems to me it would be a cruel mockery to send them out into the world without this shield from imposition and without this weapon to force their way to self-support and independence.

Nothing can be more consistent, then, than to insist upon the teaching of English in our Indian schools. It will not do to permit these wards of the nation, in their preparation to become their own masters, to indulge in their barbarous language because it is easier for them or because it pleases them. The action of the conference, therefore, surprises me. It will be observed that 'textbooks in the vernacular' are what are prohibited and 'oral instruction'; the 'entire curriculum' must be in English. These are the terms used to define the elements of an ordinary secular education and do not refer to religious or moral teaching. Secular teaching is the object of the ordinary Government schools; but surely there can be no objection to reading a chapter of the Bible in English, or in Dakota if English could not be understood, at the daily opening of these schools....

To WILLIAM P. LARKINS

Washington, *April* 14, 1888

I must ask you to excuse me from my engagement with you this morning. When I made it I did not know who you were nor the object of your request. I have learned both from Mr. Martin's letter and am satisfied I can improve my time much more profitably at this extremely busy period than by talking politics with you.

To GOVERNOR FITZHUGH LEE [1]

Washington, *April* 15, 1888

I have been hesitating a good deal about the kind of a reply I should send to your kind and considerate letter of the 7th instant, and the doubts I have entertained on the subject must serve as an excuse for my silence up to this time.

I don't think I ought at this time to write anything explaining my message to Congress, for the purpose of publication. I labored hard to make the demands simple and plain and I have heard from many sources that I succeeded in doing so. Any attempt to make a public explanation would now be greatly misrepresented and misconstrued, and might do more harm than good.

The conversation I had with you some time ago furnishes all the aid to interpretation that can be desired, and taking it as your cue I don't see why you might not satisfy any honest doubter as to my position upon the question referred to in your letter.

I said to you in substance that I was speaking in my message of the two modes of taxation — one through an internal system and the other

---

[1] Lee (1835–1905), a nephew of Robert E. Lee, was governor of Virginia from 1886 to 1890, and in Cleveland's second Administration was consul-general in Havana.

through a tariff upon imports. The latter, because it unnecessarily burdened the people in their means of living, I especially desired to present in all its inequity and injustice. In contrasting the two I spoke of one as not being a charge on the necessaries of life and easily borne; and then characterized the other as most needing the attention of Congress. I never dreamed of anyone construing my language as an expression of hostility to any modification of the tobacco tax. On the contrary, I wrote in full contemplation of the fact that any adjustment of the tariff and the reduction of receipts from taxation might involve such a modification. I am devoted to an effort to relieve the people from their unjust burdens under the guise of taxation for the support of the Government, and if the rest of our people are inclined to be as moderate and conciliatory as I am, we shall accomplish this — the best and highest purpose that can engage the attention of the people and especially of those entrusted with the management of public affairs.

I am not willing that this letter shall be published and intend it as an aid to you in recalling the conversation we have had — which conversation together with what I have here written ought, it seems to me, to enable you to so interpret the message as to meet the allegations of those who seek to misrepresent my position.

To Federal District Attorney Owen A. Galvin
Washington, *April* 18, 1888

Information has reached the Treasury Department that a large number of foreigners and aliens have lately been brought into the State of Massachusetts under contract for labor and service and especially for the purpose of manning American fishing vessels which are intended to be engaged in taking fish in the neighborhood of the Canadian coasts. It seems quite certain that such aliens and foreigners have in some cases been brought in by the procurement of parties owning such fishing vessels in Boston and Gloucester.

The importation of these aliens and foreigners not only tends to the displacement of American labor, but it is positively prohibited by our laws. Penalties are provided for aiding in any way or encouraging such importation, and punishment as for a crime is provided for the actual bringing in of these parties.

Many of the aliens and foreigners who have thus been imported upon vessels arriving at the port of Boston have been returned to the country from whence they came pursuant to the laws referred to; and in some cases it is feared that such return has been prevented through false statements made by the parties who have thus been brought in.

I desire to enjoin upon you the prompt and efficient execution of these laws, by the strict enforcement of the penalties and punishments therein provided. You will at once confer with the Collectors of the Ports of Boston and Gloucester and obtain such information, touching violations of the law mentioned, as they may have at hand. The special agents who have been detailed for the investigation of these matters will be directed to report to you; and if, in the prosecution of the offenders mentioned, you require further assistance, it will be furnished upon your application.

MRS. CLEVELAND *to* MRS. MAGGIE NICODEMUS

Washington, *June* 3, 1888

I can only say in answer to your letter that every statement made by the Reverend C. H. Pendleton [1] in the interview which you send me is basely false, and I pity the man of his calling who has been made the tool to give circulation to such wicked and heartless lies. I can wish the women of our country no greater blessing than that their homes and lives may be as happy, and their husbands may be as kind, attentive, considerate, and affectionate as mine.

To WILSON S. BISSELL

Washington, *June* 17, 1888

It seems quite a long time since I have written to you, and on this hot Sunday morning I have seated myself at Oak View to 'drop you a line.'

The political turmoil has not fairly begun yet. In point of fact the campaign thus far as I see it is very quiet. I sometimes think that perhaps more enthusiasm would have been created if someone else had been nominated after a lively scrimmage at St. Louis. I mean to be as good a candidate as I can and after the people have done their voting shall be content, and more so in case of success because my reluctance to again take on the burden has been fully considered, discounted, and dismissed, and because I am sure in being a candidate again I am but answering the demands of public and political duty. These feelings can and do exist

[1] A Baptist clergyman of Worcester, Massachusetts, who had attended a church conference in Washington and on his return had circulated silly stories of Cleveland's brutality to his wife.

without the least lack of appreciation of the honor and satisfaction which a nomination tendered in the way mine has been should awaken.

The first important questions to be settled are the selection of the heads of the National Committee and your State Executive Committee. If anyone has any very clear ideas on these subjects I am not aware of it.

I appointed Mr. Harmon upon a railroad commission, as you requested, and received a letter thanking me for it. I made an order a few days ago removing the pension office from Syracuse to Buffalo to take effect July 1.

I suppose the *News* will occupy in this campaign about the place the *Telegraph* did in the last. Its acknowledged grievances are the appointments of Sackett as postmaster in Buffalo and a man it did not favor at Leroy. The fact that I appointed to place one of its editors at Butler's request and the further fact that I kept McIntosh's uncle in office at New York until his death a week or two ago count for nothing even with people who see nothing in politics except such personal advantages as they can get out of it.

A number of people have spoken to me of the fine appearance the Cleveland Democracy made at the Convention.

The notification committee will be here on the 26th instant and their message will be delivered on the afternoon of that day. I wish you could be here. Is it not possible for you to come? I had a nice visit with Scheu, Fuchs, and Larry, and afterward with Dayton and Forsyth.

What vacation do you expect to take this summer? I can hardly calculate to get away before the middle of August and incline to the Adirondacks; but I am so bothered with urgent invitations to go to all sorts of places at all sorts of times, that I don't make any arrangements for real recreation. It is possible that I shall go to Ohio in September. If I do I have promised to go to Kentucky on the trip.

My wife sits by me and bids me send to you her affectionate regards. I tell you, Bissell, I am sure of one thing. I have in her something better than the Presidency for life — though the Republican party and papers do say that I beat and abuse her. I absolutely long to be able to live with her as other people do with their wives. Well! Perhaps I can after the 4th of next March.

I shall be glad to hear from you at any time and often and should be especially delighted if you could be with us on the 26th.[1] Won't you come?

[1] Notification meeting.

in the *North American Review* I am charged with the declaration that 'I believe in Free Trade as I believe in the Protestant religion.' In answer to your inquiry as to the truth of this allegation, I have to say that I never made use of that expression or one anything like it. The statement you quote is a pure unadulterated fabrication. While it would be in vain to attempt to meet or refute every false statement coined or forged to serve the purposes of misrepresentation in the heat of a political canvass, the friendly spirit of your inquiry has led me to make this emphatic denial.

To CHAUNCEY F. BLACK [1]

Washington, *September* 14, 1888

The papers which you kindly sent me for my perusal touching the scope, method, and purposes of the association of Democratic clubs have strengthened my belief in the extreme importance of such organizations as have been thus associated.

The struggle upon which we have entered is in behalf of the people — the plain people of the land — and they must be reached. We do not proceed upon the theory that they are to be led by others who may or may not be in sympathy with their interests. We have undertaken to teach the voters, as free, independent citizens, intelligent enough to see their rights, interested enough to insist upon being treated justly, and patriotic enough to desire their country's welfare.

Thus this campaign is one of information and organization.

Every citizen should be regarded as a thoughtful, responsible voter, and he should be furnished the means of examining the issues involved in the pending canvass for himself.

I am convinced that no agency is so effective to this end as the clubs which have been formed, permeating all parts of the country and making their influence felt in every neighborhood. By a systematic effort they make the objects of the Democratic party understood by the fair and calm discussion of the Democratic position in this contest among those with whom their members daily come in contact, and by preventing a neglect of the duty of suffrage on election day these clubs will become, in my opinion, the most important instrumentality yet devised for promoting the success of our party.

[1] A Pennsylvania attorney, son of Jeremiah S. Black.

To GOVERNOR ISAAC P. GRAY [1]

Washington, *September* 29, 1888

I have been hoping that some errand would bring you in this direction and that I might be thus afforded a personal interview touching Indiana politics. Since, however, all reports from there represent you as very actively at work in the canvass, I am satisfied that you are employed to the best possible advantage at home.

Our Indiana friends are nearly unanimous in their expressions of the utmost confidence in the result in their State; and I am sure I ought not to distrust their judgment. I have occasionally feared, however, that they were relying too much upon surface indications and were somewhat influenced by the enthusiasm of the campaign.

One or two quite rash Indianians have informed me lately that though they did not contemplate defeat in their State, the organization of the party there was not as close and complete as it ought to be. But these reports have caused me no uneasiness, since I have been assured that you have undertaken to look to this matter. I only want to remind you that there will be, later in the campaign, an attack made upon your forces that will be exceedingly dangerous unless all our men are in line, and touching elbows. I think the feeling is quite general in these parts that you are the best reliance for that thorough organization that appears to me to be indispensable to success.

The main purpose of this letter, however, is to express my gratification and satisfaction with the assurance that you have this subject in hand. I should be glad to hear from you at any time touching the progress of the campaign.

To WILLIAM A. FISHER

Washington, *October* 15, 1888

I have received your kind invitation to join you in duck shooting the latter part of this month or the first of next; and I need hardly tell you how much I appreciate your effort to put me in the way of a little recreation, with freedom from official cares and labor. I feel very much the need of relaxation and have been long hoping that I might have an opportunity to avail myself of some such invitation as that which you so courteously extend.

---

[1] Governor of Indiana 1885–89. The campaign in Indiana in 1888 was spirited, for the Republican nominee for President, Benjamin Harrison, had pledged his party to carry it; as, with the help of unblushing bribery, he did.

I know I should enjoy the shooting very much, though I am not sure I should do myself any great credit.

It is impossible for me to say much more than this, except to add that it does seem to me that I ought to be able to take a few days at the time indicated, and that if you will let me know when the ducks are fat and plenty and tame and obliging, I will make a supreme effort to accept your invitation.

SECRETARY BAYARD *to* CLEVELAND

Washington, *October* 25, 1888

I have just received a note of which the enclosed is a copy, from Sackville-West, which will give you an idea of his fatuity in general.[1] I am disposed to think the *animus* of the letter will react injuriously upon the constructors of the plot.

To DR. S. B. WARD

Washington, *November* 6, 1888

I send you with this my check on Albany for $155.36 in full of Mrs. Cleveland's bill at Saranac Inn ($108.36) and Mrs. Folsom's ($47.00). I should have sent this before, but between Oak View and the White House I have had hard work to get my check book and the bills to be paid in the same place.

This is Election Day and at the hour I write (4 P.M.) the people have determined who they will have for their next President. You know how I feel in the matter and how great will be the *personal* compensations of defeat. I am very sure that any desire I may have for success rests upon the conviction that the triumph of my party at this time means the good and the prosperity of the country.

You see I am in a good mood to receive the returns whatever they may be.

A. B. FARQUHAR *to* CLEVELAND

York, Pa., *November* 15, 1888

... The hundreds of letters received just before the election led me to believe you would have a small majority in Indiana, New Jersey, New

[1] Sackville-West's famous 'Murchison letter' was published October 24; see the editor's *Grover Cleveland: A Study in Courage*, 428 ff. The British minister in his letter to Bayard protested that he had been betrayed in the publication of a private and proper communication, and that he had meant no harm. On October 26, by Cleveland's instructions, Bayard cabled London that the minister's usefulness had ended.

York, and Connecticut. This opinion was founded upon information gathered from the cities, especially Buffalo, Rochester, Elmira, Albany, Chicago, Indianapolis, and from my customers in the various towns through Connecticut and New Jersey. But I did not sufficiently allow for Hill trading, Grant and Hewitt quarrelling, Quay's buying,[1] and the falling off in Kings County because our friend Beecher was no more. The election was lost in the rural districts, where men could easiest be persuaded that vetoes of pensions to bummers and deserters were blows struck at our country's gallant defenders; that blackmail given to rings of mine-owners and manufacturing trusts was fostering home labor; that the rapidly growing mortgages upon their homesteads come from want of more protection; that the best advisers in questions of national economy were not disinterested students of the science, who might know something about it, but the attorneys or subsidized organs of the trusts, who appealed only in behalf of their own pockets! One week more of instruction would have given us the day; I could feel the effects from the many letters I wrote.

Last spring the people were open to conviction, and could be easily influenced; we ought to have got in our best work then. I did my best to awaken our people to the necessity of it, as your devoted friend, Frank Thorne, can tell you; but they were slow to move.

But you will conquer. Your message last December came to us as a gleam in the midst of darkness, bringing faith and hope after years of error, outlining the policy upon which shall rest the basis of our freedom and national wealth and prosperity. Its truths were not alone for this day and generation, but for all time, and all parts of the world....

To DR. S. B. WARD

Washington, *November* 19, 1888

I should certainly be glad to see you and think I shall be so far free from the constant labor necessary for the preparation of my message by the time you suggest (the Saturday after Thanksgiving) that I could give you a few lessons in the game of the period. If the message is not done then it will never be, for it must be sent in on the following Monday. So if you come on the day you specify or any day within the two or three

---

[1] Mayor Hewitt had quarreled with Hugh J. Grant, one of the chiefs of Tammany Hall; he was not renominated, ran independently, and was defeated. Matthew S. Quay, in active charge of the Republican campaign, had helped finance the purchase of many votes in Indiana and New York, the two critical States in the election.

weeks thereafter, we shall all be very glad to see you. Give my regards to Mr. Lentze and tell him there isn't the least occasion for him to break his jaw in attempting to do justice to his feelings regarding the election. It's all right.

To SECRETARY ENDICOTT

Washington, *December* 9, 1888

I have examined the case of Captain John F. Marsh, 3d Artillery, whose resignation was lately accepted, and have reflected upon the manner in which the resignation came to our hands, and I am convinced that he should be treated in another manner. In the first place, I do not think resignations should be taken in this way and held as a pledge of future good conduct. I believe it is much better to apply the rules adopted for the discipline of the army, as the occasions therefor arise, and that punishment should be the result of such application.

I did not think of this phase of the subject at first and was quite satisfied with the course pursued — especially as it seemed to be on the side of leniency. But it appears now that this officer, after a service of twenty-seven years in the volunteer and regular army, and after many instances of irregular conduct have been overlooked, by the acceptance of a resignation for a long time in the hands of his commanding officer, is at the will of such officer discharged from the army at a time and under circumstances which cause his family great distress. I am of the opinion that the course which you did not take out of kindness is the one which should be adopted, and that is, that this officer be retired for causes not incident to his service. I have to suggest, therefore, that the acceptance of his resignation be revoked and that his case be presented to a retiring board.

To JOHN G. CARLISLE

Washington, *December* 11, 1888

I have understood that you were to be in the city today. If this reaches you I wish you could call and see me before half-past four. If that is impossible, cannot you come to Oak View tomorrow? There isn't a man in the United States I should give more to see than you just at this time.

To Mr. Sherman Hoar and Others

Washington, *December* 24, 1888

I am exceedingly sorry that I cannot be present at the annual dinner of the Massachusetts Tariff Reform League on the 28th instant....

This reform appears to me to be as far-reaching in its purposes as the destiny of our country, and as broad in its beneficence as the welfare of our entire people. It is because the efforts of its advocates are not discredited by any sordid motives that they are able boldly and confidently to attack the strongholds of selfishness and greed.

Our institutions were constructed in purity of purpose and love for humanity. Their operation is adjusted to the touch of national virtue and patriotism, and their results under such guidance vouch for the prosperity and happiness of our people. And so long as the advocates of tariff reform appreciate the sentiments in which our institutions had their origin, so long as they apprehend the forces which alone can govern their operation, so long as they, in a spirit of true patriotism, are consecrated to the service of their country, temporary defeat brings no discouragement. It but proves the stubbornness of the forces of combined selfishness, and discloses how far the people have been led astray and how great is the necessity of redoubled efforts in their behalf.

To lose faith in the intelligence of the people is a surrender and an abandonment of the struggle. To arouse this intelligence and free it from darkness and confusion, give assurance of speedy and complete victory. In the track of reform are often found the dead hopes of pioneers and the despair of those who fell in the march. But there will be neither despair nor dead hopes in the path of tariff reform. Nor shall its pioneers fail to reach the heights. Holding fast their faith and rejecting every alluring venture and every deceptive compromise which would betray their sacred trust, they themselves shall regain and restore the patrimony of their countrymen, freed from the trespass of grasping encroachment and safely secured by the genius of American justice and equality.

To Lewis McMullen

Washington, *January* 8, 1889

I have received your letter, accompanied by a copy of the letter of the Secretary of the Treasury asking for your resignation, and your reply thereto. These were not needed to inform me of the difficulties existing in the administration of your office, in the way of instituting certain changes and reforms, and the correction of abuses which ought not to be longer allowed.

You may be sure that the phase that the subject has assumed is not a pleasant one; but frankness and fairness compel me to say that I have become as well satisfied as the Secretary that the change he insists upon should take place; and the condition is such that I am sure no explanation or argument can change the course determined on.

I therefore regret exceedingly that you have not seen fit to tender the resignation requested. Your positive refusal to do so has obliged me to notify you of your removal from office; and I have this day signed a paper to that effect. The Secretary has written you a letter to accompany this notice, and I fully concur in the sentiments therein contained.

To WILLIAM A. VINCENT

Washington, *January* 8, 1889

I have always said to your friends, as well as to you, that your removal from the office of Judge for the Territory of New Mexico did not in the least imply any charge or conviction of dishonesty, incapacity, or judicial misconduct. In the condition of affairs at that time I deemed it my duty to promptly pursue the course so unfortunate for you, and which was adopted by me upon the mere showing of the facts alleged, without inquiry as to your motives and purposes. My action was undoubtedly harsh, but I thought it was justified.

Often since that time, as all the facts attending the incident have become known to me, and as I reflected upon your otherwise unexceptionable judicial career, so far as it has come to my knowledge, I have been impressed by the representations of your friends that your removal had subjected you to a suspicion which was unjust and unwarranted.

So far as I am concerned, notwithstanding all that has passed, I am at this time willing to express my confidence in your ability and uprightness. There is now a vacancy in the Chief Justiceship of Montana. So far as regards your fitness, I should be entirely willing to see you in that place. I write to ask you, therefore, whether, in case I should think it well to do so, I am at liberty to submit your name to the Senate for that office. I make this proposition with a reservation, for reasons not in the least connected with your personal qualifications, and I shall be glad to know your views upon the subject as soon as possible.

To WILSON S. BISSELL

Washington, *January* 10, 1889

I have just received the check you sent me for $94.50 dividend upon my stock and I hope that the mere fact of this check passing through your hands has impressed you with the sagacity of the man who invested in that stock many years ago. You know I do not approve of any sort of speculation, but if a man must go into that kind of business I cannot for the life of me see why he should not go into something that pays.

It is about half-past one o'clock A.M. and we have had our Cabinet dinner tonight. Forty-four, I think, sat down and all were first-rate Democrats but four. Brice and his wife came over from New York and are staying with us. Saturday I mean to give a stag dinner and get together all the good people to meet him who were active in the campaign who were not here tonight and some that were here. He is a first-rate fellow and I mean to do all I can to show my appreciation of his friendship.

I am very sorry to hear that you are again afflicted with the lumbago. If I remember rightly, that is an old friend of yours whose acquaintance you had better be rid of as soon as you can.

I don't like to bother you, but I wish you would get the amount of my county taxes and tell me what it is so that I can pay them. I hope that we shall see you again before we leave.

To REAR-ADMIRAL LEWIS A. KIMBERLY

Washington, *January* 10, 1889 (cablegram)

Captain of *Nipsic* telegraphs through Lieutenant Hawley from Auckland that German ships landed forces at Samoa and engagement followed with troops of Mataafa resulting in serious German loss.[1] Germans in revenge shelling villages disregarding protests and neutral rights placing lives and property of our citizens in danger. Captain urges naval reinforcement. German Government claims that German forces were first attacked and that war exists between Germany and the Samoans who attacked her forces, but the German Government invites the United States to join in establishing order in Samoa in the common interest and gives assurance of careful respect for our treaty rights. United States have

---

[1] The United States, in common with Great Britain and Germany, held important treaty rights in Samoa. The German Government, eager to establish its sovereignty there, had exiled the King Malietoa, and its agents were acting with a high hand. Cleveland was indignant, and had Kimberly hurry to Apia with the warships *Trenton* and *Vandalia*.

informed Germany of its willingness to co-operate in restoration of order in Samoa on the basis of full preservation of treaty rights and Samoan autonomy as recognized and agreed to by Germany, the United States, and Great Britain.

Proceed at once to Samoa and extend full protection and defence to American citizens and their property. Consult with American Vice-Consul and otherwise inform yourself as to situation and all recent occurrences. Protest against the subjugation of the country and the displacement of native government by German rule enforced by German arms and coercion, as in violation of positive agreement and understanding between foreign powers interested, but inform the representatives of the German and English Governments of your readiness to co-operate in causing all treaty rights to be respected and in restoring peace and order on the basis of a recognition of Samoan rights to independence. Endeavor to prevent extreme measures against Samoans and to procure a peaceful settlement. If any arrangement can be made to that end upon the basis herein mentioned, report the same here for approval and inform us as soon as possible after arrival of the condition of affairs and the prospect of peaceful adjustment, and whether when conflict occurred Germany was acting impartially between opposing forces.

To WILSON S. BISSELL

Washington, *January* 25, 1889

Your letter is just received enclosing receipt for the county taxes on Butler Street and I must thank you for attending to the matter. I enclose you my check on Albany for $33.69, the amount of the taxes paid by you.

I hope the parties from Buffalo of whom you speak will be here Thursday evening so that they can attend the next reception. I shall be glad to do anything I can for them. It seems very strange that my term should close without your attending any of the events at the White House which are really interesting, such as receptions, dinners, etc. The last state dinner will be given to the Supreme Court one week from next Thursday (I think), and if you have any idea that you can and would like to attend, if you will let me know I will send you a regular invitation.

The paper tonight gives an account of McBride's address to Gladstone and makes especial mention of the fact that Harrison, the President-elect, signed it December 7 after his election.

I have been getting a letter or a telegram from the Exile every day asking for the return of his book. I suppose, however, he will have it in his possession by the time this reaches you or soon thereafter. I am sorry to trouble you with the thing and it seems amusing to find this man's vagaries dignified by mention in the press dispatches.

I wish you would let me hear from you soon in relation to your attendance at the dinner. I know that you will appreciate my reason for approaching you in a way which to others might seem a little queer.

Mrs. Cleveland would send her love to you if she was not in bed and asleep.

To COMMISSIONER LYMAN [1]

Washington, *February* 8, 1889

The fifteenth of February is almost here, on which date Civil Service rules will cover the Railway Mail Service. Will there be a list of eligibles on that date from which names can be selected? I have heard nothing of the report of the Commission yet. Is there a prospect of my seeing that soon? A long time has passed since I have seen or heard from you, but I have supposed that you were very much occupied upon the two matters I have referred to. I should be glad to know how you are getting on. I wish you would call and see me tomorrow (Saturday) afternoon at two o'clock.

To PRESIDENT-ELECT BENJAMIN HARRISON

Washington, *February* 15, 1889

I desire, following the formal announcement of your election to the Presidency of the United States, to congratulate you upon that result, and to assure you of my readiness to do all in my power to make your accession to office easy and agreeable. I am led to suppose that you will spend a number of days here prior to your inauguration. If such should be the case an opportunity will be afforded me of canvassing certain details connected with the change of Administration, the arrangement of which will add much to the comfort of all who are affected. I shall take your request for a special session of the Senate for granted and will, according to custom, issue a proclamation convening that body March 4 at noon.

If convenient, I shall be glad to be informed whether I shall have an opportunity to see you here somewhat in advance of inauguration day.

---

[1] Charles Lyman, appointed by Cleveland as Republican member of the Civil Service Commission, was much the strongest member of that body.

To PATRICK KIERNAN

Washington, *February* 23, 1889

In relation to the arrangement between us for the care of Oak View I have this to say:

Of course I cannot tell how long I shall own the property, though I have now no definite idea of selling it. If I should dispose of it, any agreement we make would terminate with such sale. Subject to such disposition, I propose an arrangement to continue from March 1, 1889, to March 1, 1890.

I have agreed to allow a family to occupy the house from about the first of June until some time in September of this year. They are to have the use of a horse and the buggy I shall leave on the place whenever they desire, and it is quite likely they will want to drive every day. It is expected that they will have a man-servant living with them who will harness and unharness the horse when necessary, though I expect you to feed and care for all the stock left on the place.

I will leave all the horses, cows, and other stock and animals upon the place which are now there, and the buggy called the 'farm buggy.' The latter to be used by the people occupying the house above mentioned and by you at such times as may be arranged between you and the occupants of the house. You are to carefully feed and tend all the stock and animals left on the place. Any calves now there or which may be born you may sell for veal or otherwise as you think best, except any calf born of 'Grace,' the Jersey cow from Philadelphia, is not to be disposed of without consulting me. Chickens hatched may be also sold at your discretion, but you are to have such as you want for your family use without accounting for them. You are also to have such milk and eggs as you need for family use without accounting for them. The garden is to be yours absolutely and you are to plant and cultivate the same at your own expense and pay for all the seeds and extra work for the same, but of course may have the use, free of expense, of any tools or other things left on the place for the purpose of cultivating such garden.

The occupants of the house are to have as much of the fruit growing on the place as they desire. If any remains, it is to be sold and accounted for if it can be sold to advantage. The flowers of course the occupants of the house are to have. Subject to what is written above, everything raised upon the place beyond what is necessary to feed the stock and animals is to be sold for my account by you, and a correct account kept of the same, and the money received therefor is to be paid or credited to me. I am to pay for all seeds (except those for the garden) and for all necessary extra work, but the expense of extra labor shall be kept by you down to the lowest point.

The people occupying the house will probably prove good customers for much that is raised on the place if prices are fairly arranged. The proceeds of all the things sold from the garden are yours. The proceeds arising from the sale of everything else are mine. I am to furnish everything that is fed to the stock and animals except such as is raised on the place. In addition to the privileges allowed you as herein stated, I am to pay you thirty dollars a month and you are to devote all your time and labor to the maintenance and care of the place.

Every detail cannot be stated in writing and something must be left to the good faith and good intentions of the parties. I especially desire that everything shall go on smoothly and well between you and the parties occupying the house and that there may be no misunderstanding between us.

Please let me know as soon as possible if this proposition is satisfactory. I should like your answer in writing.

VIII

WORK AND REST IN NEW YORK CITY

THE Clevelands went first to the Victoria Hotel in New York, and then to a brick and stone residence at 816 Madison Avenue, near Sixty-Eighth Street. The ex-President had arranged to be 'of counsel' with the law firm of Bangs, Stetson, Tracy, and MacVeagh, with offices at 15 Broad Street. Here he had a room, and use of the library, law clerks, and stenographic staff, but was not a partner. The greater part of his work was that of a referee appointed by the courts, and he did this entirely in his own office, hearing evidence behind closed doors. He never appeared in the courts. The cases were so arranged that his summers were free, and after some hesitation between the Adirondacks and the seacoast, Cleveland bought a vacation cottage on Buzzards Bay, near his friend Richard Watson Gilder, which he named Gray Gables. He soon became one of the liveliest and most popular members of a community which included Joseph Jefferson, and learned to spend long weeks of perfect content in fishing for bluefish, sea-bass, and tautog. One day Richard Harding Davis, son of his old friend L. Clarke Davis, editor of the Philadelphia *Public Ledger*, brought the gas magnate E. C. Benedict, owner of the handsome yacht *Oneida*, to call at Marion; and thus began one of the pleasantest associations of Cleveland's life. The first child, 'Baby Ruth,' was born to the Clevelands in October, 1891. 'I have just entered the real world,' Cleveland wrote with the deepest feeling to his old partner Bissell. Politics was temporarily all but forgotten. Yet after ten months of complete retirement from public view, he began to make numerous addresses, chiefly of a non-partisan kind; and he was received with a cordiality which showed that his influence and prestige were undiminished. Late in 1890, highly indignant with the Republicans for their passage of the McKinley Tariff, and encouraged by the crushing defeat which the Administration met in the Congressional elections of that year, he spoke more vigorously on questions of the day and was plainly in a mood to re-enter public life.

To WILLIAM F. VILAS

New York, *March* 14, 1889

General John B. Woodward, my very good friend, has an idea that perhaps my seal-brown team would suit him. I am not sure of the name of the livery-stable keeper where they are, and therefore ask you to put the General in the way of seeing the team by directing him to the place where they are kept. General Woodward is a man I should like to have the team if they will answer the purpose.

To THOMAS F. BAYARD

New York, *April* 11, 1889

Your letter was received last night and I enclose you my check for $75.93, the amount you state as my share of the cost of the good things we had on our late delightful trip.[1] I shall always remember our little outing with supreme pleasure. I am not sure that I knew before that we were all such good fellows. The meeting you mentioned when Lamar was present with me—that in the mountains—made me feel a little homesick. Mrs. Cleveland sends love to you and your household, and I need not say how heartily I join.

To WILSON S. BISSELL

New York, *April* 13, 1889

It has been quite a long time since I saw or heard from you, and so far as hearing from you goes I am suddenly sensible that I am at fault, since your last letter has thus far remained unanswered. The board you spoke of in your letter was provided for in the Democratic Tariff Bill; and as that did not pass, the Board was not organized. There is not a better man in the public service than Jewell for such a position or almost any other, but you saw how I succeeded in putting good men toward the close of my Administration in good places. Under the new order of things it seems to me that no decency can be expected, but it does seem to me that the removal of Jewell can hardly be expected at once.

I think the hardest thing I have had to do was to decline to pardon Eno before trial and while he was without the jurisdiction of the courts.[2] It would have gratified so many of my friends and would have been such a satisfaction to me that I actually felt afflicted to be obliged to refuse to interfere. I made no decision at all and did not put the application upon the files so that any future effort might not be prejudiced.

[1] Immediately following the inauguration of Harrison, Cleveland and several members of his Cabinet had gone on a trip down the Southern coast and to Cuba.

[2] John C. Eno, an embezzler of New York City.

You cannot imagine the relief which has come to me with the termina-tion of my official term. There is a good deal yet which seems to result from the Presidency and the kindness of people in a social way which keeps me in remembrance of Washington life, but I feel that I am fast seeking the place I desire to reach — the place of a respectable private citizen.

I am overwhelmed with offers of houses to live in, but I am so comfort-ably located at the Victoria [1] that I can very well take my time in select-ing a permanent abiding place.

To WILLIAM F. VILAS

New York, *April* 19, 1889

Your letter of the 13th instant should have been answered before, for it gave me great pleasure to know so directly something of you and your movements.

Dickinson came last week on his way home and was joined last Satur-day by his wife, child, and his mother-in-law. We saw them Sunday and Mr. Dickinson lunched with Mrs. Cleveland and her mother Monday, then expecting to leave here for Detroit last Tuesday. Quite late last night we were astonished to hear from Mrs. Dickinson that they were still here and that her mother was quite sick with pneumonia. Mrs. Folsom was starting to go to them when I left the hotel this morning, and I hope to hear favorably tonight when I reach home.

Of course I need not say how pleased we should be to see you again before you go to Wisconsin, and I hope it will be possible for you to stop here a day or two on the way.

I notice what you say about my pursuing the wise course in taking to work again immediately, etc. I am as pleasantly situated as possible and quite content and yet these limitations in regard to what I can or ought to do, which result from the shadow of the Presidency still about me, I often find irksome and uncomfortable.

I have made no arrangements in the direction of a more permanent habitation and think the idea of purchasing a place in the country may be regarded as altogether abandoned. The way I am pelted by real estate people puts me in mind a little of officeseeking four years ago; and to make it more pleasant, the newspapers occasionally state that I am look-

---

[1] Cleveland stayed briefly at the Victoria Hotel before taking up his residence in a house leased at 816 Madison Avenue.

ing at some property in the country, which immediately lets loose a stream of offers of that kind of habitations. I shall move very quietly and deliberately and hope to, in time, suit myself. The Bar and all others have been very kind and courteous. Mr. Choate [1] gives a dinner to me next Friday night where I shall meet thirty or forty of the best of my legal brethren; and as far as social attention is concerned, we have had a surfeit of it. And still the question, 'What shall be done with our ex-Presidents?' is not laid at rest; and I sometimes think Watterson's [2] solution of it, 'Take them out and shoot them,' is worthy of attention.

One thing I cling to with especial pleasure — the memory or rather the contemplation of the course of the last Administration and the assurance that after all we were able to do something for our country. And with this comes the thought of the devotion and affection of the men, good and true, who stood about me, and I ask myself, 'Is not this after all enough for one life?'

That Bayard business I don't know about. I understand the thing is discredited in one pretty well-informed quarter; and while things of this kind are past finding out, I mean to do as the public are sometimes asked to do — withhold my judgment.

Now about the horses, etc. I have given up the idea of ever using them again myself and they must be disposed of. I sent Wood Brothers a letter today asking them if they can sell them and upon what terms they will keep them. I also wrote them that you or Marshal Wilson would probably see them in relation to the matter. The Marshal would do anything he could to help me, but I don't know that his judgment would be any better than ours. And yet I wish, if not too much trouble, that you would see him and get his views of the best manner to dispose of this property. Maybe an auction would be best. If that plan should be adopted he would be willing, I think, to see that it was in good salable shape and attend to the preliminaries. I will write to him today. In any event, unless in view of a sale something better can be done, let it remain where it is, when you are done with it.

We have all talked and thought a good deal of our people who are left in Washington; and especially have we wished to hear of a marked change for the better in Mrs. Vilas. We all hope that the bustle and confusion

---

[1] Joseph H. Choate (1832–1917), later ambassador to Great Britain under McKinley and Roosevelt, was now at the head of the New York bar.

[2] Henry Watterson (1840–1921), for fifty years editor of the Louisville *Courier-Journal*.

of change will not defer her complete recovery and that home surroundings may have a salutary effect....

To A. A. WILSON

New York, *April* 19, 1889

I never supposed so long a time would elapse since the fourth of March without our seeing you and Mrs. Wilson. I have often spoken of it and wondered why you did not find business or pleasure in a trip to the metropolis. And to make the matter a great deal worse, I have discovered that you were here a few days ago and left without seeing any of your friends of the last Administration. Colonel Lamont and I have studied out a kind of an excuse, and unless you have that to plead you are in great disgrace. Colonel Wilson dropped in on us last evening and we had a nice visit.

I must dispose of my horses and carriages. Mr. Vilas, who you know has been using them, will leave, I expect, next week. I have written to him today and asked him to see you in regard to the matter with a view of comparing ideas with you as to the best mode of disposing of these things. I have also written to Wood Brothers, who now have charge of the property, saying that perhaps you or Colonel Vilas would call on them. Vilas and you had better meet and talk the subject over before anything else is done. If it is thought best to sell these things at auction, it should be well advertised and the property should all be put in good clean shape. If it comes to that, I am going to ask you to add to the great debt of obligation I am now owing you by attending to the details of the matter.

I see you are still retained as a part of the new and improved Administration and I feel quite proud to know that one of my appointees at the seat of government is good enough to meet the requirements of the pious and patriotic people who have public affairs in charge....

To AN UNKNOWN CORRESPONDENT

New York, *April* 24, 1889

I am applied to for all sorts of opinions and information, but I am inclined to think the question you put to me is too difficult for me to master. I am inclined to think that either at the East or West, whether a man succeeds or not depends very much upon himself. There may be a difference in opportunities in favor of the West, but hard work must be done there and perhaps much disappointment suffered and overcome. It is reasonable to suppose that the few Territories which are likely soon to become States would offer as good a field as anywhere West.

To WILLIAM F. VILAS

New York, *April 27*, 1889

The letter enclosed just arrived and all I know from what I see of it is that it is more likely to be for you than for me and you are welcome to all you can get out of it.

The beaver robe I want to keep. Some day we may want it. I don't think the bear robe is good for much if it is the one that Albert used to wear over his lap. I will put no price on it. If it is of any use to you I should be delighted if you would pack it up and take it away with you as a souvenir of Washington life. Nothing would please me more than to have you do this.

I am afraid we are not to see you before you go to Madison. I see you say nothing about it.

About thirty members of the Bar here dined me last night. It was a most gratifying affair. I am to respond to a toast next Tuesday night at the Centennial banquet. I have a great mind to put in this an advance proof of the thing. Of course you know it must not get out before Wednesday morning.

I am almost sick with a cold and have not been to my office for two days. You must let me hear from you as often as you can. I shall be lonely when you are in Wisconsin. Give much love to Mrs. Vilas and Nelly from us all.

To DON M. DICKINSON

New York, *May* 10, 1889

I was delighted to receive a letter from you a few days ago and thank you for the kind words you wrote touching my remarks at the banquet. I don't like to write it to you and yet I want you to know that I have received numerous compliments on the same score. And will you forgive me if I tell you of the amazement with which I heard the cheers of the people for me as I rode through the streets? To tell you the truth, I could see no difference between the demonstrations now and those I used to encounter when I was actually President. All this would sound foolish if written to anyone else, but you being 'one of the family' will not misinterpret it.

I am not doing very much yet, though I can see some things coming. I am not at all concerned and am enjoying my release from official care more than I can tell you. Of course I was not surprised to learn that you were tugging away again in the harness, for it is your nature, and as long as you are willing there will be plenty to put on the load.

It seemed to me rather unsatisfactory to have you and Mrs. Dickinson here a number of days in trouble and affliction, and we not able to do anything to help and comfort you. You were very much in our thoughts and upon our tongues, and if we could do nothing else, you certainly had our sincere sympathy.

Our trip to Cuba becomes, I think, a more pleasant reminiscence the farther I get from it. As Bayard says, 'we got acquainted.' I hope I shall hear from you occasionally. Please give our love to Mrs. Dickinson and Frances and believe me...

To WILLIAM F. VILAS

New York, *May 20,* 1889

It is nearly one o'clock and I have just put aside what will be a 'well-thought-out extempore speech' which I expect to try and deliver after a fashion at a Democratic dinner a week from tonight. The managers told me that they meant to try hard to have you here on the occasion. Wouldn't that be grand?

I am entirely alone tonight and that leads me to say that this condition comes from the marriage of Mrs. Folsom, which I expect took place tonight.[1] It came off a little sooner than we expected it would. She had our consent to be married in June but she went to Jackson, Mich., with the man there and the young things got in a hurry. Things are getting into a pretty tough condition when a man can't keep his mother-in-law in the traces. Mrs. Cleveland started last night to see the show.

And then Bayard! He has announced his engagement to Miss Clymer, which proves that you were right when you foretold something of the sort a few weeks ago.[2] If these things don't stop I'll be married again myself. I am rather sorry to let Mrs. Folsom go, but of course there was nothing to be said. And she will live in Buffalo — the place I hate above all others.

I am pegging away — not doing so very much law business yet, but

[1] Cleveland's mother-in-law married Henry E. Perrine of Buffalo.
[2] Bayard married as his second wife Miss Mary W. Clymer May 7, 1889.

with something to do and with much contentment. The business will come in time and I am very pleasantly situated.

Why won't you write me and tell me what you are up to? These friends here are all right, but I want to keep a good hold of you and such as you. I had a letter from Dickinson yesterday. He seems to be quite busily at work.

We all want to know how Mrs. Vilas is and Nellie and the rest. Give my love to them all. I do hope that you will be able to tell me that your hopes have been realized in regard to Mrs. Vilas's health.

To GOVERNOR DAVID B. HILL

New York, *June* 19, 1889

I have just finished reading your 'Informal Memoranda' setting forth the reasons for the non-approval of many of the bills left in your hands when the legislature adjourned, and the 'Statement' of items disapproved in the appropriation bill. I am carried back to the time I wrestled in like fashion with the jobs and extravagancies of the last days of legislative work. I can see in many of your disapprovals the motive power which will start loads of swearing and cursing, but I cannot refrain from writing you a word to let you know how I have enjoyed the persual of this first-class Executive work. 'It's mighty good reading,' and must produce some results. I miss some of the 'old soldiers' in the way of swindles and gratuities which used to make their appearance in appropriation bills every year, and I suppose they have been finally knocked out for good. Congratulating you on your safe deliverance of the tremendous work the legislature imposed upon you at a time when you should have had leisure...

To WILSON S. BISSELL

Saranac Inn, *August* 28, 1889

I should have acknowledged the receipt of $94.50 before this, but my occupations since that date have not been conducive to any letter-writing at all. I have to thank you now for your kindness in collecting and transmitting this dividend and hope that you are again reminded of my sagacity in making the investment out of which this dividend arose. Sicard has written to me about the Hadcock matter and I have answered him fully. He has since written me again transmitting a letter from Robbins which I return herewith thinking it may be of use to you in settling the matter. I don't know as I am capable of putting any price upon his services for the reason that I do not know precisely what he has done, but I am not altogether certain that the price he states is too much. At the time I started the proceedings the two canal boats, if I remember rightly, were not regarded as of any more than $6000 in value. So a large part of the final money must be for interest and costs. In these circumstances the litigation will bear pretty liberal charges. I think, however, that the firm should be well paid above all things. I insist upon it that you do not permit the idea that I am entitled to anything to stand in the way of that. And you must not be a bit embarrassed, if you think I should receive anything, about the amount, for whatever you determine in the premises will be entirely satisfactory — whether it be that I should have nothing or something.

I conclude that no county taxes were found against my Butler Street property. I expect to reach home early in September.

To An Invitation Committee of Plattsburg, N.Y.

August 31, 1889

I have received your cordial and earnest invitation to attend a tariff-reform picnic at Plattsburg on the 21st instant, and I am exceedingly pleased to learn that such an active and efficient measure is to be adopted to arouse the intelligence of the people of your locality upon a question so vital to their interests and to the good of the entire country. The time is opportune for instruction and information upon the subject of tariff reform and for the correction of misapprehension and prejudice. The question is so deep and has so much to do with the welfare and happiness of the American people that its consideration ought not to be restrained within the limits of party subserviency, and it will not thus be restrained if it is understood.

I am here merely for a day, and have made arrangements for the rest of the month, which prevents my acceptance of your invitation, but you may be sure that my sincere wish is that the picnic you prepare may be full of profit and enjoyment to the participants.

To Wilson S. Bissell

New York, *September* 11, 1889

I returned from my long vacation at midnight and seize the first opportunity which presents itself to reply to your last letter, which was forwarded to me in my wilderness retreat.

The death of your father was an entire surprise to me, as I had not heard that he was ill. I immediately thought of his oft-repeated expression that he was living on borrowed time, and when I read of his peaceful departure, I felt that there was much to comfort you and that the fact that your parents had been spared to you so long must always be to you a cause for gratitude. And yet to one so tenderly attached to his parents as you their demise — come when or how it may — must be an affliction. You need not be told how fully I sympathize with you.

I send you the Robbins note and want every cent due upon it for principal and interest deducted from the amount fixed upon as his compensation in the Hadcock case. I am very clear that nothing should be paid to the Bass estate.

I have been thinking about the books since the receipt of your letter. When I can afford it I suppose I shall have some lawbooks at my house, but they need not be a great many and I am sure I could do better by way of selection if I parted with my interest in the library at Buffalo for money. So if it is precisely the same to you I should prefer that course.

Mrs. Cleveland is in Buffalo today with her mother, where she expects to remain a week or ten days. I don't hear anything more about Ball's suit against the *Evening Post*.

I was surprised today to find a letter awaiting me containing checks for dividends upon the preferred and common stock of the B. & N.W. R.R. Co. These things make me feel quite like a man of means who has made wise investments.

To WILLIAM F. VILAS

New York, *September* 15, 1889

I returned a few days ago from the longest vacation I have ever had; and among the bushel of letters I found awaiting me I somehow looked anxiously for one from you. I don't know that I had any right to expect one, but I looked nevertheless. I've sort of hankered to know something of your doings — to that extent that I am resolved to present the question plumply to you at this time, and in this manner.

I saw Dickinson a day or two ago and he told me a little about you, but not much more than that you were 'all right.'

In these days when the people who occupy in Washington are so fast running off the rope which I believe is bound to get about their necks, I think more and more of you especially, and of the nights we spent endeavoring to give our countrymen good government. I am constantly reminded, too, of the conversations we had after the defeat of last year, in which we lamented the fact that we must leave two objects to which we had given special attention — to wit: the Indians and the Public Lands — to the tender mercies of the enemy. I used to hope that we overestimated the danger. We did not a single iota. I hardly believed that in these matters and in the matter of civil service reform such retrogression could be made in so short a time. You and others used to say that our administration of affairs would be remembered long by the American people. I could not see why this should necessarily be so; but our successors have made it so, I am sure. I feel badly and sad to see the result of so much hard labor undone; and knowing that you, as one who shared so fully in this work, must feel the same way, I sympathize with you. And yet I sometimes think that God has ordered it all for the enlightenment and awakening of our people.

I hope that you have had a good rest and that you are strong and well. I was very sorry to hear through Dickinson that you had lost one of your brothers. You have surely met your full share of such afflictions during the four years just passed. We are very anxious to know of Mrs. Vilas and I hope you have some good news for us in that direction. Mrs. Cleveland is visiting her mother and I have been entirely alone and expect to be for a week to come. We hope to be keeping house pretty soon and shall then feel more as though we were living.

I find it very hard to shake off the results of my official incumbency. It takes much of my time to answer letters of all sorts, and it really seems sometimes as though the people did not appreciate that I was no longer President. Everybody is very kind to me, but the pressing invitations to go to all sorts of places embarrass me a good deal, for I feel that I must work or be ready to work as it comes along. I am very pleasantly situated professionally and think I shall gradually get on.

I see by the paper today that Endicott is on his way home from Europe. His son is to be married October 3, I believe. Whitney is in on many things and I hope is adding to his riches. Bayard, I expect, will be married in October. Fairchild is managing his trust company in a steady and satisfactory way, though he is now temporarily at his old home, and I heard not very well.

Give a great deal of love to Mrs. Vilas and Nelly and Mollie. If Mrs. Cleveland was here she would heartily join and insist upon putting you in the batch.

To RICHARD WATSON GILDER

New York, *September* 18, 1889

I am more lame than 'I wish I was.' Experience has shown me that the house and quiet is the thing for me in this condition. The weather is bad. I have determined to keep away from the office today and dose myself. I am sorry.

I wish it was so that you could drop in and see me this evening. I should be glad to hear what you talk of at the meeting. Please present my excuses for absence.

To WILSON S. BISSELL

New York, *September* 20, 1889

Mr. Havemeyer and a man by the name of Stein have a large interest in the B. B. & K. R.R. They have been talking to me about the thing and have made me think that if there was a change of management there would something come out of it for the stockholders. I have given them my proxy to vote for me at the next election. They say you have 105 shares. Do you want to let them vote on it? They seem to think that there will be no difficulty about their getting control of a majority of the stock to vote upon. I said to Stein, who was just here and got my proxy, that I understood you to say that you had no interest now and if you had that perhaps you would not want to do anything looking to the ousting of Carter, but that I should write you and tell you what was going on.

To CHAUNCEY F. BLACK

New York, *September* 26, 1889

The subject you presented to me last evening has received my earnest, and as you requested, my 'prayerful' consideration. I believe you understood the assurances of my sincerity, when I told you that I very much desired to accede to your request and be with you in Philadelphia on the 15th of October. I feel that your earnest efforts to organize and put upon an effective basis, associations of active Democrats, entitles you to favorable hearing and to the utmost encouragement and support. These considerations have made it very hard for me to look at all the factors in the question and give them proper weight.

There is no mistake about one thing: duty and inclination dictate that I should, as much as possible, assume a modest position, free from any imputation of arrogating to myself especial influence or control. There is a great deal in this which might be amplified, but which I hope will occur to you without amplification. Present personal interests are all against my appearing in the political field. I cannot get business nor do business in that way; and I feel that I must try in every way to get on in the profession to which I have returned. Acting upon these considerations, I have declined many invitations from political and personal friends of the character you extend; and some of these declinations have cost a good deal of self-sacrifice — for I love to please my friends.

If I yield now I shall be charged with insincerity and a mean attempt in prior cases to cover sullen and ungrateful refusals, with a false picture. And so far as the future is concerned the door will be thrown wide open and I shall be helpless and bewildered.

To WILSON S. BISSELL

New York, *September* 24, 1889

...I think Sicard and you have hit upon about the right figure for the library and I shall be satisfied to receive the sum you name in full of all my interests.[1]...

To WILSON S. BISSELL

New York, *October* 1, 1889

I was away on Sunday and did not receive your check for $750 until this morning. I send you a receipt and if you want the form changed in any way, let me know and it shall be done.

George Hayward wrote me that he had a talk with Mr. Spayth, a real estate man who has sold some lots on or near Butler Street, and that he thought $125 per foot could be got for my lot next spring. So far I am in no great hurry, and probably if there seemed a chance to realize more by waiting I should do so. But I am very much obliged to you for the inquiries you made and it may be that I shall be glad to take $100 a foot for it if it is offered. I remember saying to you in one of my letters something that pretty plainly indicated that I would sell for that price, but I have more than once thought that in regard to that lot I did not at all times know just exactly what I wanted to do.

We expect to be settled in our house within two or three weeks and hope when we have a home of our own that you will be a frequent visitor.

---

[1] Cleveland received $750 for his share of the law library of the old firm of Cleveland, Bissell, and Sicard.

To WILLIAM F. VILAS

New York, *October* 17, 1889

I was very glad to receive your letter and to know that in the midst of your sorrow caused by your brother's death you had a comfort in the prospect of the complete restoration of the health of your wife.

I received also today a paper detailing the results of the work of the Commission appointed to deal with certain Minnesota Indians.

We are in the confusion of settling in our house — that is, Mrs. Cleveland is in that condition. She seems to be willing to attend to the matter and I am certain that such arrangement meets my hearty approval. The poor child goes up in good season in the morning and works hard till night and seems to be very happy over it all. I think we shall get a foothold there within a few days now. My wife has her heart set on spending next Sunday there.

I am getting on quietly and slowly — not overburdened with business, but quite contented on that score. I feel all the time the limitations and restraints which the Presidency has placed upon me and all my efforts. As an offset to this, I every moment experience the kindness and respectful consideration of my fellow-citizens, which is most gratifying. I don't think anybody ever had more satisfaction in that way.

Governor Hill captured the organization of our State completely and dictated our nominations. As you have seen, he is cutting quite a swath in Atlanta. There is no longer any doubt about his having designs on the nomination in 1892.

Dickinson is here, but expects to leave tonight, I believe. I had one or two good chats with him. He was in Washington a day or two ago and saw Mr. Bayard. I did not learn when he is to be married, but think it will be in two or three weeks. I so much wish you could come here soon. I lunched with a famous resident of Milwaukee yesterday, Mr. McClintock, and we talked about you a good deal.

This is not much of a letter, but I hope it is sufficient to put you in my epistolary debt. With much love to Mrs. Vilas and the children.

To DR. S. B. WARD

New York, *October* 21, 1889

Your letter is at hand and I enclose a check for nine dollars, the amount of Conroy's bill. Will you please give the check to Mr. Wright with my thanks for his kindness?

Mrs. Cleveland is at Lenox attending the wedding of Mr. Endicott's son. I hope she will return Friday night. Did you see an account of our outing at Saranac Inn in the New York *Times* of yesterday — Tuesday the 2d? I don't see how you make seven hunts by adding two to the score of four as it stood when we left, and I guess there is a little Adirondack arithmetic about the twelve deer, but I'll let that pass. I have received no plans of a cottage and I feel so kind of poor just now that I am almost afraid to pursue the subject.

I attended the cornerstone-laying this afternoon and it paid me to see how pleased our medical friends were to see me there. I don't think I did so very well, but I am glad I went, though I have been a little under the weather for nearly a week and didn't feel a bit like going.

And now, my dear fellow, I want to thank you for all your kindness to us during our stay at Saranac Inn and to tell you how much we all feel indebted to you for the many things you did to make our stay pleasant. You may be sure, Doctor, that there are three people who fully appreciate it and will not forget it. I don't think my dear wife ever enjoyed herself so well, and Ruth,[1] you need not be told, was happy all the time. When I think how little I contributed to the general enjoyment and how much you did, I am almost ashamed.

I think I'll enclose a slip of the few words I said today and I've a good mind to put in the story from the *Times*. I am keeping it to show Frank and if I do not send it now (and I guess I will not) I'll send it after she has seen it if in the meantime it does not fall under your eye. So please let me know if you want it.

I consider myself charged with a standing order to send Mrs. Cleveland's love to you.

To MAYOR ALFRED C. CHAPIN

New York, *October* 22, 1889

I desire from the standpoint of a personal friend, closely connected in an official way with the beginning of your public career, to express my gratification upon your renomination to the office of mayor of the city of Brooklyn.

I am not sure that this renomination, considered by itself and not for its own sake, and meaning as it must a continuance in the discharge of onerous and perplexing duties, is a thing to be desired; but it cannot fail

[1] Miss Ruth Burnett, of Southborough, Mass., a guest of the Clevelands.

to be most gratifying to you and all your friends, as evidence furnished by your neighbors and townsmen that you have displayed the ability, within your official sphere, to give your city good government and the disposition to give it clean and pure government. This ability and this disposition are infinitely more to be desired than the mere possession of a public place.

To A. D. ROCKAFELLOW

New York, *November* 9, 1889

I am such a thorough believer in civil service reform and have done so much to establish it on a firm basis and infuse it with energy that I should be very sorry to see any body of Democrats repudiate it. It is right. And Democrats can always afford to do the right thing.

To WILLIAM E. RUSSELL [1]

New York, *November* 29, 1889

I received today a copy of the Boston *Journal* with an editorial marked for especial perusal which I enclose, and the wrapper marked with a stamp indicating that the paper is sent by the Civil Service Reform Association of Boston and Cambridge. On reading the printed matter I am surprised that an association really in earnest in the matter of civil service reform and professing to be honest and non-partisan, should permit such mean, partisan, and unjust stuff to go out in its name.

To JOHN A. McMAHON [2]

New York, *November* 29, 1889

Your letter of the 26th is received. I should have been surprised by its tenor if I had not before its receipt had an intimation of its subject matter. I restrain as much as possible the feeling, almost of resentment, produced by the accusation that I have interfered or desire to interfere with, or in any way influence the action of the Democracy of Ohio in the matter of United States Senator. It amounts to an impeachment of my common sense and is as foreign to my nature as possible. It is in every sense false and I am almost ashamed to feel that there should be any necessity of putting in such a denial. If you have any curiosity to know how I feel on

---

[1] Russell (1857–96) was at this time mayor of Cambridge; in 1890 he was elected governor of Massachusetts after a campaign in which the tariff was the principal issue. Re-elected in 1891 and 1892, he became the principal leader of the sound money forces in New England.

[2] McMahon (1833–1923), of Dayton, Ohio, had been a member of the House of Representatives 1875–81, and was still prominent in Ohio politics.

this question I have no hesitation in saying that my conviction is that the Democratic representatives in the legislature of Ohio will be abundantly able to settle the question, and any outside interference should be promptly resented.

To GEORGE F. PARKER [1]

New York, *December* 10, 1889

I send the copies of the address as you requested. I am afraid you will be 'too previous' if you send them to the Pittsburgh papers today. I think it would be better to wait to mail them at such a time as will put them in the hands of the editors not earlier than Thursday afternoon. They ought not to be kicking about a newspaper office very long before the thing is delivered.

To WILLIAM F. VILAS

New York, *January* 17, 1890

Your last letter was gladly received. I am glad to hear that you contemplate a trip to the Sandwich Islands. I believe you will enjoy it and that it will do Mrs. Vilas good. Colonel Knight had told me prior to the receipt of your letter that he expected to accompany you to Florida and Cuba. Someone told me lately, or Mrs. Vilas wrote it to Mrs. Cleveland, that you were expecting to be in Washington soon. I was much interested in the information because I know we shall see you here if you come to Washington.

I am getting along fairly well. I say *fairly* well, because I am so followed by the results of the Presidency in a political and social way that I am not as free in mind as I wish I was to attend exclusively to legal pursuits. It all comes to me in the kindest possible way, but I am so constructed that I do not always enjoy the mixture of these things with what I came here to do. Our friend Governor Hill has been doing something which makes plenty of talk in Democratic circles and I suppose will add to the differences in our party in the State, which seem to be in-

[1] George F. Parker had been born in Indiana in 1847, was educated at the University of Iowa, and had been a journalist of wide experience; he was the first managing editor of the New York *Press*, 1887–88. He attached himself to Cleveland, and in 1889–92 carried on a systematic campaign of publicity in favor of the ex-President. From a small downtown office, at a cost of less than $200, he wrote innumerable letters, and saw that printed copies of Cleveland's speeches were widely circulated in newspapers and elsewhere. His reward was the consulship at Birmingham, England, in 1893–98. After writing his *Recollections of Grover Cleveland*, he died in 1928.

separable from our existence. Many think that he has finished the destruction of his Presidential aspirations, but I am inclined to think that sometimes the influences and aids which he has with him and about him are not fully appreciated. I am a simple looker-on with no ambition except the attainment of peace and quiet, and yet with an intense desire that all that we by the hardest work accomplished may not be lost to the country.

I see Fairchild and Whitney occasionally. Dickinson I have not seen in a long time. Mrs. Dickinson has, I hear, been quite sick. I hope the negotiations which I suppose are pending in regard to Nellie's making us a visit will result in her coming to us. If Mrs. Cleveland knew that I was writing she would join me in messages of affectionate remembrance to you and all your household.

To A. B. Farquhar

New York, *January 22*, 1890

Your letter enclosing one to you from Mr. Thorne, and the review of Mr. Blaine's article, is received. I had read with much interest the review in the *Globe* before its receipt this morning. I am glad to see an inclination on your part, as well as on the part of others, to expose the weakness of Mr. Blaine's position. When I read his article it occurred to me that its entire strength and value depended upon the admission or conclusive proof that certain conditions of our country at certain times had no other cause or explanation except tariff legislation. I did not think it possible that such admission or such proof was at hand; and I was quite sure that an easy and destructive way to reply to his article would be to give other and the true causes of the conditions to which he refers.

No one can read your review without plainly seeing that much which Mr. Blaine boldly asserts as obvious truth is simply bald and gratuitous assumption. This of course destroys the confidence of all in the soundness of his reasoning throughout — and ought to do so.

I return you Mr. Thorne's letter. I have often thought his place was upon the editorial staff of an active aggressive newspaper. Our cause needs more of that kind in such places. Please give my regards to Mr. Black when you next see him.

To WILLIAM A. FISHER

New York, *February* 11, 1890

I have tried hard to answer your letter before this late day, but have failed in the midst of all the things, little and great, that press upon me. My views upon the subject of ballot reform are so well known that [they] need no repetition, and I am heartily sick and tired of seeing my name in the papers. I am going to ask you to excuse me from writing a letter to be read at your meeting — if it has not already been held. Thanking you for the history of affairs contained in your letter and hoping that Maryland may maintain her Democratic position and also be at the front in the work of reform.

To MRS. ALFRED C. CHAPIN

New York, *March* 7, 1890

It is very late; but as I thought my hand was quite steady tonight, I determined to do a little fine penmanship in the redemption of a promise made to you some time ago. So I enclose the lines which Mr. Lowell wrote and which made me so grateful to him.[1] If it were not that in sending them I am keeping my word to *you*, I should feel a little bit silly, I believe. I hope you will be able to read my handwriting, for I assure you I have tired my hand to copy Mr. Lowell's words plainly.

(Enclosure)

Elmwood, Cambridge, Mass.
10th *December*, 1889

Dear Mr. Quincy:

I regret very much that I cannot have the pleasure of joining with you in paying respect to a man so worthy of it as Mr. Cleveland.

> Let who has felt compute the strain
> Of struggle with abuses strong,
> The doubtful course, the helpless pain
> Of seeing best intents go wrong;
> We, who look on with critic eyes
> Exempt from action's crucial test,
> Human ourselves, at least are wise
> In honouring one who did his best.

Faithfully yours

J. R. LOWELL

[1] Lowell's verses were read at a dinner of the Merchants' Association of Boston in December, 1889, where Cleveland made a notable speech on ballot reform.

To Joseph I. C. Clarke

New York, *March* 15, 1890

Mrs. Cleveland has referred to me your letter of this date informing her that in a voting contest to name the most popular woman in New York, inaugurated by the *Morning Journal*, her name stood at the head of the list, and asking that a silver wreath which she thus secured may be presented to her on the eighteenth instant.

Mrs. Cleveland fully appreciates the friendship which has been demonstrated in this affair and which actuates the proposal now made; and yet she hopes she may be permitted to say that she would have been better pleased if she had not involuntarily appeared as a contestant for such a prize. If she is allowed to suggest the disposition to be made of this prize, which she learns from your note depended upon the contest mentioned, her especial desire is that, instead of being presented to her, the same may be sold and the proceeds of such sale contributed to the Charity Organization Society of the City of New York.

To W. H. Clarke

New York, *March* 20, 1890

I received the dispatch signed by you and others, with pleasure, as an evidence of friendship and kindness which caused me gratification. But I know that you will not fail to understand me when I say that I am sure that there are questions and topics which press upon the minds of our people, the solution and treatment of which are of vastly greater importance than the political fortunes of any man. I do hope that the students of the University of Ohio will appreciate this fact, and will see their full measure of political duty in laboring to enforce the doctrines of true Democracy, and in retrieving the people from the delusions which beset them to their undoing. Thanking you and your associates for the kind expressions contained in your dispatch...

To J. A. Hill

New York, *March* 24, 1890

I have received your letter, accompanied by a copy of the declaration of principles of the Farmers' Alliance.[1] I see nothing in this declaration that cannot be fully endorsed by any man who loves his country, who believes that the object of our Government should be the freedom, prosperity

[1] The Farmers' Alliance was a non-political predecessor of the Populist party.

and happiness of all our people, and who believes that justice and fairness to all are necessary conditions to its useful administration.

It has always seemed to me that the farmers of the country were especially interested in the equitable adjustment of our tariff system. The indifference they have shown to that question, and the ease with which they have been led away from a sober consideration of their needs and their rights as related to this subject, have excited my surprise. Struggle as they may, our farmers must continue to be purchasers and consumers of numberless things enhanced in cost by tariff regulations. Surely they have the right to say that this cost shall not be increased for the purpose of collecting unnecessary revenue, or to give undue advantage to domestic manufacturers. The plea that our infant industries need the protection which thus impoverishes the farmer and consumer is, in view of our natural advantages, and the skill and ingenuity of our people, a hollow pretext.

Struggle as they may, our farmers cannot escape the conditions which fix the price of what they produce and sell, according to the rates which prevail in foreign markets, flooded with the competition of countries enjoying freer exchange of trade than we are. The plausible presentation of the blessings of a home market should not deceive our depressed and impoverished agriculturists. There is no home market for them which does not take its instructions from the seaboard; and the seaboard transmits the word of the foreign markets.

Because my conviction that there should be a modification of our tariff laws arose principally from an appreciation of the wants of the vast army of consumers, comprising our farmers, our artisans, and our workingmen, and because their condition has led me to protest against the present imposition, I am especially glad to see these sections of my fellow-countrymen arousing themselves to the importance of tariff reform.

To REPRESENTATIVE JOHN G. CARLISLE [1]

New York, *April* 7, 1890

Is it true that our people in the House Ways and Means Committee propose to present a tariff bill to antagonize the McKinley Bill? I do not assume to obtrude any advice upon those who are on the spot and whose judgments are so much better than mine, but I cannot help feeling some

[1] Carlisle served as a Representative in Congress until May 26, 1890, when he resigned to enter the Senate. The proposal for a Democratic tariff bill was abandoned.

apprehension on that subject. I have thought as I have seen the Republicans getting deeper and deeper into the mire that our policy should be to let them flounder.

I suppose the bill which would be presented by us would not be exactly the Mills Bill. If it is not, the cry will be raised that the passage and then the abandonment of that bill for something else shows that we do not know from one session to another what the country needs. A bill presented by us (the Mills Bill or any other) will give the enemy what I should think they would want: an opportunity to attack some other measure instead of defending their own. In this way they can shift ground and throw more dirt in the eyes of the people.

Is there not danger that it will be impossible to rally all our people in favor of a really good bill with such promptness and unanimity as will make a good showing before the country? Won't you get into all sorts of tangles among the private and local interests in our party and won't this rob us of the advantage we are now gaining from the alarming and disgusting selfish grabbing going on among our opponents? Of course I take it for granted that nothing really good coming from our side would go through — I mean something fully up to our line all the way through. If this can be done it should, for the country's good and without counting policy, for I do not think we would get any credit for it from the masses of the people, or that it would add a bit to the advantage we now hold, in a pure partisan sense.

I have no doubt that you and the rest of our people on the Committee have thought of all these things, and perhaps this is foolishly written, but I shall send it; and I enclose a letter I received as I was writing the above, as a specimen of those of a like character I receive every day.

P.S. You will see the propriety of keeping this *strictly confidential.*

To Dr. S. B. Ward

New York, *April* 16, 1890

Your letter is received. I understood perfectly well that you had kindly invited us to go with you to Saranac Inn for the spring fishing; but I did not know the exact date of your departure, and I suppose I may have spoken a little carelessly before the girls — meaning one thing and they understanding another. But we cannot go; and I am sorry for it. I am growing very anxious for a holiday and for relief from many annoying things here. We shall probably go to Marion and make quite a stay in that region.[1] We may get away in June. Possibly I may get a week or two before that, but if I do it will be in the West.

Miner's bill for the hawk is not paid. I have been waiting to hear from him on that subject and also concerning some deer's feet that he fixed for us, for which I never received any bill. I suppose he has sent you a bill for the other things, including the hawk. So I mean to ask you to pay for the bird; and I send with this $4 to reimburse you. If the deer's feet are also in your bill and you will pay for them too, I will send you the amount charged for them.

I hope that you will have very good luck fishing, but that enough will escape you to afford some sport for others who may arrive upon the scene later. Mrs. Cleveland is in bed and asleep, but I have a standing order to give you her love when I write. Please remember me to Gwindel and Banks.

To DANIEL S. LAMONT

New York, *April* 17, 1890

I am very much obliged for the trouble you have been to in this wretched business. It is exceedingly annoying to think that people will suppose that under any provocation I could use the words printed, to a newspaper man of all others.[2] And then, too, it gives Dana a chance he has never had before. I am astonished at the daring of the reporter, and somehow I do not hope that the editor will more than half set me right.

To A. B. FARQUHAR

New York, *May* 6, 1890

I thank you for your letter in its enclosures. I return you Governor Black's letter, thinking you may desire to preserve it. The newspaper article is certainly timely and ringing and deserves, for these qualities and I have no doubt for its just appreciation of Pennsylvania State affairs, all the praise Governor Black bestows upon it. But I cannot understand the allusions in his letter which seem to indicate that he supposes

---

[1] In 1889 the Clevelands experimentally occupied a small cottage near the Richard Watson Gilders on Buzzards Bay. In 1890 they went again to Marion, Massachusetts, taking a larger house. Shortly afterward they bought 'Gray Gables,' overlooking Buzzards Bay from Monument Point, and occupied it every summer during the rest of the nineties.

[2] A reporter from the *World* who interviewed Cleveland had imputed to him some abusive words regarding Charles A. Dana, editor of the *Sun*, including a suggestion that Dana was growing senile. Cleveland indignantly repudiated this part of the interview.

some course, adopted or to be adopted in regard to gubernatorial affairs in your State, has been approved by me. I have not been consulted upon the matter. I know next to nothing about the situation except that decent Republicans threaten to mutiny in a certain contingency,[1] and I have not and will not assume to know or have a settled opinion as to the best thing for our party friends to do.

This one thing I have thought and perhaps have said: If our opponents by their foolhardiness give us the opportunity which is somewhat indicated, it would be too bad to throw it away through divided counsels and personal animosities.

To Samuel W. Mendum

New York, *May* 7, 1890

I have been in my office but little since the receipt of your letter and now find it still unanswered.

I beg you not to give yourself any uneasiness about anything that has been published as emanating from you. I have seen nothing of it; and if I had I should not for a moment suppose that anything distasteful in it was intentionally supplied by you. I am not thin-skinned in such matters and I am perfectly well aware of how much liberty is taken by newspaper reporters in defiance of all truth and decency.

To Senator John G. Carlisle

New York, *May* 18, 1890

Need I say to you how delighted I am by your selection to succeed Senator Beck?[2] This was a happy household when the news reached us, and our congratulations are as sincere as they can possibly be. Somehow it seems to me that with much that is bad, one good and wholesome thing has been done. Mrs. Cleveland joins me in all this and we both send love to the Senator's wife.

To Charles L. Seeger

New York, *May* 30, 1890

Please accept my sincere thanks for a copy of the *Cyclopædia of the Manufactures and Products of the United States*. It is one of the most useful

---

[1] If Congress, controlled in both branches by the Republicans, passed a free-coinage bill which Harrison signed.

[2] James B. Beck, the Scottish-born Senator from Kentucky since 1877, died in Washington on May 3, 1890. He was a confirmed silverite, and Cleveland was relieved to have him succeeded by Carlisle, whose views on the currency he better trusted.

gifts I have ever received, and it may be a satisfaction to you to know that I have already had occasion to utilize it. Besides its practical usefulness as a ready means of information in daily affairs, its contents ought to stir the pride of every American and suggest to him that our industries are no longer infantile.

To RICHARD WATSON GILDER

Marion, Mass., *June* 9, 1890

I have just received your note and the statement of the result of the balloting at the Century Club.[1] I don't know when I have been more pleased; and somehow the thing is especially gratifying since the announcement of it is signed by so many kind and distinguished friends. I hope that if it chances in your way to do so, you will not omit telling them how I appreciated their signatures to the paper you sent me.

I started the fishing branch of the firm business today and am glad to report that the season promises well. I found here a feeling of depression in the trade, and on every side there seemed to be the gravest apprehension for the future. I determined to test the condition and am entirely satisfied that if the industry is properly cared for and prosecuted with zeal, industry and intelligence, satisfactory returns may confidently be relied upon.

I caught twenty-five fish with my own rod and reel — averaging larger than any lot we caught last season, about equally divided in number between bass and tautogs. We did not forget to send a nice mess to the Gilder Mansion. I am sorry to add that a persistent pursuit of bluefish, for two or three hours after having reached the limit I had fixed as to the number of bottom-fish, yielded no return. I renew the attack tomorrow and shall make the latter game the object of my toil.

To DANIEL S. LAMONT

Marion, Mass., *July* 6, 1890

I was delighted by the receipt of your letter, but was surprised to find how much had taken place in the summer disposition of your family and that they had settled down at the old hive. I hope that Bessie has entirely recovered her health and that you are no longer anxious about her.

In the Virginia indebtedness matter the position I have consented to

---

[1] An endorsement of Cleveland's doctrines; he did not belong to the Century, but was often there in company with friends.

assume, with Mr. Bayard, Mr. Phelps and two other equally good men, is so free from any responsibility as to any result which may be reached that it can hardly be called advisory in its nature.[1] It must be a queer man who objects to something being done to relieve the old Commonwealth of the disgrace which her present financial condition has fastened upon her. The lines within which any adjustment must be made have been so clearly fixed by the votes of the people of the State that I do not see how there can be any objection to the part I shall take. I am sure there can be no reasonable objection — and for other objections I do not care at all.

I do not assume to direct Gilder's movements and our relations are not political. I have, however, wished that for his own sake he would not be roped into too much political activity of any sort. He has not felt comfortable about the prominence which has been given him in this direction lately, and the day your letter came he wrote a letter saying that he could not serve upon the Citizens' Committee.

And now I want to write upon a more important subject than any other that will find a place in this epistle, and that is the matter of your proposed visit here. Our present location is the coolest and most comfortable in the summer that I have ever landed in.[2] I have not had one moment's discomfort from heat since I have been here. Our house is much larger than the one we had last year, and though it has the peculiarities and the deficiencies of old country houses, I believe we could make you quite comfortable. The fishing thus far has been good. Of course you know the bluefish are unreliable; but we never fail to catch some — all in sight of the house. One afternoon Gilder and I caught eighteen, another day William and I caught fourteen, and we have on other occasions in a short time caught five, six, seven, etc. Saturday afternoon we went out for bottom-fish, and going to the ground and returning we caught five bluefish. The bottom-fish I spoke of are such as we caught off of the yacht last summer, but some of them have weighed four and five pounds. Next Friday we are to try the weakfish which I understand are in the neighborhood. If they have commenced to bite they will give good sport.

Judge Pratt is at his place about three miles away. I have not seen him,

---

[1] Cleveland had consented to help clear up the difficulties attending a readjustment of Virginia's State debt.

[2] At Marion, where the Clevelands had rented a house for the summer.

but he told Gilder he was going to have me over to his trout stream. We are on the track, too, of some trout about eight or nine miles away, and during the coming week expect to know just what there is of that lead.

On the 18th of July (Friday) we have arranged to go to the Cape with Jefferson and expect to find some good sport there. We shall stay about a week, I suppose. If you are here then you can go with us.

What I should like above all things would be to have you and the Doctor come up together. I believe we could get some fun out of the thing. I have tried to put it before you just as it is, except I have not yet said what is the truth — that thus far the weather has been fine and we have not been troubled at all with mosquitoes. You will understand, of course, that conditions may change, but I feel entirely safe in inviting you here and promising you freedom from discomfort except as it is inseparable from life in such a place as this. You know one of the features of our vacation here has been a visit from you and it has occupied a large place in our pleasurable anticipations. We would be quite afflicted if we thought we should not see you and the Doctor.

Now, Colonel, will you see the Doctor and try to cook the thing up so that you can come up together? If you cannot do that, will you hold a caucus with yourself and settle the time of your coming? In any event you will let me hear from you on the subject as soon as you can?   Mrs. Cleveland, to whom I have just read the foregoing, desires to emphasize all that I have written and bids me transmit to you her affectionate regards. And when you write to Mrs. Lamont please give her our love and also to the Doctor when you see him.

To Dr. Joseph D. Bryant [1]

Marion, Mass., *July* 12, 1890

I had just answered a letter of the Colonel's, and told him to see you and look up the matter of his and your visit here, and was just on the point of writing you on the same subject (though you said you would write me first) when your letter came. I would like it very much if you and the Colonel could come together, only for the reason that I think you might both enjoy your stay here a little better if together. I don't think, though, that there is much in that, for there are no variety shows here and no Lotos Club, and I understand that Carmencita is not to dance

---

[1] Cleveland's intimacy with Dr. Joseph D. Bryant (1845–1914), who became his family physician, dated from his years as governor in Albany, and continued till Bryant's death.

here this season. The date you fix in your letter — the first part of August — will suit us first-rate and so will any other time that will suit you. We don't want you to come calculating only to stay a mean stingy few days, but we want you to make us a visit.

So far it has been very cool and pleasant here, and the fishing has been good. I know too much to promise a continuance of these things, and you, I hope, know too much to be disappointed if you don't find them, but I see no reason why we should not have some sport whenever you come up. Mrs. Cleveland sends her love to you and adds her endorsement to all I write. The sooner you come the better we shall like it, for we want to see you very much. We leave here next Friday the 18th for a trip down the Cape and shall be gone probably a week. If you were here we'd take you along.

To DR. S. B. WARD

Marion, Mass., *August* 1, 1890

As the time approaches when Adirondack arrangements should be made, your usual bother on our behalf also approaches.

We expect to reach there not later than the 1st of September and shall be accompanied by Mr. and Mrs. Robert W. Chapin of New York, our very good friends, who are delighted with the prospect of spending a little time in the woods. Mrs. Cleveland has had a very great desire to locate in one of the camps; but I am so sure that the cabin is the best thing for us that I have prevailed upon her to abandon her cherished scheme. Now, how are we to secure the cabin and our guides, etc.? I suppose we should write to Riddle, but somehow I feel safer in consulting you.

Mrs. Chapin is in appearance quite a large woman (and a very sweet one, too), though I doubt if she weighs any more than Mrs. Cleveland. Her husband I think would be called a tall man and by no means stout. I suppose when boating Mrs. Chapin would sometimes, and perhaps usually, go with me.

We need two good guides and I don't think we want Dave Cronk. I rather like Duck Derby, and though Mrs. Chapin and I and Duck would make a pretty good boatful, he has (or had) Dave's old steady boat and I think we could get on nicely in it. I have no idea as to any other guide, and am quite satisfied to abide by your judgment or Wesley Wood's on this question. I don't think we can stay more than two weeks — say until the 15th of September. I don't feel that we ought to expect to occupy the cabin year after year and pay nothing for it, and I should of course be entirely willing to rent it for the time we expect to stay there. You must not think I mean to impose on you, but I do want you to steer us in our arrangements. You see you have done so much for us in this direction in the days that are past that we are spoiled for managing our own Adirondack affairs. It will of course occur to you that we are anxious to know as soon as possible if we can be nicely accommodated at the old quarters with our guests.

Joe Jefferson [1] said a few days ago that perhaps he and Mrs. Jefferson would spend a few days with us. If he should conclude to do so, I expect we could obtain for him proper accommodations.

We are having a very good time here, but cannot refrain from pleasantly anticipating the supplemental part of our vacation which we shall spend in the woods. Mrs. Cleveland bids me transmit to you her kindest and most affectionate regards and I need not tell you that mine go too. Please give our love to the girls and Jack.

P.S. We shall stay here until we start for the woods.

To WILLIAM F. VILAS

Marion, Mass., *August* 17, 1890

Your good long friendly letter pleased me exceedingly — as every word from any of my associates in the last Administration always does. It sometimes seems to me that I do not hear from or see these companions as often as I ought; but when I remember how engrossed they all are and how completely in our lives the activities of the present crowd out the recollections which attend past associations, I cease to be surprised.

First of all I must tell you how glad you made us all by the good tidings you furnished touching the health of Mrs. Vilas. And I, who felt a little responsible for the encroachments upon your health and strength which attended your Cabinet work, was not much less pleased by the news of your own returning vigor.

I have been here since early in June, doing absolutely nothing which becomes a civilized human being. I am such a vagabond, and am so disinclined to enter again upon any kind of work, that I am ashamed and frightened. And yet I have done a power of thinking — much of it circling about my own mean little self. You are so long-suffering with me always,

---

[1] Joseph Jefferson (1829–1905), the most famous of American comedians, had a summer home on Buzzards Bay and shared Cleveland's fondness for fishing.

that I want to tell you one train of thought I very often find myself following.

To put it bluntly, I want my discharge from public and political life. Words of dismissal would be very sweet to me and I find myself asking, 'Why should I not extort them?' The very frequent expressions I hear and read looking to another candidacy cause me to inquire, 'Why should I not promptly stifle a sentiment so much at variance with all I value that is pleasant or comfortable?'

As long as this is not done, I am unable to lose sight of the possibility, or to forget that a contingency may arise, in which duty to my country and my party may require in me the elements of a popular candidacy. In the meantime a lot of dirty scoundrels are, under their own scurvy code, licensed to misrepresent me and lie about me and abuse me. Moreover, sentiment in our party upon some questions is taking such a course that it does not look as though I ought to be nominated, and as if the chances of my election were very slight. All this being considered, the question seems, 'Why should I not free myself from whatever danger there may be of my being put in the way of such a thing?' I have never said this much on the subject to any human being, but when I have mildly expressed a disinclination, I have been sometimes met with the question, 'Who else is there?' The answer is, that there never came a time when our party did not contain more than one man who could meet its wants.

I am ashamed now that I have dumped all this on you — but it is *so* much in my thought; and it doesn't seem to me that I have in my circle of accessible friends many with whom I can be confidential.

I sometimes hear your name mentioned in connection with political honors. You can hardly know how delighted I should be to see you in *any place* that would please you. But I sometimes feel that we will after all lose, as a party, all the benefit of the advantages which the last Administration, and the present one too, have presented to us.

I shall remain here until about the 1st of September — after that until the 15th of September my address will be 'Saranac Inn, Franklin County, N.Y.,' and after that New York City.

Mrs. Cleveland sends a great deal of love to Mrs. Vilas and the girls, and mine of course goes too. She says, 'Give my love to Mr. Vilas and tell him I think it is quite useless for him to struggle with the problem of my age and birthday, for it seems impossible for him to get them right.'

I have not said a word about the tarpon. That's all right, Vilas, I've got the scale and I saw mention of the catch in a newspaper before you wrote me about it. And I knew you'd have it, for I know you to be one of the 'get there' men who accomplish what they set out to do.

To DR. S. B. WARD

Marion, Mass., *August 25*, 1890

I believe that our plans are perfected for leaving here and reaching Saranac, as follows: Leaving here Friday the 29th, we shall go by the Boston & Albany road to Albany and leave there by the D. & H. at 11:20 P.M. This will bring us to Bloomingdale at 10:27 Saturday A.M. At this place we shall disembark unless we hear from you that we are somehow wrong. We expect to meet Mr. and Mrs. Chapin at Albany. We propose to give them the lower bedroom in the cottage, and I hope there will be two beds there so that they can use them if they desire.

I shall attempt to have Death and Destruction and Mrs. Cleveland's rifle sent from New York to Saranac Inn this week. If they do not arrive there in time for the first hunt, we shall have to depend on you or someone else for firearms.

If the strike or anything else interferes with our plans as outlined above, I will inform you by telegraph. Mrs. Cleveland and her mother send all sorts of affectionate messages to you and the children.

To DANIEL S. LAMONT

Saranac Inn, N.Y., *September 13*, 1890

Your letter of a recent date was gladly received. I have a lame right hand which obliges me to impress Mrs. Cleveland into my service as an amanuensis.

It was certainly very kind in Mr. Miller to offer me the tempting trip referred to in your letter; and I wish you would take an early opportunity to inform him how much I appreciate his courtesy. There will, however, on my return to the city be a number of matters which will require my immediate attention, and I regard it as entirely out of the question for me to leave home on another pleasure trip for some time to come.

The subject of the speech or interview has been seriously considered since the receipt of your letter. I am so opposed to the idea of making a speech that I do not think I could bring myself to the point. I have just declined an invitation to attend the opening of the Thomas Jefferson

Building in Brooklyn on the 23d instant which would have afforded me an excellent opportunity to say something if I had desired to do so.

The fact is, Colonel, that the inclination is growing on me, daily, to permit things other than politics to claim the greatest share of my attention, and if I had my way, and regarded personal considerations exclusively, I would now put a stop, if I could, to the mention of my name in connection with any political office. Besides my personal repugnance to the atmosphere of politics in their present phase as a question of good judgment, I am nearly convinced that my nomination again for the Presidency would result in party defeat. I do not think there is any use in mincing matters. Mr. Hill and his friends would never permit me to carry the State of New York.

But with all this I am far from believing that I have a right to set up my own judgment and wishes against those of personal and political friends, and if an interview such as you suggest would in their opinion be useful to our cause I ought to be willing to consider the subject. I expect to be in New York toward the last of next week and will confer with you immediately on my arrival.

Barring the weather, which has been as bad as it could possibly be, we have enjoyed our stay here, but we are nearly ready to go home, and think we shall not suffer from a diminution of our appreciation of the comforts of 816 Madison Avenue. Give a great deal of love to Mrs. Lamont and the children from both of us — I suppose when this reaches you, you will be reinstated as a family man.

To MRS. R. W. CHAPIN [1]

New York, *October* 19, 1890

It was very nice and sweet, and just like you, to write me to spend a Sunday at your home in Lenox; and your declaration — 'it will really disappoint me very much if you don't come' — is enough to make me rail at fate and duty. 'I am a poor miserable old man,' condemned to toil and worry; and I must close my eyes to the pleasures presented in your note, and those which it stirs my imagination to create. You have with you now by far the better part of myself; and in my loneliness and self-denial I will find solace and comfort in the hope that I am suffering somewhat for your sake...

[1] Mrs. Adele LeB. Chapin had a summer home at Lenox at which Mrs. Cleveland was now visiting.

To L. CLARKE DAVIS [1]

New York, *November* 5, 1890

The fishing rods have arrived, and I am very much pleased with them. You may be sure that I gratefully appreciate your gift of one of them, and I thank you for it from the bottom of my heart. I receive and shall cherish it with the same sentiment you express in giving it — 'in memory of a pleasant summer.' Besides this, I shall value it as a gift from the best all-around fisherman I think I ever encountered — a little expensive in the matter of bait, but successful enough to make amends. I hope we shall meet again 'on the reefs' next summer, for I know that with a rod more delicate than 'Old Pestilence' I can make a better showing.

The maker of the rods sent with them a bill for one, amounting to *five dollars*, carefully receipted and marked in the corner 'with the compliments' of Mr. Speed. I don't quite know what to do. I don't want to hurt his feelings and yet I would rather pay him. As you say you are to see him on the subject, I wish I might trouble you to do so speedily and let me know how to act. I will wait to hear from you.

Election news and fishing rods make me quite happy in these days. Did you ever see such a landslide? The congratulations and kind messages I have received from every part of the country are very delightful, but I am sometimes a little bewildered when I try to account for people 'pitching into' me so. The best thing of all is the moral awakening, and its effect, in Pennsylvania. It reinstates one's faith in human nature....

To ROBERT E. PATTISON [2]

New York, *November* 7, 1890

Though I know that you are overwhelmed with congratulations, I cannot resist the temptation to express to you my delight upon your election as governor of Pennsylvania. I have felt the most intense interest in the contest in your State, and have had great sympathy with the good people there, confronted as they were with everything bad, and this endorsed and supported by a party claiming an immense majority of the voters. It seemed to me that the condition was almost pitiable, and that the struggle between right and wrong at such odds ought not to have been forced upon your grand old Commonwealth.

[1] Lemuel Clarke Davis (1835–1900), veteran Philadelphia journalist, editor successively of the *Inquirer* and the *Public Ledger*, husband of Rebecca Harding Davis and father of Richard Harding Davis, had become a close friend of Cleveland.

[2] Robert E. Pattison was governor of Pennsylvania 1883–87 and 1891–95.

But when it came, precipitated by the arrogance of those accustomed to deceive and betray the people with impunity, I almost held my breath, and, as an American citizen proud of my country, prayed God for the people's safe deliverance and for a demonstration that they had not lost their love for honesty and right. That demonstration came; and I am now glad that issue between right and wrong was made so clearly, and that the wrong so impudently displayed the banner under which the forces were gathered. I want to thank you, as a citizen and as one of the people, for the gallant fight you made and for all that you have done in this trying hour to save the American character....

To NELSON F. ACERS

New York, *November* 8, 1890

There is no one thing of the same grade of importance which has resulted from the recent election which ought to please Democrats and decent people so much as the prospect of the retirement of Ingalls.[1] I don't know what kind of a Democrat it would be who would not labor in season or out of season to prevent the return to the Senate of this vilifier of everything Democratic, who has been put forward by the Republican party to pour out abuse too bad for even decent Republicans, and who was made presiding officer of the Senate to crown their insults to our party.

To WILSON S. BISSELL

New York, *November* 8, 1890

. Both of your recent letters have been received and you may be sure that I was glad to hear from you again. I have thought a great deal on the subject you touch upon in your last letter, and it seems to be one of the cases in which a man's consistency and adherence to principle is antagonized by kindly feelings, the love of peace, motives of policy, and a sense of helplessness.

I am afraid the candidate you mention is behind all the men of the same standing within our State in sincere adherence to *the* principle which we have in hand and which has been lately so overwhelmingly vindicated. Yet he has treated me very kindly, he is especially outspoken in opposi-

---

[1] John James Ingalls (1833–1900), a Senator from Kansas since 1873, was finally defeated this year, his place being taken by the Populist, William A. Peffer. His political demise was hailed by all reformers, for he had called purity in politics an iridescent dream. His foul personal abuse of Cleveland made his defeat particularly pleasing to the ex-President.

tion to the McKinley Bill, and other men who lagged as much as he in the beginning (like Gorman and McPherson) are now quite at the front. Besides, the Colonel thinks it is perhaps this or something worse with a row. Colonel Rice told me yesterday that he had heard that Tammany Hall might present Bourke Cockran.[1] I believe it is said in explanation of the letter which you enclose on a printed slip, and which certainly seems on its face a foolish one, that it was written to incite to effort, in the legislative canvass, the warm personal friends of the writer. Still, he is an outspoken candidate and claims that he will succeed *if the Governor does not cheat him.* This of course means that the Governor has absolutely promised that he shall have the place or at least that he so understands the situation. On the other hand, Colonel Rice says that no such assurance has been given and he personally is inclined in the same direction you are. He intimates, however, that some at least of the persons about the Governor are talking about his being buried in the Senate. One quite important Assemblyman spoke to me yesterday with some bitterness of his vote being traded off before he was elected, and I do not doubt that others will feel the same way. So the prospect is that a man will be elected subject to the objections which you suggest, and with the distinct expectation in Albany that service shall be rendered in aid of the Governor's aspirations or that the scheme will fail in a first-class row with much bitterness and recrimination. I believe that it is quite generally felt that the credit for a majority in the Assembly is due to the Governor and I think if he would take the place everyone would be content. But I am satisfied that he will not do this — first because he would be accused of treachery, and second and chiefly, because he has other ambitions.

Of one thing you may be entirely certain. Hill and his friends are bent on his nomination for the Presidency, and failing in that they are determined that it shall not come towards me.[2] You know how I feel about this matter as a personal question; but if I have pulled any chestnuts out of the fire I want those who take them to keep a civil tongue in their heads; and further than this, I don't want to see my hard work wasted and the

---

[1] William Bourke Cockran (1854–1923), the brilliant Irish-American orator, had first been elected to Congress in 1887. The office of which Cleveland is here writing was the United States Senatorship. After much hesitation, Governor Hill finally accepted the election. He was chosen for the term beginning March 4, 1891, but did not assume his duties until January 7, 1892, continuing meanwhile to act as governor. This virtual holding of two important positions, one State and one Federal, for political purposes, aroused much adverse criticism.

[2] For Hill's machinations to obtain the Presidential nomination in 1892, see the editor's *Grover Cleveland: A Study in Courage,* 470 ff.

old party fall back to shiftiness and cheap expediency. One other thing I want to say: This Hill movement is much more extended and has penetrated more quarters than many expect.

You know, I suppose, that our friends have had a kindly feeling for Flower — regarding him as a good-natured man, etc. I have an idea that there is a growing inclination, or at least a toleration, towards his nomination as Governor next year; but I do not believe it will go very far unless there is pretty good assurance of his tendencies.

I have tried to tell you all I know concerning the political topics touched upon, and I must confess my sensations on our grand victory are not without a sombre shade of apprehension. Mrs. Cleveland sends her regards to you and her love to Mrs. Bissell. I join in the latter to the extent consistent with the proprieties.

To GENERAL FRANCIS C. BARLOW [1]

New York, *November* 10, 1890

You know how much I thank you for your letter of the 6th instant, and for a copy of your letter on the pension business. I read the letter when it first appeared, and refrained with an effort from writing you then. I have now read it again with fresh interest. I believe it to be a pioneer in that kind of literature, and that the time is not far distant when others will follow, from sources as unquestioned and unimpeachable. I look for a pretty radical awakening among the people on this subject, and a thorough change in the public mind concerning it. I hope that the abuses which have been fostered and created by demagogues will not lead to injustice towards honest and worthy veterans, but I believe there is danger of it. If this is avoided (and perhaps whether it is or not) I am looking to a time when such men as you and I will be considered the old soldiers' best friends. I will not allow the sickening abuse I have been obliged to deal with, to prejudice me against all pensions; and I know such soldiers as you will not.

These last Democratic victories are tremendous, and I suppose I ought only to think of the triumph of the doctrines we have struggled for. But I cannot help reflecting upon the responsibility cast upon my party and the duty we owe to our people.

[1] Francis Channing Barlow (1834–96), a major-general in the Civil War, was a prominent Republican who had held several State offices of importance.

To WILLIAM F. VILAS

New York, *November* 11, 1890

I am at home today preparing something to say, or rather preparing myself to say something, at the Thurman banquet day after tomorrow in Columbus. In the midst of it all, I find myself thinking so much of you that I could not resist the impulse to stop and tell you in a line or two how delighted I was on all accounts, and especially on your account, that your State did so nobly last Tuesday. I know just how you feel and more than ever have tried to picture to friends your labors, your hopes and your fears.

And now, my dear friend, you know how anxious I am that there should be no ungracious lack of appreciation of the share you have had in redeeming your State. Somehow it seems to me there should be but one view in the matter. I wish everyone in Wisconsin knew as well as I do how useful you are in public place, and how much you are able in such place to further the interests of the Democratic party. If you have consented to be a candidate for the Senate [1] (and I really don't know how that is) it seems to me that Wisconsin ought to be proud to be the first to contribute to that body such new and young blood as it sadly needs and as our party needs as representative of it in high places.

I read your interview in the Albany *Argus*. I think I should have recognized it without being told the author. It was just right and spoke the 'English language.'

I certainly thought something had you wrong and that you were in the depths again when I did not hear from you election night, and I have been expecting to hear from you ever since. I know that I had no right to expect it, for I have owed you a letter some time, but I suppose, without meaning to be, I am a little selfish in the matter.

God bless you, Vilas! And if you are in the race for the Senatorship and want it, or are willing to take it, I earnestly hope for the sake of the country and our party that it will be promptly and harmoniously given to you. Mrs. Cleveland is out, but if she were here much love to all your household would go from her with this. Mine goes in all sincerity.

---

[1] Vilas was elected to the Senate and served six years from March 4, 1891, being a pillar of strength to Cleveland during the second Administration.

To WILSON S. BISSELL

New York, *November* 17, 1890

What a glorious thing it would be if you could be elected to the Senate. I have been sounding about on the subject and find this to be the present condition of the thing:

It is conceded in all quarters which my inquiries have reached that Hill positively controls the situation. The gains in legislative representation are mostly here and in Brooklyn. The members from these two localities can, if united, control the caucus within a vote or two, which of course they can easily obtain. I have not seen Weed [1] at all, but I hear that he started in the canvass upon the supposition that Hill was pledged to his candidacy. This, I believe, is not now Hill's position; but instead of openly helping him he is fighting off, as I think, to pledge Weed and such friends as he has to his (Hill's) schemes. Some think that the result of the recent elections will cause Hill to turn his eye toward the Senatorship for himself as the best thing he can now see in sight. In the meantime a good deal of talk is being stirred up in regard to Weed's tariff record; and if Hill puts him in, his own tariff reform record, he fears, is not strong enough to ward off criticism from himself. I think he is in a sort of a 'hole'; for if he takes it himself he will be accused of downright treachery to Weed. It may result in his abdication of control; and if he takes his hands really off, anything might follow. If Weed becomes satisfied that Hill is not for him and if he also sees that he cannot succeed alone, he would be apt, I think, to aid in a quarter as far removed from Hill as possible. In any event, I hope that you will give your friends free rein. I am wondering how Sheehan is going to manage matters. If your local representatives are strongly for you, as they ought to be excepting him, how is he going to deliver them in answer to Hill's demands? Charley Carey lately wrote me on this subject and is very much opposed to Weed.

The thing is not in the shape it ought to be at present, but so far as the machine part of the thing is concerned, Hill has been conceded (properly enough, I think, or did think when it was given to him) to be in control of the State politics, and to be master of the situation as such political movements usually go. The chance of a better outlook depends upon his letting the matter drift for his own safety or a protest on the part of the

[1] Smith M. Weed of Plattsburg, an old follower of Tilden who had been one of Cleveland's most loyal supporters. He became a bitter enemy of Hill when the latter cut off his ambitions for the Senatorship.

better and more consistent elements in the party that will frighten him off, and for this kind of thing you and your friends ought to be prepared. It would make me very happy if we could turn it in your direction.

To WILSON S. BISSELL

New York, *November* 20, 1890

Your letter is at hand. Of course you will not allow yourself to rely upon anything the gentleman in Albany or his friends say about their intentions.

Did you see a nice editorial in the Utica *Observer* only a day or two ago? I send you a couple of clippings sent to me today. You will see they express the same ideas, but are from widely separated points of publication. I think the opinion grows here that Mr. Hill will finally be selected, though I am looking for some sort of a sly dodge — maybe in favor of Chapin or some such man. I think the clippings I send you are remarkable as showing how staunch the feeling of the Democrats all over the country is in favor of honest tariff reform.

To HENRY WATTERSON

New York, *November* 24, 1890

Your question as to the wisdom of sending the letter, a copy of which you transmit, is a sort of a stumper to me.[1] I don't know what to think about it, and somehow I shrink from endorsing action that has for an important factor my nomination for the Presidency in 1892.

I suppose the party to whom your letter is addressed is surrounded by persons and influences which prevent his taking a very wide range of popular sentiment, and in this view of the subject what you propose to write ought to be deemed a kindly impulse; and I am sure no one can doubt the patriotic intention of the writer so far as the country and party are involved.

I like less than the rest of the letter, the prominence given to my candidacy. I do want the people to keep cool and be ready to do the best thing when the time comes. And when I intimate that there are things in your letter which ought to furnish wholesome information to its addressee, I mean to be understood as eliminating all considerations based upon my candidacy.

[1] In this letter Watterson warned Hill that the sentiment of the country demanded Cleveland's nomination in 1892, and that he was riding for a hard fall in trying to prevent it. The letter was sent, but produced no effect.

To WILLIAM D. WILLIAMS

New York, *November 27, 1890*

...We have gained the accessions to our ranks which made victory possible by being right and fighting for a principle which is in the interests of the people. If, flushed with success, we suppose that we can safely abandon our high standard and fall back to cheap partisanship, and if we permit those who look upon party largely as a means to secure and distribute party spoils to lead, we shall learn that we have only aroused the people to a watchfulness that will find us out and punish us. The chief inspiration of our late crusade and present struggle is that we are striving to benefit our countrymen and to plant our party upon principle instead of shallow expediency. My ambition will be fully satisfied if we justify the confidence the people have reposed in us.

To JOHN TEMPLE GRAVES

New York, *December 20, 1890*

We received the card of invitation to your wedding a day or two ago; and I am glad that your letter, received only a few hours ago, invites or justifies me, on behalf of my dear wife and myself, to do more than formally notice the occasion.

And first of all, let me assure you how much we appreciate the kind and touching sentiment you convey to us in our married state. As I look back upon the years that have passed since God, in His infinite goodness, bestowed upon me the best of all His gifts — a loving and affectionate wife — all else, honors, the opportunity of usefulness, and the esteem of my fellow-countrymen, are subordinated in every aspiration of gratitude and thoughtfulness. You are not wrong, therefore, when you claim, in the atmosphere of fast-coming bliss which now surrounds you, 'kinship' with one who can testify with unreserved tenderness to the sanctification which comes to man when Heaven-directed love leads the way to marriage.

Since this tender theme has made us kinsmen, let me wish for you and the dear one who is to make your life doubly dear to you, all the joy and happiness vouchsafed to man. You will, I am sure, feel that our kind wishes can reach no greater sincerity and force than when my wife joins me in the fervent desire that you and your bride may enter upon and enjoy the same felicity which has made our married life 'one grand sweet song.'

To Dr. Joseph D. Bryant

New York, *December* 28, 1890

Your Christmas presents made me very happy — all the more so because they were entirely unexpected. You see, Doctor, I am a believer in the doctrine that a man should have only his deserts; and I know I do not deserve such kindness at your hands. Even the scales you sent me cannot begin to weigh my thanks and my gratification. I suppose I must content myself with ten-pound fish hereafter. That's a little hard, but I'll try and stand it.

I somewhat expected you in tonight. I wanted to ask you if you have the least desire to go to Philadelphia with me on the eighth of January. I think the Colonel will go and I believe there is a way to come back the same night if necessary.

IX

OUT OF RETIREMENT

AT THE beginning of 1891, Cleveland plunged squarely into political affairs. On January 8 — Jackson Day — he made a speech in Philadelphia in which he denounced the McKinley Tariff, the Reed Rules, the Billion-Dollar Congress, and the policies of the Administration generally. But already the silver question was beginning to dwarf other issues. In the previous summer President Harrison had signed the Sherman Silver-Purchase Act, which required the Government to buy each month 4,500,000 ounces of silver and issue notes based thereon, which were to be a legal tender for debts. At the time this amount represented almost the entire output of the American silver mines. But a great part of Western and Southern sentiment was not satisfied, and demanded legislation which would establish the free and unlimited coinage of silver at 16 to 1; thus, in effect, forcing the United States off the gold standard, and benefiting all debtor classes by heavily reducing the value of the dollar. A free-coinage bill passed the Senate in June, 1890, and again in January, 1891, the Democrats furnishing the principal strength behind it. In the summer of 1890, Democratic conventions in nearly all the States from the headwaters of the Ohio to the Pacific, twenty-one in number, voted in favor of free and unlimited silver coinage. If Cleveland wished to be renominated by his party, it seemed expedient for him to keep silent. But he was determined to speak out. On February 10, 1891, he 'published his famous 'silver letter,' warning the nation that it would meet disaster if it entered upon the 'dangerous and reckless experiment' of free silver coinage. The ambitions of David B. Hill for the Presidential nomination were immediately stimulated. He set on foot plans for seizing the support of New York and the South in the next Democratic National Convention. Cleveland watched Hill's manœuvres with steadily rising indignation, but at first refused to make any open movement. Finally, in December he wrote his friend Bissell that the situation had become intolerable, and that the only way for decent Democrats to retain their self-respect was 'to break this thing up.'

To Daniel S. Lamont

New York, *January* 14, 1891

I have been thinking of the proposed action of the Reform Club [1] in the matter of the Senatorship; and the more I think of it the more I am convinced that the contemplated action would be in every way unfortunate — bad for the Club, bad for the cause it has at heart, and bad for the interests which many of its prominent supporters approve. It does seem too bad that an organization which is fast gaining popular confidence as an instrument for the education and improvement of our people should risk it all by such a useless and inconsistent meddling with matters out of the range of their activity. Can anything be done to avert this action?

To Wilson S. Bissell

New York, *January* 27, 1891

I enclose you a letter from a Chicago friend. I do not know why I send it, as it does not present a subject of much interest to either you or me. Unless Morgenstern has greatly changed, however, I am surprised to be told that he has been appointed Superintendent of Police. He was certainly at one time one of the most disreputable fellows that ever disgraced the force; and as I remember it, he left the force and was kept off on account of his thoroughly bad character.

I read your last letter with much interest. At the time of its receipt I had just made up my mind that the chances were that the Governor would be Senator. There is a little talk going on about our friends picking up the State organization again. What do you think of it? Do you suppose General Doyle would like to run for State Treasurer? And if he started for the nomination could he beat Sheehan in Erie County for delegates? I should not be surprised if things warmed up pretty early and I should be glad to hear from you on the topics here confidentially suggested, at some time in the near future.

To William F. Vilas

New York, *January* 28, 1891

My conservative disposition has led me to defer a reply to your much-enjoyed letter, until, without any anticipation or the taking for granted

[1] The Reform Club of New York City was an organization devoted to civil service reform, ballot reform, and, above all, tariff reform. Among its ruling spirits were former Secretary Fairchild, Charles R. Miller of the *Times*, Everett P. Wheeler, and R. R. Bowker. It had actively supported Cleveland in the campaign of 1888.

an assured future event, I could greet you as 'Senator.' This I now do with as much zest and heartiness as my affection for you prompts — and I know you will not ask a greater guaranty of the warm sentiment I this moment feel. But somehow, my dear friend, I wish the honor was greater. I wish you had come to a place which was more distinctly a reward for the public services you have rendered and can render, instead of a place which, it honestly seems to me, you honor and dignify by accepting. And yet when I really reflect upon the subject, I see that this feeling of mine is not based upon any reasoning at all, and that instead of standing for a moment the test of consideration, it has its rise in an intense personal attachment and appreciation. I am bound to confess, after all and very promptly, that no honor could be higher and no dignity greater than to stand in the Senate of the United States for the State whose growth and progress has moved in parallel lines with your own, and whose welfare and prosperity have always been so patriotically dear to you. And then, too, what a personal gratification it must be to you, as it is to me, to see in the unanimity of your selection, that your State appreciates you and your public services, and cannot be diverted from doing justice and honoring itself by curious carping.

I read your speech on accepting the caucus nomination and enjoyed it exceedingly.

My notion is that the Senatorial result in this State is the best that could have been attained. I am not sure about the after-clap, but I think quieter politics in this State will result.

I put the information you sent me in regard to Kansas dangers where I think it did good — judging by the manner our Alliance friends [1] were guarded by their constituents. It was a blessed thing to thus eliminate a dangerous demagogue and unworthy man from our public life.

I sincerely hope that business or pleasure may call you this way in the near future. We should be exceedingly glad to see you. Why would it not be a very nice thing for you and Mrs. Vilas to come and spend a little time with us? As for Mollie, she has been tried for all sorts of offences, in our family courts, and really convicted of being in town without reporting to us. Sentence has been suspended by a tribunal very much prejudiced in her favor.

---

[1] In the campaign of 1890 the Farmers' Alliance or Populist candidates made an impressive showing in Kansas. Such speakers as Mrs. Mary Elizabeth Lease and Jerry Simpson attracted national attention. The 'dangerous demagogue' referred to in this letter was of course Ingalls.

Mrs. Cleveland joins me in all I have written. She sends love and congratulations to you and all your household. You know how heartily 'I second the motion.' Let me urge you again to favorably consider the proposition to pay us a visit.

To GENERAL JAMES GRANT WILSON [1]

New York, *February* 3, 1891

Powers Fillmore was a man of the kindliest impulses and disposition, but very odd in many ways. I do not know of anybody with whom he was at all confidential regarding personal or family affairs. It was plain to see that he loved his father and fondly cherished his memory — though even that could not be gathered from any frequent conversation he indulged in concerning him. But he was exceedingly shy, and above all things, seemed to desire to avoid notice or publicity. You may not see that anything I have written accounts for his conduct in relation to his father's papers; but knowing him as well as I did, I can imagine a connection. And still I am bound to say he has acted strangely in the matter.

To E. ELLERY ANDERSON [2]

New York, *February* 10, 1891

I have this afternoon received your note inviting me to attend tomorrow evening the meeting called for the purpose of voicing the opposition of the business men of our city to the 'free coinage of silver in the United States.'

I shall not be able to attend and address the meeting as you request, but I am glad that the business interests of New York are at last to be heard from on this subject.

It surely cannot be necessary for me to make a formal expression of my agreement with those who believe that the greatest peril would be initiated by the adoption of the scheme embraced in the measure now pending in Congress for the unlimited coinage of silver at our mints. If we have developed an unexpected capacity for the assimilation of a largely increased volume of this currency, and even if we have demonstrated the

[1] A literary man of New York City, who helped edit *Appleton's Cyclopædia of American Biography*, and was seeking information for that work. Powers Fillmore, the eccentric son of Millard Fillmore, had once had apartments in the same building with Cleveland in Buffalo.

[2] The circumstances under which this famous 'silver letter' was sent, with the Democratic party apparently going helter-skelter for free coinage, and no other national leader daring to stand out against it, are described in the editor's *Grover Cleveland, A Study in Courage*, 465 ff.

usefulness of such an increase, these conditions fall far short of insuring us against disaster, if in the present situation we enter upon the dangerous and reckless experiment of free, unlimited and independent silver coinage.

To WILLIAM F. VILAS

New York, *February* 18, 1891

Your letter was received this morning.

I want to make a confession to you, though I am almost ashamed to do so. *I was a little bit afraid to open your letter* — though I had eagerly sought in the papers and had seen something from your State indicating that my good friends there were neither angry nor disgusted. Knowing how far your personal attachment carried you, I could not, however, keep out of my mind the fear that you might feel that I had done a thing which embarrassed you and other staunch friends.

You see the thing in all respects exactly as I do; and I am, as I said, ashamed that I ever feared you might for a moment put expediency before patriotic principle in your estimate of what I had done.

I have received a great many letters from all parts and very few of them indeed are otherwise than commendatory. So I am completely satisfied. Since I wrote the letter I have felt better than I have since I left Washington; and it seems to me that a weight has been lifted off and a cloud removed. I am not sure that much of this is not owing to the feeling that I am removed from the list of Presidential candidates. That is what many say; and you know I would not object to such an outcome so far as any personal reason goes. At any rate, no one can doubt where I stand so far as the measure now pending is concerned. (Note carefully the wording of the letter and see how much room after all there is for the action of judgment and conviction below the line of free coinage of the silver of the world.) I hope this crisis will not pass without further assurance being given of the intelligence, integrity, conservatism and trusteeship of our party. What a shame it would be to slip now, when so many good men, after much hesitation, are willing to trust us and join our ranks.

The most ridiculous assumption in all this matter is that the Democratic party must accept as its creed any principle implied in any measure for which Democratic Senators or Representatives see fit to vote. I had an idea they learned their lessons from the party instead of the party learning from them.

P.S. I have neglected in so many words to tell you how your letter delighted me and how much I thank you for it.

To Alfred C. Chapin
New York (after *February* 20, 1891)

I find it very difficult to reply to your letter because it is hard for me to convey to you all I feel, and at the same time be sure that the spirit in which I write is not misinterpreted. But I have determined to be entirely frank in the matter and take the consequences.

As I said to Mrs. Chapin, a man who has been in public life is a fool if he expects from all those who have been his personal friends a steady continuance of devotion and unselfish feeling. It is the saddest part of one's public life to see incidents of public duty cast a cloud over personal friendship and to feel that the steadfastness of friends is growing weak with the wear of interest or ambition. I can honestly say to you that I have learned this lesson well enough to be quite resigned, though far from insensible, to the cooling of friends. And as I am sure that no man lives who values more than I do the regard and affection of his friends, I need hardly express my satisfaction with your assurance which indicates that I have wrongly interpreted or given undue significance to certain conduct or speech which I have noticed or of which I have been informed.

So far as our political relations are concerned, it seems to me that I should find no fault with any change in this condition. I am, however, so certainly free from any political ambition and I am so absolutely without political schemes to accomplish, that I ought not to be a cause of political animosity to anyone. In these associations, if I have done a small share of the good work which you kindly put to my credit, do you not think it ought to plead in my behalf for fair treatment?

I have a distinct and definite belief that political matters and purposes can be greatly purified and ennobled. Your keen intellect and well regulated conscience peculiarly fit you to work in this direction.

For the sake of our country and in aid of your party and mine I beg of you to allow nothing to turn you from the path upon which I believe you started as you entered political life.

To WILSON S. BISSELL

New York, *March* 5, 1891

As a result or consequence of a little consultation today, I want to write you a short letter on the subject of State politics.

I believe the drift on the part of our friends is in the direction of Flower [1] for Governor — that is, if he is prepared to cast his lot with us. He will, I think, be called on to do this or decline to do it within a very short time if it is determined to make any use of him. There seems to be quite a strong opinion that in spite of any other appearance and notwithstanding anything that may be *said*, Mr. Hill wants Judge Parker.

Now comes an important point — and that is the Sheehan matter.[2] Of course I need not tell you how I stand on this matter; nor is there any doubt in other minds as to the desirability and importance of disposing in another way of the second place on the ticket. To do this Erie County must, I think, do a great deal of fighting. Is it in the power or the inclination of our friends there to refuse him their delegates?

I suppose the only new men who will be put upon the ticket are candidates for attorney-general, comptroller and State engineer — besides governor and lieutenant-governor. Is there one of these who could be put in Erie County to help the fight? For the moral effect of the thing, and to relieve decent Democrats from disgrace and humiliation, the lieutenant-governor and chairman of the State Committee ought to be especially attended to.

If you are in Albany it might be well for you to see Herrick; and if you are here cannot you call on the Colonel and me? Whatever you do I wish you would write me how our people feel there about entering upon the Sheehan fight. I think action in other quarters may be largely influenced by what is attempted there in this matter. The disposition is to begin operations soon.

To EDWARD S. BRAGG

Lakewood, N.J., *March* 9, 1891

Your letter of the 5th instant is received. I have thought until now that I might continue silent on the subject which, under the high sanction

---

[1] Roswell P. Flower (1835–99), a wealthy Democrat of Watertown, was at this time serving in Congress; he was elected governor of New York in the fall of 1891.

[2] William F. Sheehan was duly nominated and elected lieutenant-governor.

of your position as my 'fellow-Democrat and fellow-citizen,' and in your relation as a true and trusted friend, you present to me. If, in answering your questions, I might only consider my personal desires and my individual ease and comfort, my response would be promptly made, and without the least reservation or difficulty.

But if you are right in supposing that the subject is related to a duty I owe to the country and to my party, a condition exists which makes such private and personal considerations entirely irrelevant. I cannot, however, refrain from declaring to you that my experience in the great office of President of the United States has so impressed me with the solemnity of the trust, and its awful responsibilities, that I cannot bring myself to regard a candidacy for the place as something to be won by personal strife and active self-assertion.

I have also an idea that the Presidency is pre-eminently the people's office, and I have been sincere in my constant advocacy of the effective participation in political affairs on the part of all our citizens. I believe the people should be heard in the choice of their party candidates, and that they themselves should make nominations as directly as is consistent with open, fair, and full party organizations and methods.

I speak of these things solely for the purpose of advising you that my conception of the nature of the Presidential office, and my conviction that the voters of the party should be free in the selection of their candidates, preclude the possibility of my leading and pushing a self-seeking canvass for the Presidential nomination, even if I had a desire to be again a candidate....

To L. CLARKE DAVIS

New York, *March* 9, 1891

Thanks for your last letter and the clipping enclosed. You have the thing nearer right than anyone else who has written concerning my motives and sentiments touching the event of 1892.

I am in a miserable condition — a private citizen without political ambition trying to do private work and yet pulled and hauled and importuned daily and hourly to do things in a public and semi-public way which are hard and distasteful to me. I have never made a speech or written a letter except in compliance with importunities which I could not resist from those engaged in some good work or from those entitled to claim my consideration on party grounds. To refuse, as I am obliged to, the many urgent requests presented to me is as wearing and as perplexing as it was to refuse applications for office at Washington.

I am afraid you will suspect me of cant when I say to you that I am honestly trying to do some good in the world — within political lines or otherwise. But so it is. I often have a pretty blue time of it and confess to frequent spells of resentment, but I shall get on in a fashion. Give my love to your dear wife and the children.

To WILSON S. BISSELL

New York, *March* 25, 1891

I was glad to receive your letter this morning, but sorry to hear that you have fallen a victim to that mean and treacherous assailant — rheumatism. He is a mean 'cuss' and I hope you are not doomed to get on his list.

Regarding the subject of my last letter, I cannot help thinking the thing can be done and that it is necessary to the continued supremacy of our party in the State. The methods which have been lately prevalent can lead to but one end and that is disaster. The only question now in doubt is when it will come. Recent events, I am quite sure, have set the people of our party to thinking, and it seems to me that the rebellion cannot be postponed. If this is so, the question is whether the party shall stand and take it or whether we shall protect ourselves by enforcing better counsels. It is very troublesome as I look at it, and if a 'right about' is to be performed prompt action should be forthcoming. I saw Locke a moment yesterday. He is intensely enthusiastic, but I am afraid altogether too sanguine.

I am inclined to go to Buffalo at the time of the German Celebration. Do you think well of it still?

Hoping that you will speedily be on your pins again and with affectionate regards to Mrs. Bissell.

To L. CLARKE DAVIS

New York, *April* 15, 1891

I think you do well to stand by the text of the message [1] so far as my position is concerned. If there is any doubt as to the meaning of that, I have rummaged the English language with most unsatisfying results. I think in that message it was that I warned those interested in undue pro-

---

[1] The tariff message at the opening of Congress in December, 1887.

tection, that the consequence of resistance to reasonable demands might
be an insistence upon more radical reforms; but there is nothing vindic-
tive in my political beliefs on the tariff question. Did I write you how
much I liked what you wrote about Mr. Willard? I did not see him in the
play you mention, but I did see him in two others; and I think you
wrote very justly and very handsomely.

We had a very pleasant evening with your two children [1] last week.
I suppose you are already very vain on their account, and as I think we
all have a bit of envy about us, I will neither make you more vain nor expose my weakness by further detail.

But I heard from them that you were ailing and perhaps a little blue.
I am not at all satisfied with these conditions. In point of fact, knowing
your toughness, and your many surroundings tending to self-congratulation, I think both these conditions most absurd. At any rate it is your
bounden duty to recall the time-honored truth that 'good men are scarce';
and they should not only preserve themselves, but should preserve themselves in 'good shape.'

I thank you very much for the fishing suggestion; but I don't believe I
can go. If I leave the city at all before I pack up for the summer, I must
go to Buffalo for the 11th and 12th of May. I am invited to go bass fishing near Sandusky, Ohio, about the 15th; but I wrote my friends last
evening that they must let me off. In point of fact, I have some things
to close up here that ought to occupy my time until my vacation.

To WILSON S. BISSELL

New York, *April 27*, 1891

I don't want to be a nuisance nor make any unnecessary trouble for
my friends, but I do want to know *just as early as possible* what the
order of exercises will be during my visit in Buffalo.[2] Of course you know
that there are excellent reasons why a definite and fixed plan should be
laid out and adhered to.

I have written to Mr. Schmidt of the Young Men's German Association giving him to understand that after Monday evening or night, I must
spend the remainder of my time with other political and social friends.

---

[1] Richard Harding Davis and Charles Belmont Davis.

[2] Cleveland returned to Buffalo to help celebrate the fiftieth anniversary of the German
Young Men's Association, made two speeches, was cordially received, and buried the hatchet
with that city.

I did this in response to a sort of an intimation that I might be expected at the ball on the 12th.

Now the thing especially I desire to know is what 'remarks' will be expected and on what occasions. If the occasion there maybe calls for a political talk I want a hint of it. It would be all wrong for me to be 'sloshing around' and I must not do it. I shall be pleased, too, if all unforeseen and haphazard occasions can be avoided. I must not stay longer than Tuesday the 12th. Now you know what I need. Can you help me?

I am a little perplexed with things I must do and the sooner I hear from you the more I shall be obliged to you.

To WILSON S. BISSELL

New York, *April* 28, 1891

Your letter is just received and I thank you for the trouble you have taken to inform me of the plans proposed.

I do not want to ride all day on the cars and run the risk of arriving late. After a ride all day in the dust, it would be entirely out of the question for me to go directly from the depot to the Hall without dressing. I am very averse to a committee meeting me at Rochester or Batavia and to being escorted through the streets. If these things are contemplated for the purpose of having it appear that my visit was duly honored, how do you think it would answer to have it go through the press that these arrangements had been made by my friends and at my urgent request had been abandoned?

The plan floating about in my head was about this: Leave here at 9:15 Sunday night and arrive in Buffalo at 10:20 A.M. Monday. Go as quietly as possible to the Iroquois Hotel. (You might meet me at the station.) In the afternoon take a ride *with you* in the park and in the course of the drive call at my cousins' at Black Rock, on Mrs. Hayward for a moment, and perhaps on *Mrs. Wilson S. Bissell* for a brief space, in the course of which her husband and I might, could, or would take a drink. Of course I want to call on Mr. and Mrs. Perrine. I could do so that day or take breakfast with them the next morning. Go to the Hall in the morning (there would be a chance for an escort if there ought to be one), and devote myself to the German friends the rest of *the night* — or up to such an hour as will enable me to leave them without seeming to hurry away from any performance they may have on hand.

This leaves Tuesday all before me to utilize as seems best. I don't care for the Merchants' Exchange Reception. I had rather see the common people, or perhaps I should say, give such as may desire a chance to see me. If there are enough of these to justify it, *and it is otherwise thought best*, I should not object to a public reception.

After all, I want to defer to the judgment of the good friends having the matter in charge and will be content with the arrangements they make in the light of the suggestions herein contained. Do you not think if you and I ride together, etc., it will be sufficient to disprove any lies about our relations and thus save Mrs. Bissell and yourself the greater or less inconvenience of my putting up with you? I cannot stay over Wednesday but must start so that I will be here sometime that night.

If the plans are changed to meet my suggestions I shall be glad to know it as soon as possible.

To William C. Endicott

New York, *May* 4, 1891

I received Professor Hart's book [1] which you sent me and am very much pleased with it. I have just written to him expressing my appreciation.

Our house is in a condition of partial 'upturnedness,' and I write in the midst of some confusion. Mrs. Cleveland leaves this afternoon for Buzzards Bay for the purpose of pushing along some repairs to the house there. I am almost afraid that she will find the work so much behind that she will be obliged to return here instead of settling for the summer. I shall not in any event go for some time yet. We certainly hope to see you this summer at our country home, but did I not see in yesterday's paper the names of Mrs. Endicott and William and his wife among the passengers who sailed last Saturday for Europe?

Mrs. Cleveland sends her affectionate remembrances to you and her love to Mrs. Endicott wherever she is, and I need not tell you how heartily I join in every good wish for you and yours.

To Susan Cleveland Yeomans

New York, *May* 15, 1891

Your letter came duly to hand, and although I had heard that the two girls were to be married, when it was announced in cold blood and the day was mentioned, it gave me quite a start to really apprehend that you were the mother of two marriageable girls.

[1] Albert Bushnell Hart's work on *Coercive Powers of the United States Government.*

Now about our coming to the wedding. I am quite sure Frank will not be there. That may as well be considered settled. She is now at Buzzards Bay, where she will remain all summer. I shall join her just as soon as I possibly can — probably in a week or two. We are in a kind of a lonely place with no very near neighbors and I expect we shall have company nearly all the time at the house. But I want to be at the wedding and must try to get there. I sent your letter to Frank, but I think you said the ceremony would take place at noon. What are the girls' names?

I shall be at the Victoria Hotel after a day or two more in our own house. So direct me there or at No. 15 Broad Street.

To WILSON S. BISSELL

New York, *May* 16, 1891

My thoughts tonight are very completely filled with the incidents of my recent visit to Buffalo and all that was done for me by my very good friends while there. You will not think it strange, I am sure, that I am constrained to write to you before I go to bed, as the chief of them all, to thank you for your kindness and attention. The reception at the Cleveland Democracy was very pleasant and the speech of President Bissell was in exceeding good taste and in all respects very fine. I am glad I went to the ball; we came away before the banquet there began, but I had an opportunity to meet some good friends among the Germans. We stopped on the way and drank a few glasses of beer and ate some Swiss cheese which tasted very good indeed. I had a handsome letter today from President Georger and Vice-President Hammerstein.

At the ball, and as he escorted me to the carriage to go home, I had a little opportunity to talk with Charley Bishop. He told me that he heard awhile ago that Sheehan had said that he could not be nominated for mayor again. After that Sheehan came to him and complained that his wishes had not been regarded, etc., when Charley repeated what he had heard and told him that if he wanted another nomination he was conceited enough to think he could get it, etc. I said to Charley that if a political question arose he had better stand by those he knew to be his friends and who stood for the right and honest thing and that he might be perfectly sure that the other gang meant selfishness and personal ends, and that Mr. Sheehan would aim to get such control that he (Bishop) would have to get on his knees to him for anything he might want. The Mayor said

that he would be in New York the first week in June and would call and
see me; but I am very much afraid that I shall be away. I told him the
exact truth and I think he was somewhat impressed by it. Gus Scheu
went with me to the ball and he said they (he and his friends) were going
to make a big fight for the delegates and he thought they could win, but
that if they found other parts of the State wanted Sheehan for lieutenant-governor he supposed they would have to go for him, but they proposed to have the committeeman.

Watterson was in to see me day before yesterday fresh from old Dana,
and he was sure that when the time came Hill would try to nominate
Sheehan for *governor*. I take no stock in that. I believe an idea is gaining
ground that if Hill dictates the ticket too arrogantly, there is danger
that it will be beaten. I should not be at all surprised if there was a good
deal of thinking going on in the Democratic mind of the State. I don't
know that I have told you anything about the Mayor and Gus, but I
thought it best to put you in possession of it.

Remember me very affectionately to Mrs. Bissell. Give my regards to
all the friends who were so kind to me....

To Susan Cleveland Yeomans

New York, *May 29*, 1891

I leave by the boat at half-past five tonight for Buzzards Bay, where I
shall spend the entire summer, I hope, with the exception of the two or
three days I take to attend the weddings of the nieces. On that subject
I desire to say that I hope to reach Walworth on the morning of the 10th
and leave the same day in the afternoon. I have not looked up the trains
yet to see how I can make connections, etc., and if Lucius has anything
on that question (as he is apt to have) I should be glad to know what it
is. I judge from your letter you do not expect me to remain only long
enough for the ceremony, and I feel that I ought to be on my way back
as soon as possible.

Give my love to the girls and all the family.

To Daniel S. Lamont

New York, *June 9*, 1891

I saw, as perhaps I told you, Poucher and Beach the day before I left,
and they talked a good deal about State matters. They suggested that

you notify a few people to come here and consult and I promised I would communicate their ideas to you. I did not do it, and to keep my word I do it now.

My own idea is, if D-Cady Herrick was written to and given to understand that he was in charge of the movement, that he could begin to issue orders which would be accepted and obeyed with alacrity without further consultation, and thus much time be saved. I do not see why all this bother should be put upon you, but there seems to be no one else unless I write to Herrick, which I am willing to do if it is thought best.

I shall be here again early Thursday morning and remain in the city until time to go to the boat in the afternoon. If you will write me a note and direct it to the Victoria Hotel, letting me know what you want me to do about seeing you, I will get it when I arrive and stay at the hotel or come down here just as it best suits your convenience. I had rather stay at the hotel, I believe.

I must start from there as early as half-past four o'clock.

To GOVERNOR WILLIAM E. RUSSELL

New York, *June 9*, 1891

I am in town from Buzzards Bay for a day on the way to attend the weddings of a couple of nieces tomorrow, and I expect to return to my Cape home on Friday morning. I find your letter of the fifth instant on my office table.

There are very few things I would not do for you and the others for whom you speak. I want to avoid all the speechmaking possible, for in the first place I do not think I am very good at it, and secondly, during my vacation I am such a vagabond and lazy good-for-nothing, that I find any mental exercise a great effort.

Still, I should like to get your ideas a little more completely upon the subject of your letter and help the cause in any way possible. At Buzzards Bay I am only about two hours from you. I think it will be nearly or quite two weeks before we get settled in our house, though we are roosting there now after a fashion. Our unreadiness, however, need not prevent your coming to us any day next week. We can find a place to talk. I might run up to Boston if the trip would not attract too much notice and start too much gossip....

To Dr. S. B. Ward

Gray Gables, *June* 21, 1891

I was much gratified by the receipt last evening of your letter of the twelfth instant, because it furnished additional evidence of your consideration and friendship. I saw the article in the *Press* and was disgusted with the entire lack of decency of which it was a demonstration; and I was enraged that such a thing should have first appeared in that dirty and disreputable sheet.[1] Somehow it appears to me to be too sacred a thing to be mentioned in such a quarter.

All the same, my dear friend, I am the happiest man in the world — as I ought to be if the anticipation of what one has longed for as the greatest of blessings should make a man happy. My dear wife is well and as happy as I am in the prospect of rounding off and perfectly fulfilling a sweet wifehood. I believe she is glad to have you know the fact, for we both are sure that your satisfaction and congratulations are genuine and sincere.

We shall probably stay here until the middle of September — as late as we dare if we are to have a native-born New Yorker with us. Can you not come and see us before the first of September? We have first-rate fishing and excellent boating, and I believe you would enjoy a visit here. You know how delighted we should be to have you with us. Think of this, Doctor, and let me know if you will come and when. Mrs. Cleveland sends her love to you and the children and I very heartily join.

To L. Clarke Davis

Gray Gables, *June* 28, 1891

For a man that is 'a good deal in the dark' you get the situation, so far as it relates to me, just about as it is. Of course all the talk about any conference between my friends and myself, and the representation as to what took place at such a conference, is baldly imaginative; but what you reproduce on the subject comes nearer what *might* have been said at such a conference, than much else that has been published concerning my position. I am in quite a placid condition and have no desire to commit any violence upon the wishes of my party or the sensibilities of the American people. A man so tame as that is entitled to decent treatment. I cannot imagine how any good purpose is to be compassed by abusing me and I can see how much harm can be done — at least within the party

[1] Cleveland was referring to the expected birth of his first child.

to which I belong. I am trying to keep my temper and, as long as the fish bite well, shall succeed.

That reminds me. Why cannot you come to us for a few days before you 'cross the briny deep'? We can get a lot of bottom-fish here — and good ones too. The bluefish are soon to be here in paying quantity and quite a number have been already taken. We can go to Peter's Pond for black bass and — do all sorts of things.

I have tried the idea (not the bob) you sent me and I know I shall have great fun with it. Thus far the fish I got on were two big dogfish; but I shall certainly do better. I know I am to catch bluefish and bass that way, during the next week, if I can get some menhaden, which up to this time have been very scarce here. See if you can't come up and help me. Mrs. Cleveland sends her affectionate regards to you and through you to Mrs. Davis and Nora; and I join just as strong as I possibly can.

To WILSON S. BISSELL

Gray Gables, *June* 30, 1891

I am not at all surprised to learn from the newspapers and from your letters and other sources, that there is a revolt in Buffalo against the dictation of Hill and Sheehan, and the kind of politics they believe in and rely upon. I am quite certain that the same fight has begun, or will prevail, in other parts of the State. The fact is that matters have been carried on so defiantly, by those assuming to dictate in the management of our party in the State, that it is getting to be very hard to endure and submit to a continuance of the prevailing bossism, and look honest men in the face. Such men as you and I, and the thousands of other good Democrats, who believe the principles of our party mean the good of the people and honesty and fidelity in public place, cannot afford to be traded off and misrepresented by those who are in politics for what can be made out of it; and it is a disgrace for us to allow ourselves to be used to further their purposes.

I have no doubt that the movement now on foot to change the management of the party in the State will succeed. If it does I am anxious that no decent honest man shall be suspected, and left out of the fellowship of those who come to the front. I am satisfied that policy, as well as honesty, is on the side of becoming identified with the movement for a change. I think I see this so plainly, that I hope there will be no hesitation as to their course on the part of any of my personal or political friends.

I was very sorry that I was away when, as I saw in the newspaper, Mayor Bishop was in the city, for I wanted to talk a little further on this subject with him than I had an opportunity to do when I was in Buffalo. I take it for granted that he will be on the right side. His strength is in the confidence the decent honest portion of the community have in him; and it seems to me that is what he must cultivate and satisfy, if he retains his hold. I wish he knew what the other thing involves, and the price he must pay to keep on terms with those who seem determined to retain control. Their favor is only to be secured by the most abject submission to their dictation; and I know that Charley Bishop is too honest a man to agree to the conditions they would impose. Besides, if he should do this, there is no faith to be placed in their assurances. They are quite willing to use anybody and then throw him aside. From what Charley told me, I should judge that Sheehan had already made declarations, which indicate that in no event would he support him for renomination; and I think he will find his friends in another quarter when the time comes. But I don't know why I should write all this, for I expect the Mayor is now with you in your efforts to commend the Democracy to the honest decent men of Buffalo.

We are pretty well settled here, and are having a quiet, delightful, lazy time. I wish you and Mrs. Bissell could look in on us. Cannot you do this? Mrs. Cleveland sends love to you both and joins me most heartily in the wish that you might visit us....

To DANIEL S. LAMONT

Gray Gables, *June* 30, 1891

I send you a letter descriptive of a house in Orange County.

We are pretty well settled, though painters are still in the house. I tell you, Colonel, we have a nice place here and I don't think you would know it at all if you should see it — which I hope you will do before long. I wish you would come up and spend a few days with us before you come up for the long visit you have promised us. This much I will say: I never saw a place I liked so well thus far, and I never was so contented and happy as I am in these days. I have a good many schemes to carry out in the way of improving my 'Estate,' and these with my regular fishing business keep me very busy — too busy to read or write or think of politics. Parker sends me clippings and I see the *Times* every day; and a look at these keeps me informed of the amount of abuse that is showered upon me as a Presidential candidate. I hope I shall not be obliged to submit to this misrepresentation, and while no effort is made to check those who abuse me, I shall be by and by laughed at and abused more for trying for something I could not get. You know how I feel in the matter. The fight has broken out in Erie County and is growing quite hot.

I wrote Gorman,[1] and Mrs. Cleveland wrote Mrs. Gorman, inviting them here, but they both in very handsome letters replied that they could not come. If you have time and there is anything of interest to tell I wish you could write to me. Mrs. Cleveland sends her love to you and the Doctor and both your families, and so do I.

To Dr. S. B. WARD

Gray Gables, *June* 30, 1891

I was delighted with the prospect which your letter gave us of a visit from you at our summer retreat. An answer to your letter has been postponed a few days because I had a slight idea of going to Canada to fish for salmon — in which case I should not have returned before the 16th of July, and should have asked you if you could not have come to us at that date instead of the one you suggested. But it's all right now. I have made up my mind to remain here and we shall look for you on the 13th. Don't fail to tell us just when you will arrive or at least what route you will take so we can meet you.

Of course you understand that children and dogs and things of that kind never show off well when it is particularly important that they should. It may be so with 'Gray Gables.' The weather may be bad and the fish may be contrary. If so, you must take our word for the advantages and beauties of our summer home. Hoping to hear from you as soon as possible in a perfectly definite way and with the most affectionate regards to you and the children from Mrs. Cleveland....

To DANIEL S. LAMONT

Gray Gables, *July* 3, 1891

I wrote you a letter a day or two ago, and suppose you have not yet received it. I received your letter dated yesterday this evening. I should be very glad to see Dunnell and hope he will come here. He ought to let

---

[1] Arthur Pue Gorman (1839–1906), of Maryland Senator 1881–99, and 1903 until his death; he was the most astute of politicians, and Cleveland's invitation is evidence that he was becoming interested in a renomination.

me know when he expects to arrive, so that I will be at home. I am delighted with the prospect of seeing you and the Doctor at Gray Gables. You must by all means encourage the yacht trip. I promise to show you a somewhat different place from that you saw last summer.

My only thought about politics is that we are great fools if we allow ourselves to be hauled about by Hill and his gang. I know that I, who am doing next to nothing to prevent such a condition, ought not to expect others to inordinately exert themselves, but I do hope the thing will not be neglected so long that the pins will be fixed fast and strong against us. My information and my belief is that Tammany Hall will not aid us. They don't like me — never did and never will — and they will not help any movement with which my name is associated. Of course you know I am ready to take my discharge papers and be very obedient and dutiful, except in one contingency.

We were a good deal disappointed to learn that we were not to see Mrs. Lamont on her way, for we wanted to see her and to have her see how beautifully her idea worked out in altering the house.

To RICHARD WATSON GILDER

Gray Gables, *July* 3, 1891

I am much obliged to you for the clippings you sent me and I return the one on Mr. Sloane's article as you requested.

I suppose these concerning the Anti-Cleveland movement represent a feeler and the response for which it was put out. How little and frivolous all this seems to me! — not because I do not realize the importance of everything in the remotest way connected with the great office of President, but because they appear to be indices of the meanness and malice of men and politicians. So all this time I am wondering when the bluefish will be about and biting.

I am glad to hear through you and from Mr. Morgan directly that the wagon was shipped on the 20th — whatever that may signify. In the meantime our vacation is slipping away and we need the wagon every day. We have put up a nice flagstaff on the point and have a fine large flag with 44 stars upon it which early tomorrow morning will be flung to the breeze — if there is any. We are all the time happy in our Gray Gables and its improvement. Every day something new is brought to light which would, if done, add to its beauty and convenience. All, however, which I contemplate cannot be done immediately.

We hope to see you again soon. Mrs. Cleveland sends her love to you and Mrs. Gilder and the children. So do I — and especially to George.

To P. J. SMALLEY

Gray Gables, *July* 5, 1891

Please accept my thanks for your recent letter and the editorial from the *Globe*, which have been forwarded to me here. I am very much pleased with the *Globe's* article. A little more such doctrine would do a great deal of good.

It is a very strange thing that just at this time, on the very heels of a new demonstration of the strength and sufficiency of principles and beliefs which we know to be Democratic and right, there should be so much willingness to follow lights which, if not set up for our destruction, are by no means thus far recognized as Democratic, and which are by no means certainly known to be right. Every citizen who loves his country and every Democrat who loves his party, ought to pray that the question to which you refer may be considered with reference to its relations to the good of the country and the conscience of the party, rather than in the light of temporary and dangerous expediency.

To DR. S. B. WARD

On board the *Oneida, July* 11, 1891

This will be handed you by my good friend Mr. E. C. Benedict,[1] whose guests we are, on board of his yacht *Oneida*. Being in this vicinity on a most delightful cruise, he has insisted, while his guests are riding about Newport, on calling for you, hoping to take you with us and land you at Gray Gables tomorrow or Monday. I hope you will come aboard with him, as I can assure you the greatest possible enjoyment beneath the shelter of his most hospitable wing — or yacht awnings. I need not say how delighted Mrs. Cleveland and I would be to have you join us here and make the acquaintance of these very kind friends of ours.

To GOVERNOR WILLIAM E. RUSSELL

Gray Gables, *July* 23, 1891

I want to defer to the judgments formed by yourself and the friends with whom you have consulted, but I am in much doubt as to the *expedi-*

---

[1] Benedict, a wealthy gas magnate, had been introduced to Cleveland some time before by Richard Harding Davis when his yacht entered Buzzards Bay.

ency of your coming out quite so pungently at Sandwich on Saturday. All you have planned to say, so far as I have seen it, is very fine and beautiful (perhaps too eulogistic) — it is true and right; but I am thinking whether there is any necessity of stating the position on the silver question quite so pointedly, as against the fight our party are making in Ohio and elsewhere, with free coinage in their platform. Ought they to be unnecessarily embarrassed by the statements of Democratic differences; and do we want now and on such an occasion to excite their resentment?

Much mischief is going on in these days. Without the remotest shade of authority, I am told that it is announced I am to make speeches in Ohio during the pending campaign. I shall probably not go. Then the old cry will be started again, that I am selfish and not willing to help anyone but myself, and that I do not care for party success, etc. It will be nuggets for those who are putting up such jobs, if they can add to my refusal the fact that one of the planks in the Ohio platform was attacked at a gathering of my friends.

So far as this hint is personal to myself, I care nothing for the consequences suggested, but it is worth a thought for other reasons. Don't change anything on account of what I have written, unless you plainly see it is best. If you do change anything, I think the change should not amount to total abandonment but only to a toning down and reduction in strength of statements. I send to Mr. Quincy, by the mail which takes this, the manuscript of what I mean to say. I do not like it a single bit, but it must answer. Perhaps you had better read it early. Maybe after that you will think something about 'pearls before swine' in connection with the handsome things you propose to say to, and 'of and concerning' the author of it.

I expect to join you on your train when it arrives here. Cannot Mr. Joseph Jefferson do so also? Please telegraph me if he can, as soon as possible. You know, I suppose, that I shall be accompanied by a friend from New York.

To D-CADY HERRICK

Gray Gables, *July* 26, 1891

I have read and re-read your letter, and am very sorry to say that I cannot bring myself to your way of thinking. In the first place, I have no doubt that all the talk in the newspapers (originating all outside of Ohio) is for the express purpose of arousing a demand for me in Ohio[1] and affording, in case of my refusal to go, an opportunity to abuse me as selfish, etc. I am bound to be abused anyway — if not for one thing for another; but I don't want to do anything from the fear of it.

I have never been a stump speaker and do not think I should be a success in that rôle. If I went to Ohio I don't see how I could avoid going to Iowa and speaking in Massachusetts. I don't believe in speaking in a campaign when I cannot approve the entire platform. I think if I went to Ohio and ignored the silver plank or repudiated it, the candidates' chances would, if affected at all, be more hurt than helped by the insistence more than ever, on the part of the enemy, to bring it to the front, and by the resentment of the Democrats who had that plank adopted.

There would, therefore, in my judgment be no compensation for the harm I would do myself in the eyes of many good and sincere friends by doing a thing of very questionable propriety and very doubtful consistency, and a thing which would savor, in the sight of the people, of seeking after convention advantage. I doubt the expediency of putting too many eggs in the Ohio basket. Our past experience does not encourage us in that course.

To tell the truth, I think putting an ex-President on the stump in a State campaign is a poor use to put him to and that it is sure to be misrepresented and taken advantage of. It's rather against the ideas and traditions of our people. Lastly, there is a family and domestic reason why I am not willing to promise to leave home on a speechmaking trip at the time when I should probably be required to do so.

I have great faith in your judgment and dislike to differ with you or make the work you have undertaken more difficult. But I feel so sure that I am right in this matter, I would if I dared ask you to aid me in avoiding importunities on the subject. I suppose there will be tomorrow a sort of an interview sent out by Associated Press, in which I have something to say about this matter. I feel very badly and blue — for the only thing in the world I am timid about is the charge of ingratitude and want of appreciation for kindnesses done me.

[1] In Ohio James E. Campbell, who had succeeded Foraker as governor in 1890, was facing a stiff battle for re-election against William McKinley, and wished Cleveland's help. McKinley was elected.

To MICHAEL D. HARTER [1]

Gray Gables, *August* 3, 1891

Your letter came when I was away from home and I had no opportunity to answer it before the meeting of your convention. If I could have done so, I know I should not have easily replied to your suggestion. I will not conceal from you that I am much disappointed with the Ohio platform, though I suppose it is no affair of mine. Somehow the outlook depresses me, for I want very much to see Campbell re-elected as a recognition of his sturdiness and honest efforts to give his State a good clean administration. I hope all will go well and that he will be elected. I cannot rid myself of an idea that the stump is no place for an ex-President — at any rate in a State campaign. I may be wrong about this but the notion is fully fixed in my mind at present. I think too that the silver people who were strong enough to force the free-coinage plank would resent the importation of a speaker who has put himself on record as unequivocally as I have in opposition, in present circumstances, to free, unlimited, and independent silver coinage. I most earnestly hope I shall not be asked to make speeches in Ohio during this canvass.

To RICHARD WATSON GILDER

Gray Gables, *August* 12, 1891

I am much obliged to you for the opportunity afforded me to read the editorial you sent me, which I return with this. Isn't it strange that neither of the political parties see the expediency as well as rectitude of stepping boldly and defiantly to the front? We shall see what we shall see, and I think it will be a little queer.

To RICHARD WATSON GILDER

Gray Gables, *August* 18, 1891

I have read the clippings you sent me with satisfaction, and I return the same to you with this. I have frequently noticed lately the tendency to make less of the silver issue in the Southern papers, as well as in some of those published in the West. I am confidently looking for a return to common sense and conservative ideas in certain quarters. Some people, I think, will be directed to a proper frame of mind by appeals to their

[1] Michael Daniel Harter (1846–96), a merchant of Mansfield, Ohio, served in the House of Representatives 1891–95, and became a favorite of Cleveland's.

reason. Others will better appreciate the arguments which a thorough thrashing suggest.

In the meantime a great deal is going on among machine politicians; and plans are on foot to rid the Democratic party of the *incubus* which in the seclusion of Buzzards Bay ought, according to their usual calculation, to be counted as perfectly harmless. If there were not features and incidents connected with all this which are exasperating and shamefully beastly, the entire manifestation would be only ludicrous.

I have a reel and rod here belonging to you, which if we don't see you very soon I will send to you. We are expecting you over; and all send love to all.

To DANIEL S. LAMONT

Gray Gables, *August 30,* 1891

Your letter of a recent date came duly to hand and I thank you for it and the clippings accompanying it. Someone sent me some items from the *Courier* a few weeks ago similar to those you sent me.

All this is very well, but I do not notice in your letter any reference to the visit which we thought you had promised to make us and which we have been confidently calculating upon. I know it is not always easy to break away from family and other pleasant surroundings to make visits, but I hope it is not necessary to tell you how delighted we would be to see you here and to assure you that we will do all that is possible for your enjoyment. We shall not leave here until the middle of September or a little later. Perhaps you will be leaving Sorrento early enough to permit you and Mrs. Lamont and the children to stop a little while with us on your way home. There is no politics in the atmosphere of this place, and we can promise you that you will not be annoyed at all with the anxiety of anyone here on political subjects or movements. The trout season closes September 1, but I believe we can find good bass fishing and *smooth* and successful sea fishing....

To WILSON S. BISSELL

Gray Gables, *September 9,* 1891

I understand you are at home again. The last time you wrote me, you suggested that I should do something to head off, if possible, any outside pecuniary interference in Erie County political movements. It so happened that shortly after the receipt of your letter I was, in the most propitious manner, thrown in the intimate company of a former business partner and present close friend of the aspirant for the governorship you mentioned. He promised to write a strong letter in the tone of your suggestion. I have seen him within a few days and he said he wrote the letter and received a very satisfactory reply thanking him for the hint, etc.

I received some clippings you sent me concerning the contest in Buffalo. It seems to me that the plans of Mr. Sheehan are too bold and barefaced to receive the approval of the members of our party there. I have been utterly amazed by the extent to which the attempt has been pushed to supersede all pretence of fairness and popular freedom by arbitrary and personal methods. I do not believe it will do.

We shall return to New York the last of next week after spending a delightful vacation here....

To OSCAR S. STRAUS

New York, *September* 27, 1891

I have a suspicion that you had much to do with the formation of the silver plank in the platform adopted at Saratoga. I am so well satisfied indeed that you thus merit my thanks as a citizen who loves the honor of his country and as a Democrat who loves the integrity of his party, that I desire to tender them in this frank informal manner.

To GEORGE F. PARKER

New York, *October* 3, 1891

A few minutes after midnight last night a little, strong healthy girl arrived at our home.[1] I am not of course anxious that it should be treated as a matter of public interest, but I should like the *Evening Post* people to know — to the end that if they desire to do so they may announce it this afternoon. Such a course might serve to embarrass such Sunday morning papers as might contemplate making an exclusive sensation of it.

To MRS. RICHARD WATSON GILDER

New York, *October* 3, 1891 (telegram)

Mother and daughter doing well. Our little girl came last night.

[1] Later named Ruth Cleveland.

To GEORGE S. HORNBLOWER

New York, *October* 6, 1891

I scarcely do anything just now but read the kindest messages of congratulation and receive in every possible way manifestations of the kindness which pervades the people of the land. And yet nothing has come near touching me so much as the incident of today relating to the gift [1] your little daughter sent to mine. I do not know why you did not leave the doll with me. Nothing could have been more dear to the mother than the doll which a little girl, *and your daughter*, was willing to give up to our new baby.

I do not want your child to feel that her gift was not valued for what it was worth. It meant so much to her that it means a very great deal to us. I wish we could have the doll and that its precious little donor could receive our heartfelt thanks, with the assurance that when our child first plays with a doll it shall be with the one she gave her. Of course if we are to have it, it must be in the exact shape it was in when I saw it today.

To DANIEL S. LAMONT

New York, *October* 13, 1891

I cannot get the Massachusetts matter out of my head. The more I think of it the more I am convinced of the importance of helping that canvass.[2] I saw Mr. Grace today and he said he would gladly do something and that he would like to be called on to contribute. I don't know how under Heaven I can afford it, but if a fund is started $250 may be put in for me. I will not speak to Whitney about it, but I wish you would if you have not — $10,000 to pay the taxes for our poor voters there, who without such payment will be disfranchised, would, I believe, insure carrying a State as important to us now and in the future as any State can possibly be.

I am so poor myself that I don't think it looks well for me to ask other people to give. If anything is done it must be done at once and certainly not later than the 20th of this month.

---

[1] A much-tousled and soiled doll, which Hornblower, one of the leading attorneys of New York City, had carried away with him.

[2] In this election, which resulted in the choice of William E. Russell as governor, the tariff had been made the principal issue.

To GOVERNOR WILLIAM E. RUSSELL

New York, *October* 16, 1891

I am sorry to say that all calculation or hope of my being in Boston before election must be abandoned. I see plainly enough now that the plan discussed a little when you were here cannot well be carried out. I wrote to Quincy last night to say to him that something more would be done in the direction desired when I saw you last. I did not, however, write him anything touching the Boston visit. I know it is not necessary for me to express the deep interest I take in the success of your ticket, for you know already that I regard it as important to all the people of the land.

To WILSON S. BISSELL

New York, *October* 21, 1891

The house is perfectly quiet — at ten o'clock. I have just been up to find my wife and child sleeping and the nurse too. Only our mother-in-law awake.

I feel an impulse to write to you. And I feel too that unless I make an effort, I shall write in a strange fashion to you. I, who have just entered the real world, and see in a small child more of value than I have ever called my own before; who puts aside, as hardly worth a thought, all that has gone before — fame, honor, place, everything — reach out my hand to you and fervently express the wish — the best my great friendship for you yields — that in safety and in joy you may soon reach my estate.[1]

I think a great deal about you and your dear wife just now. I think a little of your anxiety and suspense, a little of the cloud that must pass over her, but a great deal of the joy and happiness that will come to both of you when anxiety and suspense are over and the cloud is past.

Give our love to Mrs. Bissell, and let me know when you are made happy.

To JOHN McCONVILL [2]

New York [no date; probably late October, 1891]

I am a staunch believer in the doctrine of Home Rule, and have not failed to appreciate the labors in the cause of the man whose services you

---

[1] Bissell, who had married Louisa F. Sturges in 1889, was also expecting his first child.

[2] This letter was written to be read at a memorial meeting for Charles S. Parnell, who died this year.

propose to commemorate. For what he accomplished and sought to accomplish for Home Rule, he deserved to be honored by all those who love a free and representative government; but his aim and purposes had their rise so completely in patriotism, and his unselfish love for his countrymen was so conspicuous and disinterested, that the reverence and devotion due to the memory of a patriot must always be associated with his name. The influence of his example surely ought not to be lost upon those who take up his work, to which he so thoroughly consecrated his efforts and aspirations.

To WILLIAM C. ENDICOTT

New York, *November* 3, 1891

I was at Gray Gables last Saturday and saw that the vines you kindly sent to us had been set out according to my directions. I hope and expect that they will do well and add much to the beauty of the place. Please accept our joint thanks for your kindness in giving them to us.

I had a nice evening with the young Democrats of Boston after my visit to Buzzards Bay. I was delighted with the spirit and vim they were exhibiting in the campaign and I am sure they deserve victory, for which I am praying today. I have thought, in the main, that we should certainly carry New York, but at times I have very uncomfortable misgivings. It is settled at this moment one way or the other.

Mrs. Cleveland and Ruth have gone out riding. If they were here they both would send much love to you and Mrs. Endicott. You know how sincerely mine goes with this.

WILLIAM C. ENDICOTT *to* CLEVELAND

Salem, *November* 7, 1891

Your pleasant and *cheerful* letter of the 3d instant was duly received. You were then in the dark as to the result of the election. How satisfactory it is! New York, Iowa, Massachusetts, while the loss of Ohio (uncertain at the best) perhaps will bring our Silver Democrats to their senses.[1] We did not do as well with the Legislature as we hoped, for both houses are against us: last year the Senate was a tie. The State is so gerrymandered that it will take a long time to make headway against such odds. But great changes are going on, and for the first time I have

---

[1] In New York the Democrats elected the Flower-Sheehan ticket in the fall of 1891, Flower getting a plurality of almost 50,000 and Sheehan of less than 35,000.

personal knowledge of changes among a class of Republicans hitherto very hostile to us. The cities are becoming rapidly Democratic, being equally divided between the parties. Salem has always been a Republican stronghold. In 1888 Russell was defeated by something over 700 majority — in 1889 by 350 — in 1890 by 200, and this year by only 11 votes.

I was sorry that I could not see you when in Boston, had I known that you were there on Sunday I should have seen you; but I was told you were to return to New York by the night train. You did good service here, and gave great pleasure and satisfaction to the Democrats. We never have had so well organized a party before, and the credit is due to the young men, to Burrell, Quincy, Matthews, Williams, Hoar [1] and others too numerous to name — and, what is quite a novelty in politics, they are fair, honest, and just, as well as able.

I am glad to hear that the vines arrived in good order. If any of them fail let me know, as we have an abundance of them. I also have quite a number of young catalpa trees; they too thrive vigorously, I know, at the Cape. I will send you a few in April. They flower abundantly in June, and are very fine when in bloom....

To E. C. BENEDICT

New York, *November* 9, 1891

If you have nothing else to do tonight and want to play a *game or two* of cribbage, I have a board and a pack of cards here and a few shiners.[2] Mrs. Cleveland says, 'I wish Helen would come with him.'

To E. C. BENEDICT

New York, *November* 21, 1891

I've got ten more shiners. If you will come up tonight and can win them, you can put them in the contribution box tomorrow.

To E. C. BENEDICT

New York, *November* 30, 1891

When you left my house on the 26th instant I was two shiners in your debt. On the 28th at your house this indebtedness was increased to eight shiners. I send you with this seven shiners and one dull dime.

[1] Josiah Quincy of Boston, George Fred Williams of Boston, and Sherman Hoar of Concord were the most important men in this list.

[2] That is, bright new dimes used for wagers in cribbage.

When you see the latter coin it will indicate to you that I have at last been obliged to draw upon my reserve fund. Considering the time and effort you have expended in bringing about this result, I hope that you will find satisfaction in its accomplishment.

I beg to suggest, however, that a few of the shiners which came originally from you were spent by me for carfare.

To WILSON S. BISSELL

Lakewood, N.J., *December* 4, 1891

I read this morning the account of your so-called Democratic primaries and the astounding fact that your vote was rejected. I don't think there ever was a more discouraged and disgusted Democrat than I am today.

Hill's performances in Albany, the late proceedings of the State Committee, the squabble for Speaker in Washington,[1] and the general recklessness of our party everywhere almost convince me that we are either rushing to overwhelming defeat or the people are heedless of everything political that will happen. Was it for this that we braved temporary defeat in order that we might stand on principle? And what becomes of all our fine promises to the people? If we have much more of the work that is now disgracing us, and the people do not resent it, I shall think the people are not worth saving or serving.

I still think Mills will be elected Speaker and with that we may pull ourselves together. Without that I feel that everything is cut loose.

To GOVERNOR WILLIAM E. RUSSELL

Lakewood, N.J., *December* 9, 1891

The proposition you make in your letter of the 4th instant was laid before me some time ago. I was not at all inclined to entertain it then and for additional and different reasons I am in no mood to do so now.

In my present depressed condition I would not undertake to give my assurance as to the present position and tendency of the Democratic party so far as they are dependent upon the influences and men apparently controlling it in the atmosphere I breathe. I am afraid that my confidence in the organization has led me to make all the guarantees to

---

[1] Cleveland had hoped to see Roger Q. Mills of Texas (1842–1911), who had served in Congress since 1873, and was loyal to him and tariff reform, elected Speaker; instead, the prize went to Charles F. Crisp of Georgia (1845–96), who had entered Congress in 1883, was a prominent free-silver man, and supported Hill for the Presidential nomination.

the good people of the land that I am willing to be answerable for. My faith in the principles of our party and in the sincerity of our rank and file is as strong as ever; but in what manner these principles and men. are to be represented or *mis*represented, which makes the position of the party, I am, until further developments, unwilling to assert. I hope, my dear friend, you fully understand my meaning and motive. The detail of this note is for you alone.

To WILSON S. BISSELL

Lakewood, N.J., *December* 12, 1891

Occupying the position I do in my personal relations to political affairs, and in my complete lack of political ambition, I do not feel that I ought to bother you or other friends with my views on the situation. And yet it is hard to refrain from doing so occasionally, in view of the fact that I have every possible desire to see our party succeed on decent honest lines, and have a strong disinclination to being exhibited at the tail end of a procession which means the betrayal of the principles we profess and the deception of the people. It seems very ridiculous for the State of New York to claim any sympathy with the professed aims of the National Democracy, and to still be content to follow the lead of Hill, Murphy [1] & Co.

Sheehan has been boasting in Washington of the unanimity of New York for Hill. Governor Francis of Missouri told me day before yesterday that Sheehan told him that Hill would have every delegate with possibly the exception of six. He had in his pocket, and displayed, a caucus ticket used at Buffalo headed 'Cleveland ticket.' Dickinson of Michigan was here today and said he heard Sheehan asserting about the same thing which Francis reported. I enclose you a letter I received yesterday from Niagara County.

It seems to me that the only way for a decent Democrat to live in New York and maintain his self-respect, and at the same time stand by his party, is to break this thing up. I believe it could be done by creating an understanding between the districts outside of New York City and McLaughlin [2] and the Kings County Democracy. This is of course for

[1] Edward Murphy, Jr., a wealthy brewer of Troy (1836–1911), who was a political partner of Hill and the Tammany leaders, and who had been chairman of the Democratic State Committee since 1887.

[2] Hugh McLaughlin was political boss of the Brooklyn Democracy.

you alone at present. I wish you would turn it over and tell me what you think of it.

To L. Clarke Davis

I am at fault in neglecting to acknowledge before this your letter of a few days ago, and to thank you for it and the extract from your paper which you enclosed. Such mischievous publications as that which you corrected seem to be just now the stock in trade of that sweet-scented journal the *World*, and are intended primarily to maintain its reputation as a sensation and scandal monger, and secondarily to annoy its victims.

Your letter of yesterday came this morning. When I wrote the letter to Canton, Ohio, I was very careful to *write plainly;* and I also enclosed a separate note to the addressee of my letter, telling him that I was tired of seeing letters I wrote, made ridiculous by *incorrect publication*, and asking him to take a little pains to have this latest production printed as it was written — if it was printed at all. I was amazed to see afterwards in the newspapers, that I had intimated that our countrymen ought not to be 'deceived through blunders' — though I wrote 'deceived through blindness.'[1] I am not inclined to find much fault with this, and am not sure but the printer was nearer right than I was — since I have lately occasionally had a fear that the people with whom I affiliate politically, as well as those whom we ought to try to convert, are as apt to be deceived by the 'blunders' of Democratic leaders as by their 'blindness.'

The editorial you sent me in your last letter, has a whole lot of sense in it — necessarily so because you wrote it. If I were to make any comments there would be two of them: 1st, I think the tariff question, in its present situation, involves something more than mere business policy. It seems to me that it has a decided moral aspect and cannot be separated from the kind of morality which a great and just government ought to teach its people by example and precept. 2d, When we can inaugurate a system of protection which 'coddles none and protects all,' I want to talk further with you on this subject, with a bottle of whiskey and two tumblers in our immediate vicinity.

These things will do in their way; but of course you understand that you have an engagement to fish with me next summer. There must be

---

[1] All Cleveland's letters were written in longhand, and many were not too easily legible.

no mistake about that — whatever becomes of the tariff question. With much love from all our household to you and all yours.

To E. C. BENEDICT
New York, *December* 18, 1891

I would go to your office to see you if I did not fear I would interrupt you in a busy hour.

You have spoken of my engagement to 'preach' in Brooklyn next Monday evening; and in connection with that circumstance, have with characteristic courtesy invited me to spend the night at your house. I do not see how that can be done without making you a great deal of trouble, with almost no compensation — even in the way of 'shiners.' I expect to 'preach' in the city of New York on the evening of the 8th of January, when I believe I could go to you much better. I want to break into No. 10 [1] very much indeed some night. I shall stay at Lakewood tomorrow, leaving here today by the 1:30 train. I will be in my office as early as half-past ten o'clock Monday and I wish I dared ask you to come and see me between that hour and half-past three....

To DR. JOSEPH D. BRYANT
Lakewood, N.J., *December* 31, 1891

I put my hand on my heart and simply say 'I thank you.' I am quite overcome by this last demonstration of your kindness and friendship. I can add nothing — unless it be the assurance that hereafter on our many cruises in the *Helen* — and I hope they will be very many — we shall not hunt among the lunch to see if William has forgotten to put *it* in, nor shall you ever have to ask the second time for 'a light.' One other thing I may say: I'll have matches without too much brimstone on the ends.

The Clevelands are at present the healthiest and happiest family in the world; and the entire 'gang' send lots of love to you and Mrs. Bryant and Florence.

To RICHARD WATSON GILDER
Lakewood, N.J., *December* 31, 1891

Your Christmas present to me came from the city here, only yesterday. I am very much delighted with it. Do you know, my 'old partner,' that

---

[1] Benedict lived at 10 West 51st Street; late in 1892 Cleveland removed to No. 12, the house next door.

when I am hunting in the past for pleasant things, I always stop and take a long retrospective rest on the *Allie*[1]? Of course you — sick or well — are the chief figure in the foreground of my view: and next comes Captain Ryder. This picture helps me to fill in all the details. The old man looks as though he was considering the propriety of 'taking a kind o' slant and going around agin.'

You know how fully I appreciate your thoughtfulness and kindness in sending me a memento I prize so much.

To DANIEL S. LAMONT

Lakewood, N.J., *February* 8, 1892

I returned last Wednesday evening and though I should have been glad to see you, I was actually pleased to learn that you had gone to Old Point for rest and recuperation. Knowing you as well as I do I am entirely satisfied that you did not start a bit too soon. I hope you will remain until you are entirely reinstated in health. I spent a couple of hours in New York on Thursday, but saw no one but Parker. Today I have been there with about the same result. I have not seen Whitney and really know but little of what is going on in political matters except what I see in the papers. You know, of course, that is a good deal; and I am impressed with the belief that the meeting of protestants to be held this week [2] will be a very large one and that it *may* have a far-reaching result. I have no doubt you see the papers and are posted. I do not expect to go to the city again this week. One of the *World* editors was here to see me Saturday and had a good deal to say. He wanted me to say something for him to publish, but I did not see that it was in any way profitable.

We had a good time in the South and I wish you had been with us. The Philadelphia people, Harrity,[3] etc., did not come as they expected to today. The Adjutant-General of the State (McClelland) died. I shall go to Ann Arbor for the 22d. I wish you were here and wanted to go with me. I have done nothing yet by way of preparation, but expect to begin tomorrow if I can bring myself to it. Mrs. Cleveland says, 'give my love to the Colonel.' The baby is well and as happy and jolly as she can be.

[1] The fishing vessel owned by Cleveland's friend Captain Ryder in Buzzards Bay.

[2] Hill's friends had called a 'Snap convention' for February 22, 1892, to elect national delegates. Cleveland's friends thereupon called an 'anti-snap convention' which met in Syracuse at the end of May to elect a contesting delegation.

[3] William F. Harrity of Philadelphia, one-time postmaster of that city and nominal manager of Cleveland's campaign in 1892.

To L. CLARKE DAVIS

Lakewood, N.J., *February* 17, 1892

I wish you had been with us in Louisiana, though the shooting was not the best in the world and the fishing was *nil*.

I thank you for the clippings you have lately sent me and [the] copy [of the] letters. A certain gentleman is, I think, much mistaken when he supposes (if he does) that the movement to which he refers is one of Grace & Company. I know but little of its details and inner manifestations but I am told that it means a great deal. As I look back seven years and recall the steps by which the present condition in this State has been reached and then consider the boldness and utter disregard of all party decency which characterize present movements and intentions, I am utterly amazed, and shall be more so if it turns out that the end of the rope has not been reached. Republicans in Pennsylvania have had experiences which may permit them to comprehend the situation, but I know the people in no other State at present can. I am not involved in the way of personal feeling except so far as I may have cause to be ashamed of the morals of my party.

I am going to Ann Arbor on Saturday to talk to the students of the University there on the 22d. Perhaps I will send you in confidence an advance copy of my 'remarks.' It is not in type yet. Please give my affectionate regards to Mrs. Davis and Nora.

To W. H. BLACK

Lakewood, N.J., *February* 20, 1892

I will not attempt to conceal the gratification afforded me by the message you transmit from the Cleveland Club of Atlanta. I have received so many manifestations of friendliness from the people of Atlanta that I cherish toward them the warmest gratitude and liveliest affection.[1]

I cannot say that I am certain I deserve all the laudation contained in the resolutions of your club. I can say, however, that I find a sense of great satisfaction in the reflection that I have been permitted to aid somewhat in restoring to the people in a large section of our country their standing and position in our common American citizenship — not nominally and barrenly, but substantially and potentially. For whatever I

[1] A strong Hill movement was on foot in Georgia; but Hoke Smith and John B. Gordon of Atlanta led a stronger Cleveland movement, and on May 18, 1892, Cleveland captured most of the Georgia delegates to the Democratic National Convention.

have done in this direction I have abundant reward, in the prosperity of your people, which doubles our national prosperity, in the cheerful co-operation of your people, which insures a lasting national brotherhood, and in the appreciation by your people of all that has been done in their behalf.

After all, I look upon their beneficent accomplishments as resulting from the appreciation of true Democratic doctrines; and I believe that one who, in public place, submits himself to their guidance, will find it easy to do justice and to subserve the interests of all his fellow-countrymen.

To WILSON S. BISSELL

Lakewood, N.J., *March* 1, 1892

Confidential

I want to thank you more fully than it has been heretofore done, on behalf of our entire household, for the very fine hams you sent us. They are kind o' like old times and we are enjoying them very much. That picture of your baby is the cutest thing I have seen in a long time. I think she looks very much like her father and it seems to me you have not heretofore — at least when I have been along — made half enough fuss over her.

I arrived home [1] Thursday morning — quite tired and with my hand a little lame but feeling pretty well. My trip has started up a number of invitations from colleges, etc., in different parts of the country, but I intend to 'stay put' now for a while. I had a very warm invitation from Yale this morning.

The protesting movement seems to move on without much abatement. It's wonderful how well the situation in New York is understood in every corner of the land. If things go on I shall not be surprised if Tammany Hall hears some very plain language next June. The question in my mind now is whether it would not be better for the Convention in May to send a *committee* to Chicago instead of *delegates* claiming admission. I think little or nothing is being done of a practical character in New Jersey, Indiana, or Connecticut. These States, with New York, it is calculated will constitute the stock in trade of the forces and influences which called the midwinter convention.

Within the last day or two I have heard quite a little talk about my

[1] From Ann Arbor, Michigan.

doing something. Some want me to write a letter denying that I have withdrawn, etc. Others rather hint that I should do something still more pronounced. A letter might be carefully written that would steer clear of anything like self-assertion and which might still plainly present the fact that I did not intend, for personal reasons and to satisfy personal inclinations, to abandon those enlisted in a cause to which they deem me useful.

My personal desire you fully understand; but I am going to tell you how I think the matter may progress. Congress will do about all the fool things it can, nearly or quite (so far as they can) committing the party to the silver craze and puttering with tariff reform until it is tired and sick as an issue. When the Convention meets, the representatives of the party will perhaps see the condition — that they have nearly lost the only issues upon which there is the least hope of carrying the country. If they do they will see that they must have a man who in his person and record represents exactly the things so nearly thrown away and the direct opposite of all that they have tried to do. If such a man is nominated, the Democratic masses and the honest men of non-Democratic affiliations will feel so relieved and so happy in the prospect of political salvation that an enthusiasm will be furnished to the campaign that will be irresistible.

If matters should take on such a complexion, present politics would be brushed aside without any ceremony. A good sound new man might just fit the situation.

The people in the Eastern States, especially Massachusetts, are very much roused and I should not be surprised if they spoke quite emphatically very soon. Every man in this State ought to be well considered.

To Justice L. Q. C. Lamar

Lakeview, N.J., *May* 1, 1892

First of all I must tell you how pleased I am with the report I have from the press and other sources concerning your improved health. I hope and pray that you are on the road to complete recovery, and great public usefulness.[1] You will not, I think, consider me effusive if I say that it seems to me that the love of friends ought to make you well — though I do not exactly see how this result is worked out. I need not say how delighted I was to hear from you again in your own hearty, kindly

---

[1] Justice Lamar died in Vineville, Georgia, on January 23 following.

style. And I was especially touched with your letter, written, as it was, when you were so sick.

I have within the last few months passed through much that has been trying and perplexing to me. The office of President has not to me personally a single allurement. I shrink from everything which another canvass and its result involves. I know what another election means, and I know as well the dark depths that yawn at my comfort or my desire. My discomforts arise from a sense of duty to honest people and devoted friends. I am alone with my own thoughts and with the apparent trust and confidence of my countrymen. Am I mistaken in all this, and are my country and my party prepared to discharge me from service? One thing I know. Forces are at work which certainly mean the complete turning back of the hands on the dial of Democracy, and the destruction of party hopes. Is it ordained that I am to be the instrument through which Democratic principles can be saved — whether party supremacy immediately awaits us or not? If folly is to defeat us in any event, ought I to be called upon to place myself under the falling timber? This last consideration smacks a little of care for self, which perhaps ought to be discarded.

You shall know, my dear friend, my inmost thoughts. I shall be obedient to the call of my country and my party. Whatever happens no one shall say that I refused to serve in time of evil, or abandoned those whom I have been instrumental in calling to the field. If I am given my discharge I shall thank God most fervently. I can easily be disposed of, either by the selection of a candidate more available, or by the adoption of a campaign policy on the financial question which I am not willing to further. In the first case, I shall be a happy helper; in the second, I shall sadly await the announcement of a party defeat which will be predetermined.

Our Southern friends, if they persist, will be left alone with their free-coinage heresy. The West is slipping away from their side. The danger is that another Southern idea, and a charge of heedlessness for the public safety on the financial question, will do service in the place of the memories of the Civil War. The question is often and justifiably put by friendly Southerners, 'Can Cleveland carry New York?' The answer is ready as to Cleveland, or any other man, if the Democracy is at all weak on the coinage question. As one who loves his country, and believes that her interest is bound up in Democratic supremacy, I am most uncomfortable and unhappy in the fear that the South will not see till too late the danger of their marring all.

If I should read this letter, I hardly think I should send it; but it goes laden with affection, and the most tender memories.

To E. C. BENEDICT

New York, *May* 3, 1892

Strictly confidential

I see in the papers this morning an account of how Bill Eaton and his friends called a convention (at Norwalk, I believe) and elected fourteen delegates to the State Convention, and that they propose to have the aforesaid 'Bill' preside over the last-named convention.

If you are as much surprised as I am by this news, I think it would not be amiss for you to let Mr. Davis Clive understand that you are watching movements in your State, by sending him a laconic — *very* laconic — expression of your surprise.

To MICHAEL D. HARTER

New York, *May* 7, 1892

All my friends (and you are certainly one) know how I feel about the Presidential nomination in the mere *personal* phase of it. But when I make up my mind to retire and not permit my friends and the people to longer consider my candidacy, such men as you will know it first; and will not need the information gabbled by busy-bodies who go about and tell what impression was left on their alleged minds, by something I may have said or that they think I said.

To LOUIS R. EHRICH

Lakewood, N.J., *May* 8, 1892

If I have not until now answered your letter of March 25, and I am not entirely sure whether I have or not, it must be attributed to the fact that I did not know what to say on its receipt, and to the further fact that soon thereafter the position of the silver question was so changed that the suggestion contained in your letter lost much of its immediate importance. The action of Congress on this subject and the declarations contained in recent State platforms cannot fail to reinforce your faith and mine in the potency of reason with the American people. These things make me love my countrymen, if possible, more than ever. What a shame it is that such a good people should ever be made the victims of demagogues. I want to thank you most sincerely for sending me your book on *The Question of Silver* and your late speech on the same subject. You know I regard your plain way of dealing with this matter as having had much to do with correcting popular misapprehension.

To Dr. Joseph D. Bryant

Lakewood, N.J., *May* 10, 1892

I was glad to hear that the rods arrived at your house safely — though I did not see how it could be otherwise, for I attended to the matter myself. Your statement that you had not heard from the Colonel disappointed me, for I certainly thought when I saw or heard from you I should hear from him. I am extremely anxious to know how he is getting on.

It has been an astonishing thing to me that the changes in the Health Board have not attracted more public attention and comment; and I have felt like congratulating you that such was the case. I suppose when the time comes the members of the Board will have to take their turn. I am glad for your sake that Dr. Janeway [1] shot off his charge in the *Sun*, where the public do not look for anything in the way of honest reform. I think you and Jeremy Martin are not very well matched, but I suppose you know exactly what you are about.

We are as well as we can possibly be; but as Mrs. Cleveland says she intends to write you tomorrow, I will leave details on that subject to her after confessing, as I hereby do, that in the matter of the baby's vaccination there is a bare possibility that you knew better what to do than I did.

If we carry out present plans, we shall move from here a week from next Monday the 23d, and stay in New York a few days before starting for Gray Gables. Some night this week, after Tuesday, when I am engaged for a dinner, would be a good time for us to have our German.

---

[1] Dr. E. G. Janeway, who later assisted Dr. Bryant in the operation on Cleveland's jaw in 1893.

X

RENOMINATED AND RE–ELECTED

WITH surprisingly little difficulty, Cleveland was renominated at
Chicago on June 23, 1892. Hill had hoped that by bold and dramatic action he might first gain the New York and Georgia delegations, and then sweep other States into his net. But his 'snap
convention' in New York alienated a multitude of fair-minded Democrats, while in Georgia the Cleveland forces under Hoke Smith
utterly defeated him. When the Convention met, Tammany Hall
made a defiant stand against Cleveland, culminating in a memorable
two-o'clock-in-the-morning speech by Bourke Cockran just before
the voting began; but only one ballot was necessary. William C.
Whitney, who had been active at Chicago, was finally prevailed upon
to take charge of the campaign. He brought to the task all his usual
dash and fervor. The principal worry of the party leaders at first
was whether they could carry New York State in the face of Hill's
sulkiness and the covert hostility of Tammany. Always conciliatory,
Whitney made friendly approaches to the Hill-Tammany group —
to Richard Croker, Edward Murphy, Jr., of Troy, who was State
Chairman, and William C. Sheehan. He besought Cleveland to do
likewise, even writing a letter for him to send to Murphy; but
Cleveland refused to follow any such course. His native independence of spirit rebelled, while he felt that it would be treachery
to his Mugwump and 'anti-snapper' friends to take off his hat to
Tammany Hall. In the end he did nothing more than attend a
famous dinner-conference which Whitney arranged at the Victoria Hotel with Croker, Murphy, and Sheehan. Here he declined to
promise any patronage to the Hill-Sheehan group, and delivered an
ultimatum — if the regular Democratic organization of New York
refused to support him, he would give up the nomination. The up-
shot was half-hearted support on the part of Hill and Tammany.
All the circumstances of the campaign were favorable to Cleveland
and against Benjamin Harrison, the Republican nominee. Industrial
conditions were bad; the West was seething with discontent, and the
Populist party there cut heavily into Republican strength; an outburst of labor violence at Homestead, Pennsylvania, helped to
crystallize sentiment against some of the corporations which
profited from the Republican tariff; and in Illinois and Wisconsin
feeling on the parochial-school issue assisted the Democrats.

Cleveland won by a plurality of almost 400,000 in the popular vote, and had 277 electoral votes against Harrison's 145.

To WILLIAM F. VILAS

Lakewood, N.J., *May* 12, 1892

I cannot do less than say to you that some very warm friends think there should be a touching of elbows among those who think as you do on the Presidential question. This was spoken of particularly by Harrity of Pennsylvania the other day, evidently with the view of my suggesting it in other quarters.[1] I understand that Stevenson will soon be in Washington; Dickinson goes from Michigan, Harrity from Pennsylvania, Morss from Indiana, Frank James from New Hampshire, Doran, I believe, from Minnesota. McPherson can be trusted and quite likely will go from New Jersey; Matthews, mayor of Boston, and John E. Russell from Massachusetts; Haney, mayor of Providence, from Rhode Island; Smalley can tell who the right man is from Vermont, etc.

I am sticking to my text and doing nothing. I only write this because I think unless there is some recognition of each other throughout the country the good friends who are so devoted to me may get a little lonely and feel a little forlorn. I have had positively nothing to do with the May Convention movements except to commend the utmost discretion and moderation whenever I have had an opportunity. Neither side do much talking, and I see no indications of heat or rage.

I expect to go to Buzzards Bay the last of this month for the season. This will not look like insensibility or a lack of appreciation of the efforts of friends, will it? I don't want to be accused of that....

To A. K. McCLURE

New York, *May* 28, 1892

I was delighted to receive a copy of your book,[2] and shall enjoy reading connectively the recollections and incidents which I have occasionally

---

[1] There was a decided 'touching of elbows' by Cleveland's friends prior to the national convention. On June 9, 1892, Whitney held at his New York house a conference of a dozen leading Cleveland supporters, including William F. Harrity of Pennsylvania, S. E. Morss of Indiana, Josiah Quincy of Massachusetts, W. L. Wilson of West Virginia, Don Dickinson of Michigan, Francis Lynde Stetson of New York, and William F. Vilas of Wisconsin.

[2] *Recollections of Half a Century*. McClure was founder and editor of the Philadelphia *Times*.

glanced at in the *Times*. I thank you most sincerely for thus kindly remembering me.

I cannot but think that the perils attending the May Convention [1] are overestimated in some quarters. I am not in the council of the promoters of the movement, but judging from the character and motives of the men who will probably direct it, and their appreciation of the absolute necessity of coolness and discretion, I am led to hope that no disastrous consequences will flow from it. At any rate, I suppose the convention must be held and I expect delegates will be sent to Chicago; and I am very clear that the situation will be made worse by the expression of too much apprehension concerning the affair.

To WILLIAM C. ENDICOTT

New York, *May* 30, 1892

Your very hearty letter came to hand yesterday and I thank you for your kindness and thoughtfulness in sending the trees and shrubs to Gray Gables. The man there wrote me that they had arrived, but hearing nothing concerning them I thought they had been sent by a nurseryman with whom I had a contract to replace some dead ones which he had set out. They have been cared for and though probably not put in place yet, will be in a day or two. We go tomorrow to Gray Gables and I have been preparing to start, which has kept me up till it is now past two o'clock in the morning. I am exceedingly sorry that we shall not be here to see you, and then we have a truly wonderful BABY we want to show you; but we will wait until you return, when we hope you will look in on our summer home....

To CHARLES S. FAIRCHILD

Gray Gables, *June* 10, 1892

My vacation thus far has been spent principally in bed trying to worry out an unwelcome visitor in the shape of an attack of rheumatism. I have been the most of today 'up and around,' and consider myself pretty near right again. I want to congratulate you on the recent event at Syracuse, and compliment you on first-rate generalship.

[1] The anti-snapper convention.

To WILSON S. BISSELL

Gray Gables, *June* 11, 1892

I have been laid up with rheumatism ever since I arrived here and am only just around and able to write a little. It is a curious fact that your letter came yesterday just as I was about writing to you on the subject it embraced.

I am delighted to know that you are going to Chicago, for if my name is presented there, and there is any danger of my nomination, I shall feel very safe and comfortable if a few such good and discreet friends as you are on the spot.

In the first place, my dear fellow, I have no particular 'views' as to plan of action — at any rate, except in a very general way. There was to be a sort of conference in New York a day or two ago, but I have not heard what, if anything, was done. I am quite sure the details are receiving attention.

You may not understand and perhaps will not entirely approve the way the thing has drifted; but I have been fully convinced that nothing better could be done in this thing than to have Whitney pretty well to the front in the matter of management and organization. In point of fact, it has already gravitated to that point. Associated with him from New York State, I hope, will be Bissell, D-Cady Herrick, Tracy, Stetson and such others as are like-minded and are wise and useful. There will be a great many first-rate men among the May contestants, but I expect they will understand that they should not be too prominent in the counsels of my friends. You ought to be a means of communication between such counselling friends and the May people who go from Buffalo. I had a letter from Locke at the same time I received yours on this subject. I wish you would see him and tell him, as nearly as you think best, what the plan is and that plans in my behalf will probably be concocted in Whitney's headquarters, and intimate to him that they can be learned through you. Say to him, if you please, that I may not be able to write to him. If I do it will only be to ask him to confer with you.

I am thinking some of being in Boston after the first day of the Convention 'on the quiet' with a friend not at all related to politics and have any dispatches deemed necessary sent to him and signed in an assumed name. I have not matured that scheme yet, but if the newspapers are on the alert they can get any message sent to me here before it reaches me.

One reason why I hope the persons I have mentioned will work together is found in my anxiety about the platform of the Convention. Of course as a Democrat I want a good platform for the success of the party; and if I should chance to be in any way related to it, it must be sound — especially in the money plank. If the nomination to the Presidency passes by me, I shall be anything but disappointed or afflicted; but for the nomination as for anything else I cannot forego my opinions nor appear to shuffle or falter on the financial question. Now on this subject I shall feel like relying very much indeed on the judgment of yourself and Stetson and Tracy and Vilas and Quincy and such people.

I cannot write more. I hope that every friend of mine at the Convention will feel easy regarding me and my fate. While I want to do my duty to my party and the good people of the country, I am still perfectly sincere in saying that the result which would bring to me the greatest personal gratification would be the nomination of some other good man and good Democrat. And this is quite consistent with my great satisfaction and gratitude for all that is done for me.

STATEMENT TO THE PRESS [1]

Gray Gables, *June 22, 1892*

I should certainly be chargeable with dense insensibility if I were not profoundly touched by this new proof of the confidence and trust of the great party to which I belong and whose mandates claim my loyal obedience. I am confident that our fellow countrymen are ready to receive with approval the principles of true Democracy and I cannot rid myself of the belief that to win success it is only necessary to persistently and honestly advocate those principles.

Differences of opinion and judgment in Democratic Conventions are by no means unwholesome indications; but it is hardly conceivable in view of the importance of our success to the country and the party that there should be anywhere among Democrats any lack of harmonious and active efforts to win in the campaign which opens before us.

I have therefore no concern on that subject. It will certainly be my constant endeavor to deserve the support of every Democrat.

[1] Cleveland was nominated at dawn on June 22.

To E. C. BENEDICT

Gray Gables, *June 29,* 1892

I believe Mrs. Benedict has written Mrs. Cleveland saying that she cannot come to see us just now as we hoped. I wish you could come up Saturday night or Sunday and *bring Whitney with you.* I want to see him very much and if he wanted to have his coming kept quiet, the yacht would be such a nice quiet way to drop in.

I will write him tonight and simply say that if you ask him to come I hope he will do so.

If all this cannot be brought about I wish you would, if you can, tell me when you expect to come as I may want to go back with you.

To WILSON S. BISSELL

Gray Gables, *June 30,* 1892

I was delighted to receive your letter yesterday and thank you for it. I think the way you looked into my hand in the matter of dealing with certain parties is 'perfectly lovely,' as the ladies say.

I will not attempt to tell you even a small part of what is in my mind and heart in the way of admiration and gratitude for all that was done at Chicago. All was superb, and it was almost uncanny to sit here at the end of a wire and see and hear and feel and know it all as it transpired.

Of course my duty now is to be as good a candidate as possible and do all I can to aid success. I do not think Murphy[1] or Sheehan should be at all prominent in the campaign. In point of fact, I think neither of them nor any of that kind of thing should have the least direction of it.

But I do think — indeed I know — that Whitney should nominally if not really and actively be at the head of the committee to manage the national campaign. I have regarded it as exceedingly desirable on my own judgment, and the letters I have received within a few days, and the expressions I have heard made, convince me that it is more essential and vital to success than any one thing.

This brings me to the main purpose of this letter. I want you and all the men who worked with him at Chicago to write to him and insist upon his conducting the campaign or at least allowing the use of his name at

[1] Edward Murphy, Jr., who served five terms as head of the State Committee, and Lieutenant-Governor Sheehan, were as sulky as Senator Hill himself. They insisted upon being prominent in the State campaign, and there was serious danger that they would knife Cleveland. Murphy became United States Senator, 1893–99.

the head of the campaign organization. I expect to see him soon and will urge it as far as I can in decency, but I don't want him to feel, if he does it, that he is doing it entirely at my personal solicitation. Will you write him at once? I will immediately urge Dickinson and Vilas to do so. Some of the Boston people were here last Sunday and I suppose they have written already.

Someone told me you were suffering at Chicago from a fall. I hope nothing in any way serious has come of it. I don't see how your baby got 'them teeth.' Ours could have plenty of them, I suppose, if she wanted them, but she don't eat any roasted beef or things of that kind — so what's the use?

It may be that I shall go to New York soon. If I do I shall let you know — hoping I may see you there. The date of notification is not settled, but I suppose will be soon. Mack [1] of the Buffalo *Times* telegraphed me yesterday asking me when the sub-committee of which he is chairman could see me and I replied I'd notify him later — thinking I might see them when I was in New York. My own idea is that the notification need not be hurried. On the other hand, I am decidedly of the opinion that it should be delayed until things and people are a little more settled. I have never received so many and such warm congratulations, but thus far not one from any State official in New York and almost none from the Hill following. This is queer, and I think it will be a good thing to let them dwell awhile with their *alleged* reasons and consciences. God bless you and your dear wife and baby. We all send love to them and you. I hear Ruth crowing and carrying on now.

To WILLIAM F. VILAS

Gray Gables, *June 30*, 1892

Your letter received yesterday impressed me very solemnly and it has put many thoughts in my mind. I confess we have seen strange things of late and it seems that a higher than man's power must be taken into account if any explanation is reached.

I feel now that it is an exceedingly high duty to do all that is within legitimate human reach to win success in November. To this I shall address myself with all the intelligence and worldly wisdom I possess.

I am quite sure that the campaign can be influenced, if not controlled,

---

[1] Norman E. Mack (1858–1933), founder and editor of the Buffalo *Times* and long prominent in Democratic politics.

by forces and methods not usually known or much utilized. One thing, I hope, will not be urged upon me and that is trip-making and speech-making.[1] I believe the imagination of the people is in just the right condition regarding the nominee.

But really the point of this letter is to urge upon you the importance of Mr. Whitney's being put at the head of the Campaign Executive Committee or the National Committee. This also is a matter of sentiment and imagination as well as a matter of vital practical importance in my judgment. I am confirmed in my opinion by numerous letters lately received from hard-headed working and loyal Democrats.

I think he will not be entirely willing to take such a place, but if your judgment accords with mine I want you to write him a letter urging him to assume the position. If those who stood with him during the battle of Chicago insist that he shall take further responsibility in the conduct of the war I hardly think he can refuse. I have written to Bissell and Dickinson on this subject. Some of the Boston people were here a few days ago and were, without my prompting, very desirous and anxious that this end should be reached, and said they would write to Whitney urging it immediately they reached home. If you approve I hope you will not only write yourself, but instigate others who have influence to do so.

I want to see you very much, and if I go to New York soon (as I expect to) I shall notify you in the hope that you may run over.

To NORMAN E. MACK
Gray Gables, *July* 4, 1892 (telegram)

I would be glad to see you and your associates if they desire it any day this week if you will notify me in advance, but I am now prepared to fix upon the twentieth of July and the city of New York as the time and place, details to be arranged by a local committee, and Mayor Grant or Mr. Whitney may be consulted for information concerning them.

To MRS. MARY FROST ORMSBY
Gray Gables, *July* 6, 1892

Mrs. Cleveland has referred to me your letter informing her of the organization of a 'Frances Cleveland Influence Club.' It is by no means pleasant to dissent from the methods which sincere friends adopt when

---

[1] Cleveland made but one public appearance, his speech of acceptance in Madison Square Garden.

their efforts not only demonstrate their friendliness, but when they also seek to subserve the public good and are, therefore, engaged in a patriotic service. It is, however, impossible for us to approve the use of Mrs. Cleveland's name in the designation of clubs assigned to do political work. We trust you will not undervalue our objection, because it rests upon the sentiment that the name now sacred in the home circle as wife and mother may well be spared in the organization and operation of clubs created to exert political influence.

To REPRESENTATIVE MICHAEL D. HARTER

Gray Gables, *July* 7, 1892

I was very much touched by that portion of your recent letter which refers to your prospect of re-election, and by the fear you express that the path of duty may lead away from a continuance in public life. Do you know that I cannot help thinking that it will after all straighten out?

If the Democratic House of Representatives permits a free-silver bill to go to Mr. Harrison for his veto, those responsible for it will in my opinion stand a chance to gain the same splendid notoriety as the man who burned the temple of Diana.

To WILLIAM BACK

Gray Gables, *July* 11, 1892

I am almost ashamed to yield to your request to deny a statement so silly and absurd on its face as the one you send me. However, as this is the second application... I think it best to end the matter, so far as it is possible to do so, by branding the statement in all its details and in its spirit and intention as unqualifiedly and absolutely false.[1] I know Cardinal Gibbons, and know him to be a good citizen and a first-rate American, and that his kindness of heart and toleration are in striking contrast with the fierce intolerance and vicious malignity which disgrace some who profess to be Protestants. I know a number of members of the Presbyterian Church who were employed in the public service during my Administration, and I suppose there were many so employed.

I should be ashamed of my Presbyterianism if these declarations gave grounds of offence.

[1] A statement that Cardinal Gibbons had exerted pressure on Cleveland against the appointment of Protestants in certain branches of government service.

To SENATOR DANIEL W. VOORHEES [1]

Gray Gables, *July* 11, 1892

... I remember conversations with you during my residence in Washington, indicating how I felt about a continued incumbency in the Presidency. I doubt if you recall it, but I said once to you that I was willing 'to be the ploughboy,' and make way for another to harvest. I remember, too, how earnestly and with your big-hearted and peculiar generosity you antagonized the idea.... I am extremely anxious to be elected. I want to carry Indiana. I do not for a moment suppose I can do this without your help. I hope that you will give the ticket the benefit of your experience and familiarity with Indiana politics. I say I 'hope' you will do this. That is not the word I should have used. I ought to have said, I 'know' you will.

To GOVERNOR WILLIAM E. RUSSELL

Gray Gables, *July* 13, 1892

Your letter of the 11th instant is at hand and I have just received the invitation you refer to from the citizens of Gloucester. I should of course be glad to attend their celebration and we should consider a trip to your Magnolia home the pleasantest incident of the trip. The emergencies of the campaign are, however, so entirely beyond human calculation that I do not feel that I can make an engagement so long in advance.

Everything I hear about the canvass is encouraging, but I am aware that my information should be somewhat discounted. I am bothering myself a good deal concerning what I shall say at the notification next week. It seems to me something more is necessary in this case than the usual pretty and complimentary talk. I am troubled with the tariff plank and think our people invited a false issue when they denied the constitutionality of protection.

I expect to consult with Quincy tomorrow. I wanted to see you on the subject very much indeed, but did not feel justified in asking you down in this busy time for you.

---

[1] Voorhees (1827–97), a resident of Terre Haute, was one of the Democratic war-horses in Indiana; he had been elected to the Senate in succession to Oliver P. Morton, and sat there continuously from 1877 to a month before his death.

To R. R. BOWKER [1]

Gray Gables, *July* 15, 1892

Your note of July 4 was read with great satisfaction. I desire to thank you for the kind and hearty expressions which it contains. My judgment is all at sea on some of the topics which you suggest, but I have no doubt you yourself will be able to arrive at a very just and wise conclusion concerning them.

Mr. Winslow Warren of Boston, in a recent conversation, expressed considerable anxiety as to a certain class of independent voters who had not come so far over to the Democratic ranks as to be reached by Democratic agencies, but who he thought might be reached and kept in line through another independent organization. I was unable then, as I am now, to give an opinion at all valuable on that subject. I believe, however, a meeting of some of them has been held, and if I understand it rightly it has been determined that any organization made should be an exceedingly quiet, unostentatious one.

I have thought a good deal on the subject of the election of Senators by the people, but not enough to be certain that I have seen all the reasons which tell for or against the change, but I must confess that I have a strong leaning at present in favor of it. It may be, however, that on further reflection I would find this to be a mere sentiment and not well supported.

I expect and hope that I shall spend the summer here substantially. I do not anticipate more than an occasional absence. I should of course be very glad to see you at any time.

To CLARK HOWELL [2]

Gray Gables, *July* 16, 1892

The receipt of your recent letter has gratified me exceedingly. It has a tone of true Democracy about it, and is pervaded with the sort of Democratic frankness which is very pleasing.

I think the underlying principle of party organization is what you so admirably express as an acceptance of the arbitrament of the National Convention. On the other hand, it is as fully the duty of one opposed to

---

[1] A New York publisher and writer, born in 1848, and long prominent in tariff reform and civil service reform. For Cleveland's letter of this date to Henry Watterson, see Addenda.

[2] Owner of the Atlanta *Constitution*, a newspaper of free-silverite tendency which had supported Hill for the nomination.

shut his mind and heart to any feeling of irritation or resentment that might be allowed to grow out of opposition based upon honest judgment and a conscientious desire for party success.

I am not surprised, though I am gratified, by the announcement that from this time to the close of the campaign your own service and the incaluable influence of the *Constitution* will be devoted to the fight for Democratic success. It honestly seems to me that Democrats who are not at this time loyal to the cause are recreant to their country. Personal advancement of man is nothing; the triumph of the principles we advocate is everything.

Hoping that we may congratulate each other on a glorious result in November...

To William F. Vilas

Gray Gables, *July* 24, 1892

I have been home from New York only a few hours. I received your letter in the hurly-burly of my stay there. Our friends all say that the campaign starts very well indeed in New York, but I think there are dangers which ought to be guarded against, and to tell you the truth I do not feel as fully as many do, that we can rely upon all the professions that are made in certain quarters of loyalty and devotion.

I wish I could see you. I would be delighted if you could come up here. You know I am watched like a suspected criminal. If you should leave Boston at 9 A.M. you would arrive here about 10:45, and if on that train (and some others) you should tell the conductor that you wanted to go to Gray Gables you could pass the station of Buzzards Bay and the train would be stopped just a little farther on and upon my premises. I would meet you there. Of course whatever train you might come on I would meet you there or at the station. A very pleasant way to come up is by the Fall River boat leaving New York at 5:30 and 6:15 P.M., arriving here on the same train, I think, which leaves Boston at 9 A.M.

I want to urge upon you the importance of getting a branch of the National Committee opened at the West. I write this upon the theory that such a thing would help in our efforts to carry your State and Illinois, etc. If it would not tend in that direction my argument and claim on that subject fail. Illinois is very anxious for it and Dickinson told me he was intending to urge it before the Committee. I should not be at all surprised if Indiana, Wisconsin, and Illinois *were absolutely necessary to*

our success; and I am quite certain that a good prospect to win the election without New York *is the best way to get the electoral votes of that State.*

Whitney is working night and day very hard to secure the support of Tammany Hall and the Hill men. He thinks he is succeeding perfectly. I wish I could feel so.

Don't misconstrue me. I merely do not think it amiss to have as many reasons as possible to induce certain Democrats to be honest and to give them a hint that it is barely possible that treachery might fall short of accomplishing its designed purpose.

I wish I might hear from you if I do not see [you]. If Mrs. Vilas or either of the girls are with you, I am commanded by Mrs. Cleveland to say that we should be very glad to see them with you. She sends love to them present or absent, and so do I.

To WILSON S. BISSELL

Gray Gables, *July 24, 1892*

Personal

I have just this moment arrived home from New York. I went to Greenwich Friday and spent the night and left there Saturday (yesterday) morning on Mr. Benedict's yacht. We lingered on the way to fish a little and spent last night at New London. But fishing or eating, reading or drinking, asleep or awake, my mind has been on one thing constantly — and that is the situation politically in the city, county, and State of New York. *The thing is not right* — that is, in my judgment. I believe there is a lot of lying and cheating going on and unless the complexion changes we shall wake up, I think, the morning after election and find that we have been fooled by as base a set of cutthroats as ever scuttled a ship.

The one of my friends at the front in the city of New York is Mr. Whitney. He is as true as steel and is devoting himself night and day to the work. But his labor is altogether in the line of pacification and everything he does tends to persuading the men of Tammany Hall and those who belong to their gang, to vote the Democratic ticket. In the meantime my friends are entirely ignored or treated as if they deserved punishment. This is on the theory, as he says, that my friends we have anyway, and the point should be to gain the support and votes of those who were not my friends at Chicago, and who were 'beaten and humiliated.'

The campaign is to be kept in the hands of men who have solemnly declared that I cannot carry New York. Do you suppose that Hill wants to see me elected? Look at the men through the State whom he has been building up for two years and who are on the local committees. They will, I suppose, insist stronger than ever upon managing the campaign in their localities, and when the disaster comes will lay it on the May Convention people. *They* will feel that I have deserted and betrayed them, because they are not consulted. Gilsey has been more of a friend to me than any of the rest; and the Sagamore Club is under his domination. The demonstration there was as much more hearty than that at the Garden the night before, as you can imagine. I only mention that as an accident.

This is not the way I talk to others — *only to you.* Lander, the Treasurer of the National Committee, was a sympathizer with the May movement. There are a number of other little things which show the direction of the wind. I cannot tell you anything like all of them, but the atmosphere at the present time is not at all right. You will see Sheehan on the Executive Committee, and then I believe the effort will be to let the ticket drop and hide their responsibility for it. If this is the result, Whitney will be as badly fooled, or worse, than anybody else; but you see when a man is thoroughly saturated with pacification he doesn't suspect these things. Why should I bother you with all this? Simply because I want to tell someone how I feel. I have thought of a way, I believe, to mend matters. You know Illinois and some of the other Western States want a branch of the National Committee located at Chicago. They say they will pay their own expenses and contribute besides to the general committee. This is opposed by Indiana because she wants to be considered the Western battlefield and thus have large sums of money sent there. Wisconsin and Illinois combined cast the same number of electoral votes as New York, and I believe with proper effort can be carried. There is nothing in the world that will make the Hill Democracy hearty and honest in the campaign as surely as the conviction that the country can be carried without them.[1]

I have not been consulted at all — or scarcely at all — about the conduct of the campaign, but I mean to favor the scheme of a Western branch to the very utmost. Of course all possible must at the same time be done to carry New York and Indiana. It's a funny thing for a man to be running for the Presidency with all the politicians against him.

---

[1] Cleveland actually carried Indiana, Illinois, and Wisconsin in 1892, and would have won without the electoral votes of New York — which he also carried.

W. C. WHITNEY *to* CLEVELAND

New York, *July 29,* 1892

Things are looking well, in my opinion. I have been smoothing out the recalcitrants and have got far enough to begin to look in the other direction a little. The Republicans are still running after their disaffected and with no apparent result. Elmira I have taken in hand this week. I had an interview with Arnot and have asked him to send two men to see me and it will straighten that town out. That was the worst place, perhaps. I do not know what the Syracuse people mean by talking about being overlooked. They are not eligible to any positions, not being on the National Committee.

I am to meet Grace this afternoon at four and shall give a dinner next week to them and Harrity so as to make them feel as though they knew him. If things shape up as we expect, the campaign work will be in the hands of Harrity, Quincy, Dickinson, and Whitney — four Cleveland men if there are any — and we shall have the prestige of a united party. I consider that we are doing great work in removing from the canvass the blight which dissension brings in the way of discouragement. You can jog my elbow, if you see something wrong. I push ahead in what I deem the important thing at the time. I want responsibility put on these people. I want it their fight. We will handle it, but they can be put where they will by election be tearing mad, and if so, we will win anyhow. I go to Newport tomorrow or Saturday night.

P.S. Miller [1] of the *Times* dines with Harrity here tonight.

To CARTER H. HARRISON [2]

Gray Gables, *July 29,* 1892

Mr. George F. Parker has edited a book made up of my speeches, letters, messages, etc. I have had next to nothing to do with its preparation and have not even examined it with any care, though a copy has been sent to me. I am very much afraid you will consider it presumptuous, but I want to send you my copy of the book. I am thinking a good deal lately about the relations between labor and capital and the condition and prospects of our laboring men. When in Washington I sent to Congress a

---

[1] Charles R. Miller (1849–1922), editor of the New York *Times*.

[2] Carter H. Harrison (1825–93), after service as Representative in Congress and Mayor of Chicago, was at this time owner and editor of the Chicago *Times*. Cleveland was anxious to have his support.

message on the subject of arbitration as a means of adjustment of labor troubles which I wish you would look at, as well as some other references to the general subject to be found in the book I send. I know you are interested in this topic. I wish the Democracy might carry your State in November, and I believe it would be done if you willed it so. I should be very glad to hear from you on the situation, and if you come East I would be happy to have you call on me. We have cool weather here.

P.S. You will find the message on arbitration also in the book I sent you containing my public papers.

To FRANK P. POSTON

Gray Gables, *August* 7, 1892

In reply to your letter of the 13th instant, I beg you to believe that I am in no wise wanting in sympathy for your family and friends of your brother, nor do I forget in the situation there is a perfect excuse for conclusions arrived at without absolutely cool judgment; but I address you in the hope that, notwithstanding all this, you may be able to take a more reasonable view of my conduct. I have been amazed beyond expression at the misinterpretation which has been placed upon my letter written to Mrs. White. I cannot conceive what there is in the minds of the people of your locality which leads them to give it a meaning so entirely foreign to my intention, and so entirely beyond its just interpretation. This is the first reply which I have thought fit to make to the frequent criticisms of my action in this matter....

Have you and others who are inclined to criticize my action for a moment reflected upon the fact that my letter was written in response to the pitiable plea of an apparently heartbroken woman, setting forth in a manner most impressive the reasons why the life of her uncle should be spared? Have you and my critics overlooked the fact that I absolutely declined to interfere with the Governor in behalf of this man? Have you and they forgotten the courtesy and consideration which gentlemen in the North, as well as in the South, consider due to the appeal of a woman? Has it entirely escaped your attention that the letter was dictated simply and solely by the sympathy which every true man ought to feel for a woman in distress? I do not overlook the fact that in the closing paragraph of the letter I did say I felt there might be extenuating circumstances....

In response to your suggestion that this act of mine may result in the loss of Democratic votes in the pending campaign, you will pardon me, I hope, if I say that when political expediency forces me to be discourteous to a distressed woman, I am prepared to retire from politics.

WILLIAM C. WHITNEY *to* CLEVELAND

New York, *August* 9, 1892

I hoped to have run across and had a talk with you yesterday, but the fates were not propitious.

I am going to enclose you a letter from Horace White just received because it represents current talk here. These people are using your polite letters of acknowledgment in such a way that it will lose you in a short time that position you have that we talked about when we were considering whether you had better make yourself common in the campaign. Already a man said to me the other day he found himself thinking, 'Oh, another letter from Cleveland,' and didn't read it. Being on commonplace subjects, they are necessarily not specially important. Can't you devise some way of preventing their publication? You are losing from it now. Do as I do; let them go unanswered until after election, or let the answer be an acknowledgment only.

These are suggestions only, but I suppose no one but myself would tell you that everybody mostly is regretting your being ever before the public except when you strike a blow — and justify the attitude in which you have come to stand in the public mind.

The *Sun* and *Tribune* publish them all now daily; at least the *Sun* does and I saw a lot in the *Tribune* a few days ago. Trying to use your ordinary correspondence to familiarize the public with you in a commonplace character — that is the way they are using it.

I had Mowry and Parker and Herrick down last week and they agreed on certain names for me to try to get on the State Campaign Committee. Mowry and Jim Stevens and Mr. Browne and Cord Meyer were among them. Unfortunately I was taken at last with so bad a headache, I concluded to go to bed and wrote Murphy instead. He selected some that I named — the above four and Griffen and Jimmy Martin and some other whose name I have forgotten.

Murphy did not on Thursday, when I saw him, refer to Sheehan, but I have no doubt they are in good faith in putting Sheehan there — so far as that goes. Sheehan talked well at the meeting of Campaign Committee on Thursday. We passed several hours together in informal talk and all seemed to indicate loyalty and growing confidence.

If you think well of it I wish you would write Murphy a note in a friendly spirit, and say that — well, let me make the suggestion on a separate sheet. Will be over to see you Monday next, I think.

. (Enclosure)

Dear Murphy:

As I am the candidate and you are the State Chairman can't you come into the Harbor some day and pay me a visit? Whitney will manage to bring you, I imagine, if you can come.

I regret very much to hear that your other daughter's health is requiring your attention.[1] I hope it is nothing that will cause you anxiety.

We are entering upon a campaign which in my honest judgment is full of the gravest consequences to the people of this country. I cannot feel that it is personal to me. It is for or against the triumph of Democratic principles that we are enlisting. Let us all sink our personal differences in the greater interests involved. I shall do so myself and to those who work now for the triumph of our party and its principles, I shall look for my friends, irrespective of differences of opinion heretofore held. It shall never prejudice a man in my mind hereafter that he opposed my nomination if he stands by the party and works for success in this fight.

If we will all do the same and present a united front to the foe, we can win easily in my judgment. I shall rely upon you to second my efforts in this behalf.

You may think it cheeky — my suggesting — but it is to get the tone in which I hope you will write to him. I know he is surprised and disappointed you haven't dropped him a line. He thinks you and he are great friends. Don't do anything unless you go as far as this.

To Senator William F. Vilas

Gray Gables, *August* 9, 1892

I enclose you a letter just received from the editor of the Appleton *Volksfreund.* I take it for granted that you know something of the paper as well as its management. I do not think it would be wise for me at this time to answer the questions which he propounds. I cannot judge whether in any event it would be worth while for anyone to do so. I suppose that

---

[1] Murphy had just lost a daughter by death.

this is a subject which must be treated of in my letter of acceptance; and it will be a very delicate operation. So far as I have thought upon the subject at all, it has been my idea to adhere to previous declarations and to treat the subject as one having relation to a condition, but which still permits the wholesale denunciation of Republican protection as a theory. Of course, my notions on the treatment of this subject are indefinite and crude as yet, but it occurs to me that, if it is important at all that this letter should be answered, you might say something to the writer which would cover the ground, based upon your own ideas of my opinions, and of what exact position the Democratic party ought to assume. I do not like to trouble you with this, but if there is no importance to be attached to the letter, it can be disposed of without trouble.

The more I think of it the more I am convinced that your State and Illinois should take their places this fall as Democratic States. I understand, though it is not yet made public, that a movement will be inaugurated to raise funds for the express purpose of aiding doubtful Western States; and so far as I have expressed an opinion on the subject I have maintained that the effort should be confined to these two States. If this plan is consummated, it may perhaps prove to be a very welcome assistance to our friends there in the contest.

Inasmuch, however, as thus far it is only proposed, and inasmuch as my judgment in the matter of confining it to the two States mentioned may not be adopted, you will see the propriety of receiving this information for the present as if intended for you alone.

The scheme will originate and be pushed by the New York *World* and other Democratic newspapers, and will, I expect, be entirely free from any tendency to newspaper booming.

The information I get from the country at large is in the main encouraging. Our friends in New York calculate on a united and successful effort to carry that State handsomely. Reports from Indiana are quite satisfactory. Our friends in the Southern States are evidently much frightened and I am afraid not entirely without foundation. Confidentially, it is my opinion that if they had had some idea of the practical precautions, which were necessary to avoid the condition they now find themselves in, and if real Democrats there had early attempted to stem the Alliance [1] tide instead of drifting with it, our situation would now be

---

[1] The Farmers' Alliance had originated in the Southwest and was stronger in the South than anywhere except a few trans-Mississippi areas.

very different. I cannot now convince myself that any Southern State, with the traditions of the Democratic party before it, remembering all that the National Democracy has done for their people, and appreciating the dangers that must follow a Democratic defeat, will desert the standard. Still, the condition there is not free from danger. I should be glad to hear from you at any time on the political outlook....

To WILSON S. BISSELL

Gray Gables, *August* 10, 1892

There is an old story which you have doubtless heard, but which was fixed in my mind by the fact that it is the only story I ever heard Chapin of Brooklyn tell. A frontiersman had occasion to leave his cabin and his wife and children for a number of days and nights. When he returned, he found that his house had been burned and the mutilated and charred remains of his family were scattered about the ground. He leaned upon his gun in silence for a moment and then remarked with earnestness, 'Well! I'll be damned if this ain't *too* ridiculous.'

I felt like saying just that when I read in the paper yesterday morning that Sheehan had been appointed chairman of the State Campaign Committee. My condition is not improved by receiving a letter from Whitney today in which he suggests the form of a most abject and humble letter for me to write Murphy, amounting to a prayer for his support. I'll see the whole outfit to the devil before I'll do it. Somebody must be crazy, and unless the people of the State take matters in their own hands some people stand a right smart chance to get left — and I am one of them. I expect to see Whitney on Monday. I am glad it is not today — for I don't believe I could hold myself in.

To JULIUS CHAMBERS

Gray Gables, *August* 12, 1892

I have received your letter of August 9, asking for one of Mrs. Cleveland's photographs to reproduce in *Once A Week*. I fully appreciate your consideration in bringing this matter to my attention before the publication of a picture of my wife. I am exceedingly anxious to shield her as much as possible from any notoriety, and especially such as is connected with a political campaign. The New York *World* has lately published a number of her pictures, and notwithstanding good intentions, has greatly annoyed both her and myself; and I ask you as a special favor to forego carrying out your design.

WILLIAM C. WHITNEY *to* CLEVELAND

New York, *August 22,* 1892

I thought I might get over to see you this week, but my spirits go down so when I let go and get away — aside from the detail that I am without the necessary force to break engagements here and go. There is nothing to say so far as I can recall. Hill has declined to go in on the advisory committee.

But I think we have all the rest of them — his friends from end to end — and I shall lay down on them pretty soon and either bring about a breach between them and Hill or bring Hill into line. If you hear from Murphy, I wish you would let me know what he says and keep me posted generally on their movements so far as you see them.

The policy of getting everybody upon whom Hill relies and nullifying him is the true policy both for now and for the future. It is no use to say not trust any of them. We have got to trust them; they have the organization and the power and by trusting them we can make them pull straight.

P.S. I wish you would do as much reconciling of recalcitrants as you see your way to do. You can do much more with a word than I can with a speech.

To M. SHELLEY

Gray Gables, *August 22,* 1892

Your letter of the 12th instant is at hand. In reply I have to say that I have not the least idea what 'your worthy friend' meant when he declared that 'I had been the medium through which 20,000 families were made homeless and had lost their all fighting for their rights.' I am perfectly well aware that I have been the means of saving some homes to my countrymen and have tried very hard to make the burden of their lives easier. I am amazed at receiving from the Southern country letters containing charges like that which you bring to my attention. I am surprised, first, at the ingenuity necessary for their concoction without the least semblance of foundation. I am more amazed that, with my record before the people of this country, such baseless lies should be deemed sufficient arguments to prejudice me, and the cause which I for the time being represent, in the minds of the Southern people.

WILLIAM C. WHITNEY *to* CLEVELAND

New York, *August* 30, 1892

I received your two letters with the checks, which I have used as requested. You will have recognized your contribution in the *World* as from '*A Friend of the Cause.*'

As to writing Murphy, you may be right — the sequel will tell. I cannot but record my judgment that it is a great error — perhaps a fatal one. You do not realize, I think, that you were nominated against the united voice of your State organization and that their pride is in a state of serious irritation from that cause. I think it is for you to send for them and remove the feeling as much from their minds as possible. You cannot carry this State without that feeling is removed, and they are working warmly for the success of the ticket.

It is idle to talk of Massachusetts and the West. I know you and I agree that the fight is upon the old lines — with a *possibility* of outside surprises. I have laid down on my friendships and worked night and day to bring this about.

If you think best not to write a friendly letter to the chairman of your State Committee, who has come in and is acting in your interest to straighten out difficulties, I had better stop where I am. We must differ radically.

Isn't it possible for you to move to some place more accessible? I could not get away this Sunday on account of the Alabama men being here Saturday, but conferring by letter is a little difficult. We need all the time to be in closer relations to you. You could help the campaign very much by being where men could see you now and then. Your personal influence is lost where you are and it is a great element in the campaign.

I have not expressed any approval of any requests for speeches from you. The North Carolina man spoke of his desire, but no one said a word of approval or disapproval. As to the State bank matter I cannot find where it would benefit us specially. I think you can help by a restatement of the silver matter.

In the South the impression of you got by the people is that you do not appreciate their suffering and poverty (and these are the real sources of the Alliance movement) and have your ideas formed by Eastern money power, etc. — *the usual twaddle.* I think, having this in view, you might write on the tariff and on silver in a mood sympathetic to them and make a great change in the South. As you said to me, it is unaccountable what ideas they get and where they get them.

CHAIRMAN W. F. HARRITY *to* CLEVELAND

New York, *September* 1, 1892

... As you may surmise, we are somewhat concerned about the Peck report,[1] chiefly because of its supposed significance in that Mr. Peck is generally regarded as a friend and follower of Senator Hill. My own judgment is that Senator Hill and Chairman Murphy should be invited to participate actively in the campaign. Such an invitation should be extended in some authoritative way, although no invitation whatever should be necessary. I very much fear that if Senator Hill maintains his present attitude, it will have a very prejudicial effect upon our campaign. I am not entirely clear as to who should extend the invitation or how it should be given, but I am reasonably certain that they will need to be asked to take an active part before they do so. This is particularly true of Senator Hill. This is the thought that is in my mind, and it occurs to me to respectfully submit it to you.

I hope to be able to give myself the pleasure of seeing you at an early date if you will find it entirely convenient and agreeable....

To D-CADY HERRICK

Gray Gables, *September* 3, 1892

I want to see you very much indeed. Cannot you come to me some day next week? You can take a train from Boston at 9 o'clock A.M. and tell the conductor that you want to stop at Gray Gables and he will let you off just after passing Buzzards Bay, at a little station at the entrance to my land and less than half a mile from my house. I will meet you there....

To WILSON S. BISSELL

Gray Gables, *September* 4, 1892

Your letter is received. I feel very gloomy and very much provoked and am not sure that I ought to write to you in such a mood. The policy of truckling conciliation which has characterized the campaign thus far has resulted in its legitimate fruit, and I am urged now to send for Murphy and Sheehan and conciliate them. Whitney wrote me a letter he wanted me to send to Murphy and I declined to do it, whereupon he wrote me a very petulant and unpleasant letter. He was here yesterday and we had

---

[1] Charles F. Peck of Hornellsville was Commissioner of Labor in New York State, and though a Democrat, mysteriously published at this juncture a report on industry and the tariff favorable to the Republicans.

a little talk — nothing unpleasant, but I can see that he is not satisfied and he seemed to be on the point of exploding. He professes to feel that the campaign is in a very dangerous shape, and more than half intimates that unless I get into personal relations with these men I will be defeated. I told him I would go to New York whenever he desired and meet them and be as agreeable as I could, but I would not pledge myself to do their bidding in case of success. I further told him I did not want to annoy him, but that I did not have a particle of confidence in Sheehan and that I thought he would use any money or power that was put into his hands for the election of members of Assembly to the end that Flower might be made Senator and he Governor. I believe Tammany and Kings will do as well as they can, that the electoral tickets will be elected for the legislative tickets in the rural districts, and that if I am defeated in the State it will be claimed as further proof of my unpopularity, which will be urged as an explanation of the result. The neglect of everything except tickling these men amounts to a craze at headquarters, and in the meantime the campaign, it seems to me, limps and halts.

I curse myself for getting into this scrape and would get out of it today if I could. I will not give up my old friends for the gang, and yet I do not see why the latter want me to conciliate them unless they mean by that an assurance which they will regard as a promise of exclusive favor and influence.

Cannot you come and see me for a day? We are easily reached from Boston.

To Don M. Dickinson

Gray Gables, *September* 5, 1892

Confidential.

I received a letter from Whitney a few days ago and had a talk with him Saturday. As a consequence of these combined incidents, I am thoroughly miserable and depressed and feel very much like doing a desperate thing. I am thinking very hard, and the thing that troubles me more than all others is the duty I owe to such good sincere friends as you. I feel as though I *must* see you.

I wrote Parker last night and said to him that I wanted you to come to me; but I write this to inform you as heartily as I can my aim in this matter. I know I am a very great trouble to you, but if I can have a good talk with you perhaps we can remedy that condition.

And, my dear fellow, if you do come, I beg you to come in a mood to believe that I am not always wrong and that I ought to be allowed to emerge from this campaign still deserving, in some degree at least, the respect of those whose good opinion I prize more than any office or honor, and still preserving to some extent my self-respect. If you cannot come or prefer that I come to you, I will do so promptly on hearing your desires.

To D-CADY HERRICK

Gray Gables, *September* 6, 1892

Confidential.

I received yesterday a telegram from Mr. Whitney asking me to be in New York Wednesday or Thursday of this week. I expect, therefore, to start for New York tomorrow (Wednesday). I have no idea how long I shall remain, but it might be so that I could see you there if you could make it convenient to come down; at any rate, I thought I ought to let you know so that if, by any chance, in response to my letter you contemplated coming up this week, you would not make your journey without seeing me. I imagine that the object of this visit is to try to induce people in the Democratic management of the campaign in New York State to assist in electing the Democratic ticket.[1]

To WILLIAM REED

Gray Gables, *September* 7, 1892

Your letter of September 3rd is received. I have a great many letters commending to my attention all manner of projects, so that it is utterly impossible for me to examine their merits, to say nothing of entering into them. I cannot find the material which you sent with your first letter, and it is therefore impossible for me to return it to you. I noticed your gratuitous and petulant reference to my coolness since I learned that your scheme was connected with the G.A.R. Such an intimation does me great injustice and is very discreditable to you.

[1] This visit resulted in the Victoria Hotel Conference, held September 8.

To EDWARD M. SHEPARD

Gray Gables, *September* 14, 1892

I have received your letter of September 10, and thank you for it. During my recent visit to New York I learned from Mr. Villard [1] the situation regarding Mr. Schurz, and the speech which he had hoped to deliver. I am glad to learn from you that it will soon be presented to the public in as good a form as is possible in the circumstances.

I hardly know what to say in response to your suggestion that I exert some influence on Mr. Stevenson [2] in regard to his letter of acceptance. If I could see him, I am sure it would be easy for me to convey to him the ideas which I agree with you are important, without the least chance of misinterpretation. It may be that I shall have an opportunity to do this before he writes his letter. If it appears that I shall not meet him, I will carefully consider some other means through which a hint may be given him.

I should certainly be glad to receive from you any thoughts you may have upon the subject of my letter of acceptance. I have not yet begun it, though of course I have given it some thought.

Confidentially, I desire to say to you that the prevailing idea with me at present is to make the letter very short, even at the expense of failing to dwell upon some subjects which many good friends would deem important and would be of the opinion should be elaborately treated. I cannot but think that I am in a position upon the important questions involved in the present campaign to enable me to write such a letter without damage to the canvass. Indeed, it seems to me it would be an excellent stroke of policy, after Mr. Harrison's long and dreary deliverance. I should like your ideas on this subject. I shall be pleased to have you suggest anything else which is in your mind concerning the subject-matter of the letter.

WILLIAM C. WHITNEY *to* CLEVELAND

New York, *September* 15, 1892

The more you can be here now the better for us. Every day men are here whom I would like you to see and I want to confer with you all the

[1] Henry Villard (1835–1900), railway-builder and financier, supported Cleveland as offering the surest protection against the free-silver movement. Carl Schurz had written a campaign speech which illness made it impossible for him to deliver.

[2] Adlai E. Stevenson was Democratic candidate for Vice-President.

time now. Your last visit did a world of good. But for it we should be in bad now.

Hill is thoroughly mad now. Madder at his own people than at us. They are pressing him on all sides and telling him he can't play fast and loose, etc. He has declined to see me. I haven't asked him, but he sent that word to me. I have warned Sheehan to see his speech before it is delivered and he intends to. Frank Locke came here this week and went and called on Sheehan and told him he was satisfied and should disband his committee. Ellery Anderson and Sheehan are working together, and are pleased with each other. I do not doubt now but we shall have the full organization strength on election day. That is the way it is working now. Hill can't do much if he should feel inclined.

We may meet our first setback today in Alabama. I see Chris Magee is there, and our plans may fail. Watch the result of their convention today. The New Jersey nomination is a good one. If he runs, it will tend to restore the confidence of the general public. I wouldn't come down temporarily, but would move as soon as I could. We need you all the time. Can't you get a place at Lakewood?

To LAMBERT TREE [1]

Gray Gables [undated; about *September* 20, 1892]

I have received your letter of the 15th and thank you for it. I was very glad indeed to learn that ex-Mayor Harrison is so solidly in the fight, and I believe his efforts cannot fail to be productive of good results.

The complaints you make regarding the course of the *Herald* I do not quite understand. I have seen a good many editorials from that paper lately, and it seems to me that they are doing grand service. I do not know when I have seen more pungent, energetic editorials than these. I am a little disappointed to learn that there is the least possibility of Judge Gresham's not pursuing the course which all of us have expected that he would follow, and was only awaiting his time to do so. I am exceedingly anxious that his friends and the people generally should hear from him, and I cannot appreciate any objection to his doing so.

I shall write to Mr. Walsh, not only on account of your suggestion, but in the performance of a pleasant duty which I had anticipated before receiving your letter, for I certainly was very much pleased with the

[1] Lambert Tree (1832–1910), capitalist and lawyer, had been circuit judge in Illinois 1870–74, and minister first to Belgium and then to Russia in Cleveland's first Administration.

editorials he wrote and thought that he deserved from me an acknowledgment. I am getting very much in the mood of expecting, confidentially, that the Illinois Democracy will carry their State; the more I think of it the more I am convinced that it might, and — if you will pardon me for saying so — that it ought to be done. Of course, at this distance I cannot appreciate the difficulties you have to overcome and perhaps make a wrong estimate of them, but it does look to me as though the opportunity was a very good one. I have read within a day or two that Altgeld gave the most encouraging account of what he saw in his trip through the State, and predicted with the utmost confidence his election by quite a large majority. He is inclined to make a difference of 15,000 votes between his and the electoral ticket, but thinks, so far as I can learn, that there is a good chance of both being carried.

I note the expression of your hope that soon the Western branch of the National Committee will be established on lines which will make its work effective. I had supposed that by this time it was established on precisely those lines and was already doing first-rate work.

Whatever may happen, I know that your personal efforts will be earnestly and efficiently devoted to the success of the ticket, and relying a good deal on your judgment makes me anxious to hear from you again on the outlook. I hope you will gratify me with a word now and then, as you find it convenient.

To RICHARD WATSON GILDER

Gray Gables, *September 25,* 1892

I have read the article you were good enough to send me with a great deal of interest. It is ably written, but somehow it strikes me that the author has a most sublime or unusual faith in Republicans when a chance to promote party ends presents itself or that his judgment is a little warped by his appointment as Chief Supervisor. Perhaps he supposes that other officials appointed under such a thing as the Force Bill would be as fair and honest as he. All this is evidence of a kindly judgment and disposition, but my idea of Republicanism leads me to the belief that the entire plan is bad and that its operation would be simply atrocious.

I finished my letter of acceptance early this morning — three o'clock — and Dickinson was here today and left for New York tonight with the letter in his pocket. I suppose it will appear in the newspapers Tuesday morning. I hope you will like it. If you do not, I hope you will try to realize some of the difficulties and perplexities attending its preparation.

I expect to leave here for New York next Thursday night and shall probably remain there some time. I don't know when we shall be settled there — some time in October, I expect. My judgment is decidedly in favor of my making my headquarters here for some time to come. I *know* it would be good politics for me not to go to New York for good until nearly the end of the campaign, but I don't seem to be running things much.

Take my advice, my dear friend, and *never run for President.* Mrs. Cleveland and the BABY are as well as possible and both would send love if they were awake. I wish you were here to fish a day with me and go to New York with me Thursday night.

To A. B. FARQUHAR

Gray Gables, *September 26,* 1892

Personal.

I have received your letter of the 23d instant and desire to thank you for it. I expect my letter of acceptance will appear in the papers either tomorrow or next day. I hope that on the whole it will be satisfactory to you and to other good friends. The news I receive from New York is of the most encouraging description. I have myself no doubt that we shall in November next present a solid and a united front to the common enemy. I can see no reason why we should not carry the State by a very handsome majority....

To DON M. DICKINSON

New York, *November 21,* 1892

I said to the clerk of the Arlington Hotel some time ago that I would probably stop at that hotel when I went to be inaugurated. I do not expect to be in Washington more than one night before I sleep in the White House. I suppose that the management of the Arlington expects to reserve rooms for me. It was exactly like your kindness and thoughtfulness to engage the rooms you mention for me....

I expect to go away tomorrow. I don't feel altogether comfortable, but there is no reason why I should bother you with my troubles. I only wish God would put it in my power to make known to the Democratic party what the last election means.

I want you to see to it that you get well seated. With love to Mrs. Dickinson and Frances....

To SENATOR WILLIAM F. VILAS

New York, *December* 12, 1892

I saw Mr. Wall today and sent you a message by him intended to indicate to you my very great desire to see you and 'talk it out' with you. By a considerable coincidence I find here, on my return from my office this evening, your exceedingly gratifying letter indicating your desire to talk it out with me. In this condition of affairs there should be nothing in the way of our pleasing each other and each one himself. I am at leisure to you at any time, day or night; and the more of the time you will occupy the greater will be my satisfaction. I want you, however, to come directly to my house and stay with me....

I thank you most sincerely for the kind things you write concerning my Saturday evening's speech. I think it is the last public political utterance I shall make until I speak on the steps of the Senate March 4, 1893. I appreciate gratefully your offer of hospitality when I shall arrive at Washington. I suppose I must consider arrangements as made for a very brief hotel stay at the Arlington, prior to my settlement at the White House. I shall not enter upon the many things I have to say to you now — reserving all until I see you....

XI

THE YEAR OF THE PANIC

CLEVELAND was inaugurated on March 4, 1893, before a shivering audience standing on ground white with snow. In his brief inaugural address he promised that he would maintain the standard of the currency against any debasement or depreciation; that he would support economy and civil service reform; that trusts and monopolies generally would be curbed in so far as the Federal power could reach them; and that the tariff would be reformed in the interests of the people. He had chosen a Cabinet that was quite equal in ability to his first. Breaking all precedents, he named a member of the opposition party — Walter Q. Gresham of Indiana — to be Secretary of State. The Secretaryship of the Treasury went to John G. Carlisle, the Secretaryship of War to the faithful Lamont, the Secretaryship of the Interior to Hoke Smith, and the Attorney-Generalship to Richard Olney. It was well that Cleveland was surrounded by a strong group of men, for weeks before he entered office it was evident that a financial and commercial storm was approaching. The causes of this impending crisis were partly international, for the 'Baring panic' of 1890 had been severely felt, and there had been crises in Australia and parts of Europe; but they were partly rooted in the unwise financial practices of the United States ever since the Civil War. The banking system was defective; the Sherman Silver-Purchase Act of 1890 was inflating the currency by about fifty millions annually; the heavy appropriations of the Harrison Administration had dangerously depleted the Treasury; and the steady growth of free-silver sentiment in the West and South had aroused grave fear of the destruction of the gold standard. Cleveland was faced with a demand from two quarters for a special session of Congress. One group wished it held to reduce the tariff; another group demanded it to repeal the Silver-Purchase Act and thus avert the worst consequences of a panic. After some hesitation, Cleveland decided to call Congress in August to repeal the Silver-Purchase Act. He thus deliberately sacrificed his best chance of obtaining that full and satisfactory revision of the tariff for which he had so long argued. In July, under circumstances of careful secrecy, he underwent an operation for carcinoma of the jaw. While still recovering from this, he returned from Gray Gables to open Congress. Under the leadership of William L. Wilson, the silver repeal bill easily passed the House. In the Senate the struggle was close and prolonged; at one time almost everyone but Cleveland gave up hope for an unconditional repeal, and a proposal for a compromise was signed by 37 of the 44 Democrats in the Senate. But Cleveland refused to listen to this, and on October 28 the desired legislation passed. By this time the panic had prostrated all American business, but the gold standard seemed in less peril. When the regular session of Congress met in December, Cleveland confronted it with a demand for immediate tariff legislation.

To JOHN G. CARLISLE

Lakewood, N.J., *January 22,* 1893

Your letter was handed to me after I had left home to go to Fremont,[1] and I only returned from there last night. Though I was very glad to read your reassuring words, I confess I am not as hopeful as I would like to be. My belief is most confident that if the question could be presented to both houses for a vote, the result would be favorable.

I have been thinking lately what a shame it is that you and I must worry so much over a thing that ought to be a subject of the same importance to every man who loves his country and every Democrat who loves his party. I was beginning to ask myself why at this time we should be called upon to encounter the indifference and opposition of those in our party who, on every ground, ought to be laboring for the suspension of the purchase of silver. Its continuance, without even the promise of cessation, undoubtedly endangers the prosperity of the country; and it certainly threatens with disaster the Democratic party and the incoming Administration. I don't like to think that there are alleged Democrats in Congress who do not desire the success of our Administration, but it is hard to keep such thoughts out of my head.

I have made up my mind not to submit to this without at least giving some sign that I understand the situation.

If the silver business is not in some way adjusted before the 4th of March, the question will present itself whether a special session ought not to be immediately called after that date, for the consideration of the subject; and whether in the meantime the distribution of patronage ought not to be entirely and absolutely postponed. One thing may as well be distinctly understood by professing Democrats in Congress, who are heedless of the burdens and responsibilities of the incoming Administration

[1] Cleveland had attended the funeral of Rutherford B. Hayes in Fremont, Ohio.

and of the duty our party owes to the people. They must not expect me to 'turn the other cheek' by rewarding their conduct with patronage.

I wish I could see you soon. We are on a direct line from Philadelphia. I enclose you a time-table from which you can see that you can leave Philadelphia at 3:45 and arrive here at 5:45. If you had rather visit us in New York, I will stay all night there for that purpose if necessary. If you can do either, please let me know here in advance, so that I can clear the track of engagements....

To L. Clarke Davis
Lakewood, N.J., *January* 25, 1893

I don't know what to write. I would be glad to help Parker in any proper way and it would please me to have him succeed in his venture. I see him very often and he ought to know my gait pretty well. At the same time I don't propose to tell him or anybody else anything I ought or want to keep to myself. Of course what he writes will be apt to be nearer the truth than any of the other reporters' stuff I see from day to day. Whether he can [get] material enough and of a character to be interesting or profitable from a newspaper point of view, I do not know, but I should suppose that could be judged from the samples he is prepared to show.

Bayard came to me night before last and left this morning. We had a very frank and unrestrained talk, as we have always had, and so far as he can do so, he has, like the good patriotic friend he is, left matters almost entirely in my control.

I am dreadfully perplexed and bothered. I cannot get the men I want to help me,[1] but strange to say, my greatest trials come through those professing to be near and attached friends, who expect things. I hope the skies will lighten up by and by, but I have never seen a day since I consented to drift with events that I have not cursed myself for yielding; and in these particular days I think I curse a little more heartily than ever. This is strange talk and perhaps seems ungracious and unappreciative. It is nothing of the kind. It presents only the personal side of the matter; and sometimes, when I feel that perhaps I may after all be the instrument of doing good to the American people whom I know I love, I am quite happy.

[1] Cleveland wanted Bayard for the Secretaryship of State, Fairchild for the Secretaryship of the Treasury, and George Gray of Delaware for the Attorney-Generalship; and all three declined.

To Judge Walter Q. Gresham [1]

Lakewood, N.J., *January 25,* 1893

Will you accept the place of Secretary of State in the incoming Administration?

You will doubtless be surprised by this proposition, but I hope you may see your way clear to accede to my request. You know enough of Cabinet duties to make it unnecessary for me to enlarge upon their character or scope.

I fear that your sensitiveness concerning the view that may be taken of your acceptance of the position, in connection with your prior political affiliations and the part you took in the late campaign, may cause you to shrink from a fair consideration of this subject. I beg you, however, to believe that your sturdy regard for political duty and your supreme sincerity and disinterestedness, seen and known of all men, are proof against any and all unworthy suspicions or malicious criticisms. In really a great emergency, the country needs your services in the place I ask you to fill. In an effort to subserve the interests of my countrymen, I need you.

Can you not come to us? Hoping for an early reply, I am...

To Judge Walter Q. Gresham

Lakewood, *February* 6, 1893 (telegram)

Every consideration of my duty and personal inclination constrains me to ask a reconsideration of the subject referred to in your letter.

To Judge Walter Q. Gresham

Lakewood, N.J., *February* 9, 1893

Confidential.

Your letter of the 7th instant came to hand two or three hours ago, and causes me the greatest satisfaction. I know perfectly well that only considerations of patriotism and duty have constrained you to accede to my wishes, and I assure you this vastly increases my appreciation of what you have done. Do you not think I (or you) had better, in a matter-of-fact and unsensational way, give the fact to the public that you have

[1] Gresham (1832–95), an Indianian, had been Postmaster-General and Secretary of the Treasury under Arthur, and had been supported by several Western States for the Republican Presidential nomination in 1888. He was a firm believer in the gold standard and low tariffs, and he had come over to Cleveland in 1892.

accepted the place? If you deem it best that I give it out, I wish you would simply send me a dispatch of some sort to that effect, put in a way that no one need to understand it but me.

Ordinarily, of course, the names of the Cabinet officers would go to the Senate and be confirmed March 5. If you could continue to act as Judge after confirmation, matters can take the usual course, and the State Department be left in the hands of those at present in charge, until you are ready to take possession; otherwise your name need not be sent in or confirmed until your judicial work is done. Of course conditions exist which may render it desirable that you assume charge as soon as possible; but this must yield to your desire and convenience or to the duties of your present position.

Mr. Carlisle writes me that Senator Morgan would be glad to see me or my Secretary of State, before he leaves for Paris to attend the Bering Sea Arbitration. Unless you desire to see him, I do not see why your work should be interrupted for that purpose. Perhaps I will ask Carlisle to see him or see him myself. I would certainly be exceedingly glad to have a chat with you between now and the 4th of March and hope that your work will so close up as to enable you to come to me.

I have settled, I think, on five members of the Cabinet. I mean to have Carlisle for the Treasury — Lamont for War — Bissell (of Buffalo, one of my oldest friends and former partner) for Postmaster-General, and Hoke Smith of Georgia (a very able representative of the new and progressive South) for Interior. This leaves Navy, Attorney-General, and Agriculture still to be selected. I want George Gray, Senator from Delaware, to accept the Attorney-General's place, but he has thus far, strangely enough, declined. If there was a first-rate man in Alabama, Mississippi, or that neighborhood, I would like to consider him. If not, I am prepared to take a man from almost any quarter.

I offered Agriculture to Bliss of Iowa; but he and his friends are reckoning on his making a successful canvass for United States Senator next fall and he declined my invitation. The Navy ought not to be a very hard place to fill, but I have not just the man in my view yet. It is barely possible that I may induce Senator Gray to take the Attorney-Generalship after all, but I hardly expect it. I would be very glad to receive any suggestions you may make concerning incumbents for these vacant places. Now that I have secured the head of my Cabinet, I feel that it should be completed as soon as possible.

If your leisure and convenience permit, I hope you will write to me. Please address me by letter or dispatch at this place.

To RICHARD WATSON GILDER
Lakewood, N.J., *February* 18, 1893

I return you the letter which you sent me to read. It looks to me now as if the Commissioner of Internal Revenue would hail from outside of Kentucky. Our friends must go a little slow there. I wonder if I am to be called on to wade up to my ears in the political disturbances of all the States. I like my 'friends'; but if I am to be charged with the care of them in every locality and against all attacks, I shall certainly find no time to do anything else. But I suppose we shall manage it in some fashion.

To DANIEL S. LAMONT
Lakewood, N.J., *February* 19, 1893

The Attorney-Generalship is not closed and Mr. Olney can have it if after full consideration he feels it is the one he should accept.... All this is written in subordination to my main idea that Mr. Olney is so desirable a man to have in my Cabinet that I am certainly willing to leave the choice in the two places to him.

Now what if he declines both? I believe that you had better enlist him to actively and aggressively operate with us on John Quincy Adams in an effort to induce him to accept the Secretaryship of the Navy.[1] I believe it would be the best thing left for us.

To DANIEL S. LAMONT
Lakewood, N.J., *February* 19, 1893

If in your opinion it is necessary and [you] will telegraph me to that effect, I will go up tomorrow evening and join in the consultation — though I do not want to go unless you deem it quite essential. If I should go, I would stop at the Victoria, arriving there about 9 P.M.

Carlisle tells me that Parsons, a correspondent for a Chicago newspaper, told him that Fairchild and Lettenchafer were very much offended at an interview they had with me and gives details that make it absolutely certain that someone who was present has been retailing accounts of what took place when I was there.

[1] The Secretaryship of the Navy went to Hilary A. Herbert of Alabama.

I am trying very hard to keep cheerful and in a most irritating and per-plexing situation. I am only partially successful, and I am constantly wondering why there are not, within the circle of my life, more Lamonts and Dickinsons. And this reminds me of another confidential mission I want you to undertake for me.

Will you go to Belmont and Company and see if they can arrange for the purchase [1] *abroad* of say fifty millions of *caisse* bonds (but within the declaration of the Sherman Act of the intention of the Government to maintain the parity between the two metals and undoubtedly as good as if formally payable in gold) with interest at 3 or 4 per cent? I want in the transaction the *actual gold* brought from abroad and put in our Treasury, and I want it done promptly and in such manner that the par value of the bonds shall be forthcoming to us free from commission. Of course we do not commit ourselves to the issuance of these bonds. We may be an-ticipated or the necessity of such action may be averted. I only want you to find out in the most confidential way possible what can be done if the contingency arrives.

To DANIEL S. LAMONT

Lakewood, N.J., *February 23*, 1893

I enclose a letter from Dickinson which explains his dispatch of yester-day. I have telegraphed him accepting the suggestion and man with thanks.[2] This I suppose ends the private secretary business. A dispatch from Olney came this morning confirming his of yesterday and adding, 'that if you can possibly excuse me I want to be excused — please wire me your decision.' Of course I can do nothing now but stick to the thing.

Gresham writes that he will be at my office Friday morning (tomorrow) to get any word that I may have for him. I shall write or telegraph him and ask him to come here Saturday and trust Carlisle, whom I expect that afternoon. I wish to avoid any mistake. You should try to see him at the Buckingham before he goes downtown in the morning and tell him what I want. Have him telegraph me tomorrow if he will come and when. It may be possible that I shall want to make hotel arrangements for him.

I received a nice dispatch from Carlisle this morning cordially approv-ing yesterday's appointment. Don't fail to come down Monday. Why couldn't you stay overnight?

[1] Cleveland meant the *sale* abroad.
[2] Don M. Dickinson had suggested a friend, Henry T. Thurber, to be Cleveland's private secretary.

To RICHARD WATSON GILDER

Lakewood, N.J., *February 27,* 1893

I expect to see you this evening and did not suspect any such conspiracy as was developed when the beautiful gift [1] sent to me by yourself and your 'pals' reached my hands. I don't know what to say to 'you fellows' — and no wonder, for I never had so fine a present before. I can only say that I am perfectly delighted and that this reminder of real friendliness comes to me at a time when my surroundings do not indicate that all friendship is sincere and disinterested. I thank you from the bottom of my heart.

I wanted to tell you that we expect you and Mrs. Gilder to go with us to Washington next Thursday. A train of three special cars will start from Jersey City (Liberty Street Ferry) about ten o'clock A.M. You should take the boat that leaves the New York side at 9:45. The train will come here and pick us up and from here we will go to Washington by way of Elizabethport, etc. Your baggage must be ready and in the hall, perhaps three feet and two inches inside the door of your house, at seven o'clock in the morning — certainly not later than seven o'clock and seven minutes A.M. — and a wagon will call for it. It will be well to put on the trunk a card or tag inscribed in legible characters with the name of the owner and his destination in Washington. We shall arrive there between six and half-past six P.M. You will probably hear from Colonel Lamont on this subject as well as other details of the expedition. Please let us know if we may expect you.

To E. C. BENEDICT

Lakewood, N.J., *February 27,* 1893

I am a very happy man tonight; and the thoughts of all that await me are for a time at least banished by the grateful sentiment that possesses me. I am delighted by the receipt of the beautiful gift [1] that has just reached me from these good and disinterested friends. To my dying day I shall cherish this gift and it will always be a reminder of the friendships that are after all the dearest and best things in life.

I can now give you the correct time on the trip to Washington . . .

---

[1] His friends Gilder and Benedict gave him a gold watch with a photograph of Mrs. Cleveland and their daughter Ruth on the inside of the case.

To CARTER H. HARRISON

Washington, *March* 10, 1893

Your letter is received. I am in the midst of much turmoil and perplexity and know but little of the complications which attend the local contest in Chicago. The fact, however, that quite serious divisions exist among our Democratic brethren there makes it a very delicate matter for me to do or say anything that may be construed as an interference. I am by no means unmindful of your exceedingly valuable service in the last national campaign, and I assure you that I entertain for you the utmost personal friendliness.

SENATOR DANIEL W. VOORHEES *to* CLEVELAND

Washington, *March* 20, 1893

I do not feel that the sun ought to go down before I convey to you my earnest and grateful appreciation of your kindness and courtesy today in the appointment of Mr. Risley.[1] I thank you most sincerely, not only for the appointment itself, but also for the exceedingly kind and handsome manner in which it has been made. You have indeed made me very deeply and permanently your debtor, and it will be one of the principal pleasures and purposes of my life, and at every opportunity, to recognize and justify, as far as may be in my power, the generous confidence and friendly regard you have extended to me.

Permit me to subscribe myself, with the highest respect and esteem, very faithfully your friend.

To MR. LEO OPPENHEIM

Washington, *April* 15, 1893

An advertisement recently published in the Albany *Evening Journal* signed by you introduces the name of Mrs. Cleveland in a most indecent way. I suppose we must always have among us dirty and disreputable fellows; but I shall be surprised if you find such advertising profitable among the residents of so respectable a city as Albany.

[1] Cleveland was wooing Voorhees, who was chairman of the Senate Finance Committee, to support of a repeal of the silver-purchase clause.

To SENATOR WILLIAM B. ALLISON [1]

Washington, *April* 18, 1893

I have received your resignation as Commissioner of the International Monetary Conference, which convened at Brussels on the 2d day of November, 1892. Your colleagues have also placed their resignations in my hands. I assume that this action of the Commissioners indicates their disposition to leave me unembarrassed if I should desire to designate other persons to attend as delegates the adjourned meeting of the conference on the 30th day of May next.

The ability and character of the Commissioners originally selected, their knowledge concerning the subject to be treated, and their familiarity with the discussions which have already taken place at the conference, make it exceedingly important that they continue the work upon which they have entered. I shall certainly be personally gratified if they consent to do so. I hope, therefore, that I may be allowed to decline an acceptance of your resignation as Commissioner, and that the country and the objects of the conference may have the great benefit of your continued service.

FRANCIS LYNDE STETSON *to* CLEVELAND

New York, *April* 20, 1893

The situation here tonight is such that I do not feel it consistent with my personal regard for you and for your Administration, to withhold the expression of my opinion (even though unasked and irresponsible) upon the financial question.[2]

Gold today has gone to a premium. This is a fact (though not generally observed), inasmuch as sterling bills have been sold for gold at a lower price than for currency. There is a general feeling of alarm, not among the Republicans alone, but among your warm and sincere supporters; and this feeling is not confined to Wall Street, but is affecting the mercantile community, which is unable to obtain the necessary banking accommodation, and consequently feels not merely alarmed but a severe pinch.

The situation is such that no careful observer will be astonished at a

---

[1] Allison (1829–1908) had been a Senator from Iowa since 1873.

[2] Secretary Carlisle made an unwisely ambiguous statement on April 20 that he would pay demands on the Government in gold 'so long as it has gold lawfully available for the purpose,' and this aroused fears that the nation would go to a silver basis. But the diary of Charles S. Hamlin shows that Cleveland had approved this statement, and must share responsibility for it.

pronounced and serious panic at any moment. This being the situation, the question comes, first, as to what is its cause, and second, as to what is its remedy. The cause, of course, is to be found originally in the Bland Act of 1878; but at present and immediately it exhibits itself in the uncertainty as to the course which the Administration is to take. Whether rightly or wrongly, it is generally believed that the Treasury Department is contemplating the payment of silver certificates in silver, thus destroying the parity of the various classes of what is considered public money.

It is most important that, as suggested in your inaugural address, the Executive power of the Government should be exerted to avert such a disaster as seems now to be impending, and that the policy of the Administration should be made known as soon as possible. The uncertainty is almost as dangerous as any step. The remedy for the situation is thus indicated: Every dollar of the $100,000,000 gold reserve should, in my opinion, be expended in meeting the government obligations, rather than that, for the mere purpose of keeping in hand and intact a reserve intended to provide for the full redemption of government obligations, those obligations, or any part of them, should now be discredited....

ANDREW CARNEGIE *to* CLEVELAND

New York, *April* 22, 1893

You know that for several years my chief anxiety in public matters has been in regard to the 'silver question,' and that I stated in the *North American Review* that if I were called upon to vote for a Free-Trade Democrat who supported sound money, or a Tariff Republican who was not sound upon money, I should vote for the former. Perhaps this will excuse me in your eyes for venturing to address you at this juncture.

I have not gone down to my office since the day I had the pleasure of meeting you on the Elevated Railway — many months ago — but the position of affairs called me down yesterday. Let me assure you that, in my opinion, the decision to pay notes in gold saved this country from panic, and the entire confusion of its industrial interests.[1] From my own experience I can tell you that foreigners had taken alarm and had begun to withdraw their capital in gold. Unless all doubt is put to rest, there is still great danger of the country being drained of its gold. Had Secretary

---

[1] Cleveland had given out a reassuring statement on payments in gold. This was more formally made in the note given below.

Carlisle's statement been unequivocal, this trouble would not have arisen. All excitement can be allayed and the crisis safely passed by a simple declaration from you. If I might suggest, somewhat like the following: 'As long as I am President of the United States, the workingman is going to be paid in as good a dollar as the foreign banker is.' I think this would also be good politics....

To THE UNITED PRESS

Washington, *April* 23, 1893

The inclination on the part of the public to accept newspaper reports concerning the intentions of those charged with the management of our national finances seems to justify my emphatic contradiction of the statement that the redemption of any kind of Treasury notes, except in gold, has at any time been determined upon or contemplated by the Secretary of the Treasury or any other member of the present Administration. The President and his Cabinet are absolutely harmonious in the determination to exercise every power conferred upon them to maintain the public credit and to preserve the parity between gold and silver and between all financial obligations of the Government....

To CHARLES N. PLUMMER

Washington, *May* 3, 1893

I was very glad to receive your favor of the 21st of April, and thank you for the kind words which it contains. I am pleased to comply with your request, and to assure you that the work of the Rhode Island Radical Peace Union, in so far as it tends toward the ideal of universal peace, has my hearty support and approbation. The abolition of war, as a means of settling disputes among the nations, at first the dream of the philanthropist, now seems to be getting every year nearer and nearer a reality; and it is to be hoped that our nation will do much in the future, as in the past, to hasten the day when the desire for peace shall be more prevalent among the nations of the earth. With best wishes for all agencies tending to this end...

To THE PUBLIC

Washington, *May* 8, 1893

It has become apparent after two months' experience that the rules heretofore promulgated regulating interviews with the President have wholly failed in their operation. The time which, under these rules, was set apart for the reception of Senators and Representatives has been almost entirely spent in listening to applications for office, which have been bewildering in volume, perplexing and exhausting in their iteration, and impossible of remembrance.

A due regard for public duty, which must be neglected if present conditions continue, and an observance of the limitations placed upon human endurance, oblige me to decline from and after this date all personal interviews with those seeking appointments to office, except as I, on my own motion, may invite them. The same consideration makes it impossible for me to receive those who merely desire to pay their respects, excepting on the days and during the hours especially designated for that purpose.

I earnestly request Senators and Representatives to aid me in securing for them uninterrupted interviews by declining to introduce their constituents and friends when visiting the Executive Mansion during the hours designated for their reception. Applicants for office will only prejudice their prospects by repeated importunities and by remaining at Washington to await results.

To JAMES J. HILL

Washington, *May 29,* 1893.

I learn that your friends and neighbors intend to celebrate the completion of the Great Northern Railroad to the Pacific Coast, early in June. I cannot permit the occasion to pass without extending to you my hearty congratulations upon the achievement which is so entirely your own and which is related in such an important manner to the progress and prosperity of the section of the country with which you have been so prominently identified. While your friends sound your well-deserved praises, I cannot but think that the most pleasing thing about the celebration to you will be the feeling that you have contributed so largely by your intelligent activity to the development of our country's material interests. You surely ought to enjoy your neighbors' congratulations; but the monument which you have erected must in all time to come be a source of gratification to you and to all who appreciate your sterling qualities.

To POSTMASTER-GENERAL WILSON S. BISSELL

Washington, *June* 7, 1893

I have seen Senator Mills and he feels so deeply and sadly in respect to his son-in-law, and he is such a thoroughly sincere and useful friend, that I cannot do otherwise than to express the hope that conditions with his relatives may remain unchanged. Internal Revenue Collector Fitch has resigned. I have the application for the successorship here and would be glad to talk the matter over with you tomorrow afternoon.

SECRETARY WALTER Q. GRESHAM *to* CLEVELAND [1]

Chicago, *July* 3, 1893

I am about to leave on the 5 P.M. Limited for Washington. Was not able to buy a ticket for Saturday or Sunday. During the three days that I spent in Indiana I heard nothing indicating the existence of a free-coinage sentiment in that State. It looks like the vote of Indiana would be solid for repeal of the Sherman Law. I think the silver men realize that their cause is doomed. Your proclamation was received with great demonstrations of satisfaction in this part of the country. I am glad that you took the step — although I realize that all this financial trouble is not due to the Sherman Law.

There is no foundation for what we heard about an effort to organize an anti-Administration party in Illinois. *The people are with you.* There is no doubt of it....

J. L. M. CURRY *to* CLEVELAND

Asheville, N.C., *July* 4, 1893

... You may recall that, a few weeks before the election, after much travel and conference in Tennessee, Alabama, Georgia, and North Carolina, I wrote to you that the vote of those States was certain for you, as it was impossible to seduce the Alliance men from the Democratic party and their confidence in you. Subsequently, when travelling together to President Hayes's funeral, I had the temerity to express the opinion that in the filling of offices, the Alliance men and Populists who voted for you were more worthy of recognition than those who, while never departing from our organization, yet maligned you, and sought by sinister means to deprive the party and the country of your leadership. The farmers in

---

[1] Cleveland underwent his jaw operation on July 1, 1893. For the next month he wrote almost nothing, and the gap is filled with letters to him.

the South, I could not speak for the West, had unshaken faith in your integrity and ability, and were tempted, temporarily, from their allegiance because of the terrible paralysis which had befallen agriculture.

This introduction is to excuse me (1) for making a statement and (2) for offering a suggestion. First: Many of the men, bitterly hostile to your nomination, some of whom are now Congressmen, foreign ministers, consuls, collectors, postmasters, marshals, district attorneys, will 'knife' you at the first opportunity. Some of the aspirants for leadership, claimants of statesmanship — it were easy to name them — hate you because with tact and courage and statesmanship and reliance on the masses, you led the party and the people away from them, to living, practical issues, to higher altitudes of principle. You are now leading them to an abandonment of the 'silver craze,' to the advocacy of a safe and honest financial policy. They acquiesce *ex necessitate*, but it is not human nature to love the man who has exposed their demagoguism, their shallow sciolism. Second: — The suggestion which is the main object of this letter. Let me beg you, in your message to the extra session, to discuss, clearly and *fully*, the silver question, so that the people, who trust and honor you, may see the utter deceptiveness of the remedies that have been commended as specifics for their distressing poverty. You always state great constitutional and economic truths with clearness, in axiomatic, quotable phrases, which stick in the public memory, but what is too clear in your mind for argument may not be understood by the masses. In a somewhat protracted life, much given to study of political questions, I have never known as much ignorance, appeal to prejudice, perversion of the facts, shallow sophistry, fallacy of argumentation, as have been used in public debate and by press to delude and mislead the people. More than any other American, you can write what will be read and accepted.

My motive or purpose in writing so frankly will not be misunderstood. The letter requires no answer. It is the patriotic utterance of one who, for nine years, has not for a moment, or a hair's breadth, deviated in his devotion to you.

SECRETARY JOHN G. CARLISLE *to* CLEVELAND

Washington, no date [*July*, 1893]

Personal.

Crisp has been here today in answer to my telegram and we have had a very satisfactory interview. He says he wrote Mr. Straus some time ago that he (Straus) must understand that the question as to the chairmanship of the Committee on Ways and Means was an open one until after the election of Speaker.[1] Of course I cannot write all that was said, but the substance is that he will give us a satisfactory organization. I urged the importance of five committees: 1. Ways and Means; 2. Appointments; 3. Banking and Currency; 4. Coinage, Weights, etc.; 5. Rules, and I believe he will make them all to suit us.

There is one point upon which he is not in entire accord with my views of policy. He thinks the repeal of the Silver-Purchase Law and the repeal of the 10 per cent tax ought to be included in the same bill; that is, he thinks the measure would command more votes in that form. He thinks also it would be bad policy to repeal the Silver-Purchase Law and fail to repeal the other, and that Representatives from the South could not sustain themselves at home if such should be the result. But my opinion is that he will support the two measures on separate bills if he is satisfied that they will be stronger in that form. Cliff Breckinridge is here, but I have not yet had an opportunity to have an interview with him. He sent a message to me by Logan today that I need have no fear about his vote — that he would be 'all right.'

This has been a very hard day — the weather is hot, the crowd has been large and eager, and there has been a great deal of work to do in order to get ready to leave tomorrow.

Mrs. Carlisle has been laid up with rheumatism, but will be able to start tomorrow.

SECRETARY JOHN G. CARLISLE *to* CLEVELAND
Washington, no date [*July*, 1893]

Crisp was interviewed before he left Georgia and stated that he had received a telegram from me asking him to come here. The consequence was that all our movements were closely watched, but I think the newspapers will not learn much. I send some clippings from the *Star* of this evening which may interest you.

Every day strengthens the opinion I expressed to you two or three weeks ago — that the so-called silver men will propose and insist upon free coinage at a new ratio, say 20 to 1, and this, I think, is the strongest

---

[1] Carlisle was supervising preparations for the special session of Congress which began August 7. William L. Wilson of West Virginia was appointed chairman of the House Ways and Means Committee, which was to draw up a tariff bill.

position they can take to prevent their former supporters from deserting them.

I received another telegram this afternoon from Fairchild about Lyon, the Surveyor at New York. He still refuses to comply with the request of the Commission. Chenowith is here and wants to be Director of the Mint.

FRANCES F. CLEVELAND *to* GOVERNOR WILLIAM E. RUSSELL
Gray Gables, *July* 31, 1893

As the housekeeper, I think it is my privilege to thank you for the delicious salmon which came to us from you several days ago. I say several days — when you and I know exactly how long ago it was — because it makes it seem as if I had been more prompt in expressing our great satisfaction and gratification.

The President has not been writing at all since he came up for his much-needed rest, or he would have taken the matter into his own hands and told you of the pleasure you have given us — long before now.

He came here completely worn out, and with an unusually bad attack of rheumatism [1] besides. We have made him give up entirely to resting — and he is already another man. If the country hadn't been so inconsiderate as to get up this financial trouble, which necessitated the early session of Congress, and he could get another month here away from worry, I think he would be thoroughly rested. As it is, we insist upon his returning when he gets things running in Washington.

To JOSEPH JEFFERSON
Gray Gables, *July* 31, 1893

Dr. Bryant left us last evening. He especially requested me to express to you his thanks for your thoughtful invitation to accompany you tomorrow, and his assurance that nothing would have pleased him more than the acceptance of your courtesy if it had been possible. Please accept my thanks also for your kind attention to my guests at a time when I was unable to personally entertain them as I desired.

I am delighted to know that your vacation is doing so much for you. I wish I were in better condition to return to my work.

[1] A certain amount of innocent mendacity was required to keep news of Cleveland's actual condition from reaching the public.

To SENATOR WILLIAM F. VILAS

Gray Gables, *August* 13, 1893

I have been very much disturbed since I saw you last with your Senatorial associates. What troubles me is the proposition that a compromise should be made, merely for the sake of having something passed without Republican help. It hardly seems to me that any arrangement can be made with all of our side that will not disgust and disappoint the people who have trusted us. I am very sorry that a committee was appointed.

I still believe it would be better for those of our side who believe in unconditional repeal,[1] to offer a bill for that purpose and support it. If we do not, I am afraid such a bill will be offered from the Republican side. If that should occur, the sound men on our side would perhaps be found following Republican lead instead of obliging sound Republicans to fall in behind them. I cannot help but feel that there is great danger of our friends the enemy gaining more credit with the country than we. Thus far I do not see that we are a particle ahead — so far at least as the Senate is concerned.

I am very certain that this is not the time to play for partisan position. Another thing is equally certain. If we, who are charged with the responsibility, inaugurate the measure of relief, our countrymen will give us full credit for it and will not inquire whether Republicans helped us by their votes or not. If a measure that in the eyes of the people promises relief is not passed, we cannot escape condemnation. The fact that a compromise measure has been passed won't satisfy our people if the measure don't suit them — even though it was passed by Democratic votes alone.

I want to do my Democratic best; the only way in my opinion to help or save the party is to be right on the question now before Congress.

To HENRY T. THURBER

Gray Gables, *August* 17, 1893

I send you by the mail that takes this a quantity of nominations, pardons, etc. I have an idea that the postoffice nominations, so far as they nominate parties who have been appointed during the recess, ought to state that fact. It is done in all the other Departments. If the Postmaster-General thinks it best to add such a statement as I suggest, there is room left for it above my signature in those I have signed. You have

[1] Of the Sherman Silver-Purchase Act of 1890.

in your custody an appointment of a man named Du Bellet as consul to Rheims. It was held up. I wish you would deliver it to the State Department to be held or delivered as is thought best in that Department.

I am improving fast, but I feel very often that I ought to be in Washington.

To HENRY T. THURBER

Gray Gables, *August* 20, 1893

I send you with this four packages of nominations, etc. A suggestion has been made to me, which I think should be carried out as far as possible, considering the large proportion of nominations already sent in. If there are some nominations that the Senators who are inclined to be mean, as well as opposed to what we want, especially desire, it might be well to postpone sending in such nominations until my return. This, of course, is confidential, but I don't want you to act on your own responsibility in the matter. If you see any chance to carry out my idea I want you to consult with the head of the Department to which the nomination is related. If it is not approved in that quarter, let the plan be abandoned. It is, however, my judgment that we ought not to incur too much fatigue in our efforts to gratify at this time those who bitterly oppose our political attempts to help the country and save our party. I was pleased at your canvass of Senators, but very much surprised to see that you had put Faulkner and Pugh [1] in the negative column, for I had relied on both of them as being right. I am not willing to give them up yet.

Of course you will carefully keep the statements of recommendations, etc., attached to the nominations I send you from the Interior Department. I expect to return to Washington in a week or ten days, and I should hardly think it would pay to send me any more nominations after you receive this unless it is something especially important. I have been a little under the weather during the last week, which has interfered with my recreation, but I hope to make it up in the next week.

To DON M. DICKINSON

Gray Gables, *August* 25, 1893

Your letter was received yesterday and I need not say that I was glad to hear from you again. I have not been real well this summer, but am

---

[1] Charles J. Faulkner (1847–   ) was Senator from West Virginia 1887–99; James L. Pugh (1820–1907) was Senator from Alabama 1880–97.

much better now, and while I feel that I could stand even a little more vacation than I have had, I believe I shall soon return to my work in pretty fair condition. I am willing to do anything you want me to do about the portrait and Mr. Ives.

I am disturbed by that part of your letter which refers to the Supreme Court Justiceship. I want to agree with you in all things of this kind, but your ideas and mine relating to the availability of Mr. Hornblower [1] are not in accord. I know him well, and while I have not made up my mind fully in the matter, I do not believe there is in the State of New York a Democratic lawyer better fitted for the position. You will, I know, agree with me that a man should not be rejected for the place simply because corporations are among his clients, and I hope you will agree with me that in these days of wildness, conservatism and steadiness should not be at a discount.

I think I can see daylight in the financial matter, though this and other things have perplexed me almost to death. I should be glad to have your ideas in detail regarding the Supreme Court Justiceship. The matter ought to be settled very soon.

Please give my most sincere regards to Mrs. Dickinson and my love to Frances. Mrs. Cleveland joins me in this and desires to include you in her remembrances. You know my affection for you.

To SECRETARY JOHN G. CARLISLE [2]

Gray Gables, *August* 28, 1893 (telegram)

You and the rest of the Executive family will please accept my congratulations and gratitude upon today's consummation.

JACOB H. SCHIFF *to* CLEVELAND

New York, *August* 29, 1893

Scarcely more than three months ago, alike with many others, I despaired of the possibility of an unconditional repeal of the purchasing clause of the Sherman Act, and submitted to you, if unconditional repeal could not be carried, the desirability of a compromise measure to save the financial fabric of our country from destruction and to insure the continuation of gold payments by the United States Government.

Though hardly more than three months have since elapsed, every

[1] William B. Hornblower was duly nominated to the Supreme Court.
[2] The Silver-Purchase Repeal Bill passed the House on August 28 by a vote of 239 to 108.

measure to restore silver has been defeated and unconditional repeal has been passed by the House by enormous majorities, while it is not likely that the Senate will close its ears to the voice of public opinion expressed with such tremendous force.

The country is to be congratulated that you, Mr. President, while others doubted and despaired, did not falter, and succeeded in carrying the adoption of the only measure which will restore the confidence at home and abroad which the country so sorely needs, and insure a return to prosperity in the not far future. Permit me to congratulate and to thank you, and to assure you of my high respect.

To Richard Watson Gilder

Washington, *September* 1, 1893

I left at Gray Gables a half-written letter to you. It was to thank you for your very kind note and to tell you how grateful your words of approval are. I meant also to say to you that it is very likely that I shall nominate the gentleman from Rhode Island [1] to Italy. He is thoroughly qualified and much that has been said about him is very unjust. I am not at all coerced and if I do it I shall be altogether to blame, except that some friends I value very highly and to whom I ought to be grateful want the appointment made. There is positively nothing in the talk about a promise in return for a subscription and he himself has been so unjustly treated that it seems to me it will be agreeable to vindicate him so far as his appointment will do it.

I don't know now much you care for this, but I do hope if the thing is done you will wait and see. I am always glad to please you and to agree with you.

To Thomas F. Bayard [2]

Washington, *September* 11, 1893

I received today your letter of September 1st and thank you for it as well as for two or three preceding it and thus far unacknowledged. I especially want to thank you for the splendid picture of yourself you sent. I think it is the best and most faithful likeness I have ever seen.

I can well believe how interested you are in the subject just now oc-

---

[1] James J. Van Alen, a friend of Whitney who had made a large contribution to the Democratic campaign fund.

[2] Bayard, declining a reappointment as Secretary of State, served as our first Ambassador to Great Britain, 1893–97.

cupying the time of the Senate. The action of the House was wonderfully gratifying and the majority we secured was beyond our expectations, and to me was a demonstration that behind these direct representatives of the people there was a sentiment that actually *drove* them to duty.

The Senate is making a shameful display, but no one doubts that we have a good sound majority when the vote comes. With this conceded by all, the result hangs on, keeping back the day of better things. I shall not be much surprised, however, if the break occurs and a vote is reached sooner than the most of us expect. Isn't it queer that Voorhees and Gorman should be the leaders in a cause in which I am so vitally interested? 'Strange bedfellows!' They are, I believe, both working well, but every day is an anxious one for me, fearing that something may occur to distract time and attention from the pending topic....

Day before yesterday (the 9th) my wife presented me with what is always called, I believe, 'a fine baby.'[1] It's a little girl and they do say it's a healthy one. The mother is as well as she can be, and Ruth thus far seems to think the newcomer's advent is a great joke. You were only one of many who were trapped by a fool of a newspaper man into the premature expression of kind congratulations. I laid yours away and applied it to the event of last Saturday.

The report you saw regarding my health resulted from a most astounding breach of professional duty on the part of a medical man.[2] I tell you this in strict confidence, for the policy here has been to deny and discredit his story. I believe the American public and newspapers are not speculating further on the subject.

The truth is, officeseeking and officeseekers came very near putting a period to my public career. Whatever else developed found its opportunity in the weakened walls of a constitution that had long withstood fierce attacks. I turned the corner to the stage of enforced care-taking almost in a day. And this must be hereafter the condition on which will depend my health and life. Another phase of the situation cannot be spoken of with certainty, but I believe the chances in my favor are at least even.

I have learned how weak the strongest man is under God's decrees and I see in a new light the necessity of doing my allotted work in the full apprehension of the coming night.

[1] Cleveland's second child, Esther, was born in the White House September 9, 1893.

[2] This breach was always attributed to the dentist present at Cleveland's jaw operation, Dr. Ferdinand Hasbrouck.

You must understand that I am regarded here as a perfectly well man and the story of an important surgical operation is thoroughly discredited. I think I never looked better and I am much stronger than I have lately been. You have now more of the story than anyone else outside of the medical circle. Mrs. Cleveland sends love to you and Mrs. Bayard and with mine added in plenteous degree I am...

To MRS. JOHN G. CARLISLE

Washington, *September* 14, 1893

Jane is a very pretty name and there is no living person whose name I would rather our new baby should bear than yours. The responsibility of selecting her name was put upon me long before her birth and I feel that responsibility very much indeed. It may be very disappointing to those still alive whose names are passed by, but I have determined to ignore mother, grandmothers, and great-grandmothers and avoid all jealousy by going back to Biblical times. I mean to call the little girl Esther. It is a favorite name with me and associated in a pleasant way with things I remember besides the hanging of Haman.

You are the first one in the world, except her mother, to know the name of our second child. I hope 'Jane' can wait.

To GOVERNOR W. J. NORTHEN [1]

Washington, *September* 25, 1893

I hardly know how to reply to your letter of the 15th instant. It seems to me that I am plainly on record concerning the financial question. My letter accepting the nomination to the Presidency, when read in connection with the message lately sent to Congress in extraordinary session, appears to me to be very explicit. I want a currency that is stable and safe in the hands of our people. I will not knowingly be implicated in a condition that will make me in the least degree answerable to any laborer or farmer in the United States for a shrinkage in the purchasing power of the dollar he has received for a full dollar's worth of work or for a good dollar's worth of the product of his toil.

I not only want our currency to be of such a character that all kinds of dollars will be of equal purchasing power at home, but I want it to be of such a character as will demonstrate abroad our wisdom and good faith,

[1] The free-silverite governor of Georgia.

thus placing upon a firm foundation our credit among the nations of the earth. I want the financial conditions and the laws relating to our currency so safe and reassuring that those who have money will spend and invest it in business and new enterprises, instead of holding it. You cannot cure fright by calling it foolish and unreasonable, and you cannot prevent a frightened man from hoarding his money. I want good, sound and stable money and a condition of confidence that will keep it in use.

Within the limits of what I have written, I am a friend of silver, but I believe its proper place in our currency can only be fixed by a readjustment of our currency legislation and the inauguration of a consistent and comprehensive financial scheme. I think such a thing can only be entered upon profitably and hopefully after the repeal of the law which is charged with all our financial woes. In the present state of the public mind this law cannot be built upon nor patched in such a way as to relieve the situation. I am therefore opposed to free and unlimited coinage of silver by this country alone and independently, and I am in favor of the immediate and unconditional repeal of the purchasing clause of the so-called Sherman Law.

I confess I am astonished by the opposition in the Senate to such prompt action as would relieve the present unfortunate situation. My daily prayer is that the delay occasioned by such opposition may not be the cause of plunging the country into deeper depression than it has yet known, and that the Democratic party may not be justly held responsible for such a catastrophe.

To RICHARD WATSON GILDER

Washington, *October* 8, 1893

I am not willing that you should believe that I have nominated a man I knew or supposed to be unfit to an important place either because he contributed largely to the last campaign or because I was overpersuaded.

I have not the slightest doubt of Mr. Van Alen's entire fitness and I am sure that it will before long be generally accepted. His contribution, since it did not induce his appointment, is, it seems to me, irrelevant. I have not seen printed nor have I heard a single thing (that I did not know to be false) which militates against the propriety of his selection. I have made no excuses to anyone, and no explanations. I hardly know why I write this to you unless it be that I am not willing so good a man and so good a friend should be grieved on my account. I believe this act of mine will fully vindicate itself; but the incident demonstrates how readily prejudicial newspaper chatter is picked up and scattered.

I am suffering many perplexities and troubles and this term of the Presidency has cost me so much health and vigor that I have sometimes doubted if I could carry the burden to the end. My determination is to live, and I believe God has put the belief in my mind that I can still be of use to my country.

Whatever happens I am grateful and happy in my home. Mrs. Cleveland and both children are as wel as they can be....

To Don M. Dickinson

Woodley,[1] Washington, *October* 9, 1893

Your very kind letter was received today and I thank you for it from the bottom of my heart. I am very much depressed. I feel that I am looking full in the face a loss of popular trust in the Democratic party which means its relegation to the rear again for many years if not its disruption. I am feeling, too, the punishment of again occupying the office of President without the previous advice and consent of the United States Senate. This is perhaps something I deserve and I do not complain on my own account. I am only sorry that this cause of offence should imperil the good of the country.

One phrase in your letter touches me deeply and gives voice to a thought that has frequently entered my mind of late. I mean the statement that some who should actively help 'pass by on the other side.' I suppose I know exactly what you mean. I feel that when I go beyond my Cabinet my situation is a most forlorn one — more so than even you suspect.

My good friend, of one thing you may be sure. On the question now awaiting solution I shall be right. I am not discouraged and so far as I am concerned the fight will continue until no further fight can be made. I wish there were about twenty Dickinsons in the country.

Whatever happens, my wife and two children are as well as they can be.

To Dr. Kasson C. Gibson [2]

Washington, *October* 14, 1893

I hasten to announce that you have scored another dental victory and a greater one than has before attended your manipulation of my corpus.

[1] A house not far from Oak View which Cleveland leased and held during his second Administration.

[2] The dentist of New York City who fitted a rubber jaw to Cleveland.

The new plate came last night. I looked at it quite askance — in point of fact with disfavor. I put it in this morning. It is now about 11 o'clock at night. I have worn it all day with the utmost ease and comfort without a shred of packing of any kind. I took it out to cleanse it after break-fast and lunch, but found very little on or behind it, that needed atten-tion. My wife says that my voice and articulation are much better than they have been for a number of days. I have not had the plate out since dinner.

I feel very well as you may suppose over my new machine. The double-header, as I call it — the one you built up and afterwards cut down — I cannot make work very well, but the new one promises to be such a comfort that I expect to get on nicely with it and the old stand-by you first made. If I could only regain my strength and hearing I should feel quite like myself. I think unless improvement sets in respecting these things soon, I shall go to New York soon and spend a day among the Doctors. If I go of course you will have due notice, for I shall want to see you.

Give my affectionate regards to J. D. B.[1] when you see him and believe me with thanks for your care and thoughtfulness...

P.S. The instrument you sent me for holding cotton is just what I wanted.

To Oscar S. Straus

Washington, *October 20*, 1893

Your letter was received today. I need not tell you how much I value your friendship; and I hardly need confess how touched I am by the mani-festation of affection afforded by the solicitude you evince in the Van Alen matter. I am amazed by the course pursued by some good people in dealing with this subject. No one has yet presented to me a single charge of unfitness or incompetency. They have chosen to eagerly act upon the frivolous statements of a most mendacious and mischievous newspaper, in an attempt to injure a man who in no way has been guilty of wrong. I leave out of the account the allegation that his nomination was in acknowledgment of a large campaign contribution. No one will accuse me of such a trade and Mr. Whitney's and Mr. Van Alen's denial that any such thing existed in the minds of anyone concerned, I believe to be the truth. I think it would be a cowardly thing in me to disgrace a

---

[1] Dr. Bryant.

man because the New York *World* had doomed him to disgrace. Since the nomination was sent in, I have left the matter entirely to the Senate, and I hear that the nomination was confirmed today. This ends the matter. I am entirely content to wait for a complete justification of my part in the proceeding.

I am sorry you regard this matter as so unfortunate, and if anything could have induced me to turn away from a course which seemed to me so plainly just and right, it would be my desire to satisfy just such good friends as you have always proved yourself to be.

CHARLES FRANCIS ADAMS, JR., *to* CLEVELAND
Boston, *November* 18, 1893

I do not suppose you or Secretary Gresham have much time in which to read letters; but I wish to trespass on whatever time you do allot to that work, to express the deep sense of respect, not to use a stronger term, I feel for the position the Administration has taken on the Hawaii question.[1]

Of the right and wrong of the question I know little; I do know that it requires courage in a public man to do what he is persuaded is right, when so doing is tantamount to a defiance of 'jingoism.' I remember no stand taken by a Government so morally sound and dignified as that now taken by Secretary Gresham and your Administration, since the similar stand taken some years ago by Mr. Gladstone towards the victorious African Boers. It is not easy to see how the United States can protest against the policy of force in their dealings with semi-civilized natives and races, if we ourselves are quite unable to resist the temptation to have an occasional hack at them on our own account.

To JAMES J. VAN ALEN
Washington, *November* 22, 1893

The Secretary of State has submitted to me your letter of the 20th instant in which you tender your resignation as Ambassador to Italy. I hasten to express my earnest wish that you reconsider this conclusion. The sentiments contained in your letter do credit to your conscience and

---

[1] The circumstances under which Cleveland withdrew from the Senate the pending treaty of annexation with Hawaii which the Harrison Administration had left there, and sent a special commissioner to the islands who reported that the American representatives in the islands had committed a grave wrong, are explained in the editor's *Grover Cleveland: A Study in Courage*, 549–62.

Americanism, but you must allow me to dissent from their application in this case.

I did not select you for nomination to the Italian mission without satisfying myself of your entire fitness for the place. I am now better convinced of your fitness than ever. You know and I know that all the malignant criticism that has been indulged in regarding this appointment has no justification, and that the decent people who have doubted its propriety have been tricked or have missed the actual considerations upon which it rests. We should not yield to the noise and clamor which have arisen from these conditions.

My personal preference should enter but very slightly into your final determination; but so far as I have such preference, it is emphatically that you accept the honorable office conferred upon you and vindicate by the discharge of its duties the wisdom and propriety of your selection.[1]

To WILLIAM C. WHITNEY

Washington, *December* 1, 1893

I have this moment finished my message and lose no time in writing you on the Van Alen matter. I thought when I received his first letter that my reply, informing him that his resignation was exactly what I did not want and that so far as my desires were deemed of any importance they could only be hurt by his not going to his post and doing well, would end all talk of resignation. I was therefore profoundly amazed when I read his second letter.

I have thought a good deal about it since in the light of your note to me. I have concluded either that he has not a proper apprehension of the situation and the conduct it demands, or that you have discovered something in him that satisfied you it would not do to risk him in the place. I don't want to urge him to go merely for my sake and against his judgment or inclination, for in that event I should be afraid he would not be in a mood to do as well in the place as he ought. It seems to me, therefore, that I am left to be suspected of appointing a man out of sheer stubbornness if nothing more, and after defying much criticism, figuring around to bring about his resignation — while he will be accused of

---

[1] Van Alen replied to this letter on November 25 that for reasons which 'were reached only after long and serious consideration of the subject, I feel that I cannot accept the high office to which I have been appointed.'

fighting for a high office for the sake of a personal triumph and then casting it aside.

I suppose you desire his resignation to be accepted and I expect you are actuated by friendliness in all you do in this matter. Relying upon this interpretation of what has taken place and with an earnest desire to meet your wishes, I accept Mr. Van Alen's resignation and consider the incident closed. Never having heard from Mr. Van Alen in any manner before his late letters since I sent his name to the Senate, I write to you instead of to him.

P.S. I shall mail a formal acceptance of Mr. Van Alen's resignation to him tonight.

To SECRETARY HOKE SMITH [1]

Washington, *December 20*, 1893

Here are two bills which I want very carefully examined in your Department and reported out as soon as possible. What is the use of allotting small parcels of land to Indians and at once allowing railroads to cut them up by their rights of way? At this rate the Indians to whom land has been allotted will soon be on our hands as paupers. I think the Indian Commissioners should be consulted in regard to the bill (S. 1021).

[1] Hoke Smith (1855–1932), owner and editor of the Atlanta *Journal*, was Secretary of the Interior, 1893–96, and Senator from Georgia, 1911–21.

XII

A SEA OF TROUBLES

IN 1894 the industrial prostration and the human suffering which resulted from the depression were greater than ever. Cleveland from beginning to end of the year had to contend against a sea of difficulties. Great areas of the country were seething with discontent; his own party was becoming more and more insubordinate; the financial situation of the Government remained alarmingly precarious; industrial troubles were cropping forth. Early in the year the gold reserve in the Treasury dropped to a level which threatened the gold standard, and Cleveland had to sell $50,000,000 worth of four per cent bonds to avert the peril. This bond issue proved a mere stopgap. By November the gold reserve was again at a dangerously low ebb, and that month a second issue of $50,000,000 worth of bonds had hurriedly to be disposed of. Meanwhile, the President had aroused the enmity of many Southern and Western members of Congress by vetoing a bill which provided for the coinage of the silver seigniorage and other loose bullion in the Treasury — enough for an additional $55,000,000 in silver dollars. During the first six months of 1894 he bent his principal energies to an attempt to carry a tariff revision bill through Congress. This measure, known originally as the Wilson Bill because William L. Wilson of the Ways and Means Committee was its principal author, passed the House without great difficulty. But in the Senate it encountered a coalition of eight high-tariff Democrats and the protectionist Republicans. This coalition was able to defy the President and House. The Wilson Bill was thoroughly rewritten, being amended some six hundred times — for the most part to raise its rates. The resulting Wilson-Gorman Bill was not so high as the McKinley Tariff, but was higher than the previous Republican tariff under Chester A. Arthur. Cleveland denounced it in wrathful terms, and, refusing to sign it, let it become law without his name. While the Tariff Bill was going through Congress, he was struggling with the problems offered by Coxey's Army and the other labor or 'commonwealer' forces, and by the Pullman strike in Chicago. The former proved less serious than had been anticipated. Coxey's motley array gradually disintegrated and only a few hundred men reached Washington. But the Chicago strike was a desperately serious affair. Recent evidence shows that Cleveland wished to avoid any drastic Federal intervention. But his impetuous and hot-tempered Attorney-General, Olney, who had been closely identified with railroad interests, determined to smash the strike; he created a situation which seemed to make it necessary to use Federal troops to preserve law and order; and against the protest of the Illinois authorities — Governor Altgeld and Mayor Hopkins — troops were thrown in. The year closed with the Western revolt rising to higher intensity than ever. In the fall elections the Administration suffered a heavy defeat, both House and Senate passing into Republican control.

To RICHARD WATSON GILDER

Washington, *January* 4, 1894

I really don't know when I have been so delighted as when I received your exceedingly handsome and valuable Christmas gift. Somehow I cannot help the feeling that I do not deserve such kindness at your hands and yet it is most pleasant to be reminded of your friendly remembrance. I can do no more than thank you from the bottom of my heart.

We have given our Cabinet dinner tonight, at which we had forty-six guests. It was a very pleasant occasion, though I could not keep out of my mind some pretty serious thoughts. John E. Russell [1] and his wife are with us and she was telling us after the departure of our other guests that when she was pointing out to one of her neighbors her husband's seat, he said, 'I can see Mr. Gilder, but I do not see Mr. Russell.' So you were suggested to me.

I am thinking these days that I have my full share of perplexities — indeed, I am never without them — and I am also thinking that they can be met in but one way, and that is by keeping the heart and conscience right and following their lead. Give my love to Mrs. Gilder.

To SECRETARY HILARY A. HERBERT

Washington, *January* 10, 1894

I have examined with care the report of the board appointed by you to investigate the irregularities in the construction of steel armor at the Carnegie steel and iron mills and the assessment of the damage sustained by the Government on account of deficiencies in the quality of the armor which was affected by such irregularities. I have also examined the evidence and the documents which form the basis of the Government's

---

[1] John E. Russell (1834–1903) of Massachusetts served in Congress 1887–89, was a Cleveland delegate at the Convention of 1892, and was an unsuccessful candidate for governor in 1893 and 1894.

claim for damages. I am satisfied that a large portion of the armor supplied was not of the quality which would have been produced if all possible care and skill had been exercised in its construction. I am of the opinion that under the terms of the contract between the Government and the company this constituted a default entitling the Government to damages.

It is, however, an exceedingly difficult matter to extract from the facts developed a satisfactory basis for the assessment of such damages; and, inasmuch as my decision in the matter is final, I am naturally anxious to do justice to the company and to avoid presumptions against it not fully warranted. The award of the board, although exhibiting an honest desire to meet the case fairly, does not satisfy my inclination to give the company all reasonable benefit of the indefiniteness of the proofs obtained. It appears that the first irregularities of construction were discovered about November 3, 1892. September 16, 1893, some intimation of such irregularities reached the managers of the company, and a letter is produced whereby one of the superintendents is enjoined to greater care in the preparation of the armor. I am willing to assume that the faulty construction began November 3, 1892, and was concluded September 16, 1893. On all the armor manufactured for the Government between these dates, I think 10 per cent from the price should be deducted.

The amount so manufactured is reported to be 2,647,937 tons, and its value $1,404,849. Ten per cent of this value is $140,489, and this amount, in my opinion, should be forfeited to the Government.

To SECRETARY HOKE SMITH

Washington, *January* 20, 1894

I believe I said to you that I would give you an opportunity to see the amendments proposed to civil service rules affecting the Indian School Service before I acted upon them. Therefore I send them with this. I am quite convinced that they should receive my approval. I am surprised and chagrined to learn that teachers in the Chiloco School were made assistant teachers in towns near by, and very much to the advantage of a niece of the Commissioner of Indian Affairs; and I am very willing to do what I can to prevent such things in the future. I would be glad to have you return the papers accompanying this as early as possible, with such suggestions as occur to you.

Senator John T. Morgan *to* Cleveland

Washington, *January 22*, 1894

It appears that Mr. Peckham [1] is to have intense opposition. Mr. Brice is quoted as saying that *he is a crank*, and that he bolted the ticket and voted for Warner Miller for governor, etc. I give you this early information so that no miscalculation may be made in preparing for the contest. I suppose that Judge Peckham [2] would not aid in his brother's defeat.

To E. C. Benedict

Washington, *January 22*, 1894

I was glad to hear from you in such a pleasant way and to know that you were to have a vacation. I am sure it will do you great good. We certainly expected to see you here during the winter, but there are more coming — I hope.

It has occurred to me that during your absence there might be a necessity, or at least it might be best, to know who to communicate with in regard to my matters and interests, now in your hands. I wish you would make me a statement of the present condition and tell me who to apply to, in your stead, if it is thought best to do anything with the securities by way of sales or in any other manner. I cannot write more, but we all send love to you all.

To E. C. Benedict

Washington, *January 25*, 1894

A green investor, I suppose, had rather have 'cash money' when it is tight than to have anything substituted for it. At any rate, that is my case, and if you please I would like my dividends and the proceeds of the scrip dividend sent to me. At what dates is interest due on the bonds?

Mr. Lambert Tree of Chicago, minister to Belgium during my last Administration, sails on the boat with you February 1. I told him you were going and he said he was glad, for you were 'first-rate company.' I guess you met him at the Convention.

I must prepare for a big reception which begins in about half an hour

---

[1] Cleveland's nomination of William B. Hornblower to the Supreme Court was defeated in the Senate in January, 1894. He then nominated Wheeler H. Peckham, another enemy of Hill, who was also defeated.

[2] Rufus W. Peckham, who had been a judge of the New York Court of Appeals.

and cannot extend this scrawl. You know how heartily I wish for you a safe and enjoyable trip and how sincerely I send love to all your household.

To Joseph H. Choate

Washington, *January* 27, 1894

You can do what I deem to be a great service to the country and add very much to the prospect of a high honor coming to the Bar of New York, if you will immediately write a letter to Senator Hoar representing to him the good things you know concerning Wheeler H. Peckham's fitness for a place on the Bench of the Supreme Court.

You can hardly conceive what little and mean things have been and will be resorted to in an effort to defeat him. One pretext is that he has an infernally bad temper, and there is an inclination in certain quarters to hide behind this pretext. I suppose, of course, there is nothing in this allegation. If I am right in this supposition, I wish you would negative the charges and speak of Mr. Peckham's ability in such a way as your knowledge of the man justifies.

Let me suggest that it would be very well indeed if you could convey to Senator Hoar, or have presented to him, Mr. Evarts's good opinion of Mr. Peckham, as well as your own. I wish Mr. Carter would also write. I desire Mr. Peckham's confirmation. First, on account of his merits and fitness, and second, because I want the appointee to come from the New York Bar *and I have no names in reserve which represent it.*

Joseph H. Choate *to* Cleveland

New York, *January* 30, 1894

I duly received your letter this morning, and have done as you desired and so has Mr. Carter. Indeed, we were fully alive to the urgency of the matter and are ready to do all in our power to promote Mr. Peckham's confirmation. The suggestion that his temper is not judicial is without foundation. When it comes to forming legal or judicial decision, he can lay aside all personal inclinations and political bias as successfully as any man I know. He has won his high place in the profession by his own merits and his fitness for the place to which you have nominated him is universally recognized by the profession.

It is true that he always says what he means, and is all the better for that. I do hope that the Senate will feel its way clear to confirmation.

To WILSON S. BISSELL

Washington, *February* 15, 1894

I want to suggest that when you see the gentleman we referred to in our last conversation, you set forth fully the situation here and the little party cohesion there is and the present danger that the Ship of Democracy which has weathered all storms will sink through the mutiny of those on board. If the thing is saved at all, it must be by a quick and radical change of direction.

To E. C. BENEDICT

Washington, *February* 16, 1894

I enclose another letter of introduction. I hope that no thief will succeed in borrowing money on the strength of the good character guaranteed by the stolen document. You are not the first man who has lost his 'character' when away from home.

I am overwhelmed with work and vexation. Political affairs look more squally every day. Harrison and Vance of Connecticut were in a day or two ago. Vance said they did not propose to run you unless there was a good show of election. I judge there is a little sentiment for the old ticket again, but I am inclined to think that as yet it is not strong. You will be at home in time to learn the trend of events. I need hardly say to you 'Look out!' Clarke Davis is still quite sick.

We are all well. Mrs. Cleveland sends love to you all, and I join.

To EDWARD M. SHEPARD

Washington, *February* 20, 1894

Is it Henry I. or Henry J. Hayden? I am afraid we are not exactly on the right track. I am willing to be very radical — even to the exclusion of Hayden if strength lasts. The more radical we are, however, the more important it is to get perfectly fit men. To select any but the best possible persons in point of ability for the discharge of duty is to do the persons selected a positive damage — subject them and the appointing power to defeat and humiliation and put weapons in the hands of those who oppose us.

I am afraid Green is not the man to prosecute criminals effectively. If Healy did not vote for Democrats, etc., is it safe to choose him? For heaven's sake don't give advantages to the enemy. If you have in mind anyone as good as Hayden with anything about him that is desirable that Hayden has not, I shall be gratified if you suggest him. Where is Bennett (or Burnett)? Has he dropped out? Let me hear from you at once.

To L. Clarke Davis
Washington, *February* 25, 1894

When I came here I knew perfectly well that there were schemes, ideas, policies, and men with which and with whom I should be obliged to do battle, and hard and trying battle. I thought the right must win, and perhaps I relied too sentimentally upon the right to win. I thought the men who professed to be willing to fight with me were sincere and earnest.

I still believe that right will win, but I do not now believe that all who loudly proclaimed their desire for better things were in earnest. At any rate, not a few of them are doing excellent service in the cause of the worst possible political methods, and are aiding in bringing about the worst and most dangerous political situation....

To Charles H. Fairchild
Washington, *March* 9, 1894

I was glad to learn from your letter received yesterday that you had so far recovered your health. I hope it may speedily be completely reinstated. So that you shall not outdo me in frankness, I am constrained to say that your letter greatly disappointed me.

I have been very unjustly treated by some people who march under the banner which you so nobly bear, but I have relied upon your knowledge of conditions here and of me to save any misunderstanding between us in regard to our respective motives and purposes. So I am disappointed in gaining some practical suggestions from you. I gather from your letter, however, that you would approve the nomination of Mr. Macfarlane. I shall send his name in today. Mr. Ottendorfer is extremely and constantly persistent for the nomination of Mr. Grosse for Internal Revenue Collector, and I am told will be very much hurt and offended if it is not done. His paper already indicates, I am told, some restlessness.

Necessarily I have passed through a sort of a hide-thickening process; but in the midst of vicious attacks from quarters not unexpected, I am very desirous of holding, if I can, the friends whose encouragement and support I not only need but *deserve*. So while I have great misgivings as to Mr. Grosse's business capacity, I shall also send his name to the Senate today....

To DON M. DICKINSON

Washington, *March* 18, 1894

I was very much touched this morning when I found on my breakfast table your beautiful remembrance of my birthday. These are days of especial perplexity and depression and the path of public duty is unusually rugged; therefore it is that any proof of the continued confidence and affection of friends is intensely welcome. I thank you from the bottom of my heart.

To EDWARD M. SHEPARD

Washington, *April* 4, 1894

I enclose a letter I received lately from Mr. Grace. I remember Mr. Searing's visit to me after election and the independent stand he took against the candidacy of Mr. Murphy [1] for the United States Senate. His election, I see plainly now, was the greatest blow given to Democratic decency and Democratic hopes and aspirations in the direction of good government. I shall never fully forgive McLaughlin [2] for his refusal to take hold of the opposition.

All these things make me turn with some warmth towards those who took the right side on that question. I should be very glad if something could be done for Mr. Searing.

To E. C. BENEDICT

Washington, *April* 10, 1894

It is very late, but before I go to bed I mean to send you a 'greeting home' and say a word to you about Willimantic. I have received the papers you sent me and am of the opinion that the man selected by us ought not to be appointed. I also think the other man (Webb) ought not to be appointed. I am here where I see all the things done and attempted to be done in the way of appointments in Connecticut, and I tell you if we don't look out, we shall fritter away the Democratic majority we have in that State. I have never known such recklessness as I see now

---

[1] Cleveland had made public and private appeals against the election of Edward Murphy, Jr., to the Senate by the legislature which met in January, 1893, but in vain.
[2] 'Boss' Hugh McLaughlin of Kings.

in the recommendations of persons for office. The mistake we were led into at Willimantic we will try to correct. We were led into it through such men as Mr. David A. Wells. The thing will not be properly corrected until our friends there suggest to us the name of some clean bright man whom we can substitute. It should be a new name. Pigott insists upon the appointment of a saloonkeeper as Collector at New Haven. Of course I will not do that.

To E. C. BENEDICT

April 15, 1894

I should be delighted to see you and have been rather expecting your advent almost daily. I don't want you to come here on any political matters connected with Connecticut offices and I hope you won't do so....

What Mr. Harrison says about Mr. Wells is true to an extent of other men in the State. The Governor, Lieutenant-Governor and I are quite sure Mr. Davis recommended a saloon-keeper for Collector at New Haven, and between you and me I don't think Webb is the man for postmaster of Willimantic, even if he did go to the Convention. Mr. French was almost entirely responsible for the appointment of Meade as Consul at San Domingo, who I now understand only avoided disgracing us there by dying. French is one of the best men in the world. What I want is somebody in Connecticut who knows the men applying and who knows their character and who believes it is better politics to appoint a fit man than to appoint one merely and solely on the score of partisan activity.

I hope you will come and see me — the sooner the better — but if anyone is to come here on political business I beg you not to join them.

HORACE WHITE *to* CLEVELAND

Washington, *April* 16, 1894

... I was in the company of a Republican Senator this afternoon — one of the foremost of them.[1] He said that it was God's mercy to the country that you were elected President in 1892 instead of Harrison or any Republican because no Republican President could have procured the repeal of the Sherman Silver Act, however strongly he might have tried. He added his belief that no other Democrat than yourself *would* have done it. It was his opinion that if that act had not been repealed we should now be a ruined people. Which is my opinion also.

[1] This Senator was Allison of Iowa.

To EVERETT P. WHEELER

Washington, *April* 16, 1894

I thank you from the bottom of my heart for your letter in the New York *Times* today. It is very refreshing, in the midst of much misconception and prejudice and ignorance and injustice, to know that there are some who are inclined to be just and fair.

There never was a man in this high office so surrounded with difficulties and so perplexed, and so treacherously treated, and so abandoned by those whose aid he *deserves*, as the present incumbent. But there is a God, and the patriotism of the American people is not dead; nor is all truth and virtue and sincerity gone from the Democratic party. The delay may be discouraging and our faith may be sorely tried, but in the end we shall see the light.

To CHAUNCEY F. BLACK

Washington, *April* 18, 1894

I have carefully read the communication you lately placed in my hands setting forth the future purposes and present needs of the National Association of Democratic Clubs. The achievements of this organization should be familiar to all who are interested in the continuation of Democratic supremacy and should enlist the encouragement of those who appreciate the importance of an effective dissemination of Democratic doctrines.

Your association has done much by way of educating our people touching the particular subjects which are recognized as belonging to the Democratic faith; but it seems to me that its best service has been an enforcement and demonstration of the truth that our party is best organized and most powerful when it strives for principles instead of spoils, and that it quickly responds to the stimulus supplied by an enlistment in the people's cause.

This acknowledgment of the important services rendered to the advancement of true Democracy suggests that the National Association of Democratic Clubs, and any other Democratic agency, should labor unceasingly and earnestly to save our party in this time of its power and responsibility from the degradation and disgrace of a failure to redeem the pledges upon which our fellow-countrymen trusted us with the control of their Government. All who are charged, on behalf of the Democratic party, with the redemption of these pledges should now be impressively reminded that, as we won our way to victory under the banner of tariff reform, so our insistence upon that principle is the condition of our retention of the people's trust, and that fealty to party organization demands the subordination of individual advantages and wishes, and the putting aside of petty and ignoble jealousies and bickerings when party principles and party integrity and party existence are at stake.

I cheerfully enclose a contribution to the funds necessary to carry on the good work of your organization, with a hearty wish for its continued success.

To RICHARD WATSON GILDER

Washington, *May* 3, 1894

It seems to me that your unceasing acts of kindness to me keep me in a constant state of 'thank-you'ness. The books you sent me certainly constitute a delightful and valuable gift, and though you know what a complete loafer I am during the summer vacation, I promise you now and here to return here next fall with the contents of these volumes in my mental man. Mrs. Cleveland, I know, will read them before I do. I thank you from the bottom of my heart for putting them in my hands. I thank you too for the opportunity to read the forthcoming article on the Consular Service. Nobody would be better pleased than I to see it reasonably hedged about.

We are getting on pretty well. In the sphere of public affairs I feel that I had my full share of trouble and perplexity, but I have never lost hope and have never doubted that the end would compensate for all. This will certainly be so and even today the clear sky is showing. The American people ought to have learned a valuable lesson. I don't know whether they have or not.

I wonder if a *true* history of the last fourteen months will ever be written. It is crammed full of instructive things.

I wish you'd say to Mrs. Gilder that I am thinking of her proposition. Give her my love too — also George.[1]

---

[1] George Gilder, small son of R. W. G., and a great favorite of Cleveland's. He once electrified a circle which was praising Mrs. Cleveland's beauty by saying he considered Mr. Cleveland better-looking.

To SENATOR WILLIAM F. VILAS

Washington, *May 29,* 1894

I am sorry that the vast Hawaiian situation was talked today. The thing I care the most about is the declaration that the *people* of the islands instead of the *Provisional Government* should determine the policy, etc. I do not care much what is said or not said concerning annexation.

I see that you expect to offer a substitute Thursday. Can you not nail the endorsement of the Provisional Government, by putting in its place the more American and Democratic reference to *the People* as the source of power and control?

To L. CLARKE DAVIS

Washington, *June 5,* 1894

I have just read your letter and snatch a moment to write a word in reply. There can be no doubt as to the... utter discomfiture of those who seem to have an idea that mendacity and nastiness are prime factors in newspaper journalism. I am exceedingly anxious to see the dirty scoundrels who are now in the hands of the District Attorney here severely punished. I think it is most important to the public service, to popular decency, and to the usefulness of journalism.

Part of the Gray Gables caravan started yesterday — house equipage and common specimens; more will move tomorrow — the choicest animals — and Jumbo [1] will remain here until the weather is warmer. Brad, my man, tells me the fish are very plenty on the ledges, but I expect by the time I reach the scene of action they will all be 'in deep water' or somewhere else. All the same, 'we'll get 'em.'

I shall not be at all surprised if I can leave here for my vacation early in July. If I discover that this must be postponed, I shall get away for a week or so then. When do you expect to go up?

To CHARLES W. ELIOT

Washington, *June 29,* 1894

May I write you in strict confidence? I have now thrust upon me the selection of a Superintendent of the Coast and Geodetic Survey. I would like very much to select a man whom the scientific people of the country would recognize as related to them, and yet I must have good administra-

---

[1] Some of the nieces and nephews of Cleveland sometimes called him Uncle Jumbo.

tive ability. I do not feel that I can do without the latter qualification, and I know it is not easy to find it joined to scientific attainment. Can you make a suggestion that will aid me?

I believe the methods of the establishment ought to be improved, and for that reason I think it best to look outside of those connected with it. I hope you will not think me troublesome. I come to you because you yourself combine in such a marked degree the qualities I seek as to make me hope there is in the range of your acquaintance someone whom you can recommend.

To COMMISSIONER CHARLES LYMAN

Washington, *June 29*, 1894

After much reflection I have fully determined that it is my duty to ask for your resignation as Civil Service Commissioner. I desire, however, to give you an opportunity, before leaving your present position, to make arrangements for other employment, and so shall be satisfied if the place is at my disposal on the first day of September next.

To WILLIAM L. WILSON

Washington, *July 2*, 1894

The certainty that a conference will be ordered between the two houses of Congress for the purpose of adjusting differences on the subject of tariff legislation makes it also certain that you will be again called on to do hard service in the cause of tariff reform.

My public life has been so closely related to this subject, I have so longed for its accomplishment, and I have so often promised its realization to my fellow-countrymen as a result of their trust and confidence in the Democratic party, that I hope no excuse is necessary for my earnest appeal to you that in this crisis [1] you strenuously insist upon party honesty and good faith and a sturdy adherence to Democratic principles. I believe these absolutely necessary conditions to the continuation of Democratic existence.

I cannot rid myself of the feeling that this conference will present the best, if not the only, hope of true Democracy. Indications point to its action as the reliance of those who desire the genuine fruition of Democratic effort, the fulfilment of Democratic pledges, and the redemption of

[1] The situation presented by the complete rewriting of the Wilson Tariff by a small group of Senators under Gorman, who held the balance of power.

Democratic promises to the people. To reconcile differences in the details comprised within the fixed and well-defined lines of principle will not be the sole task of the conference, but, as it seems to me, its members will also have in charge the question whether Democratic principles themselves are to be saved or abandoned. There is no excuse for mistaking or misapprehending the feeling and the temper of the rank and file of the Democracy. They are downcast under the assertion that their party fails in ability to manage the Government, and they are apprehensive that efforts to bring about tariff reform may fail; but they are much more downcast and apprehensive in their fear that Democratic principles may be surrendered.

In these circumstances they cannot do otherwise than to look with confidence to you and those who with you have patriotically and sincerely championed the cause of tariff reform within Democratic lines and guided by Democratic principles. This conference is vastly augmented by the action under your leadership of the House of Representatives upon the bill now pending.

Every true Democrat and every sincere tariff reformer knows that this bill in its present form and as it will be submitted to the conference falls far short of the consummation for which we have long labored, for which we have suffered defeat without discouragement, which, in its anticipation, gave us a rallying cry in our day of triumph, and which, in its promise of accomplishment, is so interwoven with Democratic pledges and Democratic success that our abandonment of the cause of the principles upon which it rests means party perfidy and party dishonor.[1]

Our topic will be submitted to the conference which embodies Democratic principle so directly that it cannot be compromised. We have in our platforms and in every way possible declared in favor of the free importation of raw materials. We have again and again promised that this should be accorded to our people and our manufacturers as soon as the Democratic party was invested with the power to determine the tariff policy of the country. The party now has that power. We are as certain today as we have ever been of the great benefit that would accrue to the country from the inauguration of this policy, and nothing has occurred to release us from our obligation to secure this advantage to our people. It must be admitted that no tariff measure can accord with Democratic

---

[1] This was the phrase which stung Gorman, Brice, Smith, Caffery, and other protectionist Democrats in the Senate to anger.

principles and promises, or bear a genuine Democratic badge, that does not provide for free raw materials. In the circumstances it may well excite our wonder that Democrats are willing to depart from this the most Democratic of all tariff principles, and that the inconsistent absurdity of such a proposed departure should be emphasized by the suggestion that the wool of the farmer be placed on the free list and the protection of tariff taxation be placed around the iron ore and coal of corporations and capitalists. How can we face the people after indulging in such outrageous discriminations and violations of principles?

It is quite apparent that this question of free raw materials does not admit of adjustment on any middle ground, since their subjection to any rate of tariff taxation, great or small, is alike violative of Democratic principle and Democratic good faith.

I hope you will not consider it intrusive if I say something about another subject which can hardly fail to be troublesome to the conference. I refer to the adjustment of tariff taxation on sugar. Under our party platform, and in accordance with our declared party purposes, sugar is a legitimate and logical article of revenue taxation. Unfortunately, however, incidents have accompanied certain stages of the legislation which will be submitted to the conference that have aroused in connection with this subject a natural Democratic animosity to the methods and manipulations of trusts and combinations. I confess to sharing in this feeling; and yet it seems to me we ought, if possible, to sufficiently free ourselves from prejudice to enable us coolly to weigh the considerations which in formulating tariff legislation ought to guide our treatment of sugar as a taxable article. While no tenderness should be entertained for trusts, and while I am decidedly opposed to granting them under the guise of tariff taxation any opportunity to further their peculiar methods, I suggest that we ought not to be driven away from the Democratic principle and policy which lead to the taxation of sugar by the fear, quite likely exaggerated, that in carrying out this principle and policy we may indirectly and inordinately encourage a combination of sugar-refining interests. I know that in present conditions this is a delicate subject, and I appreciate the depth and strength of the feeling which its treatment has aroused. I do not believe we should do evil that good may come, but it seems to me that we should not forget that our aim is the completion of a tariff bill, and that in taxing sugar for proper purposes and within reasonable bounds, whatever else may be said of our action, we are in no danger of running counter to Democratic principle. With all there is at stake, there must be in the treatment of this article some ground upon which we are all willing to stand, where toleration and conciliation may be allowed to solve the problem, without demanding the entire surrender of fixed and conscientious convictions.

I ought not to prolong this letter. If what I have written is unwelcome, I beg you to believe in my good intentions. In the conclusions of the conference touching the numerous items which will be considered, the people are not afraid that their interests will be neglected. They know that the general result, so far as they are concerned, will be to place home necessaries and comforts easier within their reach and to insure better and surer compensation to those who toil.

We all know that a tariff covering all the varied interests and conditions of a country as vast as ours, must of necessity be largely the result of honorable adjustment and compromise. I expect very few of us can say when our measure is perfected that all its features are exactly as we would prefer. You know how much I deprecated the incorporation in the proposed bill of the income tax feature. In matters of this kind, however, which do not violate a fixed and recognized Democratic doctrine, we are willing to defer to the judgment of a majority of our Democratic brethren. I think there is a general agreement that this is party duty. This is more palpably apparent when we realize that the business of our country timidly stands and watches for the result of our efforts to perfect tariff legislation, that a quick and certain return of prosperity waits upon a wise adjustment, and that a confiding people still trust in our hands their prosperity and well-being.

The Democracy of the land plead most earnestly for the speedy completion of the tariff legislation which their representatives have undertaken; but they demand not less earnestly that no stress of necessity shall tempt those they trust to the abandonment of Democratic principles.

GOVERNOR JOHN P. ALTGELD [1] *to* CLEVELAND

Springfield, *July* 5, 1894 (telegram)

I am advised that you have ordered Federal troops to go into service in the State of Illinois. Surely the facts have not been correctly pre-

---

[1] John P. Altgeld (1847–1902) was the Democratic governor of Illinois 1893–97. For the controversy between him and Cleveland over the use of Federal troops in the Pullman strike in Chicago, see the editor's *Grover Cleveland: A Study in Courage*, 611–628.

sented to you in this case, or you would not have taken this step, for it is entirely unnecessary, and, as it seems to me, unjustifiable. Waiving all questions of courtesy, I will say that the State of Illinois is not only able to take care of itself, but it stands ready to furnish the Federal Government any assistance it may need elsewhere. Our military force is ample, and consists of as good soldiers as can be found in the country. They have been ordered promptly whenever and wherever they were needed. We have stationed in Chicago alone three regiments of infantry, one battery and one troop of cavalry, and no better soldiers can be found. They have been ready every moment to go on duty, and have been and are now eager to go into service, but they have not been ordered out because nobody in Cook County, whether official or private citizen, asked to have their assistance, or even intimated in any way that their assistance was desired or necessary.

So far as I have been advised, the local officials have been able to handle the situation. But if any assistance were needed, the State stood ready to furnish a hundred men for every one man required, and stood ready to do so at a moment's notice. Notwithstanding these facts the Federal Government has been applied to by men who had political and selfish motives for wanting to ignore the State Government. We have just gone through a coal strike, more extensive here than in any other State, because our soft-coal field is larger than that of any other State. We have now had ten days of the railroad strike, and we have promptly furnished military aid wherever the local officials needed it.

In two instances the United States Marshal for the Southern District of Illinois applied for assistance to enable him to enforce the processes of the United States Court, and troops were promptly furnished him, and he was assisted in every way he desired. The law has been thoroughly executed, and every man guilty of violating it during the strike has been brought to justice. If the Marshal of the Northern District of Illinois or the authorities of Cook County needed military assistance, they had but to ask for it in order to get it from the State.

At present some of our railroads are paralyzed, not by reason of obstruction, but because they cannot get men to operate their trains. For some reason they are anxious to keep this fact from the public, and for this purpose they are making an outcry about obstructions in order to divert attention. Now, I will cite to you two examples which illustrate the situation:

Some days ago I was advised that the business of one of our railroads was obstructed at two railroad centres, and that there was a condition bordering on anarchy there, and I was asked to furnish protection so as to enable the employees of the road to operate the trains. Troops were promptly ordered to both points. Then it transpired that the company had not sufficient men on its line to operate one train. All the old hands were orderly, but refused to go to work. The company had large shops which worked a number of men who did not belong to the Railway Union and who could run an engine. They were appealed to to run the train, but flatly refused. We were obliged to hunt up soldiers who could run an engine and operate a train. Again, two days ago, appeals which were almost frantic came from the officials of another road stating that at an important point on their line trains were forcibly obstructed, and that there was a reign of anarchy at that place, and they asked for protection so that they could move their trains. Troops were put on the ground in a few hours' time, when the officer in command telegraphed me that there was no trouble, and had been none at that point, but that the road seemed to have no men to run trains, and the sheriff telegraphed that he did not need troops, but would himself move every train if the company would only furnish an engineer. The result was that the troops were there twelve hours before a single train was moved, although there was no attempt at interference by anybody.

It is true that in several instances a road made efforts to work a few green men and a crowd standing around insulted them and tried to drive them away, and in a few other cases they cut off Pullman sleepers from trains. But all these troubles were local in character and could easily be handled by the State authorities. Illinois has more railroad men than any other State in the Union, but as a rule they are orderly and well-behaved. This is shown by the fact that so very little actual violence has been committed. Only a very small percentage of these men have been guilty of infractions of the law. The newspaper accounts have in many cases been pure fabrications, and in others wild exaggerations.

I have gone thus into details to show that it is not soldiers that the railroads need so much as it is men to operate trains, and that the conditions do not exist here which bring the cause within the Federal statute, a statute that was passed in 1881 [1861] and was in reality a war measure. The statute authorized the use of Federal troops in a State whenever it shall be impracticable to enforce the laws of the United States within such States by the ordinary judicial proceedings. Such a condition does not exist in Illinois.... To absolutely ignore a local government in matters of this kind, when the local government is ready to furnish assistance needed, and is amply able to enforce the law, not only insults the people of this State by imputing to them an inability to govern themselves or an unwillingness to enforce the law, but is in violation of a basic principle of our institutions. The question of Federal supremacy is in no way involved. No one disputes it for a moment; but, under our Constitution, Federal supremacy and local self-government must go hand-in-hand, and to ignore the latter is to do violence to the Constitution.

As Governor of the State of Illinois, I protest against this, and ask the immediate withdrawal of the Federal troops from active duty in this State....

To GOVERNOR JOHN P. ALTGELD

Washington, *July* 5, 1894 (telegram)

Federal troops were sent to Chicago in strict accordance with the Constitution and laws of the United States, upon the demand of the Postoffice Department that obstruction of the mails should be removed, and upon the representations of the judicial officers of the United States that the process of the Federal courts could not be executed through the ordinary means, and upon competent proof that conspiracies existed against commerce between the States. To meet these conditions, which are clearly within the province of Federal authority, the presence of Federal troops in the city of Chicago was deemed not only proper, but necessary, and there has been no intention of thereby interfering with the plain duty of the local authorities to preserve the peace of the city.

GOVERNOR JOHN P. ALTGELD *to* CLEVELAND

Springfield, *July* 6, 1894 (telegram)

Your answer to my protest involves some startling conclusions and ignores and evades the question at issue — that is, that the principle of local self-government is just as fundamental in our institutions as is that of Federal supremacy.

First — You calmly assume that the Executive has the legal right to order Federal troops into any community of the United States, in the first instance, whenever there is the slightest disturbance, and that he can do this without any regard to the question as to whether that community is able and ready to enforce the law itself. Inasmuch as the Executive is the sole judge of the question as to whether any disturbance exists in any part of the country, this assumption means that the Executive can send Federal troops into any community in the United States at his pleasure, and keep them there as long as he chooses. If this is the law, then the principle of self-government either never did exist in this country or else has been destroyed, for no community can be said to possess local self-government if the Executive can, at his pleasure, send military forces to patrol its streets under pretence of enforcing some law. The kind of local self-government that could exist under these circumstances can be found in any of the monarchies of Europe, and it is not in harmony with the spirit of our institutions.

Second — It is also a fundamental principle in our Government that except in times of war the military shall be subordinate to the civil authority. In harmony with this provision, the State troops are ordered out to act under and with the civil authorities. The troops you have ordered to Chicago are not under the civil authorities, and are in no way responsible to them for their conduct. They are not even acting under the United States Marshal or any Federal officer of the State, but are acting directly under military orders issued from military headquarters at Washington; and in so far as these troops act at all, it is military government.

Third — The statute authorizing Federal troops to be sent into States in certain cases contemplates that the State troops shall be taken first. This provision has been ignored and it is assumed that the Executive is not bound by it. Federal interference with industrial disturbances in the various States is certainly a new departure, and it opens up so large a field that it will require a very little stretch of authority to absorb to itself all the details of local government....[1]

To GOVERNOR JOHN P. ALTGELD

Washington, July 6, 1894 (telegram)

While I am still persuaded that I have neither transcended my authority nor duty in the emergency that confronts us, it seems to me that in

---

[1] Altgeld went on in his reply to use other arguments. He declared that the officers who had called for troops were all Federal appointees; that most of them were removable by the Federal Executive; and that the Executive could bring about a request for troops at will. He asserted that the arrival of Federal troops had been an irritant because it excited the indignation of many Illinoisans who believed in local self-government.

this hour of danger and public distress, discussion may well give way to active efforts on the part of all in authority to restore obedience to law and to protect life and property.

To E. C. BENEDICT

Washington, *July* 6, 1894

Your letter just read. I return Mr. Flower's, which you enclosed. I know Mr. Farrell *very well indeed*. What an illustration of the stage we have reached in conception of public duty the Governor's letter presents! Instead of writing me himself, he beats about the bush and tries to rope you into the chestnut-pulling business.

I have no intention of bothering you about my trip to Gray Gables — if I make one. It is impossible to see now when, if ever, I shall be free.

To SENATOR WILLIAM F. VILAS

Washington, *July* 23, 1894

Fearing I may fail to see you before you go to the Senate (though I am attempting to do so), I write this to say that the balance of my judgment is that if your motion in its present shape is ruled out of order, it would best subserve the purpose we wish to gain to accept the situation with perhaps such a statement as you happily suggested a day or two ago. I am quite clear in this opinion in the light of the *very dark incident* bearing on the situation.[1]

One's judgment, of course, on so delicate a subject may be at fault, but I am half converted to the belief that the best if not the only chance for us is to let the matter go to the conference again without instructions.

It is only fair to say to you that this was emphatically insisted on in an interview I had this morning and a *certain gentleman*[2] *knows I am* making this suggestion to you. Perhaps I ought not to have said to him that I would present the subject to you, but I did so; and the understanding is that we are all to take hold after the remission of the matter to the conference. He says he thinks it would be criminal for us to go away without passing a bill.

[1] By the 'very dark incident' Cleveland probably referred to the violent attack Senator Gorman delivered upon him this same day.

[2] Senator James K. Jones (1839–1908), of Arkansas, who delivered Cleveland an ultimatum stating that the tariff bill must be taken as it stood, or lost entirely.

To SENATOR WILLIAM F. VILAS

Washington, *July* 25, 1894

My callers this morning came to see me on behalf of *an officeseeker!* The question that ought to fill Senatorial minds at this time was not discussed in the least, nor spoken of. Everything stands, so far as I know, in the same condition as when I saw you last, except my wonder constantly increases at the seeming lack of appreciation of the importance of being right on the free raw materials question. I never was as certain of anything in my life as I am that a wrong treatment of this subject will be the cause in the near future of many long Democratic faces.

To WILLIAM L. WILSON

Washington, *August* 13, 1894

I suppose a man depressed and disappointed may write a word of sympathy to another in like situation.[1] We both hoped and wrought for better things, but, now that we know our fate, I shall not let a moment pass before I acknowledge the great and unselfish work you have done in an attempt to bring about an honest and useful result.

Much has been developed which has shocked and surprised you and me, and I have within the last hour found myself questioning whether or not our party is a tariff-reform party. This, however, is only temporary, and such feeling is quickly followed by my old trust in Democratic doctrines and the party which professes them.

But I only intend to express my sympathy with you and my gratitude for the fight you have made for real, genuine tariff reforms. I hope now that you will be mindful of yourself and that you will try and repair a strained mental and physical condition by immediate care and rest.

To PRESIDENT SANFORD B. DOLE

Washington, *August* 17, 1894

Great and Good Friend:

I have received your letter of the 7th ultimo, by which you announce the establishment and proclamation of the Republic of Hawaii on the 4th day of July, 1894, and your assumption of the office of President, with all the formalities prescribed by the Constitution thereof. I cordially reciprocate the sentiments you express for the continuance of the friendly re-

---

[1] On this day a caucus of the House Democrats decided that the only course was to accept the Senate amendments and pass the tariff bill in its mutilated shape.

lations which have existed between the United States and the Hawaiian Islands, and I assure you my best wishes for your personal prosperity....

To REPRESENTATIVE THOMAS C. CATCHINGS [1]

Washington, August 27, 1894

Since the conversation I had with you and Mr. Clarke of Alabama a few days ago, in regard to my action upon the tariff bill now before me, I have given the subject further and most serious consideration. The result is I am more settled than ever in the determination to allow the bill to become a law without my signature.

When the formulation of legislation which it was hoped would embody Democratic ideas of tariff reform was lately entered upon by the Congress, nothing was further from my anticipation than a result which I could not promptly and enthusiastically endorse.

It is therefore with a feeling of the utmost disappointment that I submit to a denial of this privilege.

I do not claim to be better than the masses of my party, nor do I wish to avoid any responsibility which, on account of the passage of this law, I ought to bear as a member of the Democratic organization. Neither will I permit myself to be separated from my party to such an extent as might be implied by my veto of tariff legislation, which, though disappointing, is still chargeable to Democratic effort. But there are provisions in this bill which are not in line with honest tariff reform, and it contains inconsistencies and crudities which ought not to appear in tariff laws or laws of any kind. Besides, there were, as you and I well know, incidents accompanying the passage of the bill through the Congress, which made every sincere tariff reformer unhappy, while influences surrounded it in its latter stages and interfered with its final construction, which ought not to be recognized or tolerated in Democratic tariff-reform counsels.

And yet, notwithstanding all its vicissitudes and all the bad treatment it received at the hands of pretended friends, it presents a vast improvement to existing conditions. It will certainly lighten many tariff burdens that now rest heavily upon the people. It is not only a barrier against the return of mad protection, but it furnishes a vantage-ground from which must be waged further aggressive operations against protected monopoly and governmental favoritism.

[1] A Confederate veteran (1847-1927) who was Representative from Mississippi from 1885 to 1901; he had urged Cleveland to sign the Wilson-Gorman Bill.

I take my place with the rank and file of the Democratic party who believe in tariff reform and who know what it is, who refuse to accept the results embodied in this bill as the close of the war, who are not blind to the fact that the livery of Democratic tariff reform has been stolen and worn in the service of Republican protection, and who have marked the places where the deadly blight of treason has blasted the counsels of the brave in their hour of might.

The trusts and combinations — the communism of pelf — whose machinations have prevented us from reaching the success we deserved, shou'd not be forgotten nor forgiven. We shall recover from our astonishment at their exhibition of power, and if then the question is forced upon us whether they shall submit to the free legislative will of the people's representatives, or shall dictate the laws which the people must obey, we will accept and settle that issue as one involving the integrity and safety of American institutions.

I love the principles of true Democracy because they are founded in patriotism and upon justice and fairness toward all interests. I am proud of my party organization because it is conservatively sturdy and persistent in the enforcement of its principles. Therefore I do not despair of the efforts made by the House of Representatives to supplement the bill already passed by further legislation, and to have engrafted upon it such modifications as will more nearly meet Democratic hopes and aspirations.

I cannot be mistaken as to the necessity of free raw materials as the foundation of logical and sensible tariff reform. The extent to which this is recognized in the legislation already secured is one of its encouraging and redeeming features; but it is vexatious to recall that while free coal and iron ore have been denied us, a recent letter of the Secretary of the Treasury discloses the fact that both might have been made free by the annual surrender of only about seven hundred thousand dollars of unnecessary revenue.

I am sure that there is a common habit of underestimating the importance of free raw materials in tariff legislation, and of regarding them as only related to concessions to be made to our manufacturers. The truth is, their influence is so far-reaching that, if disregarded, a complete and beneficent scheme of tar'ff reform cannot be successfully inaugurated.

When we give to our manufacturers free raw materials we unshackle American enterprise and ingenuity, and these will open the doors of foreign markets to the reception of our wares and give opportunity for the continuous and remunerative employment of American labor.

With materials cheapened by their freedom from tariff charges, the cost of their product must be correspondingly cheapened. Thereupon justice and fairness to the consumer would demand that the manufacturers be obliged to submit to such a readjustment and modification of the tariff upon their finished goods as would secure to the people the benefit of the reduced cost of their manufacture, and shield the consumer against the exaction of inordinate profits.

It will thus be seen that free raw materials and a just and fearless regulation and reduction of the tariff to meet the changed conditions would carry to every humble home in the land the blessings of increased comfort and cheaper living.

The millions of our countrymen who have fought bravely and well for tariff reform should be exhorted to continue the struggle, boldly challenging to open warfare and constantly guarding against treachery and half-heartedness in their camp.

Tariff reform will not be settled until it is honestly and fairly settled in the interest and to the benefit of a patient and long-suffering people.

To CAPTAIN ROBLEY D. EVANS [1]

Gray Gables, *September 3, 1894*

Your letter is at hand and I enclose you my check for $23.69 for the expenses of my last trip to Gray Gables on the *Rogers*, when you were with us.

The freedom from work and worry which I am now enjoying is very grateful and was, I am sure, very much needed. We are catching quite good strings of bottom-fish. The weakfish we have not tried since they acted so badly when you were here. I have, however, an account against them which I propose to make them settle. I do not know as I shall be able to go with you after birds at Bailey's Island, but I am so anxious to do so that I shall feel grateful to you if you will give me the opportunity. I would like all the notice it is possible for you to give me....

[1] Cleveland's friendship with Evans (1846–1912) dated from the first Administration, when Secretary Whitney restored him to a post from which the Arthur Administration had dropped him.

To CAPTAIN ROBLEY D. EVANS

Gray Gables, *September 13, 1894*

I hardly know what to say about the North Carolina trip. My gun and shooting suit are in Washington. Of course I had rather go there and get my things and start from there, on some accounts, than to go any other way, though I could send for them and start from Boston or New York or some other point. The trouble about that plan is that it is worth sometimes all my life is worth to travel alone in a public conveyance. Isn't there some way I can go from here in a lighthouse boat and so avoid that annoyance, or if I will come to New York can I take one there?

I am not at all sure that Secretary Lamont would decline an invitation to go with us if we could have smooth water. I see him almost every day. Of course I should rely on you for cartridges, mosquito protection, and all that sort of thing. I ought not to leave here and go there unless there is a good prospect for birds, though of course I know the uncertainties of that business. I could have my man William go to Washington and get my things and meet me with them in New York. I wish you would cook up a plan that seems to you the best and submit it to me, as soon as possible, by wire if necessary.

To SECRETARY WALTER Q. GRESHAM

Gray Gables, *September 19, 1894*

Your letter came duly to hand and I was very glad to hear from you. In a letter received from Secretary Carlisle tonight, he says you are looking very well. I am pleased to know that your little vacation has done you good, for I think it was quite time for you to have a 'let-up.'

Herbert has been here and I told him about the Walker affair. Since he left I have written him to leave the matter *in statu quo* until the Cabinet has another chance to discuss it. In a reply received yesterday he of course agrees to this and indicates that he feels as the rest of us do as to the merits of the case. I send you some clippings from the *Journal of Commerce* of yesterday. Somebody sent me the paper and I send you all the portions marked. I think you were exactly right when you expressed the opinion that the appointment of Furbish was a mistake.

I am enjoying my vacation hugely and am almost up to the old standard in strength and ability to work. Unless I am absolutely needed in Washington, I intend to prolong my rest into October.

To CAPTAIN ROBLEY D. EVANS

Gray Gables, *September 25, 1894*

I enclose you my check for $9.63, the expense of my last trip here on the *Rogers*, as advised in your letter of the 20th instant. Captain Schley and his boat left here this afternoon. He came here Sunday bringing Mr. and Mrs. Carlisle.

It looks to me as though we might as well as not settle on giving up our North Carolina trip. I am afraid the flies and mosquitoes will continue to largely outnumber the birds. I think if we go that both the Secretary of War and Dr. Bryant would go with us. I shall not, however, calculate at all on going. I am having a pretty good time here and catching some pretty good fish, though I have not yet found any bluefish or weakfish. If anything new turns up in regard to the trip, of course you will let me know. If I go I shall start from Washington and return there.

To SECRETARY DANIEL S. LAMONT

Gray Gables, *September 28, 1894*

I think I ought to tell you that the prospects are not very strong in favor of the North Carolina trip. The latest news from there represented the birds as scarce and the mosquitoes and flies as very plenty indeed. Unless these reports are changed, we shall not start. And yet if proper word should come, we might start upon quite short notice. I should go to Washington and start from there.

I am farming and building principally now. I have been so engrossed with these occupations that I have not thought of New York's political complexion until today, when the strange situation broke upon me.

Here is the Democratic party pledged to tariff reform as its stock in trade and as the issue upon which it won success. And the Democratic party of the State of New York nominates for governor a man [1] who openly and at every turn tried to defeat it and who has studied to oppose a Democratic Administration. New York Democrats hug to their bosom Hill, Sheehan, and Murphy, whom they have so lately repudiated. For lieutenant-governor a man is nominated [2] who is a protectionist Democrat and absented himself rather than vote for our tariff bill.

Thomas Myers, Ed Bacon, and John Sullivan (Internal Revenue

---

[1] David B. Hill was nominated (though he continued to hold the office of United States Senator) and defeated. Levi P. Morton succeeded to the governorship.

[2] This was Daniel N. Lockwood of Buffalo.

Bureau Collectors) send congratulations to Hill, and all the Democrats in the country seem at this moment to think they are to be saved by returning to the wallowing in the mire.

Of course there will be a sober second thought that will influence voters after a while, and it will probably be discovered that a shouting, dancing convention does not elect its nominees, but the thing as far as it has gone bodes no good to the country or party.

It may be that I shall stay here until the 10th or 15th of October. Do you think I ought to do so? I expect Gibson tomorrow. Can you not write me a letter?

Francis Lynde Stetson to Cleveland
Tuxedo Park, N.Y., October 7, 1894

Of course I will respect your confidence, and of course I share your anxiety for our party. Its situation in New York seems to me hopeless for a variety of causes and reasons.[1]...

It seems to me that as a result you will be left free to make a fight for civil service reform, which I should be glad to see you push almost to its extreme. This is the one mark you can now leave on the country. You can do it with Congressional help, which you cannot get, though you need it, for tariff or currency reform.

By the way, Senator Higgins told me at Saratoga that Gorman told him that Vest and Jones (who were there also) said the silver men of all parties had made up their mind to force a free-silver bill next session. They expect your veto, but do not care for it, as they are making the plan for 1896, when the Silver party shall have swallowed the Populists as the Republican party did the Free-Soilers.

We are on the eve of a very dark night, unless a return of commercial prosperity relieves popular discontent with what they believe Democratic incompetence to make laws, and consequently with Democratic Administrations anywhere and everywhere. It is clear to my mind that no form of tariff legislation is going to satisfy or affect public demand or discontent. Time is the only alleviator, and a good deal of time too....

---

[1] Stetson went on to state some of these reasons. The party, he wrote, had never included a majority of New York voters; it had always contained a considerable number of men who preferred protection to tariff reduction; and it had made an irrevocable blunder in choosing Edward Murphy, who was hated by all liberals, as State Chairman.

To RICHARD WATSON GILDER

Gray Gables, *October* 12, 1894

From something Mrs. Cleveland said to me, I fear, as much as fear can displace astonishment, that you went away from here feeling uncomfortable on account of my very poor joke about the Stevenson Cabinet.[1] My position is such a grievous one and my work is so altogether gloomy, that I suppose I never ought to attempt pleasantry.

You will perhaps concede my privilege of saying things quite direct about the Democratic party. Concerning that party as represented by its organization in the State of New York and perhaps in other quarters, I said that the logical thing for me to do, if I were to be in agreement with the conduct of that organization, was to resign and hand the Executive branch to Mr. Stevenson; and then, to relieve this statement of seriousness, I committed the great indiscretion of attempting a joke by saying that when the contingency arose I would try to get you a place in the new Cabinet.

I am very sorry and will steer clear of rocks of that kind in the future. I hope it is not necessary for me to assure you how much I am comforted by your constant and disinterested friendship and how much I am encouraged, or at least saved from utter discouragement, by any approval I am able to win from you and men like you. I know, too, there is a God, but I do not know His purposes, nor when their results will appear. I know the clouds will roll away, but I do not know who, before that time, will be drowned in their floods.

To SECRETARY DANIEL S. LAMONT

Gray Gables, *October* 12, 1894

I have been feeling for the last day or two that I ought to be in Washington taking my share of the work and perplexity with the rest of you, notwithstanding the pleasant assurance in your letter that I am not needed and its hearty repetition by Secretary Gresham this morning.

I am ashamed to confess it, but the truth is I caught a mean cold nearly two weeks ago which hangs on to me in a most persistent way. The weather has just cleared off after a hard storm and I am quite certain it will be fair for some time to come. The baby has just cut her first tooth, and I suppose it would be well to give her as much of the cool pleasant

---

[1] Vice-President Stevenson had surrounded himself with a coterie of free-silver men who were dubbed the 'Stevenson Cabinet.'

weather now prevailing here as possible. I am dreadfully depressed about the political situation and want to keep as far away from it as possible. I am undoubtedly wrong as usual, but I don't see how anybody who knows what Democratic principles are or cares to see them prevail can support the man that the Democratic organization of New York State has defiantly and impudently attempted to crowd down Democratic throats.[1] What claim has he to the support of men who desire the ascendancy of Democratic principles and why should decent Democrats desire to strengthen the power of the gang who laughed in their sleeves every time they gain these decent Democrats' support? Are they any better than they were or do they show any disposition to invite harmony by the recognition of the men they have so long and so outrageously abused? Look at the Convention — Hill in the chair and Sheehan chief manager. The success of Hill would mean a stronger and more unrelenting fight against the Administration and against every effort to redeem Democratic pledges.

I say again I suppose I am wrong, but while I am perfectly willing to attend my own funeral, I am not willing to aid in bringing about the funeral of the splendid and generous men I have asked to share with me the work and responsibility of the Administration. If it is thought to be politic or a duty to others, I can maintain silence if I am permitted, but if I am forced to speak I shall say what I believe in straight United States language. It is a delusion to suppose that any profession of support, or actual aid by our friends, will be appreciated or recognized. If Mr. Hill is defeated in the State of New York, it will be said the Cleveland or Administration men did it, no matter how great their labors in the campaign and no matter how completely Mr. Hill and his friends may know of their labors. One of the purposes of the nomination was undoubtedly to thus put us in the wrong, whether we desired it or not.

You seem to think there is no chance for Hill's election, but I do not suppose he accepted the nomination until he had from the liquor dealers, or some section of the Republican party, or some church influences, or from the manufacturers he has aided in protecting, some assurances which encouraged a hope for his success. After all, everyone must follow his own judgment in the matter and should have only his own idea of duty to answer.

Mrs. Cleveland now talks about the 20th. I am complicated by an

[1] Cleveland is, of course, referring to the nomination of Senator Hill for the governorship.

armory opening in Brooklyn which I have declined and might want to stay here a day or two longer than that. Do you think I can properly do so?

To SECRETARY DANIEL S. LAMONT

Gray Gables, *October* 15, 1894

... Dr. Bryant has asked us to stop over with him and dine and go to the theatre. Mrs. Cleveland must stop at Greenwich and cannot see her way clear to leave her babies, but I ought to see the two doctors anyway and have written Bryant that I would join him Wednesday next and stand by him Wednesday night. We expect to start from here next Tuesday night and go all the way home by train, arriving in Washington Thursday afternoon.

The Doctor said [something] in his letter that led me to think he hoped to have you and Mrs. Lamont there at the same time. As the girls say, 'that would just be too lovely for anything.'

Isidor Straus has written me asking for a letter of endorsement for Nathan's candidacy.[1] I don't know what to do, I ought not to meddle, but Nathan has always been my friend and I like him very much. I'll be mighty glad when this election is over.

To NATHAN STRAUS

Gray Gables, *October* 18, 1894

My personal friendship for you and the many kindnesses I have received at your hands make it almost impossible for me to do otherwise than comply with your request and give public expression of my support of your candidacy. I have, however, determined to ask you to give another proof of your friendly consideration by relieving me of the embarrassment of such compliance.

As I understand the Constitution and laws, I cannot regard myself as a voter in either the State or city of New York. Considering this fact and the Democratic complications and differences existing in the State and city, in connection with the general subject of the propriety of Presidential interference with the people's suffrage in any event, I desire to avoid any active interference with the local politics of New York.

I am very much troubled by the fear that you will not regard my de-

[1] Nathan Straus was given the Democratic nomination for mayor of New York in 1894, but finally declined. William L. Strong, nominated by a reform committee, was elected and began a much-needed house-cleaning.

termination, so far as it relates to your candidacy, as consistent with my professed friendship. If I could vote in New York City, the personal relations existing between us and my firm conviction that if elected mayor of the city, the duties of the office would be performed with fidelity and in furtherance of the interests of the people, would induce me to cast my ballot for you with the utmost pleasure and satisfaction; but in existing circumstances I cannot make any public announcement to that effect upon the assumption that the canvass would be influenced thereby.

To SECRETARY HOKE SMITH

Gray Gables, *October* 18, 1894

Somehow it seems to me that we can get up a better Commission than you suggest if we put our heads together, which we will have an opportunity to do in a few days. I confess I have no one in mind and I think your judgment in the matter is perhaps the best guide, but I do not hanker much after Governor McC—— and I am afraid there would be a little too much Utah in it. At any rate, it will keep until my return and we can discuss the matter.

I have two commissions here made out for land officers in California. I want to talk with you a little about the Gray influence in California matters. I am afraid it is not entirely healthy.

I feel that I have had a very long vacation and ought to be at work, though I know I never needed a vacation so much as when I left Washington. I am afraid that we are going to have a depressing time politically, but I think there never was a time when patriotic men and Democrats had need to stand steadier at their guns. Please convey to Mrs. Smith affectionate remembrances from both Mrs. Cleveland and myself.

To E. C. BENEDICT

Washington, *October* 30, 1894

The action you report in your last letter is heartily approved, and I hope soon to hear of further like action.[1] I am certainly very appreciative of your kindness in these matters, and know perfectly well that you have been actuated solely by a generous desire to help me. I sometimes have a fear that you may be annoyed by my references to my matters in your hands; but I have not been able altogether to refrain from expressing a desire to have the affairs closed up. Some of my reasons for this

[1] From this time Cleveland relied more and more upon Benedict's advice in investments.

desire I cannot, and do not wish to, explain even to you. I am very far from happy in these days, and, rightly or wrongly, I shall feel relieved when I receive the very satisfactory profit upon my investment arising from a sale. But above all things, I don't want you to feel the least bit bothered or annoyed....

To CAPTAIN ROBLEY D. EVANS

Washington, *December* 7, 1894

I return General Alexander's letter and thank you for the opportunity to read it. I shall not wade about in the marshes much, *probably*, but I have sent for my rubber boots which come a little above the knees. As usual when the time is drawing near to start, I begin to feel that perhaps I ought not to go; but I guess I'll hold to my intention.

What worries me is to settle how we shall dispose of all our game. According to my count we shall have enough of game and fish to supply any civilized country on the globe. However, if I should stop shooting after the first day or two, I suppose the situation would be relieved.

To RICHARD WATSON GILDER

Washington, *December* 26, 1894

I was very much troubled by your thoughtful and valuable Christmas remembrance and I thank you for it from the bottom of my heart. I hope in days to come we may together explore the nooks of my lunch basket on the shore of Peter's Pond or in some other carefree spot.

I am so depressed during these days [1] that the thought of my lack of deserving any thoughts of my friends is strangely mixed with the gratification caused by the evidence that you *have* thought of me. I am sure I never was more completely in the right path of duty than I am now and I am sure I never did better public service than now; but it is depressing enough to have no encouragement from any quarter. I believe I shall hold out, but I doubt if I shall ever advise anyone to lose the support of party in the hope of finding support among those who beyond partisanship profess a patriotic desire for good government.

I want now to live until my task, undertaken to suit good people, is done, and until your work for the public good is also done; and then I want to see much of you and as much as you.

---

[1] The continued financial troubles of the Government, the necessity for another bond issue in 1895, and the heavy defeat administered the Democratic party in the fall elections, all acted to depress Cleveland.

XIII

GOLD AND VENEZUELA

CLEVELAND'S second bond issue to maintain the gold reserve of the Treasury, made late in November, 1894, proved the briefest of stopgaps. It sustained the credit of the Government for only ten weeks. By January 24, 1895, the gold reserve was down to $68,000,-000, though $100,000,000 was generally considered the minimum of safety; the drain on the Treasury was steadily continuing, while gold exports were large; and a third sale of bonds was imperative. Cleveland and Carlisle had asked Congress for legislation which would enable them to bring out bonds on more favorable terms, and to require the payment of all important customs duties in gold. By the time the silverite majority in Congress defeated this proposed legislation, an alarming crisis was at hand. The reserve on January 31 fell to $45,000,000, and a few days later the amount of gold coin in the sub-treasury at New York dropped below $9,000,000. There was imminent danger that the Government would have to suspend gold payments and go to a silver basis. Cleveland had to accept the harsh terms offered by a syndicate of New York bankers headed by J. P. Morgan and August Belmont, who paid $65,116,244 in gold for $62,000,000 in four per cent bonds purchased at 104½, at the same time engaging to stop the export of American gold to Europe. The measure was one of the most unpopular of his Administration, for the syndicate made a large profit and Cleveland was denounced as being in league with the 'money power' of Wall Street. But he took the step only upon absolute compulsion, after prolonged bargaining with Morgan and his associates; and by it he saved the gold standard, for the reserve was brought up above $107,500,000. Early in 1896 a fourth and final bond issue, this time of $100,000,000, was sold at public subscription, and thereafter the Treasury was in a position to resist all attacks. During 1895 the President had numerous other problems to face. Late in the spring the Supreme Court by a narrow decision, after one justice had changed his mind on the subject, declared the income tax which was a feature of the Wilson-Gorman bill to be unconstitutional. This unhappy decision aroused wide resentment among the agrarian and labor masses, who paid an unfair proportion of the national taxes. The weak efforts of Attorney-General Olney to prosecute the trusts broke down in the Supreme Court, which made an adverse decision on the evidence he presented against the Sugar Trust; and this again aroused widespread resentment. Late in

May Secretary Gresham died, and Olney became Secretary of State. During the summer he and Cleveland pressed the British Government to reconsider its refusal to arbitrate the disputed boundary between Venezuela and the British Government, a subject which concerned the United States under the Monroe Doctrine. After irritating delays, Great Britain refused. Cleveland then sent Congress a message in December in which he asked authority to appoint a commission to determine the true boundary, saying that the United States would maintain this line when fixed. The provocative and undiplomatic language of this message, which caused a brief war scare, was in the first instance from Olney's pen.

To E. C. BENEDICT

Washington, *February* 3, 1895

I think I have not written you since the receipt of your letter on business quite a while ago. I want to say now how well satisfied I am with the outcome and how fully I appreciate the trouble you have been to in managing in your line the business entrusted to you. Of course I accept without the least question your judgment in regard to the Natural Gas bonds and stock and am entirely willing to hold that property as an investment if you still think well of its permanent desirability. You must understand me, however, that whatever happens I shall be content — only expecting from you the benefit of your judgment upon the conditions now appearing. What do you think about sending the bonds and stocks to me to 'stick away'? If there is any reason in my interest or yours why you should retain them, of course do so. You know rich investors like me have to keep an account of income in these days.

I feel the money in your hands belonging to me ought to be invested in something which will bring returns, but of course I do not know what to do in that direction. I cannot get it out of my head that New Jersey Central stock is cheap, but why I think so I am utterly unable to say. Would it be too much trouble for you to give me a statement of the amount you now have on hand of mine?...

To AMBASSADOR THOMAS F. BAYARD

Washington, *February* 13, 1895

First of all I want to thank you from the bottom of my heart for several very kind and very comforting letters I have received from you. I have been dreadfully forlorn these many months, and sorely perplexed and tried.

Think of it! Not a man in the Senate with whom I can be on terms of absolute confidence. Our Wisconsin friend and former asssociate seems somehow to be cowed, and our Delaware friend [1] has only spasmodic self-assertion and generally is in doubt as to the correctness of what I do or want to do. Not one of them comes to me on public business unless sent for, and then full of reservations and doubts. I am on the whole glad you are not among them. Your efforts to stem the tide would only hurt and grieve you. And yet I must not forget the opportunity you would have to add glory to your patriotic career and raise the hopes and inspire the faith of your country-men. I am sorry the malevolent change in our public life since you and I worked together here has been made known to me. I am sure you cannot fully realize it.

I have at my side a Cabinet composed of pure-minded, patriotic, and thoroughly loyal men. I sometimes feel guilty when I recall the troubles I have induced them to share with me. In our hand-to-hand conflicts our triumphs are many, but I am afraid as we triumph our party loses and the country does not gain as it should; and yet what would the condition be without us?

You may be surprised to learn that in all the darkness I have never lost the feeling that the American people and I have a perfectly fair understanding.

I do not believe you will think me vain and foolish if I say to you that I ought to be and am profoundly grateful for a guidance which has thus far kept me from pitfalls. God knows I cannot bear mistakes now.

Our friends at the Capitol have blindly wandered into a close trap on the financial question. Today the House Ways and Means Committee expect a bill for gold bonds and the Senate is thrashing about in a way that is pitiable. In the meantime the Administration is lightened from a heavy load by our last arrangement for the procurement of gold. I have not a doubt that we shall be free from anxiety on that score for a good long breathing spell.

That trouble over, another looms up. I do not see how I can make myself responsible for such a departure from our traditions as is involved in an appropriation in the Diplomatic bill, for building a cable by the Government to Hawaii. The Senate has thus amended the House bill. The House will stubbornly oppose and resist it and I hope it will be dis-

[1] That is, Senator Vilas of Wisconsin and Senator George Gray of Delaware. Gray honestly and openly disapproved of some of Cleveland's acts.

posed of in conference and rejected. If it is not, another conflict will be forced upon me. I hear today that the claim is made that I have heretofore expressed myself favorably towards such a scheme. I suppose this claim is based upon references to the usefulness of telegraph communication between us and Hawaii in my annual messages of 1886 and 1888. Whatever inferences are attempted to be drawn from those expressions I do not believe we should in present circumstances boom the annexation craze by entering upon Government cable building.

I long for the 4th of March to come with no necessity in sight for a special session. We shall not need it for the purpose of making another effort to bridge or cure financial troubles.

I need not say to you that I shall be delighted at all times to hear from you. I am surprised to see how sensibly the English papers treat our situation as manifested by the clippings you sent me. I trust you will be alert to discover any growing inclination in England to deal with the silver question internationally, and advise us if you see a propitious opening.

Mrs. Cleveland and the babies are well. God be praised for that! I often think that if things should go wrong in that end of the house I should abandon the ship. If she were not in bed and asleep Mrs. Cleveland would send her love to you and Mrs. Bayard. Mine goes anyway.

JACOB H. SCHIFF *to* CLEVELAND

New York, *February* 15, 1895

Some day the country will wake up to a sense of what it lastingly owes you for having saved its honor and for having made a return to more prosperous conditions at least possible. Meantime permit me to give expression to the admiration and satisfaction I feel, in common with many others, for the far-sighted statesmanship, patriotism and courage you are exhibiting in these most trying and critical times through which the country is passing.

To CHARLES S. FAIRCHILD

Washington, *February* 16, 1895

I enclose a speech on the financial and currency question made in Congress a few days ago by Mr. Patterson of Tennessee.[1] He is a man who has seen his way from silverdom to a better abiding place and is not

---

[1] Josiah Patterson (1837–1904) of Memphis, a Confederate veteran who served in the House 1891–97.

ashamed to confess it. His speech was spoken of by those who heard it as quite able and I asked him to send me two or three in pamphlet form. It strikes me as a good presentation and it has occurred to me that, coming from a Southern man, it might be a good document to circulate at the South.

I am entirely certain that section can be dislodged from their association with the West on the currency question. They have heard but one side and there is plenty of proof at hand that they will respond properly if the other side is made plain. A campaign of education such as was waged for tariff reform would produce quick and abundant results — in the South especially.

I know how easy it is to say these things and how hard it is to do the work. I know the Reform Club has a committee charged with this subject of distributing sound doctrine and I send Mr. Patterson's speech thinking some use could be made of it.

To E. C. BENEDICT

Washington, *February* 20, 1895

I thank you most sincerely for clearing up my affairs in such a satisfactory way. If you please, you may send the 'documents' to me directly.

I enclose you six dollars in currency. My remembrance was that I owed you that sum, but I have always inadvertently neglected to send it when I was writing. I think you ought to charge me interest unless our unwritten law allows the debtor to be without default if the settlement of one season's losses [is made] before the next season sets in. On this theory I have just saved my bacon, and shall have a stern chase before me when we cut for deal the next time.

I am ashamed to say that I cannot put my hand on your last letter tonight. I have put it somewhere very carefully, I am quite sure, but at this moment I cannot tell where it reposes. I expect it will turn up, but in the meantime may I ask you to duplicate the figures it contained? It exhibited the amount you had received, the amount paid to me on my account, the amounts paid for my securities and especially the small balance I owe you. It was all very interesting to me and made me feel kind of wealthy and moneyed-like. I ought not to ask you to be bothered again on account of my carelessness, but I must at all events have the amount of my indebtedness to you so that I can pay — which I will do instanter.

We are having a nice visit with Helen, though the social whirl takes her a good deal away. She pays as she goes and has told me to say to you that 'the board agrees with her first-rate.'

P.S.... After sealing and directing my letter to you and doing a good deal of work I left my table after one o'clock to go to bed. After reaching my bedroom I hunted my pockets again for your letter and found it tucked away in a wrong envelope. I have come back to the office and lighted up again to send you a check which I enclose. This makes irrelevant a good deal of my letter, but I will not rewrite it.

To E. C. Benedict

Washington, *February* 25, 1895

I have received today the bonds and stock you kindly purchased for me and I enclose you herewith the receipt for the same.

I desire to express again my gratitude to you for all you have done for me in the transaction of this business. I shall take your advice and not be too anxious to see quotations. If, however, I occasionally bother you with inquiries as to the value and prospects of my property, you must remember that half the fun of holding stock and bonds is to see if their value increase or decrease. In one case a calm satisfaction intervenes — in the other the exhilaration of hope and expectation.

If you are going out of active business, which I earnestly hope you will do, you have certainly done a very sensible thing in purchasing the Americus Club property.[1] I say this without reference to your having made a good or bad bargain, but with some regrets that you are to leave the old home which you have made so delightful. I am glad because your new purchase will give you pleasant occupation in its improvement and embellishment. I do not believe your active nature would find contentment in the entire lack of busy effort. You have earned just such a respite as you desire, and I hope you will live long to enjoy it.

I am thankful to you for the encouraging words you write me in regard to my course in financial matters. Such expressions are my only comfort, except my wife and babies, in these troublous perplexing days. The next week will be especially harassing and anxious; what will follow may add to my burdens. Do you know, my dear Commodore, that I have never been so sure that there is a high and unseen Power that guides and

---

[1] The Americus Club was Tweed's old organization, and its property was at Greenwich, Connecticut.

sustains the weak efforts of man? I feel it all the time and somehow I have come to expect that I shall find the path of duty and right, if I honestly and patriotically go on my way. I would be afraid to allow a bad, low motive to find lodgment in my mind, for I know I should then stumble and go astray.

I am conscious of being somewhat in a moralizing mood tonight. Perhaps it's not amiss, but I ought not to inflict it on you.

I saw Mr. Scott of Chicago this afternoon and he pleased me very much by saying pleasant things of you. He sailed with you on your last trip abroad. Give my love to all your household.

To Dr. S. B. Ward

Washington, *March* 19, 1895

Your kind letter and congratulations received today caused me extreme gratification and I thank you most sincerely. I have not seen the newspaper reference touching Mrs. Cleveland to which you refer, but I can guess what it is. You write, 'In that event of course I have nothing further to say.' On that theory, I am afraid you will have to follow the example of the member of Assembly from Buffalo, during my stay in Albany, who notified the Speaker that he would 'withdraw further remarks.'

I would be delighted to meet you and the fish at Saranac this spring, but I honestly do not see any chance of doing so. I suppose we shall start our Massachusetts establishment about the first of June; and if I can go anywhere in May I am already booked for a trip to North Carolina after birds and fish. I believe my last outing was taken just in time to save me from a kind of breakdown. I am bound to acknowledge that fifty-eight is not forty-eight — by a long shot. I sometimes absolutely long for mountain air again and I should be very unhappy if I thought I should never share it again with you.

Please give my love to the girls and Jack.

To Don M. Dickinson

Washington, *March* 20, 1895

You made me very happy on my birthday in the receipt of the volumes you kindly sent me.[1] I know that I shall be much entertained and in-

---

[1] A set of the *Greville Diary*, which, as Dickinson wrote, contained much history paralleling that of Cleveland's Administration.

structed by their perusal, and I promise myself the pleasure of reading them at an early day.

Somehow the kindly congratulations and remembrances of friends were peculiarly gratifying to me on my latest birthday. I suppose it is accounted for partly by the fact that as we grow older kindness touches us more nearly, and perhaps another reason, in my particular case, is found in the fact that I have had some occasion to feel unusually forlorn during the last year. Troubles in official duty follow each other thick and fast, and we are out of one perplexity to immediately face another.

I tell you, my friend, there is no doubt about Divine Providence and there is no doubt that if deserved, His care and guidance will be constantly at hand.

You don't know what a comfort Gresham is to me, with his hard sense, his patriotism and loyalty. It is but little for me to say that I would trust my life or honor in his keeping at all times. I have some other good men about me and I am constantly thinking that enmity and evil and misfortune must overcome eight more good true ones (nine with Thurber) before my discomfiture can be accomplished. We shall work the problem out.

I only intended to thank you for your birthday gift. I am sincerely grateful. Give my affectionate regards to Mrs. Dickinson and my love to my Democratic girl and believe me...

To GEORGE GILDER [1]
Washington, *March* 21, 1895

I was very much pleased with the pen you sent me for a birthday present, and I am using it for the first time in writing this letter to you. It is so much nicer than any other pen I have, that it will take me a little while to get used to it.

I want to thank you very much indeed for remembering my birthday and for the handsome present you gave me.

I hope I shall see you sometime during the summer.

To RICHARD WATSON GILDER
Washington, *March* 23, 1895

I am exceedingly grateful for your remembrance of my birthday in such a pleasing and substantial manner. The books you sent me shall be

---

[1] The small boy before mentioned.

the first taken up for thorough perusal in that future time, so much desired, when I shall have opportunity to do at least a little reading.

As day after day passes, full of trouble and annoyance with such small surface results, I find myself again and again saying, 'How flat, stale, and unprofitable!' If occasional words of encouragement did not reach me like a breath of fresh air in this dreadful atmosphere, I would be in danger of sinking into a condition of mere anxiety for my release from the things that surround me here. But two years more will quickly pass.

I hope you will make it your business to secure for yourself a good holiday this summer. It's one of the things you need. I am looking forward to the first of June as the time I hope my vacation will begin. I was very much touched by George's gift and I am much comforted by his steadfast friendship. I flatter myself it takes a pretty good man to gain and keep the good opinion of such a boy. Please give my love to Mrs. Gilder.

To CHARLES S. FAIRCHILD

Washington, *March* 25, 1895

Mr. R. H. Clarke,[1] I understand, will go to New York this evening to confer with certain parties there in relation to an attempt to start an aggressive movement in the South on the subject of sound money. He sends me word that he wants to talk with you, among others, but has not the advantage of your personal acquaintance.

I have no information concerning the details of his plan, but can do no less for so good a man than to say to you that few if any men in Congress from the South (I think I may say no Representative from the South) has a better appreciation of public duty or sounder ideas on public questions. Without any prompting and, so far as I have been able to see, without any reference to selfish interests, he has been faithful and sound among many faithless and unsound. There is no man in Congress whom I hold in higher esteem and if anything is to be done to win his section back from error and misconception it must be done through just such men.

I cannot and do not ask you to devote any time to such affairs, but if you see Mr. Clarke I want you to know what manner of man he is. He represents in Congress the district including the city of Mobile, and was re-elected last fall on a sound-money issue.

[1] Richard Henry Clarke (1843–1906), of Mobile, Alabama, a Confederate veteran and lawyer who served in Congress 1889–97.

STATEMENT ON THE REVEREND MR. LANSING'S
ACCUSATION OF INTEMPERANCE [1]

Washington, *April* 7, 1895

This is simply an outrage, though it is not the first time a thing of this kind has been attempted. I cannot avoid a feeling of indignation that any man who makes claims to decency, and especially one who assumes the rôle of a Christian minister, should permit himself to become a disseminator of wholesale lies and calumnies not less stupid than they are cruel and wicked.

I easily recall other occasions when those more or less entitled to be called ministers of the Gospel have been instrumental in putting into circulation the most scandalous falsehoods concerning my conduct and character. The elements or factors of the most approved outfit for placing a false and barefaced accusation before the public appear to be, first, someone with base motive sufficient to invent it; second, a minister with more gullibility and love of notoriety than piety, greedily willing to listen to it and gabble it; and third, a newspaper anxiously willing to publish it.

For the sake of the Christian religion, I am thankful that these scandal-mongering ministers are few, and on every account I am glad that the American people love fair play and justice, and that in spite of all effort to mislead them they are apt to form a correct estimate of the character and labors of their public servants.

NOTE ON THE REVEREND MR. LANSING'S RETRACTION

Washington, *April* 11, 1895

While his so-called retraction is an aggravation of his original offence, I am willing that his further punishment should be left to his conscience and the contempt of his neighbors and the American people.

To a CHICAGO GROUP [2]

Washington, *April* 13, 1895

If the sound-money sentiment in the land is to save us from mischief and disaster, it must be crystallized and combined and made immediately

---

[1] The Reverend Dr. Lansing at a conference of the Methodist Episcopal Church in Salem, Massachusetts, had accused President Cleveland of intemperance. In a later statement he declared that there was a conflict of evidence on the subject, and he could not decide between the opposing sides!

[2] A business group who had invited the President to attend and address a sound-money gathering in Chicago.

active. It is dangerous to overlook the fact that a vast number of our people, with scant opportunity thus far to examine the question in all its aspects, have nevertheless been ingeniously pressed with specious suggestions, which in this time of misfortune and depression find willing listeners, prepared to give credence to any scheme which is plausibly presented as a remedy for their unfortunate condition.

What is now needed more than anything else is a plain and simple representation of the argument in favor of sound money. In other words, it is time for the American people to reason together as members of a great nation, which can promise them a continuation of protection and safety only so long as its solvency is unsuspected, its honor unsullied, and the soundness of its money unquestioned. These things are ill-exchanged for the illusions of a debased currency and groundless hope of advantages to be gained by a disregard of our financial credit and commercial standing among the nations of the world.

If our people were isolated from all others and if the question of our currency could be treated without regard to our relations to other countries, its character would be a matter of comparatively little importance. If the American people were only concerned in the maintenance of their physical life among themselves, they might return to the old days of barter, and in this primitive manner acquire from each other the material to supply the wants of their existence. But if American civilization were satisfied with this, it would abjectly fail in its high and noble mission.

In these restless days the farmer is tempted by the assurance that though our currency may be debased, redundant, and uncertain, such a situation will improve the price of his products. Let us remind him that he must buy as well as sell; that his dreams of plenty are shaded by the certainty that if the price of the things he has to sell is nominally enhanced, the cost of the things he must buy will not remain stationary....

It ought not to be difficult to convince the wage-earner that if there were benefits arising from a degenerated currency they would reach him least of all and last of all. In an unhealthy stimulation of prices an increased cost of all the needs of his home must long be his portion, while he is at the same time vexed with the vanishing visions of increased wages and an easier lot. The pages of history and experience are full of this lesson.

An insidious attempt is made to create a prejudice against the advocates of a safe and sound currency by the insinuation, more or less directly made, that they belong to financial and business classes, and are therefore not only out of sympathy with the common people of the land, but for selfish and wicked purposes are willing to sacrifice the interests of those outside their circle.

I believe that capital and wealth, through combination and other means, sometimes gain an undue advantage, and it must be conceded that the maintenance of a sound currency may, in a sense, be invested with a greater or less importance to individuals according to their condition and circumstances. It is, however, only a difference in degree, since it is utterly impossible that anyone in our broad land, rich or poor, whatever may be his occupation, and whether dwelling in a centre of finance and commerce or in a remote corner of our domain, can be really benefited by a financial scheme not alike beneficial to all our people, or that anyone should be excluded from a common and universal interest in the safe character and stable value of the currency of the country....

If reckless discontent and wild experiment should sweep our currency from its safe support, the most defenceless of all who suffer in that time of distress and national discredit will be the poor, as they reckon the loss in their scanty support, and the laborer or workingman, as he sees the money he has received for his toil shrink and shrivel in his hand when he tenders it for the necessaries to supply the humble home. Disguise it as we may, the line of battle is drawn between the forces of safe currency and those of silver monometallism.

To WILLIAM GORHAM RICE [1]

Washington, *April 20*, 1895

Present appearances indicate that I shall need you in the Civil Service Board early in May. I ought perhaps to say to you *in the strictest confidence* that you will probably be associated with Mr. Procter, now at the head of the Board, and a Republican member as yet not determined on. I shall hope with this reorganization to secure a harmonious and effective Commission, which will furnish guaranty of no relaxation in the way of enforcing strictly the Civil Service Law, and that important extensions may be made in its operation. I think you and your colleagues will find plenty to do.

[1] Mr. Rice, who had been assistant to both Governor Cleveland and Governor Hill at Albany, served as Federal Civil Service Commissioner 1895-98. The chairman of the Commission was J. R. Procter of Kentucky.

COMMISSIONER THEODORE ROOSEVELT *to* CLEVELAND

Washington, *April 23*, 1895

Mr. Wyman has shown me your letter requesting his resignation. I venture to write to you again on the question of the organization of the Commission. I am now about to leave it, and my sole desire is to see it put on the most efficient footing possible, so as to work for the best advancement of the cause. Of course the better the Commission is, and the more the cause is advanced, the greater the credit that rightfully attaches to your Administration.

In Mr. Procter you have literally an ideal head of the Commission. In courage, integrity, and capacity to do this very work, he could not be surpassed. For the Republican member of the Commission Mr. Bellamy Storer [1] would make another ideal appointment if he could be persuaded to take it. As you may perhaps remember, he was the only man from Ohio of either party who in the House voted in favor of your gold bond resolution, and he defended it most ardently in a speech in Cincinnati afterwards. He is a singularly high-minded man, and his appointment would be of especial consequence in view of the fact that the next Congress will be Republican. Plenty of Republican spoilsmen will wish to attack the law and will wish to attack your Commission. Their teeth will be drawn by the appointment of a man like Storer. He is of all others the one best fitted for it if he will take it.

For the third member, Mr. Hill, one of your own appointees, now in the Department of Agriculture, would admirably round out the Commission. He is an ardent Democrat from the Far West, a man who on the stump and in his paper has advocated free trade, sound money, and the other principles of the Democratic party which you especially represent. He is an ardent civil service reformer, and he has, what is very necessary in this Commission, a thorough practical knowledge of departmental and office business. If you had three such men you would, without exaggeration, have the best Commission there has been since the law went into effect.

I shall send you my formal letter of resignation in a day or two. I am waiting to hear from Mayor Strong whether he wants me on May 1 or May 6. [2]

[1] The third membership in the Commission went to J. B. Harlow of Missouri.

[2] Roosevelt had been chosen Police Commissioner of New York City in the reform administration of Mayor Strong.

To GOVERNOR J. M. STONE [1]

Washington, *April* 26, 1895

Your letter of the 21st instant is at hand. I do not feel inclined to find fault with your criticism, but I think the matter you refer to should be judged in the light of the circumstances existing at the time the things were done. I never had an idea of building up or fostering a personal following, but so far as politics should properly influence me in making appointments I have tried to be Democratic and not proscriptive. I am glad you are frank enough to admit your participation in bringing about a condition in officeholding which may not be all that could now be desired.

Whether those appointed to places shall, in speech and action, behave decently toward the Administration under which they hold office must remain, to a large extent, a matter of taste and good breeding. There are, however, some officials who devote themselves so industriously to vilification and abuse of those under whom they hold office as to indicate that their fidelity cannot be trusted for the performance of their duties in a manner creditable to the Administration and who apparently assume that they may spend the time they owe the public service in doing political mischief. In the interest of good government such officeholders must not be surprised if they are summarily dealt with.

When I received your letter I had just finished reading a letter of yours in which you explain to the citizens of Mississippi your views on the currency question. It seems to me you have in that letter contributed in the best possible style and in a most valuable way to the fund of argument in favor of sound money. I have never ceased to wonder why the people of the South, furnishing so largely as they do products which are exported for gold, should be willing to submit to the disadvantages and loss of silver monometallism and to content themselves with a depreciated and fluctuating currency, while permitting others to reap a profit from the transmutation of the prices of their productions from silver to gold. I hope this letter of yours will be given the widest possible circulation, especially among our Southern fellow-citizens, and that they will be permitted to see the pitfall which is directly before those who madly rush toward the phantom light of free, unlimited, and independent silver coinage.

If we, who profess fealty to the Democratic party, are sincere in our

[1] John M. Stone, governor of Mississippi 1890-96.

devotion to its principles, and if we are right in believing that the ascendancy of those principles is a guarantee of personal liberty, universal care for the rights of all, non-sectional American brotherhood, and manly trust in American citizenship in any part of our land, we should study the effects upon our party and consequently upon our country of a committal of the national Democracy to this silver aberration.

If there are Democrats who suppose that our party can succeed upon a platform embodying such a doctrine, either through its affirmative strength or through the perplexity of our opponents on the same proposition, or if there are Democrats who are willing to turn their backs upon their party associations in the hope that free and unlimited and independent coinage of silver can win a victory without the aid of either party or organization, they should deceive themselves no longer, nor longer refuse to look in the face the results that will follow the defeat, if not the disintegration, of the Democratic party, upon the issue which tempts them from their allegiance. If we should be forced away from our traditional doctrine of sound and safe money our old antagonists will take the field on the platform which we abandon, and neither the votes of reckless Democrats nor reckless Republicans will avail to stay their easy march to power. This is as plain as anything can possibly be.

It, therefore, becomes the duty of every Democrat, wherever he may be, to consider what such a victory would mean, and in the light of a proper conception of its results he should deliberately shape his course.

To SECRETARY HOKE SMITH

Washington, *May* 4, 1895

As the commissioners to negotiate and treat with the five civilized tribes of Indians are about to resume their labors, my interest in the subject they have in charge induces me to write you a few words concerning their work. As I said to the commissioners when they were first appointed, I am especially desirous that there shall be no reason in all time to come to charge the commissioners with any unfair dealing with the Indians, and that whatever the results of their efforts may be the Indians will not be led into any action which they do not thoroughly understand or which is not clearly for their benefit.

At the same time I still believe, as I have always believed, that the best interests of the Indians will be found in American citizenship, with all the rights and privileges which belong to that condition. The approach to this relation should be carefully made and at every step the good and welfare of the Indian should be constantly kept in view, so that when the end is reached citizenship may be to them a real advantage, instead of an empty name.

I hope the commissioners will inspire such confidence in those Indians with whom they have to deal that they will be listened to and that the Indians will see the wisdom and advantage of moving in the direction I have indicated. If they are unwilling to go immediately so far as we may think desirable, whatever steps are taken should be such as to point out the way and the results of which will encourage these people in future progress. A slow movement of that kind, fully understood and approved by the Indians, is infinitely better than swifter results gained by broken pledges and false promises.

To CHARLES S. FAIRCHILD

Washington, *May* 6, 1895

Your letter is just received. I am much obliged to you for attending to the matter and am sorry I was so thoughtless as to entirely miss the possibility of your being out of town.

I confess I acted a little hastily in the matter of the resignation; but it seemed to me on the instant, that some allowance ought to have been made for my seeming neglect. I sometimes fear that I am 'losing my grip' a little, and feel that I am as nearly insane as a sane man can be. It certainly never occurred to me how far-reaching the effect of my resignation might be.

I would like to resume my non-resident membership in the club, and will do so if it will be agreeable to the organization. I enclose my check for $100 to aid the sound-money propaganda.

ANSWER TO A REQUEST FOR CLEMENCY FOR W. CALVIN CHASE

Washington, *May* 8, 1895

It is conceded that this convict maliciously published an outrageous libel in a newspaper which he controlled and used, in this instance at least, as a dirty weapon to satisfy his personal rage and revenge.

This crime is a most detestable one. It has become so common and is so seldom punished that I cannot reconcile executive clemency in the case here presented with the duty I owe to decent journalism, the peace of society, and the protection of those constantly subjected to libellous attack.

To E. C. BENEDICT

Washington, *May* 9, 1895

Your letter came yesterday and the check you enclosed was a most gratifying surprise. In computing my wealth I have always felt that the time had not arrived to put any specific present value on the stock which you assumed as dividend-paying. I shall be obliged to exercise much self-restraint to keep out of foolish extravagance to which I shall be tempted by this sudden change in my pecuniary condition. I will adopt your suggestion and send my certificate with this so that the stock can be transferred to my name. I have still twelve or fifteen thousand dollars which ought to be earning something. Do you want to suggest any future investment? I find I am developing quite a strong desire to make money, and I think this is a good time to indulge in that propensity.

The *Oneida* never figured in an invitation so tempting as your letter contains. I wish I could say now that I would avail myself of it and fix on a date. This, however, I cannot do. The Secretary of State is ill and public affairs are not as settled and unruffled as I could wish. I will, however, continue to think and plan and communicate with you further, perhaps. If I could go nothing would suit me better than to have Dr. Bryant go too. If the Secretary of State were well enough it would be a great benefit to him if he could take the trip. His improvement to a sufficient extent to permit this is, however, extremely uncertain.

I forbear enlarging on the tarpon question, and only suggest a wise forbearance on your part, to the end that you may not be suspected of being a victim of 'buck fever' which transformed to your disordered gaze a large mullet to a hundred-pound silver-king. In these days of hypnotic mysteries nothing of this sort need surprise us.

To CHARLES S. FAIRCHILD

Washington, *May* 9, 1895

You are quite right about the certificate; and if you will take it in your own name and hold it for me I shall be glad. I don't think any too much of my purchase and shall probably want to sell before very long. This condition makes it more satisfactory to me that the shares were $50 instead of $100, as I supposed. When you get the certificate may I ask you to write me something — just a note — saying you hold it for me? I find at fifty-eight I am thinking much more of mortal contingencies than in earlier years.

I want to write something to you quite confidentially. Affairs in Venezuela are liable to assume a condition calling on our part for the greatest care and good management.[1] Do you happen to recall anyone who would do well as our representative there in such a contingency? I think I ought to send someone there of a much higher grade than is usually thought good enough for such a station. The salary is only $7,500, and I believe Caracas is a fair capital to live in.

To E. C. BENEDICT

Washington, *May* 14, 1895

I received your letter and the certificates, for which I thank you. I have got some work to do at Gray Gables this summer — that is, I want to do some work — and I am not sure that I can undertake it unless I can make some money to meet the expense of my contemplated improvements. I've got some already made, but I want a little more. If I don't get it in the way I propose, I shall not grieve, and I want you to agree not to laugh. I want you to buy me 100 shares of Rock Island and keep it until you hear from me further. I enclose a blank check which you may fill up to pay for the purchase, and let me know how much you fill in so that I can put it on my stub. Of course this is *between us*.

Dr. Bryant was here Sunday and seemed very much in the mood for the trip you suggest. I am still unable to say whether I can go or not.

To SECRETARY HOKE SMITH

Washington, *May* 16, 1895

I have been presented with a soft-shelled turtle from Georgia. Can you or any other Georgian within your reach tell us how it should be cooked?

To E. C. BENEDICT

Washington, *May* 17, 1895

I am of the opinion that you and I are both a little cranky. You are constantly trying to do kind things for those you like by stealth; and I am

---

[1] Secretary Gresham had been working upon a message regarding Venezuela to be presented to the British Government, and Cleveland was growing determined to bring the matter to a head.

not willing that you should give me money 'cold out of hand' without the assumption on my part of any risk or expenditure. I am quite content to join you in anything you undertake because I think your judgment is good and because I know you would not let me into anything which is objectionable on grounds of propriety. It's an ungracious thing to interpose any objection to your scheme which, so far as it involves me, is based upon nothing but the utmost kindness, but somehow I don't feel comfortable about it in the way you put it.

Cannot we compromise the matter in some way? For instance, can I not put in your hands or become responsible for a moderate sum which in case of an unprofitable turn will limit my loss, and which in case of a profitable turn will have some relation to my share of the winnings? I will ask no questions and will especially agree to laugh as heartily in one case as the other.

I know you can fix it in some way so that your kindness will shine out as brightly and be appreciated as fully as if you had your way, and at the same time enable me to feel much more comfortable than I would under your plan. One of the best things in our relationship is the entire frankness of our association. On that line I make these suggestions, feeling sure that you will understand me and humor my notion.

Public affairs are still in such condition as to prevent any certain calculation as to the time I can leave here. Mrs. Cleveland and the babies will go early in June, I suppose, and it is barely possible that I can go with them.

I am surprised to hear that you had to 'manage' to get a sound-money declaration in your State. I sometimes pinch myself to find out if I am dreaming when I see some of the Democratic performances now going on in certain quarters. I cannot believe that our party will be committed to free and unlimited independent coinage, but I am afraid there will be such nibbling and fussing with it that we will be discredited and suspected, however much next year we protest the soundness and safety of our views. I am sometimes very blue in the fear that the damage is already done.

Talking about making money makes me wish for an opportunity to avail myself of that unfailing resource, the cribbage board, with you on the opposite side of the table. Mrs. Cleveland sends love to you and your household. So do I.

To JOHN S. MASON [1]

Washington, *May 20*, 1895

I regret that my official duties oblige me to decline the courteous invitation I have received to attend the annual banquet of the Democratic Editorial Association on the 24th instant. This reunion of Democratic editors will, I am sure, be an enjoyable occasion to all who participate; but I shall be much disappointed if the fellowship and interchange of sentiment it will afford do not stimulate the zeal and effort of the fraternity there assembled, in behalf of the Democratic cause and Democratic principles.

Our party is so much a party of principle, and its proper action and usefulness are so dependent upon a constant adherence to its doctrines and traditions, that no tendency in our ranks to follow the misleading light of a temporary popular misapprehension should go unchallenged. Our victories have all been won when we have closely followed the banner of Democratic principle. We have always been punished by defeat when, losing sight of our banner, we have yielded to the blandishments of un-Democratic expediency.

There is a temptation now vexing the people in different sections of the country which assumes the guise of Democratic party principle, inasmuch as it presents a scheme which is claimed to be a remedy for agricultural depression, and such other hardships as afflict our fellow-citizens. Thus, because we are the friends of the people and profess devotion to their interests, the help of the members of our party is invoked in support of a plan to revolutionize the monetary condition of the country, and embark upon an experiment which is discredited by all reason and experience, which invites trouble and disaster in every avenue of labor and enterprise, and which must prove destructive to our national prestige and character.

When a campaign is actively on foot to force the free, unlimited, and independent coinage of silver by the Government, at a ratio which will add to our circulation unrestrained millions of so-called dollars, intrinsically worth but half the amount they purport to represent, with no provision or resource to make good this deficiency in value, and when it is claimed that such a proposition has any relation to the principles of

---

[1] Read at a dinner of the Democratic editors of New York State held in New York City on the night of May 24, 1895; John S. Mason was chairman of the Association.

Democracy, it is time for all who may in the least degree influence Democratic thought to realize their responsibility.

Our party is the party of the people, not because it is wafted hither and thither by every sudden wave of popular excitement and misconception, but because, while it tests every proposition by the doctrines which underlie its organization, it insists that all interests should be defended in the administration of the government without especial favor or discrimination.

Our party is the party of the people because, in its care for the welfare of all our countrymen, it resists dangerous schemes born of discontent, advocated by appeals to sectional or class prejudices, and re-enforced by the insidious aid of private selfishness and cupidity.

Above all, our party is the party of the people when it recognizes the fact that sound and absolutely safe money is the lifeblood of our country's strength and prosperity, and when it teaches that none of our fellow-citizens, rich or poor, great or humble, can escape the consequences of a degeneration of our currency.

Democratic care and conservatism dictate that if there exists inconvenience and hardship, resulting from the congestion or imperfect distribution of our circulating medium, a remedy should be applied which will avoid the disaster that must follow in the train of silver monometallism.

What I have written has not been prompted by any fear that the Democracy of the State of New York will ever be an accomplice in such an injury to their country as would be entailed by the free, unlimited, and independent coinage of silver; nor do I believe that they will ever be so heedless of party interests as to support such a movement. I have referred to this subject in the belief that nothing more important can engage the attention of the American people or the national Democracy, and in the conviction that the voice of the Democrats of New York, through its press, should constantly be heard in every State.

W. H. MERRILL [1] *to* CLEVELAND

World Editorial Rooms, *May 21, 1895*

Don't be too easily discouraged in your endeavor to enlighten newspaper men as to the law and its bearing! I was misled, evidently, by the

---

[1] Chief editorial writer of the New York *World*, who had been harshly criticizing Olney for failure to press the anti-trust cases.

statement in your first letter that 'another decision on the same law, and covering the *same ground*, and holding *precisely the same doctrine*, was made by Justice Jackson,' etc. I should have remembered the advice of President Wheeler [1] to me, in the Constitutional Convention: 'Stick to the statutes — scan the decisions — take nothing for granted.' I will have the Jackson decisions looked up.

I quite agree with you that suits cannot well be brought in the face of decisions (except of lower courts, perhaps) or for the sake of a sensation. But I candidly say that one case successfully prosecuted against a trust would greatly help the Administration and the Democratic party. I fully believe that you would gladly achieve such a triumph for the people. And if the *World* can help you it will. We furnished the evidence and made the case on which the coal combination was knocked out by the Attorney-General in New Jersey; and I have instructed our legal and detective departments to see if a good case cannot be made up either under the Sherman or the Morgan Law.

It was a close case for the income tax, but 'twas better that the remnant should go with the rest — 'the tail with the kite.'

To JUDSON HARMON [2]

Washington, *June* 5, 1895

There are substantial reasons for my desire that you regard the contents of this note entirely confidential.

A readjustment of my Cabinet consequent upon the lamented death of Judge Gresham, makes it necessary for me to select a new Attorney-General; and after much reflection, I am very clear in the opinion that your acceptance of the position would insure the best possible results to the public service, and be in every way a most desirable consummation. Will you join us? The office is well equipped with Holmes Conrad of Virginia as Solicitor-General and Mr. Dickinson of Tennessee and Mr. Whitney of New York Chief Assistants. Inasmuch as there is less than two years remaining of the term of this Administration, I do not see why, if you accept the place, your private practice could not be kept somewhat in hand during that time. I know that you could be of great service to

---

[1] William A. Wheeler (1819–1887), president of the New York Constitutional Convention of 1867, and Vice-President of the United States 1877–1881.

[2] Harmon (1846–1927), an attorney and former judge resident in Cincinnati, Ohio, was Attorney-General under Cleveland from June 8, 1895, to the end of the Administration.

the country in the position, as well as to the party to which we both belong — now, in my opinion, in great need of steadying influences. If my personal desires can add anything to the more important considerations involved, you may be sure they are strongly enlisted.

I am naturally anxious to learn your determination as soon as possible. If you consent to accept the position will you please telegraph me these words: 'Your information is correct. J. H.'? If, as I hope will not be the case, you feel obliged to decline, will you wire me as follows: 'He cannot go. J. H.'?

To E. C. BENEDICT

Washington, *June* 9, 1895

I was very glad to receive your letter. You are quite right in supposing that Judge Gresham's death [1] is a great affliction to me. His companionship and constant loyalty largely constituted all the comfort that came to my official life.

If you are in real earnest in what you say about the *Oneida* in connection with my trip to Gray Gables and if you are sure it won't bother and interfere with you, I am inclined to make a proposition. A week from tomorrow, June 17, I want to start. Olney lives at Falmouth in the summer and he will probably go with me. Dr. Bryant expects to come here and start with me also. It may possibly be that Thurber will want to go to Marion at the same time. Now what do you think of joining the party and going with us on *my* yacht the *Oneida*?

If you agree, where do you think the yacht had better take us on, and at what hour in the day? I suppose we shall go in a special car from here and will have our baggage in the car. The Doctor is only coming down with his wife and daughter and for the purpose of starting with me, and if he knew where the yacht would be he might have his trunk sent to it and thus save the trouble of bringing it here. It would be well, I suppose, to take a train from here that will arrive at such an hour in New York as will coincide with the time the yacht should start.

It rather seems to me just at this point that I am a little forward in suggesting all these details before I am sure that the trip can be undertaken as proposed. At least I think you should now have an opportunity to express your views.

[1] Secretary Gresham died in Washington, May 28, 1895.

To JUDSON HARMON

Washington, *June* 9, 1895

I received your dispatch yesterday afternoon and your letter today, with very great satisfaction. I congratulate you upon the complimentary manner in which your appointment has been received by the country, though I believe the people and the Administration are most to be congratulated on the event. Let me just mention, in passing, that the statements I have seen in one or two papers to the effect that this or that man was invited and declined, are absolute inventions of silly newspapers who are piqued because their guesses were all wrong.

I have signed and sent your commission to the Department of Justice, where it awaits you. I supposed you would come here and qualify and would not care to have the commission sent to you. I suppose Mr Olney will qualify as Secretary of State on Monday. The Solicitor General acts in his place until you are installed, so the business of the office does not call for any haste on your part. It is not unlikely, however, that both Mr. Olney and I may leave town a week from Monday (the 17th) on our vacations, and of course we would be glad to see you before we start.

To E. C. BENEDICT

Washington, *June* 13, 1895

I now intend to leave here on the Pennsylvania road at 7:05 A.M., reaching New York towards 1 o'clock, I believe. Dr. Bryant and perhaps Thurber will be with me. Mr. Olney will not make one of the party. Is this a proper arrangement, and what do you want us to do when we reach New York?

To LIBRARIAN A. R. SPOFFORD [1]

Washington, *June* 15, 1895

I am informed through the Treasury Department that embarrassment has been caused by your neglect to file the accounts required by law. I am also of the opinion that some confusion exists in the affairs under your charge which ought to be remedied. I have therefore directed —— who is the bearer of this note and an agent of the Treasury Department to make an examination of your accounts and methods, to the end that

---

[1] Ainsworth R. Spofford (1825–1908), who was librarian of the Congressional Library, 1864–1897, was one of the most venerable and respected figures of Washington. His age explained the confusion of his accounts.

they may be correct if faulty and the interests of the Government if necessary fully protected.

I request you to render Mr. —— all the assistance possible.

To KOPE ELIAS [1]

Gray Gables, *June 20*, 1895

I have read with very great interest and satisfaction the clippings you sent me from the Charlotte *Observer*. Such able presentations of the arguments against the dangerous and delusive notion of free and unlimited silver coinage cannot fail to arrest the attention of men as intelligent as those making up the population of North Carolina. I look upon those who take such an active and earnest part as the editor of the *Observer* in clearing away the fallacies and correcting the misapprehensions so prevalent just at this time and circling about the subject of our currency, as true patriots, who will in due time see with pride and satisfaction the happiest results from their patriotic labors. The American people are still sensible and honest and cannot be misled to their undoing.

To E. C. BENEDICT

Gray Gables, *June 30*, 1895

Your letter is received. I have no doubt the launch will often fit my case, but I want, so far as is consistent, to be true to the *Ruth* and therefore do not intend to see her superseded. The launch I must regard as a sort of extravagance for me, so I hope you will not allow her cost to be increased on account of any embellishment, ornamentation, or extra fitting. Of course, as you say, the concern would be of little use to me unless it was easily managed and easily cared for. I am much obliged to you for undertaking the matter on my behalf and hope that I may soon be in possession of my new idea.

I won seventy-five cents from the Doctor Wednesday, and Thursday — the last day we went together — the game was drawn. We intend to go tomorrow, when I expect my seventy-five cents to be more or less in jeopardy.

To ATTORNEY-GENERAL JUDSON HARMON

Gray Gables, *July 2*, 1895

I received your letter last night and had great satisfaction in telegraphing you this morning that I approved your recommendations. The action

[1] A North Carolina supporter.

you propose is in exact line with my efforts to do something solving the Indian problem in a sensible, decent, and Christian way. Send up the commission for Mr. Horton and I will promptly sign and return it.

I am glad to know that the prospects are brightening in Ohio. Of course you know that the objects and purposes of the Senator [1] are entirely selfish and cold-blooded, but no one ought to be hindered at this time who stands for sound money — though it is hard for me to overlook the exasperating and negatively damaging position this gentleman occupied when lately the cause sadly needed friends in the Senate. I hope no such good man as Campbell will be sacrificed — that is, I hope the State ticket will be justly and fairly treated. Another thing may as well be understood at the start. Mr. Lou Bernard cannot be assistant postmaster at Cincinnati. Whatever else happens this will not be done. I know I am right in this matter and some day all such Ohio Democrats as you are will see it.

You have invited a frank statement on my part concerning your participation in the Ohio campaign. I have always been quite a stickler for quite moderate or at least unobtrusive interference on the part of Cabinet officers. I confess, however, that just at this time the interests involved are of such high importance that to render aid in their cause seems to me a patriotic duty.

Whatever any of us can do by way of exercising quiet influence ought to be done, and if your neighbors and friends in Cincinnati are desirous to hear from you (as of course they are) and if a first-rate opportunity offers, I would be pleased to have you make them a speech, but my notion is it would be best to stop at that.

I am a little worried about one thing, not related to your Department.[2] Carlisle and Olney are in my neighborhood. Where will you be for the next two weeks and where is Wilson?

To JOSEPH H. CHOATE

Gray Gables, *July* 4, 1895

The case of Dr. Kershaw has not yet reached me. When it does you may be sure I shall examine it with the utmost care and with as little check to my natural inclination to save the name and reputation of the

---

[1] Calvin S. Brice (1845–98) of Lima, Ohio, who, after mismanaging Cleveland's campaign for re-election in 1888, sat in the Senate 1891–97.

[2] The Venezuelan question.

accused, as a proper regard for the public service will permit. Such cases are among the most perplexing things that fall to my lot.

I am inclined to think that the papers will present every consideration necessary to inform me fully of the merits of the case; but if I see on any points in the investigation that a verbal representation will assist me, I will avail myself of your offer to wait upon me for the purpose of thus supplementing the record and documents.

To SECRETARY HOKE SMITH

Gray Gables, *July* 5, 1895

I return the memorandum you sent me relating to the Choctaw tribal dissolution. I am not sure that I understand the situation well enough to make suggestions that will be of any value, but I have noted on the papers a thing or two that occurred to me. It seems to me that if the lands including coal lands are to be divided equally, it will be a little queer to have coal-mining going on, on a man's allotment, and he be prohibited from receiving any of the royalties. The terms of the purchase of town-site land should be such that all the money would fall due during the continuance of the tribal relation, so that everything could be cleared up at that time and the United States be discharged from its guardianship.

To JOSEPH JEFFERSON

Gray Gables, *July* 10, 1895

I am told that you sometimes find recreation in the rod and reel. I think it not amiss, therefore, to suggest a locality or spot where you might be able to find some sport in the direction mentioned. On the Sandwich road, a mile or two from Bourne, is a sort of abandoned farm, now owned by that universally popular veteran comedian Joseph Jefferson. This farm was originally purchased, I think, by Mr. Jefferson on account of a trout stream running through it; but lately he seems to have lost conceit with it and now pretty thoroughly neglects it. I am told he is a little capricious that way.

However, we will let that pass, since a friend visiting me and I took eight (8) as handsome trout as you would wish to see in a whole season out of that selfsame stream, this afternoon, in a short time. At the point where a railroad crosses the stream seems to be the spot where the fish congregate — though other places near-by will yield good results. Almost anybody about Bourne can tell you where the Jefferson farm is; and I am sure the owner would not object to your fishing there.

I enclose a poem which I received in my mail this evening. I see Mr. Jefferson is referred to in its well-worn lines.

To DON M. DICKINSON

Gray Gables, *July* 31, 1895

We are very late in acknowledging the receipt of the beautiful flowers you sent Mrs. Cleveland with your congratulations on the birth of our new girl. It was very thoughtful and we fully appreciated this additional evidence of your attachment. The baby is as well as can be and her gain in weight is constant and said to be unusual.

I read with much interest the letter you wrote on the subject of the Loyal Legion Speech. I was glad you wrote it. In due time it will be found that the Administration has not been asleep. The devils that were cast out of the swine centuries ago have, I am afraid, obtained possession of some so-called Democratic leaders. Good times and justification of Democratic policy, with gifts in their hands, are driven out from the Democratic camp. If there were a penitentiary devoted to the incarceration of those who commit crimes against the Democratic party, how easily it could be filled just at this time.

To ATTORNEY-GENERAL JUDSON HARMON

Gray Gables, *July* 31, 1895

My judgment is that we had better send Mr. Wallace's candidate to Alaska as district attorney, if on the papers and representations you are satisfied with his testimonials of fitness. I regard Mr. Wallace as quite reliable.

I am a good deal annoyed by the situation of the sugar bounty question and Comptroller Bowler's position in relation to it. I have always expressed the opinion that, in view of the fact that the McKinley Law provided that the bounty should be paid for a certain number of years — in so many words or in effect — sugar producers had more than an ordinary right to rely upon the payment of the bounty during that time. Having relied upon the permanency of the bounty to the extent provided by the limit fixed in the law, it has always seemed to me that when the bounty was swept away in the midst of the producing season and after

expense had been incurred on the faith of the promised bounty, equity
and justice dictated some reimbursement of the loss sustained by reliance
upon the promise of the Government. I don't call this a bounty but
reimbursement. I hold the belief that the money appropriated by way of
such indemnification should be paid, and I am very earnest in this belief
and I think I am perfectly consistent in claiming at the same time to be
one of the strongest opponents of bounties in the country.

I have no idea that there is any constitutional objection in the way of
the Government's doing a thing so clearly in the line of equity and good
conscience, as is this indemnification to the sugar producers who have
incurred expense they would not have incurred except for the Government's invitation. I thought the question all out before approving the
appropriation; and while I esteem Mr. Bowler as an excellent and careful officer, I do not think that in this case he is called on to override the
Congress and the President on a question so entirely judicial as the constitutionality of this provision.

Even if he should think it his duty to take up the judicial question of
constitutionality, I am by no means certain that he would find in the
decision of the District Court of Appeals justification for deciding against
the appropriation. Before he assumes such a responsibility (if in any case
he should assume it) he should have, it seems to me, the judgment of the
highest court upon the exact point. He certainly has not the former and
I do not believe the judgment of the Court of Appeals covers the phase
of the bounty question now presented.

I cannot but feel the greatest anxiety on this subject, for I have been
an openly avowed advocate of this measure of restitution; and until I
get new light, shall continue my efforts to bring it about whoever with-
stands. I am not at all adverse to Mr. Bowler's knowing my views.

To ATTORNEY-GENERAL JUDSON HARMON
Gray Gables, *August* 6, 1895

I was a good deal relieved by your last letter. I telegraphed Senator
Caffery on Sunday, that I hoped he and his associates would be temperate
and patient. I did this from a desire to prevent hasty talk and action,
which might make it less easy for the Comptroller to do the thing which
seems to me proper.

I telegraphed the Honorable Josiah Patterson of Memphis, asking him
to suggest a sound and able man for district attorney, to succeed Taylor,

deceased. I received a reply yesterday in which he said he was in consultation with our friends, and would present a name within forty-eight hours. His time is nearly up, but I have not yet received his suggestion. I shall be very much inclined to follow it when received.

In the matter of the marshalship in Oklahoma, I believe all of the judges and many others strongly urge the appointment of Charles L. Stowe....

I would be very glad to see you here, and discuss these subjects, early next week or Saturday of this week. You can get here quite readily and quickly by taking a steamer at Nantucket for Woods Hole and taking the train there. Tell the conductor you want to get off at Gray Gables and I will meet you there. The little depot is partly on my land. The car-ride time is not much more than half an hour. If you could spend two or three days you would please us greatly. I understand, however, how much you are likely to begrudge any of your vacation time with your brothers; and therefore, if you prefer it, you may write what you have to say upon the subject I have opened up. I would be glad to hear from or see you, as soon as convenient — inasmuch as I am convinced that early action will save us both annoyance.

I cannot close without again assuring you that we should be very much pleased if you concluded to come here. If you do so, notify me of the hour or train. If you come Saturday, you would of course spend Sunday with us and as many more days as you can afford.

I go to Falmouth tomorrow to fish with Secretary Olney.

To JOSEPH JEFFERSON

Gray Gables, *August* 13, 1895

I am glad you are home again with improved health. I will be indeed most happy to go with you next Monday and will endeavor to see you soon and settle details. I start very early tomorrow to fish a pond near Falmouth with Mr. Olney. I had a delightful day's trout fishing at Maple Spring last Thursday. I have never seen so many trout anywhere else. We caught one squeteague this morning in the 'narrows.'

To JOSEPH JEFFERSON

Gray Gables, *August* 20, 1895

When I arrived home last evening my family had received the welcome intelligence that Dr. Bryant would reach here this morning. I shall of course desire to invite him to fish with us Thursday and I have already asked Mr. Thurber to join the party. I write this because if there is any earthly thing you want me to do which you did not want me to do before, I beg you to let me know.

To Senator William F. Vilas

Gray Gables, *August 25,* 1895

I lost no time after the receipt of your first letter, and after discovering Senator Edmunds's [1] whereabouts, in writing him as persuasive a letter as it was possible for me to construct, asking him to accept the position of deputy water commissioner and explaining as fully as I could the nature of the duties it involved. After some delay, caused partly by the tardy receipt of my letter, his reply came — full of interest and zeal, but conveying his positive declination based upon reasons so related to his daughter's health that I could do nothing but admire his parental tenderness and solicitude.

He suggested that someone, preferably a Democrat, from New York State be selected. I have racked my brain on that scent and cannot think of any New York Democrat prominent and fit that would be at all likely to be fair and uninfluenced by Erie Canal or railroad notions.

About a week ago Senator Edmunds wrote me another letter indicating that he was still importuned on the subject and repeating and emphasizing the reasons for his declination. I wrote him last night and received your second letter today. I disclaimed in my letter to the Senator any movement on my part to press the matter upon him after his first reply, told him all the names that had occurred to me, and invited further suggestions.

Of course I need not tell you how troublesome the affair is — not less so by reason of Mr. Angell's [2] attitude, which I fully understand and approve. Three names have been in my mind lately, to wit: Andrew D. White of Ithaca, New York, ex-President of Cornell University; Simeon Baldwin of New Haven, Connecticut — I think was judge in that State and now or formerly a law professor in Yale College; Henry O. Kent — of Manchester, New Hampshire — surveyor or naval officer at the port of Boston under our previous Administration.

[1] George F. Edmunds (1828–1919) of Vermont, with whom Cleveland had clashed vigorously in his first Administration, sat in the Senate from 1866 to 1891, resigning for reasons connected with his daughter's health.

[2] James B. Angell (1829–1916), president of the University of Michigan.

I am hesitating about approaching any of them now, thinking something better might occur to me. Unless Mr. White is appointed I think it must go to New England. I expect to see Mr. Olney this week and shall ask a suggestion from him.

To ATTORNEY-GENERAL JUDSON HARMON
Gray Gables, *September* 5, 1895

Of course it is very exasperating for Judge Toulmin [1] or any other federal official to make an ass of himself and exhibit utter and complete insensibility to common decency and propriety. It may be because I am a little used to it, that I am rather of the opinion that the chase after him would turn out a skunk-hunting excursion.

If a letter should be written calling him to account, he would probably answer it after the style of a silver lunatic and publish both letters and invite a controversy, while cutting up capers before a packed jury. If he should be turned out, the Republican and Populist majority in the next Senate would probably roll this 'persecution for opinion's sake' like a sweet morsel under their tongues, and perhaps reject the nomination of a successor. I have always regarded a judicial officer in a very different way from an executive officer when considering removals from office, and have uniformly made removals of judicial officers only for causes affecting competency in the discharge of judicial duty or conduct which disgraced the bench.

I do not know who this fellow is and until your letter came did not know or had forgotten that there was any such man holding a federal judgeship. I am open to conviction, but on the information presented I incline to the opinion that this game isn't worth shooting.

To JOSEPH JEFFERSON
Gray Gables, *September* 11, 1895

Arrangements for tomorrow's fishing trip to the 'pond in the direction of Plymouth' are all completed, and we are to leave Buzzards Bay on the train for Wareham, a few minutes before seven A.M. Secretary of War Lamont will accompany us, and the plan is to stay all night at the pond and take in the early fishing Friday morning.

We are to take with us each his favorite rod and reel, whatever is deemed

---

[1] Apparently H. T. Toulmin of Mobile, Alabama, at this time judge of the Federal court of the southern district of his State.

actually necessary to a very plain existence overnight away from home, plenty of hope and expectation, and thousands of that philosophy which consoles and cheers at the close of an unsuccessful excursion, if we have been preserved from accident and have had a good outing.

To SECRETARY RICHARD OLNEY [1]

Gray Gables, *September* 12, 1895, 5 A.M.

This is the day we start early for our fish with Mr. Collector Warren. I suppose we shall return early tomorrow afternoon. I hope to see you before you return to Washington, but do not want you to put yourself to any trouble on that score.

I write now to say that I do not think the young man we were talking about (Phillips) will do at all. Besides the difficulty we were speaking of arising out of his mother's relations with a certain Mr. Butler, I learn that he is a good deal of a club man, and, what is a settler with me, that his close intimates are John Hay, Henry Adams, Cabot Lodge, and such.

I would feel very unhappy if anyone with such associates, who wish nothing but ill for the Administration, were connected with the State Department. I have told the Secretary of War to say to Herbert when he returns to Washington that there is no chance for his son-in-law and that he had better not further ask his appointment. Cannot you find some good young man in Boston or elsewhere whom you can swear by?

If I don't see or hear from you to the contrary, I will send the Civil Service orders to Washington as soon as I get back from my trip.

To SECRETARY RICHARD OLNEY

Gray Gables, *September* 15, 1895

I knew perfectly well that there were a great many consulates compensated only by fees, and it was very stupid in me not to recall that condition when we were talking about our Civil Service scheme. I believe the order would be pretty nearly right if it included all consuls paid by fees and all paid by salary of $2500 or less, excluding fees. You will see I have blundered away at the order you drew on that basis. This, however, is merely suggestive.

I see the resignation of our Swiss Minister is announced in the papers

---

[1] Olney, in whose rugged strength Cleveland reposed the greatest confidence, had at once succeeded Gresham as Secretary of State.

today. Unless something on the whole more desirable occurs to us, I am sure ex-Congressman Charles Tracey of New York is worth serious consideration in connection with this place — though I do not know that he would take it. If Uhl should chance to fancy it, I should be delighted to give it to him if you thought well of it. Tracey is in every way up to it and his wife is an accomplished and refined lady. Both are Catholics and they have a number of children, some of them old enough to profit by a stay of eighteen months at the Swiss capital. However, these are only hints. Something better may occur to us.

I see the Mora claim is paid. I hope you will have a safe deliverance in the matter of distribution.

To Secretary Richard Olney

Gray Gables, *September 20,* 1895

I return your Civil Service order with suggested changes which if not necessary might, I think, be made on the score of exactness and certainty.

We do not intend, I believe, that salary of say $2000 and fees in addition of say $525 should, because the compensation by way of salary and fees amounts to over $2500, be beyond the scope of the order. Of course I do not overlook the third paragraph, but I am anxious to have no room left for a claim of uncertainty. My idea is, and I suppose yours is also, that when a salary is attached to an office that should govern without any reference to any fees that may also be attached to the office; and that fees are not regarded except when they constitute the entire compensation.

I hardly know what suggestion to make about the Solicitor. It would be a first-rate stroke if we could find a good man with a good Democratic name and lineage. I suppose Judge Jackson's son would hardly do. There are reasons why just at this time I would like to see such an appointment made. Perhaps Harmon could make a good suggestion, or at least tell you all about young Jackson. You know we had him under advisement for district attorney in Ohio. There is a young man named Lehman who within a year or two left Iowa and went to St. Louis — a very able man. Eckles,[1] I think, knows him well. Of course I would not object to either of the men you mention, but if by a little waiting we can strike something distinctly Democratic, I should like it.

[1] James H. Eckles (1858–1907) of Chicago, Comptroller of the Currency.

sation plainly called for such a disclosure. All the same, however, he struck me as he did you and his statements impressed me very much. I want to think your proposition over a little.

I have not felt first-rate for two or three days, but expect to be all right tomorrow. Ruth seems to be a little ailing and Mrs. Cleveland has the idea strongly in her head that I ought not to start from here until the 12th. I am not sure I shall submit, but I have considerable work here (official) that I can do better before I return than after.

I have no doubt Mr. Uhl has formed a just and correct judgment of Faison. I had much rather have it, as to the merits of a man for the solicitorship, than Dickinson's. Northern and Southern standards concerning legal ability are widely different. I want you to have the man you fancy, but if I were you I should look sharply at all sides of a candidate from Tennessee, both as a lawyer and as to political affiliations.

If Mr. Uhl wants or will take the Swiss mission I should be much gratified to give it to him. I will write and tender it to him tonight.

To SECRETARY HOKE SMITH
Gray Gables, *October* 4, 1895

I expect to be in Washington in ten days or about that time, and immediately upon my arrival, if not before I leave here, I desire to confer with somebody duly authorized and settle upon an exact and fixed scheme involving every detail of my visit to Atlanta. I have already in conversation with you said that my stay in the city must be very short, and a definite programme may save me from some embarrassment and prevent the making of plans on my party which might interfere with the calculations of the managers of the Exposition.[1]

I have had a long vacation and begin to feel that I should be at work again.

To SECRETARY RICHARD OLNEY
Gray Gables, *October* 6, 1895

I enclose this with my note in the Hansen and St. Clair matter, as a sort of an unofficial communication, of a personal nature.

If we send a man to Cuba, I have an idea that the Secretary of War has one about him who would exactly fill the bill. I refer to Major Davis,

[1] Cleveland, with Vice-President Stevenson and six members of his Cabinet, visited the Cotton States Exposition in Atlanta on October 24, 1895.

an officer who has done considerable inspection work for the Secretary and performed for him other duties of a delicate nature.

I shall be in Washington, I expect, on Tuesday morning — the 15th. If you can give me until that day to finally make up my mind about sending a man, I shall be glad, though I may give you my conclusion sooner by wire or letter. In the meantime, if you think well of it, you might confidentially sound the Secretary of War on the subject. In such matters in dealing with such countries as Spain a military title helps. It may possibly be, however, in this case we might better stick to the civilian side. I suggest Major Davis more on account of what I suppose to be his personal qualities than his military connection.

It is very provoking to have such matters as the Venezuela affair prematurely and blunderingly discussed in the newspapers. It would be easy, I know from personal experience, to so discourage the approach of news gatherers and news harvesters as to be free from their vexatious intermeddling, but human nature and the desire to tell something is strong in official station as everywhere else.

To SECRETARY RICHARD OLNEY

Gray Gables, *October* 6, 1895

I spent yesterday and last evening until late in a patient and thorough examination of the applications for clemency on behalf of St. Clair and Hansen, the two men convicted in California of murder at sea. I confess to a feeling of disappointment when I was obliged to deny relief. The facts of the case left no doubt in my mind that an atrocious murder was committed by these two men and another; and every consideration of public duty forbade my interference with the just punishment attached by law to their crime.

The British Ambassador presented a petition and letters from the Lieutenant-Governor of Canada and some good people living at St. John's in behalf of Hansen, and the Danish Minister represented his Government in asking clemency. I shall return all the papers by the mail conveying this note. I think you have in your office the original documents, or at least the original communications presented by the ambassador and Minister. If not, they or copies of them are among the papers sent to the Executive Mansion.

I wish you would promptly communicate to the diplomatic officials I have mentioned my determination assuring them that it would have been

more agreeable to me if I could have reached a conclusion favorable to the benevolent and humane sentiments submitted through their mediation.

To ATTORNEY-GENERAL JUDSON HARMON

Gray Gables, *October* 7, 1895

I enclose you two letters received tonight asking appointments to the vacant judgeship in the Indian Territory. I do not suppose either of the persons to whom these letters relate ought to be very seriously considered.

I want you, however, to be thinking of this subject with a view of a selection for the place. I do not know how the Chief Justice is made under the law of last winter in such a contingency as is presented by the resignation of Judge Stewart, who, I think, was made Chief Justice by the statute. I am uncertain whether we now appoint a Chief Justice as such or merely a judge, leaving the Chief Justice to be designated in some other way — as by the three judges.

With Stewart there as Chief Justice, I thought we could safely appoint Springer and Kilgore — though I had grave misgivings as to the latter. With Stewart out and the other two in, the Chief Justice should be an exceptionally good man in every way, and he should have, in my opinion, some judicial experience so that he could easily take and hold the head of the Court and have all the control and influence that should belong to the place *in the existing circumstances*. If we could find a good big lawyer for the position, judicial experience might be dispensed with, but I should feel safer with it.

I shall be in Washington early next week and we shall then talk it over.

To BOOKER T. WASHINGTON

Gray Gables, *October* 9, 1895

I thank you for sending me a copy of your address delivered at the opening of the Atlanta Exposition.

I thank you with much enthusiasm for making the address. I have read it with intense interest, and I think the Exposition would be fully justified if it did not do more than furnish the opportunity for its delivery. Your words cannot fail to delight and encourage all who wish well for the race; and if your colored fellow-citizens do not from your utterances gather new hope and form new determinations to gain every valuable advantage offered them by their citizenship, it will be strange indeed.

To SECRETARY RICHARD OLNEY

Gray Gables, *October* 9, 1895

By the same mail that brought your letter I received the Boston *Herald* of today, from which I clip the following: 'A Confidential Agent Needed' — Washington dispatch dated October 8. 'Secretary Olney seriously considering sending confidential agent to Cuba, etc.' It seems to me this 'beats the very devil.'

At first blush I do not think General Schofield is the best man in sight; but perhaps he is. I have a notion that he would not see all that he ought to see.[1]

To SECRETARY HOKE SMITH

Washington, *October* 25, 1895

I have just seen in the New York *World* a dispatch to the effect that the managers of the Exposition have by a unanimous vote fixed a Cuban day; and this information is accompanied by sensational expressions by individual members of the Direction of the Exposition, with references to my visit and your presence in Atlanta at this time.

Naturally I am somewhat surprised and disturbed by the intelligence, because I understood you to say that nothing of this kind was contemplated. I am very far from any desire to interfere with the feelings or sympathies of our people as individuals, though these often make the path of duty hard especially in its relations to our conduct toward other nations. The Exposition, however, in its purpose, in government participation and aid, as well as in other attending incidents, has so much of governmental and official flavor attached to it that I cannot but think, if the directors have taken the action indicated, that they have made a mistake which will perhaps prove detrimental to the sound and beneficial effects we all wish to attend their efforts.

Of course it is quite likely the report may be false, but if true we feel here that this action has been taken without properly considering all that it invites.

To SENATOR DAVID B. HILL

Washington, *November* 18, 1895

Secretary Lamont has shown me your letter to him, and I appreciate your willingness to come to Washington to confer with me if thought

[1] No confidential agent was sent.

desirable. There is only one matter which I desired to talk with you about that I think, to save you the trip here, and especially in view of your expected absence from the opening of Congress, I ought to write you about. All other things will as you say 'keep' until you arrive here.

I have been a good deal bothered about a nomination to the United States Supreme Court — not because I have had much personal doubt as to the best selection under all the circumstances, but on account of other considerations outside of absolute fitness.

Of course I want to nominate a New Yorker; and my mind has been constantly drawn to Judge Peckham [1] as the best choice. It seemed to me a short time ago that I ought to know whether or not he would accept the plan, and I wrote to him asking the question. After some reflection he replied in the affirmative. So you see I am committed to the nomination. I think the place should be filled by a confirmed nominee as early as practicable and I want to send in the name as soon as the Senate meets.

I suppose, in your absence and with a lack of knowledge on the part of the Committee as to your feeling in the matter, it might and would be laid over until your arrival.

Have you any desire as to the time of sending in the nomination? I think the Court needs him and I would be glad to have him qualified very early if you could find it consistent and agreeable to pave the way for it in your absence. I need hardly say to you that this is entirely confidential except as you may see fit to confer with Judge Peckham himself.

SECRETARY JOHN G. CARLISLE *to* CLEVELAND

Washington, *November 23,* 1895

The gold reserve on the 1st day of February, 1894, when the bids for the first sale of bonds were opened, was $65,438,377; on the 24th of November, 1894, when the bids for the second sale were opened, the reserve was $57,669,701. You already have the amount at the date of the last issue of bonds. I will try to come out tomorrow afternoon for a short interview.

[1] This was Rufus W. Peckham, brother of Wheeler H. Peckham, whose nomination had been defeated the previous year. He was called Judge because he had sat in the State Court of Appeals. Hill liked him, and his name was promptly confirmed.

To SECRETARY RICHARD OLNEY

Washington, *December* 3, 1895

I want very much to go away this week Thursday and stay until next week — say Friday or some such matter. Can I do so? I will have all the nominations to go in signed and they can be sent in by instalments during my absence. The only thing I am hesitating about is the state of some things in your Department.

You cannot receive anything from Bayard or Sir Julian before the early part of next week.[1] Why can you not put the thing in your pocket, so that no one will know you have heard it read or at least that you have it in possession, until I return? In the meantime, if its transmission should be accompanied by any particular message, you can, if you have time, be blocking it out. If I were here I would not be hurried in the matter even if the Congress should begin grinding again the resolution-of-inquiry mill.

To SECRETARY DANIEL S. LAMONT

Washington, *December* 4, 1895

I have read every paper in the Walker retiring case and approved the finding of the Board, though I am astonished at the letters I find from officers associated with him in his last duty, testifying to his conduct, habits, professional ability, etc. However, I am getting more and more accustomed to such things in Army and Navy matters.

I see the record is only signed by the president and recorder of the Board. Is that enough? I am sure in Navy cases the entire Board signs. I have no book at hand to look at on the question and it would not be at all the thing to have this officer years hence claim pay on the ground of ineffective retirement.

To SECRETARY RICHARD OLNEY

Washington, *December* 25, 1895

I was glad to receive your note and its enclosure, and am satisfied, if not intensely gratified that... one commissioner has been settled upon.[2]

[1] An answer was expected from Lord Salisbury to the drastic note on the Venezuelan question — Olney's 'twenty-inch gun' — sent him by the American Government in July.

[2] Cleveland was selecting a commission to ascertain the true Venezuelan boundary, and did so with less consultation of Olney than this letter indicates. The list included David J. Brewer, Richard H. Alvey, Andrew D. White, Frederic R. Coudert, and Daniel Coit Gilman.

I was also glad to receive the letter from Boston, for it adds to the satisfaction I was experiencing by reason of a forcible return of my first determination not to select the gentleman referred to. I arose this morning firmly resolved to eliminate that name from the list. I have sent Mr. Thurber to New York to see the other gentleman who telegraphed me last evening late that he could not come here on account of his son's sickness. If he accepts, my judgment is decidedly in favor of selecting the Chief Justice of the District's Court of Appeals as the third member. I have sent for him. I expect to hear from New York before I go to bed, and if I can see the third party suggested we might announce the Commission tomorrow morning. I have entirely given up the scholastic and diplomatic idea. Of course I shall be pleased to know the progress of your thought on the subject.

To Ambassador Thomas F. Bayard

Washington, *December 29,* 1895

I thank you sincerely for the hunting stool you kindly sent me, and I hope I may have abundant occasion to recall by its use your thoughtfulness.

I am very sorry indeed that I cannot fully understand your very apparent thought and feeling on the Venezuelan question; and you must believe me to be entirely sincere when I say that I think my want of understanding on the subject is somehow my own fault.

You cannot fail to remember my inclination, during my former incumbency of this office, to avoid a doctrine which I knew to be troublesome and upon which I had nothing like your clear conception and information. I knew that your predecessors for many years, and you as well, regarded the Monroe Doctrine as important, and I supposed that when it was frequently quoted by you and them in treating of this very question of [the] Venezuelan boundary, it was so quoted because it was deemed to have relation to that question. Not being able to perceive how a doctrine would have any life or could do any good or harm, unless it was applicable to a condition of facts that might arise, and unless when applied all consequences must be appreciated and awaited, I was quite willing, if possible within the limits of inflexible duty, to escape its serious contemplation.

I remember too how kindly and considerately you used to speak of and treat the people and governments of South America, though fully understanding their weaknesses and faults, and how much through your treatment of them these countries became attached to the Administration. Very few incidents attended my last coming to Washington more pleasing than the heartiness with which the representatives of Central and South America welcomed me. These considerations are not, however, of importance, since in an application of the Monroe Doctrine, though another country may give the *occasion*, we are, I suppose, not looking after *its* interests but *our own*.

Events accompanying the growth of this Venezuelan question have recently forced a fuller examination of this question upon me and have also compelled us to assume a position in regard to it. I am entirely clear that the Doctrine is not obsolete, and it should be defended and maintained for its value and importance *to our government and welfare*, and that its defence and maintenance involve its application when a state of facts arises requiring it.

In this state of mind I am positive that I can never be made to see why the extension of European systems, territory, and jurisdiction, on our continent, may not be effected as surely and as unwarrantably under the guise of boundary claims as by invasion or any other means. In 1888 you called Mr. Phelps's attention to the apparent enlargement of Great Britain's boundary claims between the years 1877 and 1887, and I think within a year you have referred us to the same or other enlargements. I have not failed to notice the stress laid by Lord Salisbury upon the fact that settlements have been made by British subjects whose allegiance might be disturbed if England's insistence was found to be incorrect.

We do not say either that Great Britain's boundary claim is false, nor that the enlargement of her claims toward the centre of Venezuela, as now known, is unjustifiable beyond a doubt, nor that the settlements upon the territory claimed by Venezuela have been brought about or encouraged while delay in settling the boundary has been prompted or permitted; nor do we attach too much prejudicial importance to other facts and considerations within our view, but we do say that these things and others furnished a controversy in which we were interested, that this controversy was complicated by facts so disputed that it presented a case which of all cases that can be imagined should be subjected to the sifting and examination which impartial arbitration affords.

The refusal to refer the question to such determination was intensely disappointing. It was disappointing because we cannot see the force of the reasons given for refusal.

After a little hesitation, just here, I shall mention another reason for disappointment and chagrin, which I believe to be entirely irrelevant to the case and which has had absolutely nothing to do with any action I have taken. It would have been exceedingly gratifying and a very handsome thing for Great Britain to do, if, in the midst of all this Administration has had to do in attempts to stem the tide of 'jingoism,' she had yielded or rather conceded something (if she called it so, which I do not) for our sake. In our relations with her we have been open, honest, and fair, except as to settling or providing for the adjustment of claims for Behring Sea seizures. I am ashamed of the conduct of Congress in that matter, but it is understood everywhere how persistent the Administration has been in efforts to have the right thing done.

The insistence upon a principle or the assertion of a right should be the same in the case of England as Chili; and I do not see, the necessity actually arising, that former relations or anything of that sort should prevent action or change the course of action, except that good relations, etc., might induce a nation to acquiesce in arbitration when not obliged to do so, in aid of the ascertainment of facts which a friendly power felt should be developed to relieve it from embarrassment.

Great Britain says she has a flawless case. Our interest in the question led us to ask her to exhibit that case in a tribunal above all others recognized as a proper one for that purpose; and this was done to avoid a wrong procedure on our part in a matter we could not pass by.

Great Britain has refused our request. What is to be done? We certainly ought not, we certainly cannot abandon the case because she says she is right, nor because she refuses arbitration. We do not threaten nor invite war because she refuses — far from it. We do not propose to proceed to extremities, leaving open any chance, that can be guarded against, of a mistake on our part as to the facts. So instead of threatening war for not arbitrating, we simply say, inasmuch as Great Britain will not aid us in fixing the facts, we will not go to war, but do the best we can to discover the true state of facts for ourselves, with all the facilities at our command. When with all this we become as certain as we can be, in default of Great Britain's co-operation, that she has seized the territory and superseded the jurisdiction of Venezuela — that is a different matter.

I feel that I would like you to know precisely what is in my mind and therefore I have hastily written you, without the least hint of it to any person whatever and without the least consultation.

It seems as if all the troubles and perplexities that can gather about the office I hold were just at this time making a combined assault.

XIV

BRYAN AND McKINLEY

THE year 1896 was dominated by the Presidential campaign. During the early weeks, thanks to British moderation, the flurry of panic and jingoism caused by Cleveland's Venezuelan message rapidly died away. Lord Salisbury's Government consented to arbitration under certain restrictions and in the end the British received most of the territory in dispute. The last bond issue excited less antagonism than its predecessors, in part because it was so successfully floated by popular subscription. By maintaining a bold front to Congress, the Administration checked a constant succession of attempts to embroil the United States with Spain over the Cuban rebellion; and it trod a path of careful neutrality, though it was unremitting in its efforts to induce the Spanish Government to remove the abuses which had caused the revolt. But while Cleveland was thus successful in some of the principal features of his policy, he was steadily losing control of his party. For a time he hoped that the sound-money element in the Democracy might, by energetic crusading in the South, maintain its dominance. He tried to raise money in the North for a systematic campaign, encouraged friendly members of Congress to speak in the South, and sent Carlisle to make a series of addresses in border cities. As the States began to hold their conventions, he and his Cabinet watched the election of delegates with a certain hopefulness. At the very least, they believed that it might be possible to hold more than a third of the members of the National Convention, and thus deadlock it against a radical free-silver nominee. But they were struggling against a movement too powerful to resist. Here and there, as in Michigan, a victory was gained. But most of the States of the South and West joined headlong in the silver movement. By failing to stop the talk of a third term for himself, Cleveland chilled such men as Senators Brice and Hill, and unintentionally handicapped his own followers. William C. Whitney took a special train of sound-money Democrats to the Chicago Convention, and thought that he might bring about a last-minute rally for the nomination of ex-Governor William E. Russell of Massachusetts. Within half an hour after arriving, he knew that his venture was hopeless. Cleveland watched in disgust from Gray Gables as the silverites triumphed, adopting a free-coinage platform and nominating William Jennings Bryan. The Republicans had already named William McKinley on a sound-money platform. It was impossible for Cleveland to support either of the principal candidates. He encouraged the formation of a Gold Democratic party, which met in convention in Indianapolis and nominated John M. Palmer of Illinois. All the members of the Cabinet except Hoke Smith supported Palmer; and when Smith came out for Bryan but not for Bryan's platform, Cleveland forced his resignation. The election of McKinley was a profound relief to the President. He spent his last months in the White House dealing with comparatively minor problems; though he still had to struggle against Congressional attempts at intervention in Cuba, and vetoed a bill to check immigration by a literacy test.

To SENATOR DONELSON CAFFERY [1]

Washington, *January* 5, 1896

I have read today in the *Congressional Record* the debate in the Senate on Friday concerning the financial situation and bond issues. I am amazed at the intolerance that leads even excited partisanship to adopt as a basis of attack the unfounded accusations and assertions of a maliciously mendacious and sensational newspaper.[2]

No banker or financier, nor any other human being, has been invited to visit Washington for the purpose of arranging in any way or manner for the disposition of bonds to meet the present or future needs of the gold reserve. No arrangement of any kind has been made for the disposition of bonds to any syndicate or through the agency of any syndicate. No assurance of such a disposal of bonds has been directly or indirectly given to any person. In point of fact, a decided leaning toward a popular loan and advertising for bids has been plainly exhibited on the part of the Administration at all times when the subject was under discussion.

Those charged with the responsibility of maintaining our gold reserve, so far as legislation renders it possible, have anxiously conferred with each other, and, as occasion permitted, with those having knowledge of financial affairs and present monetary conditions, as to the best and most favorable means of selling bonds for gold. The unusual importance of a successful result, if the attempt is again made, ought to be apparent to every American citizen who bestows upon the subject a moment's patriotic thought.

[1] Donelson Caffery (1835–1906) served in the Senate, 1892–1901, and while disagreeing with Cleveland on the tariff, gave him general support on currency issues.

[2] The New York *World*. But Joseph Pulitzer's campaign against another sale of United States bonds to a Wall Street syndicate was patriotic and well-intentioned, and he did much to make the public sale which soon took place a success.

The Secretary of the Treasury, from the first moment that the necessity for the sale of another issue of bonds seemed to be approaching, desired to offer them, if issued, to the people by public advertisement, if they could thus be successfully disposed of. After full consideration, he came to the conclusion, with which I fully agree, that the amount of gold in the reserve being now $28,000,000 more than it was in February last, when a sale of bonds was made to a syndicate, and other conditions differing from those then existing, justify us in offering the bonds now about to be issued for sale by popular subscription.

This is the entire matter, and all these particulars could have been easily obtained by any member of the Senate by simply inquiring.

If Mr. Morgan, or anyone else reasoning from his own standpoint, brought himself to the belief that the Government would at length be constrained to again sell bonds to a syndicate, I suppose he would have a perfect right, if he chose, to take such steps as seemed to him prudent to put himself in a condition to negotiate.

I expect an issue of bonds will be advertised for sale tomorrow, and that bids will be invited, not only for those now allowed by law, but for such other and different bonds as Congress may authorize during the pendency of the advertisement. Not having had an opportunity to confer with you in person since the present session of Congress began, and noticing your participation in the debate of last Friday, I have thought it not amiss to put you in possession of the facts and information herein contained.

To CHARLES S. FAIRCHILD

Washington, *January* 7, 1896

Your letter is received. The time fixed for receiving bids was supposed by us to be none too long if we were to avoid the accusation of curtailing the opportunity of ordinary people to subscribe. Of course, except in that view, it was immaterial what limit was determined on as far as we were concerned. Mr. Stillman [1] seems to think the instalments are pretty close together. If it will help matters at all, that can be modified.

I believe, with the help of the banks, trust companies, and such financial agencies, this effort by way of popular loan will succeed. Without such aid I am not very sanguine. I think it would be an excellent thing if such assistance were to be heartily forthcoming. Why cannot such in-

---

[1] James Stillman (1850–1918), head of the National City Bank.

stitutions as yours do the business for those who you learn would like to purchase for a reasonable commission or profit?

I am very anxious to have the thing succeed, but am not willing to depart from the idea of a popular loan. If its success depends palpably on the aid financial institutions and financiers alone can give, such an outcome would be very far from an *unmixed evil*...

To CHARLES S. FAIRCHILD
Washington, *January* 12, 1896

It is horribly late and I am awfully tired.

I can only thank you for your letter and the efforts you contemplate in the interest of our bond sale. Your ideas about inviting withdrawal of gold for greenbacks, it seems to me, present the subject in a sort of new phase and I am afraid would produce confusion of ideas and perhaps new carping and opposition.

We are determined here to do everything possible to alleviate the feared disturbance caused by drawing the unit of gold we want from its present holders, whether the plan be by extension of the time of payment or otherwise. I have already written one or two of our friends that the period between the instalments of gold might be extended and I have invited suggestions as to what extension should be made and intimated to Mr. Stewart that your knowledge of Treasury loans would make you a good man to advise with.

To SENATOR GEORGE F. HOAR
Washington, *January* 14, 1897

I had an interview with Sherman Hoar today, and then, having been informed of your interest in the retention of the postmaster at Worcester, I hasten to assure you that he will not be disturbed during the present administration of the Postoffice Department. Your desire in the matter and his faithful performance of the duties of his office, I regard as sufficient reason to determine the question in his favor. I have heard this evening that he has just suffered a severe affliction in the death of his wife, which, in addition to all other reasons, ought to entitle him at this time to kindly consideration.

J. Pierpont Morgan *to* Cleveland

New York, *January* 14, 1896

I have to acknowledge with many thanks your kind note of the 10th, which, however, only reached me yesterday. My letter of the 4th conveyed to you every assurance that I can now offer of my co-operation in the negotiation of the bonds.

So far as regards the first point you raise, the management of the details of the subscription, payment of instalments, etc., no one appreciates more the difficulties to be encountered, nor should they be underrated; at the same time, in my opinion, they are easily overcome by the Secretary of the Treasury availing himself of all expediencies which experience and precedent make available for such transactions. I might here add that I should be extremely glad to be of any service in suggestions on these points. As regards the second trouble to which you allude in the terms of the advertisement, I think they should be remedied at once. The most important one is the amount of the first instalment, which must be provided for and met before the confidence which the negotiation is sure to inspire can make itself felt.

I would therefore urge that the first payment be limited to the premium upon the bonds, and the subsequent payments should follow at intervals of fifteen days to the amount of ten per cent. The only objection to this course is that the first payment would not be sufficiently large to replace any drain upon the gold reserve, but this, it is safe to say, is only in theory, for experience has shown that there will be a large amount of bonds for which subscribers will desire to pay in full at once.

I do not quite agree with you about the impossibility of allowing gold to remain in the banks subject to call. As you probably know, this has always been done and never without good results, and, whilst I appreciate that money paid into the Sub-Treasury cannot be transferred back to the bank, the original payment can be made to the banks and the bonds left as collateral for the deposit. To my mind such a course is absolutely essential to the successful working of the liquidation of the subscriptions.

I would add that my services are in every way at your disposal and that of the Secretary of the Treasury, and, if I can be of assistance at any time, I shall be glad even to go to Washington, and I suppose, now that the matter is practically 'res judicata,' my doing so would not excite undue comment or curiosity.

I will avail myself of this opportunity to enclose you a circular letter which I have today sent to the participants in the syndicate, accompanied by a notice of its dissolution, and which I cannot but feel will, not only advance the interest of the loan, but will also tend to aid in restoring confidence. I have expressed to Messrs. Stewart and Stillman my views as herein contained, and they will doubtless communicate with you on the subject.

AMBASSADOR THOMAS F. BAYARD to CLEVELAND [1]

London, January 29, 1896

I need not tell you how much you have been in my mind since Congress met and especially since your special message of December 17. Since then I have your kind letter of December 29, and twenty times I have endeavored to write a *full* reply, but could not. Nor shall I now take up the entire question, but will send you some comments upon its present and practical aspects — which I rejoice to say have many features of hopeful adjustment on lines that fully accomplish the wish and purpose that I am sure lie closest to your heart, the maintenance of friendly competition in the onward march of civilization of the two great branches of English-speaking people.

I have diligently supplied Mr. Olney with the published expressions of the leading men and journals here — and you have been informed, of course, of the confidential tentative suggestion for a settlement of which Lord Playfair was the proponent. The progress of these suggestions has been somewhat checked by Mr. Olney's apparent subtraction of Venezuela's consent or co-operation from the plan of submission to arbitration — by which I mean that in what has passed in the exchange of telegrams between Mr. Olney and myself, Venezuela seems to be eliminated, although by your message she was distinctly a controlling and independent factor in the settlement of her boundaries.

It is an encouraging feature, and one highly honorable to Great Britain, that there is a ready and friendly co-operation between both political parties to promote an amicable and honorable adjustment of all difficulties with the United States. There is not the slightest wish to embarrass the Government or to make political capital out of present international difficulties — certainly not where the United States are concerned. In proof of this I enclose reports of a speech made two days

---

[1] From the Bayard Papers at the Bayard family home near Wilmington, Delaware.

ago by Mr. Chamberlain, Colonial Secretary, and the day after one by Sir Henry Fowler, the late Secretary for India (and a very statesman-like man), in which the Monroe Doctrine is stated with satisfactory precision and fullness. Whatever else may come of this incident it is certain that the preservation of the continent of South America from European occupation or colonization has been secured.

I also send you Mr. Smalley's latest report to the London *Times* from Washington on the general subject. The prejudices of this gentleman are very decided, and he will not see that which he does not wish to see; and therefore I do not expect him to confess that the most persistent reason for hatred of Great Britain in the United States is the protective alliance of which McKinley is the chief exponent and old Mr. Morrill of Vermont the venerable head. I do not know whether Mr. Smalley has been to see you or whether he has presented a letter of introduction I gave him to you. The tone of his despatches since he went to Washington give me the impression that he has presented it, and certainly his expressions on your position have greatly changed.

Have you considered the expediency of a tribunal of six? — two from your present Commission, two British, and two Venezuelan members with power to select an umpire, or in case of non-agreement to have him named by the President of the Swiss Republic. The private rights of settlers and occupants *bona fide*, and within a reasonable period of occupation and ownership, should be protected by the usual and proper safeguards.

They are hard at work preparing a very full Blue Book, and a very able and learned lawyer, Sir Frederick Pollock, is in charge of the work. The late attempt to stampede the Boers and overthrow their government in the Transvaal has thrown a flood of light on the buccaneering methods by which empire is sought to be extended, and has brought the British mind to consider more intelligently the process by which private conveyances of land are transformed into international transfers of sovereignty. If I am not greatly mistaken, the law that will be laid down in the trial of Dr. Jameson and his brother brigands will tell strongly against some proposed boundaries in Venezuela.

As I close this letter Mr. Olney's cable of yesterday (the 28th, arriving here at 9:30 P.M.), conveying the suggestion of a new commission, has arrived and I have written for Lord Playfair to come and hear it. I send you by this post a *Times* with a speech by Sir Michael Hicks-Beach, the

Chancellor of the Exchequer, in admirable tone, and very timely. I will telegraph Mr. Olney as soon as I have seen Playfair.

On the Armenian question there seems to be an insanity on both sides of the Atlantic, and some of the propositions reported from the United States would wrap the world in flames if carried out. A voluminous Blue Book on Turkish affairs is announced this morning, which I shall send to the State Department by this post. Every now and then the tide of civilization seems to ebb, and mankind go backward.

I hope your health is maintained — it is most important to our country that it should be.

To the REVEREND CHARLES WOOD
Washington, *February* 1, 1896

I want to be very frank with you in the matter of the candidacy of Mr. Davis for the West Point chaplaincy. A bill is pending in Congress changing the tenure and somewhat the character of the office. Until this proposed legislation is disposed of, no selection will be made.

I feel that I should say to you what is in my mind in regard to Mr. Davis when the time for appointment arrives. There is not in my opinion the slightest prospect of his securing the place. Without explaining here the reasons for this opinion, I am quite willing to say to you as his friend that none of them are to his discredit. It was entirely right and proper for him to desire the position and for you, his friend, to second his desire, but I am not particularly pleased to learn that the Secretary of War is daily bombarded with that kind of support and endorsement that usually characterizes the chase for offices not at all like chaplaincies. It would be more of a relief to me than you can imagine, if all this were discontinued. Some day you will understand all this better.

To E. C. BENEDICT
Washington, *February* 11, 1896

Thurber is away today and I cannot lay my hand on the official notice of my election as an honorary member of your yacht club. It has, however, already remained too long unacknowledged, and rather than wait until his return I have determined to send you my acceptance instead of another officer of the club to whom perhaps it might be more properly addressed. If you think it should be done another way, please do me the favor to indicate it. I thought that I directed that the notification be left on my table for personal action, but after a thorough search in its confusion I cannot find it. So I suppose Thurber must have it.

AMBASSADOR THOMAS F. BAYARD *to* CLEVELAND

London, *February* 12, 1896

Personal

... Venezuelan envoys here, and the administration of their affairs, especially in this unsettled region now in dispute, have left a most unpleasant odor in men's nostrils. It has come to be well understood that *anything* in the way of governmental concession is for sale in that country, and the envoys here have usually been the brokers. Speculators in the United States have thrust their soiled hands into the business, and sought to embroil the United States in sustaining their corrupt contracts. I enclose copies of the notes that I exchanged with the Foreign Office in relation to documentary evidence to aid the investigation of the Boundary Commission. You will approve, I am sure, the comments in Parliament on the creation and objects of the Commission.

To DON M. DICKINSON

Washington, *February* 18, 1896

I have just returned from our last Cabinet dinner; and Colonel Lamont has sent me this moment a letter which he told me, at the dinner, he had received from you for my perusal. I cannot delay an instant my reply. The letter indicates your extreme and thoughtful friendliness, but I hasten to correct some impressions upon which it seems to be based.

Mr. Quinby's occupation of the mission at The Hague has been so satisfactory, at least as far as I know, that I would be sorry to have him relinquish it. There is no one in the world that I would care to put in that place in his stead. As to Mr. Thurber, I can honestly say that of all things you have done for me, I regard your suggestion of his selection as private secretary the most useful and fortunate. He has plenty of ability, good discretion, a pure heart and conscience, unquestioned honesty, sufficient tact, and is as loyal and devoted a helper as I ever had about me. This latter quality I have learned to appreciate more and more as the difficulties, perplexities, and treacheries of my present situation have more and more closed in about me.

I have never been so depressed as now in my view of the affairs of my country and party. I have never felt so keenly as now the unjust accusations of political antagonists and the hatred and vindictiveness of ingrates and traitors who wear the stolen livery of Democracy. If in the prevalence of widespread infidelity and untrustworthiness I should meet the necessity of filling the place now occupied by Mr. Thurber, I should feel forlorn indeed.

You know my supreme faith in the American people. While I believe them to be just now deluded, mistaken, and wickedly duped, they will certainly return to sound principles and patriotic aspirations, and what I may suffer in the period of aberration is not important.

I have studied laboriously to discover or imagine what, if anything, is in the minds of those who assume the rôle of Democratic leaders. Hatred to the Administration seems to be the only sentiment which pervades their counsels. It is absolutely certain that this issue will not wear during the campaign nor lead to success. It will be the irony of fate if in the hour of defeat, thus invited, the air is filled with Democratic clamor accusing me of destroying party prospects. And yet this is precisely what I expect. I have a consciousness within me, however, and an experience behind me that will permit me to bear even this injustice with resignation; and I will patiently wait for the final verdict of my countrymen, which will certainly in due time be returned.

I cannot be mistaken in believing that if the Democratic party is to survive, its banner upon which shall be inscribed its true principles and safe policies must be held aloft by sturdy hands which, even though few, will in the gloom of defeat save it from the disgraceful clutch of time-serving camp followers and knavish traitors.

To E. C. BENEDICT

Washington, *February 21, 1896*

I hope you will not be annoyed by the interpretations and inferences which have lately been indulged in upon the basis of your alleged third-term interview. Inasmuch as those things have a tendency to make us both appear ridiculous and in view of your disposition to be courteous to all you meet, including newspaper scavengers, I am in a position to assure you in the most positive way that those latter animals cannot be trusted, and that any indulgence shown them will only lead to complications and embarrassments, constantly growing worse. I have followed your suggestion and written a note to Mr. Hayden.

To SECRETARY HOKE SMITH

Washington, *March* 7, 1896

I have under consideration, as you know, the amendment and codification of the civil service rules, and I desire at the same time to extend the service to the utmost extent compatible with an effective and orderly administration of public affairs. I am inclined to the proposed amendment of rules to provide for the inclusion of all employees and officers of the Government that are embraced within the limitations of the Civil Service Law, and to provide for such exceptions as are suggested by experience and familiarity with administrative duties.

Will you please, at your earliest convenience, suggest to me the places in your Department which in your opinion ought, for the good of the service, to be excepted, with a brief statement of the reasons for such suggestions? In doing this you will bear in mind that abundant provision will be made in the rules for filling vacated places in the higher grades of the service by promotion and transfer, and that examinations to test fitness for certain positions which at first might appear to be difficult have been demonstrated to present no serious obstacle in actual practice.

To RICHARD OLNEY

Washington, *March* 16, 1896

It occurs to me that the letter of condolence to the Queen of England which I enclose is a little cold and formal as proposed, and I have taken the liberty of suggesting, as you will see, some alterations. The changes, as you sometimes say, will perhaps do 'to amend by,' if you agree with me that *in present circumstances* [1] a little warmth of statement would improve it.

I wish I could see you sometime today to suit your convenience. I am not sure that we ought to lose the opportunity afforded us by the Hoar resolution of inquiry to say a little something about Cuban affairs.[2] In a talk with Senator Gray this morning he suggested the possibility of a substitute resolution which would eliminate the disputed points of the pending resolutions and reduce the utterance to a mere expression of Congressional sympathy.

---

[1] Parliament had just met, and negotiations for the reference of the Venezuelan boundary to an arbitral tribunal were still pending.

[2] Hoar's resolution of March 9, 1896, called for the postponement of an embarrassing concurrent resolution which declared that the United States should be prepared for intervention; and it asked the President to transmit to the Senate his information on the Cuban revolt.

To DON M. DICKINSON

Washington, *March* 19, 1896

I was made very happy yesterday by the receipt of the painting you sent me of the duck hunter. It is a very *relieving* picture to look at, and every time my eye falls on it in these dreadfully dark and trying days I say to myself, 'I wish I was in that old fellow's place.'

Two things I am longing for — the adjournment of Congress and the 4th of March, 1897. I honestly believe the present Congress is a menace to the good of the country if not to its actual safety. If the Democratic party was in proper condition and inclined to half behave itself, the wildness and recklessness of the Republican Congress would turn many thousands of recruits to our party; but every day develops more and more plainly the seeming desperation and wickedness of those in the Senate and House for whose conduct our party will, I suppose, be held responsible.

I am positive there is but one chance for future Democratic successes — a perfectly and unequivocal sound-money platform at Chicago. If this means the loss of votes, present defeat, or even a party division, the seed will be sowed from which I believe Democratic successes will grow in the future. But I must not be morbid on this subject. All the same, it is outrageous that Democracy should be betrayed 'in its hour of might.'

To DON M. DICKINSON

Washington, *March* 25, 1896

I want to thank you for your exceedingly friendly and comforting letter. It contained some suggestions which have come near my mind many times, but which have been denied free admittance, because they rudely attacked the notions I love to entertain concerning friendship. I can only say, now that you have aroused me from pleasing dreams, that I cannot dispute you in your characterization of the character of political friendship as I must see it in this atmosphere.

I do not think I should have written you to say this after two o'clock in the morning if I had not something much more important on my mind.

The extreme importance to the country and to our party of a clear, distinct, and unequivocal declaration on the money question at Chicago oppresses me. I do not believe that any of us who desire the welfare of the country or the life of our party can excuse any relaxation of effort to bring about the result suggested. If our prospects look dark, that should stimulate action instead of tempting to inaction. Who can tell what change may be brought about in three months? Besides, I do not believe the real condition of silver prospects are by any means up to the volume of bluster and brag we hear. I shall not be surprised to see the silver forces in the South attempt to throttle all the sound sentiments, if in a minority in any State, by the application of the unit rule. If they do, the same medicine should be administered to them in every State where sound money gains a majority of the delegates.

We can survive as a party without immediate success at the polls, but I do not think we can survive if we have fastened upon us, as an authoritative declaration of party policy, the free coinage of silver. Can there not be a majority at hand of sound-money delegates sent from Michigan to Chicago?[1] I am by no means certain that we can be beaten next November if we can get such a platform deliverance.

To the REVEREND WILTON MERLE SMITH

Washington, *March* 26, 1896

I have been very much tempted lately to ask you to come and see me, and give me your advice as to the West Point chaplaincy. I am very anxious to make a good appointment to this place, for I fully realize the extended influence for good the right man can exert among the cadets and among the men in the Army over whom they will, later on, be placed. The appointee should be a man who will readily adapt himself to the ways and disposition of the boys, and thus gain their confidence and attachment as well as their respect, and thus pave the way to effective religious teaching. Of course he must also be a good preacher. In short, I have said more than once, in canvassing the matter: 'If we could get such a man as Mr. Smith or Mr. van Dyke or Mr. Wood, we'd have it about right.'

I don't want to be unduly denominational in the matter, but our Episcopalian friends have, in some way, secured more than their share of chaplains in the Army and Navy; and we poor Presbyterians have been rather 'badly left.' So I would not object, other things being equal, to seeing one of *our people* in this place. I know the instructors at West Point have rather settled on Mr. Shipman, the gentleman of whom you write; but my judgment in the matter is still unhampered.

[1] Dickinson and his friends made vigorous efforts in Michigan, and when the State Convention met in Detroit on April 29, the gold men carried their platform and chose 17 of the 28 national delegates.

I think the man most prominently mentioned among Presbyterian applicants is Mr. Imbrie — a Princeton man whom I suppose you know and who is very well spoken of by Dr. van Dyke and by Dr. Ward. The latter has made some inquiries for me and his report is favorable; but with all this, I confess I have slight misgivings. I feel that I cannot afford to do anything but the best thing, if I go contrary to the wishes of the instructors, and yet I am not prepared to swallow the dish they have prepared without looking at it.

What do you know about Mr. Imbrie? Can you give me any advice in the matter? You must know just what I want — a man that will be a teacher to the boys and a companion as well. If he enjoys a game of baseball or football or if broken fingers or a broken nose indicate that he *has* enjoyed these sports, so much the better. I think Mr. Shipman is very good, but I would not object to 'working in' a Presbyterian. If you can give me your views I shall be very grateful.

I am having a dreadful time here. The atmosphere about me, except in the home end of the house, is very unwholesome; but I am waiting for the return of reason, which my faith in the American people teaches me will certainly be forthcoming. In the meantime I am anxiously looking to the adjournment of Congress as a relief from dangers that threaten the country.

To THEODORE ROOSEVELT

Washington, *March* 26, 1896

Your letter commending the son of Nicholas Roosevelt as an applicant for a cadetship in the Naval Academy arrived the day after an appointment had been made to fill the only vacancy at my disposal. The son of a poor widow was selected, whose husband died in the naval service, and I am quite certain that young Roosevelt's name did not appear in the long list of applicants. I have written to his mother suggesting that it be placed there for future consideration. I note with pleasure what you write with regard to the Venezuelan affair and thank you for it. It has taken a little time and strength for the good people to understand our position in the matter, but as usual they are 'coming around.'

It seems to me that you and I have both been a little misunderstood lately.[1]

[1] Roosevelt had been under heavy attack as Police Commissioner for his strict enforcement of the Sunday-closing law for New York saloons.

Don M. Dickinson *to* Cleveland

Detroit, *March* 31, 1896

... Regarding Michigan, I will face about and do my best. I appealed to Whitney and to Lamont, long since, stating that I was being written to from all directions and that unless I could give advice on lines of some policy to be pursued by your followers, I should publicly and privately assume that I would take no part or interest in the campaign. This announcement I had made when your note was received. I also wrote both that if I could have notice *then*, I could take an honest-money delegation to Chicago even from 'free-silver Michigan.' Since then I had felt that I did not care to labor for a Convention the outcome of which would be Mr. Morrison or a like nondescript, and an overwhelming defeat — even on a sound platform. It seemed to me that if a bad defeat was to come anyway, it had better be *with* the crank platform, as well as with a candidate who would not carry a Northern State, and probably not half the South. It seemed to me that a bad defeat with a good platform would encourage our worst element and depress our best, whereas the same defeat when the silver men had their way would enable us to rally under the banner of sound principles, and reorganize the party after election....

And so, if your mind is made up that you want this contest made, I will do my part, which shall be my best. I may not do as well as if I had commenced sixty days ago or thirty, and may not make much noise about it, but if the outcome is a majority of our delegation (from 'free-silver Michigan') for an honest financial standard and against the coinage of silver, I suppose it should be satisfactory, with what I may be able to do elsewhere. There are some pretty serious handicaps in this State, where in districts discrimination has been made, in this miserable patronage business, against the Administration and in favor of 16 to 1, to the humiliation of our friends. This is notably so in western Michigan and in the second city — Grand Rapids, where we had our strongest allies. The sound-money men are all demoralized and out of service, while free silver is in full control of all the organizations, all the offices, etc. But we will buckle to and do our duty from now on, as *you* see it.

To George F. Parker

Washington, *March* 31, 1896

I have received your letter informing me that the Birmingham Dramatic and Literary Club intend to celebrate the birthday of Shakespeare on the 21st of April, and extending to me, on behalf of the club, an invitation to be present on that occasion.

Everything that tends to keep alive the memory of Shakespeare, and preserves a proper appreciation of his work, challenges my earnest interest and approval; and though I cannot be with you on the occasion you contemplate, I am glad to know that our American people are to be prominently represented in the celebration.

There is much said and written, in these days, concerning the relations that should exist, bound close by the strongest ties, between English-speaking peoples, and concerning the high destiny that awaits them in concerted effort. I hope we shall never know a time when these ennobling sentiments will be less often expressed, or will, in the least, lose their potency and influence. Surely, if English speech supplies the potency of united effort for the good of mankind and the impulse of an exalted mission, we do well to fittingly honor the name and memory of William Shakespeare.

To SECRETARY RICHARD OLNEY

Washington, *April* 9, 1896

I suppose the Havana matter must wait, now that we have entered upon it by way of Virginia.[1] I last night went through the Salisbury letter which I enclose. You will see that I have made some suggestions in pencil — some of them perhaps worthy of consideration. The shading of your reference to the influence of party considerations in our Administration, and the insertion somewhere of the idea imperfectly outlined in my memorandum on page 12, are especially commended to your attention. I wish you would consider also, *in connection with such an addition*, whether the claim I have *queried* on page 9 could not be safely omitted. I think, too, that perhaps the bias paragraph on page 11 might be amended so that it would not be stated quite so baldly.

I have just received and partly read the letter from the Spanish Committee. Is it worth considering whether they can be utilized through a communication made by them to the Government of Spain on our lines?

---

[1] The 'Havana matter' was the resignation of our consul-general in Havana. His place was filled by Fitzhugh Lee of Virginia.

To E. C. Benedict

Washington, *April* 30, 1896

just received your letter and write in very great haste to say
r full consideration I have determined that I cannot attend the
a College affair. Of course I would be glad to meet the wishes of
York friends who are especially interested in the occasion, and
unmindful of the proprieties which weigh in favor of my yield-
request made. There are reasons, however, which to my mind
ly forbid my taking part in the exercises. I will write Mr. Coudert
want to thank you for the hospitalities you offer and to assure
they present inducements more alluring than any other involved
vitation.

about my steam launch? Must I have a man to run it, and if so
a man on very reasonable terms to do that and perhaps make
useful in other ways besides? If you can will you put me in the
securing such a man? If things get cheap, I suppose I have
or so which ought to be earning me something. Can you make
gestions in that direction? At odd moments — they are rare —
blic duties do not engross my thoughts, I find my mind wander-
e direction of my future home and means of livelihood.

To E. C. Benedict

Washington, *May* 7, 1896

you would write to Secretary Herbert and tell him what you
me, and I can second your request. Of course I do not know what
encies of the service may be. We shall have to yield to the condi-
they happen to be adverse.

advice in regard to investments I have no doubt is very good and
to say 'go it' at once. I see Indianapolis Gas bonds quoted at
. Are they 6 per cent bonds? If so, why would they not be on
le better for me? They would pay more than five and a half per
the investment, as I figure it. These stocks that pay so well
ttack....

To L. Clarke Davis

Washington, *May* 14, 1896

fact that such silly things as are contained in the clipping you
can find a place in *any* newspapers, indicates one of the strangest

stirring them to action. Michigan seems to be the only State where work
was needed and forthcoming.

Events sometimes crowd closely upon each other and much may be
developed within even four weeks.

Don M. Dickinson *to* Cleveland

Detroit, Michigan, *June* 12, 1896

Your letter of the 10th instant is received as I am about leaving for
Chicago to meet Harrity.... I never knew that atmosphere of Washington
to be anything else than discouraging and depressing when there is anything to be done requiring courage and work. Kentucky was bad, of
course, but it was only a skirmish as compared with the field. Success
can only be accomplished at Chicago.

We have the National Committee and the right with us, and the outside delegations of good men will be worth more than all the free-silver
shouters in the Southern delegations to the Convention. We must bear
in mind, too, that the other side have not our good Convention workers
and fighters in their crowd. Vest is no good, even to talk, outside the
quiet Senate. Blackburn has no method whatever, and so far as his noise
is concerned, by the time the work gets on he will be out of condition sure.
On the other hand, we have all the best workers and fighters. Tammany
will send the most experienced men who ever went to a Convention.

Tillman [1] and Altgeld, in Convention and in evidence, will be worth
everything to us in discrediting the opposition, and in shaming their
delegations into coming over to decency. I hope Maryland will distinctly
discredit the Gorman influence and keep him away. Brice has played the
cause false. He desired the result in Ohio. The whole aspect may be
changed by the result of the Republican Convention....

To the Democratic Voters [2]

Washington, *June* 16, 1896

I have made no figures as to the probable action of the delegates already chosen to the Democratic National Convention, but I refuse to
believe that when the time arrives for deliberate action there will be

[1] Benjamin R. Tillman (1847–1918) of South Carolina, was governor of South Carolina
1890–94, and United States Senator from 1895 to his death.

[2] Published in the New York *Herald* as a result of the urgings of the Chamber of Commerce
of the State of New York and other gold-standard advocates.

about the size of a small pea. This indicates how completely I have been on the gold standard. I've got the gold in my possession. What shall I do with it?

To DON M. DICKINSON

Washington, *June* 10, 1896

I so fully approve of your suggestions concerning delegations of sound and solid men to attend the Convention as non-delegates, with a view to exerting wholesome influence on delegate sentiments, that I immediately began to agitate the subject in question where I thought it would effect the best results. My ideas seemed to meet with much approval and I had some assurances of co-operation, though I am bound to say to you that they were even then accompanied with that sort of reserved enthusiasm which seems to have for the most part characterized all movements in favor of sound financial policy. Since the receipt of your letter, however, events have occurred so discouraging to the cause of sound finance that I am afraid the efforts promised will not be made. The fact is, people whom I see here who believe with us appear to be thoroughly impressed with the idea that nothing can be done to stem the tide of silverism at Chicago.

I believe I am by nature an undismayed and persistent fighter and I do not believe in giving an inch until we are obliged to; and yet it is hard to call on friends to maintain a struggle which seems so hopeless. It does not seem to me that there should be any relaxation in the effort to prevent our party from entering upon a course which means its retirement for many years to come. If we cannot succeed in checking the desperate disease, perhaps a demonstration can be made which will indicate that a large section of the party is not infected. I don't know how this can be done, but I very much desire that we shall not all have to hang our heads when our party is accused of free-silverism.

Of course I have never seen anything like this craze before, but my faith in the American people is so great that I cannot believe they will cast themselves over the precipice.

But there is our old party with all its glorious traditions and all its achievements in the way of safe and conservative policies, and its exhibitions of indestructibility. Is it to founder on the rocks? Will not sanity return before we reach the final plunge? While I am not completely discouraged, I confess the way looks dark. The most astounding feature of all this matter is the lethargy of our friends and the impossibility of

developments of the insanity that seems just r...
American people.... 'The American people are ...
lieve that fully, though I confess I have mome...
sometimes of distressing misgivings. I am prayin...
infection may pass away leaving life and hope o...
the meantime, the brood of liars and fools must ...

To DON M. DICKINSON

I steal a moment from working hours to writ...
cannot longer refrain from expressing my thanks,...
crat, to you and those who worked with you, for t...
of the 29th of May in Michigan.

Whatever else may be done before July 7 to sa...
party, the result of the Michigan Democratic St...
must be, looked upon as the most important i...
crowd the intervening time. I know you do not ...
mention, when so many have done so well, but I ...
prouder than ever I am of your friendship, and ...
men of the material in Stevenson's constructio...
country have better cause for self-congratulation...

New York hangs fire and delays speaking,[1] thou...
thing, and though she now owes that speech to t...
I am much humiliated that she should be content...
ground by the same dickering, petty, ignoble, cri...
confront us 'in our hour of might' at Chicago. ...
harmony and the false pretence of compromise wi...
path of those who may fight valiantly and well as...

Thanking you and trusting you, and with sincer...
Stevenson...

To DR. KASSON C. GIBSON

This morning about an hour ago, there came ...
right under jaw, next to the dead tooth you fixe...

[1] Had Hill and the other New York leaders wished to aid Clevela... an early convention and had it adopt a vigorous gold-standard plan... was not held till June 24, when it voted a weak platform which... the standard money of the country.

I have...
that afte...
Columbi...
my New...
I am no...
ing to th...
inexorab...
today. ...
you that...
in the i...
What...
can I ge...
himself ...
way of ...
$10,000...
any sug...
when p...
ing in t...

I wis...
want do...
the exig...
tions if ...
Your...
I ought...
107–108...
the who...
cent on...
invite a...

The...
send m...

To E. C. BENEDICT

Washington, *April* 30, 1896

I have just received your letter and write in very great haste to say that after full consideration I have determined that I cannot attend the Columbia College affair. Of course I would be glad to meet the wishes of my New York friends who are especially interested in the occasion, and I am not unmindful of the proprieties which weigh in favor of my yielding to the request made. There are reasons, however, which to my mind inexorably forbid my taking part in the exercises. I will write Mr. Coudert today. I want to thank you for the hospitalities you offer and to assure you that they present inducements more alluring than any other involved in the invitation.

What about my steam launch? Must I have a man to run it, and if so can I get a man on very reasonable terms to do that and perhaps make himself useful in other ways besides? If you can will you put me in the way of securing such a man? If things get cheap, I suppose I have $10,000 or so which ought to be earning me something. Can you make any suggestions in that direction? At odd moments — they are rare — when public duties do not engross my thoughts, I find my mind wandering in the direction of my future home and means of livelihood.

To E. C. BENEDICT

Washington, *May* 7, 1896

I wish you would write to Secretary Herbert and tell him what you want done, and I can second your request. Of course I do not know what the exigencies of the service may be. We shall have to yield to the conditions if they happen to be adverse.

Your advice in regard to investments I have no doubt is very good and I ought to say 'go it' at once. I see Indianapolis Gas bonds quoted at 107–108. Are they 6 per cent bonds? If so, why would they not be on the whole better for me? They would pay more than five and a half per cent on the investment, as I figure it. These stocks that pay so well invite attack....

To L. CLARKE DAVIS

Washington, *May* 14, 1896

The fact that such silly things as are contained in the clipping you send me can find a place in *any* newspapers, indicates one of the strangest developments of the insanity that seems just now to be afflicting the American people.... 'The American people are good people.' I still believe that fully, though I confess I have moments — only moments — sometimes of distressing misgivings. I am praying now that the prevalent infection may pass away leaving life and hope of complete recovery. In the meantime, the brood of liars and fools must have their carnival.

To DON M. DICKINSON

Washington, *May* 31, 1896

I steal a moment from working hours to write this, because I feel I cannot longer refrain from expressing my thanks, as a citizen and a Democrat, to you and those who worked with you, for the splendid achievement of the 29th of May in Michigan.

Whatever else may be done before July 7 to save the country and the party, the result of the Michigan Democratic State Convention will be, *must* be, looked upon as the most important incident of all that will crowd the intervening time. I know you do not want the least invidious mention, when so many have done so well, but I must tell you how much prouder than ever I am of your friendship, and how glad I am to know men of the material in Stevenson's construction. No two men in the country have better cause for self-congratulation.

New York hangs fire and delays speaking,[1] though she can say but one thing, and though she now owes that speech to the party and the cause. I am much humiliated that she should be content to be kept in the background by the same dickering, petty, ignoble, criminal figuring that will confront us 'in our hour of might' at Chicago. The treacherous cry of harmony and the false pretence of compromise will still, I fear, be in the path of those who may fight valiantly and well as you have done.

Thanking you and trusting you, and with sincere remembrances to Mr. Stevenson...

To DR. KASSON C. GIBSON

Washington, *June* 9, 1896

This morning about an hour ago, there came out of a tooth in my right under jaw, next to the dead tooth you fixed up, a piece of gold

---

[1] Had Hill and the other New York leaders wished to aid Cleveland, they would have called an early convention and had it adopt a vigorous gold-standard plank. Instead, the convention was not held till June 24, when it voted a weak platform which endorsed gold and silver as the standard money of the country.

about the size of a small pea. This indicates how completely I have been on the gold standard. I've got the gold in my possession. What shall I do with it?

To Don M. Dickinson

Washington, *June* 10, 1896

I so fully approve of your suggestions concerning delegations of sound and solid men to attend the Convention as non-delegates, with a view to exerting wholesome influence on delegate sentiments, that I immediately began to agitate the subject in question where I thought it would effect the best results. My ideas seemed to meet with much approval and I had some assurances of co-operation, though I am bound to say to you that they were even then accompanied with that sort of reserved enthusiasm which seems to have for the most part characterized all movements in favor of sound financial policy. Since the receipt of your letter, however, events have occurred so discouraging to the cause of sound finance that I am afraid the efforts promised will not be made. The fact is, people whom I see here who believe with us appear to be thoroughly impressed with the idea that nothing can be done to stem the tide of silverism at Chicago.

I believe I am by nature an undismayed and persistent fighter and I do not believe in giving an inch until we are obliged to; and yet it is hard to call on friends to maintain a struggle which seems so hopeless. It does not seem to me that there should be any relaxation in the effort to prevent our party from entering upon a course which means its retirement for many years to come. If we cannot succeed in checking the desperate disease, perhaps a demonstration can be made which will indicate that a large section of the party is not infected. I don't know how this can be done, but I very much desire that we shall not all have to hang our heads when our party is accused of free-silverism.

Of course I have never seen anything like this craze before, but my faith in the American people is so great that I cannot believe they will cast themselves over the precipice.

But there is our old party with all its glorious traditions and all its achievements in the way of safe and conservative policies, and its exhibitions of indestructibility. Is it to founder on the rocks? Will not sanity return before we reach the final plunge? While I am not completely discouraged, I confess the way looks dark. The most astounding feature of all this matter is the lethargy of our friends and the impossibility of stirring them to action. Michigan seems to be the only State where work was needed and forthcoming.

Events sometimes crowd closely upon each other and much may be developed within even four weeks.

DON M. DICKINSON *to* CLEVELAND

Detroit, Michigan, *June 12,* 1896

Your letter of the 10th instant is received as I am about leaving for Chicago to meet Harrity.... I never knew that atmosphere of Washington to be anything else than discouraging and depressing when there is anything to be done requiring courage and work. Kentucky was bad, of course, but it was only a skirmish as compared with the field. Success *can* only be accomplished at Chicago.

We have the National Committee and the right with us, and the outside delegations of good men will be worth more than all the free-silver shouters in the Southern delegations to the Convention. We must bear in mind, too, that the other side have not our good Convention workers and fighters in their crowd. Vest is no good, even to talk, outside the quiet Senate. Blackburn has no method whatever, and so far as his noise is concerned, by the time the work gets on he will be out of condition sure. On the other hand, we have all the best workers and fighters. Tammany will send the most experienced men who ever went to a Convention.

Tillman [1] and Altgeld, in Convention and in evidence, will be worth everything to us in discrediting the opposition, and in shaming their delegations into coming over to decency. I hope Maryland will distinctly discredit the Gorman influence and keep him away. Brice has played the cause false. He desired the result in Ohio. The whole aspect may be changed by the result of the Republican Convention....

To the DEMOCRATIC VOTERS [2]

Washington, *June 16,* 1896

I have made no figures as to the probable action of the delegates already chosen to the Democratic National Convention, but I refuse to believe that when the time arrives for deliberate action there will be

---

[1] Benjamin R. Tillman (1847–1918) of South Carolina, was governor of South Carolina 1890–94, and United States Senator from 1895 to his death.

[2] Published in the New York *Herald* as a result of the urgings of the Chamber of Commerce of the State of New York and other gold-standard advocates.

engrafted upon our Democratic creed a demand for the free, unlimited, and independent coinage of silver. I cannot believe this, because I know the Democratic party is neither unpatriotic nor foolish, and because it seems so clear to me that such a course will inflict a very great injury upon every interest of our country which it has been the mission of Democracy to advance, and will result in lasting disaster to our party organization. There is little hope that as a means of success this free-silver proposition, after its thorough discussion during a political campaign, will attract a majority of the voters of the country. It must be that many of the illusions influencing those who, now relying upon this alleged panacea for their ills, will be dispelled before the time comes for them to cast their ballots, which will express their sober second thoughts. The adoption by the Democracy of this proposition would, I believe, give to our opponents an advantage, both in the present and future, which they do not deserve.

My attachment to true Democracy is so strong that I consider its success as identical with the promotion of the country's good. This ought sufficiently to account for my anxiety that no mistake be made at our party Convention. In my opinion no effort should be spared to secure such action of the delegates as will avert party demoralization. It is a place for consultation and comparison of views, and those Democrats who believe in the cause of sound money should be heard and should be constantly in evidence. A cause worth fighting for is worth fighting for to the end.... I hope I may not be blamed for saying this much at this time, in the interest, as it seems to be, of the grand old organization, so rich in honorable traditions, so justly proud of its achievements, and always so undaunted and brave in its battles for the people's welfare.

To DON M. DICKINSON

Washington, *June* 17, 1896

Yours at hand. Delaney has been telegraphed. Henry will be all right, and of course Ransom will do as we desire. He was here a few days ago full of disgust and discouragement. He said he would be this way about Convention time, and he seemed indifferent whether he went or not. What do you want us to do about him? I did not know the Oregon man was in the service. We will follow any suggestions you make regarding him.

Wallace told me yesterday that Whitney told him last Saturday that he would leave for Europe today; but from a dispatch he sent to Lamont today I think he has changed his plans and I would not be surprised if you saw him in Chicago. Old 'Do' was in today. What a trump he is! A few more Dickinsons and Dorans would save our party. He is quite determined that he will not go to the Convention, but I hope he will 'turn up.' He says it looks as though the best he could do in any event would be to gain a compromise that would be of no use, etc. I have no idea how Whitney will be 'hitched up' and with whom if he goes.

General McCorkle of West Virginia was in today. He says a great deal can be done with his delegates and he is willing to go and take others. I asked him to write to you and he said he would. If this outside attendance looks hopeful our friends will need headquarters, but I suppose you will not do anything in that direction until matters 'shape up' a little more.[1]

To E. C. BENEDICT

Washington, *June* 19, 1896

The Hahnemann statue bill was objectionable in a number of particulars: 1st. — It may well be said that the statues erected here at the nation's capital should be in commemoration of national heroes, or at least those who are of our people and have performed deeds of national renown. 2nd. — Before any statue is erected here there should be an approval of its artistic merit. I hear the complaint that some already erected are justly criticized for their inferiority. 3d. — It is questionable whether public funds should be appropriated for the erection of a statue of this description. On the whole, the resolution of Congress on this subject, it seemed to me, would establish a precedent or a number of precedents that could not fail to be vexatious. No one made any objection to its approval.

I understand the engineer at the White House would like to spend his vacation at Gray Gables. I have not spoken to him about it yet. We know him, he is a nice fellow, I believe, and as there is nothing for him to do here I am inclined to take him up with me. At any rate, I think you had better tell Mr. Elliott that I have made other arrangements. It is

---

[1] Dickinson wrote Cleveland on June 20 that he still had hopes of the National Convention, but that 'all arrangements and plans and work are about paralyzed by the reports, *and worse than all, the fact,* of the attempted reincarnation of the Bunco-Steerer by Mr. Whitney.... Mr. Whitney had no real intention of going to Europe. That was for effect, and the Bunco-man was to be summoned, and they together were to take charge of the sound-money movement.' As he explicitly added that he would rather vote for Hill than the Bunco-man, by the latter he apparently meant Brice or Gorman.

very kind of you to offer to take up the launch and I am glad to know that Mrs. Benedict has planned to visit Mrs. Cleveland. I do not think I can leave here before the last of June and I hope Mrs. Benedict's visit will not at all depend on my movements and that when she finds it convenient she will start.

Are you calculating to intervene in my transportation? Of course you know how unwilling I am to be of any trouble to you. I think I ought to spend a day in New York on my way.

I am thinking of selling some bonds and stock of the Southern Railway soon. How is this done? Can I do it through your firm? Do I have to send them on before they are sold?

To JOHN C. SHEEHAN

Washington, *June 22*, 1896

I regret that I am unable to accept the courteous invitation I have received to attend the celebration by the Tammany Society of the 120th anniversary of American independence.

The situation that confronts the country and the Democratic party at this time invests with unusual impressiveness this commemoration of our beginning as a nation. When, as appropriate to the occasion, our stupendous advancement is recalled, the fact should not be overlooked that our progress has not been by chance, but is the result of wise observance of the monetary laws which control national health and vigor; and while we contemplate with pride the commanding place we occupy among the nations of the earth, we should not forget that this has been gained only through a jealous preservation of financial soundness and a careful maintenance of unsuspected public credit.

The high and firm financial ground which we have thus far been able to hold should not have been abandoned in the pursuit of a policy never attempted without national injury, and whose bright promise of individual benefit has never been fulfilled.

If there is anything in present conditions that impeaches experience and indicates that we can safely change our present high financial standard for the free, unlimited, and independent coinage of silver, this should be made plainly apparent before such a radical departure finds a place in party creed.

The tremendous consequences of a mistake in dealing with the financial question now pressed upon us as Democrats should constantly make us thoughtful and solicitous. I am confident, therefore, that the voice of the Tammany Society, always potent in party council, will not fail to be heard in warning and protest on an occasion which especially inspires patriotism, and at a time when the felicitations of our people appropriate to Independence Day are mingled with apprehension.[1]

To DON M. DICKINSON

Washington, *June* 27, 1896

Would you undertake to act as Chief Counsel for the United States before the arbitrators to determine the damages we should pay for the sealers, vessels, and catches seized by us in Bering Sea in which we were found to be in the wrong by Paris Commission's award? A young man by the name of Lansing [2] who is quite familiar with the details will assist. *Confidentially*, I may say to you that Judge Putnam of Maine will be our arbitrator. I do not know who will be appointed by England. I think there will be in the neighborhood of twenty claims to be tried involving largely the question of value with the usual *queer* conflict of testimony. There may be a few questions of law involved and the question of speculative damage may arise.

I suppose the inquiry may begin during the summer or early in the autumn. Hearings will be had in Alaska and probably in California. Of course the time necessary to complete the work must be uncertain. If I were obliged to guess, I might say two months. The compensation is also unfixed. I should say, if you undertake it, you might earn $10,000 or

---

[1] The situation when this letter to Tammany Hall was written is described by Charles R. Lingley in *Since the Civil War*, 333, 334:

'For some years influential silver advocates had been associated in the Bimetallic League, an organization which supported the free coinage of both gold and silver. Among its members were prominent Democrats, Republicans, and Populists, especially from the Western States, and some of the foremost labor leaders. At one of its meetings in 1893 it was determined to invite every labor and industrial organization in the country to send delegates.... A silver convention in 1894 was attended by a thousand delegates. From the point of view of party harmony the subject was a nuisance. Democratic State conventions were badly divided. Thirty of them adopted resolutions distinctly favorable to free coinage, and fourteen opposed. The fourteen included all the northeastern States, together with Michigan, Wisconsin, and Minnesota. Such Gold Democrats as President Cleveland sought to stem the tide, but Cleveland's control over his followers was rapidly dwindling, and it seemed likely that the silver element of the party might reach out to seize the organization and displace its former leaders.'

This letter was Cleveland's last public appeal before the Democratic Convention. It was read at the annual Tammany celebration of Independence Day, July 4, 1896.

[2] Robert Lansing, later Secretary of State.

$15,000. The appropriation already made to cover all our expenses of the arbitration is, I believe, $75,000.

I've now made all the guesses I ought to in the matter and would be glad to hear from you on the subject at Buzzards Bay as soon as possible. If you prefer it for any reason, it will be precisely as well to write to Mr. Olney.

To SECRETARY RICHARD OLNEY
Washington, June 29, 1896

I am not sure that I told you definitely what my vacation plans are. I start for Buzzards Bay tomorrow morning at seven o'clock. If there is any subject you desire to discuss with me before I leave, I will be quite at your service from now until a quarter after one or at any time after eight o'clock this evening. I have engagements with the Secretary of War and Postmaster-General this afternoon. You spoke of my having the cipher of the State Department.

I hope we may have diplomatic exercises with the fish in and about Buzzards Bay at times during the summer.

To SECRETARY RICHARD OLNEY
Gray Gables, July 4, 1896

You can say with entire safety that I will return to Washington before the 1st day of November and that any engagements made on my behalf for that day or thereafter will be met (D.V.).[1]

I suppose we will have to do something by way of entertaining Esquire Li Hung Chang. How would it do to fire off a bunch of fire-crackers?

The fishing on the Bay is first-rate. I have been after them twice already with good success. I'll save a few for you if I can.

P.S. I've received the cipher. I think I can study it out if necessary, but I had rather talk 'United States.'

To ATTORNEY-GENERAL JUDSON HARMON
Gray Gables, July 8, 1896

Your letter concerning the Oklahoma judge is at hand. I remember when the first mutterings against him came to our ears they did not seem quite substantial and specific enough to make it certain that they did not originate in the inevitable discontent of certain members of the bar. One

---

[1] *Deo volente.*

queer thing which I remember in connection with the matter was the fact that Speed, a former Republican district attorney who recommended Scott when he was appointed, appeared in the front rank of his enemies when complaints were made. I think as the matter now stands you had better carry out your idea as expressed in your letter, and write to him suggesting his resignation. It seems as though the very devil was in these territorial judgeships.

To Secretary Richard Olney

Gray Gables, *July* 13, 1896

The Putnam Commission just received will go, in the same mail which takes this, to the White House and will be sent immediately to you 'personally' if you are at the Department, and without giving it to the press. You can do that when you desire.

If Lord Salisbury's dispatch takes you a little 'sudden' and you want to make some sort of reply before determining definitely what the response should be, can you not send him a kind of waiting, promising dispatch that will make the record as complete as possible and yet indicate that more will follow? I suppose it is too much to hope, but I wish we could reach some point in that matter.

I am thinking a great deal about Cuba, but am as far as ever from seeing the place where we can get in.

I would like very much to read the Duke of Argyle's book on the Turkish question and wish you would send it to me.

I am so dazed on the political situation that I am in no condition for speech or thought on the subject. It is certainly an ill wind that blows no good to anyone. Has it occurred to you that in view of the outcome at Chicago no one can be fool enough to charge against this Administration the disasters that await the Democratic party? [1]

To Secretary Daniel S. Lamont

Confidential.   Gray Gables, *July* 15, 1896

I have given the subject broached in your letter much thought. I really do not see what I can properly do or say. Those who controlled the Convention displayed their hatred of me and wholly repudiated me. Those who at the Convention differed with them seem to have thought it

---

[1] On July 8 the Democratic Convention in Chicago had adopted a free-silver platform, and on July 9 it had nominated Bryan for President.

wise to ignore me in all consultation, fearing probably that any connection with me would imperil success. I do not say they were not right. I only say that events have pushed me so much aside that I do not see how I can be useful in harmonizing or smoothing matters.

I have an idea, quite fixed and definite, that for the present at least we should none of us say anything. I heard from Herbert today. He says he has declared he will not support the ticket. I am sorry he has done so. We have a right to be quiet — indeed, I feel that I have been invited to that course. I am not fretting except about the future of the country and party, and the danger that the latter is to be compromised as an organization.

I suppose it has occurred to you that since the Chicago Convention there cannot be a fool stupid enough or malicious enough to attribute to the present Administration any calamity that may befall the organization of the Democratic party. While I would be willing to incur that accusation to save or benefit the party in a good cause, what is the use of inviting such an accusation by saying something which at this time can have no influence for good? I feel well out of it by the condemnation I have received at the hands of those who have managed affairs, and by the nomination of men whose personal hatred of me seemed to be a prerequisite for Convention honors. Others who fought on the other side were not anxious to see me gain anything from the outcome, whatever it might be.

I am receiving a good many letters from all sorts of people which confirm me in the belief that whatever the rest think they ought to do, I ought to keep silence — at least until conditions change. In the meantime I am having some good fishing and promptly attending to all official work sent to me.

To SECRETARY HOKE SMITH

Gray Gables, *July* 15, 1896

... I am a good deal dazed politically, but my judgment is that it is best for the present to think much and *talk none.*

To SECRETARY RICHARD OLNEY

Gray Gables, *July* 16, 1896

Macgrane Cox is a gentleman living in Orange County, New York, a lawyer by profession and I think has an office in the city of New York. He was a candidate for District Attorney for the Southern District of New York and presented some very fine endorsements which are now on file in the Department of Justice. He would like to be appointed Minister to Guatemala and saw Thurber a few days ago on the subject. I know him slightly and am very favorably inclined to his selection.

Thurber by my direction has written to him suggesting that he go at once to Washington to see you, and I suppose in a few days he will present himself. I want you to see him and look him over carefully. In the meantime I hope you will examine the recommendations he filed when an applicant for the other place. I would not be surprised if your brother Peter knew him. He talks French and reads and writes (I believe) Spanish. Consul-General Williams would like the appointment and I send today to the White House to be filed with you his letter and some others asking for the place. Power of Louisiana I think fairly well of, but when you go down there you hardly know what kind of an animal you may strike. Boyd Winchester of Kentucky was one of our Ministers from 1885 to 1889 and did creditably. He is in need of a place too, but Kentucky has had *so much* that I hardly think his appointment would be the best that could be made. I am inclined to believe Coxe is the best in sight. At any rate, I hope you will see him and let me know what you think of him. The Bowen business I do not like at all.

I am looking for the advance sheets of the correspondence between you and Lord Salisbury.

I am a little surprised at Consul-General Lee's dispatch. He seems to have fallen into the style of rolling intervention like a sweet morsel under his tongue. I do not think the purchase plan would suit at all, though it is perhaps worth thinking of. Many of the fairest talkers in favor of intervening (Sherman, for instance) are opposed to incorporating the country into the United States system and I am afraid it would be entering upon dangerous ground. It would seem absurd for us to buy the island and present it to the people now inhabiting it, and put its government and management in their hands. According to my remembrance, Lee's reference to Jackson's recognition of Texas is not fortunate.

I do not like the suggestion of a man-of-war, etc., though of course prudent measures might well be taken to provide in good faith for the safety of our people and interests in case Spain failed in that behalf; but I do not want *now* anything of that kind made a convenient excuse for trouble with Spain.

I am very glad to hear that you are likely to be released next week. The fishing in the Bay is first-rate, but I am afraid it is a little slow in the ponds.

To E. C. BENEDICT

Gray Gables, *July* 17, 1896

I am itching to own three hundred shares of Chicago Gas in addition to the two hundred you now hold for me, and unless you know something bad about it I wish you would buy it for me.

I received a bill of lading today for ten barrels of oil which I am advised have been shipped by your direction to me. I don't quite know what it means, but am very much pleased to know that I am to have it. I thank you for thus providing me with a surely good quality and am prepared to pay the bill on presentation. My launch is improving every day and I take lots of comfort with it. I think my engineer is getting a good hold of it.

We have had three days of good squeteague fishing and go again to-morrow. We are the first to get hold of them and are keeping very quiet about it. We caught fifteen today and repeatedly wish you were along. I don't know how long they will hold on. The bottom-fishing has been good too. *Come up!* I think I shall attend poor Russell's [1] funeral next week some day and have promised to leave here next Friday night and stay till Saturday evening. But I'll be glad to see you any time.

To DON M. DICKINSON

Gray Gables, *July* 19, 1896

I received two letters from you last night.

I was very much pleased to read the passage which referred to a possible trip in this direction, but I did not like the way you put it — that is, the intimation that you might 'run up to Thurber's.' I want you to run up here. It's easier to reach this place than Marion and I'll see you get to Thurber's if you want to go there. Besides, perhaps Thurber will be here Tuesday. He said he would come if he didn't have to go to New York to meet his sister.

[1] Ex-Governor William E. Russell of Massachusetts died at Little Pabos, Quebec, on July 16.

Why don't you start Tuesday evening by boat or train and reach here Wednesday morning? We have plenty of trains and all of them stop at Gray Gables for our family and guests. Telegraph whether you will come by boat or train, and if by train, when you leave Boston. In either case, tell the conductor before you get to Buzzards Bay that you want to come to Gray Gables and the rest is easy. Our little station, you know, is a mile or two below Buzzards Bay on the Woods Hole Branch and it may be you will have to step from one car to another at Buzzards Bay.

Having thus imparted to you my anxious desire and given to you the above specific instructions, I shall expect to hear from you by wire tomorrow (Monday) or Tuesday. I do not care who knows you are coming. Indeed, I wish everybody knew it. I send this to Boston for mailing tonight so that you can get it tomorrow when you arrive in New York.

P.S. I go tomorrow to the Russell funeral and shall remain overnight, I suppose, in Boston.

To RICHARD WATSON GILDER

Gray Gables, *July* 20, 1896

I see you are having considerable to say about overcrowded houses since your return from abroad. There's a house up here which is not overcrowded, but which I think you should examine. Indeed, I shall not feel safe and comfortable until you do.

I have supposed, of course, you would be up and have been expecting some intimation from you on that subject, though I suppose for a while after your return to the country you would submit to the 'damnation grind' of waiting work. I think now, however, it is about time for you to bust the harness and cut for Buzzards Bay air. We shall all be very glad to see you at any time.

I am just about starting to attend ex-Governor Russell's funeral. What a loss! There are few men in the country who, it seems to me, could not have been better spared. Mrs. Cleveland and her mother, who is with us, send affectionate remembrances. Our youngest — a year old a few days ago — just proudly trotted past my window.

HOKE SMITH *to* CLEVELAND

Washington, *July* 20, 1896

I have been confined to my room for several days or I should have written to you sooner.

I am deeply distressed by the action of the Chicago Convention, and by the situation it has produced.[1] Just indignation at first led me to feel that I should openly oppose the nominees, and this seems to be the course that will be pursued by the other members of the Cabinet. But an earnest desire to reach a conclusion which will be in the line of my real duty has satisfied me that I cannot pursue such a course.

All through the campaign, in a number of speeches, I urged my hearers to pledge themselves in advance to support the nominees of the National Convention, and I frequently pledged myself to do so. Besides, this is a contest against a Republican candidate, and I cannot, even by failing to vote, aid him. The local situation is such in my own State that I consider the protection of person and property involved in the local Democratic success, which can only continue through Democratic organization.

I would strike my own people a severe blow if I repudiated a nominee of a regular convention, thereby setting a precedent for disorganization. While I shall not accept the platform, I must support the nominee of the Chicago Convention. I have not reached this conclusion without pain. I realize fully the probable consequences, for, of course, I understand that you should be surrounded with men who support the view which you may take upon so important a subject. I would not have written at this time, but would have, with great propriety, waited your action, except for the fact that the *Journal* will tomorrow declare in favor of the ticket nominated in Chicago, and this will be accepted as an expression for myself. I should have delayed any expression by the *Journal*, but the action of Secretaries Herbert and Morton prevented further silence.

Now, Mr. President, permit me to express from my heart my deep appreciation of the privilege of association with one so wise, brave, and patriotic. Whatever happens, I shall cherish it as the most valued portion of my life, and I can never cease to be devotedly loyal to you.

To SECRETARY HOKE SMITH

Gray Gables, *August* 4, 1896

I suppose I should have replied to your letter of July 20 before; but to tell you the truth, I have delayed and hesitated because I could not satisfy myself as to what I should write.

[1] It was impossible for Hoke Smith, as owner of the Atlanta *Journal*, to avoid taking a position on the nomination of Bryan; and he believed with many other Southerners that any division of the Democratic party which would bring back Republican domination in his State would be a calamity.

I have determined to say to you frankly that I was astonished and much disappointed by your course, and that I am by no means relieved by the reasons you present in justification of it. When you addressed the citizens of your State so nobly and patriotically, you were discussing the silver question alone; and when you assured them that you intended to support the nominee of the National Convention you could certainly have intended no more than to pledge yourself that, in case you were overruled by the Convention *in the question under discussion*, you would accept your defeat and support the platform and candidates which represented that defeat. This — considering your strong expressions on the silver question, your earnest advocacy of sound money, and your belief in its transcendent importance — was going very far.

You surely could not have intended to promise support to a platform directly opposed, not only to sound money, but to every other safe and conservative doctrine or policy, and framed in every line and word in condemnation of all the acts and policies of an Administration of which you have from the first been a loyal, useful, and honorable member. You could not have intended a promise to uphold candidates, not only pledged to the support and advancement of this destructive and un-Democratic platform, but whose selection largely depended upon the depth and virulence of their hatred of our Administration. I say 'our' Administration because I have constantly in mind the work we have done, the patriotism that has inspired our every act, the good we have accomplished, and the evil we have averted in the face of the opposition of the vicious forces that have temporarily succeeded in their revolt against everything good and glorious in Democratic faith and achievement.

It is due to our countrymen and to the safety of the nation that such an Administration should not be discredited or stricken down. It belongs to them and should be protected and defended, because it is their agency devoted to their welfare and safety. None can defend it better than those who constitute it, and know the singleness of purpose and absolute patriotism that have inspired it. You say, 'While I shall not accept the platform, I must support the nominees of the Chicago Convention.' I cannot see how this is to be done. It seems to me like straining at a gnat and swallowing a camel.

The vital importance of the issues involved in the national campaign and my failure to appreciate the inseparable relation between it and a State contest, prevent me from realizing the force of your reference to the 'local situation.' I suppose much was said about the 'local situation' in 1860.

I am perfectly satisfied that you have been influenced in the position you have taken by the same desire to do exactly right that has guided you in all your acts as a member of the Cabinet. You know how free my association with my official family has been from any attempt to influence personal action, and how fully that association has been characterized by perfect confidence and a spirit of unreserved consultation and frankness. In this spirit I now write. I have no personal grievance that anyone need feel called on to even notice. My only personal desire is to make as good a President as possible during the residue of my term, and then to find retirement and peace; but I cannot believe that I will do my duty to my countrymen and party, either as President or citizen, by giving the least aid and comfort to the nominees of the Chicago Convention or the ideas they represent.

To ATTORNEY-GENERAL JUDSON HARMON

Gray Gables, *August* 5, 1896

I have examined the Union Pacific Railroad matter quite carefully, and in the light of your last letter I think we can do something in the direction suggested. I wish I could see Olney, Carlisle, and you together in conference on the subject. I hope that Mr. and Mrs. Carlisle will visit us soon. If you could manage to come up at that time I could get Olney here and we could go over it. If, however, there is no hurry this will not be necessary. I think if Carlisle is in Washington you had better see him and find out when he is coming and arrange to meet us here. Of course we would be glad to see you anyway, and there are some things besides Union Pacific affairs I would like to discuss....

To the NEW YORK 'EVENING POST'

Gray Gables, *August* 7, 1896 (telegram)

It is absolutely untrue that I have given any advice touching the course of the Indianapolis conference.[1]

---

[1] A conference of Democratic National Committeemen who believed in the gold standard was held in Indianapolis early in August, and called a Gold Democratic Convention to meet there on September 2.

To SECRETARY DANIEL S. LAMONT

Gray Gables, *August* 9, 1896

Mr. Olney was here today, and read to me your letter to him touching the visit of Li Hung Chang.[1] He will telegraph you today or tomorrow approving your suggestion to call General Merritt east to take charge of certain movements. Inasmuch as our visitor will not come in any official capacity, I do not think our highest general should attend him. I will say to you *confidentially* that I propose to be in New York about the time the great Chinaman arrives, and have him presented, receive from him the letter he brings from his Emperor, and return to Buzzards Bay at once. The citizens of New York, I am afraid, will not have much opportunity to lionize, but I hope whatever is done will be just the thing. Of course I shall take no part in it.

Mrs. Bryant wrote to Mrs. Cleveland a day or two ago that the Doctor hoped to come to Gray Gables the middle or the last of the coming week. Why cannot you join him? I want to see you very much indeed about two or three things, and whether you come with the Doctor or not, I hope I may have a conference with you as soon as possible. Herbert was here with Olney today and I hope to see Carlisle and Harmon before many days. I am sure that our cool air would do you good. There is a matter I ought to act on within the next week, concerning which I feel that if possible I must have your advice.

I do not desire to interfere or interrupt any plans you may have in mind promising more recreation or enjoyment, or which you may consider more in the line of duty, but if you can come you know how glad I and all our household will be to see you. I can promise you, according to all indications, first-rate fishing, and I am in no mood to pester you with political talk, though I would be glad to hear whatever you have to say on that subject. No one is inviting me to bother my head about politics and I am very glad of it.

To SECRETARY HOKE SMITH

Gray Gables, *August* 16, 1896

The correspondence which has lately passed between us has reached such a stage that there seems to be nothing left for me to do but to accede to your desire to retire from the Cabinet.

---

[1] The famous Chinese statesman, now seventy-three, had been sent by the Empress Dowager to the coronation of Czar Nicholas II, and had continued around the world in a triumphal tour.

Availing myself of the considerate suggestion contained in your last letter that I indicate the date when this separation shall occur, and desiring to meet your convenience in the matter of a speedy release, I am led to ask you to postpone the relinquishment of your official duties under the resignation you have tendered until the first day of September. I hope I need not say how deeply I regret your retirement, and how much I appreciate the devotion, industry, and ability which have characterized your discharge of duty as a member of my official family.

With the sincere wish that success and contentment may attend you in your future way of life....

To ATTORNEY-GENERAL JUDSON HARMON
Gray Gables, *August* 18, 1896

Your last letter is at hand. I still think you can do [no] better than to pitch upon Keaton in Oklahoma. I am so anxious to give the people there the best judge their bar can supply and I was so impressed with the idea that for a judicial position, especially considering the atmosphere there, financial ideas ought to count less than in other cases, that I am inclined to risk Mr. Keaton, in view of my belief that he is an honest, self-respecting, decent man, who will aim to be a good judge and will be willing to forego political controversy and blackguardism....

I like your letter on the Chicago platform very much.

To JOSEPH JEFFERSON
GRAY GABLES, *August* 19, 1896

Last night after a late return from a 'good outing' at Big Sandy I found a telegram from Charley asking when and where he could see me today. It was too late to make a reply by telegraph, and thinking his dispatch indicated his presence in the neighborhood today and yet of course uncertain whether he has left New York or not, I write this to ask you to say to Charley, if he is accessible to you, that I should be happy to see him if he can call at any time after six o'clock this evening. I must take my Attorney-General out on the bay to fish today.

D. B. GRIFFIN *to* CLEVELAND
Indianapolis, *September* 2, 1896 (telegram)

You will be nominated tomorrow unless you make definite refusal. We strongly urge that you communicate privately, to be used publicly if necessary, with some friend on the ground. Otherwise every indication is that you will be nominated by acclamation.

To D. B. GRIFFIN

Gray Gables, *September 2*, 1896 (telegram)

My judgment and personal inclination are so unalterably opposed to your suggestion that I cannot for a moment entertain it.[1]

To SENATOR WILLIAM F. VILAS

Gray Gables, *September 5*, 1896

Your letter reached me a day after the appointment you referred to had been made. I had an intimation like that contained in your letter prior to the disposition of the matter, but I could not for the life of me see how delay would aid in the cause you and I have so much at heart, and I did see plainly that the conditions of judicial business were such as to make early action quite desirable. If, however, I had received your letter a little earlier, I might have regarded the affair in a different light. I am sure that I have selected the best men in the localities and that they are sound on the 'main question.' I do not think any of the other aspirants were in that state of mind or that any anticipation of selection would have made them so.

I am exceedingly angry and humiliated by the course of some of those now holding office under the present Administration and am considering the question of my duty in the premises, very anxiously. I suppose many of those who are behaving badly were appointed at the request of good friends who would now be offended if a proper corrective should be applied. I am hesitating, but it need not surprise some of those people if they run against some unpleasantly sharp corners.

I am delighted with the outcome of the Indianapolis Convention and as a Democrat I feel very grateful to those who have relieved the bad political atmosphere with such a delicious infusion of fresh air. Every Democrat, after reading the platform, ought to thank God that the glorious principles of our party have found defenders who will not permit them to be polluted by impure hands.

It is a very delicate matter for me to decide upon the course I ought to pursue in regard to any public declaration touching the matter of the

[1] John M. Palmer (1817–1900) and Simon B. Buckner (1823–1914) of Illinois and Kentucky respectively, were nominated.

convention just held. You know I have six months more of official life, during which time all I can do of public duty must be done in co-operation with those in another branch whom perhaps I ought not to further irritate. It may be, too, that inasmuch as one element in the stock in trade of the reactionists is hatred and opposition to the Administration, I might aid them by entering the lists and thus giving force to the argument upon which this opposition is based. On the other hand, I rather desire to speedily cast in my lot with those who have come to the rescue of Democracy. But why is anything now needed from me to make known my position? For years, officially and unofficially, I have, in season and out of season, declared my opinions on the subject of sound money and Democracy.

I shall continue to seek for the path of duty and good judgment.

To SECRETARY DANIEL S. LAMONT

Gray Gables, *September* 6, 1896

I was glad to receive your last letter and thank you for it. It is pleasant to hear from you occasionally such news as I should not otherwise obtain.

I have written to Professor Bern asking him to take a place on the Commission and to also aid me in the selection of the other two members I am to appoint. I mentioned to him that Coolidge of Chicago had been favorably presented to me, and another man from New York whose name did not occur to me, but might be Morrison who was on the Bridge Commission. (I mislaid somehow the memorandum of those names you gave me.)...

Mr. Harmon has written me a letter, which I cannot lay my hand on now, in which he says that a United States Senator from Wyoming or Montana tells him that the Surveyor-General of that State, named Thompson, I believe, is transcending all decency in his abuse of the Administration and the President generally. I don't know what, if anything, should be done with such a fellow, but I think it is a shame to have one holding office under us carry on in this fashion when so many good men receiving no benefit at our hands and asking none are laboring in our defence and in defence of the policy we are endeavoring to uphold for our country's good. If you are willing to take the trouble, I wish you would see Harmon and Francis and have this allegation investigated.

I am delighted with the result of the Indianapolis Convention. Its platform is the best possible statement of the true doctrines of Democracy and makes all those who believe in and love the grand old organization feel that they still have a home.

I am gratified to know that you are willing to declare your sentiments and the quicker and stronger you or any other member of the Cabinet speak, the better I shall like it. My notion is that the tune should be, or at least one note of it, that the Indianapolis platform and the candidates are Democratic and the Chicago platform and candidates are not.

I am perplexed concerning the course I should pursue. My inclination, of course, is to join the chorus of denunciation, but I am doubtful as to the wisdom of such action, in the light of a chance that it might do more harm than good. My position cannot be misunderstood by any man, woman, or child in the country. I am President of all the people, good, bad, and indifferent, and as long as my opinions are known, ought perhaps to keep myself out of their squabbles. I must attempt to co-operate with Congress during another session in the interest of needed legislation, and perhaps ought not to unnecessarily further alienate that body and increase its hatred of me, and if I take an actively and affirmatively aggressive position, it may aid the cause we have *not* at heart by increasing the effectiveness of the cry of Presidential interference. In addition to all this, no one of weight or influence in political matters has advised me to speak out — though I shall be surprised if Palmer does not urge it soon.

If you say anything I do not care how plainly you present the inference that I am in accord with your views. Write me again when you can, come and see us again if possible, give our love to Mrs. Lamont.

To W. D. Bynum

Gray Gables, *September* 10, 1896

I regret that I cannot accept your invitation to attend the notification meeting on Saturday evening. As a Democrat devoted to the principles and integrity of my party, I should be delighted to be present on an occasion so significant, and to mingle with those who are determined that the voice of true Democracy shall not be smothered, and who insist that its glorious standard shall be borne aloft, as of old, in faithful hands.

To ATTORNEY-GENERAL JUDSON HARMON

Gray Gables, *September* 13, 1896

... I have only seen a portion of your letter on the anarchistic portion of the Chicago platform. If you have the full text convenient I wish you would send it to me. The Administration seems to be pretty well 'out' for the third ticket, and I am glad of it. I think it will delight me hereafter to remember these things. (I put this in English, as I am a little rusty in my Virgil.)

I asked the Secretary of War to talk with you and the Secretary of the Interior about the ill-mannered and pestilent Surveyor-General of whom you wrote. There is an impudent Auditor in the Treasury Department named Baldwin, who is talking silver very bravely in Maryland. I am growing very sick of this business and am inclined to deal with some of these fellows as they deserve.

To ATTORNEY-GENERAL JUDSON HARMON

Gray Gables, *September* 21, 1896

Your letter and the nomination for Keaton were received this morning. I have signed the commission and it will go to the Executive Mansion by the same mail that carries this. I am very well pleased with this appointment on all grounds — a minor one being that if we find it necessary for proper reasons to deal in the way of discipline with any of our officers who chance to be of the silver persuasion, the contemporaneous appointment of one of that sort will negative any allegation that we are persecuting that class for their opinions....

I am glad you are doing so much to prove the sincerity of our professions in regard to unlawful interference in Cuban affairs.

To SECRETARY RICHARD OLNEY

Gray Gables, *September* 24, 1896

I enclose you the letter you sent me a few days ago. I think the course you suggest is the best one to be pursued. Another meeting could, I suppose, result in nothing better than the note you contemplate, while it might give life to embarrassments which are at present dormant.

It is hard to restrain oneself on this cursed Turkish question, but we must do so, I suppose. Of course you will not repel the idea he [1] advances

[1] The British Ambassador.

any more decidedly than necessary, and will speak of protection to our people very distinctly indeed. We don't want *him* to have any excuse for saying that we are in the least unmindful of the duty that rests upon us — even if his country is backward in doing hers.

To E. C. BENEDICT

Washington, *October* 28, 1896

Your letter was received this morning, and I am much obliged to you for the assurances it contains. Will not the deal said to be in process of consummation touching the Southern Railroad help the price of my bonds and stocks? I hope so. As for the other, I am very content and pleased at the prospect and am satisfied that I can profitably wait before making a snap for bonds, which of course I have always intended to do at some time. I cannot make myself believe that the election will go wrong next Tuesday. It involves so much that any possible chance of an adverse result cannot fail to make thoughtful citizens anxious; and yet I am inclined to think as a matter of cold judgment that there will be something of a landslide in the right direction.

I do not see why those bass at New Rochelle could not have been on hand a day or two earlier, but I suppose they will work that way at times until the end of the chapter. You don't know how much I am delighted with my Isaak Walton. I prize it more than any book I have, except my mother's Bible, and I am as grateful to you as I can possibly be. I don't see anything in it about catching tautog, but I suppose the author died in ignorance of Buzzards Bay and Plum Gut.

I don't often do such things but I've an idea that I may enclose my Princeton speech.[1] It was a great occasion.

To E. C. BENEDICT

Washington, *November* 8, 1896

You hold 600 shares of Chicago Gas stock which belong to me. If you will buy on my account 600 shares of Southern Railway preferred, you may hold both stocks as security for the outlay until such time as I desire to sell and settle. If you are willing to do so and it accords with your judgment, you may increase the purchase to 1000 shares.

---

[1] Cleveland spoke at the sesquicentennial celebration at Princeton in October, 1896, when the college became a university.

To PROFESSOR ANDREW F. WEST

Washington, *November* 8, 1896

I want to write you a little bit confidentially; and I write to *you*, because I do not know a better-natured man to bother with a private matter.

Mrs. Cleveland and I, naturally enough, are casting about for a resting place where we can settle with our three babies after the fourth of next March. Somehow for the last few days the idea has entered our minds that we might be very comfortable and satisfied at Princeton. This may be only a passing notion which will disappear when other schemes crowd in.

I think I would like to buy a house in which I may live and die (if I could afford it), having plenty of room and a fair share, at least, of the conveniences of modern existence; and in this home I want to be free from all sorts of social and other exactions that might interfere with the lazy rest which I crave. This house must be one which can be maintained cheaply. These personal considerations, except the last one mentioned, are not, however, so important as the following:

For my wife and children I want some ground about the house, a pleasant social life, a healthy and comfortable climate (especially in the winter), and good school advantages. The second and last of them I consider assured at Princeton, but its weather — cold and damp, cold and dry, or temperate with dampness or cold — I know nothing about.

Will you take the trouble to write me all you know of all these matters? If you happen to know of a house and lot which you think might suit us and which could be bought reasonably, I wish you would mention it. If not, perhaps you will give me the name of someone acquainted with such matters. I fear I am asking too much from you. Mrs. Cleveland desires to be remembered and we both are very glad we attended Princeton's Sesquicentennial.

To ALEXANDER E. ORR

Washington, *November* 16, 1896

... Recent events may well cause those who represent business interests to rejoice on their escape from threatened peril. But while they have abundant reason for rejoicing and can view with greatest satisfaction the support they have given the cause of sound money in the contest lately waged against it, I earnestly hope that in this time of congratulation it will be remembered that absolute safety will only be secured when our financial system is protected by affirmative and thorough reforms.

To ATTORNEY-GENERAL JUDSON HARMON

Washington, *November* 17, 1896

Judge Charles C. Nott having served as a Judge in the Court of Claims for more than thirty years, I am contemplating his promotion to the Chief Judgeship of that court, made vacant by the death of Judge Richardson. I am impressed with the belief that the selection of Judge Nott for that place would subserve the public interest and be a just recognition of long and valuable service.

I desire, however, before finally determining upon my course in the matter, to have your opinion in answer to the following question: Would the retirement of Mr. Nott as Chief Justice of the Court of Claims, upon his attaining the age of seventy and before he had served ten years as Chief Justice, deprive him of the benefit of Section 704 of the Revised Statutes, providing for the continuance of salary to a judge retiring at the age of seventy, after having held his commission at least ten years? I should be glad to receive your opinion on this question at your earliest convenience.

To RICHARD WATSON GILDER

Washington, *November* 20, 1896

You are quite right. There are now three projects, in fact, to serve me up and help people to breast or dark meat, with or without stuffing.[1] The one I have heard the most of was when I last got sight of it, running towards Prof.——, the man who made the motion at Princeton.[2] I've forgotten his name. I don't know in the shuffle what will become of me and my poor old battered name, but I think perhaps I ought to look after it a little. I shall probably avail myself of your kindness.

To E. C. BENEDICT

Washington, *November* 22, 1896

We have been casting about in the Munich matter, and recalling my last conversation on the subject with the Secretary of State, I am a little afraid that the selection is forestalled, though I am not certain.

---

[1] That is, three plans for writing magazine articles about Cleveland.
[2] Woodrow Wilson.

My purchase of Southern Railroad was for two purposes — to reduce, if I made profits, the price of the bonds I hold, and to realize on them at a favorable time and put the proceeds on a home. I bought and have held the Chicago Gas for the latter purpose only. My doubt now is whether I had better not sell Chicago Gas and pay for the other and hold on to that until I need it to pay for a residence — which of course will be a very modest one.

I have, however, concluded to ask you to receive and credit me with the Chicago Gas dividend and permit matters to remain as they are for the present. I suppose subjects that will rightly or wrongly affect prospects and prices will be mixed and uncertain for quite a time, but I must take those things as they come. My necessities and desires point to paying for a home and in some way having invested enough bonds to yield an income upon which I can quietly and economically live. I am by no means certain that I can bring about these results, but all my efforts are aimed at their accomplishment. I am obliged to stare in the face the probability that my earning days of activity are past, and I must act accordingly.

As far, therefore, as bond investments are concerned, I am inclined to let well enough alone until the question of a home is settled, and I can see more clearly my exact situation.

To E. C. BENEDICT

Washington, *November 26, 1896*

Your old friend has been appointed Consul at Munich.

I wish you would sell 1000 shares of Southern Railway preferred stock you hold for me and remit the net proceeds. I don't like the appearance of things as they are, or may be, related to that stock, and I want the money *at once* to help pay for my new home which I expect is as good as bought today *for cash*. I am entirely satisfied to get out with a little loss. I hope you will sell and remit to me as soon as possible.

To E. C. BENEDICT

Washington, *November 27, 1896*

After I went to bed last night, it occurred to me, for the first time, that my request to sell at a loss certain property which I had not paid for, and remit the 'net proceeds' to me, was a decidedly cool proposition. I laughed to myself at my stupidity, but now hasten to tell you that without much reflection, and with a head full of other matters, I acted on the supposition that the Southern Railroad stock was not only mine, *but wholly paid for*. Finding this morning that I would not need the money until the latter part of next month — say December 20 — I telegraphed to withhold action, if none had been taken, until you could hear from me.

I do not think the stock will improve much, for some time at least. I see it is about 28 today. I think the way to do is this: If you have sold the Southern Railroad, sell also the Chicago Gas and reimburse yourself and remit me the balance. If you have not sold, all the same, *sell both*, square up the account, and remit. I shall make a fair profit at that and certainly have the money necessary to pay for my home when the time for payment arrives, and shall not be in your debt.

This ought to satisfy me, and it does satisfy me, though I think Chicago Gas promises far better than the other. The latter averages in cost to me about $53\frac{1}{2}$.

I don't mind telling you, as the fourth person that knows it, including Mrs. Cleveland and myself, that I have dared to bargain this morning for a home in Princeton, New Jersey, where I expect to live the remainder of my life, and at its end be laid to rest.

To HOKE SMITH

Washington, *December* 21, 1896

I was on the point of writing you when your letter of the 19th arrived. I need not say that your kindly expressions and continued friendly interest are most gratifying.

We shall have our Cabinet dinner on the evening of January 7, 1897. I have conceived the idea of having as guests on that occasion those friends who have been associated with me as Cabinet officers in both my terms as President, so far as possible. It would especially gratify me if you and Mrs. Smith would join us. Will you do so? I think, on the plan suggested, a very pleasant and compatible company would be gathered with very little if any outside reinforcement.

With affectionate remembrances to Mrs. Smith...

To RICHARD WATSON GILDER

Washington, *December* 27, 1896

I was very much touched to receive on Christmas Day your beautiful and valuable gift, made more impressive by the sentiment suggested on the card accompanying it. Of all men in the world you know best that I do honestly try to 'keep the compass true,' and I am convinced that you appreciate, better than others, how misleading the fogs sometimes are. I frequently think what a glorious boon omniscience would be to one charged with the magistracy of our nation. I can only thank you from the bottom of my heart for this last of many proofs of your friendship, and assure you of the comfort and encouragement it has been to me. I should be afflicted if my barometer ever indicated anything but 'clear weather' in our relations.

I have been afraid sometimes since I left you here a week ago that you might not feel like bothering us too much in the preparation of the article you had in proof. I want to say to you that you must draw on us to any extent you desire to make the article suit you. Of course your magazine instinct fits you to judge as to the items that will interest readers, but you must understand that anything, personal or otherwise, that would be at all suitable for such publication is at your disposal. For example, I have been sometimes surprised and irritated by the accusation or intimation that I lacked in appreciation of friendship and did not recognize sufficiently what others did for me. Of course this is as far from the truth as it can be and can only have its rise in a refusal on my part to compensate friends by misappropriation from the trust funds of public duty. To this I plead guilty on many charges; but no one is more delighted than I when friendship and public duty travel in the same way. Would it add a bit to the interest if the reader was given a little more of a peep at the home life and the sustaining influence of wife and children — working in the remark I have many times made in dark and trying times of perplexing affairs, in answer to inquiries after the welfare of my family: 'They are as well as they can be. It is this end of the home that troubles me. If things should go wrong at the other end I would feel like quitting the place for good'?

Having made these suggestions I am so impressed that they are useless and foolish that I feel like telling you to utterly disregard them, except as they indicate my willingness to do anything you wish in the premises.

A few days ago Mr. Gardiner Hubbard and Mr. McClure (of *McClure's Magazine*) called on me and said Carl Schurz was to write an article for that magazine on the Administration; and they wanted to know if Mr. Cox could take some pictures, etc. Of course I could not object, but the *Century* article was spoken of and Professor Wilson's too. They seemed to understand or to know about both, and thought Mr. Schurz could hold his own with anyone in the same field. I suppose his article will be far removed from the track of yours. I was delighted in my late interview with Mr. Schurz to see that he had recovered from his Venezuela scare and was quite satisfied apparently with the civil service reform situation. He is a good and useful man and I am always pleased to have him friendly, but as I told him once, he is 'a hard master.' I only hope he will gain the best information obtainable and be just. I know he will try to be.

This is a horribly long letter. Give my love to Mrs. Gilder.

To E. C. Benedict

Washington, *January* 1, 1897

It is nearly one o'clock A.M. and I have had a hard day — among other things having shaken hands with about seven thousand people. I do not feel that I ought to go to bed, however, without thanking you for your very kind and interesting letter.

I am better satisfied with my last message than with any other that I have ever written. What I wrote about trusts and combinations was prepared with great care to avoid misconception, and I am convinced that the growth and operation of such as are specified should be guarded against to the end that the passion and prejudice which have lately shown such a threatening front should not be given unnecessary aid to activity and mischief. I have no idea that we will disagree on that point.

You have, from intimations I have given you and otherwise, a better appreciation of my condition than any other man, I think. I appreciate that my day for earning money is past — at least that is the way I consider the subject — and I am a little perplexed to know just how I am to secure a sure and safe income to meet the expense of living in a way which has been heretofore permitted by my earnings and which my situation towards the American people seems to demand. I am not afraid of the attempt and I ask no quarter, but the fact that in the course of nature a young family may be left dependent on my present care and economy cannot, of course, be banished from my mind. I only state this to you for the purpose of accounting for the bother I have caused you sometimes in asking your advice and seeking your aid in my affairs.

You speak of an investment you lately made and say you were thinking of me at the time and that I can help myself to some of it. I see it has risen in price since then and of course I ought not after my delay to avail myself of your offer. I confess I have been thinking about bonds and income by way of interest, but as I said in my former letter I am willing to abide by your judgment and will do whatever you suggest, or will keep what I have to invest to a more convenient season. I understand perfectly how difficult it is to make a good guess in such times as these and such as are likely to stay with us.

I beg of you, my dear Commodore, not to be bothered with my little affairs, but if you do anything for me and want money please let me know just how much. I am very green in all those things.

To RICHARD WATSON GILDER

Washington, *January* 16, 1897

I enclose the slip you kindly sent for my perusal. I like it and am glad that you have kept so well within bounds.

Of course you know what my desire would be in regard to biography, etc. I have been so prodded by public duty for a number of years past that I have had no opportunity to look after the preservation of anything that might be useful in writing history. 'Things done are won, but joy's full soul lies in the doing,' has perforce been the motto over my mantel. It is late to gather things, but I thank you for your hint and will as far as possible act upon it.

I feel in this matter as I do in regard to my White House portrait. I am not anxious to have one on exhibition, but if it is insisted on I naturally would be glad to be represented in a way that would be recognizable. One of the last things I shall do will be to put the Eastman Johnson portrait in the garret entirely out of sight.

To E. C. BENEDICT

Washington, *January* 31, 1897

I enclose you check for $6412.50 in payment of the balance due you on our last transaction, excepting interest, which if I should attempt to adjust I would probably get astray. That can be adjusted hereafter, I suppose. There has a thing occurred within the last day or two which will raise the price of Northern Pacific securities. I believe they have appreciated some under suspicion that something might or had happened, which is undoubtedly an accomplished fact.

It seemed good to see you all on Friday night and I am now glad I went to the Doctor's show — though it did seem a dreadfully hard thing to do. No living human being could have induced me to undertake it but the Doctor — or you. You were good enough to speak of the Florida trip — a thing which I did not think you had kept in mind. I am inclined to start on inauguration day for a duck hunt in Southern waters, to be gone a week or ten days. That is the only expedition I have really planned, though a gentleman has insisted that I shall go to Monroe, Michigan, and shoot with him in the latter part of March. And then Jefferson and I have talked a good deal about fishing together for trout on the Cape early in the season — April, I believe.

We propose now to get well settled in Princeton before the 4th of March. In fact, I think the wife and babies will be actually living there and that Mrs. Cleveland will return here a few days before the curtain falls to be on the stage in the last scene. Immediately after the new President is sworn in, I want to leave on my trip, and perhaps at an earlier hour in the day she will go to the Princeton house *for good*. Now you know I want to do anything you plan for me, but I insist that you shall not put yourself out on my account or change any plans to please me.

To SECRETARY RICHARD OLNEY

Washington, *February* 6, 1897

I can't get it out of my head that it would be a good thing if you would ask Senator Hill to call on you either at your house or office between now and Monday noon and talk with him about the arbitration treaty. I suppose he still wants to be in a position to say he has not conferred with me. This leads me to suggest that you see him instead of doing it myself.

I had a despatch a day or two ago from Dr. Shakespeare, who attended the Paris health conference for us. He is now in Europe and intimated that he would like to attend the Florence conference as our representative. I don't care much whether we are represented there or not, but Shakespeare would be a first-rate man to go.

To GEORGE CARY EGGLESTON [1]

Washington, *February* 14, 1897

Your letter enclosing the interview you manufactured from the conversation (ostensibly on public business) which I had with you a few days ago is received. I should not notice either the letter or the publication except to guard against any inference which you or others might seek to gain from my silence.

[1] Well-known author, at this time editorial writer for the New York *World*.

You gained access to me upon the theory that you desired to confer upon a subject pertaining to executive duty, in which you were personally interested. I was more willing to see you because I knew something of you before you made your present editorial connection and believed you to be a gentleman. In the course of our conversation you took pains to assure me that you had not come with any idea of a newspaper interview.

I hardly need to add that when I saw the published account you gave, in a twisted and colored form, of our conversation, I was astonished and indignant. Nothing could have been more disreputable and ill-bred. There is a slight compensation in the fact that I shall not need another lesson to guard me against such an imposition in the future.

To SECRETARY RICHARD OLNEY

Washington, *February* 28, 1897

Coudert is at the Arlington and has a case in the Supreme Court to-morrow.[1] I have written to him asking if he will call tonight between 8 P.M. and 2 A.M. If I get his answer soon, I will write you further. It might be well for you to drop in sometime this evening if you do not hear. I like the Dickinson suggestion the best and perhaps we could get him here by telegraph tomorrow. If we conclude to do that, we can get along with Coudert by consulting him generally on the subjects without asking him to go.

If possible, we certainly should designate the man and not *embarrass our successors* with it.

How would it do to ask the Spanish Minister to have the beginning of the investigation postponed till we are prepared to appear?

To A. B. FARQUHAR

Washington, *March* 3, 1897

I have seen a copy of your 'reminiscences,' and as a last request before I leave my office, I have to ask you that you do not publish the paper.[2] There is too much personal friendliness in it, and I am quite sure occasion would be made to unpleasantly attack both of us.

---

[1] Cleveland, who had lost faith in Consul-General Fitzhugh Lee, wished the eminent lawyer Frederic R. Coudert to go to Havana on a special mission of conciliation.

[2] Probably one of the principal reasons why Cleveland wished Farquhar's article suppressed lay in its gross inaccuracies. It saw the light in *Harper's Weekly* immediately after Cleveland's death.

To NATHAN STRAUS

Washington, *March* 3, 1897

I am just leaving for the Capitol where I am to relinquish my office. I write this last of my communications while in public life, to say to you that I shall never fail to remember and gratefully appreciate the many acts of friendliness and kindness which I have received from you and to express the sincere wish for your future prosperity and happiness.

XV

WHILE REPUBLIC TURNED TOWARD EMPIRE

CLEVELAND, greatly pleased by the reception he had been given at Princeton in the autumn of 1896, and disliking to take his three small daughters to a large city, secretly purchased a house in the university town shortly before his term expired. Mrs. Cleveland put it in order while he made a short fishing trip along the Southern coast just after March 4, 1897. He quickly took a happy and prominent place in the life of Princeton. Various members of the faculty, notably Andrew F. West and John Finley, came to be numbered among his closest friends; he accepted an honorary degree in 1897, and was prominent on nearly all university occasions thereafter; and he was held in great esteem by the students. On October 15, 1901, he became a trustee of the university, and till his death performed the duties of the post with earnestness and fidelity. His influence, usually conservative in nature, was felt on all matters of university policy. In 1899 an alumnus founded the Henry Stafford Little Lectureship on Public Affairs, which Cleveland immediately accepted, delivering in 1900 his first two lectures — an account of his struggle with the Senate over the Tenure-of-Office issue. The next year he lectured on the Venezuela boundary question, and in 1904 on the Pullman strike. Until after 1900, however, Cleveland showed a strong inclination to keep out of the public gaze. He believed that the general public looked upon him with indifference or hostility; he was completely estranged from the regular Democratic organization, controlled by Bryan and his friends; and he regarded many of the new currents in American life with amazed indignation. The jingoism which swept the country into the Spanish War, and the wave of imperialist feeling which led the majority of Americans to support a policy of overseas expansion, caused him the deepest misgivings. He believed that the McKinley Administration showed lamentable weakness in yielding to the war spirit, and still more lamentable short-sightedness in catering to the demand for new territory. A querulous and critical tone marks many of Cleveland's letters in these years. When Bryan was renominated by the Democrats in 1900 on an anti-imperialism platform, many of the ex-President's former associates supported the Nebraskan. Carlisle and Olney were among those who at least preferred Bryan to McKinley. But Cleveland could not swallow the renewed demand in the Democratic platform for free-silver coinage at 16 to 1, and voted for neither ticket. He found comfort and employment in these years in family life — his first son, Richard, was born in the fall of 1897, and his second, Francis, in the summer of 1903; in fishing and hunting; in legal work, for he sometimes acted as consultant in important cases; and in increasingly numerous contributions to magazines.

To E. C. Benedict

Princeton, *March* 19, 1897

I saw my new home for the first time yesterday, having spent more time on my North Carolina trip than I anticipated. I was very lame and exceedingly perplexed during the last week of my stay in Washington and postponed replying to your letter until I reached here, thinking I could do it more satisfactorily. So I attempt it now in an unsettled house, with plenty of hammering, etc., sounding about me and your letter *not* before me, with all my care to have it constantly at hand.

I am a little afraid I cannot take the Florida trip with you. It don't seem exactly right for me to leave home so soon again and escape all the work of settling. If I went anywhere I ought to go to Buzzards Bay early in April in pursuance of an arrangement to trout-fish with Jefferson at that time. I must be in New York on the 23rd of April and must have a few days to myself before that day. In view of all these things don't you think I had better give up the idea of my joining you on your cruise?...

To Andrew F. West

Princeton, *March* 23, 1897

I have been here almost a week and have not seen you yet. How am I to get on in this way? Unless I see you within a very 'brief period' I shall pull up stakes and clear out.

To Richard Watson Gilder

Princeton, *March* 23, 1897

I want to see you — a little especially. Why cannot you come and spend Sunday or at least Sunday night with me? I shall be out Saturday evening, but that will make no difference, for perhaps you would go with me. I am to attend the Nassau Club for the first time after my election to membership. You can take the five o'clock train from New York either Saturday or Sunday and return as early or late the next morning as you like or you may leave in the evening. Telegraph me if you can come, and if you can come when you will leave New York.

To E. C. BENEDICT

Princeton, *April* 2, 1897

I discovered after you left yesterday that you had not taken with you a 'perfect wealth' of fine cigars which you brought. I don't think you can afford that on $2 winnings. If, however, you intended to leave them, I thank you most sincerely. If not, I will send them to you by express. We got the pony out of the cars and on *terra firma* with some difficulty, and today has been pony day here.

To CHARLES S. FAIRCHILD

Princeton, *April* 2, 1897

Yours of March 30 is received. I am perfectly willing to say something at the dinner on the 24th if I can do any good in that way. The matter of the limitation of speeches which you suggest is in my opinion absolutely essential and ought to be strongly insisted on unless you are willing to go well into Sunday. I believe I can deliver what I have to say in fifteen minutes at most. Carlisle writes me he is going and I suggest that some latitude be given him.

I think 'Present Problems' is as good as anything for me to wrestle with, but to tell you the truth I am going to find it difficult, I am afraid, to be prudent and say just what I would like to say. I am very much disgusted with the Silver-Democratic leaders and am not inclined to credit them with sincerity or convictions. I am near the point of believing them to be conspirators and traitors and, in their relations with the honest masses, as confidence sharks and swindlers.

I don't suppose that the diners will all be Democrats and so a man can't cuss both parties as at present controlled, and yet it is not perfectly easy to see how a Democrat can condemn his party organization and steer clear of being struck in the face with the suggestion that the way out is to act with the Republican party. But we will have to get along with it somehow.

To RICHARD OLNEY

Princeton, *April* 6, 1897

I have thought many times lately that about the most pleasant thing that could occur to me would be a good chat with you, and a sort of comparison of notes upon the course of those things which, thank God! we have not now to manage.

I have been a little amused at the cackling over eggs that were substantially in the nest before we left the scene, like the release of Americans in Cuba, etc., but have been on the whole much gratified by the apparent conviction among the people that the new Administration after all could find but little to amend. You know what I hope will be the result of the Senate's tomfoolery in the arbitration treaty business. I am satisfied I can indulge in the hope I have expressed to you without the least unpatriotic feeling, and I do want this Senate to get the hot end of the poker as long as present influences control it.

We are pretty well settled here and have a very homelike home. I wish you could see it and its occupants about this time or a little later when the grass and leaves are more advanced. It looks quite like spring here already and the last few days have advanced matters very much indeed. If you should be called to New York, it would be very easy for you to come to us. It's only a matter of about an hour and a half. Thus far I have not had the season of leisure which I thought would immediately come to me here; but I expect it is not far off.

I see from the Baltimore *Sun* that Mrs. Olney is getting ready to join you. Upon this I extend my hearty congratulations. If you can have any fun with my catboat *Ruth* this summer at Falmouth, I wish you'd let me know. I should be dreadfully pleased to hear from you.

To Richard Watson Gilder

Princeton, *April* 13, 1897

I want to thank you for sending me the volume of poems, *For the Country*. I have read them with much profit, and have derived from them not a little wholesome inspiration. You know I am not very demonstrative in such matters, but I must tell you how these poems have supplemented and increased my appreciation of your useful and valuable life and work. I read last night the address delivered at the Lowell Commemoration in Boston last February, and was delighted to see that a beautiful oration closed with noble words written by you. I suppose you have seen the oration of which I speak, delivered by Professor James Taft Hatfield. You see I have accepted the invitation to attend the Grant Monument exercises. I am inclined to think I shall not leave New York after the Reform Club dinner, until the other affair takes place. Of course I would be pleased to be under your charge on the 27th, but feel that I must consider myself absolutely subject to the orders of those having the engagements in hand.

To RICHARD OLNEY

Princeton, *April* 14, 1897

I was delighted to receive your letter, and of course we are much pleased with that portion of it which encourages us in the hope that we may soon see you. I expect to go to New York a week from Saturday (the 24th) to attend a dinner of the Reform Club in the evening. I suppose I must also attend the Grant Monument ceremonies on the 27th, the next Tuesday I shall probably remain in New York from the 24th to the 27th. On that day or the next I may go in Mr. Benedict's yacht up to Gray Gables for a day or two. Carlisle and Wilson [1] will be at the dinner and one or both of them may possibly go in the yacht with me if I go.

Mrs. Cleveland now expects to join me in New York on Monday the 26th and stay over Tuesday, I suppose — or perhaps returning Thursday afternoon. I don't know where we shall stop — perhaps at Benedict's, 10 West 51st Street. If these plans are carried out there will be, you see, no trouble in our meeting in New York even if your view of our new home should be postponed for a short time.

Carlisle spent a day or two with me last week and I enjoyed his visit very much. What an able good man he is! I honestly believe I am feeling the need of mental rest more and more as time goes on. I am thinking a little of something to say at the dinner, and it's like pulling teeth to get anything together.

I congratulate you on the tariff on cranberries. The Dingley bill has not done anything for me yet and therefore I am still 'agin it.'

I was surprised to read Roosevelt's letter, though you will remember I expressed some fear that B—— might find out about the correspondence. I guess the world will move on.

To E. C. BENEDICT

Princeton, *April* 16, 1897

Yours of the 13th is at hand.... Mr. Carlisle will be in the city to attend the dinner and will remain until Grant Day. Mr. W. L. Wilson will be at the dinner, but I do not know whether he will remain over or not. Mr.

[1] Carlisle had returned to the practice of law in Washington and New York; William L. Wilson had become president of Washington and Lee University.

Olney will be in New York on the 26th and 27th to see his wife on shipboard for a trip abroad.

I am ashamed to confess it, but the truth is, I am not getting the rest and freedom I crave, and somehow my mental works and nerves are not in first-class condition. It would be very nice if after the Grant ceremonies you could take Olney, Carlisle, and me on board the *Oneida* for a trip to Gray Gables. If Olney went he would probably remain in Massachusetts and the remainder of the party could saunter back as we pleased. I have a notion that Carlisle would like to go, though of course I have not assumed to present the matter to him in the shape of an invitation. I beg you not to consider this suggestion important enough to make any change in other plans you have in contemplation.

To JOSEPH JEFFERSON

On Board the *Oneida*, *May* 3, 1897

At a council of war just held, my friends have decided that they had better stay by the ship and perhaps fish for tautog. I will, however, go with you and will meet you at 'the Corners' at 9 o'clock tomorrow morning unless you think an earlier start is necessary. I will leave Brad at home to wait on the tautog fishermen. If you have two landing nets you had better take them, though I have one somewhere. I may not, however, be able to find it. My other tackle I hope to find or put in commission.

To WILLIAM GORHAM RICE

Princeton, *May* 17, 1897

My daughter Ruth is in the midst of so much that engrosses her mind and hands that she finds it difficult to command sufficient time to thank you for the wood-sawyer you kindly sent to her. I have half a notion, too, that she has a slight lack of confidence in her penmanship.

At any rate, she has this moment enlisted me in her service and bids me thank you and to say to you that when the saw-man came it was a little hurt but not bad, and that she fixed it and now it goes all right. Her mother has smuggled it out of sight during the last day or two and when it again appears it will be quite fresh and new again. Mrs. Cleveland and I, with all kind wishes to you and Mrs. Rice, thank you sincerely for thus remembering our little daughter.

To RICHARD OLNEY

Princeton, *May* 17, 1897

I have just read your letter. Scruggs has been here with an unsealed letter to me from President Crespo of Venezuela [1] offering to me and asking me to accept the position of counsel for his country in the arbitration. Mr. Scruggs *approves* the suggestion and would *concede* me first place. Of course the thing is ridiculous, but I gravely told him that while at first sight my judgment was against it, I would consider the matter. I did this to get time to talk with you about the phases that cropped out during my talk with Crespo's envoy. He came with this letter open and unsealed and furnished me with a translation of it — I am quite sure he said made by himself.

He said he had consulted with the Venezuela Government about counsel in addition to me and that he had suggested Senator Morgan, Phelps, and Edmunds. These things and others made me fear that perhaps he really had influence with our friends and that there might be danger of their going into the arbitration with a misfitting outfit. I am not sure that you would feel that you ought to bother at all with any further steps in the matter, but if you should desire to do anything that may be properly done to avoid a false step now, I thought you ought to know what I have here written. I told Mr. Scruggs that I would quite likely deem it best to communicate my decision directly to President Crespo, but I would at once inform him (Scruggs) what my conclusion was.

I hate to see a botch made of it now and I don't know as we can or ought to do anything. I don't know about Andrade as well as you do, but except in clear cases I think they will all stand watching....

To PRESIDENT JOAQUIN CRESPO

Princeton, *May* 20, 1897

I have received your letter sent to me by the hand of Mr. Scruggs, and beg to assure you that I fully appreciate the confidence and friendliness exhibited by your request that I should act as counsel for Venezuela in the arbitration proceedings to settle the boundary dispute between your country and Great Britain.

---

[1] General Joaquin Crespo had in 1892 become virtual dictator of Venezuela. He had been ruler of the country when in April, 1895, the Venezuelan authorities had arrested two British police inspectors, and through its minister in Washington, Andrade, had pressed Cleveland to bring the boundary question to an issue. Cleveland therefore knew a good deal regarding him.

I have considered the subject in all its phases, and have determined to ask you to permit me to decline your very flattering offer. In reaching this conclusion I have been greatly influenced by the belief, that in view of all the conditions, I could not be as useful to the interest of Venezuela in the capacity mentioned as another might be. I trust my extreme desire that the Venezuelan cause may not lack the best possible presentation will excuse the suggestion that I would not for a moment regard myself so well qualified for the important duty as such distinguished advocates among my countrymen as Mr. Choate, Mr. Coudert, or Mr. ex-Senator Edmunds.

To RICHARD OLNEY

Princeton, *June* 19, 1897

You needn't put on any airs because you are settled on Cape Cod. I'll open up there myself in a few days — and I've got a degree that I'm going to bring with me. There may be 'others' — I presume there are — but there are no rivals of my gown, hood, and cap; and the Latin investiture of the degree was to my certain knowledge faultless. I wonder if Brad and Jim Jones ought not to have some sort of a degree, so that you and I might feel a little more at ease with them.

The Cleveland caravan starts in sections, beginning tomorrow and ending with a last detachment Tuesday or Wednesday. Mrs. Cleveland and the children, etc., will probably arrive at Gray Gables Wednesday or Thursday by yacht and I hope to arrive there by the same conveyance a day or two afterwards. The railroad people very kindly say they will stop trains at Gray Gables this summer for my family and visiting or departing friends.

Did you ever see such a preposterous thing as the Hawaiian business? The papers I read are most strongly opposed to it, and there ought to be soberness and decency enough in the Senate to save us from launching upon the dangerous policy which is foreshadowed by the pending treaty; but I am prepared for almost anything.

Mr. Bayard spent last Sunday night with me. Our recent negotiations with Great Britain were only once referred to in the most casual way, strangely enough, and our (mostly *his*) talk was entirely free from any embarrassment.

To PAUL KERSH

Gray Gables, *June 29,* 1897

My love of true Democracy is so intense, and my belief in the necessity of its supremacy to the welfare of the country is so clear, that I cannot fail to sympathize with every effort to save the principles of my party from threatened abandonment. I believe the very existence of true Democracy, as an agency of good to the American people, is in the hands of those who are willing to be guided by the declaration of principles announced by the National Democratic party.[1] It is a high mission to thus have in keeping the life and usefulness of the party which has deserved so well of our countrymen, and the important consideration involved should surely stimulate to patriotic effort. The work before us rises above partisan triumphs and its rewards. The question is, Are we doing our duty to our country and to the principles of our party? No success worth the name can be reached except by the path of principle. I hope the National Democrats of Iowa will not fail to exhibit to their fellows in every State the bright light of true Democracy.

To E. C. BENEDICT

Gray Gables, *July* 18, 1897

Your letter was duly received and I thank you for the correction of the account so much in my favor.

I see you have been having a 'season of weather' since I last saw you. We also had two days and more of steady gale, but it has cleared off very nicely and Brad and I have resumed our piscatorial duties. The squeteague are in. I caught fifteen yesterday.

We are to have a day at them Wednesday with the Jeffersons [2] and Mr. Wood of Boston and perhaps ex-Postmaster-General Wilson. I hope you will come up soon and try them. I'd like it just as well if you and I could make the party and perhaps one or two more. You needn't wait for the new yacht — the *Oneida* is good enough for me. I had a letter from a man a day or two ago saying the *Hermione* — the Henry L. Pierce yacht — could be bought for $55,000. I shall not buy her, but she is a beauty.

By the way, talking of yachts — I am having the devil's own time with my launch. I have had but one satisfactory time with her since I came and that was the day after I arrived when Brad ran her. I get so

[1] That is, the Gold Democrats.
[2] Joseph Jefferson and his son Charles.

cursed mad every time I go out that I almost swear I'll never go in her again. I think I would lay her up if I had not loaned my catboat to Olney for the summer. It needs something done to it that the boy they sent up don't know enough to do. He says himself that an expert ought to overhaul it and that he has written the company to that effect. He had only been in the shop three weeks, is evidently afraid to take the machine apart, and I am *afraid* don't know much about running the boat. It goes pretty well after it starts, but it's enough to make a man jump overboard to see this young man start it. I think he is a nice fellow and perhaps could get along if he had a little instruction about this particular boat.

I am very certain that no one would buy any such a boat if all he knew about them was derived from the action of mine.

To E. C. BENEDICT

Gray Gables, *July* 22, 1897

I enclose you a check for $10,375 as advised by your letter of the 20th instant. I am very much pleased to see that the banks are taking hold of the reserve matter in a patriotic way and moving in a definite direction that will lead to a better condition of confidence. Somehow I cannot yield to fright and my faith in the saving common sense of the people will not permit me to suppose that our finances are to be undermined. I have ten or fifteen thousand dollars now that I would like to invest if I knew where to put it.

We caught eighteen squeteague today. I wish you would give me an intimation in advance of the time you will come up so that I can be at home. With love to all and many thanks for the valuable and timely present which demonstrates your extreme friendliness...

To JOSEPH JEFFERSON

Gray Gables, *July* 31, 1897

I have an idea that this afternoon the squeteague will be on the alert looking for shrimp and such food. At any rate, I mean to test the question and shall start from here *at half-past one* P.M. for the grounds — or rather the waters — where they *may* be found. Will you join me? If Charley is still with you I would be very glad to have him come too.

The fishing is frequently the best on the last of the incoming tide. If we wait for that, it will be a little late when we return, and I hope you will dine with us. Of course, however, we can discontinue fishing when we see fit. I speak of this matter so that if you think you will want to fish a *little late*, there will be no anxiety at home on your account. Please send a verbal answer by the bearer of this.

To DANIEL S. LAMONT

Gray Gables, *August* 1, 1897

Your letter enclosing Mr. Chamberlain's came last night.[1] I have written Mr. Chamberlain thanking him for his work on the *Public Papers*. They arrived at Princeton a day or two after I left and remain there unpacked. I have never seen a copy and do not expect to until our vacation is over about the first of October. Even then there will be but little need of unpacking them, as but few people care for that sort of literature in these days. As far as I can see, the tendency at present is to enjoy being humbugged by the Administration now in power and to forget or decry all that was done by the last one. Of all weak milksop things it seems to me the Democratic press, so far as it comes under my observation, is a prize winner.

I am glad you are enjoying the summer so well and heartily commend your good sense in taking a good long well-deserved vacation. I hope, however, you will give Gray Gables a little of it. We are having very good fishing. I had a letter from the Doctor a couple of days ago. He says he is better and he contemplates another visit to us, though he is not very definite as to the time. I expect Captain Evans and Lamberton during the month and I hope Professor West will spend a few days with us.

Secretary Gage [2] called last Wednesday. I think he is a good man — quite frank and outspoken about public matters — and I don't think he would have been much out of place in *our* Cabinet. Will you please remember me affectionately to the Chief Justice? We are all as well as can be, and the entire household send much love to you and yours.

To WILLIAM GORHAM RICE

Gray Gables, *August* 1, 1897

I have received your letter and the accompanying documents and thank you for them. It seems to me there is a very little bit of humbugging

---

[1] Eugene T. Chamberlain, formerly of the staff of the Albany *Argus*, who had served Cleveland loyally in his campaigns, had now compiled his public papers.

[2] Lyman T. Gage of Chicago, Secretary of the Treasury under McKinley.

going on just now in the civil service conduct of the new Administration; but the people and press I suppose like it, and the idea seems to be that this fills the bill.

Your report and what fell from Secretary Gage when I saw him a few days ago satisfies me that this Administration has not sacrificed itself for the cause. He seems to be a frank man and I believe he will do the very best he can....

I am glad you have remained on the Commission. I cannot help speculating on the promptness with which your report would have been presented to the President if it had been made to the Commission prior to the 4th of last March. However, I am not fretting over these things, but am trying to be very modest and quiet and out of everybody's way. I sometimes wonder at the lying and abuse aimed at me, but the days pass with no great disturbance on that account. The account is much more than balanced by the pleasures of a delightful home life, and the love of wife and children. I cannot, of course, forget duty to country and party, but in the councils of both I seem just now to be an unwelcome guest.

To Kope Elias

Gray Gables, *August* 1, 1897

I desire to acknowledge your recent friendly letter and thank you for it. You say the 'advance agent of prosperity has not struck the South.' It seems to me that the people of that locality are doing all they can to bar the gates to that desirable visitor, as long as they persist in attacking every safeguard of enterprise and business activity. Help may come to the South in spite of false and dangerous theories, but I believe a short and safe road to its prosperity will be found in a return to the solid ground of tried and true Democracy.

To Judson Harmon

Gray Gables, *August* 3, 1897

Now that I have you located in such a way as to offer a prospect that a letter from me would reach you and not be unwelcome, I cannot longer refrain from writing you to say how much your letter, received long ago, gratified me and how pleased I was to know that you were regaining your former professional status, after your unprofitable connection with the Cleveland Administration. That Administration seems at present to be so little in the minds of the people and its achievements appear to be so nearly forgotten that I feel like apologizing to all the good and true men who cast in their lot with it.

As usual, you have done the sensible thing in taking a good vacation at the seashore, and I doubt not you and your family are getting a full share of the vigor and recuperation which the sea air affords. I wish you could come down and see us before your vacation ends. We are as well as can be. In fact we do little else but keep well. I have seen less of Olney than usual for the last two weeks and I suppose from that he has business on hand.

Political affairs do not seem to clarify. It seems to me that in Ohio better than anywhere else the bogus Democracy has turned itself up for a sound spanking. The thing that strikes me with amazement is the gullibility of Democratic newspapers and men that want to be sound and yet do not see the mischief and humbug of the Maryland platform. When anything straight, honest, or truly Democratic emanates from Mr. Gorman, neither you nor I will 'be there to see.' I feel very badly over the whole situation. I have made up my mind, however, that I can afford to submit to much misrepresentation and abuse without a murmur, as long as I am absolutely certain that I have done all I could for my country, and all for my party I could do with a clear conscience.

To RICHARD OLNEY

Gray Gables, *August* 12, 1897

I have been waiting what seems to me to be a long time for an excuse to write you. I am not sure that I have a very good one now, but I cannot refrain from sending you the enclosed clipping from the Baltimore *Sun* of yesterday. You have doubtless seen many newspaper comments of a like tenor, but what I send emanates from such a careful, conservative source as to make it quite significant.

Of course you and I are too patriotic to gloat over the condition, and you no doubt feel as much humiliated as I do by the silly exhibition our Government is making in its conduct of foreign affairs. I am willing, however, to confess to enough of the 'old Adam' to feel a little bit of satisfaction in a situation that crowds this bitter dose down the throats of the dirty liars who attempted so hard to decry and depreciate your dignified, decent, and proper management of our foreign relations. The present Administration must soon find that the Executive Department cannot drift through public duty on a wave of applause and adulation and that the day comes when popular tickling and humbug will not do....

To DR. KASSON C. GIBSON

Gray Gables, *August* 24, 1897

Your letter is received and I am glad you are giving yourself a vacation, though sorry we are not to see you at Gray Gables. The knife came also and I have delivered it to Brad with appropriate ceremonies. He is very much pleased with it and asked me to convey to you his thanks. He immediately began to calculate upon a plan to preserve it from damage in salt water and 'keep it true.'

To E. C. BENEDICT

Gray Gables, *August* 30, 1897

I wrote you last evening that I might be able tonight to make a little report on the fishing question here. A friend who had been visiting me and I breakfasted at half-past six this morning and started for the fishing grounds immediately afterwards. We fished all day and had disgustingly poor luck. We did capture one big tautog, but our whole catch was so small that I don't want to indulge in that sport for a time to come. It must be that they will begin again, but until conditions change I can promise nothing in the fishing line here. In view of the situation as I have stated it and the further fact that we are likely to have guests in the very near future, I suggest that about the 15th of September would probably allow better fishing and more freedom to me in testing that question with you, than an earlier date. We shall break up here the last week in September....

To W. J. CURTIS

Gray Gables, *September* 1, 1897

Your letter was received some time ago. I have hesitated in replying to it, because of a disinclination to volunteer advice in the present extraordinary and distressing political situation.

I am, however, a Democrat who refuses to be dismissed from adherence to my party principles, and I am a New Jersey Democrat who ought not to refuse participation in the political counsels of my neighbors. With you and many other good Democrats of our State, I am certain that the platform adopted last year at Chicago utterly fails to represent our party principles and announces a political creed totally at variance with our Democratic teaching. We cannot approve such a platform either as citizens or as intelligent men. Our party is to us something more than a name without meaning, character, or mission; and our fealty to party rests upon something higher and better than an instinct to blindly follow adventurous leadership, heedless of consequences or destination.

The doctrines and conduct we insist upon as truly Democratic are rejected in many localities by those claiming to represent our party organization; and yet there can be no doubt that if Democracy ever again resumes its place as a patriotic, useful, and successful political agency, it must cease to wander and return to the old path, diligently seeking the old landmarks.

In the meantime, those who still hold to the true Democratic faith must staunchly keep their course, and refuse all alluring concessions that mean only faithless surrender. We must not be ashamed to be counted, always insisting on our title of true Democracy, and constantly vindicating said title by our aggressive courage. We should thus labor, patiently awaiting the time when the principles we strive to protect and keep alive will again rally to their support a united, beneficent, and triumphant party.

To Don M. Dickinson

Princeton, *October 20,* 1897

I was very glad to receive your letter written just as your duties in behalf of the Government before the Bering Sea Claims Commission had been discharged. I have not been entirely ignorant of the faithfulness and zeal of your service and I need not tell you how proud and gratified I have been when I have received information of your conduct. I have something on the subject from a quarter that you will greatly appreciate. I will send it to you — but not now. I want to thank you for the complete manner in which you have vindicated the choice of counsel by the last Administration.

We are pretty well settled here again after a delightfully restful summer at Gray Gables. I have just finished a sort of *thing* — I believe it is called an address — which I am to deliver before the college the day after to-morrow. Somehow I am not satisfied with it at all, but it will have to answer, I suppose. Maybe if it is printed in good shape so that your eyes will not be injured by reading it, I will send it to you. It will perhaps indicate how a man falls off after he passes the sixtieth milestone — sometimes. I received a printed brief in the Bering Sea business, but it was in reply to your [plea] and therefore not as plain standing by itself as it might be to one having no facts nor even the brief it replied to, at hand. I read it, however, and saw in it plenty of evidence of hard intelligent work. I am watching the political fracases in New York City and Maryland with a good deal of interest. I am such a political outcast these days that the rôle of looker-on seems quite a natural one; and yet I feel that matters are brewing that may bring decent men into activity again....

To E. C. BENEDICT

Princeton, *October* 31, 1897

Of course we are all happy here in these days. We are happy because we have a child [1] and 'he's a buck, all right'; but not less happy because the mother seems to be getting on so splendidly, and there does not appear an unfavorable thing in the conditions surrounding either mother or child. We have been much pleased with the very numerous and hearty congratulations we have received testifying in a most delightful manner to the kindness of the people and their friendship for us. Your telegram was the most amusing we received, and of course intensely gratifying as proof of sincere and disinterested friendship.

They all say here that the youngster looks like me. That, of course, is all nonsense, but just as soon as his mother is well enough to be about, I should be glad to have your unbiased judgment on that question. A few moments ago, when I told Mrs. Cleveland I intended to write you she bade me especially to give you and your household her love, and to say to Mrs. Benedict how delighted she was with her handsome gifts for the boy.

I received a letter from President Wilson of Washington and Lee University a few days ago in which he spoke in a complimentary way of an address I lately delivered at Princeton. He thought it ought to be illustrated, and among other things said: 'I would put our good friend the Commodore in as one who knows how to "give gifts that exalt humanity."' I repeat this to you so that you can see how appreciative he is.

Our extension is substantially complete. The billiard table is up and the light will be put in tomorrow, I expect. So I am nearly ready for you, with the baby and billiards and of course cribbage.

I must have some money pretty soon, and I suppose I must sell something, though 'I don't know what to discard. I want to keep them all.'

---

[1] Cleveland's son Richard Folsom had just been born.

Chicago Gas seems to be working up again. How would it do when it gets to par or a little above to sell it or at least part of it?

To WILLIAM F. VILAS

Princeton, *November* 8, 1897

I was delighted to receive your exceedingly hearty and friendly letter and thank you most sincerely for your kind wishes for me and my son. He is a strong sturdy little fellow and his mother has been so free from all untoward incidents that she is sitting up today in strength and comfort. I try to be very grateful for all this; and I fully agree with you in your estimate of the infinite distance between the joys and comforts of a happy home and the transient gratification that in best conditions wait upon the honors of official place.

I congratulate you upon the marriage of your son and the satisfaction it brings to you; for I suppose, next to watching the growth and development of our children, their happy settlement in new family selection is cause for parental joy. The thought sometimes comes to me with a tinge of sadness that such a joy may not be in store for me. I do not know, however, why in the midst of all the happiness I now have I should dwell on such thoughts.

Thus far I have no lack of employment. My books and papers are yet in considerable confusion and a most voluminous correspondence gives me plenty to do. Applications to write and to speak are more numerous since I left Washington, I believe, than in all the remainder of my life. I don't know what to make of it, but I have thus far almost invariably declined their requests. The day before yesterday I was applied to for an article to be published in the *North American Review* touching political conditions. I am almost considering whether I can concoct anything in that line that can possibly be of benefit to the country or our party. I hardly think I shall attempt it, but I am very much afraid that the events of last Tuesday will lead the Democracy deeper in the mire of free silver. If it does, I can see nothing in the future but disastrous defeat if not destruction....

To RICHARD OLNEY

Princeton, *November* 11, 1897

I welcomed your letter yesterday right heartily, and it was as good a substitute probably as you could offer for a personal visit, which I hope is postponed only for a short time.

I wish I could write something satisfactory to the ladies of your household touching our new boy. This I cannot do on my own responsibility, for I agree with you that when they count but two weeks as the period of earthly experience, all babies are very much alike, both as regards their looks and conduct. As sort of second-hand information, however, I venture to say that the female members of our household declare that this particular child looks like his father, that he has blue eyes, a finely shaped head, and bids fair to be a very handsome and a very distinguished man. I have no doubt this is all true, because a neighbor lady who was today admitted to a private inspection of the specimen told me he was 'the loveliest thing' she ever saw. We have named him Richard Folsom — my father's first name and my wife's father's last name. Some good friends thought we ought to call him Grover Jr.; but so many people have been bothered by the name Grover, and it has been so knocked about, that I thought it ought to have a rest.

On the whole, I think I am pleased with the results of the election, but I am very blue indeed about the general outlook for our country and our party. I don't see where we are going to land.

I was very much pleased with your speech on Storrow. It is very refreshing to read a statement on such an occasion so true and just and yet not overdrawn and sickish. I am thoroughly disgusted with Hannis Taylor.[1] I'd give a month's salary as President if I was in the White House and he was in Madrid. What a satisfaction it would be to bounce him! It is an aggravating thing to have to put up with his general inefficiency, and find out at last that he is not even a gentleman. Well! He's another of our Southern men of 'high character' who if appointed 'will reflect credit on the Administration.' He wrote me that he intended to come to see me. I hope he will not come.

I see Lee has gone back to Cuba. There's something queer about all that business. How differently the present Administration is treated, though pursuing the same policy as the last. I suppose something will come of it, 'some of these days.'

We are all well. Mrs. Cleveland sits up a good deal....

To RICHARD WATSON GILDER

Princeton, *November 20*, 1897

I have been wanting to write to you ever since the election, but to tell you the truth, I have not known what to write; and I have learned to say

[1] Hannis Taylor of Alabama had been appointed Minister to Madrid by Cleveland in 1893.

nothing when I am in that condition. I see by the papers, however, that you have not worked yourself sick and that you and your co-workers are not extinguished. I am very glad to hear these things.

I have just read something that was sent me by its author which I enclose together with the letter that accompanied it. Your thoughts have probably been so much in the same direction that you may not be as much interested as I was; but to my mind the paper presents the *utility* of art and culture in a new and most useful way. What we need in this country is reconciliation and some common plane of brotherhood between the rich and poor.

The *North American Review* wants me to write an article on the political outlook or something like that, but after pretty full consideration I am nearly at the point of declination. I have not consulted you about it because I have supposed the *Century* would not want anything of that sort from me in any event. I have about made up my mind that just now no very great number of my fellow-citizens care to hear or read what I might say or write. If I can ever do any more good in behalf of my countrymen, I do not think the time is *now*.

Mrs. Cleveland sits by me as I write and sends love to Mrs. Gilder. The 'young fellow' is asleep upstairs. I think, as you say, that we struck the name pretty nearly right, 'grandfather or no grandfather.' There are others.

To RICHARD OLNEY

Princeton, *December* 4, 1897

I am in a little bit of trouble; and as usual in such cases I go to you for help.

I have received an invitation signed by a number of good Boston people, asking me to attend a banquet celebration in honor of the memory of William E. Russell, on his birthday, in January. My invitation is accompanied by the information that you too have been or will be invited.

You know I was exceedingly fond of Russell; and my attachment for him is well known by all his friends in Boston. I don't exactly like to be accused of refusing to encourage a manifestation in his memory. But I am superlatively anxious to avoid as much as is possible and decent all participation in public or semi-public occasions, and I am not entirely satisfied that the conditions justify the local friends of Russell in expecting me to go to Boston to attend this affair. Besides, the invitation is strenuously seconded by President Eliot in a personal letter; and I have a deep and lasting grudge against him. I cannot help suspecting a Harvard boom wherever he appears, and I am an awfully stiff and vociferous Princetonian.

Do you expect to attend this thing? Have you any objection to giving me a little confidential hint of the aspect my relations to the contemplated event assume in your view? You know how fairly you can deal with me; and I am anxious to know from some good frank friend on the spot, whether I can, without too much impropriety, follow my very strong inclination and decline this invitation.

I am expecting to go South on a gunning trip next Friday, the 10th instant, and hope it will be convenient for you to reply to this before I leave. I shall be absent about ten days. We are all well — the boy is beginning to look quite human — and Mrs. Cleveland sends affectionate messages to you and the ladies of your household, and I second them most heartily.

To E. C. BENEDICT
Princeton, *December* 31, 1897

I am the only one out of bed in the house; and in about half an hour the year 1897 will disappear in the darkness of the past. I want to wish you a Happy New Year before I go to bed, and to write you the only letter I have written today. I said to my wife when she bade me 'good night' that 'old '97' had treated us very well and I felt thankful. I want you to know that in thinking of the pleasant things of the year, you are prominently present; and that your kindnesses and those of your household are gratefully remembered; and we fervently hope that the coming year will be full of happiness and comfort for you and all you hold dear....

To RICHARD OLNEY
Princeton, *January* 16, 1898

When I saw a newspaper announcement that you were coming to New York to attend a New England dinner, I managed to get three thoughts in my mind: 1st, That the announcement was probably a lie; 2d, That if not, you contemplated doing a very handsome thing that would not be half appreciated; and 3d, That if you came to New York we should see you here. We did not see you; I looked in vain in such New York newspapers as I saw for an account of your speech and Colonel Lamont told me that you were not called on until one or two o'clock. This disgusted me very much. *Per contra*, however, I heard that the affair was very uninteresting and that the only good speech made was yours.

Of course the pension vetoes could be easily arranged and published. But who would want them after they were published? Perhaps a dozen newspaper men. It might be well, if anything of the kind is done, to trace the vetoed cases and see how many succeeded after veto and in subsequent administrations. But I have an idea that there are not many people who care to hear from me at this time. That's why I stay at home and mope.

I am drifting along, doing no work and yet puttering at something all day long. My wife and little children are sources of constant and increasing comfort and I follow my inclination in refusing all invitations to attend public dinners and to make speeches. I have not reached the point where I can do some reading, but perhaps that will come about in due time.

Ex-Secretary Francis [1] was here today and I had a good visit with him. I have not seen or heard from Carlisle in a good while, but I suppose he is well settled in New York. Bissell came to see me the day before New Year's and seemed very happy and content. Wilson, I imagine, is well satisfied with his work. It is certainly precisely fitted to him. Give our affectionate remembrances to Mrs. Olney and Mrs. Minot and write me as often as you can.

STATEMENT TO ASSOCIATED PRESS

January 24, 1898

I do not believe in discussing matters of this kind [2] as a private citizen. I do not care, however, to be misrepresented. I will, therefore, say that ever since the question of Hawaiian annexation was presented I have been utterly and constantly opposed to it. The first thing I did after my inauguration in March, 1893, was to recall from the Federal Senate an annexation treaty then pending before that body. I regarded, and still

[1] David M. Francis of Missouri, who had succeeded Hoke Smith as Secretary of the Interior when the latter resigned in 1896.

[2] President McKinley had negotiated a treaty for the annexation of Hawaii in June, 1897. It was now before the Senate and was meeting with much opposition. Finally its supporters had to give it up, and annexation was effected by joint resolution in July, 1898. This letter of Cleveland's was evoked by a misleading statement from Senator Morgan, who favored annexation.

regard, the proposed annexation of these islands as not only opposed to our national policy, but as a perversion of our national mission. The mission of our nation is to build up and make a greater country out of what we have, instead of annexing islands.

I did not suppose that there was anyone in public life who misunderstood my position in this matter. It had been said that I was partial to the former Hawaiian monarchy and desired to see it restored in order that I might treat with it for the purpose of annexation. How could I have had such an idea if I regarded annexation as contrary to our national policy? The same answer can be made to the statement that my opposition to Hawaiian annexation was based merely upon dissatisfaction with the treaty pending before the Senate at the time of my second inauguration. I was opposed to annexation as such.

In regard to the Hawaiian monarchy, aside from any question of annexation, and without harboring any previous designs of restoring that monarchy, I investigated the relations of our representatives to its overthrow. This investigation satisfied me that our interference in the revolution of 1893 was disgraceful. I would gladly, therefore, for the sake of our national honor and our country's fair name, have repaired that wrong.

In regard to the Cuban question, my position was fully made known to Congress in the various messages in which the subject was discussed. I was opposed to the recognition of the belligerency of the island, and my position was perfectly well known. Indeed, so very unmistakable were my views on the subject that I was time and again threatened by frenzied men and women with dire calamities to be visited upon myself and children because of what they saw fit to assert was my enmity to the Cuban cause.

My position on all these questions was made perfectly clear in the official documents of the time, and there can be no possible mistake. It is difficult for me to understand Senator Morgan's evidently wrong impressions in regard to my position. Indeed, it is one of the strangest things of these strange times that my position in these matters should be called into question.

To E. C. BENEDICT

Princeton, *February* 6, 1898

It is very unbusinesslike for me to be still in default of an acknowledgment of your last letter and its enclosures. They came duly to hand and were very much appreciated. I have heard you say that a joint account began with two fathers, and quite often ended with none. I must say that I like the joint account which has one careful father and an uncle who wishes it well for what he may make out of it. I, as such uncle, am certainly much obliged to the Dad in this particular instance.

A week or two before the receipt of your letter I received a copy of the circular you sent me in regard to launches. I was looking it through in a listless sort of way, when I saw a picture of a boat that looked familiar; and upon further examination discovered to my great gratification that the motive power most approved by the important builders represented by the pamphlet was alco-vapor. I believe this thing will 'go' some of these days and be profitable. I am thus reminded that if I can afford to keep my launch, I must make early arrangements to secure someone to run the engine. I want some such a man as one of your sailors, that knows or can learn at the shop of the company before the 1st of June how to manage the machine and take care of it, and who besides will be able and *willing* to do any kind of work about my place as in any way related to fishing. I do *not* want any more such boys as I have had.

Can you, through some of your men, put me in the way of the person I need? If I have one who claims to be in any degree an engineer, he will not be willing to do the other things I want of him. So I have made up my mind that I can be best suited by an active intelligent sailor, with wit enough to run and care for the launch, and not too nice or too lazy to do anything else I desire him to do....

To Daniel S. Lamont

Princeton, *February* 7, 1898

I am almost ashamed to bother you with the contents of this letter; but I don't know how I can avoid it and you must bear with me — remembering that we are all called on occasionally to bear each other's burdens.

The trouble is this: An old Buffalo acquaintance (who calls me 'Grover') by the name of J. W. Close has just left me. He has a frog which he has invented, and is naturally most enthusiastic over it, as the best railroad appliance of the kind ever conceived by the brain of man. Of course I know nothing of such things; and I am afraid its mere mention will bore you as much as the constant offer of 'game preserve' land and appurtenances does me. Mr. Close has been a mechanic and worker in iron all his life, I think, and I suppose has some skill in that direction. He goes from here to New York; and I could not do less than promise him that I would write to you and ask you to see him. Will you please do so? If you will I shall be gratified.

To E. C. BENEDICT

Princeton, *February* 9, 1898

Your letter was received an hour or two ago and I hasten to reply and correct an error you have fallen *into* — either by reason of my carelessness or bad penmanship. I intended to say in my letter, that as I had given up my engagement in New York for the 12th, I could *not* accept your kind offer of hospitality. It would never do to disappoint the good people who invited me to attend their meeting, and yet be found in New York or its vicinity visiting friends. Besides, I was visited last night by a rather unwelcome guest in the form of my old enemy the rheumatism who tripped up my right foot. I have taken large doses of medicine today, and though I am much better tonight and have fair prospects of wriggling away from my antagonist's hold, I cannot calculate upon much activity in the next few days.

I am in very active business now — all owing to the farm I bought.[1] I didn't know it was loaded. Every mail brings new applications for employment from gamekeepers, farmers, builders, masons, and landscape gardeners — as well as offers to furnish us with all sorts of wild animals ranging from buffaloes and bears to chipmunks. I have sixty acres of land to sell....

To RICHARD OLNEY

Princeton, *February* 16, 1898

I received your Chamber of Commerce speech promptly and read it with much interest — agreeing entirely with the gentleman who heard it and pronounced it the only redeeming feature of that feast of reason. Your letter which followed the transmission of the speech in some unaccountable way was mislaid here so that I did not see it until a few days ago. The copy of the ex-Minister's letter which you enclosed interested me very much — especially his reference to the Consul-General. If the

[1] Cleveland had purchased a little farm of some sixty acres a few miles from Princeton for use as shooting headquarters.

President stubs his toe on him, as I think he will, he cannot say he ran on it without warning.[1] . . .

It has undoubtedly occurred to you that popular sentiment seems to be vindicating our ideas on certain unfinished public business. All the influence of this Administration appears unable thus far to bring to a successful issue the Hawaiian monstrosity; the delectable Lodge is still howling, apparently to no purpose, for the passage of his immigration bill even in a modified form; if the President's backbone holds out, our Cuban policy will, I believe, be fully justified, our treatment of Union Pacific affairs has been outdone, though in a very questionable way, and the idea seems to have entered into many minds that there are pension frauds. As parties now organized, however, neither side is inclined to even whisper approbation of our work.

Did you ever know of such an asinine exhibition as Gray, Lindsay, and Smith [2] furnished in their votes on the Teller resolution? Poor Gray! I remember he told me months ago that his State would elect another free-silver Senator. I am very tired of good, *weak* fellows who are everybody's friend.

I said a little something in the press about old Morgan's nonsense. It was done just about the time your letter was written and I suppose you had not seen it when you wrote. Mrs. Cleveland sends affectionate remembrances to you and your household — in which I join.

To WILLIAM RANDOLPH HEARST [3]

Princeton, *February* 28, 1898 (telegram)

I decline to allow my sorrow for those who died on the *Maine* to be perverted to an advertising scheme for the New York *Journal*.

To RICHARD OLNEY

Princeton, *March* 4, 1898

As I put down 'March 4' it has somehow a familiar look, and I recall the fact that a year has passed since we laid down the hardest and most

[1] On Inauguration Day in 1897, Cleveland had specifically warned McKinley that he placed little trust in Consul-General Fitzhugh Lee in Havana, yet McKinley had retained him.

[2] George Gray of Delaware, United States Senator 1885–89; William Lindsay of Kentucky, Carlisle's successor in the Senate 1894–1901; James Smith, Jr., of New Jersey, Senator 1893–99.

[3] Hearst had asked permission to add Cleveland's name to a long list of prominent men who had endorsed his popular subscription for a memorial to the sailors lost in the *Maine*.

unappreciated work of our lives. The year has not brought to me the rest and comfort I anticipated, but a glance at the current events of American public life causes me to feel pretty well satisfied with my condition.

I see you delivered a lecture at Harvard after all. I saw editorial comment on it in the New York *Evening Post* and Brooklyn *Eagle* and an extract from the lecture itself in one of them. I do not believe they taken altogether give a very clear idea of what you really said or meant. I wish I could see the lecture entire.

The Iroquois Club of Chicago — a Democratic organization made up of decent people — have had an election of officers lately which involved in the most unequivocal manner the issue of sound money and the gold standard. The election resulted in a decided victory for the right side; and the Club proposes to have a kind of celebration dinner and meeting late in April. They have urged me to attend and speak, and it does not seem to me I ought to refuse. How can I profess to be a believer in sound money and sound Democracy and still be constantly running away when such believers propose to stand up and be counted? I have substantially agreed to attend and the prospect is at this early day a nightmare. It may be the last time I shall talk sound Democracy to Democrats, and I would be glad to say something useful and timely. I cannot bring myself to talk that kind of harmony which is a genteel name for a cowardly abandonment of conscience and conviction and yet I fully appreciate the volume of abuse likely to be aroused if another course is pursued. I would like the benefit of any suggestions you may see fit to make.

Mrs. Cleveland has this moment come in with the New York *Herald* of this morning from which I cut the editorial I have mentioned. They all seem to treat the lecture a little gingerly, as though the writers did not quite know what to make of it. It is evident that it will give rise to comments and discussion that will result, I think, in good.

I wish I could see you. Mr. and Mrs. Carlisle spent Sunday with us. Mrs. Carlisle appeared better than we were prepared to find her and the visit seemed to do them both good, while it gave us much pleasure. We are all well with the unimportant exception of an attack of gout or something of that kind directed at the head of the house. Mrs. Cleveland sends affectionate regards to your household; and so do I.

To RICHARD OLNEY

Princeton, *March 27*, 1898

I only yesterday had an opportunity to read your address, and I assure you I did so with great satisfaction. When you intimate that the late Mr. G. Washington ever said anything that can be outgrown or that by any chance does not fit every phase of our nation's life, why — I just want a little time to consider that proposition. You see that comes pretty near being treasonable and a fellow shivers a little as he puts his foot in.

I was delighted to see that the newspaper attempt to give readers in brief an idea of the address had absurdly miscarried. They had entirely missed its drift and gave no hint of its best features. The touch-up of Eliot on the Venezuelan business was perfectly neat and the isolation of ridiculous tariff legislation and navigation laws was grandly instructive, and ought to be useful. Of course I assume that your ideas of co-opera-tion with other nations will be criticized as leading to entangling rela-tions, etc., but that will be because your real meaning and its limitations are not rightly understood. As one of your fellow-citizens who has been benefited by the address, I thank you for it.

Notwithstanding warlike indications, I cannot rid myself of the belief that war will be averted. There would be infinitely more credit and politi-cal capital in avoiding war when so imminent than to carry it on even well. And then there is Spain's condition and the reflection that may come to her that 'the game is not worth the candle.'

Some of these days I am intending to begin my preparation for my Chicago engagement. I don't know where I'll come out. There's no dearth of things that might be said. I am longing to be at Gray Gables. How do you feel about Falmouth?

To WILLIAM F. VILAS

Princeton, *April 1*, 1898

I am laid up with the rheumatism — or whatever else it may be called. I would give a round sum to see you — first, because I am always glad to see you, and secondly, because I would be glad to talk with you, especially about the Chicago meeting and banquet on the 23d. I received an hour or two ago a letter from Mr. Eddy suggesting that you and I speak in the afternoon and that I would be expected to consume an hour. I im-mediately wrote to him in reply that I would do nothing of the sort and

I supposed perhaps I might fill up forty or forty-five minutes and maybe fifteen at the banquet.

Now I want to tell you how my (alleged) mind is tending so far as I am able to discover — though I have not entered upon the real work of preparation — and then I want you, *as usual*, to help me out by giving me some ground to tumble around on.

My inclination is to attempt, in the best way within my reach, to show that the Chicago platform does not announce Democratic principles and that the organization of the party is not at present engaged in the furtherance of Democratic success: that in point of fact it is being propelled on all lines but those that are truly Democratic. I don't know how I can succeed in making this out in an effective way, but in no event will my attempt involve a thorough or lengthy discussion of any particular heresy, as I think it will be sufficient to characterize them and then show how un-Democratic they are in the light of our party's history and tradition.

I expect a good many adherents of the Chicago platform and the present party organization look upon me as the worst rebel because the most ungrateful; and therefore it has seemed to me that I could thus 'take the bull by the horns' better than others less steeped in guilt. I only fear I cannot get just the right grip on the bull.

What do you think of my plan, and do you not think that if carried out, abundant ground will be left for you and others to indulge in the most valuable work of showing the dangerous and mischievous inherent character of the error which the Democracy is called on to support? Mrs. Cleveland just came in where I write (and swear a little at my ailment) and bade me expressly to give her love to you and Mrs. Vilas. I hope I need not say that mine goes too.

To E. C. BENEDICT

Princeton, *April* 6, 1898

... I am trying very hard to do something in the way of getting my thoughts together for use at Chicago — with indifferent success. If we should be in the midst of war on the 23d, perhaps the thing will be postponed or abandoned, as the greater city celebration has been.

I wish the President would stand fast and persist in following the lead of his own good sense and conscience; but I am afraid he intends to defer and yield to Congress. I cannot yet make myself believe there will be war. If there is and it is based upon present conditions, the time will not be long before there will be an earnest and not altogether successful search by our people for a justification.

I wish you would convey to Mrs. Benedict my sincere thanks for the delicious salmon she sent me. I am enjoying it very much indeed at my breakfasts, but am enjoying much more and at all times the assurance of her thoughtful remembrance.

To E. C. BENEDICT

Princeton, *April* 14, 1898

Your letter of the 11th is received. Yesterday it was determined to postpone the Chicago affair. This action is in accordance with my clear judgment, and I suppose was due largely to my insistence. I am now entirely free until the early days of May and perhaps for a somewhat longer time — depending upon the day finally fixed for my Ohio fishing trip. With these introductory statements, I express with much enthusiasm the hope and expectation that we may see you here soon. I suggest next week as a most opportune and favorable time, and that the particular day can perfectly well be fixed by regarding solely your own convenience.

I am surprised to learn how correctly, according to my standard, you have diagnosed the Americo-Spanish situation. My judgment that we would have no war was predicated upon the anticipation that we would continue to hold a position from which we could honorably and consistently meet any conditions that gave the least promise of a peaceful outcome. It seems to me, however, that we have allowed ourselves to be crowded away from that position and that we face today a sad, afflictive war, that our own people will soon look upon as unprofitable and avoidable, and which, in the sight of contemporaneous judgment and history, may seem unjustifiable. Of course we, the people, have but one thing to do, however, when the storm is upon us, and that is to stand by the action of our Government, and hope that the issue and all its results will be more beneficent than the most conservative contemplate.

Are you putting your yacht in commission? Hoping to hear from you soon and that you will fix an early day for your visit to us...

To DAVID M. FLYNN

Princeton, *May* 2, 1898

I am not sure that I can be of service to you in advising your course in beginning the study of law. I do not know anything about the correspondence system of which you write. Next to entering a law office and studying under the direction of a good practitioner or attending a course of law lectures, I should say the best way to begin is faithfully to apply yourself to the study of such elementary books as Blackstone's *Commentaries* and Kent's *Commentaries*.

To RICHARD WATSON GILDER

Princeton, *May* 23, 1898

... Your fish story is all right. The drawing you send me is conclusive. So is the fact that you have eaten the fish. Certainly a fish could neither be laid on a paper and its outline traced, nor be eaten, unless it was caught. And then, too, I am a fisherman and never, never doubt a fish story that another fisherman tells.

The letter of Mr. Waring presents greater difficulties. It is impossible for me to attend a dinner in New York next Friday. I have a job on hand that I must do at once and I am all cluttered up with lots of things.

The atlas volume of the *Century Dictionary* arrived just as I was leaving home. It is a beautiful and very useful thing and I thank you for it. I don't know why you should be so kind to me, and I do hope this last evidence of your kindness will not only lead to a proper appreciation of your friendship (though I doubt if that could be greater), but will be the means of driving into my head some idea of geography, on which I am in a sad state of benightment. I have already carefully studied it....

To MASTER WILLIAM C. F. FARNELL

Princeton, *May* 24, 1898

In your debate you should present your own argument — not mine or anybody else's. It's all right for you to hunt for facts upon which to base your argument, but the argument should be of your own manufacture. I have no doubt that by writing to some member of Congress whom you may know or whom someone else may interest in you, you could obtain some speech lately made in Congress against the increase of the navy that might contain helpful facts. Representative Holman of Indiana,[1] now deceased, made many such speeches.

To RICHARD WATSON GILDER

Princeton, *June 20*, 1898

Your letter has just arrived. We are in the pangs of closing up and preparing to leave day after tomorrow morning. In the meantime there's that miserable Lawrenceville business for tomorrow.

You are as kind as you can be about the book matter; but I'm agin you. No one wants to read anything from me in these days, and I think I am 'the smartest man in America' to root out the truth in that regard in opposition to the opinions of my friends who generally know a great deal more than I do.

The Self-Made Man, you know, was published in book form by or through the solicitation of your friend Mr. Dole. As far as I can learn, it has sold very poorly indeed — and so would any other book made up of my writings. I think perhaps I have written some things worth reading, but that is not to the purpose. The firm that Mr. Dole was acting for (I can't think of the name) copyrighted *The Self-Made Man*.

The talk I am to give the Lawrenceville boys tomorrow is constructed with the idea of suggesting to them some reflections which I hope may be useful — that's my entire purpose. I don't know whether the thing is good or not, but my wife says it is. At any rate, it is a comfort to me in one way. It is probably the last of that sort of work that I shall bother with. I have not been applied to from any direction for an advance copy for publication....

To RICHARD OLNEY

Gray Gables, *July 8*, 1898

It was very good of you to call the other day and I feel that it was very bad of me to be away from home. I hope you will try again soon and that if possible you will give me a hint of your coming. I am such an idle loafer. We receive news today that trains are to stop at Gray Gables to accommodate us and those coming to us or leaving us. So you can come and go on any train passing our way.

I am very much saddened by this new affliction to poor Carlisle — the

[1] William S. Holman of Indiana, a Democratic member of Congress for thirty years between 1859 and 1895, and known as a Treasury watchdog.

death of his remaining son and child. He certainly is having his full share of sorrow. I hope to have him here during the summer.

Hawaii is ours. As I look back upon the first steps in this miserable business, I am ashamed of the whole affair. However, I know of nobody who can stand it better than I. That's one way of looking at it — and perhaps as comfortable, and as good a way as any other.

To RICHARD WATSON GILDER

Gray Gables, *July* 23, 1898

Thanks for the new 'spinner.' It strikes me as a killing device; and I am sure everything is fair against such a mean, tricky fish as a black bass. I am a little afraid that parts of the machine are too finely and delicately constructed to survive unimpaired a tough struggle with a vigorous bass; but I am going to a pond this afternoon where I know there are large fish and perhaps shall have the good fortune to test this matter.

Professor West has been here with us for a few days, but intends to leave next Tuesday.

Mrs. Cleveland just came in my door from her salt bath and expressly bids me to give her love to you and Mrs. Gilder, and I put mine in with it.

I hope you will drift this way during the summer. By the way, how pleasant days fly. Mrs. Cleveland quite startled me today by suggesting that we had been here within a day or two of four weeks.

To JUDSON HARMON

Gray Gables, *July* 24, 1898

I thank you heartily for sending me a copy of your address before the Ohio Bar Association. I had seen pretty full extracts from it published in the newspapers, but I enjoyed all the more the opportunity to read more of it. I want to congratulate you with all my heart upon your presentation of a matter of the highest importance to our country in a masterly way, and upon your recognition that 'one's duty to his country-men is to give warning of danger when he believes he detects its approach.'

Have you seen Wilson's address somewhat in the same direction delivered on Founders' Day (July 1, I believe) at the Chicago University? Carlisle writes me that something from him of the same kind will appear in *Harper's Magazine* for August. So with my little drive at the thing in my talk at Lawrenceville on the 21st of June, I think the last Administration is pretty near right — as usual.

I am going down to fish with Olney tomorrow. I have not seen him for a long time, but he wrote me some time ago that imperialism had gone far in advance of what he said in his address at Harvard. This whole thing is very clear to me and very sad too. By the time disgust for the rascally Cubans becomes more general and death in battle and by disease has made thousands of American households dark, I shall be prepared for a revulsion of feeling that will start the general and ominous inquiry as to the justification and necessity of this war and as to the consistency of its prosecution with its declared purposes. We should all wish that this may be otherwise; but can we confidently expect it?

We are all well and enjoying our stay here to the utmost. Are you not coming in our direction this summer? Of course I need not tell you how glad we should be to see you.

To E. C. BENEDICT

Gray Gables, *July* 24, 1898

I received a day or two ago a notice that my application for government bonds had been refused — also a check for $200 as a return for my deposit. I sent the entire batch to your firm today. Judging by what I see in the papers, it does not seem to me that you are likely to fare any better than I. If you don't, what is to be done with me?

I may fail on bonds, but I want you to understand I do not fail on squeteague. On Friday Professor West and I started early and began fishing at the four buoys at 8:30 A.M. At 10:30 we had nine fine fish and the tide turned. As it was too early to go home, we went over to the Neck (after trying Abial's with poor success) and attempted to catch a few bottom-fish. They acted very badly, and as it got to be about one o'clock and our bait nearly gone, we were about to start home when Brad said he saw a squeteague break water. Of course that was absurd with the tide running out, fast, and at a place never suspected of squeteaguishness. He, however, put over a float and a chug and in two or three minutes landed a good one. Then we went at it in earnest and landed fourteen in less time than I ever caught the same number. I don't know whether the prevalence of these fish there under the conditions named was accidental or whether it is an habitual thing. If the latter, it is a mighty good joke on you and me and all of us who have been waiting about there for bottom-fish that would not bite. In a day or two we shall see what it all means. The next time you come up perhaps we will have made some progress in developing the best fishing here. If squeteague can learn this sort of a game, then why not bluefish and striped bass?

We go tomorrow to Falmouth to fish with Mr. Olney. How did you get through the fog last Wednesday night? It was thick in here early the next morning....

To E. C. BENEDICT

Gray Gables, *July* 28, 1898

I received your letter last evening when I came home from a bass pond and I telegraphed you this morning that I could not go to Barnegat. The fact is I have so much to do here, and so many good friends come to see me here, that it is difficult to get away. Then, too, for me to go to Barnegat seems like going back home to 'go a-fishing.' Last of all, I had a letter from Huntington this evening, and like a sensible man and a good fellow, he confesses that he does not feel like urging me to take the trip in present conditions....

I wrote Wilson a short time ago and invited him to visit us. A letter from him tonight indicates that he will come the latter part of next week. He is with Isidor Straus at West End, New Jersey. I suppose you cannot turn your face in this direction before the 8th or 9th of August. I would, of course, be glad to see you then or any other time; and if you could come about the day I indicate you would do a very handsome and kind thing if you would indicate it to Wilson (Honorable William L.) at the address I have given, and offer to bring him up. I give you this hint because I know how much you admire Mr. Wilson and because I know how much good it would do him. I understand from his letter that the time of his coming is not important to him. I said something in my letter to him about the Maine trip, but on reflection I do not see how I can well go. I believe he would be glad to entertain such a proposition and I wish he and Carlisle could go.

The Princeton assessor rather insists upon my making a regular return and I shall do so.

To DON M. DICKINSON

Gray Gables, *July* 31, 1898

It has been a long time since I have heard from you and I have determined to make an epistolary attack upon you, hoping thereby to hear something directly from you.... Public affairs and politics have gained such a start of me that I despair of catching up with the procession; and yet I am intensely interested in both. I do not know where we are tending, but it seems to me there is a general cutting loose and that conservatism is at a great discount. It would, however, be strange, I think, if the sober second thought and patriotic common sense of our countrymen did not assert themselves in time to avoid disaster....

To PROFESSOR JOHN GRIER HIBBEN

Gray Gables, *September* 22, 1898

I want to thank you for your two letters and the information you have furnished me concerning the farm and Mr. Vroom. I am the more appreciative of the latter, because I can get next to nothing from Mr. Vroom himself, except twaddle about his school and irrelevant protestations of his good motives. As nearly as I can guess from what he writes, he expects to derive what he needs for the purposes of his school from charitable donations. This phase of the subject adds to my irritation and annoyance. I am determined that *he* shall not maintain a farm school for boys on the farm while it belongs to me. I have offered to give him five hundred dollars if he will vacate the place with every vestige of his school. If he accepts this offer he will do a wise thing and I shall be properly punished for my foolishness in expecting a thoroughly impractical man to satisfactorily manage a farm.

I leave this unpleasant topic, however, to express my thanks for the delicious tobacco you sent me — which I am at this very moment enjoying. I think it suits me better than any I have ever smoked; and I am willing to concede that though I can *perhaps* land a six-pounder better than you, I am not 'in it' with you when it comes to the selection of smoking tobacco.

We have not had exceptionally good luck in fishing since you left us, though we have caught some good ones — such as I very much hoped would attack you. We have given the Bay fishing a rest lately, but I expect an old fishing comrade here tomorrow or Saturday when the contest will be renewed with vigor and determination....

To JOHN G. CARLISLE

Princeton, *October* 21, 1898

Your letter is just received. I have no reason to believe that I shall be in New York soon. Indeed, I do not contemplate going there at any particular time.

I would like to talk with you a few moments very much indeed. I am invited to preside at a Democratic meeting in Trenton. They have made a good platform and I am told have nominated first-rate candidates. The campaign is run on State issues exclusively. I consider what has been done by the New Jersey Democracy as a long step toward political sanity and I am not sure that I ought not to do anything I can do to aid in party harmony on proper lines. But there's one thing I don't exactly hanker after. The election of a majority of Democratic members to the Legislature means the selection of the present Democratic United States Senator for another term.

What do you think of the suggestion of my presiding at this meeting? I don't really want to do it, and I intimated that my interference might do more harm than good. It may be that the project will be abandoned. If it is not, I rather hate to appear to shirk political duty. Cannot you drop me a line as soon as convenient giving me a hint as to how the thing strikes you? [1]

I cannot tell you how much I was gratified with your 'expansion' article. I can't for the life of me see how such a thing can be insisted on in the face of such a plain exposure of its danger and the national inconsistency it entails. It often seems to me that the ears of our people are closed to reason.

We are glad to hear that Mrs. Carlisle is gaining in health and spirits, and Mrs. Cleveland joins me in affectionate expressions to both you and her.

To A. B. FARQUHAR

Princeton, *November* 13, 1898

I thank you for your letter and the accompanying copy of your address. I am amazed beyond expression to see that so little impression is made upon our people by such reasoning as you put forth. It seems to me that every consideration against this fatal imperialistic folly has been presented to our countrymen; but they do not seem inclined to weigh them.

[1] Carlisle wrote advising him not to preside, and Cleveland followed the advice.

The question has, in these circumstances, become a football of politics; and I am afraid its rush will not be stopped until the politicians are made to see that it will become a dangerous thing to trifle with — I mean dangerous *for them*.

To Dr. Joseph Leidy

Princeton, *December* 22, 1898

Newspaper perversity has never been better illustrated than by the manner the press has treated my alleged connection with the so-called Farm School in this neighborhood. From the first to last I have been opposed to the ill-advised project of a young man with more zeal than sense, who was in occupancy of a small farm belonging to me — where he insisted on making his foolish venture. He moved from my premises about the 1st of November and I suppose the school has collapsed. Whenever I have had opportunity I have disclaimed all connection with the affair, since the day it was started; and yet the clipping you send me purports to originate here, where the facts are well known, and speaks of the school farm as something which I in company with others undertook early in the summer!! The salvation and the education of boys without advantages, but who have in them the elements of useful men, is an intensely interesting work, and if conducted on a practical basis would, I believe, yield as good results as any benevolent undertaking that can occupy the attention and efforts of philanthropic men. Owing to my supposed connection with the project here, I received a few communications from those engaged in the management of such institutions which I believe were in successful operation.

A start ought not to be made without a considerable fund secured in advance, and the co-operation of men especially fitted for the work.

To Daniel S. Lamont

Princeton, *December* 31, 1898

I want first of all to thank you for your very agreeable remembrance of me on Christmas. The cigars are very fine indeed, but I was only suspicious of you as the donor until a day or two ago, when I discovered your card stuck to the top of one of the boxes in such a way as eluded my prior examinations.

As to the portrait, I cannot see why even you should want it. Your request seems a little to me like asking me to sit in a dentist's chair and be operated on, but I'll tell you, one thing is mighty certain; if you want me to sit for my portrait, I'll do it very cheerfully and without the least suspicion of preference concerning the artist or the time when his performances shall begin....

To CHARLES S. HAMLIN [1]

Princeton, *January* 2, 1899

I was glad to receive the account you sent me of the discussion of Imperialism at the Young Men's Democratic Club. I am so intense in my opposition to the sort of expansion now facing us that I have no patience in dealing with it. I suppose the exhilaration of this intoxication will prevent our people from appreciating, for a long time, the sadness and depression that must follow such a condition. With sincere New Year wishes...

To EDWARD M. SHEPARD

Princeton, *January* 12, 1899

Your letter arrived at a time when I had just arrived at a conclusion upon the [same] proposition submitted to me by Messrs. Hinrichs and Healy. With a full realization of the fact that my relations with Mr. Bayard and my love for him should constrain me to join with enthusiasm in any movement to honor his memory, I have determined to decline participation in the meeting suggested. I cannot detail all my reasons for this conclusion; and I hope my justification does not require it. I will say, however, that I have been controllingly influenced by a clear negative conviction on the following proposition contained in your letter to me: 'Whether amid all the present din and noise, a worthy presentation of Mr. Bayard's career and services can be fittingly heard is possibly open to doubt.' Unpleasant suggestions of 'pearls' and 'swine' *will* obtrude themselves.

My pride and self-conceit have had a terrible fall. I thought I understood the American people.

To DANIEL S. LAMONT

Princeton, *January* 16, 1899

I suppose I am indebted to you for a copy of *David Harum* which I received a few days ago. I thank you most sincerely for it; and I have

[1] Charles S. Hamlin (1861–), a Boston attorney, had done brilliant service as Assistant Secretary of the Treasury 1893–97.

testified my appreciation and enjoyment of it by reading it faithfully until I finished it. I think, Colonel, it is one of the many compensations of our rural bringing-up that we can understand and enjoy such a book; I expect there are lots of city-bred people who cannot.

I had a special delivery letter from Bacon this morning full of the project of my becoming president of the American Surety Company, if it could be brought about. He wanted me to meet him in New York today. I don't suppose the thing could be accomplished if I wanted the place ever so badly; and if it could I don't think I ought to undertake the work and live here. So I have telegraphed and written Bacon to that effect. I see your name in the list of trustees and that is the reason why I tell you of a thing which came to me as 'private and confidential.' I wish you would not speak of it to Bacon unless he opens the way — though I do not think he has intended to keep it a secret from you. It was certainly extremely kind of him.

While writing this letter Professor Libby came in and I gave him a note of introduction to you. I do not indulge in this as often as I have opportunity, but Libby is a hard-headed, sensible fellow who knows precisely what he wants and won't bother you very much, I think. He has a telephone project that I believe is a very good thing and which will come to the front one of these days in great shape.

When are you coming up with your artist? I shall be away I expect from Thursday P.M. of this week until Monday P.M. of next week — the latter three days in New York or its neighborhood.

To JOSEPH JEFFERSON

Princeton, February 1, 1899

The fish arrived on the 30th of January — two days after their shipment — in first-rate condition, having encountered quite cold weather on their way North. We have already tested the quality of the 'snappers' to our very great satisfaction, and propose on Friday evening to utilize one or more of the sheepsheads at a little dinner function which we contemplate.

We are very grateful to you for this kind remembrance of us, and to the other members of your fishing party who contributed to your benevolent project. I thank you also for suggesting a short stay with you in Florida later in the season if you find a quiet and 'fishy' spot — though I am by no means certain that I can avail myself of such an invitation if it comes. I am very busy doing nothing or next to nothing.

To CAPTAIN ROBLEY D. EVANS

Princeton, *February* 18, 1899

I was very glad to get your letter, for it was the starting point of my plans. I communicated with the Commodore at once and told him what you wrote and asked him to confer with Captain Gordon about the prospects of duck, etc. The date of departure which you mention — the last week of February — suits me exactly, and I am quite sure will suit the Commodore, unless he is prevented by the illness of his daughter, who is now sick, but he thinks not seriously. I want to be away very much during the first days of March — but this is distinctly *between us*.

And now I am going to presume upon our friendship to take a liberty with you. The Commodore and I have been written to by Colonel William L. Brown of the New York *Daily News*, suggesting the giving a dinner to you and utilizing the occasion by at the same time *presenting you with something*. The Commodore in the heartiest way expresses his delighted readiness to co-operate in doing you honor in any way entirely agreeable to you; and you need no assurance of my feelings on the subject. Neither of us has made any reply yet.

I have my own ideas of this everlasting dinner-giving and sword presentations, etc.; and if I were you I had rather 'stand pat' than to 'draw' for any of these things. I may be all wrong in this; but there is another question: Do you want to go into such a matter under the auspices suggested? Bill Brown is one of the best fellows in the world; and when he starts to do a thing, he 'bores with a big auger'; but after the Schley, Sampson, and Phillips affairs do you want to follow with a dinner and presentation of the sort now suggested? Brown spoke of my making *the* speech or *a* speech. I never was more sincere in my life than when I say that would be a mistake; because it would give rise to ill-natured remarks that could as well be avoided as invited. Now, if you don't look right into my heart, and do not understand just what is passing in my mind and appreciate all I feel, you are a 'mean old cuss.' And that's all I have to say, except to ask you to give me a hint of how you feel as soon as convenient.

To E. C. BENEDICT

Princeton, *February* 19, 1899

Your last letter, enclosing Captain Brown's, which I herewith return, arrived yesterday. I wrote Captain Evans at once, and taking advantage of our friendly relations, I wrote quite frankly — which I found rather a delicate task. I had just received a letter from Colonel Brown similar to yours, and therefore could deal with the subject in a double-headed fashion — for you as well as myself. I told him I had my own ideas of the presentation and banquet business, and if I were in his place I should prefer to 'stand pat' on the honors he had. I added that I might be all wrong on that point, but there was another feature in the affair and that was whether after the Schley and Sampson and Phillips affairs he wanted a dinner and presentation gotten up under the auspices proposed. I said also that it was with the utmost sincerity that I suggested that my participation in making a speech of presentation would invite some ill-natured criticism that might as well as not be avoided. I asked him to tell me as soon as possible how he felt about it. I am of the opinion that the thing had better not go on, but of course Evans himself is the only one who can decide the question. He wrote me that he was to be in Cincinnati on the 22d and I hope my letter will reach him and be answered before he leaves. Perhaps you can wait a few days longer before answering Colonel Brown and if I get a reply from Evans I will telegraph you in a way that *you* will understand if nobody else what he desires.

If our plans prosper we ought to start not later than next Sunday or Monday, I think.

To E. C. BENEDICT

Princeton, *February* 22, 1899

Frank Hastings has this moment left us. I enclose you the Gordon letter and memo and also one from Captain Evans, which please read and return to me. I was very much relieved to receive the Captain's letter this morning, as I very much feared that mine written to him might in some way cause him to feel unpleasantly. You will observe that he does not say the project has been, or even will be, abandoned. I hope, however, it will not be pushed farther. Perhaps you will have to temporize with Colonel Brown by saying that you cannot definitely decide the question of your co-operation without being more fully informed of the details of the scheme, and an assurance that they are quite agreeable to Captain

Evans. My letter from the Colonel was so much later than yours that I can delay my answer — though I would like to send it before we leave for the South — if we go.

On this latter topic I have to say that 'as at present advised,' I shall refuse to go without you. I have made no plans by way of arranging for transportation on any particular day, though I suppose it is not necessary to give the railroad a very long notice. Colonel Lamont is to attend to that branch of the business. I have declined one or two invitations on the theory that we would be gone by the 2d of March for ten days or so. The 2d is a week from tomorrow (Thursday), and perhaps then or before, you will feel easy enough about Helen to start. We haven't secured our fourth man yet. I think General McCook is the best all-around candidate in sight and perhaps I will meet Evans on his return to Washington next Friday (the 24th) with a letter suggesting that he communicate with the General on the subject. Captain Ackly would be first-class, but there is danger that he cannot leave Washington. If there happens to come an early day when you can determine whether you will feel easy to leave home some time soon, I wish you would indicate it to me by telegraph....

To CAPTAIN ROBLEY D. EVANS

Princeton, *February* 28, 1899

About whiskey — I will take one of my big glass jugs containing two quarts, or perhaps another package I happen to have, containing, I think, two gallons. I'll look out for it anyway.

To RICHARD OLNEY

Princeton, *March* 19, 1899

It seems to me that a long time has passed since we have had direct communication with each other; and I am determined to re-establish the carriage of mails between us if possible. I hope this can be done without troops, or any interference with the domestic affairs of the States.

Did you ever, 'in all your born days,' see such goings-on as have been exhibited at Washington during the past year? I am in a constant state of wonderment, when I am not in a state of nausea. Sometimes I feel like saying 'it's none of my business'; but that's pretty hard for me to do, though it would be comfortable if I could settle down to that condition.

The Democratic party, if it was only in tolerable condition, could win an easy victory next year; but I am afraid it will never be in winning condition until we have had a regular knock-down fight among ourselves, and succeeded in putting the organization in Democratic hands and reviving Democratic principles in our platform. I don't think the kind of 'harmony' we hear so much of will bridge over our difficulties, and I don't believe our people, notwithstanding the disgust the Administration is breeding, are ready to accept Bryan and the Chicago platform; and if they are, what comfort is there in that for decent, sound, Democrats? One thing I regard as absolutely certain: If the plans of those now in charge of our party management are not interrupted, the dishes served up to us will be Bryan and the Chicago platform. To suppose anything else will occur in the contingency suggested is to ignore every indication in the political sky.

Other questions, however, of the utmost importance confront us. Bryan is alive and his followers active, numerous, and determined; but is Jim Jones alive, and are the bass in Long Pond numerous, and will they in due time prove active and determined? When do you go to Falmouth? I intend to leave here for Gray Gables as early as possible and I now hope to become established there early in June, and to cut Commencement exercises here....

To RICHARD OLNEY

Princeton, *April* 12, 1899

I returned Monday from a trip of two or three days to Gray Gables and its vicinity — mostly the vicinity. I fished a couple of days for trout down West Barnstable way with very fair success and came away without doing anything in regard to the matters about my place which furnished the pretext for my journey.

You speak of the Zorn portraits. They are both in Boston, I suppose. Mrs. Cleveland's has had a great deal of supplemental work done on it in the way of improving the likeness and I think may be regarded now in every way a success. I shall be glad, however, to have your judgment on it, as I fear my opinion and satisfaction may arise from the growth I have seen from a bad likeness to at least a fair one. As for my ugly mug, I think the artist has 'struck it off' in great shape. He is quite a genius and would make a great picture of you if he had the chance. I believe, however, you had a good one painted for your home when in Washington.

The 'round-up' and slaughter of Philipinos seems to go merrily on.

Of course it has little of glorious war about it, but perhaps it's good practice for our army — though they must have grown quite skilful in hitting on the run, since I see one of our soldiers writes that the difference between shooting at Philipinos and jack-rabbits consists in the fact that some jack-rabbits escaped, but no Philipinos. All the same, anybody who says this is not a Christian nation or that our President is not the very pink of perfection of a Christian, is a liar and an un-American knave. And the poor old Democratic party! What a spectacle it presents as a tender to Bryanism and nonsense! If there should be a glimmer of re-turned Democratic sense between now and the next National Convention, it might at its best (or worst) result ascend (or descend) from Bryan to Gorman — nothing better, in my opinion.

I hope now to leave here for Gray Gables early in June, though I may be disappointed in this.

To E. C. Benedict

Princeton, *April* 16, 1899

Your letter is at hand. I fully appreciate your kindness in signing my name to the document which will develop me into a stockholder in the new Trust Company....

I want to thank you especially for the pleasure you gave me in putting the yacht in commission to take me to Gray Gables, and enabling me to have a trout fish. If I thanked you for all the things of this kind you do for me, I should be giving out a constant stream of gratitude — like Jake's blower when it *works* — but the trip last week was so thoroughly enjoyable, that I feel like making special mention of it. I want you to fix a time in the near future when you will come and spend a little time with us. How would it do to come early in this week or next? I think we shall have some decent weather now and my luck is fair in cribbage and billiards.

I have been hoping that I might be a little more sure of 'where I was *at*' after the two Jefferson dinners in New York; but I fear I am as much at sea as ever; and to tell you the truth I don't get very much comfort from Croker's testimony before the Investigating Committee — do you? I sometimes fear that your 'orphans' will not decrease for the next year or so....

To JUDSON HARMON

Princeton, *April* 17, 1899

I was very glad to see your familiar handwriting again. I am afraid you will be a little impatient with my treatment of the subject suggested in your letter, but I shall be entirely frank and confidential with you. I have a reluctance I cannot overcome to making public speeches — especially just at this time. I do not believe this can be justly attributed to a lack of patriotism, a willingness to shirk duty, or actual laziness; but the aversion is so strong that it has led me to decline every invitation which I have received during a long period, except in two cases occurring here at home.

I am not the sort of man people want to hear in these days. My beliefs and opinions are unsuited to the times. No word that I could speak would do the least good, and the announcement that I was to address my fellow-countrymen on any subject whatever would be the signal for coarse abuse and ridicule. I am content in my retirement and am far from complaining of my elimination from public thought or notice; but I cannot see that I ought to uselessly give an opportunity to those who delight in misrepresenting and maligning me. You know me too well to imagine that such a consideration would have a feather's weight with me if over against it there was the slightest possibility of my being of service to the country in these perilous days. Indeed, I would gladly do such a service. The time may come when I can see such an opportunity, but I cannot now; and it may be that this opportunity will more surely come to me if I am silent now.

If I did not feel like making this statement to you, which is in the nature of a confidential confession, I should still be obliged to say to you that I have plans and engagements for next month such as make it impossible for me to make a further engagement for any particular day in that month....

To E. C. BENEDICT

Princeton, *April* 19, 1899

Your letter was received this morning. You have no idea how rich I feel, and how much pleased I am with the operations and success of the partnership. It seems to me I know of one *joint account* which did not start with two fathers and end with none — as I have heard you describe their usual fate. Recalling your threats of ruin, I have felt all along like the giddy girl who, when a good man asked her if she had been ruined, said, 'Not yet, but I hope to be,' and it seems I had it right. As near as I can make out, I have in the hands of the firm of E. C. Benedict & Co., after paying for my Trust Company stock, over $20,000; and like every silly fellow who suddenly becomes rich, I want to buy something — that is, with all but about $10,000 of it. But perhaps I can wait until I see you.

I am under an engagement to go to Ohio bass fishing, some time in May — but whether it will be late or early in the month is uncertain. I must keep myself in readiness to start on pretty short notice, I fear; and am thus prevented from making any other engagement until the date for my bass trip is fixed. I have hoped, too, that if I tried the trout in May, it would be on Cape Cod....

To JOSEPH JEFFERSON

Princeton, *June* 16, 1899

It is early in the morning, but the caravan starts at nine o'clock for Gray Gables and I could not sleep with such a thing impending. We shall linger over Sunday at Greenwich and reach God's Country, I should think, Tuesday evening, or Wednesday evening at the farthest. We shall take passage in the *Oneida* at Greenwich. But I did not intend to give you so much of our itinerary. I wanted to merely tell you how sorry I am that I did not see you on my recent visit to Gray Gables — especially now that I know how near I came to it. When seven o'clock came without hearing from you, we concluded you had stayed another day in Boston, and that we had better get beyond the lighthouse, on our way home, before dark.

I am very glad to hear such good reports about the trouting and the fishing generally, and I hope to enjoy many an 'outing' — as well as successful fishing days — with you during the summer. Did it ever occur to you what a fortunate thing it is that you and I jointly are able to appreciate and enjoy a regular out-and-out 'outing,' undisturbed by the question of fish captured? How many of our excursions have been thus redeemed! It really seems to be a kind of a low, sordid view to take of our excursions, to measure their success by the number of poor, slimy fish we are able to exhibit. Still we will not scorn them, and I have quite a lot of new-fangled gear for their capture....

To RICHARD OLNEY

Gray Gables, *September* 12, 1899

Your letter is at hand. It gives me a better opportunity than I had before to say something to you in explanation of the inquiry I made of you just before we separated about your near horse. Brad has been suggesting to me all summer that one of my working horses ought to be replaced by a better one. This I think might be so, if I could see just where enough team work was done during the winter to justify the expenditure. I think Brad would like to have a *little better roader* for his *own convenience.*

Sometimes, however, I have thought I would buy another horse if I could get one at a low price. This led me to make the inquiries I have referred to. I had no idea you and Brad had discussed the subject, as appears to be the case from what he now says. He talks as if he had asked you about selling your horse, and seems to think it is just the horse I want. I don't suppose he has any idea of buying a horse himself. That I would not like at all. I have written all this to introduce the statement that when I inquired about the cost of your horse, it was merely to get the benefit of your experience on that point, as some evidence of what the expense of a horse might be if I concluded to buy one. I was not 'sneaking around' with the thought in my mind that you and I would ever talk horse trade.

I was surprised to hear from Brad that you are willing to sell your near horse. If I get one I want a strong sound horse that will do team work with another — a little plowing and considerable drawing of heavy loads — and that I can also drive single through the woods or anywhere else on excursions, and that I can hitch to a tree and find him there when I am ready to go home, and that will take me home in fairly good time....

To E. C. BENEDICT

Gray Gables, *September* 23, 1899

Your letter received; and I send this morning by express your tackle box and fishing rod and reel. I only opened the box sufficiently to put the reel in and a newspaper to keep the tackle from shaking too much. I had already taken the rod apart, given the line a good drying, and put all away carefully. We went to Abial's yesterday, caught a few good fish, and would have caught an enormous quantity if the wind had not driven us away and if you had not carried away the net we use to put them in when caught. The wind is in the northeast this morning, but we shall start out soon, I suppose, but shall probably be obliged to throw our fish back for the want of something to keep them in.

Doctor and I went to the marshes the day after you left and brought home twenty-three good birds....

To BOLTON HALL

Gray Gables, October 8, 1899

Your letter and the statement of the belief of the proposed American League have been forwarded to me. I think the statement is the best I have seen on the question of anti-expansion as it is at present exhibited to us. The concluding paragraph comprises, in my opinion, the pith of the matter. The use of power in the extension of American institutions presents an inconsistency whose evil and dangerous tendency ought to be apparent to all who love these institutions and understand their motives and purposes.

I have no objection to being among those who subscribe to the statements you send me. If it is altered, however, I desire to be advised of the change before I am recorded as an adviser.

To E. C. BENEDICT

Princeton, October 25, 1899

I have been home a couple of days; and though there are a peck of letters — more or less — to be answered, I am determined that no more time shall pass before I assure you that 'I still live.'

I hope by this time that you have recovered from the strain put upon you by your determination to see the boat-races through; and I am glad that for your persistent devotion you saw one good race at the end. I am very glad, too, that our people are treating Sir Thomas so handsomely. He seems to me to deserve it.

I remained behind at Gray Gables to do just a little more fishing and shooting — though neither pursuit paid very large compensation. The fish were not numerous, but I caught a tautog that weighed a little more than ten pounds and Brad caught one that weighed eight. Almost Brad's last word to me was a request that I ask you if you wanted him to send to you the net Brown made for you and the plant. The latter appeared to be in fine shape when I saw it last. It was put in Brad's cellar just before I left.

To Richard Watson Gilder

Princeton, *October* 27, 1899

I hardly know what to say in reply to your kind letter. Your friend speaks of a business presidency, as I understand. I have lately declined an offer of such a position to which was attached a very large salary, because I did not think I could do all the situation demanded and make the project a success. I am afraid I should come to the same conclusion in considering another proposition. I am not happy in the thought that sometimes crowds into my mind, leading to the fear that my working days are over; though I know that in every way limitations hamper me. Yet I also know I ought to earn something if I can; and I am not sure that I am justified in *drifting* the rest of my life. I wonder if I might not have just a little hint of the kind of position your friend has in mind, before I positively say I cannot take it.

One or two other things I want to submit to you. I have promised the faculty of the University here, that sometime in the spring — probably in March — I would give two quite easy-going talks to the students or some of them. I am now annoyed to find that these talks are frequently spoken of as a 'course of lectures'; and newspapers and magazines are after me for opportunity to publish these 'lectures.' Professor Perry,[1] the new editor of the *Atlantic*, has applied; and my old clerk O'Brien has written me in behalf of the Boston *Transcript*; and today Mr. Scott of the *Century* writes me that when published in book form he hopes they will bear the imprint of his company. This latter would, of course, please me very much indeed; but I have no idea that when my talks occur they will be found to be proper material for magazine or book publication. I have such a settled notion in this direction that I am quite inclined to do all I can to prevent the publication of them in any form.

I want to pester you with one more of my troubles and then I will let you off. Today a Mr. Barry, assistant editor of the *Forum*, called and urged me to write for his magazine an article in the direction of saving the Democratic party. I was fool enough, after as much as saying that I would not do it, to tell him I would consider it on the basis of utilizing for the purpose a speech I prepared to deliver at a banquet of the Iroquois Club at Chicago about a year and a half ago, which was abandoned on account of the breaking-out of the war. After we had reached this point

[1] Bliss Perry, who had been professor of English literature at Princeton when Cleveland arrived, was editor of the *Atlantic* 1899–1909.

in the negotiations he told me the magazine would pay me for such an article the munificent sum of $150. What do you think of that?

I wish I could see you and have a talk about these and other matters. I am not sure that the best thing I can do at present is to keep still, that I am sorry almost that I consented to talk to the college boys.

To GEORGE GRANTHAM BAIN
Princeton, *November* 1, 1899

I return the photograph proofs you sent me in another enclosure. I would be glad to see proofs of all these pictures when they are completed and mounted. I think I should have my hands full if I attempted to mention all the papers in which I did *not* want my picture to appear besides the *Journal* and *World*. These two I insist on excluding. As far as others are concerned, I think I must rely upon you to do the right thing.

To DON M. DICKINSON
Princeton, *November* 11, 1899

I have received the clippings you directed to me in your very familiar and always welcome chirography. I congratulate you most heartily on the success that has at last crowned your long and laborious struggle; and I do not doubt in the least that your success is the success of justice and equity. It has been a long time since I have seen you or heard from you except in an indirect and indefinite way.

I am living very quietly here trying very hard not to bother anyone, and wishing for reciprocity in this regard, and at the same time more anxious to see old friends than ever. I hope you will have the opportunity and inclination to call on us on some of your trips to New York. What do you make out of Tuesday's elections? Don't you, in these days, sometimes pinch yourself to see if you are awake, when you contemplate so-called Democratic management? I actually find myself wondering whether or not those who are leading us do not deliberately intend to assassinate the organization and bury it completely out of sight and for all time....

To JOSEPH JEFFERSON
Princeton, *November* 22, 1899

Your two letters of the 20th instant have been received within the last hour; and I hasten to reply so that my letter will surely reach you before you leave St. Louis.

I appreciate as much as any human being can appreciate a kindness, your suggestion that I join you at Palm Beach, about the 21st of December; and I hope you will not be discouraged by the miscarriage of your friendly designs, when I say that at this moment I cannot calculate on meeting you as proposed. I do not want to be away from home and my wife and chicks on Christmas; and I hope that early in January I may be able to join my comrades of former seasons on a ducking excursion. Such a trip I hoped could be organized for December, but a letter from Captain Evans received this morning puts an end to that scheme.

My wife says I ought not to spend December here without a change; and I suppose she is, as usual, nearly right. I have thought, however, that the time could be well spent and perhaps precaution taken against accidents, by an attempt on my part to get my alleged brain in training for my alleged lectures. However, all this is not of interest to you.

How would it do for me to postpone the further consideration of the Palm Beach matter until I know more about my ducking trip? In the meantime, if you go there as you propose, you will know more definitely concerning the lay of the land, and perhaps I might join you at some time during your stay.

I had a call from W. L. Wilson about a week ago. He was to be examined physically the next day, and seemed very much allured by the companionship with you which he would enjoy at Palm Beach. I have heard since indirectly that he had been sentenced to Arizona.[1]...

To BOOKER T. WASHINGTON

Princeton, *December* 3, 1899

My inability to attend the meeting tomorrow evening, in the interest of Tuskegee Institute, is a very great disappointment to me. If my participation could have in the slightest degree aided the cause you represent, or in the least encouraged you in your noble efforts, I would have felt that my highest duty was in close company with my greatest personal gratification. It has frequently occurred to me that in the present condition of our free negro population in the South, and the incidents often surrounding them, we cannot absolutely calculate that the future of our nation will be always free from dangers and convulsions, perhaps not less lamentable than those which resulted from the enslaved negroes less than forty years ago. Then the cause of trouble was the injustice of the

[1] Wilson was stricken by tuberculosis, and died October 17, 1900.

enslavement of four millions; but now we have to deal with eight millions, who, though free and invested with all the rights of citizenship, still constitute in the body politic a mass largely affected with ignorance, slothfulness, and a resulting lack of appreciation of the obligations of that citizenship.

I am so certain that these conditions cannot be neglected, and so convinced that the mission marked out by the Tuskegee Institute presents the best hope of their amelioration, and that every consideration makes immediate action important, whether based on Christian benevolence, a love of country, or selfish material interests, that I am profoundly impressed with the necessity of such prompt aid to your efforts as will best insure their success. I cannot believe that your appeal to the good people of our country will be unsuccessful. Such disinterested devotion as you have exhibited and the results already accomplished by your unselfish work ought to be sufficient guarantee of the far-reaching and beneficent results that must follow such a manifestation of Christian charity and good citizenship as would be apparent in a cordial and effective support of your endeavor.

I need not say how gratified I am to be able to indicate to you that such support is forthcoming. It will be seen by the letters which I enclose that already an offer has been made, through me, by a benevolent lady in a Western city, to contribute $25,000 toward the endowment fund, upon condition that other subscriptions to this fund aggregate the amount required. With so good a beginning I cannot believe it possible that there will be a failure in securing the endowment fund which Tuskegee so much needs.

To E. C. BENEDICT

Princeton, *December 22,* 1899

Your letter and subsequent dispatch are received. I was sorry to learn from the latter that General Lumbago's forces were still in your immediate vicinity, on the watch to take advantage of the slightest opportunity. I am told he is a wily cuss. I am enduring the siege undertaken by old Rheu quite comfortably, and the cowardly old duffer seems to be relaxing his interference with even the forces on foot, which are the only ones he has, at any time, had the courage to afflict.

I hope, Commodore, that you are really through your troubles. And this brings me to speak of another matter. Evans and I have it cooked up to start for South Carolina on the 10th day of January, 1900. I think it was yesterday that I heard from him, and today I have spent all the strength I had to spare in writing about transportation, camps, etc. General Alexander, who I suppose you know lost his wife within the last few weeks, is in great grief and hardly expects to join us, but has in the midst of his sorrow insisted that the usual party spend some time at the old camping ground, and some time ago had the tents put up and everything done for our comfort that could be done before the date of our departure was fixed. I have today written fully to General Alexander's agent as he bade me do. I am inclined to think that between Bob Evans and me, arrangements for the trip will be pretty well made.

All this is preliminary to the question — Will you join the picnic? If you go there will be five, I think, in the party and you will not be bothered with any preparations unless it be to provide yourself with water you can safely drink.

To RICHARD WATSON GILDER

Princeton, *December 28*, 1899

... Evidence accumulates that as you grow older you grow wiser. This is actually getting to be so rare a condition that I mention it by way of congratulating you. When you bought Four Brooks farm an indication of increasing good sense shot out very distinctly. Your present sojourn there follows in a most gratifying manner, giving promise that you will soon develop a style and degree of loaferism immensely encouraging to your friends.

I am still laid up — writing now in my nightshirt and dressing-gown. It will be five weeks next Monday since you saw the beginning. My neighbor Colonel Stockton was buried today; and I was not able to attend his funeral. I am in no condition to work; and at this rate I shall not be ready with my so-called lectures. Whatever happens, I intend to spend a week or ten days ducking next month....

To CAPTAIN ROBLEY D. EVANS

Princeton, *February 3*, 1900

I have packed up and shall forthwith send by express to you all my photographs of our South Island camp. Some of them I am sure will not be of use to you, but I want to be sure that I have done all that is possible for me to do in aid of the affair entrusted to you.

I also send with them for Miss Virginia the photograph of Mrs. Cleveland and myself, which I mentioned to you. Mrs. Cleveland is a little sedate and matronly, it seems to me. This I do not quite like, for I insist that she is better looking and as young looking as the day I was married to her. I am a modest man; but of course the main point is to have *my* picture good; and I think the artist has accomplished that.

I am not sure that Virginia will care much for it, but it is the last we have had taken. We sat on our front porch here. Mrs. C. was just starting to market and had wheedled me into going with her.

Do you remember that the Commodore took a couple of photographs of our camp on our recent trip? I don't think he is very expert and quite likely he made a botch of it. If, however, by any chance he secured a good picture, perhaps it would better suit your purpose than those I send.

I laid up again when I returned from our hunt, and today have my clothes on for the first time since the day I reached home.... My journey home and especially my experience at Princeton Junction was far more damaging than anything I encountered in South Carolina marshes.

To E. C. Benedict
Princeton, *February* 6, 1900

I am just in condition to sit up all day, after the experiences at Princeton Junction the morning I left you. I had a bad time getting over the tracks, the broken ballast stones, and a platform or two — so that I arrived at home in somewhat worse condition as to my locomotive adjuncts than when I left for the trip. In all other respects, however, I had improved largely. Last Saturday I put on my clothes for the first time since my return, and today I rode out feeling very well. I think I can see my way out of my trouble.

Within an hour or two I have received a letter from General Alexander. He has visited the camp and seems to be quite chagrined at its condition. He says he was cheated in the delivery of the tents and that he had never seen those erected at the camp. He is full of kind intentions in the matter of another visit from us and contemplates a change in the location and arrangement of the camp and the construction of better ponds and marshes for ducks. He is wonderfully kind and generous....

To EDWARD M. SHEPARD

Princeton, *February* 7, 1900

Your letter is just at hand. I have not sufficiently recovered from a tedious disability to permit my attendance at the dinner appointed for next Saturday evening. Perhaps I ought not to add anything to this; and yet I feel that I would not be candid, if I suppressed the further statement that even though the obstacle I have mentioned were not in the way, I should still be constrained to avoid appearing as a sombre figure at the feast. This is written under the influence of so strong a desire to see true Democracy rehabilitated, that it outweighs every other wish. It is written, too, I beg of you to believe, uninfluenced by the least feeling of personal irritation or resentment.

Considered in the light of judgment and expediency, I am satisfied you are wrong in suggesting my presence at your meeting of conciliation. Thousands of those who have struggled to maintain the true Democratic faith may be forgiven by the apostles of the newly invented Democracy; but it seems that I am, as yet, beyond the pale of honorable condonation. Prominent among your guests of honor there will be those who lose no occasion, on the floor of Congress or elsewhere, to repudiate me as a Democrat, and to swell the volume of 'jeers' and 'laughter' that greet the mention of my name in that connection. Perhaps they are justified; but if I have sinned against Democracy I am ignorant of my sin; and in any event, my love of country and party will not permit me to sue for forgiveness while being dragged behind the chariot of Bryanism.

I know your motives are pure and your purposes exalted. Have I not written something that should challenge your thought in support of my opinion that I would be an ill-selected guest at your dinner? If a movement shall be there inaugurated tending towards a revival of true Democracy, I shall be glad that I have taken no risk of interrupting it. If it should lead to loading more securely upon our party the fatal blunders of the Chicago platform and Bryanism, I shall be glad to have had no part nor lot in the matter.

To E. C. BENEDICT

Princeton, *February* 22, 1900

I enclose a certificate for ten shares of State Trust Company stock which I want your firm to sell for me. The quotation I saw a few days ago was 400 bid, and I suppose it ought to sell for that and perhaps a trifle more.

I also enclose you a letter demonstrating that the disadvantage of our intimacy in the matter of outside attack is not altogether on your side.

Dr. Bryant was here a couple of days ago and Colonel Lamont called today. They have cooked up a scheme to go to Florida by special car on a loafing trip — fishing if they find good places, eating in all places, and resting all the time, 'whether or no.' They want me to go, but I have not positively agreed to do so. The Colonel told me to ask you to go. I suppose the calculation would be to stay away two or three weeks, and the Colonel said it would take a week or so to make car connecting arrangements, etc. I do not understand that there would be any Mede and Persian programme laid down as to itinerary. What do you say?

I am ashamed to tell you that since I returned from the South I have been up and about, and down again, and for the last two days have been downstairs to my meals in token of a better condition again. I don't know that there is much the matter with me. I eat very liberally and sleep well, but I get lame mighty easy and a little exertion tires me. I begin to think my troubles are laziness and confinement. Excepting on our Southern trip I haven't been out of the house but five times (and then only to ride) since November 26. Isn't that ridiculous?

I have lately been 'dawdling along' with my 'job,' making short stages and slow progress. My bosses in the matter have given me an extension of time if I desire to take it; and if I should go on the trip I should do so in the hope and expectation that I would be able to take up the work when I return with renewed vigor....

To RICHARD OLNEY

Princeton, *March* 26, 1900

I returned a few days ago from a trip to Florida in the hope of finding relief from a long and vexatious attack of rheumatism, gout, or whatever else my visitation may be. I am much better — but still lame; and it sometimes seems to me I shall continue more or less lame to the end of the chapter. Just before I left I read with the utmost interest your last article in the *Atlantic*. There is no doubt about one thing, as the boys say: you can sling the English language in proper shape. The matter of the article I like, too; but I am sorry I am so antiquated as to wish we were back in our old place. However, I take comfort enough in what you say about the Philippine business to compensate for a little reserved feeling I cannot help entertaining concerning the rest. I am afraid Cuba ought to be submerged for a while before it will make an American State or Territory of which we will be particularly proud.

I have been struggling with a preparation to keep a promise I foolishly made a good while ago, to talk to the students here about something that happened 'when I was in Washington the first time.' I have gotten up a couple of poor 'talks' — all but some finishing touches. It may possibly be that I can say something that will interest and perhaps even inform these young men. If I can I shall do all I have hoped in my most hopeful moments.

I am longing for warm pleasant weather and Gray Gables....

To CHARLES S. HAMLIN

Princeton, *March* 28, 1900

I have either been laid up with rheumatism, or away from home trying to shake off my unwelcome visitor, or struggling with some work that I felt must be done — sick or well — since last November. This condition of affairs has brought about arrears in letter-writing.

We were very much pleased to learn, from your letter received long ago, that we might hope to see you and Mrs. Hamlin at our home *sometime*. We hope that trip of yours to New York which was to be the occasion for the visit will not be long delayed.

Now I have a little business to talk with you, as my Attorney and Counsellor in the matter of opposition to the Cape Cod Canal Company. From what I have heard and seen concerning your conduct of that affair, I know that your presentation was singularly good. And now I want to pay my lawyer; and for that reason I want to know what his charge is.

I had rather be left to the enjoyment of Gray Gables in the peace and quiet which made it so dear to us all — and to take the chances of a profitable sale of it, when the future shall unfold inevitable changes in our family circle — than to part with it now for almost any price. But I have found that the construction of the Canal would not be averted, and that with such construction a nuisance would be at our doors. For these reasons I made the arrangement with which you are familiar — so to speak — which seems to put me in the position of the hunter who aimed at the game so that he would miss it if it was a calf and hit it if it was a deer.

To JOHN G. CARLISLE

Princeton, *April* 10, 1900

Or course there is no truth in the stuff you send me which purports to give information as to the non-appointment of Mr. Phelps to the Chief Justiceship.

The entire story is as follows:

A number of names were under consideration — Mr. Phelps's among them. It was my duty to canvass all worth canvassing, and at the time, I thought his might be regarded in that category — though I certainly had no especial predilection for his selection. However, as a matter of duty, I sent for Senator Edmunds and consulted him confidentially as to Mr. Phelps's ability as a lawyer, his age, etc. He spoke very highly of him and said he thought he was sixty-one or sixty-two years old. He jocularly added, 'He was accused of being something of a copperhead, but I guess he was no worse than the rest of you fellows.' I may say here, by way of parenthesis, that if his age was correctly given at the time of his death he was actually sixty-six years old at the time of this conversation; and that years before then the Senate Committee on the Judiciary had adopted a rule — not always observed, however — that a nominee for a place on the Supreme Court might not be confirmed if more than sixty years of age.

I think it was a very short time after this conversation that I was waited on by quite a delegation of our Irish friends, who respectfully enough and without threats of any kind protested against the appointment of Mr. Phelps. I answered them quite impatiently, but did not think it worth while to give them any intimation as to my state of mind on the subject.

While the matter was still undetermined, Mr. Phelps called on me, and in the course of the conversation I said to him, 'Some people think you ought to be appointed Chief Justice.' I cannot recall his reply, but I think it was to the effect that he would regard it an honor or something of that kind. It could not have been anything very striking or I would remember it. At any rate, I said absolutely nothing more on the subject.

I appointed Mr. Fuller. I have always been glad I did not appoint Mr. Phelps. I never promised to appoint, I never determined to appoint him, and I was not prevented from appointing him by any threats or representations from any quarter whatever. I do not think the newspaper tale is worth a denial, but you now have all the facts.

To A. L. McLean

Princeton, *April* 12, 1900

I do not know of any constitutional or statutory provision that prevents the President from leaving the country, but it is a rule very properly and very generally observed.

To Charles S. Fairchild

Princeton, *April* 12, 1900

I am immensely obliged to you for your kind letter, and for the pains you have taken to give me so much comfort and satisfaction. Such things compensate for much ill-natured criticism and abuse.

I am very much troubled by the present condition of our party. Sometimes I wonder why I should be, when I consider how distinctly those at present managing Democratic affairs have signified that they desire neither the anxiety nor aid of such men as you and I. My Democracy is so deep-seated, however, that I cannot see my great party in the hands of charlatans and put to the ignoble use of aiding personal ambition, without positive grief.

Today I mean to write a letter which will be read, I suppose, at the dinner next week to be given by the Brooklyn Democratic Club in celebration of Jefferson's birthday. I am considering whether to content myself with a brief declamation or to 'speak some certain truths.' I am inclined to do the latter. If I do, I suppose what I shall say will be sneered at as a view from the tombs, and I condemned as a disturber of Democratic peace and an ingrate to an organization which has honored me so much and so often. On the other hand, I am constantly told that it is my duty to speak.

Once in a great while the path of duty is a little obscure.

To the Reverend E. Tallmadge Root

Princeton, *June* 2, 1900

It is not a pleasing thing to be obliged to concede that at this period of our nation's history there should be truth and relevancy in the proposition: 'The Great Need of Our Country — Reverence for Law.'

The difference between barbarity and civilization consists in the absence or existence of laws and their enforcement. American civilization requires that laws for the safety and protection of persons and property should be made and executed by those chosen for that purpose, *by the people to be affected by such laws.* This circumstance creates the demand of popular participation and consent, which increases enormously the obligation of support and obedience. These are included in 'Reverence for Law.' That this reverence is the great need of our country results from an inordinate national and individual strife to reach ends *regardless of all restraint,* and from the growth of the notion among our people that ends must be gained whether the *means* employed are justified or not.

That this tendency is extremely dangerous to the well-being, if not the perpetuity of our nation, there can be no doubt; and *when those in control of our Government can satisfy themselves in a certain course of action by saying if there is no constitutional or legal warrant for it, there ought to be, it is a short step to a feeling among the people that if the laws made for their control and guidance do not permit them to do everything they desire, such laws may be despised and disregarded....*

To Captain Robley D. Evans

Princeton, *June* 7, 1900

... I don't think I ever read more sincere and grateful expressions of appreciation and gratification than were contained in General Alexander's letter acknowledging the receipt of his cigarette case. He is full of plans to prepare a more comfortable place for us to stay and a better place for us to shoot; and I think it would greatly distress him if he thought we had made our last visit to his grounds. I hope the old crowd will meet there during the next ducking season and many times thereafter....

I returned from Bermuda a few days ago. The Commodore, Dr. Bryant and I went down on the *Oneida* — had a very pleasant time, saw a beautiful island, had a fine blow coming home, and enjoyed all the incidents of sea locomotion, though I was skipped, as usual, in the distribution of sea-sickness.

We expect to start for Gray Gables a week from tomorrow (the 15th) and spend a few days at Greenwich on our way. I am anticipating with much pleasure a visit to our summer home by you and Lamberton....

To E. C. Benedict

Princeton, *June* 10, 1900

... The Commencement fuss has fairly begun, and at nearly all hours the students sing and 'music by the band' can be heard. I shall endeavor to abstain from any part in the rumpus except on Wednesday, when I suppose I shall make my annual appearance in academic robe and cap. We professors have to do that, you know.

Some newspaper reporters came to see me about your political deliverance. I said that so far as I was concerned I had positively nothing to say, but that Mr. Benedict was abundantly able to express and maintain his beliefs on the political situation....

To LOUIS R. EHRICH

Gray Gables, *June* 25, 1900

I desire to thank you for your article 'Our Birthright of Liberty.' I have read it with much profit and pleasure, and regard it one of the most important and interesting contributions yet made to anti-imperialistic argument. What a dreadful political and party condition is upon us, when the best Democrats are in doubt as to their duty in the coming canvass!

To RICHARD OLNEY

Gray Gables, *June* 25, 1900

Your very gratifying letter reached me at Greenwich, Connecticut, where we stopped a few days on our way here. We reached Gray Gables last Saturday, and I am astonished by the improvement in my general physical condition which my short sojourn has already brought about.

You are very kind to write such consolatory words about my talk to the Princeton students, and the other people who came to hear me. Though I did not think overmuch of the thing — made worse by some exasperating misprints in the *Atlantic* — I was fully repaid for my trouble by the very close attention the students gave to what I had to say, and by the resulting feeling that I might have done them a little good. I think the second talk, which will appear in the July *Atlantic*, is the most interesting of the two. It may be that I will talk again at the college next winter. If I do, my notion is to go over the Venezuela business. Before I die, I want the correct statement of what you and I did in that matter bored into those of the American people who care to 'have it straight.' I suppose there is a good deal of material, in your head and otherwise in your possession, that would be of service in preparing such a statement; so you must expect to be drawn upon.

I hope to see considerable of you this summer and trust you can stop off on some of your trips to and from Boston, in addition to the set visits, which I anticipate.

The political situation is too much for me — that is, I cannot put it before me in any shape for satisfactory contemplation. I see Massachusetts' sweet-scented 'scholar in politics' played true to his despicable nature at Philadelphia. As for our own party, the old Adam occasionally dominates me to the extent of prompting me to second the suggestion of a queer old woman who said a few days ago, anent the *Herald's* suggestion that I run for President, 'Let them that got into the scrape, get out of it.'

I expect, as usual, that I shall be away from the house considerably, so I hope that any time you feel like calling you will if possible notify me in advance.

To Judson B. Harmon

Gray Gables, *July* 17, 1900

Personal.

I was very glad to hear from you, though it is difficult to write as full and frank a reply as I would like. Letters similar to yours come daily to me from all classes and conditions of men who still love the old faith, and who cannot plainly see the path of duty. So with the arrival of every mail I have a season of cursing the animals who have burglarized and befouled the Democratic home. I have refrained from replying to those letters, because I have not been forgiven by Mr. Bryan for lack of support in 1896; and *pending his pardon*, have no standing in the new Democracy, and cannot therefore speak from that standpoint; and if I should speak according to the principles and teachings of the old Democracy, the notions of the rank and file of the party are so mistaken and confused, that the charge against me of ingratitude, and other accusations and abuse, would do as much or more harm than good.

Of course the 'old Adam' rebels against the demagogue and insolent crusader, whose title to Democracy is far from unquestioned, but who notwithstanding assumes to say what Democracy is, and to grant certificates of membership. It is humiliating to feel that Democrats who were fighting its battles before Bryan was born should be obliged to sue to him for credentials; and as a condition of obtaining them forego all the political beliefs of former days. But personal feelings should be sacrificed if by doing so the country can be saved from disaster.

As between imperialism and a continued struggle against sound money, you and many other good and patriotic Democrats see more danger in the first. The latter and much more trouble we would surely get with Bryan. How certain can you be that he would save you from imperialism? What did he do towards that end when the treaty of peace was before the Senate; and how do you know what such an acrobat would do on that question if his personal ambition was in the balance?

My feeling is that the safety of the country is in the rehabilitation of the old Democratic party. It would be a difficult task to do this, at the end of four years of a Bryan Administration and its absurdities for which the Democratic party would be held responsible. With the defeat of Bryanism and the sham Democratic organization gathered about him, and his and its disappearance in the darkness of accused Democracy's scorn and contempt, the old guard, untainted with either Bryanism or McKinleyism, could gather together the forces — checking, through fear of the indomitable force of *true* Democracy, Republican excesses and promising to the country the conservation and safety of domestic principles.

Bear in mind that McKinleyism has not so far committed itself concerning the treatment and disposition of our new possessions that it could not be frightened into decency by the organization of an opposition resting upon sane principle, solid character, and substantial appeal to the sense and judgment of our people.

I am afraid that the Republicans cannot be dislodged until Bryanism and all in its train is abandoned if not expressly repudiated; this cannot be done until new men are at the helm of the party; and when such new men are called for, it seems to me those most useful and acceptable will be those who now decline Bryanism because it is not Democracy, and Republicanism because it is in every way and at all times un-Democratic. When the collapse of Bryanism comes, the rank and file who have been deceived and misled will in my opinion look for just such leaders. I shall remain only an intensely anxious looker-on. The activities will fall on such men as you.

I have written you my thoughts as I have to no other person. I may be all wrong, but if I am I don't intend to influence others to go wrong too. I am quite happy in political exile — or should be if I did not love my country so well. I will only add that I am not in favor of an independent Democratic ticket; and further that what I have written is for you alone.

To E. C. BENEDICT

Gray Gables, *July* 30, 1900

Just to remind you of the contrariness of fish:

Since a week ago last Friday, when we 'had company' and wanted the squeteague to behave, and five good fishermen chased them about all day to no purpose, we have until today shown our resentment by letting them alone. This afternoon, however, I thought I'd try the Four Buoys again. I started to fish at four o'clock and caught a squeteague in twenty minutes. At a quarter after six I had alone caught TWENTY-SIX (26), and stopped satiated. Brad asked to catch one before we left, which he immediately did, and we came home with twenty-seven. They did not average very large, though we weighed one that showed five and a half pounds. This is the way it goes.

I expect Mr. Carlisle and Professor West here in a day or two and I hope the fish will then behave decently. Yesterday we went after bottom-fish with only moderate success — a few tautog, one weighing four pounds, etc. I have mentioned about or quite the only fishing we have done since you left....

To LOUIS R. EHRICH

Gray Gables, *August* 4, 1900

Your letter of July 30 is received. I feel obliged to say that I must be counted out of the movement to organize a new party organization, separate and distinct from the Democracy. I love the old party too well to dissolve my connection with it — believing and hoping as I do, that when the aberration that now afflicts it shall pass away, party sense and conscience will be restored, and our people can look for safety and national welfare to the regeneration of true Democracy.

To E. C. BENEDICT

Gray Gables, *August* 16, 1900

I have thought a great deal of what you told me about our dear friend Wilson. I have hit upon a plan which I think would succeed in overcoming the difficulty arising from his delicacy and aversion to anything that looks like charitable treatment. He has often spoken of his desire and intention to write a history of the last Democratic Administration.

Why could not a moderate sum — say $5000 — be raised among his friends to be paid to him for doing such a work, in Arizona or some better climate if it can be found? It would be in the nature of a salary and could be paid to him at one time or as the work went on, as would the better carry out the scheme of giving him a change of surroundings, and as would make him feel most comfortable and at ease. He would have to be assured that it was a matter not requiring haste and hard work and perhaps it might be well to enjoin on him a stay in Arizona before he entered upon the task. Of course it would make no difference if it was never completed or even entered upon.

Colonel Lamont thought very well of the scheme and stands ready, as you do, to help in a substantial manner. He perhaps would suggest others. He is now at Sorrento, Maine, and will leave there with his family about September 1 and about that time will start on a trip to the Pacific Coast. I do hope something can be done for our friend. I have further news of his sad condition.

To A. S. ABELL COMPANY

Gray Gables, *September* 11, 1900

I hope that I have not grown heedless of any duty I owe my countrymen; but I am not inclined to publicly declare my thoughts and opinions on the political situation. This I supposed was quite clearly expressed in my note recently published in the New York *Herald*.

For a number of years I have been abused and ridiculed by professed Democrats, because I have not hesitated to declare that Bryanism is not Democracy. I have had the consolation of seeing those who professed my belief run to cover, and of noting a more headlong Democratic rush after anti-Democratic vagaries. My opinions have not changed; why then should I speak when bedlam is at its height? Perhaps I am wrong in my opinions, at any rate I should say unwelcome things; and all to no purpose except to add to the volume of abuse, which, *undefended*, I have so long borne.

I have received this morning a clipping from a German newspaper containing a note to the *Herald* with this comment: 'That was wise. That part of the American people who most need instruction at this time would not listen to Grover Cleveland, but the only thanks they would give him for his well-meant advice would be to open upon him a new bombardment of poison and dirt; the other part do not need to be taught by anyone how to vote rightly next November.' That's about it.

You are not, however, to suppose for a moment that I could be induced to do anything in aid of McKinleyism or any phase of Republicanism.

I suppose it is a case of being 'damned if I do and damned if I don't'; but I have made up my mind that I am entitled to decline enlistment in the war between Bryanism and McKinleyism. This communication is strictly confidential. It is written because I cannot ignore your letter.

To CHARLES S. HAMLIN

Gray Gables, *September* 13, 1900

Your letter of the 5th enclosing one from Secretary Gage came in due time and but for unusual occupation with guests and a rheumatic knee would have been answered before. I could not possibly bring myself to the point of accepting the President's appointment. The reasons that militated against it, I cannot explain fully by letter. I am importuned and *ordered*, to the point of unhappiness, by those who think I ought to publicly announce myself as favorable to Bryan's election. Inasmuch as I am not inclined to do this, it has occurred to me, among other things, that more significance than it deserved would be given to my acceptance of any appointment from the McKinley Administration. This, however, was only one and perhaps not the most potent consideration that influenced me.

My political thoughts are of the saddest description. I would be so glad to help the situation if I only could see the way; but I feel that I am bound 'hand and foot.' Bryanism and McKinleyism! What a choice for a patriotic American!

You were very kind to invite me over to see you; and I should have been glad to accept your invitation if it had been possible....

To WILSON S. BISSELL

Gray Gables, *September* 16, 1900

I was very glad to get your letter of the 8th. Somehow, in these days, I think I am more than ever glad to hear from old friends.

The President wrote me asking if I would accept the appointment as one of the arbitrators under the Hague Convention. In reply I wrote that my disinclination to assume any duty of a public nature was so great that I should ask him to permit me to decline the proffered honor. He replied urging me to accept the place, and informed me that ex-President Harrison had accepted, etc. Oscar Straus, who was then in Washington, also wrote seconding the President's request; and Secretary Gage wrote to Hamlin in the same way, and his letter was sent to me by Hamlin. Notwithstanding all this, I felt constrained to adhere to my determination; and a number of days before the receipt of your letter, I had definitely disposed of the matter, by writing to the President that upon re-examination of the subject I failed to persuade myself that I ought to accept the appointment.

I think the conclusions arrived at by the Hague Conference were lame and disappointing ones. I did not care to be one of a few men, the majority of whom would probably be quite under the lead of Mr. Harrison; and in my particular relation to the organization of my party, I thought it better not to hold a place under the appointment of the present Administration.

The pending campaign has brought upon me much unhappiness. First there came numerous letters from apparently honest Democrats in every part of the country, asking my advice as to how they should vote. These have been largely succeeded by persuasions and demands from self-styled rock-ribbed Democrats, that I should publicly declare myself in favor of the ticket of the 'party which has so greatly honored me'; and in many cases the insistence is made that a word from me would insure the success of the ticket. With these came appeals from anti-imperialists asking all sorts of things. Through all this I have maintained silence, except to say that I have nothing to say. To four letters, I think, from people I could not ignore, I have written my views. I cannot write or speak favorably of Bryanism. I do not regard it as Democracy. But many good party men do. I cannot conceive that anything I might say would better conditions or change results. It would add to the volume of abuse which for a long time has been hurled at my 'defenceless head,' and by a bare possibility destroy an opportunity for usefulness in the future. I have some idea that the party may before long be purged of Bryanism, and that the rank and file, surprised at their wanderings, and enraged at their false leaders, will be anxious to return to the old faith; and in their desire to reorganize under the old banners will welcome the counsel of those who have never yielded to disastrous heresy. This may never be; or it may be that, however complete the return, those who now refuse to aid in the struggle made in the name of Democracy, whether for right or wrong, will still incur Democratic hatred and distrust. Still it is worth all, to be conscious that at all times one has been consistent and patriotically Democratic. I have not seen Olney but once this summer. I put the matter before him as I have to you. He expressed his inclination to vote for Bryan, and suggested that those who did so might better secure the confidence of the party in the future. He may be right on this proposition, as *there may have been something more in his mind than there was in mine.* It seems to me strange that a man who in my judgment is largely responsible, through his *Atlantic* article, for the doctrine of expansion and consequent imperialism, should now be so impressed with the fatal tendency of imperialism as to be willing to take Bryanism as an antidote. But the times are as full of strange and untoward things as they can be; and no one can foretell the issue. I cannot believe Bryanism will win. I am sure Democracy if it was in the field would win: and in any event we shall the most of us, I think, be surprised at the number who will follow the spurious banner to the polls.

We have had many good friends with us this summer, and but for the disgusting things I have referred to, our stay here would have been exceedingly pleasant to me. Dr. Bryant and Mrs. Perrine are here now. Mrs. Cleveland has taken a little trip visiting friends, and will be absent for a week yet....

To Don M. Dickinson
Princeton, *October* 12, 1900

I enclose you a copy of a note I have mailed today to Sir Wilfrid Laurier.[1] I shall be glad if it helps in the least to bring about the desired result.

I am still pestered to death nearly with appeals 'to come out for Bryan' and for advice 'how to vote.' It is surprising how many letters I receive purporting to come from people who opposed Bryan in 1896 and are supporting him now. A comparative few of my correspondents ask me to publicly oppose Bryan. Since, however, I cannot do what the large majority desires, and since I am very far from wishing to affirmatively aid McKinleyism, I have thought I might satisfy my conscience and avoid the accusation of open and pronounced ingratitude by keeping silence. This is a thing very hard for me to do at a time when I am so clear in my convictions; and occasionally I am very restive. You see there are millions of our fellow-citizens who believe that the organization now sup-

---

[1] Dickinson wished to have Laurier make an address at the University of Michigan; and Cleveland wrote the Canadian statesman telling him how much he had enjoyed his own visit to Ann Arbor.

porting Bryan is the same that on three occasions nominated and supported me; and it is hard for them to reconcile my silence, and would be more difficult to reconcile my open and avowed opposition, with a proper appreciation on my part of the honors and favors freely accorded me by Democracy in the past.

On the other hand, the day I hope is not far distant when sanity will succeed insanity and the Democratic masses will cry out for deliverance from Bryanism and a resurrection of true Democratic faith. If the day dawns there must be those untainted with heresy to hold aloft the standard. I do not assume for a moment that I shall or can be one of these; but perchance I may encourage and rejoice. You can hardly believe [how] deeply I am concerned lest I should miss doing that which is best for my country and — what in the present emergency seems to me almost the same — best for my party....

To RICHARD OLNEY

Princeton, *October* 16, 1900

I am very grateful for the document you sent me in the Venezuela matter, and appreciate the pains you have taken to supply my wants. I see there is a perfect skip between my 'warlike' message and the dispatches that immediately preceded it in date (November and December, 1895), and the very mild and bland note of Mr. Bayard to Lord Salisbury, dated February 27, 1896, proposing, on behalf of his Government, an entrance forthwith *at Washington* upon negotiations 'to constitute a tribunal for the arbitration of the boundary between British Guiana and Venezuela — *which seems to be almost unanimously desired by both the United States and Great Britain.*' I thought there was something between those two things — on our side, at any rate.

I see, too, that dispatches leading up to the treaty as furnished terminate with yours of July 13, 1896, suggesting sixty years' occupancy as evidence of right — or rather proof of title. This was the first suggestion of any definite period as related to this branch of the subject; and my remembrance is that there was considerable interchange before a conclusion was reached. I have published volumes of our *Foreign Relations* for 1895 and 1896, but they appear to contain but very little not included in the document you sent me. I had an impression that not only the Venezuelan treaty but the general arbitration treaty had been made public.

I think I can manage the matter I have in mind, if I really undertake it, with what I have — though, of course, the more complete one's material, the better and more comfortably he can work. It's a great satisfaction to have 'chapter and verse.'

Just before I left Gray Gables I read an editorial in the Boston *Herald* referring to Mr. Foster's book and saying that it would be issued this week. I immediately wrote to the publishers asking them to send me a copy as soon as the book was out. I am expecting it daily.

To E. C. BENEDICT

Princeton, *October* 16, 1900

We have been here almost a week, and are fully settled again. I intended to get at work immediately, at some jobs that confront me; but I find that it takes a little time to get tame after the summer's revel....

Commodore, I am sometimes a little troubled over this election business. This, of course, is in confidence. We are all influenced in our judgment by what we see immediately about us. Calculating by all rules and reasoning that approve themselves to me as safe and sensible, I cannot see how anything dangerous can happen; but I have a short season of doubt and apprehension every day after reading my mail. My letters come from such a variety of people, in such different stations, and many of them are so earnest, and indicate that the objections and oppositions to all that is implied in imperialism are so deep and deliberate, that I sometimes wonder if more is not going on in the minds of the people than we have any idea of. This feeling is only temporary; for the moment I take a pencil and make figures, I come to the same conclusion — 'It is impossible' — that is, unless Illinois and Indiana part their moorings. I shall be glad when the election is over....

To DON M. DICKINSON

Princeton, *October* 18, 1900

...I am just starting to attend 'Billy Wilson's' funeral — a sad errand. A good man dies when his country and friends need him desperately.

In April or May, 1897, or somewhere about those months, the Reform Club had a dinner in New York for the avowed purpose of crystallizing sound Democratic sentiment and, as I understand it, of making a stand against Bryanism. Carlisle, Wilson, Turner, Caffery, Patterson, Shepard,

Bynum, and I spoke. De Witt Warner, at present a Bryan fugleman, *presided*.

I spoke of 'True Democracy' and did not mince matters at all in my condemnation of Bryanism and all it implies, and as vigorously as I could I tried to set forth its dangers to the country and true Democracy. I noticed that many of my auditors seemed to look aghast at my boldness, and I noticed afterwards that my declarations and those contained in the better speeches made on the occasion attracted but little public attention.

I think the chairman or secretary of the Sound Money Committee in Missouri sent me a little pamphlet containing all these speeches which I thought I put aside for future use as a reference; but after a pretty thorough rummage I cannot find it.

In present conditions and if my position is of the importance that many suppose it to be, a republication of the speech I made at that dinner might be useful. I don't see how an honest man holding the view I there expressed can favor Bryanism now....

THEODORE ROOSEVELT *to* CLEVELAND

Albany, *November 22, 1900*

During the last campaign I grew more and more to realize the very great service you had rendered to the whole country by what you did about free silver. As I said to a Republican audience in South Dakota, I think your letter on free silver prior to your second nomination was as bold a bit of honest writing as I have ever seen in American public life. And more than anything else it put you in the position of doing for the American public in this matter of free silver what at the time no other man could have done. I was delighted to find that Governor Shaw of Iowa had just the same feeling about it that I had, and made an even fuller acknowledgement of the debt due to you in one of his speeches at which I was present. I think now we have definitely won out on the free-silver business and therefore I think you are entitled to thanks and congratulations.

To CHIEF JUSTICE MELVILLE W. FULLER

Princeton, *November 25, 1900*

I am very desirous of having a chat with you on political topics especially and many other topics in a more general way; and I had hoped to do this in combination with an errand to your court which I thought of making. It happened in this way: I have been employed as counsel in a case which has interested me immensely on account of the questions involved and some peculiar circumstances connected with it. A motion is to be filed next Monday, December 3, in your court for a writ of certiorari, in the hope that the cause may be at another time heard there on its merits; I had nearly consented, on the earnest persuasion of my client (who has more confidence in my legal ability than he ought to have), that I would personally appear at the court on the motion. However, after a full conference and co-operation with other counsel employed in preparation of the petition and brief, I have thought it more appropriate that Mr. Custer of Chicago, one of my associates, should file the papers. In the meantime, I have pledged to my client my life, my fortune, and my sacred honor that our application will receive proper consideration — though I know your court must be greatly annoyed by the number of similar applications, and averse, without good reason, to thus add to its calendar. Every counsel, I suppose, is convinced in such applications that his case is exceptionally meritorious; and I may be as much mistaken as many others — but nothing short of an adjudication of the highest court of the land will convince me of it.

It occurs to me that I have inordinately extended what I intended merely as an explanation of my failure to see you next week. I find I am more fully possessed by my case than I supposed.

To JOHN G. CARLISLE

Princeton, *December* 14, 1900

... It's very queer that so long a time has elapsed since we have met or communicated — though I have heard about you sometimes. I was pleased very much by your interview given out just after the election. Though I thought at the time it was about right, I have been more and more convinced ever since that it hit the nail quite squarely on the head. I was very much encouraged at first by the tone of some of the Southern papers, but I am not now feeling so well, since I see that many others of them are still inclined to play the fool and ass. I am actually ashamed to read some of their editorials indicating that they are willing to profess to believe that the South is not getting its share in the *control of the Democratic party* — and this at a time when so many good Northern Democrats are attempting to repair the damage which has been visited upon the party largely through the solidity and preponderating influence of the Southern contingent in the present organization.

It appears to me to be a question whether sense or nonsense will prevail in that quarter. It may be that the weight of sentiment will settle on the right side. If it does I can see a bright prospect for rehabilitated Democracy — otherwise a longer flounder in the mire of wilful defeat....

To the EDITOR OF THE ATLANTA *Journal*
Princeton, *December* 24, 1900

I do not like to be called upon to deny or notice anything the *Constitution* may charge against me, but since you seem to be disturbed by its statement that I voted for McKinley, I am willing to say absolutely and *sans* reservation that it is not true. I will be drawn into no further discussion on account of the *Constitution* nor into any further denials of its untruths.

To DON M. DICKINSON
Princeton, *December* 28, 1900

Since I received your telegram on election night, giving your idea of the result, I have heard nothing from you .... I hope in the coming year you and I will see brighter political skies, for I know we both love our country. I think things look brighter for a Democratic return; and I say this not only in spite of but because I am just now in the current of abuse again for my devotion to true Democracy; and aside from this I hear, on the other side, such expressions that convince me that with all the abuse of me there is an increase in the conviction that Bryanism and Populism must be cut out of our party organization. As compared with this, the abuse of me is as dust in the balance.

I don't know what you think of my deliverance upon the 'Plight of Democracy,' but I am sorry I wrote it. I shall appear in one more article, 'The Young Man in Politics,' and expect to subside for a time at least and make room for abler attempts than mine can be.

XVI

CLOSING SCENES

CLEVELAND was greatly touched, as the years of retirement passed, by evidences that after all he was held in high regard by the American people. He spoke more and more frequently in Eastern cities, always to appreciative audiences, and when he went to St. Louis in the spring of 1902 to attend the dedication of the Louisiana Purchase Exposition, he received a striking ovation. Not a few voices even proposed him for President in 1904. This was absurd, for his health had become infirm, and he suffered greatly from frequent attacks of rheumatism and stomach trouble. Nevertheless, his renewed influence enabled him to play an important rôle in the campaign of 1904. Though his personal preference was for Olney or Gray as the Democratic nominee, he early came out for Alton B. Parker; for he saw that Parker offered the best means for uniting the conservative Democrats. When the Convention met, it reverted with enthusiasm to some of Cleveland's principal doctrines, and by a decisive vote acquiesced in Parker's telegram stating that he regarded the gold standard as irrevocably fixed. Cleveland made two speeches and wrote several magazine articles in behalf of Parker, and felt his defeat by Roosevelt as a heavy blow. A few months later the ex-President entered upon his last public service. The famous life insurance scandal broke upon the public in the spring of 1905; in an effort to stabilize the Equitable Life, which was the centre of this scandal, Thomas Fortune Ryan purchased control at a cost of some $3,500,000; and in order to reassure the public, he entrusted the reorganization of the company to a board of trustees composed of Cleveland, Justice Morgan J. O'Brien, and George Westinghouse. The principal task of these three men was to select a large number of new directors, and to impress upon them the necessity of devoting time and hard work to their offices. When the reorganization had been completed, Cleveland continued to serve three of the largest life insurance companies as a referee in a certain group of disputes, while he subsequently became head of the Association of Presidents of Life Insurance Companies. But his health gradually became worse, till in 1907 he was incapacitated much of the time. He had been sorely stricken in the first days of 1904 by the death of his eldest daughter, Ruth. In consequence of this he gave up Gray Gables, and spent his last summers instead in New Hampshire, finally buying a house there near Tamworth. Much time was also spent at Lakewood, New Jersey, and some in Florida. Early in the spring of 1908 he suffered a prostrating series of gastro-intestinal attacks, and on June 24 died at Princeton. He was buried there two days later.

To J. STERLING MORTON

Princeton, *January* 14, 1901

I returned yesterday after a two weeks' absence from home; and have this moment learned, through the last issue of the *Conservative*, of the death of your son Carl. Both Mrs. Cleveland and I are saddened by this intelligence and hasten to express our heartfelt sympathy with you in your great grief. The exceptional tenderness which I recall existing between you and your son, while it cannot fail to add sharpness to the first stages of your affliction, must aid in the future your comfort and alleviation. In days to come, all that he has been to you and all that you have been to him will be gratefully remembered, while a sad pride will come to you in recalling what he has been to others and how well he met every duty of life.

To E. C. BENEDICT

Princeton, *February* 10, 1901

... I fully approve of the way you let me into the cyclone of Wabash. Gresham used to say on certain occasions, 'The Wabash is rising.' These words have now a new significance to me, and I am just reckless enough to say, 'Let her rise.' I believe I have heard you and Larry say something about 'overstaying the market,' and I am glad to note your statement that you are informed the move upward has just begun.

I think I intimated to you once that we possibly might not be at Gray Gables this summer. A short time ago I had an inquiry about the place looking to renting it, to which I replied that I didn't see how I could quite bring myself to the point of going elsewhere for the season. The matter has just been renewed in such a way that I am considering it seriously. I have sometimes thought that a summer spent more inland and in a higher altitude might be well for me as well as my wife and children; and with the rent I could get for Gray Gables it would not be a bad scheme on the money side of the question....

To E. C. BENEDICT

Princeton, *February* 17, 1901

... If you and I were speculators instead of steady-going investors, I think I would suggest that one of us buy a moderate amount of something, and having thus prepared the way for a decline, that the other sell a large quantity of the same thing short, and divide the profits. It must be that such a scheme would work....

To E. C. BENEDICT

Princeton, *March* 3, 1901

I shall do all I possibly can in a substantial way, and supplement it by merely suggesting the cause [1] to perhaps half a dozen friends. I certainly cannot do less. All but you whom I shall address, or to whom I have already written, are among those whose relations have been closer with Mr. Wilson than yours; and I remember how generous you were on one occasion to our friend in life....

I am thoroughly sick of my work preparatory to my platform appearance;[2] and somehow I seem to be generally out of sorts in a mental way; but what you write about your sister's patience and uncomplaining faith, together with a renewal of my own firm faith on the subject, have made me more confident than ever, that happiness and contentment are but relative terms which define conditions attainable in every environment....

To RICHARD OLNEY

Princeton, *March* 3, 1901

Does the within circular appeal to or impress you at all? If it does not, please ignore it entirely — that is, regard it as never having been sent. I could not refuse to do what I could; and I did not desire to refuse, for I am much interested in this project of commemorating the public services of Mr. Wilson — as well as the purity of his personal character. I am such a poor beggar, however, that I shall only contribute all I can myself, and present the cause to a very few that I hope may not be irritated and annoyed with it.

I have been struggling with the Venezuelan boundary question, with a

---

[1] A fund to endow a chair in Washington and Lee University in honor of William L. Wilson.

[2] His lectures on the Venezuela question on the Henry Stafford Little lectureship at Princeton.

view of talking to the students and others about it on the 27th and 28th instants. I have in my narrative just reached the time when your twenty-inch gun [1] was fired; and I am provoked to find that if I had looked at that fulmination in the beginning, I could have stolen a great deal from that which would have improved my recital of facts and saved me a world of trouble. Can you tell me without bother who made the first 'nibble' at arbitration as between us and Great Britain, and how it was done? I find something from Sir Julian [2] that indicates there had been previous personal interviews on the subject, your inquiry what Lord Salisbury meant by 'settlements,' and something from Mr. Bayard to Salisbury, speaking of arbitration as an end desired by both countries; but I do not find among the papers that I have anything embodying the first advance in that direction. Don't take any trouble in the matter, for I can get on without the information by a general statement that a movement was made, etc. I would not desire, in any event, to make a prominent point of the matter; but I suppose I am right in my recollection that England moved first.

In reviewing the subject I am surprised to find how mean and hoggish Great Britain really acted; and I like old Mr. Salisbury much less than I did. I have had Mallet-Prévost here and am glad to find that Venezuela did pretty well in the arbitration, after all; but what a disgusting story he told about the way the award was reached.

I saw the *Atlantic* yesterday. If you have seen it I want to ask you if you ever read anything quite so absurd as the article on McKinley as President;[3] and what an outrageous suppression of truth there is in the reference to the statement of the Pacific Road's indebtedness. I thought Woodrow Wilson's preceding article on the 'Efficiency of Democracy' was a close second. I only read the two articles and laid down the book entirely satisfied.

To E. C. BENEDICT

Princeton, *March* 24, 1901

Your last letter came duly to hand. I was sorry I could not be with you over Sunday at Indian Harbor, but the last work on my lectures would not

---

[1] Olney's note to Lord Salisbury on the Venezuelan question in the summer of 1895.

[2] Sir Julian Pauncefote.

[3] Written by Henry B. F. MacFarland; a piece of fatuous eulogy, asserting that 'The story of the United States in the summer of 1898 is as dramatic and as brilliant and as glorious as any that history tells.'

permit it. The final ceremonies will take place next Wednesday and Thursday night, and then I shall breathe freely again.

I have such a fixed idea that one summer away from salt water will be good for us all that I regard the next summer so spent as a settled thing. It is altogether likely that we shall be neighbors of Mr. Gilder in the Berkshire region within three or four miles of the New Haven Railroad and about two hours from Greenwich. I don't see anything to prevent our having some good fishing bouts together during the summer if my yacht is in order.

I see 'the Wabash is rising.' I'm not afraid of wet feet; and then we've got rubbers, you know. I note certain mysterious hints you throw out in regard to some wealth I am not to know about just yet. I don't think you ought to do that sort of thing. I am already under such obligations to you for known kindnesses that I am afraid if you indulge in secret kindnesses I shall have more of obligation on my shoulders than I can bear.

To DANIEL S. LAMONT

Princeton, *March* 26, 1901

I enclose a circular which shows you that I am on the committee attempting to raise $100,000 to endow a chair in Washington and Lee University in honor of our friend Wilson. I am such a poor one to beg that I have thus far done nothing; and if it was for myself instead of the memory of a dear, dead friend, I would go hungry before I would annoy you. It seems to me that Wilson deserves some token of remembrance from the great and vital interest which he served so well, and I am sure such a sentiment will naturally be intensified in the cases of those who were personally associated with him.

I have modified my notions somewhat in regard to the particular project now pending, and think on all grounds this endowment ought to be accomplished. At any rate, I mean to help — though I fear but little — to the very last cent of my ability.

Now, Colonel, you know the chief object of this note. There are but very few to whom I shall present this matter, for I can hardly bring myself to speak of it even to as intimate a friend as you. If you are inclined to help, I hope you will let me forward your contribution. If not, I pray you not to be impatient of this application. I wonder if Whitney could not be induced to do something for this cause.

I am 'up to my ears' in preparation for my lectures. It sometimes seems that I must give up the job. I keep at it every day and every night, but my progress is very discouraging. I am afraid I shall be obliged to keep 'pegging away' pretty steadily until the things are thrown overboard on the evenings of the 27th and 28th of March.

To RICHARD OLNEY

Princeton, *April* 15, 1901

I am not certain that I ever thanked you for your last letter, in aid of my Venezuelan talks. I rather slid over the particular branch of the subject to which your letter was related, without attempting to indicate directly whether we or Great Britain made the first advance towards arbitration. I am satisfied now that would have been the best course to take, even if I had been perfectly informed concerning the matter. The so-called lectures were very well received, I thought, and they are to be published in the June and July issues of the *Century Magazine*.

We have definitely determined to spend our summer vacation among or near the Berkshire Hills in Massachusetts. I know we shall miss very many things that we have greatly enjoyed at Gray Gables; but I have an idea that a summer 'off' inland and in higher atmosphere may be well for Mrs. Cleveland and the little ones — to say nothing of the economy of the change. I have rented Gray Gables to Mrs. Keyes of 88 Commonwealth Avenue, Boston. I do not expect I can keep away from there all summer....

To DON M. DICKINSON

Princeton, *April* 27, 1901

I have just received and read your article in the *Inlander* on the study of the law, and if you were concerned in putting it in my hands (though I do not recognize the handwriting of the address), I want to thank you for it. Your article is the best thing on the subject I have ever read. I suppose I am influenced in this opinion by the fact that the ideas you express are those which have been floating about in my brain for a long time, but which I could not formulate as well as you have if I should try until the end of my allotted days.

We have had such a vile 'spell of weather' here that living has been a grief and good spirits exceptional and difficult.... I have kept fairly well through it all — though constantly inclined to depression and profanity.

It's a little comforting to see the end of Bryanism in politics, but on the Democratic side I am constantly asking, 'What next?'

In your last letter you asked about the phrase 'perfidy and dishonor.' It was used in a letter to Mr. William L. Wilson just as he was going into a conference on the tariff bill. The letter will be found on page 309 of the *Public Papers* for the last Democratic Administration and the words are at the close of the sixth paragraph. I suppose you have the volume referred to — if you have not I would be glad to send it to you. I am wondering when the crash that must follow our present madness will come, and how far-reaching its results will be....

To CHARLES S. HAMLIN
Tyringham, Massachusetts, *August* 18, 1901

Your letter is at hand. You are very kind to invite us to visit you and you may be sure we would enjoy seeing you and yours in your summer home; but you know how well all become fastened and how the days pass during a summer sojourn. I have been on two fishing trips to Gray Gables, lasting in one case one day and in the other two days. Mrs. Cleveland starts with one of the children on Tuesday the 20th for perhaps a week's visit to the old home on Buzzards Bay. Perhaps you can see her then.

I saw a mention of the Governor scheme in a newspaper quite lately, and was immediately subjected to conflicting emotions regarding it. I have not the slightest doubt of the benefit to the morale of the party which your candidacy would bring about. I believe it would hasten the day when Democracy in Massachusetts would be respected and trusted again. We shall have great opportunities when that day arrives. It has not, however, yet dawned; and I have no idea that there is a Democrat in Massachusetts that can carry the State this year. Thus convinced, my mind instantly fell foul of the question, what would defeat mean to you?

Would you be kept in line for a better opportunity in the future or laid aside? I don't like to see you beaten; and in any event I don't think the Massachusetts Democracy has behaved well enough to deserve the sacrifice of as good a man as you merely for the sake of aiding it in a restoration to popular confidence — *and there an end* — so far as you are concerned. And perhaps, too, the rebound might be greater if the party was allowed to play the fool a little longer. This is a cold-blooded suggestion and only made in the light of your situation. I don't want to see you made a pack-horse and turned out uncared for afterwards. Of course the silver craze is done for; but there is a lot of meanness yet, among those who have been shouting for it. They probably will try to get back into full communion with restored Democracy, but with as little relinquishment of the 'old grudge' against the Democrats as will serve their purpose. This will all be knocked or thrashed out of them sometime, and I hope speedily. When days are brighter we shall need some good man to put forward; and then I do not want to see you treated as a '*has been.*' If you think the party in the State is reunited and ready to make a strong pull unanimously and heartily, that's one thing; but if they want you to help bridge them over to a better standing simply and solely, it seems to me that is quite another.

I don't know why I have to preach to a man who is cool enough and wise enough to see all the elements involved better than I can....

To E. C. BENEDICT

Princeton, *October* 8, 1901

I have taken a great liberty with you and perhaps with your money. I should have asked your participation in a scheme, hatched a couple of weeks ago, I think, to give General Alexander [1] a bridal gift. General McCook has the thing in charge, and the matter has gone so far that the gift has been selected — but not seen by any of us except General McCook; and in view of the fact that General Alexander was married last Tuesday, October 1, I have written McCook today suggesting that the gift be appropriately marked with the addition of the initials of the five donors (McCook, Benedict, Evans, Lamberton, and myself) and shipped at once to General Alexander at Georgetown. The present is to be a handsome silver cake tray and the cost will be one hundred dollars, with the cost of engraving and express charges added....

I am afraid, Commodore, that I cannot go to Gray Gables again this season. I have agreed with Mr. Carnegie to make an address on Founders' Day at the Carnegie Institute early in November, and with the inevitable interruptions that must occur, I feel that I ought not to take the time for such a trip. Besides, I am afraid it is too late for assured good fishing....

---

[1] Edward Porter Alexander (1835–1910), Confederate general of artillery, and a government director of the Union Pacific Railroad during part of Cleveland's first Administration, owned North and South Islands off the South Carolina coast, where Cleveland often went duck-hunting. In 1901 he married Mary L. Mason.

To OSCAR S. STRAUS

Princeton, *December* 24, 1901

Your letter of the 18th instant is at hand.[1] Illness has confined me to my room for almost five weeks, and I am now hardly able to sit up and write this.

My desire for the quiet and comfort of absolute retirement from public or semi-public service is very strong and grows stronger as the days pass. I should without hesitation yield to this and decline your request that I accept a place among those who are to seek the promotion of industrial peace by friendly intervention in troubles between employers and the employed, if I were not afraid that I should thereby disregard an important duty. My reflections have made it clear to me that I should accept the place assigned to me, and I do so with an earnest wish that those selected to actively represent the purposes and activities of your conference may not labor in vain....

To JOHN URI LLOYD [2]

Princeton, *December* 31, 1901

Yesterday there came to me your last book, *Warwick of the Knobs*, for which I also thank you most sincerely. I have examined it sufficiently to know that I shall be much interested in its careful perusal; and I am especially gratified to see that in it you have carried out the intention you had in mind when I saw you last, looking to some explanation of certain religious beliefs peculiar to the section of Kentucky of which you write. I shall begin the reading of the book today or tomorrow.

I have been confined to my room for about six weeks. What is left of my illness is due, I suppose, to an attack of gout (or something of that kind) which took advantage of a feeble condition from another cause to fasten itself upon me. I am hoping to celebrate New Year's Day (tomorrow) by going downstairs; but somehow I don't gain strength as I ought.

To JUDSON S. HARMON

Princeton, *January* 7, 1902

I was glad to read your letter a few days ago. Somehow as I grow older, I prize more every indication of the remembrance of good and

---

[1] Straus had invited Cleveland to accept a place on the industrial relations committee of the National Civic Federation.

[2] John Uri Lloyd (1849–1929), at this time professor of chemistry in the Eclectic Medical Institute of Cincinnati, had written several popular novels.

constant old friends. The errand part of your letter, however, was not so pleasing. To a man who wants above all things to be amiable and good-natured, the necessity of declining requests such as you present, based upon friendship and esteem, is anything but gratifying.... I am sincerely sorry, therefore, that I must decline the invitation you convey. My illness has been of such a sort as allows but slow recuperation. Though I am now getting on nicely, I have not been out of the house for more than six weeks. I hope towards the last of the month to take a trip South. It is expected, I suppose, that I shall deliver a couple of lectures here early in the spring. Perhaps I will give them up; if I do not, their preparation will be all the mental labor I shall undertake in the near future. To all this add my unconquerable and growing disinclination to speech-making of every kind and variety, and it seems to me that you have reasons as plenty as blackberries why I cannot be with the good people of the Commercial Club on the 22d of February.

I have been quite annoyed lately by a feeling of uncertainty as to whether I answered your letter written to me soon after your State Convention. I was exceedingly interested in the account you gave of the proceedings and I was very much afraid that the narrow margin against the endorsement of free silver was a bad omen. I do not see how we are ever to regain the confidence and support of the people sufficiently to win in a national election until we clear ourselves from... the control of the men who have disgraced and discredited us. And inasmuch as this resuscitation is of necessity a slow process, it seems to me that the sooner a beginning is made the better. Of course I am a mere looker-on; but I am intensely desirous to live [long] enough to see true Democracy redeemed and triumphant....

To RICHARD OLNEY

Princeton, *January* 7, 1902

I am not sure that all afflictions have their compensations — but I am certain that the illness which has recently overtaken me brought its compensation in that it furnished the occasion for the extremely friendly letter you wrote to Mrs. Cleveland. It seemed good to see your handwriting again about our house — though I confess it is almost too legible to look real natural.

I am getting on very well. Though I haven't been out yet, I can stump about the house quite well and am anticipating with much pleasure a duck-shooting trip to South Carolina, which is sort of set down to begin in about two weeks. I am inclined to believe this sickness is 'a judgment on me' for abandoning Gray Gables last summer. I do not mean to invite another such judgment in the same way.

If I attempt to give any so-called lectures this spring, I mean to talk about the Chicago riots. I believe at the request of one of the Houses of Congress you prepared a sort of history of that affair on the reasons and justification of our interference. My remembrance is a little hazy as to the legal steps, injunctions, and certificates of inability to serve or enforce which preceded *troops*. Possibly I may not feel like preparing these lectures. I shall not do so unless I can make plain the entire matter....

To A. B. FARQUHAR

Princeton, *January* 21, 1902

I have only sufficiently recovered from my illness to be about a little, and ride out in a limited way. Tomorrow I hope to start on a trip to the South, in the expectation that my health will be largely reinstated by the outing.

I received your letter yesterday, and am much impressed by the manner in which you discuss our relations and our duty to Cuba. The arguments used in opposition to the tariff concessions she implores, based upon our material interests, are fallacious, mistaken, and misleading, while their source and the agencies of their propagation and spread cannot fail to be recognized by every honest, patriotic citizen with shame and humiliation.

It seems to me, however, that this subject involves considerations of morality and conscience, higher and more commanding than all others. The obligations arising from these considerations cannot be better or more forcibly defined than was done by President Roosevelt in his message to Congress, nor better emphasized than has been done by Secretary Root. And yet Congress waits while we occasionally hear of concessions which rival sugar interests might approve in behalf of trembling Cuba. I do not believe that nations, any more than individuals, can safely violate the rules of honesty and fair dealing.

Until there is no escape, therefore, I will not believe that, with all our fine words and lofty professions, our embrace of Cuba means the contagion of deadly disease.

To RICHARD OLNEY

Princeton, *February* 8, 1902

I am extremely grateful for your kind letter; but I reproach myself for the trouble a suggestion of my wants has caused you. My stay in South Carolina was cut short by a physical condition which gave emphasis to the proposition that home is the best place for a man who is a little sick. I have not been out of the house since my return — ten days ago. I am not really sick, but am lame, a little weak, and I think a little lazy. It is not likely that I shall deliver my 'lectures' this winter; but if I begin their preparation I shall find the way much easier than I expected — thanks to your kindness. I hope I shall be able to try another trip next week, and perhaps after that there may be more vigor and energy aboard.

I have been very much interested and sometimes amazed by the eddies and currents in public affairs. If we only had a little bit of the old style of Democratic leadership, I believe we might confidently hope to see the disturbance settle our way; but good Heavens! what can we look for under the management of Bryan and Jones and Stone [1] and such haphazard blunderbuss shooters?...

I had a nice visit from Mr. Carlisle two or three weeks ago. I think he is doing well — which gratifies me very much because I think he deserves it....

To DON M. DICKINSON

Princeton, *February* 8, 1902

I hope I need not assure you that I was glad to hear from you after a very long silence, and to know that the cloud caused by your son's illness was passing away. I am exceedingly gratified, too, to learn of your professional activity and the trust and confidence your industry and ability have inspired. I think if I am ever tempted to be envious it is when I compare my condition to that of those who are still in the enjoyment of life's labors and activities....

Do you know anything about Mount Clemens for gout and rheumatism? Perhaps I'll have to go to some sort of springs or something of that kind. It will be hard for me to get up my courage to the point, for I dreadfully hate to leave home and shrink from meeting strangers. I often think it hardly worth while to tinker up the old hulk.

[1] James Kimbrough Jones (1839–1908), was Senator from Arkansas 1885–1903; William Joel Stone (1848–1918), was Senator from Missouri from 1903 to his death.

Isn't it a shame that the old Democratic party is in such a wretched condition to retake its abandoned vantage-ground? No punishment or humiliation would be too great for those who have betrayed the best cause and the best fighters that ever met an enemy or won a battle. What an inspiration it would be to hear Democratic leadership proclaim, 'Bryanism is not Democracy.'

To E. C. Benedict

Princeton, *February* 13, 1902

I am off, I suppose, tonight for a club in Virginia where there are apt to be ducks in the vicinity. I don't know whether I shall shoot or not, but I hope I have spirit enough left to defend myself against a duck or goose either, if I am attacked. I haven't been out but twice since I returned from South Island, but I hope I shall not break up another excursion as I did a short time ago.

There's a fellow by the name of Frederick Upham Adams, the author of *The Kidnapped Millionaires*, whose intimacy I don't really hanker for. He's induced me to say something pleasant about his book and now he is sending a thing to the newspapers for comment and publication, entitled 'Is Grover Cleveland a Radical?' and calling attention to the fact that I endorse all the silly things in his book. This is nothing but an attempt to excite curiosity and perhaps increase the sale of a book which converted me to radical ideas. I consented to the publication of what I wrote, but I gave him no permission to enlarge and misinterpret what I wrote.

To Dr. John M. Reiner [1]

Princeton, *May* 3, 1902

Your letter is at hand. I have just returned home after a prolonged absence and am fairly overwhelmed with arrearages of correspondence and other work. I cannot certainly say that I will be here all next week, but I do not now know of anything that will take me away — especially in the early days of the week. I would be glad to see you on any day I am here, to suit your convenience.

I hope you will not take it amiss if I add the expression of my hope that you do not desire to ask me to deliver an address or attend Commencement Day exercises. I have already been obliged to decline many such

[1] John M. Reiner was president of the College of Saint Thomas of Villa Nova, at Villa Nova, Pennsylvania, which was giving Cleveland a degree.

requests, and a number more await declination among letters still un-answered. It is impossible for me to consider such a proposition.

To Dr. John M. Reiner

Princeton, *June* 5, 1902

Your letter is at hand. What I shall say at your Commencement exercises will consist of but few words — partly addressed to the president of the college, and partly to the graduating students. It will not deserve the title of an 'address,' and I have not thought it would be worthy of publication — at any rate, before its delivery. Perhaps we had better hold that subject in abeyance for the present.

Mrs. Cleveland will accompany me; and we shall plan to go to Mrs. Wilson's home at Rosemont for luncheon immediately after the Commencement exercises. I would be glad to have you write me as soon as possible the hour appointed for the beginning of these exercises and their probable duration so that I may complete arrangements for our travel to and from Villanova.

To Judson S. Harmon

Gray Gables, *July* 15, 1902

I want to thank you for giving me the opportunity to read your tribute to Mr. Wald. It seems to me sincere, finely worded, and in every way admirable.

It has been a long time since I saw you, though I have occasionally heard of you through New York friends. Well! Our Cabinet circle has suffered from death's invasion; and Wilson and Morton have led the way to safe retreat. My first Cabinet, as organized when I took office, are all gone except Whitney and Vilas. Somehow these things set one to thinking, and ought to tighten the ties between those of us who remain.

Olney stopped over to see me a few days ago. I had not seen him for about two years; but we were not here last season.... So far as I can see, Democratic harmony is not flourishing very much, though there seems to be a great addition to the number of those who desire to find the old path again. There is to be a dinner here in Massachusetts, the latter part of this month, at which it is expected that Bryan, Senators Bailey and Carmack [1] (of Tennessee), and Edward M. Shepard will speak. Olney

---

[1] Joseph Weldon Bailey (1862–1929), was Senator from Texas 1901–13; Edward Ward Carmack (1858–1908), was Senator from Tennessee 1901–07.

has declined, but I believe Hamlin expects to attend. He wants to run for Governor in this State. I do not look for much good to result from the affair....

To RICHARD WATSON GILDER

Gray Gables, *July* 27, 1902

Your letter was received yesterday. I do not recall the incident Mr. Nelson [1] refers to — that is, in just the way he puts it.

I made a nomination once in New Jersey which caused Senator McPherson [2] to give me notice that he would thereafter make no recommendations for appointment in his State — to which I replied that I would get along without that assistance. I knowingly and deliberately sent two nominations to the Senate very much against the wishes of both the Senators [3] from Missouri. Both gave out that they would thereafter in no way indicate to me any wish concerning appointments in their State. I never saw Senator Vest in the White House afterwards. Senator Cockrell came once at my request and in the course of the conversation gave me the same notice as Senator McPherson had and got the same answer. I may have said at some time the thing referred to about losing a State, etc., but I am quite certain I never said it to the Senators of the State in question. I am anxious to have Mr. Nelson's article a bold and pungent one. He cannot make it too severe. Of all things that can be imagined as absurd and inconsistent with the theory and proper operation of our Government, the Senate as at present, and for years past, organized, reaches the extreme.

I wrote an article for the *Saturday Evening Post* [Philadelphia] which appeared sometime in April last entitled 'The President and His Patronage,' which I hope Mr. Nelson has seen. It might give him a hint or two. If an article is to appear in the *Century* intending to inform our people of Senatorial abuses, it ought to be so thorough as to leave nothing further to be said. The combination among the members of that body to oppose any Presidential nomination distasteful to the Senators of a State is not put any too strong by Mr. Nelson and can be abundantly established by instances.

[1] Henry Loomis Nelson (1846–1908), journalist and author, who was editor of *Harper's Weekly* 1894–99.

[2] John Rhoderic McPherson (1833–97), was Senator from New Jersey 1877–95.

[3] Francis Marion Cockrell (1834–1915), was Senator from Missouri 1875–1905; George Graham Vest (1830–1904), was Senator from Missouri 1879–1903.

To Professor Andrew F. West

We shall all be very glad to see you; and the earlier you come the better we shall like it.

I especially want to see you soon. I have been blundering away at my Wilson inauguration task;[1] and the more I tug at it the madder I become at you and the others who managed to get me into the scrape. You are not to understand that I intend to go to the length of venting my outraged feelings by inflicting upon you personal violence — and yet you are not entirely safe. I hope so long as you are my guest, at least, I shall be able to restrain myself. If you have Randolph with you, we shall be very glad to see him too.

I want your judgment on the plan I have blocked out for what I am to say when Wilson is inaugurated — and I don't want any feeling about it either. If I am on a wrong tack I want to set my sails differently and go to work again. I want to be early about it, for I have another thing to do of a similar sort and I may get sick or some other mischance might intervene later on....

To E. C. Benedict

... So far as I can hear, Brad and I are the only persons who have lately caught any tautog worth talking about. We have had some very fine catches by dint of bait other people don't seem to get. If you can come up towards the last of the coming week, I think we can give you some good fishing. We shall be away (Brad and I) on Thursday (the 20th) at an 'Old Home' performance at Sandwich. Next week, beginning with the 1st of September, we shall have, I expect, a pretty good houseful of guests, but you know you are welcome at any time.

I have been thinking a great deal lately about the business and financial outlook. If the coal strike and some other matters don't change soon, I believe there will be serious trouble before we are six months older. I don't like to see so many things depending on one man's nod.

---

[1] Woodrow Wilson was inaugurated president of Princeton University on October 25, 1902, with an important address by Cleveland.

To PRESIDENT THEODORE ROOSEVELT

Princeton, *October* 4, 1902

I read in the paper this morning, on my way home from Buzzards Bay, the newspaper account of what took place yesterday between you and the parties directly concerned in the coal strike.[1]

I am so surprised and 'stirred up' by the position taken by the contestants that I cannot refrain from making a suggestion which perhaps I would not presume to make if I gave the subject more thought. I am especially disturbed and vexed by the tone and substance of the operators' deliverances.

It cannot be that either side, after your admonition to them, cares to stand in their present plight, if any sort of an avenue, even for temporary escape, is suggested to them. Has it ever been proposed to them that the indignation and dangerous condemnation now being launched against both their houses might be allayed by the production of coal in an amount, or for a length of time, sufficient to serve the necessities of consumers, leaving the parties to the quarrel, after such necessities are met, to take up the fight again where they left off 'without prejudice' if they desire? This would eliminate the troublesome consumer and public; and perhaps both operators and miners would see enough advantage in that to induce them to listen to such a proposition as I have suggested.

I know there would be nothing philosophical or consistent in all this; but my observation leads me to think that when quarrelling parties are both in the wrong, and are assailed with blame so nearly universal, they will do strange things to save their faces. If you pardon my presumption in thus writing you, I promise never to do it again. At any rate, it may serve as an indication of the anxiety felt by millions of our citizens on the subject. I have been quite impressed by a pamphlet I have lately read, by a Mr. Champlin of Boston, entitled, I believe, 'The Coal Mines and the People.' I suppose you have seen it.

To E. C. BENEDICT

Princeton, *October* 20, 1902

I am glad you have it in mind to clean house a little when prices recover somewhat. It seems to me you calculate on the right basis when you

---

[1] In May, 1902, a strike had begun in the anthracite coal fields; it was now threatening widespread suffering; and on October 3, Roosevelt presided over a conference of operators and union leaders at the temporary White House in an unsuccessful attempt to bring about peace.

anticipate a fair appreciation in the immediate future and then — something else. Especially will this be the case, I believe, in securities dependent in any important degree upon coal operations and transportation. Of course there may be something you know and I do not which counterbalances what appears on the surface. Somehow I think United States Steel may not be in the category so far as recession is concerned.

What you write about our joint operations makes me feel as though some distant relative had died and left me something. I saw Laurence Hutton this morning and he invited me to dinner Saturday night and said he should invite you. We (Mrs. Cleveland and I) must go out to dinner Friday night. That makes it a little awkward about entertaining friends at home that night. If, however, you choose to come Friday, we have a place for you. I think perhaps you would enjoy it more to come Saturday morning early enough to attend the inauguration exercises at 11 A.M. and stay over Sunday with us and as much longer as you can. We have a ticket for you to the ball and the football game in the afternoon if you care to go. Hutton's dinner Saturday night you would enjoy if he don't overlook the invitation. Tom Reed, T. B. Aldrich, Stedman, Mark Twain, and 'such' will be there. I know he intends to have you among those bright lights.

To the REVEREND CHARLES WOOD

Princeton, *November 2, 1902*

A colored minister by the name of Anderson has pestered me nearly to the point of collapse to get me to preside at a meeting in Philadelphia in behalf of a manual training school he has in charge — called, I believe, the Berean Training School. Of course this is a good cause if it is in good hands; and I want to do what seems to be my duty in this matter — but the colored man as well as the white man is mighty uncertain.

I am told by Mr. Anderson that Booker Washington will attend his meeting if I do. This makes the matter more troublesome; but I think the prominent cause of my disinclination to attend this meeting is the exaggerated and foolish idea Mr. Anderson has that my attendance would result in the collection of large sums of money for his school. I know he will be disappointed in this and I shall be proportionally embarrassed. Would you object to writing me what you think of the school project and whether this meeting is something I ought to attend?

The sooner you can do this the more certainly will you save my reason
— if not my life.

STATEMENT TO THE NEW YORK World

November 23, 1902

My opinions on political matters are well known, and I should hesitate
to make any further statement were it not for the urgent solicitation of
the *World*, which is pursuing an editorial policy that must, in my judgment, tell for Democratic success and the public welfare. Moreover,
what I say to the *World's* representative will, I know, be entirely free
from the outrageous attempts lately made to represent me as endorsing
not only un-Democratic policies, but men who have unfortunately gained
temporary Democratic notoriety.

It seems to me that the Democratic situation is such as to awaken the
satisfaction and hope of every thorough and consistent Democrat. Our
party has certainly regained its old-time fighting condition and recovered
the morale that promises old-time success and prestige.

I think, however, while we can safely assume that we are not immediately threatened with a repetition of un-Democratic heresy, there
are palpable dangers to be avoided if the rejuvenation of Democracy is
not to be obstructed. The movement toward this rejuvenation tends to a
complete abandonment of our late yielding to the temptations of expediency, as against a firm adherence to Democratic doctrines.

The condition necessitates, in my opinion, both in the enunciation of
platform principles and the selection of candidates, a sturdy and determined march to the goal of substantial and thorough Democracy. In
other words, I believe that if the Democratic party is tempted, under a
mistaken apprehension of the meaning of the revival of true Democratic
sentiment, to stop short of this goal, and temporize by presenting to the
people platform, principles, and candidates not entirely in keeping with
an absolutely changed policy, it will satisfy them that it cannot safely
be trusted.

Such a situation cannot better be described than by the homely illustration of a man sitting down between two chairs. Such behavior would
discourage sincere and thoughtful Democrats now hopeful and expectant,
and repel a large independent contingent who seek relief from the heedless arrogance of the Republican party.

It may as well be fully understood that any party promising such relief cannot calculate that the people are in the mood to be deceived or cajoled by the tricks of expediency. The movement now under way must be pursued with thoroughness, consistency, and honesty. There need be no fear that a radical return to true Democracy is dangerous to Democratic success. The history of the party abundantly shows that it is only departure from principle and yielding to temptations of expediency that have brought disaster.

The hope of the Democratic party lies in the inevitable discovery by our people of its beneficent aims and purposes. Already the beneficiaries of the high protective tariff are so reduced in number, and the benefits derived from protection are so palpably lessened, even as applied to the selfish interests of those who have heretofore insisted upon its continuance, that they are inclined to receive with favor the adoption of the Democratic doctrine of a tariff for revenue.

The popular apprehension of the evils of aggressive expansion, and its incompatibility with what has always been regarded as safe Americanism, is constantly growing and cannot fail to become, in the near future, a most important factor in the political thought of our people.

The tremendous growth of trusts, the immense business aggregations and the manner in which they stifle healthful competition and throttle individual enterprise cannot long pass unheeded by the voters of the land. The stupendous governmental extravagance that now prevails must at length be appreciated by the people as not only a drain upon their earnings and accumulations, but as a most pernicious example calculated to undermine the love of wholesome economy among our citizens.

These topics and others which might be mentioned, and the abuses connected with them, should be bravely and uncompromisingly dealt with by the Democratic party, as they all involve Democratic principle. We should have sufficient faith in the intelligence and right-mindedness of our countrymen to arouse a confident anticipation that they will speedily confide the treatment of these vital questions to the party which satisfies them of its intention to deal with them in an honest, unequivocal, and patriotic manner.

I see only hope and confidence in the future of Democracy, out this hope and confidence are based entirely on the belief that the party will be true to itself and true to its profession of devotion to the welfare of the people.

To A. B. Farquhar

Princeton, *December* 28, 1902

I want to thank you for your letter and for the enclosed copy of your argument on the eight-hour law. I have read both with very great interest. I recognize fully your ability, from actual experience and personal observation, to deal with questions related to the welfare of employers and employees; but these questions have taken such form and have assumed such proportions that I find it difficult to form a satisfactory conclusion on all the phases of the subject.

If there could only be the mutual forbearance and co-operation which it seems to me should naturally exist between capital and labor, how completely our troubles on this score would vanish. I was interested but much surprised to hear the arguments on the labor side which were presented at the recent meeting of the Civic Federation. They did not strike me as being very impressive; and some things insisted on by representatives of labor unions seemed to me rank and indefensible industrial heresy. I believe it would be a tremendous gain if the entire matter could be removed beyond the reach of designing and reckless demagogues. I hope conditions may be improved; but I am not certain how it can be done.

To E. C. Benedict

Princeton, *January* 5, 1903

I don't see any 'stupidity' in the manner of making out our cribbage account as it appeared before your alleged correction.... The 'dirty paper,' as you call it, was intended, I suppose, to show all the games not settled up and balanced, as they were consecutively played. You will see on the left half of the paper after the footings for 1897 and 1898... that there are two other footings for each of us representing games for 1899 — 471 and 488 — and *for part of 1900* — 512 and 484. These are carried up on the right side of the paper and added together, making an aggregate 983 and 972 (your credit of 17, of course, was carried in the item of 488 against 471). The remainder of the games played in 1900 were added to this aggregate, and at the end of that year the account stood for the two years 1350 for me and 1296 for you; and this difference of 54 games was settled by handing me back my check....

To LINDSAY RUSSELL

Princeton, *January* 9, 1903

I am in full sympathy with the purpose of the Pilgrim Society and heartily approve the formation of an American Branch in New York. I shall not be able to attend the meeting for that purpose next Tuesday.

I have a reluctance to joining an organization when unable to devote my time to its objects; and in this case I cannot hope to devote any time or attention to the contemplated new organization. I think it would be better to secure more active charter members than I would be. If, however, with a full understanding of these things, it is thought best to include me among the charter members, and if the object of the organization is fully stated as being 'the promotion of Anglo-American good-fellowship,' I cheerfully consent.

To KOPE ELIAS

Princeton, *January* 12, 1903

Your exceedingly friendly letter came duly to hand. I want you to understand how fully I appreciate your devotion to me, and the readiness you have always shown in championing my interests.

I do not feel as you do, on the subject discussed in your letter; and you must not think it ungracious for me to tell you so. I consider my political life as ended. While I do not feel obliged to tell my thoughts to all who seek to know them, it is only fair and just for me to say, to so good a friend as you, that in present circumstances the idea of another candidacy seems to me to be absolutely out of the question, impossible for every reason, a sufficiently controlling one being the fact that I cannot conceive of a situation which would induce me to accept another nomination. One of the most ardent hopes of my life is to see our grand party regain the confidence of the people, and again win victories; but my place must hereafter be in the ranks.

This letter is for your personal information, to the end that your friendship for me may not lead you into a position of embarrassment.

To E. C. BENEDICT

Princeton, *January* 18, 1903

I received a few days ago your check for seventeen dollars, in full of an account which I am glad to know is adjusted without resort to legal investigation. I forbear to comment on the fact, disclosed by your letter, that your check was not drawn until you had counselled with the eminent lawyer retained by you to advocate and defend your cause in cribbage complications. I am constrained, however, to congratulate myself upon the submission of my claim, and your inadmissible pretext of defence, to Mr. Carlisle's keen sense of right and justice....

I have nearly given up the Florida idea — unless I am driven to a warmer climate by stress of weather. It seems sort of selfish to go entirely for my personal comfort, leaving my family to fight the battle with cold weather alone; and I cannot figure out how I can take them all with me. There is nothing that presents anything like the same allurement to me as a retreat *somewhere* that would give me freedom from nagging annoyances and exhausting importunities. It is quite evident to me, however, that I must get on as well as I can and take what comes....

To EDWARD M. SHEPARD

Princeton, *February* 6, 1903

I want to thank you for your hearty and courteous tender of the hospitality of your home on my contemplated visit to Brooklyn, on the 8th of March.

When Mr. Harrity and his party saw me here, Mr. Straus invited me to go to his house in New York; but the matter is still unsettled — and can remain so, if you are willing, until we can judge better of the necessities and the conveniences of the case.

I leave tomorrow for Florida in company with a very close and dear friend who has been sentenced to banishment there for a while. We both expect to be home again about the 1st of March. I cannot, however, put entirely out of mind the thought that in just such a case our return home is subject to some uncertainty. If a longer stay than I have indicated looms in sight, I shall promptly inform Mr. Hinrichs, and I hope they will proceed without me. This can be done without risk, for I believe I have never been useful in any attempts to aid enterprises of the kind projected, by taking such a part as is proposed.

My love for Mr. Beecher and my regard for friends who have interested themselves in establishing a memorial to him, are abundantly sufficient to insure my attendance at the meeting on March 8th if I can get there.

To JOSEPH GARRETSON

Princeton, *February* 6, 1903

I have received your letter of the 4th instant asking me on behalf of the [Cincinnati] *Times-Star* for an expression regarding my intentions as related to the next Democratic nomination for the Presidency.

I cannot possibly bring my mind to the belief that a condition or sentiment exists that makes any expression from me on the subject of the least importance.

To FRED W. HINRICHS

Princeton, *March* 3, 1903

I have only just returned from Florida. I have had almost no opportunity to prepare anything for next Sunday and I am a little afraid that I cannot do better than to bring my manuscript of my small address with me when I reach Brooklyn. I will do the best I can. I gather from something contained in a letter from Mr. Straus that the exercises will take place in the evening. Will they?

I intend to stay with Mr. Straus. I shall probably go to New York Saturday night, and if I cannot send my manuscript in before, it can be obtained on my arrival.

To E. C. BENEDICT

Princeton, *March* 29, 1903

Until I saw Mr. Truesdale and the receipt of your letter a few days ago, I had been wondering for a long time whether you had returned from your trip to South Carolina, which a previous letter forwarded to me when in Florida, informed me you were about to take.

It would be foolish and insincere for me to disclaim the pleasure I derive from the kindly sentiments of my fellow-citizens which come to me from many quarters. It seems to me, however, that I have expressed myself with sufficient clearness to enable all who believe in my sincerity to understand how settled is my determination to spend the remainder of my days in the ranks of private citizenship. I can understand why the dirty little scoundrel who is allowed to scatter filth through the columns of the Louisville *Courier-Journal*,[1] and a few vile imitators, pretend to misunderstand me; and I am not inclined to give them the satisfaction of plainer speech. I doubt if the time will ever come when a more explicit

[1] The reference is to Henry Watterson, who ceased friendly relations with Cleveland in 1892.

declaration will be necessary for the satisfaction of my friends and the decent people of the country. When in my judgment that time has arrived, such a declaration, in my own way, will be forthcoming.

Mrs. Cleveland has shown me your letter to her received last evening. We were very glad to hear such favorable reports from Mrs. Benedict, though Louise yesterday afternoon did not express herself on the subject to Mrs. Cleveland in the most encouraging way — we fear based on later information. You may be sure we are earnestly hoping that she will return in greatly improved condition.

The St. Louis Exposition managers expect that someone will accompany me. I have already asked Mr. Oscar S. Straus and he says he will go. Of course it is not anticipated that I will confine myself to one companion. I hope I need not assure you that I would be very glad to have you join us. The plan at present is to start April 28 on a train which I think leaves New York about noon. However, all that can be more definitely arranged hereafter. I would be glad to know as soon as possible that you will certainly go....

To E. C. BENEDICT

Princeton, *April* 22, 1903

Your letter is just received. I am glad to know that the plans for our start and housing at St. Louis [1] are so well arranged and so well understood. I will join the party already on board the train, at its arrival at Princeton Junction (9:57). I *may* have another passenger with me. Mr. Clarke Davis will join the party at Philadelphia.

My plan has been from the first to leave St. Louis on Friday, May 1 — the day after the exercises in which I expect to participate — and arrive home Saturday evening or Sunday morning, depending on the time of day we leave St. Louis.

An examination of the time-table sent to me illustrating our route does *not* disclose the fact that we pass through Indianapolis. The last place mentioned on the table before St. Louis is Vincennes.

So far as I am informed, the party (unless you are excepted) are desirous of returning as soon as possible. Friday will be devoted to Foreign Representatives and Saturday to Governors. The President will leave Thursday night; and I don't see why the management should not be glad

[1] Cleveland spoke at the dedicatory exercises of the Louisiana Purchase Exposition on April 30.

to have the ex-President out of the way as soon thereafter as possible. At any rate, Mr. Francis [1] (and I suppose everyone else prominently concerned in the affair) understands perfectly that I am to leave on Friday, May 1.

To JOHN T. MCCUTCHEON [2]

Princeton, *May* 8, 1903

I desire to thank you most sincerely for the book of cartoons you kindly sent me a few days ago. I assure you it does more than furnish me and my family 'with a few moments of amusement.' Its possession furnishes proof of friendly remembrance which is a lasting gratification.

I think you have quite lately executed the best cartoon in which I appear that I have ever seen. I refer to that one in which I am represented as 'not a candidate' in four different phases or stages. I have been immensely amused by it — especially by the changing expression of the main figure, and the others as well.

Hoping that my behavior will always allow me to be amused or instructed by your pictorial work. . . .

To RICHARD W. KNOTT [3]

Gray Gables, *July* 4, 1903

Your letter and the editorial from the *Evening Post* accompanying it have been forwarded to me here, and I thank you most sincerely for both. I am especially gratified by your just explanation in the editorial of the cause and justification of my course in submitting to the special session of Congress in 1893 the financial crisis — even though it postponed, and perhaps injured, the cause of tariff reform.

I have always regarded this as the most self-sacrificing and patriotic service I have been privileged to render my countrymen in all my public career; and I have been profoundly astonished to see how it has been perverted, by what you aptly call 'the babble of political assailants,' to the uses of malicious misrepresentation and downright lying.

To MRS. JOHN GRIER HIBBEN

Gray Gables, *July* 18, 1903

I sent you a telegram this morning that a tramp boy [4] had trespassed

[1] David R. Francis was president of the Exposition.
[2] The distinguished cartoonist of the Chicago *Tribune*.
[3] Editorial writer for the New York *Evening Post*.   [4] Cleveland's second son, Francis.

upon our premises. He was first seen and heard at 10 o'clock A.M. (I hear him now), and I sent the despatch a few moments thereafter, to Redfield, where, according to the itinerary you sent me, you were to be from the 5th to the 20th instant. I have heard since that there was difficulty in transmitting the despatch from Camden to Redfield; and I shall not be surprised if this letter or the newspapers give you the first information touching today's important event.

The shameless naked little scoundrel weighed over nine pounds. Richard was very much tickled as long as he thought it was something in the doll line, and was quite overcome with laughter when he found it was 'a real baby.' He and I have been planning for the amusement of the new-comer when he shall arrive at Richard's present age. He denies with considerable warmth any intention of taking him by the hair and throwing him down. In point of fact we have agreed upon no particular line of conduct, except an engagement on Richard's part to teach the young brother to swim if all goes well.

The dear mother is as well, apparently, as possible; and seems to me very self-conceitedly happy — as if she thought she had done a good job. She sends her love — and so do I. And we both include the Professor.

To RICHARD OLNEY

Gray Gables, *July 23*, 1903

In as many languages as are spoken in the wilds of Africa, my youngest son insists that I must promptly convey to you his thanks for the very handsome present you sent to him. He bids me to say to you besides that not only he but his posterity will hold in grateful remembrance the donor of this useful gift. The mother of the boy, in a language I have learned to heed, commands me to say to you that she appreciates, as deeply as her son and his posterity can possibly do, this evidence of your continued friendship; and last, but I hope not least, the glad father joins in the chorus. I am sure you will be glad to learn the mother and child are doing 'as well as can be expected.'

To JOSEPH JEFFERSON

Buzzards Bay, *September 16*, 1903

By a change in our plans quite suddenly made, we find ourselves in the confusion of preparation for leaving here for Princeton in about an hour. I am sorry I cannot take you by the hand as I say 'Good-Bye.'

I cannot leave without telling you in this cold way how much I have enjoyed your companionship during this vacation time, and how large a figure you will be in the pleasant retrospection. I can hardly believe our summer's stay here is over; but I suppose these vacations will seem shorter and shorter until the end of the chapter. With affectionate regards, Mrs. Cleveland and I bid you and Mrs. Jefferson and your household good-bye — in the hope that Fate will be kind to us all, and permit us to meet when summer comes again.

To Oscar S. Straus

Princeton, *October* 6, 1903

Your letter is just at hand. I am sorry to disappoint you in anything; but you really must 'let me off' from the Civic Federation meeting in Chicago. My plan as settled upon is to arrive in Chicago Wednesday morning, the 14th, attend the dinner of the Commercial Club that evening, and start on my return trip Thursday afternoon as early as possible. I have partly agreed to attend a lunch Mr. Eckels wants to give before I start. There are good reasons why this plan must be exactly carried out.

I ought perhaps to add that I am not in a good mood to attend the Federation meeting. I am doing quite some perplexing thinking in these days. I hope my extremely kind feeling towards labor organizations, etc., will hold out; but it is just now sorely tried.

To St. Clair McKelway

Princeton, *November* 25, 1903

I have waited for a long time to say something which I think should be said to you before others. You can never know how grateful I am for the manifestation of kindly feeling toward me on the part of my countrymen which your initiative has brought out. Your advocacy in the *Eagle* of my nomination for the Presidency came to me as a great surprise, and it has been seconded in such a manner by Democratic sentiment that conflicting thoughts of gratitude and duty have caused me to hesitate as to the time and manner of a declaration on my part concerning the subject — if such a declaration should seem necessary or proper.

In the midst of it all, and in full view of every consideration presented, I have not for a moment been able, nor am I now able, to open my mind to the thought that in any circumstances or upon any consideration I would ever again become the nominee of my party for the Presidency. My determination not to do so is unalterable and conclusive. This you at least ought to know from me. I should be glad if the *Eagle* was made the medium of its conveyance to the public.

To DANIEL S. LAMONT

Princeton, *November* 30, 1903

I received your letter (without date) an hour or two ago. I was very much surprised to gather from it that you were not aware of my McKelway letter published in the *Eagle* on the 27th. I waited as long as I could without much advice or apparent interest on the part of friends as to the time or manner in which I should speak. Of course there was but one thing to say, and I thought I saw that longer delay would subject me to embarrassment I did not deserve.

Do you think that in view of my elimination from Presidential discussion Mr. Laffan[1] would care to see me? If so, of course I would be glad to meet him....

To JOSEPH JEFFERSON

Princeton, *February* 3, 1904

Our good friend Mr. Gilder has been in a bad way for a number of months. His trouble seems to be of a rheumatic character and though he has improved somewhat his amendment is slow. He rides out every day, I believe, and walks out a little. What he needs now more than anything else is a short sojourn in a climate so warm and sunny that he can be much in the air without exposure and have opportunity to loaf and bask. If it was so that he could be with you at Palm Beach a little while, I am sure it would do him a world of good. He is evidently casting about for somewhere to go; and Mrs. Cleveland has just received a letter from him in which he says rather pathetically that the doctors think Lakewood will not do and that Stuart is too damp, etc.

Of course no suggestion has been made to me, but I cannot help telling you these things. He is able to take care of himself and would, as you know, make no trouble. I do not know that he would feel that he could go to you at Palm Beach; but I hope I am not doing an improper thing to

---

[1] William M. Laffan, associated with Charles A. Dana on the New York *Sun* after 1877, was owner of that newspaper from 1902 to his death in 1909.

intimate to you that an invitation urging him to do so would do him good even if he could not accept it....

To John G. Carlisle

Princeton, *February* 18, 1904

The supplementary report of the Attorney-General arrived in due time, and I am much obliged to you for it. I certainly thought I had acknowledged its receipt until I received your note a few minutes ago. Again I am obliged to recognize the advance of mental weakness which age invites....

I see this morning's *Herald* contains quite a long quotation from my *Saturday Evening Post* article on Democracy's opportunity. Do you know that, in spite of all self-argument and the approval of good friends, I have not at all times been free from misgivings concerning that article; and yet the activity of the Bryan-Hearst outfit goes far toward relieving my doubts. In any event, such Democrats as you and I are entitled to make our position understood as distinctly and *fightingly* opposed to any more Democratic fool business. It is not pleasant to be accused by others, or to suspect oneself, of insisting upon a position the party will not reach: but the sun is not clearer in bright noonday than is the proposition that any lesser position in the coming fight would result in another defeat so crushingly that our party organization could hardly survive it.

I am so sure of this, and I am so attached to the principles of true Democracy, that I utterly refuse to be a party to the crime of their betrayal. And I am in very comforting company as long as such men as you do likewise.

To Mr. G. Epps Tucker

Princeton, *February* 20, 1904

I have read your letter of the 5th, describing your pointer dog and setting forth his special capacity as a duck retriever, with a great deal of interest, and I am very much obliged to you for giving me an opportunity to become his owner. The truth is, however, that my duck shooting is confined usually to one trip during the season, and I do not think that it would be fair, either to me or to the dog, if I should become his proprietor for the slight period of time which I could devote to our joint recreation.

To DANIEL S. LAMONT

Princeton, *February* 28, 1904

I am surprised at the contents of your letter. Fanning came here Thursday before I heard from you with a letter from McKelway more superlative and commendatory than I had ever seen, assuring me that nothing that passed between us should be published unless I agreed to it, and indicating, I thought, that his purpose was more to have a chat with me than to interview me. Mr. Fanning certainly seemed like a decent fellow and in reply to his question on the subject I said I had nothing to say for publication. I talked quite freely to him and he did not appear to be a very decided Parker boomer.

My notion is that if there is to be an effort to get our party in any kind of promising shape there ought to be a movement in a hard-headed sensible way. Perhaps Parker has such a start that he would be the best one to concentrate on. You know my idea has been that Olney or Gray would suit present conditions best. I want you to tell all who talk 'Cleveland' nonsense that it is a waste of time that might be profitably spent in other ways.

I would not accept a nomination if it was tendered to me — which of course it cannot be — and I don't want to be considered as a defeated candidate for nomination. I am content. I want to see the party succeed, but I hope there will be no idea of playing any kind of trick on me.

To RICHARD WATSON GILDER

Princeton, *March* 11, 1904

I am very sorry to read between the lines of your letter that up to the time it was written your improvement in health had not been 'by leaps and bounds.' In this particular instance I think what 'they say' is correct; and I hope and believe that on some fine morning, after a longer stay in Florida, you will wake up and find you have left your present old bore of a companion, Bad Health, in the rear.

I note what you say of Leupp's [1] book and my letter. I do not care to see any more of the book than I have seen in the papers. I am not at all surprised that he turns up an entirely headless Roosevelt tenter.

I am amazed at Roosevelt. He seems to have thought it a proper thing,

[1] Francis E. Leupp, one-time Washington correspondent of, the New York *Evening Post*, in whom Cleveland long reposed special trust; at this time Commissioner of Indian Affairs under Roosevelt.

not only to make quite a general exhibition of my letter, which he should certainly have regarded strictly personal (unless I consented that it should be otherwise treated), but as I understand it has permitted his ready Glorificator to put it and its surroundings in an entirely false light.

I did not keep a copy of my letter, but have obtained one in a quarter far removed (in point of space) from the White House. It speaks for itself, and I would not, if I could, take from or add to it. I am not sorry that this incident and one or two others like it have effectively put me on my guard against writing letters of any description to Mr. Roosevelt. The letter referred to is, I am told, already in one or more newspaper offices; and its publication, I understand, is threatened when in the opinion of Roosevelt's tenters the psychological moment arrives — if it ever does.

I must for the present withhold assent to your suggestion that my letter be published in the *Century*. I hardly think the time will ever arrive when 'the game will be worth the candle,' but if it does I shall quite likely think it well to make the letter more understandable, by publishing one or two I have received from the White House with some explanations of my own.

There are some people in this country that need lessons in decency and good manners. Perhaps you will think, after reading this, that I am one of them....

To RICHARD WATSON GILDER

Princeton, *March* 21, 1904

I have received Morley's *Life of Gladstone* and I desire to thank you for it from the bottom of my heart. Somehow I don't get much chance to read now-a-days; but this book I shall read.

I hope by this time the good effects that should result from your stay at Palm Beach are beginning to appear. I have faith in the possibilities of the place in that direction, but I have not as much faith in your ability to be a loafer, nor in your good sense when the question of health and too much work is to be considered. When will you learn that there is a line which marks the limit of needed and safe work?

I am feeling very much gratified by the turn political affairs are taking — in a personal selfish sense. I am quite sure that I am to be eliminated by the course of events and without volition or action of my own. More Cleveland luck!...

To WILLIAM B. HORNBLOWER

Princeton, *March* 29, 1904

I thank you for the pains you have taken to put in my hands the book I need. I expect to receive it today.

In reply to the other matter contained in your letter, I have to say that I have had doubts as to Mr. Parker's being the very best candidate in sight, considering all things; but I am not very strong in these doubts. One thing is certain, I think. He is clean, decent, and conservative, and ought on those grounds to inspire confidence in quarters where it is sadly needed if our party is ever going to be a political power again. It is in my view immensely important that the same portion of our party should be as united on a decent candidate as circumstances will permit — to the end that the movement now threatened in the direction of insanity and indecency may be run over and killed 'beyond recognition.' In this view it should be taken into account that Parker's candidacy has such a start and has so many elements ready to support it in the Convention that he appears to present a better rallying point than anyone else.

Personally I would prefer Olney or Gray; but they do not seem to me to be under much headway. I believe if I were in your place I would signify a disposition towards Parker.

To EDGAR GARDNER MURPHY

Princeton, *April* 9, 1904

I have received your letter of the 2d instant and its enclosure having reference to an organization of those who are interested in the prevention of abuse of child labor. This is a topic which appeals very strongly to me, and although I am unable to promise any time or attention to the project, if the mere use of my name will be any advantage to the enterprise, I gladly consent to become a member of the National Committee.

To GEORGE F. PARKER

Princeton, *April* 22, 1904

I did not remember that anything was said when you were here looking, in a definite way, toward my making a statement in the shape of an interview touching the political situation. I certainly do not want to do so at present. I am satisfied that in every view my silence is best in present circumstances. If a time should come when I can convince myself that any good purpose would be subserved by a renewed publication of my opinions or sentiments, I certainly would be glad to have your assistance and advice.

The situation would not be improved by anything from me now. I have a great disinclination to appearing too frequently in the newspapers in the rôle of 'guide, philosopher, and friend.'

To RICHARD OLNEY

Princeton, *May* 7, 1904

I am sending you with this under separate cover a copy of the *Saturday Evening Post*, containing a sort of a history I have prepared of the bond issues during the years you and I were wrestling with divers things. It has seemed to me that this and some other incidents of that period ought to be set forth before those most intimately related to them made their final exit from life's stage; and in default of the assumption of this work by those who might do it better, I have undertaken it. I wish you could find time to look over my bond issue history I send you.

Last Monday night I gave a sort of a lecture here on the railway strike or Chicago riots of 1894. My audience seemed to be very much interested, and I have a notion that the subject was treated fairly thoroughly. The lecture will not be published until it appears in *McClure's Magazine* for July. Inasmuch as you are frequently mentioned in this story, I hope you will read it.

I have treated now of four important incidents of my Presidential career: The contest with the Senate for the possession of Executive papers, the Venezuelan affair, the bond issues, and the Chicago strike. I would like to take a whack at the Hawaiian matter, but I doubt if I will.

I have made an arrangement with the Century Company for the publication in book form of the things above-mentioned which I have already written. What do you think of that? I think but very little of the scheme, but in the business part of it I have decidedly the long end of the lever, and I should like one copy of the book for my descendants. I can't see that the sales will amount to anything, but in a pecuniary way I am not much involved in that condition.

I am sorry we are not to be at Gray Gables this season. We expect to be very much secluded in the hills of New Hampshire. I don't know who will occupy Gray Gables.

I have wanted to write you on politics; but to tell you the honest truth I have been hoping that matters would take such a turn that it might be to *your advantage*, if we could both say I had no hand in advancing your name, so far as consultation with you was concerned. I think there's a chance for a mix-up yet.

To E. Prentiss Bailey

Princeton, *May* 11, 1904

I don't know of anything which has lately touched me so nearly as the receipt of the photograph of my mother which you thoughtfully sent me. I cannot tell you how glad I am to receive it and how much I value it. It is by far the best representation of her features that I have ever seen; and while I have, of course, her picture, this fills a want I have often lamented. Assuring you of my extreme gratitude and appreciation for this renewed evidence of your personal friendship...

To the Reverend Charles Wood

Princeton, *June* 2, 1904

I am writing to all the members of our Committee on Standing Committees of the Board of Princeton University trustees, and to President Wilson, suggesting that in view of the vacancies in the Board we recommend the continuance of our Standing Committees as they now exist, reduced in membership by such vacancies. It is of course impossible to apportion committee membership now among the trustees as they will be made up after these vacancies are filled; and if a readjustment is to be made, it can only be done intelligently when all the available material is in sight.

Will you please indicate in a word your approval or disapproval of this plan?

To Daniel S. Lamont

Princeton, *June* 2, 1904

I was very much interested in your last letter and in the two you enclosed me later. Our friend in Cincinnati evidently heard quite a buzz from the bee;[1] and I can see considerable sense in Wrightman's prognostications — except so far as he involves me in his plans. I gave the

---

[1] Judson Harmon hoped for the Presidential nomination.

interview to the *North American* for the sake of saying that I did not advocate Parker on any other ground except the lead towards him which made him the best to concentrate on to avoid a worse thing, and the further ground that his nomination would leave behind us the kind of nonsense that has lately afflicted us.

I still think he will be nominated; but I cannot feel sure of his election. Isn't it surprising how much childish foolishness there is abroad in our party — even after the two thrashings we have had? I am afraid another would only produce discouragement instead of reformation.

P.S. Of course you will understand that I was a good deal misrepresented in the *North American* interview — *as usual.*

To CHARLES S. HAMLIN

Princeton, *June* 23, 1904

Your exceedingly kind letter is just at hand, and I know that I need not tell you how fully we appreciate your willingness to serve so completely the West Ossipee immigrants. A few days ago the Superintendent of the Boston & Maine wrote me that one of the best of the road's coaches would be reserved for our exclusive use — and this I thought was all that was needed to secure the most comfortable possible travel from Boston to West Ossipee.

I must not omit to mention here that Mrs. Cleveland and Mrs. Finley have *each* the most wonderful baby in the world, and that both (the mothers not the babies) have expressed their preference for the ordinary day coach because it gives opportunity for the deposit of their prodigies '*length-wise on the seats.*'

Mrs. Finley's brother, A. A. Boyden, is to be in Boston next Monday and will join the party there on the arrival of the train Thursday morning and go with them to West Ossipee. To him has been assigned the duty of attending to the transportation of the persons and luggage across the city, and looking after the hungry ones. Thus you see with your thoughtful offer the party's comforts are thoroughly buttressed....

To RICHARD OLNEY

Princeton, *June* 24, 1904

You had better look out. I cut the attached bit of news from the *Sun* of this morning.

Did you ever see such a boyish, silly performance as the Republican National Convention which has just adjourned? Perhaps Lodge & Co. think they can safely calculate on the stupidity of the people to elect 'Teddy'; but if our party was in proper shape I am sure the conglomeration of the apostles of all good would find themselves reckoning without their host.

Somehow I cannot at all times feel very confident of Democratic success; but I honestly think if the hint contained in the clipping I send could lead to a practical result, there would be brighter hopes than in any other condition — I mean, of course, for the country and party and not especially for the comfort and peace of the gentleman referred to.

My family go to New Hampshire next week. I expect to follow them after a day or two spent at Gray Gables.

To WILLIAM F. VILAS

Princeton, *June* 24, 1904

Your letter came to me as a breath of fresh air in stifling heat; and it has stirred within me thoughts and memories of mingled quality. The old days in Washington, when you and I were associated in high and patriotic executive work, are recalled with pleasure and gratitude, born of appreciative thought of the devotion and generous aid of those who undertook with me arduous public labor; and with these feelings comes the sad reflection, that of all those who sat with me at the nation's council board on the 4th day of March, 1885, you alone remain. It seems to me, my dear friend, that the memories of that time, with its unreserved confidences, its perplexities and its achievements for the country's good, should draw you and me close together. I have often reflected upon the fact that among the close friends I gained in public life you are in the forefront — brought nearer and nearer to me from the day you informed me officially of my first nomination, through four years of Cabinet association and four years more of accord and agreement and generous co-operation as Senator and President. Those things cannot be forgotten nor for a moment put aside; nor can we be heedless of the acute sympathy each of us has felt for the other in similar afflictions.

I am grateful beyond all expression for the vindication of my public course which the years have brought; but it only strengthens my affection for those who in dark days were steadfast.

I am much interested, and if possible more than ever so, in our party prospects. I fear that they have been somewhat marred by foolish management; but still hope that old-fashioned Democratic good sense will in due time be in the ascendant. I cannot yet rid myself of the idea that Olney or Gray might develop a better candidacy; but neither seems to get a start and Parker has a large concentration of sentiment and preference in his favor; and there will be elements of so malign a character in our Convention that perhaps the Parker solid front could not be broken without danger. There is comfort in the assurance that Parker is a clean, decent man. I suppose you recall him as the man to whom the First Assistant Postmaster-Generalship was offered in 1885 after the death of Malcolm Hay. Parker declined the offer and afterwards the place was filled, as I always thought you preferred from the first, by the appointment of Stevenson.

I have been very much relieved and gratified by the turn of affairs which has quieted all serious mention of me as a possible candidate again.

Remembering your great affection for General Bryant, I knew when I saw a notice of his death how greatly it would afflict you. I want to thank you for sending me a copy of your beautiful tribute to your friend. I read it with great appreciation of its beauty and appropriateness, and with great admiration for its author.

We are all well and in the midst of preparations to leave here for a summer sojourn in three or four days. We thought we discerned on the part of one or more of our children a sort of dread of being at Gray Gables this summer without our dear Ruth. Our children have in seasons past been so much to each other, there, that rather than subject them to any sad reminder of their sister's loss which everything there would suggest, we determined to change the scene during the present summer by taking a cottage in the hilly out-of-the-way portion of New Hampshire.

We appreciate gratefully your kind expression of a desire to see us at your home. We remember our stay there in 1887 with very great pleasure and would be glad to repeat the experience.

To GEORGE F. PARKER

Princeton, *June 26*, 1904

I leave here for the summer on Tuesday a little after noon; and I am in a confused stir making preparations. Your letter came yesterday.

I have not been able to make out precisely the object of your efforts or the purpose of those acting with you. My idea, however, has been that something of a movement was on foot to bring about another nomination than Parker's — though I have not supposed that 'another nomination' was related to my candidacy.

I cannot believe now that in the face of all I have written and said, and in view of conditions as palpable to every friend I have in the world as they are to me, there can be an intention in any quarter to attempt, by any means or in any contingency, to compass my nomination; and yet within a day or two I have read and heard some disquieting things. I want to do what I can to avoid a charge of permitting misapprehension of my position; and so I say to you as plainly as I can that all thought of my candidacy must be abandoned as absolutely and inexorably impossible.

To JAMES SMITH, JR. [1]

Princeton, *June* 26, 1904

You will, I suppose, head the delegation from my State to the St. Louis Convention. I am well aware of the favorable opinion you originally entertained touching my availability as a candidate for the Presidency in the coming campaign; and I remember with great satisfaction the friendly spirit in which you accepted the reasons I advanced against that proposition, when we met here a long time ago. My public declaration made before our conversation and the apparent reception of my refusal to be considered a candidate as justifiably conclusive, by you and other friends, have led me to regard all discussion of the matter as ended.

I have heard and read some things lately that disturb me. Perhaps that is unnecessary, but I am very anxious that there should be no misunderstanding which can be chargeable to me or to anything I may do or omit to do.

In view of all the circumstances, I have ventured to write you this, and to ask you, as representing the State of my residence, as my friend, to prevent the use of my name in connection with the Presidential nomination at the Convention. I certainly could not accept it.

I cannot think that any occasion will arise calling upon you to do me this service; but as I am just leaving here for my summer vacation, I re-

---

[1] James Smith, Jr. (1851–1927), had completed his single term in the Senate in 1899, but was still the principal boss of Democratic politics in New Jersey.

gard it as not amiss to provide against even a very slight or possible contingency.

RICHARD OLNEY *to* CLEVELAND

Boston, *July* 1, 1904

Thank you for your last favor and the amusing cock-and-bull story contained in the clipping enclosed, which but for you I should probably not have heard of.

My opinion grows stronger every day that, if we are to be saved from four and probably eight years more of Rooseveltism, it will have to be done through your agency. I am equally sure that, while the prospect of another Presidential term is not only not alluring, but in all probability positively distasteful, your patriotism is too strong to permit of your refusing to make sacrifice which the exigency demands.

I was somewhat gratified at the temper of the Harvard Law School Association as exhibited at the dinner on Tuesday last. My few feeble remarks in antagonism to Governor Taft and his programme seemed to be approved by a majority of the audience.

To ALTON B. PARKER [1]

Gray Gables, *July* 14, 1904

I received your letter yesterday at this place where I have been stranded for more than a week on my way to join my family in New Hampshire.

I am certain that no man living appreciates your situation and its perplexities better than I; and I am equally positive that no one is more anxious for your election. Of course this does not necessarily mean that I can be of any great service to you — I wish it did. I hope, however, that you will feel absolutely at liberty to command me in every way. I am not afraid you will ask me to do anything inadvisable, and if at any time I am too forward with advice or suggestions you must go your way without the least embarrassment. Your judgment is too good, I am convinced, to be interfered with by *anyone*.

Our best campaign material just now is — YOU. I mean 'You' as you are manifested to your countrymen in the despatch you sent to St. Louis. The spirit and sentiment aroused by this utterance of yours should be kept alive and stimulated from time to time during the campaign. Occasions will present themselves when you respond probably to

[1] Alton B. Parker was nominated for President by the Democratic Convention in St. Louis on July 9, 1904.

the committee on notification, and when you write your letter of acceptance. I do hope that you will insist upon a free hand in meeting these occasions and that you will not hesitate to paraphrase or give your own language to our platform, to such an extent as to convince our people that you propose to keep the reins you have in hand, and that your conception of Democratic obligations will constrain you to protect all legitimate rights, and to restrain all harmful trespass upon the privileges and opportunities promised to *all* our people under our plan of government — so far as such an exercise of power is within Executive limits. For myself, I do not think expediency demands of you the distortion of anything your judgment suggests, in deference to the South or the radicals of our party. Bryan is doing the cause much good in his present mood; and I for one hope it will continue. We need Indiana; and if the Taggart Chairmanship will help us to get it, it might be well to remember that after all the Chairman of the Executive Committee of the New York Headquarters is the important man.

I am bothered about the question of retaining your judgeship while a candidate for President; but I hope there will be a safe deliverance.

To RICHARD OLNEY

Tamworth, *July* 19, 1904

I found your letter awaiting me on my arrival here a few days ago, after a long delay caused by a vexatious and stubborn illness.

I am very much pleased with the outcome of the Convention as brought about by Providence and a gentleman living in Esopus. Such Democrats as you and I ought to be pretty well satisfied. Bryan and Bryanism are eliminated as influential factors in Democratic councils, true Democracy has a leader, and its time-honored and approved principles again are set before the people of the land without apology or shame-facedness.

If we can only keep peanut methods out of our campaign management, I believe there is a good chance to rid the country of Rooseveltism and its entire brood of dangers and humiliations. At any rate, it seems to me there can be no excuse for lack of effort or half-heartedness on the part of any true Democrat who has waited all these years for party regeneration.

You certainly ought to be proud and delighted to have found and touched the underlying sense of American decency and fairness as you did at the Harvard Law School dinner....

To CHARLES S. HAMLIN

Tamworth, *July* 20, 1904

I was taken sick on my way home and was laid up at Buzzards Bay more than ten days — arriving here only last Friday the 15th inst. I found your letter awaiting me. We are all very thankful to you for your efforts to make the family's journey here convenient and comfortable....

I am very much pleased with the outcome of the Convention. I read with a great deal of interest your statement concerning the action of the platform committee. I have no doubt of the expediency of your course. I was so hard to please that I thought the gold standard declaration recommended by the sub-committee rather a poor thing, and when that was stricken out and nothing substituted my heart sank away down to my boots. I am quite happy now because I think Parker's telegram and the action of the Convention thereon have made both the platform situation and the *candidate* situation better than they could have been made in any other way. Of course if the advantage is to continue and grow, Parker must not let down in any spot or place, but must keep alive and deepen the impression that he is in command.

I had a letter from Charles R. Codman this morning. He is anxious that Judge Parker should take strong ground on the Philippine question. I agree with him fully in his estimate of the great importance of this matter, and I have written him that you and Collins are the men to present the subject to our candidate. I hope this will be done....

To CHARLES S. HAMLIN

Tamworth, *August* 14, 1904

... When I consider the alternative presented to our people in the pending campaign and realize the consequences involved in their voting power, I am almost frightened. I am so anxious to have them well informed that they may see where their safety lies.

To DANIEL S. LAMONT

Tamworth, *August* 21, 1904

I received your letter last night. Late in the afternoon of the 17th the despatch announcing the death of Mrs. Fuller reached me and I sent a message of condolence to the Chief Justice as soon as I could. Telegrams to and from this place have to be carried some distance by messenger and usually telephoned besides; but we usually get them all right. I wrote Justice Fuller a letter yesterday addressed to Sorrento; and I am glad to learn from your letter that he will receive it there.

I am much obliged to you for your interposition with Parker in my behalf on the stumping question. I have written and sent to *McClure's Magazine* what I think is a pretty good setting-out of Judge Parker's personal characteristics, etc. I expect, however, it will not be published before October 25 in the November issue of the magazine. I have about made up my mind that I cannot write the article they are begging me to prepare for *The Saturday Evening Post* entitled, 'Why Young Men Should Vote the Democratic Ticket.' I don't see how I could discuss that question at any length without provoking some embarrassing rejoinders.

I have thought it might be well some of these days to give in an interview through the Associated Press my ideas of the duty of Gold Democrats to be active in the campaign. There are two classes of our people, who, if they balk now, will not be entitled hereafter to much consideration. I mean the conservative true Democrats, Gold Democrats, or whatever else they may be called, and those engaged in the business of the country....

The *Sun* amuses me; and I keep thinking every time I read it about the dog mentioned in the Bible who returned to his vomit and the sow that was washed to her wallowing in the mire.

To DANIEL S. LAMONT

Gray Gables, *September 22,* 1904

There were, I am quite sure, no letters or communications leading up to the 'coal letter,' as Mr. Roosevelt calls it. He had already inaugurated his interference with the coal situation, to no purpose; the operators (or at least one or more of them) had in his interview with them behaved very badly, as I thought; and I was deeply affected by the threatened distress among our people, and the disorder that might result from a continuation of the quarrel between those who should furnish coal to innocent consumers and their employees.

Thus influenced, I wrote the letter. I am not ashamed of it and I do not desire to retract one word of it. Of course Mr. Roosevelt's use of it and the publicity he has given to a communication received in the circumstances existing at the time the letter was written is a matter to be judged by the rules which should govern intercourse between gentlemen.

His conduct in this regard, however, can be better accounted for than his apparent determination to have it appear that I was willing to be one of the board of arbitrators afterwards created. Nothing would have induced me to accept such a position. He wrote me, after his failure to accomplish any result by his interview with the operators, that he had in mind the appointment of a sort of commission to inquire into the facts of the situation for *his own information and guidance*, and asked me if I would consent to act on such a commission. After serious thought and *because* the inquiry proposed could in no sense be called an arbitration, I thought I ought to consent — and I did so. Soon after an arbitration was agreed on, and I was relieved from further concern with the matter. After that Mr. Roosevelt (notably at the time the new chamber of commerce building was opened) tried to explain to me why I was not put on the *Board of Arbitration*, and I then distinctly told him that I would not have accepted the position.

My impression is that before this interview he wrote me a note of a tenor somewhat similar to his conversation in the interview referred to, which note I believe I did not answer, as I saw no profit in dwelling upon an incident so completely closed. This is the entire story as to the facts. I am not positively certain that I have all the correspondence on the subject, but I have enough, I suppose, to support the version I have given.

Since I began this letter I have seen in a Boston paper the ticket nominated at Saratoga yesterday.[1] I think it is a good one, but somehow I hoped that 'the powers that be' would see their way clear to nominate Shepard.

A man told me this morning that he saw a statement in the paper to the effect that I was to make a couple of speeches in New York and one in New Jersey. It is foolish to let such things go out, and if I cannot avoid importunity for speech-making I shall be tempted to stay here until after election. I will do all I can for the cause, but as I have said to you, I am satisfied my best service would not be in the speech-making line. Mr. Hornblower has sent my nephew up here to urge me to attend and speak at a meeting of the College Men's Democratic Club. I did not say I would go; and I am now strong in the opinion that I ought not to go.

I don't know when I will be in Princeton again; but unless something

---

[1] At their State Convention at Saratoga the New York Democrats nominated D. Cady Herrick for Governor.

unexpected occurs I shall not leave here before October 1. I wish the people at headquarters would do everything possible to prevent the report that I am to take a speaking part in the campaign. I shall not do it, and by this time that should be distinctly understood. My refusal after the statement that I am to speak is likely to be misinterpreted and to do harm — certainly more harm than good. Of course I do not assume that what I may or may not do will make any great difference; but I want to help, be it ever so little....

To JOSEPH JEFFERSON

Gray Gables, *October* 1, 1904

Doctor Bryant and I did not feel that we could let the season pass without further indulgence in the pleasures of this locality; and we accordingly came here together on the 31st day of August. The Doctor deserted a little more than a week ago; and since that time I have been stopping with Brad. The sport has not been the best on record, but our stay here has after all been very enjoyable. I am remaining until I can see the beginning of the end of the proper construction of the dam we have been trying to have built for the past two years across Cedar Pond Creek, which divides my land from that of Moses Williams....

Since writing the foregoing I have seen in a Boston newspaper your alleged statement that your professional work is ended. If this is true, thousands and thousands will feel sadness and disappointment; but one of your most affectionate and devoted friends, with implicit faith that your judgment has not led you astray, rejoices in the freedom from labor and the long vacation you so well deserve, and which your retirement would insure. It is given to but few to have their years of final rest and enjoyment so brightly illuminated by the love and respect of their fellows — and the crowning delight is that you have richly earned it. I am sure that God will continue his goodness to you; and if I may allow a selfish feeling to intrude, I hope he may grant to me in days to come a fuller measure of your intimacy and companionship which has been so delightful in the past.

All this is predicated upon the correctness of the report I have read. If (as sometimes happens) this report is untrue, I shall not be sorry; but I hope you will not deem what I have written amiss.

To E. C. BENEDICT

Princeton, *October* 16, 1904

I believe that you are sincerely desirous that I accompany you on your South American trip; and I dreadfully hate to disappoint you. Of one thing you may be certain. I appreciate to the utmost your kindness in thinking of me in connection with such a delightful travel.

Though when I received your invitation, it seemed to me that I must forego the gratification of its acceptance, I determined to take a little time for consideration before settling upon a final conclusion. The thought I have given the matter and a survey of the entire situation has, however, confirmed me beyond change in the decision that I must ask you to allow me to 'take the will for the deed' in this manifestation of your friendship. I cannot escape the positive conviction that I ought to avoid an absence from home at the time fixed, for a number of reasons, which I beg you to believe, without detailed explanation, are abundantly sufficient — or at least in my view, absolutely inexorable....

To OSWALD GARRISON VILLARD [1]

Princeton, *October* 20, 1904

I have received your letter, asking me for a contribution to the Tariff Reform supplement to the *Evening Post* which you have in contemplation. Since the receipt of your letter I have not been in condition to write such a contribution as would satisfy me or be serviceable to your undertaking. Will you be good enough to tell me the latest date on which anything coming from me would be of service, and give me some little hint of the particular line which, in your opinion, I could best pursue in what I might have to say?

To DANIEL S. LAMONT

Princeton, *October* 27, 1904

Your letter is just received. I reconsidered my consent to attend the Schurz meeting the day after I gave it and wrote both Ridder and Schurz to that effect. I received a letter from Ridder this morning suggesting that he should come to see me next Saturday; and I have just replied asking him not to come. His failure to correct the newspaper reports that I was to attend his meeting has subjected me to importunities from a

[1] At this time president of the New York *Evening Post* Company, and chief owner of the paper.

number of quarters and I have notified him that I should make a statement through the Associated Press....

I am not in good shape as to my physical condition. I am trying to keep a little quiet, to fret as little as possible, and eat but very little, hoping to straighten up and be able to keep my Newark engagement. If you have an opportunity I wish you would say to Mr. Murphy how much I would enjoy looking in on his dinner party and thank him for his friendly remembrance of me. I will write him if I can.

You speak of Knox's [1] statement in yesterday's papers. I saw it this morning. It is of a piece with the barefaced impudence which seems to be the motive power in Republican campaign effort. What is the use of trying to check it?

To E. C. BENEDICT

Princeton, *October* 31, 1904

I was sorry to feel obliged to decline the requests of good Democratic friends in Connecticut to speak in their State this week. After speaking in New York I could not decline to attend one meeting in my own State; and having consented to that, I hardly dared to make another engagement of the kind within the short time remaining before election.

I am writing you early this morning. I believe I feel better this minute than I have for a good many days. Everyone says, 'How well you are looking.' I am not sick at all, but somehow I believe I have gotten into the habit of 'grunting around.' I go to Newark next Friday evening; and that will end my speaking work — for a time anyway. I can see other things coming after that, and I intend to stop grunting and complaining and go at them.

I have pretty definitely concluded not to go to South Carolina as usual, this winter. General Alexander writes me that there is a great deal of public work going on at South Island and I think he is not very sanguine about duck conditions this season. I have also given up, for the present at least, a ducking trip to Virginia which I contemplated taking about the middle of November....

To A. B. FARQUHAR

Princeton, *December* 12, 1904

I was glad to receive your recent letter after so long a silence. The result of the election was so astounding that I have hardly sufficiently recovered

[1] Philander C. Knox, Roosevelt's Attorney-General.

my composure to contemplate the reasons which led to it or the results likely to follow it. I am such an intense and unalterable believer in the saving common sense of the American people that I cannot yet believe that the tremendous Republican majority given at the last election should be taken to indicate the people's willingness to allow the principles and practices of Republicanism to be unalterably fixed in the affairs of our body politic. I believe that the next swing of the pendulum of public sentiment will be quite to the Democratic side of the dial, and that, if Democracy is prepared to do its duty, when that time arrives, it will become again the beneficent agent of the people's salvation.

A number of the incidents involved in the election have so surprised me that sometimes, for a moment, the idea has entered my mind that a change in the character of our countrymen has taken place. This is, however, only for a moment, and the second thought immediately reinstates me in the confidence which I have always had in our people's right thinking. How the rejuvenation of the Democratic Party which seems to be absolutely essential is to be brought about, I do not know; but I am certain that in due time a way will be made plain.

To DANIEL S. LAMONT

Princeton, *January* 19, 1905

Your letter was received a couple of hours ago. I would like very much to go with you to visit our dear old friend [1] and will do so sometime, though I do not see my way clear to start this week Saturday. (On reading your letter again I think you meant some Saturday instead of next Saturday.) I am preparing to go to Philadelphia a week from next Sunday to speak before the Pennsylvania Railroad Department of the Young Men's Christian Association....

An embarrassment occurs to me. How would it look for me (or you either for that matter) to go to Washington and not call on the President? And yet I would dreadfully hate to call on him.

To RICHARD WATSON GILDER

Princeton, *January* 28, 1905

You need not thank me, as you did in your last letter, for my co-operation with you in doing something that may cheer our old friend Mr.

---

[1] Probably Chief Justice Fuller.

Moore. The kindness and thoughtfulness of it is all with you; and you were kind to me as well as kind to him, in permitting me to join you.

I want to thank you for your trouble in attempting to set Mr. Peck [1] right — (Professor Peck — God save the mark!). I never heard of him until Nelson mentioned him in connection with his stuff; and I don't care what else he is, it must be that he is a lover of falsehood, who had rather, in the cloak of history writing, put down something new and striking than to tell the truth. There is another coyote in Kansas (I think Lewis by name) who is cut off the same piece; and I suppose such yelping and snarling as theirs is history.

I honestly think, my dear Gilder, that there are things in my life and career that if set out, and *read* by the young men of our country, might be of benefit to a generation soon to have in their keeping the safety and the mission of our nation; but I am not certain of this, for I am by no means sure that it would be in tune with the vaudeville that attracts our people and wins their applause. Somehow I don't want to appear wearing a fur coat in July.

Mr. McClure [2] and all the forces about him have lately importuned me, in season and out of season, to write, say, twelve autobiographical articles, offering what seems to me a large sum for them; but I have declined the proposition. I went so far (for I softened up a bit under the suggestion of duty and money) to inquire how something would do like talking to another person for publication; but that did not take at all. I don't really think I would have done even that, but the disapproval of merely a hint that the 'I' might to an extent be eliminated made it seem to me, more than ever, that the retention of everything that might attract the lovers of a 'snappy life' was considered important by the would-be publishers.

There is a circle of friends like you, who I hope will believe in me. I am happy in the conviction that they will continue in the faith whether an autobiography is written or not. I want my wife and children to love me now, and hereafter to proudly honor my memory. They will have my autobiography written on their hearts where every day they may turn the pages and read it. In these days what else is there that is worth while to a man nearly sixty-eight years old?

[1] Harry Thurston Peck was publishing in his magazine the *Bookman* chapters later issued in book form as *Twenty Years of the Republic, 1885–1905.*

[2] S. S. McClure, editor of *McClure's Magazine.*

To E. C. BENEDICT

Princeton, *February* 5, 1905

This, though late, is intended as a hearty 'Welcome Home.' The dreadful weather abroad on the sea put you much in my mind and intensified the pleasure which the news of your safe arrival created. I returned from Lakewood yesterday after a couple of days spent with my family, and for some reason or another I am a little under the weather today.

I enjoyed reading your interviews giving an account of your trip, and I fully agreed with Professor West when he said: ' While I was reading it, it seemed as though I heard the Commodore's voice.'

I hasten to inform you, what I know you do not suspect, that while you have been absent I have grown very, very rich — beyond the dreams of avarice. I hardly know how it happened, and to tell you the truth I don't believe I am very much to blame for it; but I mean to hold on to my suddenly acquired wealth as tightly and as long as I can.

I want to see you and satisfy myself whether you really do look as well as you are represented in the papers. I expect Mrs. Cleveland and the children will be home next Thursday morning; and I wish that as soon after that as possible you would pay us a visit. I want for one thing, to find out if you have learned any new cribbage tricks on your trip. There's a lot more besides that I want to know.

To THE OUTLOOK COMPANY

Princeton, *February* 6, 1905

In my judgment a knowledge of history becomes more important with the passing of time, and it seems to me that it never was so important as in these days of stirring events and wondrous change. Many of us are obliged to confess that for one reason or another we missed opportunities to study history in younger days. However much we may now lament this, we know the only chance we shall have to remedy our embarrassing deficiency must be found in an arrangement of historical facts and epochs, in such a way as to be suited to the engrossing occupations and scant leisure of our later years. I have never seen a work that so completely answers this purpose as *The Historian's History of the World.* It is of broader importance than a mere work of reference, and yet no book of reference can be more comprehensive or easier of profitable utilization....

To JOSEPH JEFFERSON

Princeton, *February* 10, 1905

Your never-failing kindness to me and mine was again made manifest a few days ago, when some sheepshead of fine growth and in safely frozen condition arrived at our domicile. Though we have postponed their cooking until the arrival home of Mrs. Cleveland and the children from Lakewood (which occurred yesterday), the opportunities you have previously given us to test the quality of this kind of fish allow us to anticipate with certainty the toothsomeness of this last arrival. This conveys the sincere thanks of our entire family.

Perhaps it is imagination, but it really seems to me that my physical condition gives me an unusually good excuse for a stay in Florida this season. Dr. Bryant being in somewhat the same situation, we have calculated on starting together during this month for a sojourn with Mr. Bessey at Stuart.... We both would prefer stopping with Mr. Bessey to any other arrangement and hope to bring that about. The freedom from crowds of strangers and the privilege of being as uncivilized as we desire appeal very strongly to us both. This is a long introduction to a statement which I hope will not be entirely devoid of interest to you, to the effect that we may have the very great delight of seeing you in Florida during your present stay there. I hope that if we do we shall also have a fish with you....

To RICHARD WATSON GILDER

Princeton, *February* 10, 1905

Yours of the 2d instant is at hand. I have written Mr. Paine declining to enter into his arrangement. It would be a mighty hard, and I think an impossible job, for me to join an autobiographical enterprise; and in any event I would not do so without a pretty good share of the profit. This may seem a little mercenary — I guess it is — but I ought to be well paid for surrendering my judgment as to the publication in any form. Though I have written the *McClure* people that I have fully determined to decline their proposition, Miss Tarbell wanted to see me next Sunday. I sent her word I should be away from home, as I expected to be until I received yesterday an admonition that home would probably be a very good place for me, for a few days at least. I do not believe I am in condition to talk about a life history, in any phase of the subject; but I need not tell you, I hope, how glad I would be to see you at any time and talk with you about anything. I have read *The Fugitive Blacksmith*,[1] which you sent me (I suppose) and have enjoyed it very much. I am exceedingly grateful to you for the pleasure.

I received a letter yesterday from Mr. Harmon, my old Attorney-General, asking if my Venezuelan lecture had been published in any form except as magazine articles. He says that on his recent visit to England he found friends there who had never heard of it and he promised to send the matter to them; but he seems never to have heard of *Presidential Problems*. I will write him that the book can probably be obtained at some Cincinnati bookstore....

To JUDSON HARMON

Princeton, *February* 10, 1905

Your letter was received a day or two ago.

In October a book was published by the Century Company entitled *Presidential Problems*, by Grover Cleveland. It contains about 280 pages and is mostly made up of lectures delivered before our University here. The topics treated are the Independence of the Executive, built upon the dispute with the Senate touching the production of Executive papers in the beginning of my first Presidential term; and a history of the following incidents of my second term: the Venezuelan dispute, the bond issues, and the suppression of the Chicago labor riots. The book, I suppose, can be obtained at any prominent bookstore in Cincinnati; and of course it can be had by application to 'The Century Company, Union Square, New York.' I would take great pleasure in supplying your wants, but I have barely one copy of the book.

The political situation is, I fear, beyond me. If within the next eighteen months there is not a complete waking-up by our people to the fact that they have wandered far away in the darkness of strange misconception, I shall be sadly surprised and discouraged. The description you give of your Jackson Day meeting is very gratifying.

I see by the paper today that you have been appointed as special counsel in the matter of the Santa Fé Railroad rebates. I am very glad of it....

[1] By Charles D. Stewart.

To E. C. BENEDICT

Princeton, *March* 6, 1905

I obtained a copy of the foolish *Defence of Fishermen* [1] from President Finley and am sending it today, properly inscribed, to Mr. Fearing at Newport. We (my wife and I) jointly thank you for sending us a copy of Mr. Jefferson's poem; and we appreciate gratefully Mrs. Benedict's kind consideration in sending us *A New Arrival*, which I have been wanting for a number of years.

Speaking of Mr. Jefferson, I cannot escape the feeling that he is not doing as well in point of health as his friends could wish. I am bound to confess, however, that this feeling is not based upon any unfavorable information, or very well may be only a 'vain imagining' on my part.

I am so much given to that sort of thing that I have fancied myself sort o' sick for a number of weeks when in point of fact the only attacks I have are old age and laziness — greatly aggravated by importunities to 'attend things' and make speeches. Parker, who reported me to you as being 'pretty grouchy,' brought one of those importunities — hence the symptoms he noted. I am not without hope that the Doctor and I will still be able to take a short vacation together....

To MRS. JOSEPH JEFFERSON [2]

Princeton, *April* 24, 1905

I don't know when this will reach you; but I want you to know how afflicted we are with you, and how our hearts bleed for you in your inconsolable grief. God bless you!

To THOMAS FORTUNE RYAN

Princeton, *June* 10, 1905

I have this morning received your letter asking me to act as one of the three trustees to hold the stock of the Equitable Life Assurance Society which has lately been acquired by you and certain associates, and to use the voting power of such stock in the selection of directors of said Society.

After a little reflection I have determined I ought to accept this service. I assume this duty upon the express condition that, so far as the trustees are to be vested with discretion in the selection of directors, they are to be absolutely free and undisturbed in the exercise of their judgment, and

[1] One of Cleveland's own essays.
[2] Joseph Jefferson died April 23, 1905.

that, so far as they are to act formally in voting for the directors conceded to policy-holders, a fair and undoubted expression of policy-holding choice will be forthcoming.

The very general anxiety aroused by the recent unhappy dissensions in the management of the Equitable Society furnishes proof of the near relationship of our people to life insurance. These dissensions have not only injured the fair fame of the company immediately affected, but have impaired popular faith and confidence in the security of life insurance itself as a provision for those who in thousands of cases would be otherwise helpless against the afflictive visitations of fate.

The character of this business is such that those who manage and direct it are charged with a grave trust for those who, necessarily, must rely upon their fidelity. In those circumstances they have no right to regard the places they hold as ornamental, but rather as positions of work and duty and watchfulness.

Above all things, they have no right to deal with the interests entrusted to them in such a way as to subserve or to become confused or complicated with their personal transactions or ventures.

While the hope that I might aid in improving the plight of the Equitable Society has led me to accept the trusteeship you tender, I cannot rid myself of the belief that what has overtaken this company is liable to happen to other insurance companies and fiduciary organizations as long as lax ideas of responsibility in places of trust are tolerated by our people.

The high pressure of speculation, the madness of inordinate business scheming, and the chances taken in new and uncertain enterprises, are constantly present temptations, too often successful in leading managers and directors away from scrupulous loyalty and fidelity to the interests of others confided to their care.

We can better afford to slacken our pace than to abandon our old, simple, American standards of honesty; and we shall be safer if we regain our old habit of looking at the appropriation to personal uses of property and interests held in trust in the same light as other forms of stealing.

THEODORE ROOSEVELT *to* CLEVELAND

Washington, *June* 17, 1905

I earnestly hope that you can take the presidency of the commission which has in charge the Jamestown celebration. Of all the anniversaries, this is the most important to us as a nation, and it is eminently appropriate that you should be prominently identified with it. I understand that the committee will call upon you for but little work. They feel, as I feel, that your name and position would be an immense strength to them. I should of course back it up as heartily as possible.

Let me also say that I most earnestly wish you well in your work in the Equitable business. I have been very much concerned over the hideous scandal in that society, and I know you will cut to the bone in trying to get rid of all abuses. In Morton, the son of your old Cabinet officer, you will have a valuable associate.

To IDA M. TARBELL

Tamworth, *July* 30, 1905

Your letter ought to have been answered earlier; but I have been considerably perplexed lately and in no mood for letter-writing.

And now I am sorry to be obliged to say that I am suffering from an obdurate attack of laziness and aimlessness. I have pretty nearly agreed to write something during my vacation, for *Harper's Weekly*. If I can pull myself together sufficiently to do that, I shall be glad. In any event, I ought not to undertake anything else.

To a TYRINGHAM NEIGHBOR

Tamworth, *July* 30, 1905

I feel that I am highly honored by your invitation to participate in the Old Home Week, to be celebrated as accessory to the dedication of the new stone library and town building in the town of Tyringham. I deem myself all the more honored on account of the restrictive clauses contained in the invitation, and the apparently small claim I have to eligibility among 'old residents and their descendants,' for whom the occasion seems especially intended. My ancestry, though it had its source in New England, was not distinguished by near relationship to Tyringham. Nor is my eligibility made apparent by the permission contained in my invitation, to give in writing my 'special recollections as to the old paper mills, rake factories, or Shaker settlements.'

The tablets of my memory are absolutely blank so far as these things are concerned. I am inclined, therefore, to flatter myself with the belief that in the absence of Tyringham ancestry, and paper mill, rake factory, or Shaker settlements' recollections, the honor of my invitation consists in its interpretation as a certificate of my good behavior during a short sojourn in Tyringham only four years ago. This I consider a very great honor.... I, too, have recollections of the place, not so wrenching to the memory as the remembrance of rake factories, but nevertheless most delightful. I have forgotten that the days were sometimes hot, but remember well the glories of sunrise and sunset. I have forgotten that the hills were sometimes laborious and remember only the charming alternation of heights and valleys. I shall never forget the kindness and cordiality of Tyringham people nor how soon I ceased to be a stranger among them. I knew the stone library long before its completion, and I know the hard struggle of its birth. I am as well satisfied with my ability to recall these things as I would be if, instead of a library, I remembered a rake factory or an old paper mill. At any rate, I claim to hold a memory of proof that in advanced intelligence and enterprise the Tyringham of today is a splendid evolution of the more ancient town which Old Home Week will celebrate....

To FRANCIS WILSON

August 10, 1905

... I am quite willing to leave my John the Baptist letter in your hands, and my reputation, so far as it is included, to be dealt with as your judgment and friendly care may dictate. I can readily imagine the reminiscent revival of Jeffersoniana when you and the Commodore and the Senator foregathered. I am wondering if I could have made a contribution if I had been present. The trouble with me is that among the many things I remember, a majority of them depend for their delightful value upon the peculiar expression and manner of our dear friend, as they transpired, and these, of course, cannot be reproduced by anyone. I'll give you an instance.

We were fishing for weakfish — called by the Buzzards Bay fishermen 'squeteague.' He had a most exasperating habit of viciously jerking a fish after he was fairly hooked and during his struggling efforts to resist fatal persuasion boatwards. It looked to me like courting failure on the part of the fisherman to indulge in these unnecessary twitches. So on one occasion when he had a fish hooked and was enlivening the fight by terrific yanks, I said to him, 'What do you jerk him that way for?' With an expression that comprises really all there is of the story, he turned his face to me and said, 'Because he jerked me.'

What a trivial thing this is to tell, and yet I cannot recall anything that illustrates better the quickness and drollery of his conceits.

To E. C. BENEDICT

Tamworth, *September* 2, 1905

Yours of the 30th came duly, and I was glad to hear that you had settled down a little after your yachting dissipation, and that in the midst of it all you preserved enough of hard sense to do a little sensible fishing. I am told that neither cod nor mackerel fishing are intensely wearing on the nervous system.

I do not now contemplate a trip to New York for some time to come. I hope Dr. Bryant will be here in a couple of days. I have made arrangements for a camping trip immediately on his arrival. If my Gray Gables tenant leaves the premises on September 15, as he told me he expected to do, I shall try to take possession with the Doctor for a short time as we did last year. The trouble thus far has been my inability to get the latest information from Mr. Ames as to his plans. I will keep you posted.

The Clevelands furnished a first-class sensation in this vicinity about three hours ago by a conflagration which destroyed the woodshed and icehouse in the immediate vicinity of the dwelling. The fire broke out about 7 A.M. and is smoking and smouldering yet. Acts of tremendous heroism were frequent during its acute stage.

To E. C. BENEDICT

Princeton, *October* 22, 1905

I am pretty well again after a most irritating upset immediately following the sturdiness and good health of my vacation.

Next Thursday I expect to start on a trip to Nebraska for the purpose of taking part in the ceremonies attending the unveiling of a monument erected to the memory of my good friend and Cabinet companion J. Sterling Morton. I am trying to take good care of myself so that I will be in condition to go. Immediately on my return I suppose Mrs. Cleveland and I will probably go to Tamworth a few days — she to look after the house alterations and I to look after the making of a new road to avoid a tremendous hill on the old one. I hope this trip can be followed by a few days' ducking in Virginia. This reminds me that I received a letter from General Alexander giving me notice that the day for our visit to him must be fixed, to suit our convenience, for a date in December. So you see if I do all I must do and want to do I shall be quite a traveller — for me.

To RICHARD WATSON GILDER

Princeton, *November 22*, 1905

I have felt obliged to decline the invitation of the chairman of the committee to attend the dinner of the City Club on Tuesday next. I must speak a few words at the Jewish celebration on Thanksgiving Day; and few as they will be I have boggled a good deal in getting them together. And besides it seems to me that I have been in evidence lately as much as I ought to be — for a time at least. I gratefully appreciate your understanding of my case and the manner in which you shield me from importunities instead of 'setting them on.'

I am delighted with what you say about the Woman's Suffrage article and the Nebraska City talk.[1] I am not sure that the latter has been printed in full. I usually am very dissatisfied with these efforts of mine; and when so good a judge as you has a word of praise to say of them I am as pleased as a boy with a new top. I had, however, a good deal of satisfaction in the Woman's Suffrage business. I received many letters from the best sort of men — and women too — heartily approving my position and thanking me for writing the article. I am unalterably convinced that I have landed on the right side of that question.

Are you not coming to see us some of these days?

Of course you did wrong in voting for Ivins, but we need not quarrel over that. There are a good many other things we could talk about probably without disagreement. I wish you would conclude to send me the editorial for the January *Century*, which you say in your letter you 'think' you will send.

Mrs. Cleveland is out tonight and I am sitting up for her very late — for me. But there is a standing order in this house that every letter leaving it written to 'the Gilders' must convey the united love of our family to every member of theirs. So I keep the rule.

To PAUL MORTON [2]

Princeton, *December 19*, 1905

I have duly considered your letter of the 15th instant in which, on behalf of the New York Life Insurance Company, the Mutual Life In-

[1] In commemoration of the work of J. Sterling Morton, Secretary of Agriculture in Cleveland's second Administration, who had lived at Nebraska City.

[2] Paul Morton, the son of J. Sterling Morton, was now president of the Equitable Life.

surance Company, and the Equitable Life Assurance Society, you offer me the position of referee to determine disputes that may arise between the organizations mentioned concerning the allowance by their respective agents of rebates on their premium commissions.

I believe this to be a vice that can have no place in well-conducted life insurance.

I accept the proposition contained in your letter; but in doing so I assume that those for whom you speak are seriously determined to prevent the vice referred to, and will unreservedly second every effort directed to that end.

To SAMUEL POMEROY COLT

Princeton, *January* 26, 1906

A prior engagement which cannot be avoided obliges me to decline your courteous invitation to meet Commodore E. C. Benedict at dinner on the thirtieth instant — the anniversary of his return from an expedition to Brazil. I am exceedingly sorry that I must forego the pleasure it would afford me to personally add mine to the volume of good wishes and congratulations that will be extended to my old friend Commodore Benedict on this occasion.

A long and closely intimate relationship with your guest of honor has taught me that his sturdiness of character, his unrelenting activity in useful enterprise, his keenly just estimate of business honor, and the generous warmth of his devotion to personal friends, fully deserve the appropriate recognition which your hospitable thoughtfulness has designed.

To M. P. CURRAN

Princeton, *February* 12, 1906

I am glad that you have undertaken to write something in perpetuation of the character and work of my friend P. A. Collins. Those who knew him but slightly will look to the book you write for a portrayal of his honesty of purpose, his intellectual gifts, and his devotion to the duties of citizenship. But the many thousands who knew him well will think you have sadly missed the mark if you fail to make prominent his unaffected simplicity, his spontaneous kindliness, and his inherent manliness.

To E. C. Benedict

Princeton, *February* 16, 1906

We have just heard in a roundabout way that you had fallen somewhat below your usual degree of health and that your ailment was accompanied by pain. I need not tell you that this news concerns us all, and that we earnestly hope that you will find prompt relief.

I want to thank you for the book you sent me giving an account of your Amazon cruise. I was so interested in it that I read it in bed last night and early this morning — finishing it at half-past one A.M. It seemed to me that the man who wrote the introduction had hard work to restrain himself from running over the writer of the book; but the entire work was interestingly, and instructively, done.

Inasmuch as you have from time to time shown anxiety on account of my real estate enterprises, you may be relieved to learn that I yesterday closed a bargain for the sale of my farm in this vicinity. I dare scarcely breathe lest there should be a disturbance of the happy condition; but when I have delivered the deed and received the exceedingly modest cash payment, I'll feel like shouting. Isn't it a little absurd, after all I have passed through, that I should be at last beaten by a little New Jersey farm? It isn't very serious, though; and perhaps, instead of repining, 'the smartest man in America' should find cause for *cockiness* in the fact that he has sold for $1000 more than he would have taken rather than lose the sale.

I have been calculating to spend next Tuesday in New York, but to-night it is doubtful if I go. If I do, and you are well enough to play cribbage, I might stay overnight and give you a lesson or two. If I am in New York overnight I shall stay at the Buckingham.

Woodrow Wilson *to* Cleveland

Princeton University, *March* 5, 1906

I should think that a birthday would bring you very many gratifying thoughts, and I hope that you realize how specially strong the admiration and affection of those of us in Princeton who know you best has grown during the years when we have been privileged to be near you. It has been one of the best circumstances of my life that I have been closely associated with you in matters both large and small. It has given me strength and knowledge of affairs.

But if I may judge by my own feeling what a man especially wants to know on his birthday is how he stands, not in reputation or in power, but in the affection of those whose affection he cares for. The fine thing about the feeling for yourself which I find in the mind of almost everyone I talk with, is that it is mixed with genuine affection. I often find this true even of persons who do not know you personally. How much more must it be true of those who are near you.

To E. C. BENEDICT
Princeton, *March* 7, 1906

I was glad to learn from your last letter that you had so far gained the better of your ailment that its terrible pain had abated. Somehow I have not always been able to see how this so afflicted you when 'Rubins'[1] was still on tap. At any rate, it is a great pleasure to think of you as free from pain and patiently submitting to the rest cure prescribed for you.

My plans are all perfected for a Florida trip; and if nothing intervenes to prevent it, we shall start on Friday afternoon, with the intention of remaining about four weeks among the surroundings in which you spent your sixty-sixth birthday. Dr. Bryant and one of our young professors who needs the change will reinforce me in making up the party. I don't hear very good reports of the fishing, but I suppose we can get hot and perspire and loaf without that. What signifies a few fish — more or less?

I received a letter from General Alexander today. He writes of the very pleasant visit he and 'Mary' had with you and is evidently in anticipation of its repetition about April 1 when, he is good enough to express the hope, I may be with you. I would delight to see him and Mrs. Alexander, for the older I grow, the more dear and near such genuine and unaffected friends are to me. The dear man speaks with enthusiasm of the hunt we will have next fall — but who can tell what next fall will bring forth?

Tamworth affairs are chiefly in the hands of Mrs. Cleveland — all except the financial incidents and the road building. I believe there is a little nibbling at Gray Gables rental. It's a dreadful thing — the way we have turned our backs on that place, so wringing wet with good times. Of course, whatever happens I shall strive to reserve the 1st of July fish tussle, and more too....

[1] Rubins Water was much used by Cleveland for his rheumatism.

To RICHARD WATSON GILDER

Stuart, Florida, *March* 18, 1906

From the heights of sixty-nine, I write to assure you that this is a happy day in my life, and to tell you how happy I am that you have made it so — more by your own loving message of congratulation than by those you have inspired. I have been so deeply impressed by it all that I have had many struggles between smiles and tears as I read the words of affection and praise that have met me at the gate of entrance to another year. Somehow I am wondering why all this should be, since I have left many things undone I ought to have done in the realm of friendship, and since in the work of public life and effort, God has never failed to clearly make known to me the path of duty. And still it is in human nature for one to hug the praise of his fellows and the affection of friends to his bosom as his earned possessions. I am no better than this; but I shall trust you to acquit me of affectation when I say to you that in today's mood there comes the regret that the time is so shortened within which I can make further payment to the people that have honored and trusted me, and can make amends for neglected friendships.

You speak in your note to Dr. Bryant of the mode of acknowledging the congratulations that I have received. There are more than fifty of them. A majority at least I want to acknowledge entirely in my own way and in my own hand. Will it not do for me to write replies to as many as possible while here (though it will have to be done under difficulties) and postpone the others until I return to Princeton, probably the 10th of April or thereabouts? Is it your proposition to send each a copy of a reply I shall write without my signature, or to return copies here for me to sign after they are made under your direction?

It's not a very convenient place to write, but I believe I could dispose of a number of replies if it will do to defer the remainder to my return.

To ANDREW CARNEGIE

Stuart, Florida, *March* 20, 1906

I avail myself of the knowledge of your address which your letter furnishes to thank you for the package from Scotland which arrived in proper condition some time ago.[1] Despite all fanatical medical advice, I

---

[1] Carnegie's gifts of Scotch whiskey — made from the same vats which supplied the British royal family — were greatly prized by the few friends who received them.

insist upon it that at the age of sixty-nine, a man should know himself of at least one thing that meets his physical condition.

To WILLIAM F. VILAS

Stuart, Florida, *March* 24, 1906

In this rather secluded place where I have come to seek rest and recreation, many kind congratulations upon my sixty-ninth birthday have reached me. They have all been delightful and comforting to me; but none have touched me so deeply as yours. Twenty-one years is really a long time; and yet without dwelling upon their actual number how short a time it seems since on the 4th day of March, 1885, seven of the best and most patriotic men in our country joined me in the highest Executive work. It would have been strange, indeed, if the national responsibilities and perplexities of the next four years — nobly shared by all — had not grappled us together by bands stronger and more enduring than steel. It is one of the most impressive thoughts that enter my mind in these days, that of all that circle you and I alone remain. And so it is that your letter recalling this, and bringing to my mind our free, frank, and trustful association, and manifesting the same unrestrained affection as of old, comes so near my heart....

To THOMAS FORTUNE RYAN

Princeton, *April* 18, 1906

On my return from Florida a short time ago I found awaiting me a most generous supply of snake antidote, which, as I understand, is most efficacious when taken as well before as after the bite. Florida 'rattlers' are said to be peculiarly deadly, which will, of course, make it entirely proper for me to abundantly fortify myself against exposure to their attacks in case I visit Florida again next winter. In any event, I desire to thank you most sincerely for your extremely kind remembrance.

To E. C. BENEDICT

Princeton, *May* 27, 1906

It is a long time since I heard directly from you, but inasmuch as I have heard from time to time indirectly that you were well and busy, I have not been alarmed by your silence.

Mrs. Cleveland and I lately made a pilgrimage to Tamworth, New

Hampshire, our new country home. We found the work of house alteration in a satisfactory condition and the old barn was on its travels to a
location where it will interfere less with our mountain view, which is the
thing of most value in our new neighborhood. I think our premises will
be ready for occupancy next month. Mrs. Cleveland intends to begin
her occupancy with a part of our family about the middle of June. The
remainder of the household including me will be left behind for a time. I
expect to be the last one to go, as I fear Equitable matters will keep me in
this region until July as they did last year....

The thought has been in my mind considerably of late that if I could
advantageously sell Gray Gables and this property too, I might build a
house exactly to my liking on a very nice lot I have bought opposite the
rear of these premises. I don't have much idea that such cogitations
will eventuate in anything, but it's pleasant and inexpensive to do such
things *in one's mind*....

To J. Nassauer

Princeton, *May* 30, 1906

Your letter of the 16th is at hand. I am not sure that I ought to assume
to furnish a motto for your son, but am willing to suggest the following:
'Be sure that your heart and conscience are in accord with the laws of
God; and then trust yourself.'

To E. C. Benedict

Princeton, *June* 6, 1906

Yours of the 4th came yesterday; and I hasten to acquaint you with
my hopes and plans for the immediate future — so far as I have any plans
and hopes as aforesaid.

I expect to be here and kept busy with University affairs and barn-
moving, until the 18th instant when I will go to New York on Equitable
business, to remain there probably three days or thereabouts. I expect
then to come here and look after my improvements and perhaps see the
family remnant, to be left by Mrs. Cleveland, off for Tamworth. I take
it as settled, though you have not distinctly said so, that the usual 1st
of July fishing trip to Buzzards Bay on the *Oneida* will occur; and I would
be much pleased if I might be counted among those to go. After that is
over, the Doctor and I may go to see Mr. Eckels at his summer place, and
also Mr. Vilas at his home in Wisconsin — thus spending a week or ten

days. Then *I* propose to go to Tamworth as quickly as is consistent with the designs of Providence.

You will see from this that I shall probably be in your neighborhood during the two or three days immediately following the 18th instant, and shall have no very confining work to do here, prior to the start for Gray Gables — if you say we can go.

I am glad you like the portrait. All those who saw it here were very much pleased with it. It is the tenth or eleventh portrait of me that has been painted; and we of the family are unanimous in the opinion that it is 'far and away' the best of them all.

I think Gray Gables will be unoccupied this year. Please let me know if I may make plans to go to Gray Gables, with Dr. Bryant and the remainder of the old party on the *Oneida*, a day or two before July 1, and whether you would like to have me vibrate a little between Indian Harbor and New York or Princeton between the 18th instant and the date of starting for Gray Gables.

To E. C. Benedict

Tamworth, *July* 30, 1906

I wish you could make us a visit this week or next — or for that matter, almost any time best suiting your business and convenience. Exteriorly we are still in the rough; and I suppose this condition cannot be much improved until 'haying' is over. This word does not mean in these parts hard steady work in the field, having for its object the speedy cutting of meadows and storing of hay. On the contrary, it means a sort of picnic season, or a continuous and long indulgence in a kind of hay bee, with just enough of a semblance of work about it to give a slim pretext for the tiresome iteration, 'I'll see what I can do when I get through haying.'

The interior of our house is, however, in quite a livable condition. I am certain we can comfortably keep you, and I believe you will enjoy our air and mountain scenery. I am afraid to promise you such fishing as you like; but there are some pleasant excursions available — and there is cribbage, a never-failing recreation. Beyond all, and more sure than all, is a hearty and sincere welcome, which I hope may count for a great deal. Mrs. Cleveland has been made aware of the contents of this letter and joins heartily in my invitation.

To Mrs. Joseph Jefferson

Tamworth, *August* 26, 1906

I have received your letter of the 20th instant, but I hardly know what to say in reply. Of course I intend to keep the reel Mr. Jefferson gave me, as long as I live. It is obviously impossible for me now to determine how it should be disposed of at my death. Many things may transpire before that time that will naturally have an important bearing on that question.

I do not suppose you expect me to commit myself absolutely at this time. I am willing to say, however, that in no event will the request you make in your letter that the reel shall pass to your daughter Mrs. Scott be overlooked.

To W. J. Curtis

Tamworth, *September* 9, 1906

If I believed that the recent symptoms of Bryan insanity that have again manifested themselves within our party were to continue, I should feel that the time and effort necessary to the reinstatement of Democratic principles in New Jersey would be wasted. I do not believe, however, that Democracy is doomed to madness; and therefore I fully and earnestly concur in your views concerning party opportunity and party duty as they should affect the action of sincere Democrats and all conscientious honest citizens of our State.

I cannot promise to be greatly useful in the activities of the movement you suggest; but I want you to know that I am deeply interested in it, and am firmly of the opinion that it ought not to be postponed.

It seems to me that those who assume the direction of the movement should adopt one of two plans. They should either serve notice upon those in control of the State Democracy's organization that they will insist upon the presentation to the suffrages of the members of the party, as a candidate for United States Senator, of an honest, clean-handed Democrat, who believes in Democracy's time-honored, pure, and undefiled doctrines — this notice to be so reinforced by a manifestation of determination and strength as to make it influential; or they should, after careful deliberation, take the initiative in selecting a candidate of the kind described, and should thereupon aggressively and affirmatively centre all their efforts upon his election....

To E. C. BENEDICT

Princeton, *December* 9, 1906

I received your letter yesterday. At a meeting, which I immediately called, of the stockholders of the Indiana Natural Gas and Oil Company, residing at Westland in the Borough of Princeton, resolutions were unanimously and enthusiastically passed thanking you for your labor in their behalf, and extolling, as beyond their grateful expression, both the ability and generosity which have characterized your efforts. And further, the Treasurer was directed to transmit to you from the funds of the organization the sum of $112.50, by way of contribution towards reimbursing you for actual outlay in the transaction ($1\frac{1}{2}$ per cent on $7500).

I enclose my check for the amount mentioned. I am quite certain that the outcome of your management is to me, beyond all others, like ' finding money rolling up hill'; and I want you to know how much I appreciate it.

I have been re-reading General Alexander's letter. He seems to have his heart considerably set on our coming to him in January; and I dreadfully hate to disappoint him. And yet I do not feel that I can reply to his letter just now with definiteness. I intend to go to New York and spend a few days with Mr. and Mrs. Morton just prior to the Equitable election on the 19th.

I put on my clothes and went downstairs yesterday — the first time in two weeks.

To E. C. BENEDICT

Princeton, *January* 2, 1907

I received a letter from you a few days ago, and another this morning. The former was accompanied by a big check, having some relation, so far as I can make out, to a very handsome and able thing you have been able to do for the holders of Indiana Natural Gas and Oil stock. The theory and computation which brought out the conclusion that I was entitled to the cash sum represented by the check I have referred to is so far beyond me that I am convinced I have been enriched through the black arts of Wall Street. At all events, I gratefully and complacently appropriate the funds with no twinges of conscience — which I believe is the order of the day among those who condemn the acquisition of money save through day's wages.

Mrs. Cleveland and I had a hearty laugh over your supplemental lines to the graphic versification accompanying your letter received this morning—

> Friday sorry
> Yet defiant;
> Next day send for
> Doctor Bryant.

I am very much touched by the affectionate sentiment which, on the footing of this, you express; and it is a satisfaction to assure you, as I have often done before, that your kindness and friendship have for many years been among the greatest consolations of my life. And as for Dr. Bryant, I should hate myself and would expect you, who know so much of my relationship with him, to hate me, if I did not acknowledge a debt of gratitude to him which no length of years would allow time enough to repay. But with all this I am overtempted to humbly and meekly affirm that I am not so dreadfully heedless of the care I owe myself (for others' sakes) as is suspected of me; and touching the dear Doctor's accusation of indiscretion, is it not in the very nature of faithful, devoted, and anxious medical ministrations to find patients indiscreet?

I have been dressed and about the house for two days now, and begin to feel like doing something. I want to see you very much, and the quicker you can come and spend a few days with us, the sooner shall we be delighted. I shall be surprised if I do not abundantly demonstrate my ability to keep your cribbage faculties alert, and we can discuss some matters which you lately touched upon relating to the general outlook and the Southern Railway conditions especially. So why not pack up your grip and come to us as soon as you receive this?

I have carefully considered the subject of my contemplated Southern outing; and I have regretfully reached the conclusion that I must abandon all plans looking to a stay at the Santee Club or General Alexander's — for the present at least. I would, however, be sorry if my disability should affect in the least the arrangements set on foot so far as others of the party are involved.

I was in bed on Christmas Day, but dear Mrs. Benedict's present was brought up to me; and it did me good to know that I had still a place in that kindness and love too high and strong for her pain and illness to impair. I hope you will deem our entire household in time for deep and sincere holiday wishes for you all. They are much more heartfelt than tardy.

To Paul Morton

Princeton, *February* 6, 1907

I have just sent you a despatch which has brought me a great deal of regret, and a consciousness that I have caused you disappointment and embarrassment. I am altogether to blame for these and confess my fault without any claim of mitigation. If I had taken a little more time to consider the matter in all its aspects and had trusted a little more thoroughly to the soundness of my first promptings, I should have saved you embarrassment and vexation, by declining the place you offered me, at the proper time.

My interest in insurance affairs, I now realize more than ever, is related exclusively to the success and prosperity of the Equitable, and my great desire to be of service to you and Mr. Ryan as well as to the company. It is such a different proposition to make this new connection, and to be related to other companies and their officials whom I know nothing about and which have not enlisted any personal attachment, that I cannot, all things considered, bring myself to its acceptance.

I *know too that on the actual basis of service to be rendered* — that is, real work to be done — I would not earn anything like the salary offered me. I fully appreciate the generous compensation paid me for past services; but I have had no very serious twinges of conscience on account of its acceptance. Conditions have, however, so changed and the work which I might do in the future will be so much diminished that I insist upon an entire suspension of the compensation heretofore allowed me in connection with my trusteeship and refereeship, on the relinquishment of both positions. Perhaps, if continued, I ought to be reimbursed actual expenses and a fair compensation for such matters as should be submitted to me as referee.

I want you to understand that my interest in the Equitable and your success as its president and the satisfaction of my relationship with Mr. Ryan, is as strong as ever (and that means as strong as it can be); and I would be glad if I could continue a serviceable connection. In my judgment the head of the president's association would more naturally be an insurance man. I believe you do not agree with me in this.

Finally, if you will let me off from this new engagement with as much complacency as you can muster, I will be glad to render any other possible service to the institution and the persons with whom I am already associated, on the conditions which I believe you understand.

To RICHARD WATSON GILDER

Princeton, *March* 25, 1907

It was a complete misfit — a travesty on things as they should be — that I should be disporting in balmy air and all creature comforts, while you, cold, hungry and miserably forlorn, were finding your way to Caldwell, for the purpose of marking the time and place of my birth. You did what you ought not to have done. There is no process of calculation by which it can be made to appear a profitable investment for you. And yet, when men reach the age of seventy, I believe their mental movements grow self-centred to such an extent that, consciously or unconsciously, they sort of believe their gratitude to be in some measure compensatory to those who honor them or suffer discomforts on their behalf.

I am so new to this venerable age of seventy that I cannot tell at this moment how much I am under the influence of this idea. But my dear friend, one thing I know: Your kindnesses have been so many, and have extended through so many years, that the pages set apart for their record are full; and I long ago abandoned all hope of redeeming the one-sidedness of the account.

You must, I think, see how impossible it is for me to do more than to say to you that I am profoundly moved by the conception of the Caldwell incident and by the beauty of its completed manifestation. It stands for the thoughtfulness and affectionate remembrance of friends nearer my heart than all others.

To E. C. BENEDICT

New York, *April* 3, 1907

I am in the city for the day, engaged in work attaching to the new position I have assumed. An interruption during the lunch hour which makes no demand on my time gives me an opportunity to express to you my appreciation of your kindness in organizing our recent South Carolina trip and your friendly thoughtfulness in allowing me to participate in its benefits and enjoyments. I shall remember it with more pleasure and gratitude than any other of our South Carolina trips. I was so well during the outing and have felt so well since my return that I cannot help frequently indulging the hope that my seventieth birthday will be the date of my permanent escape from my old health-impairing enemy.

Many friends were kind and generous as I passed the seventieth mile-post; and somehow I am already regarding it as a small performance to do so easy a trick. But I want to say to you that the Caldwell tablet affair, on account of the fine sentiment underlying it and especially on account of the friends who originated and carried out the scheme, profoundly stirred my sensibilities. And you must allow me to express my grateful delight that you were one of the few concerned in it.

A day or two after my return I received a note from Mrs. Lamberton saying that the Admiral's indisposition was slight and apparently only temporary. And the Admiral himself in a letter shortly afterwards assured me he was in fine physical condition — all of which was very reassuring.

I have had a nibble — a kind of 'chocksie bite' — for the rent of Gray Gables and have written Crowell that if rented the launch and Brad must be reserved for the use of myself and friends for two or three days at least about the first of July and especially including that day. This is by way of notice that MY yacht the *Oneida* must not be otherwise engaged at that time. I hope that you yourself will be free to accept my invitation to accompany me on a Buzzards Bay trip, if I can find a place for you among my guests, at the time mentioned.

I have expended quite a sum of money (for me) in repairing and strengthening the buildings and appurtenances at Gray Gables and hope for some return by way of rental. The fight in the Massachusetts Legislature to keep sewers out of the waters of Buzzards Bay is on again. It looks to me as if the canal was pretty nearly an assured proposition. I am not inordinately anxious to sell Gray Gables just now, but I think as soon as I can do so on satisfactory terms it would be advisable to have its value otherwise located...

To the REVEREND DR. CALVIN DILL WILSON

Princeton, *April* 5, 1907

I have always felt that my training as a minister's son has been more valuable to me as a strengthening influence and an incentive to be useful than any other incident of my life.

To ALTON B. PARKER

Princeton, *April* 27, 1907

I am a little ashamed to confess that it was only after I was free from the immediate allurements of the project you presented to me day before yesterday that I realized the existence of certain complications which seem to make it impossible for me to take part in the Judge Wallace testimonial. My feeling in regard to the affair is as when I saw you. The thing ought to be done and well done. The obstacles that stand in the way of my participation are not related to the function itself in any way, nor to the plan of it, nor to the persons promoting it, but simply and only to considerations so far personal as to involve relations of friendship which I cannot afford to jeopardize. I am strenuously endeavoring to have my name erased from the list of those who speak in public. In pursuance of this I have very lately taxed to the utmost the generosity of one of the dearest friends, in begging him, much to his disappointment, to withdraw a request to me to make an address on an occasion of the greatest personal interest to him — appointed on a date very near that fixed for the Wallace dinner. I have not the hardihood to disappoint him and on the very heels of it to appear as a speaker on another occasion so nearly contemporaneous and seemingly less imperative.

The scores of other declinations which I am constantly sending out in response to invitations, I might face with equanimity; but there is one I cannot face and accept the one you conveyed to me.

This is a long recital, which might well have been avoided by pleading a preoccupation of time and effort. But I want you to know the entire case. And I hope you will so fully appreciate the situation that my name may be passed over in completing the arrangements for the contemplated testimonial.

To E. C. BENEDICT

Princeton, *June* 1, 1907

If you are at all curious to know how important a member of your body the right thumb is, I advise you to locate a little gout or something of that kind in its first joint. My experience within the last two weeks has convinced me that the deprivation of many things connected with my bodily outfit could be borne with more equanimity than the disablement of the end piece of my right hand. I am delighted to see how well I am writing this morning, notwithstanding bandages and liniments; and I am not allowing myself to be disturbed by apprehensions of retaliatory twinges that may follow my unwonted thumbly exertion.

The last time I heard directly from you, you were just starting for the Jamestown Exposition. The judgment of those who have been there seems to differ considerably as to its impressiveness and the prospect of its success. I wish I knew what you think of it.

I see our President has been making another 'Yes, I guess not' speech on business, corporations, etc., and has told the farmers how completely they should have the land and the fulness thereof; Governor Hughes seems to be attempting neck-breaking acrobatics; Bryan smiles at both of them while performing his continuous tight-rope dance; and Hearst in his cage of wild beasts waits his turn to surprise and shock the multitude. 'Open every hour of the day and night, gentlemen! Wonderful vaudeville performance — all seen under one tent!'

This is the 1st day of June; and it seems to me that we ought to be thinking and planning about our usual first day of July fish at Gray Gables. I have given a lease of the place in which I have especially reserved for my use the launch and the man navigating it (Brad) for the first five days in July. I understand both you and Larry are booked for the voyage, but I would like to be assured that there is nothing likely to interfere with your plans in this direction. The 1st of July falls on Monday. I have a speaking engagement in this part of the country on the 22d of June (Saturday); and I have no doubt I shall have plenty to do here and in New York to keep me in this region for another week. How would it do to start for Gray Gables on Saturday the 29th and be fully prepared to attack the enemy on Monday, July 1st? Brad writes me that the tautog are unusually abundant.

To E. C. Benedict

Tamworth, *August* 17, 1907

... Concerning... political affairs, I feel like the farmer who started at the bottom of a hill with a wagon load of corn and discovered at the hilltop that every grain of his load had slid out under the tail-board. Though of a profane temperament, he stood mutely surveying his disaster until to a passing neighbor, who asked him why he didn't swear, he replied: 'Because, by God, I cannot do the subject justice.'

To E. C. Benedict

Princeton, *September* 13, 1907

... I sometimes fear that Rubber may be caught in the tornado of industrial destruction, but I know you have good reason for the faith that is in you. At any rate, I am impressed as I have never been before that I ought to put my affairs in as snug and remunerative a situation as the uncertainties of investments will allow. I do not see any near pros-

pect of a sale of Gray Gables. It would be a relief to me if I could dispose
of it, and on all grounds I hope I may be able to do so within a fairly
reasonable time. It will be about two years before the option which I
have under my contract to convey the property at a price fixed will become operative.

I have been disabled by illness for thirteen weeks and I am anxiously
and hopefully looking day by day for marked and permanent improvement. I am not without days of welcome encouragement, but my substantial gain seems very fitful and somewhat disappointing. I expect,
however, to regain a very fair measure of health and strength *sometime*....

To GEORGE F. PARKER

Princeton, October 7, 1907

I have lately had a letter from Henry L. Nelson,[1] whom you know well
— now a professor in Williams College — informing me that he has a
commission from the *North American Review* to write something about
me, and asking me if I can furnish any material in his aid outside of State
Papers and *Presidential Problems* which he already has.

You know how thoroughly incompetent I am in this matter and how
little I know about myself; but I confess to a desire that, at some time,
there should be written, by someone, some things that will present the
personal traits and disposition that have given direction to my public, as
well as personal, conduct.

I have written to Professor Nelson telling him of the book of speeches
and letters you compiled in 1892 and saying that of all men you would be
the best to consult. If he applies to you, I shall greatly appreciate any
efforts you make in aid of the presentability of what he intends to write.

To CHARLES S. HAMLIN

Princeton, October 22, 1907

A disabling and persistent illness has not only forbidden my summer
vacation in New Hampshire with my family, but has long postponed my
acknowledgment of your kind offer of service on the trip. I want you to
know at this late day that I fully appreciate your friendly thoughtfulness.

I suppose as usual you are in the thick of the political contest now pending in your State. I need not tell you how deeply I am interested in its
progress and result. You know how firmly I believe that the consistency,

[1] Henry Loomis Nelson.

the frank honesty, and the proud patriotism of the Democratic party are bound up in its insistence upon conservative and sane tariff reform. This I am convinced is its highest mission, and this I believe is its path to success.

It would be strange indeed if the Democracy of Massachusetts should at this time lack in enthusiastic and hearty support of the issue of tariff revision which it presents so plainly under a leader so brave, wise, and steadfast; and it seems to me that the people of the State, regardless of party affiliation, should recognize that such an issue and such a leader give them an opportunity to effectively protest against the hurtful restrictions and unfair burdens which existing tariff laws inflict upon them.

To WILLIAM F. VILAS

Princeton, *December* 18, 1907

I have just finished reading your response to the toast assigned to you at the Saint Andrews Society banquet. I thank you most sincerely for sending me so much refreshment and delight. It could not be otherwise clad than in beautiful and elegant diction; but more than this, it contains in small compass so much profitable thought and clear political philosophy that while reading it I was constantly wishing that every American citizen could ponder and inwardly digest your utterances. Nor will I make concealment of the gratification with which I read what you said concerning me, and my efforts to meet the high duties placed upon me by my countrymen. It is one thing to have such things said by way of formal compliment. It is quite another thing to have them said by one who shared the responsibilities of which he speaks and from day to day knew from his own experience and inspiration that public duty is inexorable in its exactions. As the two survivors of the Administration whose public work was well done, it should delight us to remember these things.

I have not been uninterruptedly in the enjoyment of robust health for the past six months — having during the entire summer been substantially confined to my home here. I have not, however, been at all times incapacitated from work of a certain sort.

I am now thinking of a Southern trip to be soon undertaken if I dare risk myself so far away from accustomed medical care, and if I can make my absence consistent with engagements here at home.

Mrs. Cleveland bids me convey to Mrs. Vilas and you her affectionate remembrances; and you know how heartily I join. It would delight us greatly to see you both here.

To Mrs. E. L. Yeomans

Princeton, *December* 23, 1907

I hope my infrequent letters never suggest the thought in your mind that advancing years or any other thing has in the least abated my brotherly love for you. I think of you as often and as affectionately as ever; but you know, as well as I do, how easily the letter-writing habit becomes interrupted.

I am determined, in any event, that this holiday season shall not come and go without especially wishing you a 'Merry Christmas' and 'Happy New Year.' And from the bottom of my heart I hope the future holds in store for you many of these holidays full of comfort and the best gifts of God.

Our four children do not permit us to forget that Christmas is near; and there is an air of busy mystery about the house that cannot be misinterpreted.

I hope to be able to leave here on a trip to Florida early in January. After more than six months of substantial confinement here, I have made up my mind that the very best, if not the only, road to my recovery of real, useful health lies through warm weather and outdoor recreation. I hope nothing will interfere with the Florida scheme.

To Richard Watson Gilder

Princeton, *December* 28, 1907

... I am delighted with the book you sent me as a Christmas gift — *Lincoln in the Telegraph Office,*[1] and I thank you for it from the bottom of my heart. I have already read enough of it to be impressed with what it contains of a new *closeness* to a supremely great and good man. This 'closeness' grows more valuable to me and somehow, more — more — sacredly enshrined in my passionate Americanism, with every year of my life....

To John Uri Lloyd

Princeton, *December* 31, 1907

Your letter and the gift brought from far-away foreign lands, accompanying it, arrived at a time of physical inability and depression that

[1] By David Homer Bates.

hardly permitted their proper acknowledgment. I avail myself early of better conditions to assure you of the pleasure with which I read your letter, and of my grateful appreciation of your consideration. It may add something to your satisfaction to know that among the things I am allowed to eat is listed 'salad with oil dressing.' Thus it has happened that I have been enabled, through your generosity, to enjoy olive oil of unquestioned pedigree and rare delicacy, and also occasionally convince the other members of the family that my limit dish was by no means indifferent to those blessed with sturdy appetites and strong digestion.

I have not been well enough to boast of, since the middle of last June. My illness, as nearly as I can make out, has taken on an aggravated form of the kind of stomach and intestinal disorder which on one or two occasions interrupted my happiness and comfort at Middle Bass. But I am better, and I have made plans to start next Monday for a short stay in Florida. There I expect to thaw out to such an extent as will enable me to still do considerable work and play — notwithstanding the threescore-and-ten limitation....

To ANDREW CARNEGIE

Princeton, *January* 18, 1908

If in asking the question propounded in your note, you had followed the formula so often used and had written, 'If *you* were in my place what would you do' in the circumstances mentioned, I would not compete for the prize offered for the 'best answer.' Perhaps you will remember that once, while enjoying your delightful hospitality, I confessed to mental but unexpressed criticism touching the direction of your benevolences; and it may be that you will recall that I thereupon put myself under bonds never to allow myself to again harbor the thought that anyone could impose upon your own generous and correct impulses related to the distribution of your noble gifts.

But inasmuch as your question is what *I* would do if I had a certain sum 'to put to the best use possible,' I am free from the obligation of my bond. Nevertheless, I ought to tell you that I am influenced and biassed to such a degree that the question, as you have formulated it, is prejudged in my mind and that my answer is predetermined.

If I were in the fortunate condition you mention, I would unhesitatingly donate to the Graduate School of Princeton a liberal sum for its equipment and endowment. You know I am a trustee of Princeton University; and I think you know that while I fully appreciate the value of a liberal education, I cannot assume to be familiar with the usually accepted methods and direction of university and college educational affairs. Thus, when I accepted a trusteeship in our University it was with the hope that I might have opportunities for usefulness in some practical or newly started undertaking connected with university work — notwithstanding my deficiencies in educational acquirement.

I soon became very much interested in the project of a graduate school, which was then hardly more than a project floating about in the university air, with no habitation and with hardly a name. As a tremendously proud American it was galling to my pride to know how generally it was thought necessary for the graduates of our colleges and universities to take a course of study abroad before they were deemed fitted for a place in the ranks of the most advanced scholarship; and it seemed to me positively disgraceful that our country — leading in all things else — should be content to bring up the rear of the procession of nations which, with material less in quantity and by no means superior in quality, were manufacturing the best and most world-influencing scholarship. With this sort of stimulation, and believing that the graduate school project was so new, or at least so unformed, that by growing up to it, so to speak, I might be useful in its development, I accepted a few years ago the chairmanship of the Trustee Committee which has the undertaking especially in charge. Since that time the committee, with the very important aid of Professor A. F. West, the Dean of the School, have done much hard work; and though, comparatively speaking, we are still in the days of small things, we are greatly encouraged. Such members of the committee as were able to do so have by voluntary subscription so supplemented the very small sums annually appropriated by the University for the school's support that we have never been in debt at the close of the year. Three years ago one of the University, whose liberality is constantly in evidence, put us in possession of a house and grounds free of rent, where our Graduate School has since found a habitation. Of course our quarters are very limited (our rooms accommodate only twelve), but our house is constantly filled, and quite a number of those taking our course of study live in rooms outside. Thus far we have been obliged to utilize members of the University faculty for our teaching force; but I am prayerfully looking for the dawn of a day when we can have a few eminent professors and teachers exclusively our own.

Perhaps you will smile at the meagreness of our Graduate School outfit. But those of us who have been nearest to it in its struggle for life find, in what has been accomplished, in the promise of the future, and in the things to do that will make for our school a most exalted mission, abundant reason for abiding faith and persistent effort. I am sorry I cannot give you a list in detail of the rewards of place and honor that have been won by our students in fields appropriate to their endeavor. It is absolutely surprising under the circumstances what trophies have been already gained by the young men who have come to our school after graduating from other colleges as well as Princeton. We have already, in a limited way, bred some first-rate scholars. Those who have been with us have always proved cheerfully studious, ardently determined, and unremittingly ambitious. All have done credit to the school and some of them will without doubt be heard of hereafter as American-made American scholars, far above the ordinary grade of college graduates and fitted and equipped to defend on the field of research and discovery American primacy against all comers.

Money has lately been given to the University for the construction of laboratories which will soon add to the Graduate School immensely increased advantages in certain lines of study and original investigation. A bequest has also been made to the University for the purpose of erecting a building to be used in connection with the School — though this bequest when used as contemplated will supply only a beginning of the building outfit we need. I have never given up the idea that in time the Princeton University Graduate School will quite naturally become a supplementary adjunct to the Carnegie Institute in the sense that, with other similar agencies, it will carry out or greatly aid its splendid purposes; and I know this School, strongly built and entrenched, will give to Princeton University, more than anything else can, the prestige of leadership among the universities of our land.

I do not dream. These things will come to pass. I may not live to see the fulfilment; but I shall work, and hope, and believe, as long as I am certain that American brains supply as good soil for the growth of the highest and most useful education as can be found anywhere else in the world.

I have unwarrantably trespassed upon your time and patience, and I am half inclined to withhold this dreadfully long letter. I send it, long as it is, because it is written, and because I think so much of your good opinion that I do not like to answer your question as I have, without frankly giving the reasons for the faith that is in me.

With dutiful regards to Mrs. Carnegie and loving messages to the little daughter...

To A. B. FARQUHAR

Princeton, *February* 11, 1908

I have been out of health for a long time, and this condition, together with some things I had to do whether I was well or whether I was ill, has postponed until now my reply to your very kind letter received long ago.

I was very much interested in the account you give of your visit to the Hague Conference and the prospects of its action. Now that it is over, I have no doubt that at least forces have been set in motion which in time will count very largely in the prevalence of peace throughout the world and a better feeling of fraternity among all nations.

I am waiting very anxiously to see what the outcome will be of our present business perplexity and political turmoil. I have always been such an optimistic American and have always had such complete faith in the saving power of American good sense, that I cannot make myself believe but that we shall weather all storms and find the bright daylight in due time. Though occasionally a feeling of discouragement comes over me, I am glad to say it is only temporary. I wish you would send me the article you have lately written, to which you referred in your letter, entitled 'The Truth About the Tariff.' I am thoroughly convinced that the sensible thing for the Democratic party to do would be to force that as a prominent, and indeed paramount, issue in the coming campaign.

I think that I am gaining in health, though I must confess my improvement is slow; and I frequently get very impatient.

To E. C. BENEDICT

New York, *February* 28, 1908

I have something very much on my mind which had its origin in what you said to me last night and which is intensified by a conversation I had with Dr. Bryant this morning — within the last hour. It has reference to certain symptoms of your physical condition. Of course I need not tell you that his feeling as well as my feeling on this subject is based upon our deep, disinterested, and abiding friendship for you.

You know how much faith I have in this dear old medical friend. And

yet, when my present ailment reached a stage which pointed to seriousness, I took his advice and put myself in the hands of one who made a
specialty of such troubles.

I think this and my relationship to you justifies me in begging you to
take the same course. I want you to do for yourself what I did for myself. No man can give you better advice as to *whom you should consult as
a specialist* than Dr. Bryant. Will you not go to him at once and take his
advice in the premises? If a thorough examination *by one especially
qualified* points to a temporary or not serious condition, you can well feel
perfectly comfortable and easy. If by chance more is involved, you cannot know it too soon.

This 'chance' and perhaps painful or disturbing consequences are what
you should guard against. I don't know that I can say any more by way
of urging you to adopt my suggestions. They are not the product of
alarm, but have their rise in friendly interest and sound judgment — as
I understand that quality.

Will you not act promptly? Dr. Bryant will, I suppose, be in Princeton
tomorrow (Saturday) P.M. and will return here the same evening.

To E. Prentiss Bailey

Princeton, *March* 14, 1908

I have read with a great deal of satisfaction your last exceedingly
friendly letter. Regarding you as one of my oldest and best personal
friends, as well as one of the staunch political comrades still remaining to
wage warfare in the Democratic cause, your solicitude concerning my
health and the kind expressions contained in your letter are most gratifying. I often recall past political contests and those who were prominent
as leaders in days past in winning Democratic victories. I do not know
but your thoughts are often led in the same direction, and if they are you
must feel the same surprise that I did in being able to recall so few who
yet survive. It does not seem to me that the successors of these old
leaders naturally give rise to great confidence or hope. Still I cannot rid
myself of the idea that our party, which has withstood so many clashes
with our political opponents, is not doomed at this time to sink to a condition of useless and lasting decadence. In my last letter to you I expressed myself as seeing some light ahead for Democracy. I cannot help
feeling at this time that the light is still brighter. It does seem to me that
movements have been set in motion which, though not at the present

time of large dimensions, promise final relief from the burden which has so long weighed us down. I have lately come to the conclusion that our best hope rests upon the nomination of Johnson [1] of Minnesota. The prospects to my mind appear as bright with him as our leader as with any other, and whether we meet with success or not, I believe with such a leader we shall take a long step in the way of returning to our old creed and the old policies and the old plans of organization which have heretofore led us to victory.

I received a letter a few days ago from Judge Donahue of New York, an old war-horse of Democracy now eighty-four years old, but still active in the practice of his profession. He said to me that, though he was by a number of years older than I, he not only hoped but expected to live to see a Democratic President in the White House. I often think that with my seventy-one years to be completed in four days now, such a hope and expectation on my part can hardly be reasonably entertained; but I confess that I am somewhat ashamed of such pessimistic feeling when I read the cheery and confident words contained in this old veteran's letter. I do not want you to suppose that a feeling of pessimism toward political affairs is habitual with me. On the contrary, such a condition of mind is quite infrequent and so temporary that it yields quickly to a better mood and a settled conviction that our party before many years will march from the darkness to the full light of glorious achievement....

To the EDITOR OF THE NEW YORK *World*

Princeton, *March* 14, 1908

I have read your letter asking me to make a response to the following question: 'What is the best principle and what is the best policy to give the Democratic party new life?'

As a general proposition I might answer this question by saying that in my opinion this could be most surely brought about by a return to genuine Democratic doctrine and a close adherence to the Democratic policies which in times past gave our party success and benefited our people. To be more specific in my reply, I should say that more than ever just at this time the Democratic party should display honest and sincere conservatism, a regard for constitutional limitations, and a deter-

---

[1] John A. Johnson (1861–1909), a Democrat who was elected governor of Minnesota in 1904, and re-elected in 1906 and 1908, and who was exceedingly popular throughout the Northwest.

mination not to be swept from our moorings by temporary clamor or spectacular exploitation.

Our people need rest and peace and reassurance; and it will be quite in line with true Democracy and successful policy to impress upon our fellow-countrymen the fact that Democracy still stands for those things.

To George F. Parker

Lakewood, *March* 24, 1908

I do not think it would be at all profitable to follow up by formal denial the misrepresentation that has been allowed to appear in good company, so far as what I said concerning Mr. Ryan. It seems to me easy to discover how much the few words, put in for the purpose of *singling them out for editorial use*, are at variance with the purpose and intent of the interview. I intended to give evidence of Mr. Ryan's useful and disinterested conduct in affairs with which I was familiar — and I certainly had no idea of intimating that in his large affairs he acted without appreciating or caring for the distinction between right and wrong.

Nothing I said to the reporter could, with decency, truth, or fairness, be twisted to have any such meaning....

THE END

ADDENDA

ADDENDA

I

CLEVELAND'S VERSES TO DR. JOHN H. FINLEY

(Written at Stuart, Florida, on *April* 1, 1902)

1

Who leaves Princeton's classic shades,
To prowl around the Everglades?
Professor Findley.

2

Who with lithe and stalwart limbs,
Flops about and thinks he swims?
Doctor Findley.

3

Who tempts the depths of San Lucie,
With patient efforts to 'catch he'?
J. H. Findley.

4

Who dangling o'er the launch's side,
Soaks canvas shoes in saline tide?
Mr. Findley.

5

Who sits with grace and hope, elate,
Watching his spinning, whirling bait?
John Findley.

6

Who first of all, impatient, sees
The place to sink his crabs and fleas?
One Findley.

7

Who feels the strike with rapture fine,
And yanks and jerks and breaks the line?
Findley.

8

Who soundly sleeps, with heedless nod,
Bumping his head against the rod?
Why — Findley.

9

Who throwing spear with reckless aim,
Upsets the fire and scatters flame?
Of course — Findley.

10

Whose kindly heart and willing hand,
Have won the love of all our band?
And who in all our future days,
Shall we recall with tender praise?
Our Findley.

II

CLEVELAND'S STATEMENT ON THE NEW YORK *WORLD*

(Written for its twenty-fifth anniversary under Joseph Pulitzer in 1908, and here included
as a just tribute and a corrective of some of the criticisms in the foregoing letters)

I can never lose the vividness of my recollection of the conditions and incidents attending the Presidential campaign of 1884 — how thoroughly Republicanism was intrenched — how brilliantly it was led — how arrogant it was — and how confidently it encouraged and aided a contingent of deserters from the Democratic ranks.

And I recall not less vividly how brilliantly and sturdily the *World* then fought for Democracy; and in this, the first of its great party fights under its present proprietorship, it was here, there, and everywhere in the field, showering deadly blows upon the enemy. It was steadfast in zeal and untiring in effort until the battle was won; and it was won against such odds and by so slight a margin as to reasonably lead to the belief that no contributing aid could have been safely spared. At any rate, the contest was so close it may be said without reservation that if it had lacked the forceful and potent advocacy of Democratic principles at that time by the New York *World* the result might have been reversed.

In the presidential canvass of 1892, I was again a witness of the *World's* Democratic zeal and its efficient party work. In that struggle it left nothing undone that any newspaper could do to aid the cause, and it certainly accomplished much.

I have spoken specifically of the two campaigns with which I was personally most familiar, and in which I had the opportunity to share campaign activities, though I do not intend to speak of them as exceptional instances of the *World's* achievements.

III

CLEVELAND'S EXCHANGE WITH HENRY WATTERSON, 1892

(From Watterson's '*Marse Henry*': *An Autobiography*, II, 134 ff.)

HENRY WATTERSON *to* CLEVELAND

Louisville, *July* 9, 1892

I enclose you two editorial articles from the *Courier-Journal*, and, that their spirit and purpose may not be misunderstood by you, I wish to add a word or two of a kind directly and entirely personal....

During the four years when you were President, I asked you for but one thing that lay near my heart. You granted that handsomely; and, if you had given me all that you had to give beside, you could not have laid me under greater obligation. It is a gratification to me to know, and it ought to be some warrant both of my intelligence and fidelity for you to remember that the matter resulted in credit to the Administration and benefit to the public service.

But to the point: I had at St. Louis in 1888 and at Chicago, the present year, to oppose what was represented as your judgment and desire in the adoption of a tariff plank in our national platform; successfully in both cases. The enclosed articles set forth the reasons forcing upon me a different conclusion from yours, in terms that may appear to you bluntly specific, but I hope not personally offensive; certainly not by intention, for, whilst I would not suppress the truth to please you or any man, I have a decent regard for the sensibilities and the rights of all men, particularly of men so eminent as to be beyond the reach of anything except insolence and injustice. But, my dear Mr. President, I do not think that you appreciate the overwhelming force of the revenue reform issue, which has made you its idol.

If you will allow me to say so, in perfect frankness and without intending to be rude or unkind, the gentlemen immediately about you, gentlemen upon whom you rely for material aid and energetic party management, are not, as to the tariff, Democrats at all; and have little conception of the place in the popular mind and heart held by the Revenue Reform idea, or indeed of any idea, except that of organization and money....

You cannot escape your great message of 1887 if you would. I know it by heart, and I think that I perfectly apprehend its scope and tenor. Take it as your guiding star. Stand upon it. Reiterate it. Emphasize it, amplify it, but do not subtract a thought, do not erase a word....

CLEVELAND *to* HENRY WATTERSON

Gray Gables, *July* 15, 1892

I have received your letter and the clippings you enclosed.

I am not sure that I understand perfectly all that they mean. One thing they demonstrate beyond any doubt, to wit: that you have not — I think I may say — the slightest conception of my disposition. It may be that I know as little about yours. I am surprised by the last paragraph of the *Courier-Journal* arti-

cle of July 8 and amazed to read the statement contained in your letter, that
you know the message of 1887 by heart. It is a matter of very small importance,
but I hope you will allow me to say that in all the platform smashing you ever
did, you never injured nor inspired me that I have ever seen or heard of, except
that of 1888. I except that, so that I may be exactly correct when I write, 'seen
or heard of' — for I use the words literally.

I would like very much to present some views to you relating to the tariff
position, but I am afraid to do so.

I will, however, venture to say this: If we are defeated this year, I predict a
Democratic wandering in the dark wilds of discouragement for twenty-five
years. I do not purpose to be at all responsible for such a result. I hope all
others upon whom rests the least responsibility will fully appreciate it.

The world will move on when both of us are dead. While we stay, and especially while we are in any way concerned in political affairs, and while we are
members of the same political brotherhood, let us both resolve to be just and
modest and amiable.

IV

CLEVELAND AND MARK TWAIN

(The Captain Mason here referred to was Frank Mason, consul-general at Frankfort)

MARK TWAIN *to* BABY RUTH CLEVELAND, 1893

MY DEAR RUTH: I belong to the Mugwumps, and one of the most sacred rules
of our order prevents us from asking favors of officials or recommending men to
office, but there is no harm in writing a friendly letter to you and telling you
that an infernal outrage is about to be committed by your father in turning out
of office the best consul I know (and I know a great many) just because he is
a Republican and a Democrat wants his place.... I can't send any message to
the President, but the next time you have a talk with him concerning such
matters I wish you would tell him about Captain Mason and what I think of
a government that so treats its efficient officials....

CLEVELAND *to* MARK TWAIN

Miss Ruth Cleveland begs to acknowledge the receipt of Mr. Twain's letter
and say that she took the liberty of reading it to the President, who desires her
to thank Mr. Twain for his information, and to say to him that Captain Mason
will not be disturbed in the Frankfort Consulate. The President also desires
Miss Cleveland to say that if Mr. Twain knows of any other cases of this kind
he will be greatly obliged if he will write him concerning them at his earliest
convenience.

INDEX

INDEX